Information systems in business

New Edition

Bob Ritchie, David Marshall and Alan Eardley

INTERNATIONAL THOMSON BUSINESS PRESS
I(T)P® An International Thomson Publishing Company

London • Bonn • Boston • Johannesburg • Madrid • Melbourne • Mexico City • New York • Paris
Singapore • Tokyo • Toronto • Albany, NY • Belmont, CA • Cincinnati, OH • Detroit, MI

Information systems in business

 A division of International Thomson Publishing Inc.
The ITP logo is a trademark under licence

British Library Cataloguing-in-Publication Data
A catalogue record for this book is available from the British Library

First edition published by Certified Accountants Educational Projects Ltd 1993
Second edition published by Certified Accountants Educational Projects Ltd 1994

This edition published by International Thomson Business Press 1998

Produced by Gray Publishing, Tunbridge Wells
Printed in the UK by Clays Ltd, St Ives plc

ISBN 1-86152-053-0

International Thomson Business Press
Berkshire House
168–173 High Holborn
London, WC1V 7AA
UK

International Thomson Business Press
20 Park Plaza
13th Floor
Boston, MA 02116
USA

http://www.itbp.com

Contents

Preface

Data holdings and the information that may be extracted from them are now recognized as a key resource for all organizations, providing potential opportunities for competitive advantage, enhanced performance and greater efficiency in operations. Today, few organizations, whether commercially oriented or not-for-profit, can afford to ignore either these potential opportunities or the contribution that a technological approach to the management of information may provide towards their realization.

Two major themes are explored in this book. First, if organizations are to seek to exploit the full potential of the markets which they serve, senior managers must manage the information resource effectively at a strategic level. Second, the contribution that management and staff at all levels can make towards the effectiveness and efficiency of the organization's information systems is crucial in the optimization of overall performance. Hence, it is no longer sufficient to leave the planning, development and management of information systems to the so-called experts. Indeed, more recent developments in the information technologies have made information systems more accessible to all users, and encouraged the phenomenon of user computing. Thus, the contemporary concept of information technology (IT) comprises the integration of the services available through the use of computer hardware, software and communications technologies, and the relationship between these services and human users – the interface being achieved through the development of information systems.

The primary orientation of this book reflects these themes and approaches information systems planning, development and control from the management perspective. The initial chapters analyse and develop the role of information within the organization, the major characteristics of the systems which are used to handle the information resource, and the primary issues involved in managing the resource and associated systems. Because information usage is common to all organizations, the material covered up to this point may be applied equally well in the context of manual as opposed to computer-based information systems. Thereafter, the emphasis shifts to the theme of automating the resource. The material developed in the earlier chapters is consolidated in the major case study presented in Chapter 6. The major dimensions and developments in the information technologies are outlined in Chapter 7, but the emphasis is placed on both the contribution made, and the problems encountered, in their application to practical information systems, rather than on the technical and operational characteristics.

The importance of a strategic approach to systems development is then highlighted prior to focusing on the more detailed approaches to the analysis and design of individual systems. The tools and techniques used in supporting the systems analysis and design process are explored in Chapters 9 and 10. Managing the implementation and the maintenance of systems (Chapter 11) provides an appropriate introduction to wider issues and approaches to managing the total systems development project in Chapter 12 and the process of systems evaluation in Chapter 13.

The advances in computing and communications technologies have resulted in the potential for significantly larger volumes of data to be made available to a wider body of users, both within and outside of the organization. While such developments may provide considerable benefits and improved efficiency, they also represent significant threats to the security of the data, the information systems and utlimately the organization itself. These threats and the increased risks which face the organization, now require management to develop effective security and control systems. These issues and the potential responses are addressed in the concluding chapters.

The book has been designed to meet the requirements of both professional bodies (e.g. Chartered Association of Certified Accountants, Chartered Institute of Management Accountants) and the wider needs of undergraduate and post-graduate courses in business and management studies. The nature of the material covered, the primary orientation and the level would make the text appropriate for courses in the management of information systems at levels 2 and 3 in undergraduate programmes as well as providing an underpinning for post-graduate studies in the business management field. Selected chapters may equally be employed to cover specialist modules such as the strategic role of information systems, systems development and management or risk management for information systems.

CHAPTER 1

The nature of information systems

The primary objective of this chapter is to introduce the concept of an information system and to provide the necessary framework and foundations for the discussion of information systems and their development in later chapters.

Initially, we shall present a generic model of the organization. This will help you to define the major components of an organization in terms of its resources, activities and structures. These components within the model will help to highlight the major types of information and their uses.

The distinction between the terms **data** and **information** is particularly significant to the field of information analysis and information systems. The chapter will examine this distinction and establish what is required to convert data into information. We shall then identify the underlying reasons for the rapid expansion of data processing activities within organizations in response to different needs for information. The functions that information performs as a key tactical and strategic resource and as a source of added value will be outlined in this chapter and explored in greater detail in subsequent chapters.

Components of an organization

The main theme of this book is the development, implementation and operation of **information systems** within the modern organization. Throughout the book, we shall use the term **organization** to refer both to profit-orientated business and commercial organizations and to the 'not-for-profit' organizations such as public authorities, charities and voluntary organizations. As a first step, we shall therefore introduce the major component elements of an organization to provide an adequate foundation for subsequent discussions of the most common information systems. This chapter is intended only as an introduction to these major components; later chapters will fill in the detail when the context requires it.

In broad terms, organizations depend on, and are the product of, the following major components:

- purpose and objectives
- environment
- resource inputs, activities, tools and techniques, and resource outputs.

Purpose and objectives of an organization

The primary purpose of an organization is to satisfy the needs of its market or clients. If it is to survive, it ought to act both effectively and efficiently. This applies whether or not the organization is profit-motivated: in both cases, it should actively seek to meet the needs of its existing and potential clients, whether or not those clients make a financial payment for the goods or services provided. In broad terms, the explicit purpose will reflect the reasons underlying the initial establishment of the organization – although that purpose may have been modified in the light of the experience gained through its continued existence. For instance:

- a profit-orientated organization might focus on the design, manufacture and marketing of a high-quality product, such as footwear, in such as way as to provide secure and satisfying employment conditions for all employees, consistent with the need to provide a satisfactory financial return to the shareholders and owners of the business
- a not-for-profit-orientated organization might be concerned with the provision of care, welfare and support facilities – for mentally handicapped children and their parents, say – in a way which is sensitive and humane to the recipients and at the same time a socially acceptable use of that scale of resource.

The purpose of an organization should be seen as a dynamic element which is likely to evolve over time as the needs of the clients, owners and employees change. However, the purpose may not be particularly well articulated or indeed explicitly stated by the organization and may have to be inferred from the current declared values and beliefs of those managers with the power to influence its affairs.

While the purpose reflects the longer-term nature and characteristics of the organization, the objectives usually indicate the direction and level of achievement that are sought within a more foreseeable timescale. These objectives are typically divided into three categories relating to the period of time during which they are to be put into operation.

Category of objective	Typical timescale
Long term	up to 7 years
Medium term	up to 3 years
Short term	up to 1 year

These categories of objectives and the related timescales reflect the major levels of planning and decision-making activity within most organizations (covered more fully in Chapter 3). These categories are not absolute, but they provide examples of the typical life span of objectives, which may vary depending on the nature of the product or service provided by the organization. For example, in the nuclear power generation industry the long-term planning issues and objectives may cover a period of up to 20 years or more, because this is approximately the period required to gain approval for the concept and then to design and construct a new power station. However, the medium- and short-term operating objectives and planning periods in this industry may cover a similar period to those illustrated above. Alternatively, in fashion-related industries such as garment or footwear manufacture, the short- and medium-term timescales may be more condensed and changes in product specification may alter several times in a given year. Benetton, the knitted goods producer, monitors customers' colour preferences during specific seasons and dyes its assembled products to reflect that demand.

The objectives formulated by each organization will reflect a number of different dimensions which will tend to be particular to each organization and its operations but will broadly encompass the following five areas:

1. **The environment**. At an early stage in its development, each organization must decide how it intends to relate to the main elements of its environment both internal and external, for example its effect on the local ecology in terms of waste disposal or noise, or its attitude towards trades unions or staff associations.
2. **Competitiveness**. By establishing the degree of competitiveness to be adopted, the organization sets the tone for the way in which it will seek to satisfy the needs of its clients and/or the market, for instance will it seek to attain high levels of technical excellence, low prices and/or high quality in the product or services provided, or will other less tangible criteria prevail?
3. **External performance measurement**. The management team, in consultation with affected third parties, must decide the basis on which to judge the effectiveness or otherwise of the organization: in terms of the number of satisfied clients or customers, market share or sales revenues generated, and so on.
4. **Internal performance measurement**. Whether at an organizational or cost-centre level, decisions must be taken on the target level of internal efficiency. This will ultimately be reflected in the scale of profitability, or the declared costs of providing a service, or by reference to some other measure of resource productivity.
5. **The people**. Employees represent a key resource within the organization and if it is to effectively exploit that resource it must encourage a constructive framework within which the staff can make their contribution. Equally, the end consumers' needs and aspirations must be taken into account if the organization is to fulfil its purpose.

The objectives of an organization are normally related to practical performance criteria measured against a given timescale, and they are likely to be specified within one or more of the broad dimensions outlined above. Consequently, organizations tend to be simultaneously pursuing multiple objectives, each related to these dimensions. But in a number of cases the objectives pursued by an organization will not be mutually consistent. This arises because the achievement of one objective may be at the expense of achieving another: for example, gaining a given percentage of market share may be at the expense of profitability targets and inconsistent with objectives related to the welfare of key employees. Given that organizations frequently pursue multiple and often inconsistent objectives, the management must therefore make all the organization's objectives explicit and then prioritize them, recognizing the practical limits on achieving any single objective.

Organizational environment

All organizations operate in an environment with many components, each of which may place different demands and constraints on the organization. The major elements of the corporate environment are:

- **macro-economic** – factors such as the rate of inflation, the level of growth in the economy and the level of employment
- **financial** – for example currency exchange rates, interest rates and corporation tax rates
- **political** – **the policies** of the political party in power that affect the operation of the organization or its markets
- **market-based** – trends in product design, consumer tastes and distribution channels (for example childproof and labour-saving features in kitchen equipment)
- **the competition** – existing market competitors' pricing and promotional strategies, and the potential entry of new competitors
- **technological** – changes in technology (such as the development of non-flammable furniture components) which affect the technical specification of the product, the manufacturing processes or the way the organization conducts its operations
- **social** – developments in the structure, expectations and behaviour of society which may create a **demand**, say, for job-sharing or networking activity
- **demographic** – changes in the total size and composition of the population
- **legal** – existing or prospective laws, both statutory and case law, which may directly or indirectly constrain the operations of the organization, and shifts in the pattern of social attitude, e.g. in the willingness of people to use the courts as a legal remedy
- **ecological** – the effects of the organization's operations on the natural environment.

It is impossible to reflect diagrammatically the full complexity of the interaction between the organization and its environment: each of the above components is likely to interact with others to an extent greater than can be implied in a diagram. For example, changes in technology such as the introduction of new motor fuels may produce unfavourable effects on the ecology or social environment, causing sections of society to put pressure on their lawmakers. This in turn may result in legislation to limit the unfavourable consequences of the technological development. Such changes may then affect the potential of the market and influence the interaction of competitive organizations. In Figure 1.1 we illustrate how these environmental factors and the organization interact.

Complexity

Because of the number of dimensions involved, the environment in which organizations operate is highly complex. You should bear this key point in mind. You should also remember that the organization itself is an active participant in the environment, and that many of its decisions and actions may well have an

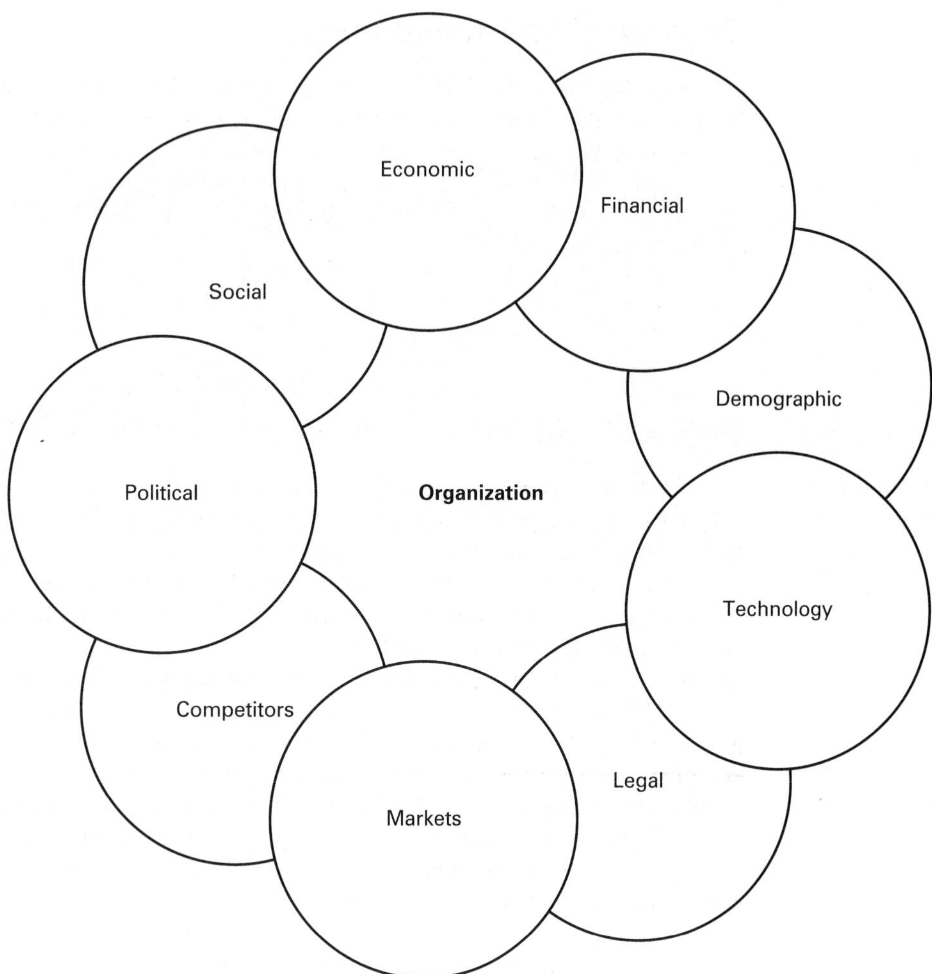

Figure 1.1 The organization and its environment.

impact on individual elements of the environment. For most organizations, these effects will be limited either to the local environment or to the industry and markets within which they operate, and there will be no material change in the national or international dimension. The main exception to this pattern will be large multinational organizations such as the Ford Motor Company or IBM, whose scale of operations and world market position allow them to have some influence on national and international environments.

Dynamism

Another important feature of the organization's environment is its dynamic nature: in other words, all dimensions of the environment are subject to continuous change. The rate of that change is variable. Some dimensions may change only relatively slowly (e.g. demographic and social factors), while other dimensions are likely to change more rapidly – for example, the economic and financial components or the actions of competitors in the market. Because our understanding of the underlying causes and mechanisms for change is still inadequate, we cannot predict accurately either the direction or the rate of change for each of the various components. There is also evidence that certain dimensions of the social and ecological environments that were previously relatively stable and predictable, such as the rate of exhaustion of rain forest resources in the Third World or the relative proportions of manufacturing and service industries in Western economies, are increasingly becoming subject to more rapid and often dramatic change.

Degree of influence

You should be aware that different organizations will be influenced by changes in particular environmental components in differing degrees. For example, changes in currency exchange rates may have a significant impact on a national distributor of imported cars but have a minimal effect on local businesses such as a suburban hairdressing salon. On the other hand, changes in methods of charging for water consumption are likely to have a greater impact on the local hair salon, if we assume that washing hair has a greater percentage impact on variable overheads than washing cars for display purposes.

The environment and the changes that occur within it provide the organization with both potential threats and opportunities. Potential threats may take the form of changes in the technology or in the manner and scale of the competition which challenge either the organization's products or its position in the market. Similarly, potential opportunities may arise from changes in technology, consumer tastes or the actions of competitors. Broadly, the management of the organization needs to be able to respond positively to the threats and opportunities posed by the environment, while seeking to maintain and achieve the declared objectives. This balancing programme must be carried out in the knowledge that the type and scope of the actions that the management may take are themselves constrained by various elements in the environment.

The environment can therefore be summarized as follows:

- it contains a very large number of components
- these components interact dynamically with each other and this results in very complex interrelationships
- the organization is itself an active participant in the environment, although its sphere of influence may be somewhat limited
- the components of the environment are dynamic, but the scale and direction of change are difficult to predict
- different components will influence different organizations to different extents
- there is likely to be a simultaneous presentation of potential threats and opportunities to the organization, which may assist or impede the achievement of its objectives

- the complexity of factors will constrain both the type and the scope of actions that management may take in responding to threats and opportunities.

The role of environmental information

The organization needs a structure which will allow ready access to information on what is happening in its environment. This process of **environmental scanning** – of collecting, interpreting and analysing information about the external environment – is an important and continuing part of any organization's overall information system, and should involve most members of the organization. (A more detailed treatment of this element of the information system is provided in Chapter 4.) The dynamic nature of the environment requires the organization's information and decision-making systems to be sufficiently flexible, sensitive and dynamic to respond effectively to the changing needs of the organization and its environment.

Organization components and structure

Any organization consists of a number of components which have been found necessary for its functioning and for the achievement of its objectives. These components may be broadly classified as:

1 resource inputs
2 primary activities
3 support activities
4 tools and techniques
5 resource outputs.

The role of management is to integrate these components effectively and efficiently in delivering the best possible level of value to the organization's clients or customers, its employees and its owners or supervisory bodies. Figure 1.2 provides a schematic model of an organization illustrating these five main components.

The organization receives resource inputs which it seeks to integrate and process to enhance the value of the individual inputs and to deliver products and services to its customers and clients. This is often termed the **added-value process**. The objective of most organizations is to provide the maximum value to their customers, consistent with the need to make some return on each transaction. In profit-orientated organizations, the aim is to undertake this 'resource conversion process' with enough efficiency to generate the profits that will reward the owners of the business for the risk involved and provide additional capital for the future development and growth of the organization. In the case of not-for-profit organizations, the objective may be to generate a sufficient operating surplus from the process to facilitate continued existence and development and to achieve other objectives.

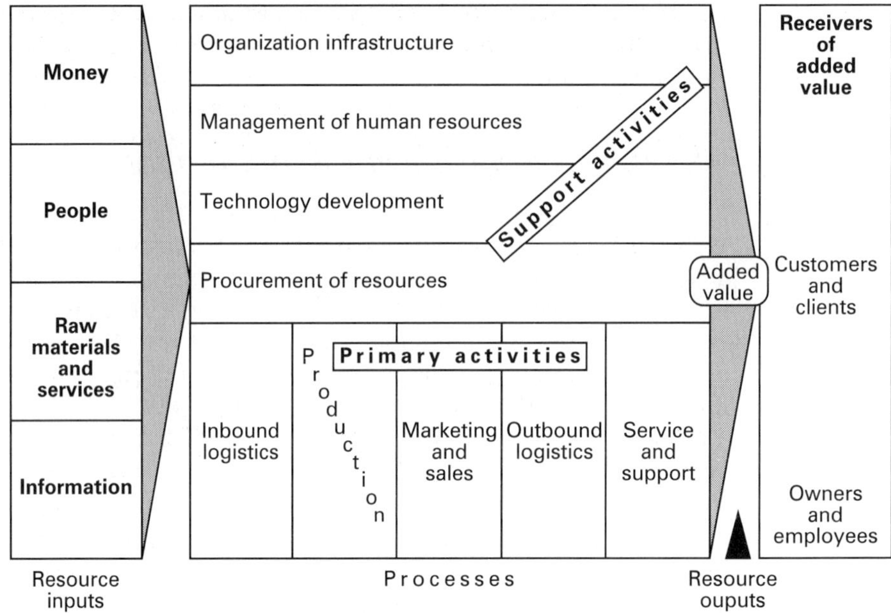

Figure 1.2 Key elements of an organization.

Resource inputs

The main categories of resource inputs are:

- **Money or capital.** This represents a key resource input as it enables the purchase of all other resource inputs. An organization not only requires the initial capital to establish its operations and to acquire the initial resources, but it also needs to generate a sufficient and continuous flow of capital to sustain its operations. We shall consider this flow of capital (or **cash flow** as it is more commonly termed) in more detail, together with its implications for the information system.
- **People** provide the necessary knowledge, skills and expertise to operate and manage the resource conversion process and to ensure that the needs of the organization's customers and clients are satisfied. This is arguably the most important resource as it provides creativity and ingenuity, but it is also the most difficult resource to manage effectively.
- **Raw materials and services.** These represent the basic inputs required for the resource conversion process. Some of these inputs, such as components, sub-assemblies and energy, may be used directly in the production of the products or services. Others, such as catering facilities and professional auditing services, provide a less direct contribution to the added-value process. These inputs are generally acquired from other organizations and will require payment for the inputs supplied from the organization's capital.
- **Information.** Inputs in this context relate to information concerning the external environment (see the earlier part of this chapter). The organization

will also require information about the three other resource input categories outlined above, for example, information on the potential sources of capital available and their respective costs; the availability of specially skilled people and the costs of recruiting and retaining them; and alternative sources of particular materials or services, with their relative merits in terms of quality, costs, delivery, and so on.

Activities

The activities of the organization can be broadly divided into primary activities and support activities.

Primary activities

These activities are directly concerned with the production and delivery of the product or service to the customer or client, including:

- inbound logistics – purchasing, goods receiving, quality inspection, warehousing and stock control of materials, and acquiring the necessary services
- operations – those activities involved in the conversion of the resource inputs into the desired products or services
- marketing and sales – market research, promotion, advertising and selling
- outbound logistics – quality inspection, warehousing, packaging, and either the delivery and installation of finished goods or the supply of the given service
- service and support – provision of after-sales service and support activities including training, fault clearance and maintenance.

Support activities

Support activities are those that are not directly involved in the production process but play an essential role in facilitating and supporting the primary activities outlined above and contribute to the overall added value process. These support activities are classified into four broad groups in Figure 1.2:

1. **Procurement of resources**. This includes the development of policies, procedures and guidelines for acquiring resources, as well as the purchasing of materials and services, raising finance, and the recruitment of personnel.
2. **Technology development** – the research, development and design of new products, manufacturing processes, and information systems.
3. **Human resource management** – the development of policies, procedures, structures and systems for the training, management and control of human resources within the organization.
4. **Organization infrastructure** – the preparation of strategic plans and corporate policies to meet the desired objectives; the development and implementation of appropriate organization structures; and decision-making, planning and control systems to achieve these.

Bear in mind that these support activities make as important a contribution as the primary activities to the effective and efficient operation of the organization, even though they are not directly involved in the production operations.

Tools and techniques

Although it may not be evident from Figure 1.2, the functioning of each element (whether concerned with acquiring resource inputs, primary added-value activities or support activities) involves the use of various tools and techniques. In fact, a wide range of tools and techniques has been developed to assist decision-makers at all levels in the organization with activities related to:

- analysis
- decision making
- planning
- scheduling
- the monitoring and control of the resources and operations of the organization.

In some cases, these techniques have been transformed into *routine* operating procedures and guidelines, while in other cases the decision-maker is required to apply the technique or tool to a *particular situation*. Examples of the former category include quality control procedures and stock control guidelines, while the latter would include capital investment appraisal decisions and product pricing policies.

All of these tools or techniques necessarily demand that information inputs operate effectively and, in most instances, the quality of the information input is a critical determinant of the potential quality of the decisions taken. Information is also required to provide decision-makers with feedback on the effects of their decisions.

Resource outputs

As we explained earlier, the purpose of any organization is to produce some form of resource output. The precise nature of the resource output, in terms of goods or services, and the recipients of the resources will depend on the nature of the organization and its purpose. We can identify four broad groups of recipient for the organization's resource outputs:

1. **Customers or clients**. Typically they receive tangible products or services and provide some form of payment in return to the organization. The exception to this may be the case of charitable and many not-for-profit organizations, where the clients provide no compensation for the products or services received.
2. **Owners or shareholders**. In the case of profit-orientated organizations, the shareholders or owners expect to receive a share of the profits generated by the operations. In the case of not-for-profit, the subscribers or owners may be satisfied with the knowledge that their financial contribution has provided some assistance to the organization's cause.
3. **Employees**. In any organization those employed will expect rewards for their contribution, in the form of either financial payments or non-financial elements such as job satisfaction.

4 **Society**. The state or community as a whole may benefit from the resources produced by organizations through either the increased wealth generated or the benefits created from the services provided by the organization.

Organizational linkages

A further feature inherent in the conduct of both the primary and support activities is illustrated in Figure 1.3 – the linkages between the various activities. Only a few of the many linkages which may exist between particular groups of activities have been shown in the diagram. For example, in more obvious linkages between the primary activities (linkage 1 in the diagram) marketing and sales departments provide information both on future demand to the production function and on earlier activities involved in inbound logistics. To take another example (linkage 2 in the diagram), information is fed back from the customer service staff to the purchasing and quality inspection activities (inbound logistics) on the incidence of faults on particular bought-in components in the product during its use. There will also typically be a number of linkages between the support activities and the primary activities (e.g. linkage 3 in the diagram, where developments in manufacturing technology resulting from the organization's research and development activities may have implications for all of the primary activities – thus, the introduction of computer-based typesetting and page layout in the production of newspapers and magazines fundamentally

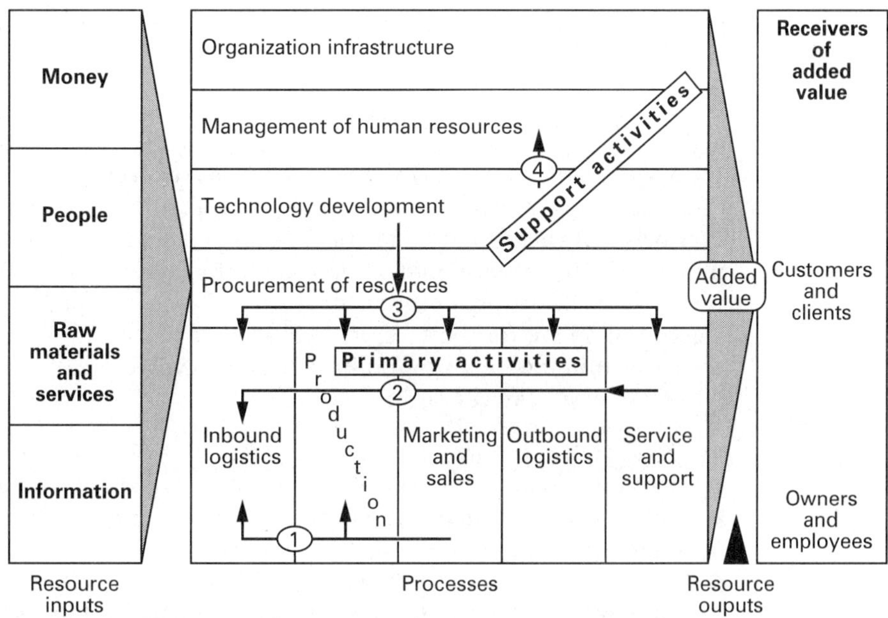

Figure 1.3 Key elements of an organization's linkages.

changed the primary activities in all the main functions and processes, including distribution, marketing and sales). There are also linkages between the different groups of support activities: linkage 4 in the diagram, for instance, shows that changes in manufacturing technology would clearly have implications for the management of human resources, for example staff training.

An important aspect of the model presented here is that particular types of activities within each block may vary between organizations, and certainly the importance and number of linkages between different activities will vary with the particular nature of the organization and its operations. Also, while there may be similarities between different organizations in terms of the primary activities, secondary activities and linkages between them, each organization is likely to have a *unique configuration* of these components. The exact configuration of the components in a particular organization will be a function of a variety of factors, including:

- the scale of the organization
- the nature of the product and production processes involved
- the type of technology used
- the nature of the market and its competitive situation
- the previous history of the organization
- the personnel employed.

In addition to this potential uniqueness, the rate and direction of change in this configuration is likely to differ between organizations.

The key conclusion for those involved in information systems development is that *no standard information system can effectively be applied to all organizations.*

The essence of information systems development is, therefore, in tailoring the information systems to meet the needs of each individual organization and to suit each organization's configuration.

Information flows and systems

The way in which an organization has previously been divided into a number of discrete groups of activities or functional units, each having the necessary linkages between them to achieve effective and efficient operations, is of particular importance in the development of information systems. In essence, the information system in an organization could equally be mapped on to Figure 1.3 or Figure 1.4. Again, for the sake of clarity, only a few examples of the information systems within an organization have been shown in the diagram.

The essential features of this model are these:

- each of the primary and support activity groupings will develop its own information system to be sufficient to support the operations of that activity
- within each of these groups there will be a number of information sub-systems
- the sub-systems within each group will rely not only on information generated within the group, but also on key elements of information provided by other groups' information systems, that is, through the linkages

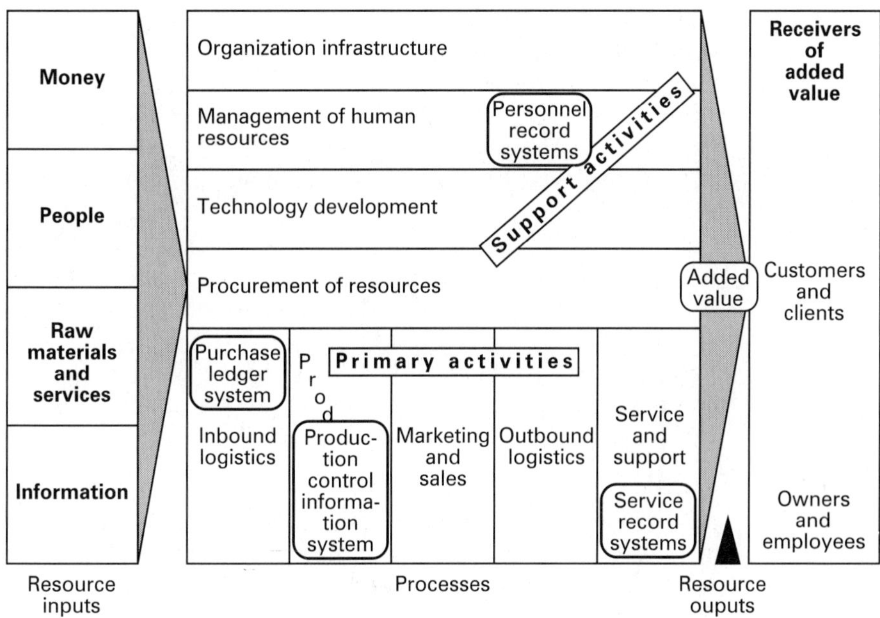

Figure 1.4 Key elements of an organization: information systems.

- certain systems operated by the support activities will encompass the whole organization and will require the input of information from each activity, e.g. the budgetary control system
- the information *system* may be based either on manual or on computer processing, while the transmission of information may be undertaken either formally or informally and use a variety of media.

We shall develop the theme of the concept and composition of information systems in Chapter 2, after distinguishing between the terms *data* and *information.*

Data and information

The terms **data** and **information** are often used interchangeably in discussions of data processing (DP) and information systems. There is, however, a key difference between the two terms which is fundamental to understanding the role and operation of information systems within organizations.

Data

The term **data** refers to the complete range of facts, events, measurements, opinions and value judgements, etc. that exist both within and outside the organization. We can classify data in an organizational context into a number of different categories or levels, as illustrated in Figure 1.5.

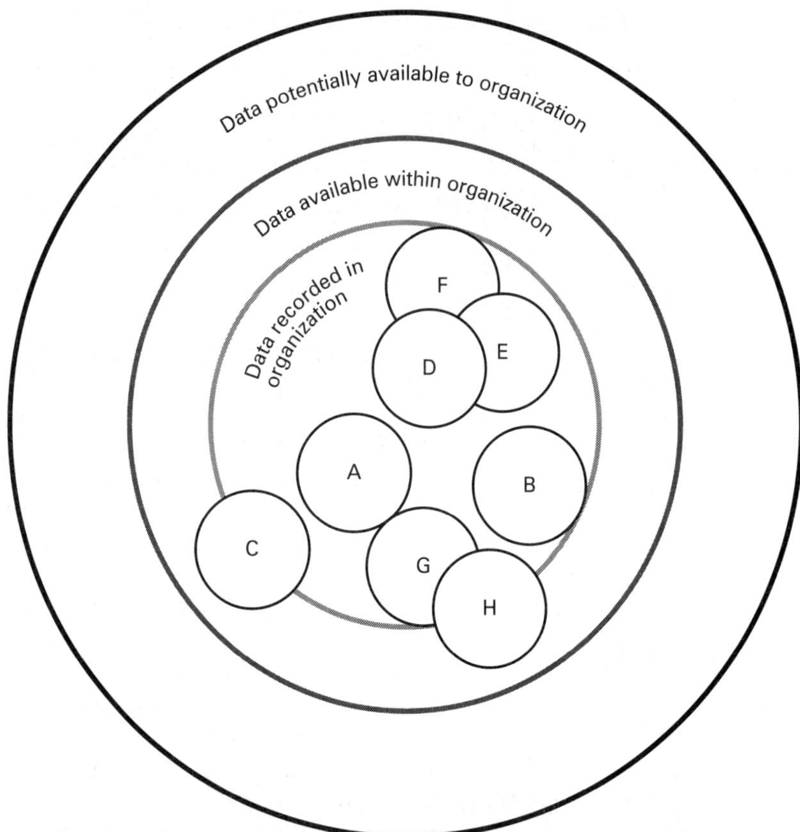

Figure 1.5 Schematic view of data and information.

Data potentially available

An infinite amount of data are potentially available to any organization. Most of these data will concern the external environment. The factors which may limit the organization's use of this potential database are:

- lack of knowledge about what information is available and where it can be located
- technical problems and the cost of locating, capturing, processing, communicating, storing and updating the data
- the low level of value that the organization may gain from the data, even if access proves possible – in other words the costs of accessing the data may exceed the value derived from the data's use.

Data available within the organization

Although an organization contains only a limited sub-set of the potential data available, the quantity of data typically held is still very large. Data exist within the organization in a number of different forms:

- **written or documentary** – textual, numerical or graphical representations
- **oral** – discussions at meetings or conversations between individuals
- **visual** – the observed actions and reactions of individuals and groups
- **subconscious** – knowledge, experience and opinions of individual members of the organization which they may apply in conducting their role and activities within the organization.

Data recorded within the organization

Only a proportion of the data available within the organization will be formally recorded and processed within the data processing activities, for the very same reasons that we identified above for the organization's limited use of the total potential database available. While the most common medium for recording an item of data is the written form, there are situations where a particular organization may find it valuable to record oral and visual forms. For example, it is common practice for organizations trading in financial securities to record all staff telephone conversations, as the majority of the organizations' business is conducted over the telephone and this provides proof of the terms and conditions of contracts made or evidence of insider dealing. Other organizations may use video recording equipment, either for security monitoring or for monitoring production operations. Typical examples of potentially valuable data held in written or graphical form within an organization include:

- the quantities of products sold during each month
- the stock levels of particular products
- the minutes of meetings held by staff at all levels
- a full employee profile including age, salary and employment records and skills
- responses to consumer research surveys
- forecasts of future market demand.

In Figure 1.5, the groups of activities or users represented by the circles A and B indicate the uses of data which are formally recorded in the organization. Group C indicates the use of some data which is formally recorded together with other data which are available within the organization but not formally recorded, for example, as expertise personal to individuals. A more common situation in practice is that represented by the user groups D, E and F: while each of these user groups requires certain data specific to its particular activities and not needed by the other users, there is also a proportion of their data needs which is common to all three user groups. This is indicated by the overlap between the three circles in the diagram. The overlap also represents the linkages between activities referred to earlier in this chapter. G and H are discussed below.

The data information conversion process

The data processing function may be viewed schematically as in Figure 1.6.

The first stage in the process is the capture and recording of the basic or raw data. The term **raw data** is used to refer to data that have not been modified or

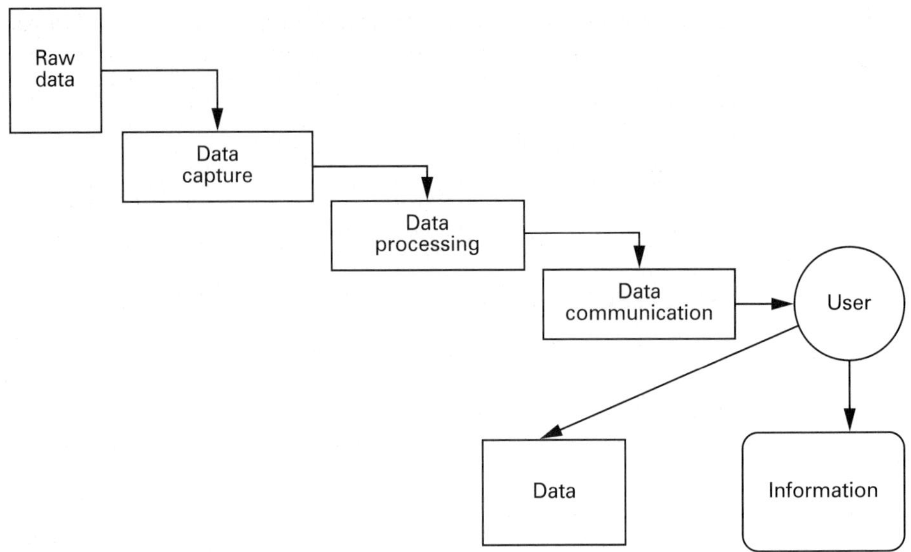

Figure 1.6 Simplified model of the data information conversion process.

processed by the organization. As mentioned earlier, data capture and storage today is typically in a written form, although the other methods of data capture are increasingly being used.

The next stage is the processing of the data into a more convenient form for the users, which may include conversion into other units of measurement, sorting, summarizing, storing, and so on.

The third stage involves the communication of the processed data to the users, which may involve textual, graphical or oral methods of communication. Up to this point, the process is still only concerned with data, although the process is developing the data into a form in which it can potentially become information. The general term applied to these activities is **data processing**.

Information

Information, as shown in Figure 1.6, can be viewed as a sub-set of the data held within the organization. This indicates that although the data processing system delivers data to the user in a processed form, only a part of this data will be converted into information; the remainder will be discarded by the particular user. In other words, all members of an organization will receive a stream of data inputs in the form of instructions, letters, statistics, internal memoranda, and so on. A proportion of this data will be either filed away automatically and never referred to or alternatively deposited in the wastepaper bin. Only a proportion of the data received will be read, used or acted on by the receiver. This will then be classified as information rather than data.

Information is that part of the total data available which is *appropriate to the requirements of a particular user or group of users*. An effective information system will therefore be one which minimizes the amount of data passing through the hands of the user without becoming information, that is, one which reduces or eliminates the contents of the data box in Figure 1.6 and increases the contents of the information box.

Certain parts of the data may be appropriate to only one user in the organization, as in the case of users A, B, C illustrated previously in Figure 1.5. Alternatively, as in the case of users D, E, and F, parts of the data are appropriate or common to all three users, while other parts of the data are specific to each individually. The third case illustrated in Figure 1.5 indicates that user H requires only part of the information that user G requires, even though they are members of the same activity group. This might represent, for example, the situation of the chief accountant as user H and the payroll clerk as user G. Further, user H, the chief accountant in this example, also relies on both formally recorded and unrecorded data from other sources in the organization outside the accounting function.

It is also important to recognize that the ways in which the items of data are presented to the various users may be differentiated to suit their particular needs. Hence, the chief accountant may require only summarized statements of salary and wage expenditures, whereas the payroll clerk will require detailed data on each member of staff. However, the relevance of items of data to the user's situation, the problem faced or the effectiveness of the data processing are not in themselves sufficient to ensure the conversion of data to information. The other key element in the conversion process of data to information is the *user* or receiver of the data.

When are data informative?

The outline model of the data processing system (Figure 1.6) indicates that only a part of the data transmitted to the user becomes information. The remainder stays in the form of data and is essentially unused or redundant as far as the particular user is concerned. This does not necessarily imply that these data items are redundant for the organization as a whole, but merely from the perspective of that particular user. However, the issue of **data redundancy** is of particular importance to the field of systems analysis and design, as high levels of data redundancy are often a consequence of poor quality systems design. Excessive levels of data redundancy imply both higher-than-necessary data processing costs and a potentially reduced quality of decision making, because the users may be required to sift through large volumes of superfluous data to find the appropriate information that they require to make the best decision.

The conversion of data to information will occur when the data received by the user enhances his or her knowledge or understanding of a situation. For this to happen, the user would need:

- to recognize that the data item received is relevant to their particular situation
- to have sufficient prior knowledge and experience to be able to use that data to enhance their knowledge and understanding.

Given that different users in an organization possess different levels of prior knowledge and experience, it follows that the same data input received by such users will not always become information. Therefore:

An item of data is only information to some of the people some of the time, and not to all of the people all of the time!

For example, consider the following data items:

1 **0111**
2 **Net present value = –£360,000**

What meaning is conveyed? The first item is the binary representation of the number 7, which would probably be understood by those familiar with the binary numbering system. The second item represents the result from a discounted cash flow appraisal of an investment, indicating that the investment concerned would generate a loss of around £360,000. Again, prior knowledge or understanding of investment appraisal will convert this from an item of data to information. Apart from the issues related to the user's prior knowledge, the conversion of data to information faces a number of other potential problems.

1 **The quality of source data**. A basic issue related to the quality of the information received by the user concerns the quality of the initial data input into the system. If, for example, the data input is poor in terms of accuracy or detail, the resulting information received by the user will be of a similarly poor quality. No matter how good the data processing system is, it will never be able to compensate for poor-quality data input. This lack of quality may result either from the quality of the data that is available to the organization (and over which it may have little or no control) or from defective data capture methods which are generally within its control. A common way of expressing this phenomenon is:

   Rubbish in = rubbish out

   Using the American terminology, this may be expressed as **GIGO**, i.e.

   Garbage in = garbage out.

2 **The processing activities**. This refers to the various ways in which the data item is manipulated within the data processing system, and includes both manual and mechanical/electronic activities. Despite the extensive development and application of electronic data processing technology, a significant number of processing activities are still carried out manually in any system. These manual activities are frequently the source of loss of quality in the data during processing, because humans are notoriously fallible when asked to perform consistently and accurately. Although many of these manual activities are being replaced by automatic systems (e.g. electronic point-of-sale recording systems), it should be recognized that automatic

systems may also lead to reductions in quality if they malfunction technically or their processing activities are poorly designed.

3 **Time**. When the data item is presented to the user, it may be inappropriate to the issues or circumstances facing the user at that particular time, but may become more appropriate at some future time. This issue of timing, in the sense of users being able to access the appropriate information rapidly as and when they require it for a particular aspect of their work, is a major reason for the development of large database storage systems and real-time computing facilities. This aspect of timing and the resulting issues of databases and real-time computing are discussed more fully in Chapters 5 and 7.
4 **Communications**. In addition to the quality of presentation, the media used to communicate the data will also have an impact on the effectiveness of the data conversion process. Apart from the technical quality of the communications system, the use of printed documents, screen displays or voice communications may be more effective for particular users in particular situations.
5 **Presentation**. The way in which the information is presented to the user may result in a failure to recognize the informative value of the data. For example, if the information is poorly presented in terms of layout quality or contains too much detail, the user may either miss the significant data or possibly abandon the task of searching for it in a mass of detail. The development of graphical and colour display systems offers potential improvements in the quality of presentation.
6 **User interface**. The quality of the interface between the user and the technology and systems providing the data has a significant impact on the effectiveness of the conversion process. In essence, this concerns the ease with which users can employ, or interact with, the technology to define their information needs and to receive the necessary information. This aspect is normally described as the *user-friendliness* of the system and is a critical feature of effective systems design. The issues associated with the design of an effective human–computer interface will be discussed in Chapter 9.

In summary, the key factors which influence the effectiveness of the data to information conversion process are:

- the quality of the source data
- the effectiveness of the processing activities
- the quality of the communications
- the degree of user-friendliness in the interface
- the level of accessibility in the presentation
- the ability of the user to gain access to the information at the right time
- the adequacy of each user's knowledge, skill and expertise to make the best use of the data.

These factors will be addressed more fully in subsequent chapters dealing with the design and development of information systems.

The value of information

When we consider the information received by each user, we can attribute different levels of value to each piece of information. An example of how the value of information may be categorized is shown in Table 1.1. While the table does not attempt to cover every conceivable permutation of levels of understanding and relevance to the user's situation, it does illustrate that the value of information is a function of both the user's understanding and the relevance of the data to the situation. Thus, no matter how important it might be to the situation that it happens to be in the right hands, it will remain as data if it is not *understood* by the immediate user.

Alternatively, where there is understanding, the more relevant the data item is to the user's situation and the greater the user's level of understanding of both the situation and the data, then the higher the information value that can be extracted will be. This will be explored in more detail in Chapter 2.

What function does information perform?

Table 1.1 indicates that there are different levels of value in the information received. In essence, if users possessed perfect knowledge about each situation faced, there would be no requirement for information. However, given that in most situations users have less than perfect knowledge, all relevant information provides an opportunity to improve the response to the situation. Within this broad role of enhancing knowledge, information may be considered to fulfil the following functions:

- **reducing uncertainty in decision making** – although it should be recognized that more information may add other possible outcomes to a situation not previously considered, thus increasing the uncertainty
- **providing error signals** which indicate any deviation from planned performance or operation, thus aiding control activities
- **providing a mechanism** for the communication of plans, forecasts, procedures, guidelines, and so on
- **supplying historical evidence** of transactions, levels of performance, results of decisions, and so on
- **reducing complexity** through enhancement of the user's knowledge and understanding of a situation.

Table 1.1 Value of information: outline classification

Level of user understanding	Relevance/importance to user's situation	Information value
None	None	None remains as data
None	High	None remains as data
Some	None	Low value
Good	Some	Moderate value
Good	High	High value
Good	Critical	Maximum value

Pressures for more information

A number of developments have generated increased demands for data and information processing within most organizations. These include:

- **Advances in processing technologies** that improve the technical capacity to capture and process data which previously proved difficult or time-consuming. For example, meteorologists are now able to capture data from weather satellites and to process national or regional weather patterns within fractions of a second. Reference to Figure 1.5 earlier in this chapter will help to illustrate the effect of these developments. Organizations are now increasingly able to extend the volume of data formally recorded in the organization (i.e. the inner circle is expanding outwards), as well as increasing their coverage of the data potentially available outside the organization (i.e. the second circle is also expanding outwards).
- **Improved methods of communication**: developments in communications technologies have provided increased scope for improved effectiveness in the distribution and exchange of information, both within and between organizations.
- **Reduced costs of processing**, storing, retrieving and communicating data and information. A consequence of developments in the information technologies has been a significant reduction in the costs of processing a unit of data.
- **Developments in information technology**, while making the technical operation of data processing inherently more complex, have also been directed towards improving the interface between the technology and its users. The primary objective is to make the technology more user-friendly, i.e. to make the use of the technology simpler and more adaptable to the style of normal human modes of operation and thought processes. Various devices including menus, graphical displays (icons) and the mouse have been developed to improve the user interface with the technology. These and similar developments which enhance the use of (and hence the demand for) information are discussed in Chapters 5 and 8. The general term for these developments is the human–computer interface (HCI).
- **The increased complexity of the environment** within which organizations operate and in which decisions are made. Decision-makers now need to consider a wider range of factors in making their decisions, which in turn generates a demand for greater information.
- In addition to the increasing complexity of the external environment, the increased **complexity of organizations themselves** creates a demand for more information. This has resulted from:
  - the increased scale of many organizations
  - their diversification into a number of different product/market sectors
  - the increasing specialization of activities within organizational functions
  - the development of alternative organization structures to facilitate effective management and control of the organization.

Many business and commercial organizations operate on a multinational basis, extending the problems of management, control and communications across national boundaries.

- **The improved knowledge, education and training** of decision-makers and users of information have resulted in a demand for more comprehensive and detailed information to assist in their organizational activities. Associated with this development are significant improvements in the fields of management and organizational research, which have produced more comprehensive models to assist in the management and control of business organizations. Such models have resulted in the development of a range of tools and techniques to aid decision making, which invariably require more comprehensive, more detailed and better-quality information in their application.
- **Greater demands** have been made of the organization **to provide more information on its operations to outside agencies** and regulatory bodies. For example, pressure for the disclosure of corporate information to shareholders and employees has been significantly increased, as have government demands on revenue, employment and statistical departments. Similarly, many organizations have increased their disclosure of information independently of mandatory requirements, recognizing the potential benefits to be gained from voluntarily providing interested parties (e.g. employees) with corporate information.

The reasons given above for the increased level of data processing and information use within organizations can be reduced to two primary causes:

- increased demand from users, both from within and outside the organization
- developments in information processing technologies and their application to meet these demands.

While it may be interesting to speculate as to whether user demand or technological development is the primary motivating factor in increasing information usage, it is inappropriate to our present discussion. Subsequent chapters will explore user needs in more detail and give attention to demands for information, developments in the information technologies and, more particularly, methods used to make the technology meet the users' information needs.

Information as a tactical resource

More recently, information has increasingly been recognized both as a key tactical and strategic resource in the organization and as a significant source of potential added value. (For a full development of the distinction between the terms *tactical* and *strategic*, see Chapter 3.) Information has always been a source of competitive advantage in the business context: for example, if a company has up-to-date information on the prices charged by competitors for their products and services, it can respond rapidly with its own price changes. If these are effectively communicated to potential customers, the company may enjoy an advantage over competitors whose pricing information is less up to date. But the real change that enhances the potential value of information is the ability of organizations to exploit this source of advantage through the use of new technologies. Thus, price lists and brochures can be amended instantly using desk-top publishing facilities and the high-quality results can be sent by post or fax to a hitlist of addresses culled from a selective database search for prospective buyers.

Information is an invaluable resource for supporting the short-term tactical decisions involved in the ongoing operations of the organization. For example, the food retailing business has long recognized that an important source of competitive advantage and higher profits is up-to-date information on demand for individual products. This resource enables management to improve their demand forecasts and ordering policies to ensure that fast-selling items are always in stock and that slow-selling items are either withdrawn or stocked in reduced quantities, thereby providing more shelf space for the faster-moving products. A key performance variable in food retailing is sales revenue and profit per square metre. Previously, a supermarket with over 10,000 product lines in stock would find it both time-consuming and expensive to monitor the stock levels of each item regularly, as this would involve the manual counting and processing of the data prior to taking decisions. The development of electronic tally systems and, subsequently, electronic point-of-sale (EPOS) systems now provides store managements with accurate data on the current stock levels and sales volumes of all items at any time during the day. This gives management the necessary information from which to make decisions that can offer an advantage over competitors. EPOS, in addition to improving information on stock movements, also increases the flexibility and speed with which the organization can change its product prices in relation to demand patterns and competitors' prices.

However, a number of potential problems are associated with the potential tactical and strategic benefits of improved information:

- the scale of such an advantage will tend to narrow as other competitors introduce similar technology and gain access to information of similar quality
- the costs of providing the information need to be offset against the benefits gained from increased revenues and profits and from reduced operating costs
- improving the quality of management information is no guarantee that the resulting decisions will maximize potential competitive advantage.

The following important points should be noted:

- information technology merely provides an opportunity to gain competitive advantage and improve operational efficiency; it does not guarantee results
- significant costs are associated with the application of information technology, not only in the equipment used but in its application and implementation
- the potential advantages that information technology offers are available to all organizations, including competitors. Thus, the real advantage to an organization necessarily arises from both successful initial implementation and sustained management development of information systems within the organization
- investment in better information systems will supply data which can be the source of better-quality information but cannot guarantee success through

better decision making. The quality of such decisions must ultimately depend on the skill and experience of the employees and on their ability to use the information system effectively.

These issues will be developed in subsequent chapters.

Information as a source of added value

Information also provides a potential source of added value to the clients and customers of the organization. The term *added value* in this context refers to the bundle of consumer needs and aspirations that the product or service is intended to satisfy; in other words, the value to be derived by the consumer from the product or service. The consumer will normally be seeking a product or service which will provide the greatest value for the least cost. The organization must therefore seek to identify these perceived sources of value and to find ways of adding to the product's or service's total value while still making a profit. For example, the following sources of information may be exploited in both the short-term (tactical) and the longer-term (strategic) situations:

- information on consumers' needs and their opinions on the organization's current products and services could lead to improvements in product design. Market and consumer research studies, together with the data held by sales personnel, may provide this information
- information on the current developments in materials, design and process technologies could lead to improved product design and quality
- quality may also be enhanced through improved communications between customer service staff and the product design and manufacturing functions, highlighting problems and defects encountered in installation and operation in the field
- improved information flows between the sales and manufacturing functions may improve forecasting and production scheduling activities, resulting in reduced delivery times
- the availability of better-quality information to management on the operations of the business may lead to better resource allocation decisions and greater efficiency, with consequent reduction in costs, improvement in profit margins, and potential reductions in product prices.

These are some of the ways in which information may provide added value to customers, resulting in greater customer satisfaction and potentially enhanced market share and profitability for the organization.

Information as a strategic resource

In addition to the short- and medium-term contribution that it makes to the organization, information also contributes significantly to its strategic development. Strategically orientated components of the organization broadly look towards future markets and usually plan over a timescale of the next five to seven years. Such planning obviously entails higher levels of uncertainty and risk, but if the management can maintain the quality of their information on potential developments and trends in the external environment, this will assist in reducing, though not eliminating, the risk elements. Equally, the availability of techniques and packages to produce rapid evaluations of the likely impact of alternative scenarios and forecasts, or to simulate future business and market operations, will provide the potential for improved strategic decisions. (For more detail, see Chapter 3.)

Information thus provides an organization with potential sources of:

- improved efficiency in resource usage
- cost reduction
- added value
- competitive advantage
- improved effectiveness
- enhanced profitability.

Summary

This chapter provided an outline model of the information system within an organization. This initial model and the associated definitions relating to the role and function of the organization and its information system will be developed more fully in subsequent chapters.

The key points covered in this chapter are the following:

- The primary purpose and objectives of an organization relate to satisfying the needs of its customers and clients.
- Organizations operate in a complex environment which is subject to continuous change and which poses new threats and opportunities.
- The role of management is to integrate resource inputs, activities, processes and structures both effectively and efficiently while maximizing the added value to the customer and client.
- Information systems perform a key role in facilitating the integration process and in supporting management.
- Information itself is a key resource for tactical and strategic decision making and is a potential source of added value.

The distinction between data and information needs to be emphasized. The fundamental role of the field of information analysis and information systems concerns the effective and efficient means of converting data to information for the whole range of users, both within and outside the organization. We have focused in this chapter on enhancing and maintaining the quality of these technological and human-based processes.

Self-test questions

1 List the main elements in an organization's environment and identify one item of data that is related to each of those elements.
2 Describe a situation in which two different users in an organization may use the same data for different purposes.
3 Explain the ways in which information may be used as a strategic resource.
4 List five factors which influence the effectiveness of the process to convert data into information.
5 What are the four main forms in which items of data are held in an organization?

Exam-style questions

1 An information system may be defined as a series of interrelated activities concerned with the conversion of data into information. Briefly discuss an outline model of this conversion process.
2 The objectives formulated by an organization will be affected by a number of factors which will be particular to that organization and its operations. Briefly describe *five* dimensions which may impinge on an organization when it is formulating its objectives.
3 The managing director of Kosmic Travel has recently read an article which suggested that information provides added value to the organization. The company operates coach tours throughout Europe and the UK. The article focused on manufacturing companies and ignored the service sector entirely. The MD has sought your advice on the ways in which the information system in Kosmic Travel might add value to the business. Provide a summary of the key sources of added value which are relevant to the type of business in which Kosmic Travel operates.

(*All answers on pages 545–547*)

CHAPTER 2

Information systems within the organization

Information has been identified as a key resource within an organization. In the previous chapter we developed a broad overview of the nature of organizations and the role of information in the continuing operation and development of the organization. This chapter begins by defining the term *information system* and explores the constituent elements of a general information system model. We then move on to:

- consider the issues associated with the use of information technologies to support the organization's information system and the implications for developing such systems effectively
- examine the main components of information technology (IT) and the nature of their interaction with a view to considering IT as a convergent technology
- use a model of the information systems development process identifying the key stages and their purposes, to structure the remainder of our discussion.

The focus of the chapter then returns to how information is used within an organization. Examining particular functions and activities within the organization leads to the identification and evaluation of reasons for information processing. We give particular attention to a key regular activity in any organization – decision making – assessing the main stages in the decision process and the implications for the organization's information processing. This analysis of the decision-making process will be developed in subsequent chapters by examining particular types of decision and their differing information requirements.

The information system – an outline model

An information system may be broadly defined as a series of interrelated activities concerned with the capture, processing, communication and conversion of data to information. The main groups of activities in an information system are shown in Figure 2.1 overleaf and are briefly described below.

Situation or problem

An information system is typically concerned with providing data on a particular situation or problem of concern to the user or organization. Some systems will be

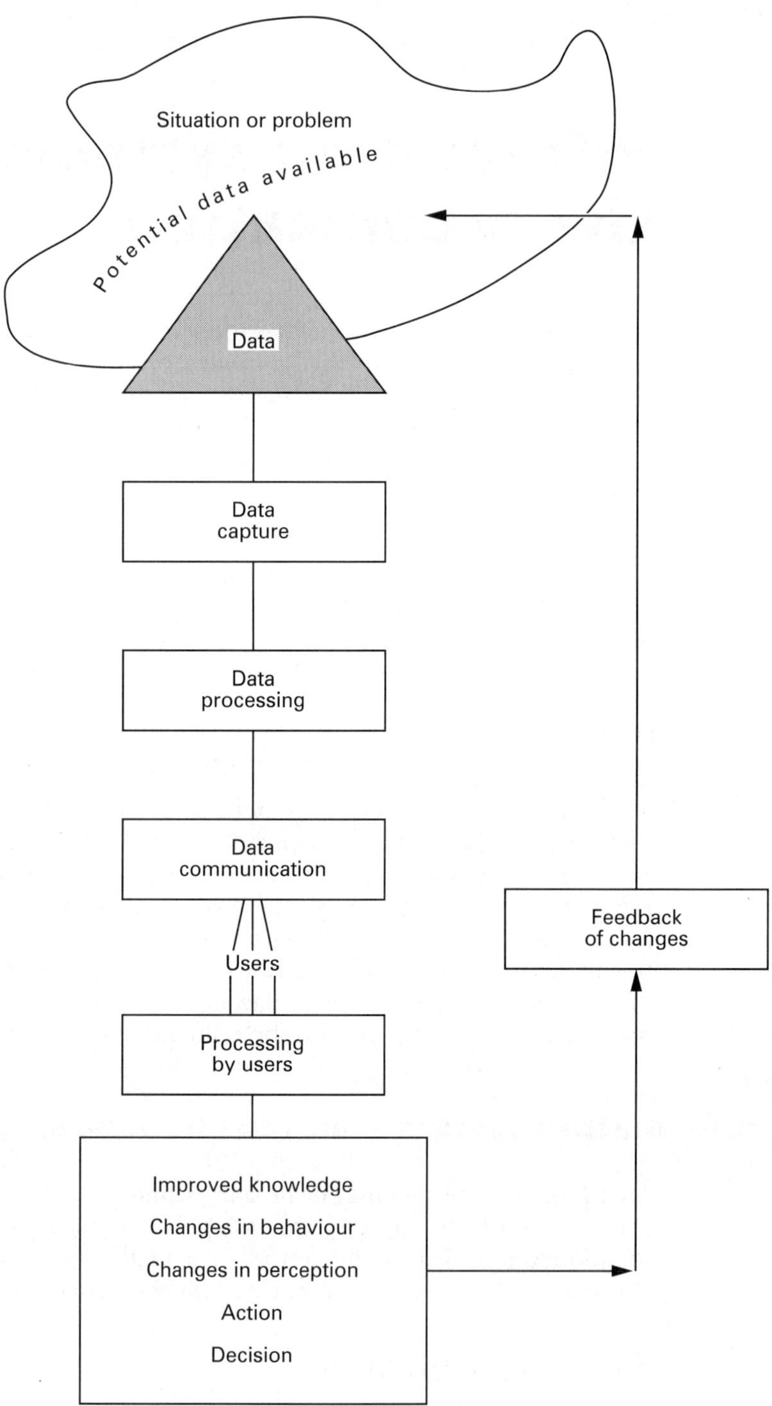

Figure 2.1 The information system: an outline model.

permanent systems, continuously and regularly collecting data relating to a particular situation: a sales order processing system, for example, will continually provide data on the organization's sales. Other systems, transient systems, may be established in response to particular needs of the organization or its users and will continue to operate only while that need remains, for example the collection of data on the effects of a disruption in the supply of key components due to an industrial dispute at the primary supplier.

A transient system may often be established on the basis of data provided by the permanent information system, which identifies a particular problem requiring more detailed data and investigation before a solution can be found. In many respects, it would be preferable to design a system which already contained all the necessary data for particular problems that arise. However, it is clearly not possible for an organization to identify in advance all the problems it is likely to face.

Data

As we saw earlier, any situation will contain a wealth of data varying in its relevance to the user's particular needs and situation. An important element in the design of information systems is establishing clearly what the data needs are for each user and designing the system to segregate the most relevant data from the less relevant or the wholly irrelevant.

Data capture

The term 'data capture' covers the processes of finding the relevant data, recording it and converting it into a suitable form for further processing and eventual communication to the user. For example, a doctor seeking to diagnose a patient's illness uses a variety of devices to measure and identify the symptoms: a thermometer, a sphygmomanometer (for blood pressure readings), and so on. The measurements are then converted to numeric values for further processing. Clearly, the quality of the measuring devices and the conversion processes used are crucial both to the quality of the data provided and to the consequent diagnoses and remedial actions. This is equally true in organizations, where the problems of measurement and diagnosis are often as complex as those facing the medical practitioner

Processing

This term encapsulates a range of actions which may be performed on the data to improve its usefulness to the users. These actions could include:

- **summarizing** – reducing the level of detail
- **arranging or sorting** into a more appropriate order – say, alphabetically or in order of size
- **storing** – collecting the data until an appropriate volume has been acquired prior to transmission to the user

- **calculating** – performing numerical calculations on the data, or converting them into more usable units – for example converting weights of inputs into monetary values
- **selecting** – providing only those data items or events which meet a particular requirement, such as details of all financial transactions exceeding £10,000.

Communications

Communicating the processed data to the user is only part of the overall communications process within the system, as communications are effectively taking place between each stage identified in the diagram. However, communication with *users* is the area that can be most clearly identified in practice. It may be carried out by any of the human senses of sight, hearing, touch or smell, or a simultaneous combination of these senses. The more usual forms of communication are visual and aural, as these senses are more fully developed and responsive in most individuals. However, individuals suffering sight or hearing handicaps often develop very responsive alternative senses to compensate for their loss.

Users

Users are themselves a critical element in the overall information system. Not only are they the primary focus of the data processing activities outlined above, but they are the essential ingredient which converts data to information and information to action through the knowledge, understanding and skills which they bring to bear on the data provided. It is only at the level of the user that the information system actually provides benefit or value to the organization: prior to this the data processing has only been incurring costs.

User processing

The users in any information system will themselves conduct further processing of the information received. In some cases, they will undertake the kind of processing activities that we outlined above: **primary processing**, i.e. calculating, sorting, selecting, and so on. In other cases, the processing activities will be related more to interpretation, application to the specific circumstances, judgement and reasoning: these can be termed **secondary processing.** A good information system ought to minimize the amount of primary information processing that users are required to undertake, allowing them to devote their skills and time to the secondary level. Developments in the field of so-called 'expert systems' are beginning to provide valuable support from the information system for this second level of user processing, particularly in situations where users apply a logical sequence of rules or procedures in arriving at their decisions.

Outcomes

The end product of any information system must be represented in some form of *outcome*. The range of outcomes will vary and may include:

- actions or decisions
- change in a situation, or change in either individual or group behaviour
- improved knowledge and understanding
- a change in the users' perception of a situation.

Ideally, the value of an information system ought to be measured in terms of the value of these outcomes. However, it is difficult to quantify the benefits derived from improved knowledge and understanding: such intangible improvements may not appear to provide any immediate economic advantage but may be evidenced only by implication, through improved performance in future time periods.

Feedback

In situations where the outcome of the information system is a specific action or decision, the user requires some means of assessing the effectiveness of the action or decision taken. This is achieved through the monitoring function of the information system, which feeds the results back to the user. This feedback activity provides the necessary loop back to the start of the outline model of the information system. The sequence of stages is continually repeated with the capture, processing and communication of further data through the system, reflecting the changing situation and problems facing the organization and its users.

Information technologies

Information systems have been (and to a large extent continue to be) dependent on manual processing methods and procedures. However, the continuing application of technologies to processing information in organizations is increasingly revolutionizing both data processing and information systems. The major current and future impact of these technologies is derived from three convergent areas:

1. computer hardware
2. computer software
3. communications.

Developments in each of these technology areas have been very significant in the last decade. The most dramatic advances have been achieved through the increased potential of each of these areas to interact more effectively and efficiently with the others, thereby producing an effect. In other words, their convergence has brought overall benefits which have surpassed those that would have resulted if the technological developments had taken place in isolation from each other.

A fourth element in this synergy is the human dimension. While developments in technology create the potential for more efficient and effective information systems, the realization of this potential depends on the degree to which people are prepared to interact with, or use, the new systems. Unless organizations make adequate plans for implementing new systems, reorientating attitudes to changing work patterns through training and skill development, actual changes in the structure and culture of organizations are unlikely to maximize the potential of the technology. Indeed, this human element may be the most important, because it can often act as a constraint on the realization of the full potential of developments made in the other three areas. A considerable proportion of the work involved in developing, implementing and maintaining information systems therefore revolves around the interface between the human dimension and the other three technological dimensions. We shall devote a considerable part of this text to addressing these issues.

Let us first consider the plus and minus factors that relate to the increased use of information technologies, identifying potential benefits and dangers.

Potential benefits of information technologies

- **Improved efficiency** in terms of time, human resource usage and costs can result in all stages of data processing and transmission, from the data source to the users.
- **Improved quality of information can be** achieved, for example in terms of accuracy, level of detail, timeliness, and so on.
- **Greater flexibility and responsiveness** to user needs can emerge: information systems may more readily be tailored to specific user requirements.
- **Increased access for users to all information** sources, both within and outside the organization, can be significant.
- **Increased efficiency** may be achieved through the sharing of common databases, either within the organization or by using external sources.
- **An enhanced degree of user interaction** may enable managers to specify information and processing needs, and to review and modify these needs as the problem or situation develops.
- **Improved effectiveness of communications** both between members of the organization and with outside organizations and agencies.

Dangers inherent in the increasing use of information technologies

- Ease of data capture and storage may lead to **a less selective approach** to identifying the information needs of users. (Possible consequences of this are high levels of redundant data within the system, and the likelihood that users will be provided with a lot of superfluous data, making the information system less effective.)
- Apparently limitless storage and processing capacity of the technology may result in **less cost-sensitive approaches** to designing and using the information system.
- Sophisticated complex user interfaces may be in advance of the skill and training levels of the personnel, resulting in **reduced levels of total system effectiveness and efficiency**.

- Specialists in system design, development and maintenance may be in danger of losing touch with the needs and expectations of users.
- Enhanced potential for flexibility in designing systems for particular user needs can result in the loss of **common standards and approaches** within an organization, thereby reducing the transferability of information processing skills.
- Improved access to databases and information sources carries with it the major problem of security, raising the issues of limiting access to data that may be considered either sensitive or confidential and preventing fraudulent transactions or acts of sabotage.
- **Decentralization of user access** and interaction with the processing and data sources can exacerbate system management issues. (In earlier times, when all the processing of user data was physically handled by the computer operations staff, for example by packs of punched cards in batch-run systems, the computer services function could monitor directly the type and volume of activity taking place. Today, however, with users accessing central data sources from remote locations, the computer services function has less opportunity to monitor activity.)
- **Increased potential for fraud** may result in systems where the possible risks have not been adequately considered in the development and design process.

Thematic conclusions

Analysing the potential benefits and dangers from the application of information technologies highlights the following fundamental issues which underlie our approach to information systems:

- the development and design of information systems must **integrate user needs fully with the technology** available: system design should be user-driven and not technology-driven
- system development and design should be **planned and managed at the strategic, tactical and operational levels**. Information systems development must be related to the organization's objectives and incorporated within its strategic plans
- to maximize the potential benefits and minimize the potential problems, the information system requires **effective management at all stages** in its development, implementation and continued operation
- information systems must reflect both the changes in the information technologies and the changing requirements of the organization and its users. Therefore, information systems need to be **continually monitored and updated**.

Information systems development model

Figure 2.2 provides an overview of the main areas and issues involved in the development, operation and maintenance of information systems in organizations.

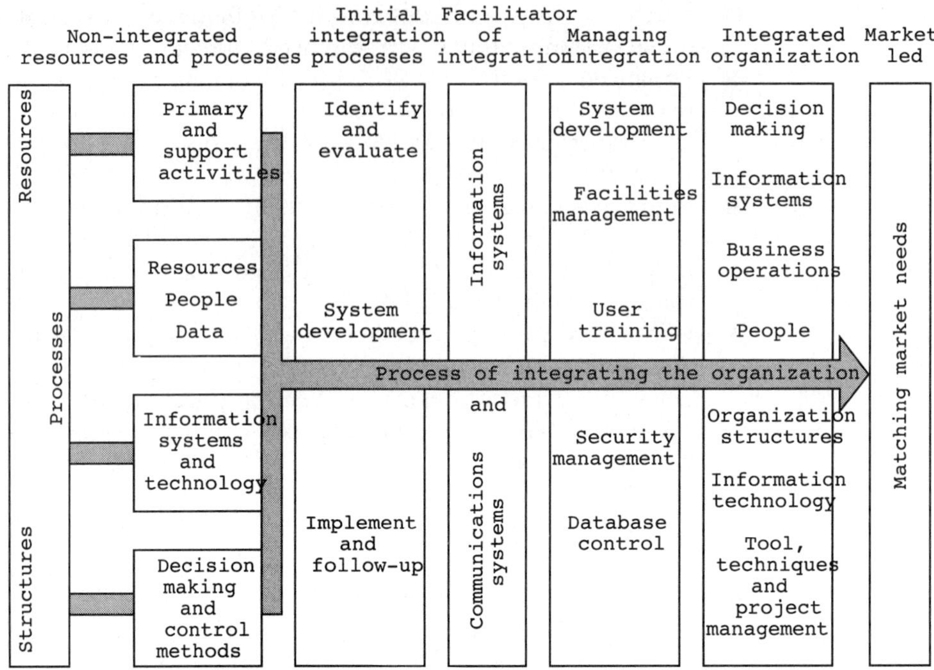

Figure 2.2 Information systems development model.

The model views information and the systems which deliver this information as key elements in the process of ensuring organizational integration, which is essential to achieving general efficiency and effectiveness. The major features of this model are outlined in the following paragraphs; a more detailed treatment of each of the areas is given in subsequent chapters.

Market-led

The primary purpose of any organization is to meet the needs of its market or clients. This applies both to profit-orientated and to not-for-profit-orientated organizations. The broad aim of all management is to optimize organizational structure, resources and operations to achieve effectiveness and efficiency in meeting market needs and in satisfying corporate purposes and objectives. The primary function of an information system in this context is to support the organization, its management and employees in meeting this broad aim.

It is important to note at this stage that the strategic development of information systems should be primarily dictated by the needs of the market, the organization's objectives and the requirements of users within the organization. The systems development strategy should not be dictated by developments in the information technologies themselves, as such developments may not be consistent with the needs of the market, the organization or its users. Many organizations have based their systems development strategies on current technological developments, only to find that they have performed less effectively and efficiently. In many cases this is because the technology has been in advance of the capacity of the organization or its users to employ or apply the latest facilities effectively.

Non-integrated resources and processes

An organization essentially comprises a series of resources, processes and structures:

- **resources**: finance, people, land, buildings, equipment, raw materials, and technical and professional services
- **processes**: a range of activities (classified in the previous chapter as primary and support activities) encompassing the production operations, decision making, planning and control. Organizations have developed a battery of procedures, tools and techniques to assist in these activities and in the general management of the processes and resources involved
- **structures**: organizations also develop a variety of structures to improve the effectiveness and efficiency of resource utilization and management of the processes. The more obvious of such structures are the division of the organization into specialist functions – marketing, finance, production, and so on, each responsible for managing particular aspects of the organization's resources and processes. Such structures may take a number of different forms, as we shall show in detail later in this chapter.

The key elements from these groups in terms of information systems development are:

- the needs of the primary and support activities
- the resources available: people, data, and so on
- management, control and decision-making requirements
- the information systems and the technology available.

Initial integration processes

The initial stages in achieving organizational integration involve the development and design of the organization's information systems.

1. **Identification and evaluation.** Analysis of the organization's information requirements is the first stage in the integration process. It is important that this process is focused on the *actual requirements* of individual users or groups of users, as opposed to merely assessing their *likely* requirements. Indeed, the whole process of systems development needs to be orientated towards user requirements from the outset and should actively involve users in the overall process. This links to the key areas identified in the previous paragraph of understanding the needs of primary and support activities, management and control requirements, and the people in the organization.
2. **Systems development**. Generally, the systems development process is concerned with matching user requirements with the potential of the technology and the data available in the most effective and efficient manner possible.

3 **Implementation, evaluation and follow-up**. The inclusion of this stage in the integration process recognizes two priorities: the importance of the *initial implementation* of an information system or sub-system, and the need to continually *review the effectiveness* of the system once it is operational. In Chapter 1 we highlighted the dynamic nature of the environment in which organizations operate. In this situation it is likely that the issues and problems faced by the organization and its members will be subject to a process of continual change, resulting in changing information requirements.
4 **Systems life cycle (SLC)**. The process of change in the situation, issues and problems facing the organization also suggests that an information system will only have a limited life cycle. The SLC concept (discussed in detail in Chapter 8) reflects this aspect, suggesting that the value of the contribution made by an information system will change as time progresses and the organizational situation changes.
5 **Facilitating integration**. The development of information and communication systems within an organization provides the potential to achieve integration. These facilities create the opportunity for the effective exchange and flow of information between users and between the organization and its environment.
6 **Managing integration**. While such information and communication systems development facilitates integration, the realization of this potential requires that these systems are effectively managed. There is hence an important functional responsibility for the overall planning, development, co-ordination and maintenance of the systems. This relates not only to computer facilities and software but to the overall management of organizational data and information flows, to system security and to the training and support of users.

The integrated organization

The outcome of the integration process based on information systems development will be an integrated organization, in which:

- problems and issues are identified at an early stage
- decisions can be taken quickly and effectively on the basis of high-quality information
- relevant information may be accessed easily and quickly to analyse decisions and decision-makers have the necessary decision support tools for this analysis
- effective communications structure permits the involvement of all appropriate people in the decision-making process
- decisions are communicated quickly and effectively in terms of new policies, guidelines, etc., allowing speedy responses to problems
- activities in diverse parts of the organization are co-ordinated more effectively with each other
- the organization is receptive and responsive to change: new systems, processes and structures may be developed and implemented rapidly and effectively in response to changing needs

- performance measurement systems are sufficiently responsive and accurate to identify early deviations from planned performance levels or objectives.

The key to achieving an integrated organization is effective information systems development, supported by continuing maintenance and sympathetic management. The achievement of this objective requires support and commitment from all members of the organization.

Uses of information

The overall use of information within any organization can be divided into the following categories:

- recording transactions
- decision making
- planning
- performance measurement
- control
- communications.

The way in which information is used in each of these activities is described in the following paragraphs.

Recording transactions

The overall process of producing and delivering goods or services to the customer or client may be viewed as an interdependent sequence of transactions or activities. Yet when we judge the nature of this process, we cannot view the organization in the abstract: it must be seen as an integral part of the environment. Thus, the range of transactions and activities encompasses both the organization's relationships with *external* organizations and persons and the *internal* operations of the organization itself. Recording the details of each of these transactions is necessary because:

- It provides a way of evidencing the nature and content of transactions with other organizations and individuals, including suppliers, customers, shareholders and employees. In some cases, there will be positive legal obligations to keep this information – a register of shareholders, for instance – but generally it is merely an advisable step: in any subsequent dispute, it reduces the risk of a court finding good records more credible and directing suspicion towards organizations with poor records.
- It allows the organization to monitor levels of resource availability and usage at various stages in the production or supply processes.
- It potentially enables the organization to identify the costs and revenues associated with each particular transaction or activity, and to attribute these to the final unit of production or service delivered to the customer or client.
- After the event, it provides recorded evidence of transactions for the purposes of accounting, auditing and, where appropriate, tax assessment.

- The quality of the record keeping and the way in which that information is used to 'image' the organization – to present or represent the organization to the public – is one of the main methods of assuring shareholders and other capital suppliers of the safety and stewardship of their capital. This also applies to state-based and nationalized organizations, which may be seen as custodians of capital from the public purse.

The process of recording transactions within an organization may be divided between the primary and the support activities involved. The distinction between these two groups of activities was presented in Chapter 1. Figure 2.3 presents an outline schematic flowchart to show the major sub-groups of primary activities conducted in an organization.

The function of **transaction processing** is concerned with recording, processing and communicating data relating to the primary and support activities involved in converting input resources into goods and services to meet customer needs. The dimensions of this data include quantitative, qualitative and financial aspects.

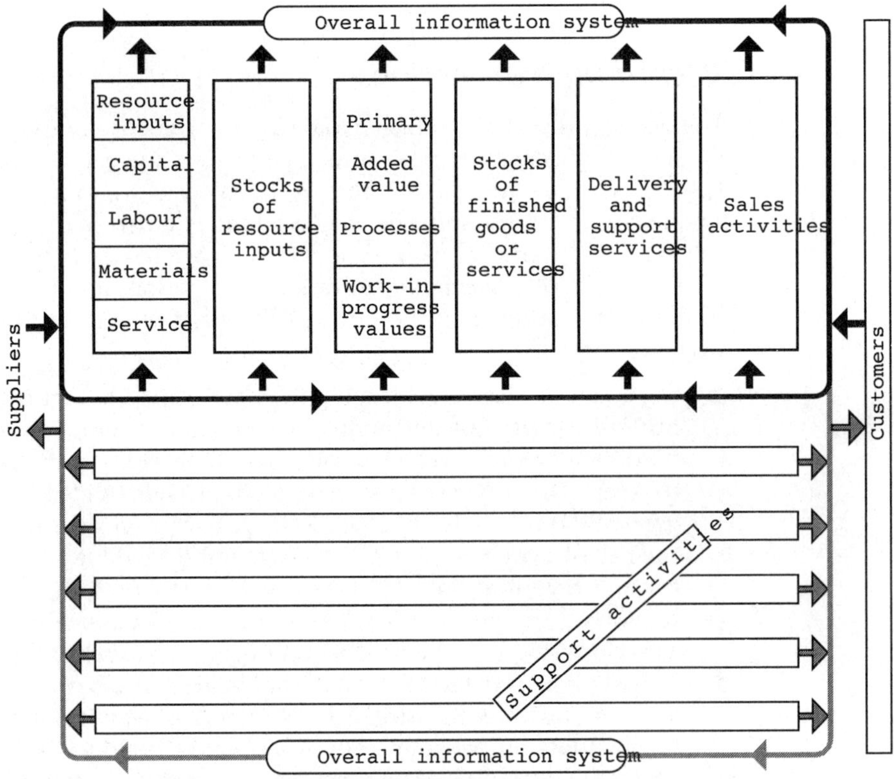

Figure 2.3 Transaction processing in the information system.

Purchasing transactions

Every organization has some degree of involvement in the activity of purchasing (or otherwise legitimately acquiring) resource inputs from outside sources. These inputs may be conveniently grouped under four headings:

- materials
- services
- labour
- capital.

In all these cases there will be some form of contractual or commercial transaction between the organization and the supplier. It is necessary to record these transactions (for the reasons outlined earlier) and to identify both the costs of the resources acquired and the costs of making the transaction.

Resource stocks

Resources acquired through the purchasing activities will not always enter the first stage of the primary processing operations immediately but will be stocked until such time as they are required. In essence, stocks of resource inputs can be viewed as a 'buffer' between the purchase transactions and the primary operations of the business. This buffer helps to ensure operational continuity in the event of delays or interruptions in the supply of inputs. Stocks are also a reflection of the economic factors involved in the buying transactions: it may prove more cost-effective for the organization to use its purchasing power to order large quantities, on an infrequent basis at high discount rates and on longer periods of credit, than small quantities on a more frequent basis but less favourable terms.

Maintaining information on current quantities and changes in stock levels is important because:

- it enables the organization to assess the quantity of particular items currently held in stock and to trigger off the purchasing process when these levels reach some predetermined minimum level, set in the knowledge of the time usually taken to restock the item
- it provides an indication of the percentage value of the organization's circulating resources held in that form, and of the cost of financing that investment
- it allows the organization to monitor the level of risk of dislocation to its functions and operations related to potential shortages of input resources.

Most organizations recognize the significant potential value of the capital resources invested in stocks. But this may equally be viewed as idle capital. The problem is that stocks represent an accumulation of resources and added value which the organization has paid for but which remain an unrealized investment. Apart from the direct financing costs involved in providing this idle capital, there may also be an **opportunity cost** in terms of the return that could be generated from the capital if it were in more immediately productive use. As a result, close attention has been given to improving the efficiency of purchasing transactions in terms of creating a continuous, regular and uninterrupted flow of inputs from suppliers. This may significantly diminish the level of investment in stocks of resources, reduce financing costs and release capital for more productive purposes. The 'just-in-time' supply systems developed by motor vehicle manufacturers involve a continuous flow of input components to the vehicle assembly plants, such that only a few hours of key resource inputs are held in stock at any time by the manufacturer. The importance of information monitoring in regard to these flows and stocks of resources is obvious, particularly as such systems expose production operations to higher risks of interruption due to delays in supplies.

The definition of resource stocks is not limited to materials and components used directly in the production operations. It must also include **capital**. Capital stocks may be represented by cash balances held in the organization itself or in its bank accounts. These stocks represent a buffer in exactly the same way as raw materials, this time standing between the purchasing and sales activities. Thus, the transactions with suppliers incur an outflow of cash payments, and the transactions with customers cause an inflow of cash receipts – yet the amounts are most unlikely to match each other in either size or timing. The organization needs cash balances to provide for potential excesses of cash outflows over inflows. It is to be hoped that these cash balances will accumulate as a result of an excess of inflows over outflows at other periods. The problem is that these cash balances, whether held as cash or bank balances, may also be viewed as idle capital as they are not generating returns equivalent to the funds invested in the organization's more productive assets.

The organization's capital may also be invested in fixed assets, including land, buildings, plant and machinery, which cumulatively represent stocks of production capacity. Information on the value, location and utilization of fixed assets is required to identify the distribution of the capital funds and to ensure their efficient utilization.

Finally, the employees represent another form of resource input which may also be reflected as a form of production capacity and in stocks of unused capacity. For example, the idle time or the under-utilized skills and abilities of employees may be considered as a form of stock worth recording.

Primary added value processes

The primary added value processes are those which are concerned with converting the resource inputs into the product outputs of the organization in the form of goods and/or services. An organization will normally be interested in recording data on these operations in terms of the quantities and costs of the labour, materials and other resources which have been input to the operations, as a basis for:

1 accumulating the costs, either for assessing and fixing the prices or for deciding what constitutes a reasonable profit margin on the products or services
2 measuring the efficiency of the individual component stages or of the whole process.

The type and quality of the information collected on this group of transaction activities will be determined by the nature of the production processes employed. These may be classified into three groups:

1. **Job processing**. This makes a single product unit the focus of attention. The organization follows the production of a single identifiable item through each of the processing stages, creating the option that the costs of resource inputs used at each stage may be charged (recorded) directly to each item or job. Each job is usually allocated a unique reference number or 'job number' and will often be related to a specific customer's order.
2. **Batch processing**. Identical product items are processed as a group through each of the processing stages. The products in each batch may be associated with the same customer's order or may relate to orders for several different customers. The usual reason advanced for batch processing is that there may be variations in the production operations required to produce either completely different products or variations on the same product design. The costs associated with preparing the machinery for each new product type or variation may make it more efficient to process a number of similar items before adjusting the machinery for the next type of product. For example, in a car plant it is clearly more efficient to paint all the 'batched' blue cars consecutively before spending time in cleaning the spray gun and changing the paint supply to paint the red cars, as opposed to undertaking these operations separately after each car is sprayed in the required colour. The data on the costs of resources used in the production operations are collected and charged to each batch of items processed. The cost of individual items would normally be assessed from the average cost of the batch produced.
3. **Flow-line or process**. This mode is used either where all the product output is the same, or where it is difficult and not cost-effective to separate the output into identifiable units. Examples include the manufacture of chemicals, nuts and bolts, and confectionery products or the provision of banking services. Costs in such cases are usually averaged over the total volume of output produced in a given time period. Efficiency measurements would also be related to the resource inputs required to produce a particular volume of outputs.

Different product costing systems have been developed to cater for each of these three types of production operations. In some organizations, it is likely that there will be a combination of two or more of these types applying to different stages of the total manufacturing or service supply process. The manufacture of mainframe computers, for example, may incorporate the following:

1. **process**: the manufacture of small transistors, capacitors and other electronic components used in computer hardware will typically involve the production of a large volume of similar components
2. **batch**: the assembly of printed circuit boards containing these electronic components. The manufacturer will assemble a variety of boards in different quantities, depending on the particular functions that each board is required to perform. Each board is likely to use the same basic components, albeit in different design configurations

3 **job**: the printed circuit boards, along with other components, will then be used to assemble the mainframe computers. Some computers may be made for stock, others may be made to order. Each of the computers which are made to order is likely to vary in terms of the composition of boards and components, depending on customer requirements, although the scale and the nature of the assembly processes would enable each item to be identified and charged against each customer's order.

The mainframe computer manufacturer in this situation may be interested in the following types of information.

Cost information

This will be determined by reference to the following elements:

- the cost of all the components used in assembling each computer: transistors, printed circuit boards, wiring, cabinets, and so on
- the labour costs involved in each stage of the manufacturing and assembly process
- the time required on each piece of plant and equipment to assess the proportion of capital costs that may be allocated to the particular product
- the degree to which the organization's support and other services are used as a basis for assessing the level of overhead costs to charge to each computer.

Efficiency measurement

The organization will be able to assess efficiency by referring to the following types of performance indicator:

- the quantity of components wasted or rejected as faulty
- the labour and machine time taken for each stage of the assembly process, often measured against a predetermined standard for the type of product
- the quantity of defects found in the finished computers which require correction or further working, and the cost of this work
- the percentage utilization of plant and equipment capacity, and data on breakdowns of plant.

The value of the resources currently committed to the production process, commonly termed **work in progress**, is also important for calculating the level of value added by the organization. The valuation process for work in progress is equally applicable to both manufacturing and service organizations – the latter requiring some assessment of the proportion which each task in hand represents of the total service provided at a particular stage in time.

Finished goods stocks

Products completing the phases of the production operations will usually become part of the finished goods stocks. As with the stocks of input resources, the finished goods stocks represent a buffer between the primary activities of the organization and outside agencies. These agencies are usually the customers or clients of the organization. The maintenance of such stocks is necessary:

- to enable the organization to respond quickly to customer requirements for particular products, which may represent an important element in the total service and added value provided to the customer
- to provide for fluctuations in demand from the market, if the pattern of market demand is likely to be uneven due to seasonal effects or unexpected variations. (Failure to maintain stocks may result in the loss of sales, particularly if the lead-times required to manufacture and deliver the products are lengthy)
- to maintain an even level of production activity or to ensure the full utilization of production capacity.

As with stocks of input resources, information on quantities and changes in stock levels is important in terms of:

- assessing the quantity of particular items held in stock, and triggering off the production process to replenish stocks when these reach a given minimum level
- providing an indication of the value of capital resources invested and the associated financing opportunity costs
- monitoring the level of risk of dislocation to the organization's sales operations and revenue generation should products or stimulus materials, for example catalogues and brochures, be out of stock.

Some organizations – shipbuilders, for example – operate their activities on the basis of only producing goods to customer orders received, which would mean that every product in the production process is designated for a particular customer. However, except in the most extreme cases, there are likely to be stocks of finished goods either awaiting completion of other goods in that order or awaiting delivery to the customer.

Delivery and support activities

From the customer's point of view, the most important features of an organization's performance, apart from the quality of the product itself, are often the delivery, installation, maintenance and general after-sales support that goes with the product. The organization will require information to monitor the costs, efficiency and effectiveness of these activities. For this purpose, its information requirements may include:

- delivery schedules, times, routes and transport costs
- if appropriate, the length of time required to install the product at a place selected by the purchaser or service receiver, and the level of any training provided to those who are to use it
- the frequency and cost of maintenance or fault-repair visits to each customer site
- the nature of the problems encountered and the general quality of the after-sales support services provided.

Sales activities

In practice, sales activities may be involved at a number of different stages in the sequence of primary activities. The customer's agreement to purchase occurs early in the sequence, and post-delivery follow-up at the end. However, to simplify the model we have used and our discussion, we shall deal with all these sales activities together at this stage. The sales activities reflect a series of transactions with existing customers of the organization as well as its potential customers. Recording the details of commercial transactions with the customer is important to the organization because it provides information on:

- the nature of the contractual rights and obligations incurred by both the seller and the buyer. (This can be particularly important, say, if the selling organization has attempted to protect its position by reserving ownership of the goods pending payment of the price by using a **Romalpa clause** in a standard form contract)
- specification of the customer's requirements which are to be met:
  (a) from existing stock
  (b) by modifying existing stock
  (c) through the primary production operations
- possible demand for resource inputs necessary to complete the order, and identification of shortages resulting from the satisfaction of the order which require replacement purchasing
- the quantities, prices and discounts agreed to facilitate the preparation of accounting records and initiate other accounting and support activities
- where appropriate, the delivery destination(s) and any other arrangements for installation and training, and so on
- the purchasing activities of the particular customer to assist the sales department's customer monitoring and progressing activities
- the transaction itself for other external purposes, for example auditing and tax assessment.

The organization will also be interested in measuring the costs involved in the sales activities, their level of efficiency and effectiveness.

An organization's information system will in aggregate terms be receiving data inputs from and transmitting to each of the six broad groups of primary activities identified in Figure 2.1. This data flow will be both concurrent and continuous across each of these groups. Figure 2.3 was designed primarily to highlight the overall transaction-based information system and its main components, and as such omits details of the essential information flows both between and within the groups. These *inter-group* and *intra-group* information flows represent the organizational linkages explained in Chapter 1. The examples given earlier in this sub-section should indicate that the information flows occur not only between adjacent activity groups but between all the activity groups illustrated in the diagram.

Support activities

The other activities which support the primary activities outlined above have been added to the primary activities in the previous diagram, as shown in Figure 2.4.

Some of the support activities are involved in directly underpinning the individual primary activities or the general operation of the organization's affairs, while others are concerned with the more general aspects of planning, decision making and performance measurement. These latter activities will be discussed under the corresponding headings later in this section. The operations and services involved in supporting the primary activities include:

1 **Marketing services.** Because commercial organizations only survive by identifying and satisfying the market, it is debatable whether this is properly a support activity. It may be better to view it as a major part of the strategic planning effort of the organization. However, pending resolution of this debate, the services comprise:
   - researching customer needs and market trends
   - planning, implementing and controlling product development, distribution channels, pricing policies, advertising and promotional strategies and other activities associated with identifying and satisfying consumer needs.

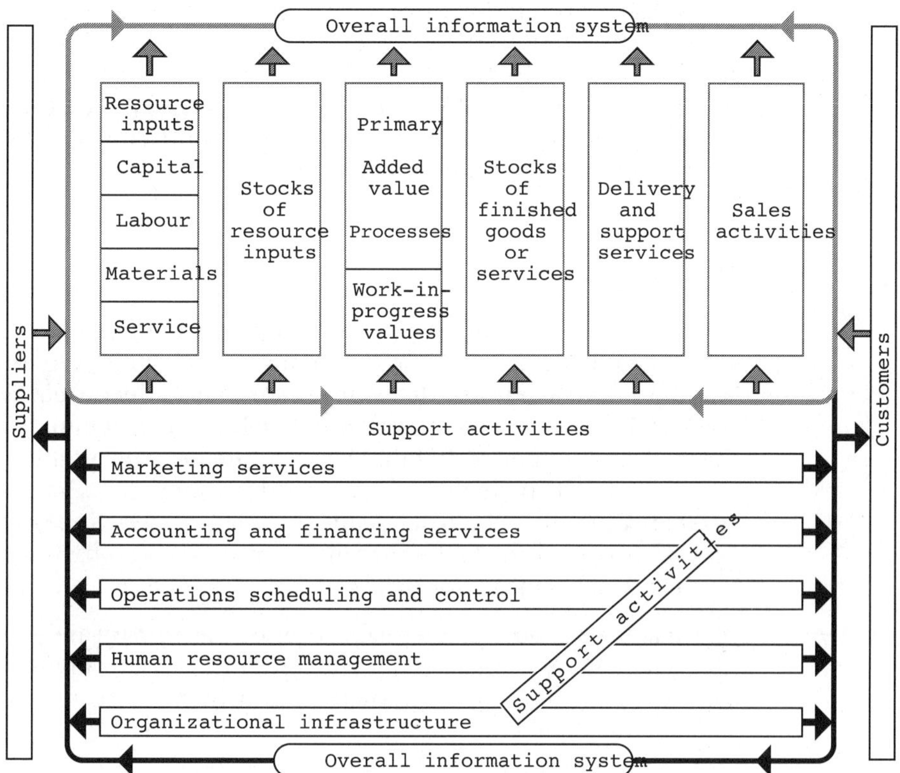

Figure 2.4 Transaction processing and the information system.

2 **Accounting and financial services** are clearly support activities and include:
   - the routine recording of purchases and the arrangement of payment for resource inputs and services
   - the raising of invoices for sales, controlling credit and progressing payment
   - ensuring that adequate funds are available at the appropriate time to make wage and salary payments for the labour resources used
   - monitoring the percentage of capital resources used effectively within the organization, and paying for all the resources in use.

3 **Operations scheduling and control** activities include:
   - planning and co-ordinating the various primary activities involved in the production process
   - establishing processing priorities for particular orders.

4 **Human resource management (personnel)** activities are now recognized as increasingly important as organizations seek to optimize their investment in human skills. The services include:
   - recruitment and training of the required personnel resources
   - providing the necessary support systems, such as medical, safety and catering services, to maintain the effectiveness and skills of the labour force
   - ensuring that proper staff development is maintained by providing continuing training and maintaining morale by seeking to ensure proper career development and advancement.

5 **Organizational infrastructure** comprises:
   - the practical activities of planning, developing and administering the organization's fixed capital resources (such as buildings and plant)
   - the less tangible (but equally necessary) resources such as those structures, systems and processes which facilitate the effective operation of both the primary and other support activities.

Cashflows

One dimension of the primary and support activities, which is not reflected in the diagram but necessarily has a significant effect on every organization, is the cashflow associated with the various operations undertaken. The overall flow of cash within the cycle of operations is a reflection, in summarized form, of all the primary and support activities. The aggregate cashflow position is compiled from data inputs which are derived from all the activities outlined above. In addition to recording the financial value of each transaction involved, **cashflow accounting** necessitates the recording of details on the timing of all the cash receipts and payments, including:

- materials, labour and services acquired for primary and support operations
- purchases of capital equipment and/or the leasing and rental charges
- payments for capital resources used, which would include interest charges and dividend payments
- receipts from the sales of goods and services.

Decision making

We now come to consider decision making in general terms, incorporating all the types and levels of decision in the organization. (The next chapter develops this further by distinguishing between the different levels or types of decision and examining their consequences for the information requirement.)

The importance of information to the decision-making process cannot be overstated. Indeed, 'The entire decision-making process can be viewed as the acquisition and processing of information' (MacCrimmon, 1977). For these purposes, the term *decision* may be defined in a number of different ways, often reflecting the situation in which the decision is taking place. However, a broad definition of the term for the purposes of our current discussion would be:

A decision is a process or a sequence of activities undertaken by an individual or groups with a view to establishing and implementing a solution to an existing or potential problem.

Three features of this definition are worth stressing:

1 decision making is a process or a sequence of activities which will not always take place in a continuous or uninterrupted fashion
2 the taking of decisions is both an individual and a group activity, with the latter likely to be more common in most organizations
3 decisions may be taken in a proactive stance for preparing solutions to potential future problems, as well as a reactive stance for resolving existing problems.

Figure 2.5 overleaf provides an outline of the main stages in the decision-making process and identifies the information inputs associated with each of them.

The decision trigger

Every decision process requires some factor to trigger or initiate the process. Data/information is the most likely trigger. For example:

- information identifying defects in components purchased ought to trigger an examination of the quality standards maintained by the particular supplier and might lead to a decision to change suppliers
- information revealing increasingly high stock levels of certain finished goods may trigger an evaluation of market demands and production levels for the product, leading to future changes in pricing, promotional or production policies
- information on future changes may also initiate the decision process. Thus, a proposal to change the technology used to produce the organization's products may require decisions on financing the capital investment, on amending the marketing policies to reflect the modernization of plant and/or product, and on training the staff who will be associated with the new technology implementation.

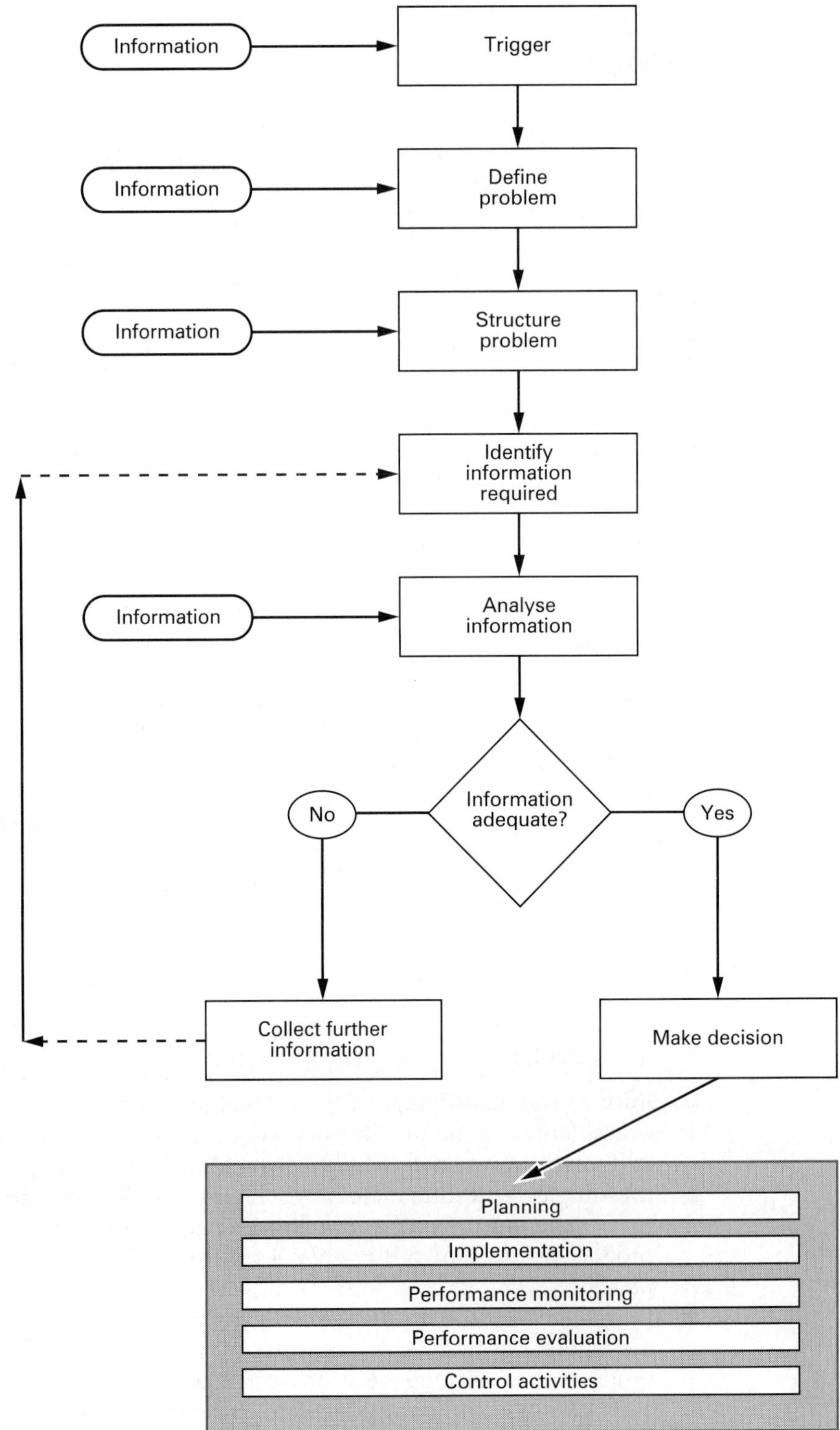

Figure 2.5 Stages in the decision-making process.

Problem definition

Having initiated the decision-making process, we may then need to define the cause of the problem. The important issue at this stage is to differentiate between cause and effect. While decision-makers may be only too aware of the effect of particular problems on the running of the organization, the effectiveness of their proposed solution will depend on how well they have identified and understood the root causal factors. For example, a reduction in the level of sales revenue may be caused by any number of factors, including changes in the total size of the market, changing consumer needs, competitors' actions influencing both price and quantity of sales, and an increase in customer dissatisfaction due to poor-quality products or support services.

The problems encountered in practice are typically complex, in the sense that there are usually several causal factors involved. Further, each factor is likely to interact with one or more of the others, making the effects of any individual factor difficult to assess. Time is also a vital variable, as the importance of individual factors may vary as the organization's situation changes. Thus, even as the decision-maker is defining the current problem, the nature of the problem may itself be changing owing to changes in the external environment. In the sales revenue example we gave earlier, the primary causal factors may have been established as the competitors' pricing policies and customer dissatisfaction with quality standards. Competitors' lower prices alone would have some effect on sales revenues, but when these are combined with customer dissatisfaction the reduction in sales may be considerably greater than if the quality standards were high. Continual changes in competitors' prices will result in a dynamic as well as a complex problem situation. In these situations, decision-makers not only need the initial information to establish the relevant causal factors but require this information continually updated to reflect changes in the problem situation.

Problem structuring

Defining the problem in terms of the primary causal factors provides the basis on which to structure the problem. This may take the form of constructing a model of the problem, highlighting the important dimensions, the scope of the analysis required and the possible types of solution. Continuing the sales revenue example above, and assuming that the problem is defined primarily as competitors' actions, we may structure the problem in terms of:

- which competitors to consider
- the parts of their activities which have some relevance to the problem
- the markets and products involved.

Once this has been done, it becomes easier to make decisions as to which techniques and tools are appropriate for analysing and resolving the situation. Two fundamental issues arise at this point.

Models

The term *model* as used in the context of problem structuring may be defined in a number of ways:

1 **The physical model**: a two-dimensional or three-dimensional drawing or physical representation of the decision problem, for example a graph showing the sales revenues of competitors in the market over the last three years, or a model of a proposed plant layout incorporating new technology features.
2 **The symbolic model**: a representation of the problem situation using symbols, equations or mathematical formulae. An example is the use of regression analysis methods to identify and express the trends in sales revenue.
3 **The conceptual model**: a representation of the situation in a less specific form, often in the mind of the decision-maker, and exploiting the available knowledge and experience of those involved. For example, the previous experience of the decision-maker may suggest the most likely reactions of the competitors to changes in price or to promotional activities undertaken by the organization. This experience may be difficult to capture in either a physical or symbolic type of model. However, as you will see later, many of the developments in supporting decision-makers are increasingly focusing on methods to capture and represent such models in a form suitable for analytical appraisal. Advances in spreadsheet software packages have provided one such vehicle for these developments.

Objectives

A vital element in structuring the problem situation is a clear and explicit understanding of the objectives which the decision is seeking to achieve. These objectives may be expressed in a number of different ways for a given decision situation. For example, in the declining sales revenue case referred to earlier, the objectives may be expressed as:

- to prevent any further decline in sales revenue
- to redress the decline in sales revenue to previous levels
- to achieve a 5% increase on the previous levels of sales prior to the decline.

Each of these objectives may be further qualified in terms of, say, the requirement that the objective should be achieved without any reduction in the profit margins per unit, or within the current sales and marketing budgets. The objectives thus not only determine the broad parameters of the potential solutions and the criteria against which each potential solution should be judged but also indicate the type and quality of information required and the depth of analysis which must be performed to verify which of the proposed solutions is most likely to succeed.

Information requirements

The major by-product from the structuring of the problem is the identification (at least initially) of:

- the information required to analyse those aspects or dimensions of the problem that are seen as important
- the information required to evaluate possible alternative solutions to the situation.

To continue our sales revenue example, the decision-maker may identify the initial information required as:

- the sales patterns for the product over the last two years
- the market shares of the organization and of each major competitor
- the organization's pricing levels over this period
- the prices of, say, the three major competitors' products over a similar period
- the cost structure of the product and the resulting profit margins.

The key factor in this identification process is the definition of the type and quality of information that will be required to support the decision making. There are many possible dimensions to information quality, including variables such as the level of detail and the degree of accuracy and reliability in the initial data. In certain cases, detailed and accurate costs and other financial information may be required to support decisions on changes to product pricing structures, while in other cases broad estimates of costs and margins may prove sufficient. This aspect of the different qualitative dimensions of the information required for different decisions will be outlined in Chapter 3.

Information analysis

The analysis of the information specified is undertaken by the decision-maker. It will involve both quantitative and qualitative approaches.

Quantitative approaches may include statistical methods such as graphical trend plotting, regression analysis or correlation analysis. This process need not be automated, and the analysis may involve a series of manual data processing activities including the sorting, coding, selection and summarizing of the data available. Following this analysis, the decision-maker may apply predetermined criteria in evaluating the situation and/or undertake some degree of **subjective evaluation** of the results produced in relation to the situation.

Adequacy of information

An integral part of the process is an evaluation by those involved in taking the decision as to whether or not the information presently available is adequate to enable the decision to be made. If the decision-makers consider that the information is inadequate, they will specify the further information required and arrange for its collection and subsequent analysis. This is represented by the loop (the dotted line) in Figure 2.5. Requests for further information may be the result of one or more of the following:

1. identifying a lack of data concerning certain dimensions of the problem. This may be due to poor initial problem specification, to inadequate information collection or to the subsequent appreciation of the importance of particular factors

2 the poor quality of the information provided – an issue addressed more fully later in this chapter
3 recognizing the need to search for further information to support and confirm a tentative decision already taken
4 a deliberate action to delay the decision and its implementation pending an assessment of potential reactions internally and externally. This may involve the decision-makers in requesting additional information that is unlikely to influence the decision taken to any significant extent.

This assessment of whether the available information is adequate should also be considered in cost–benefit terms. The decision-makers should assess the likely costs and the feasibility of collecting further information against the potential benefits arising from the above list. However, it is most unlikely in practice that the decision-makers will ever achieve the state in which there is perfect information about all the relevant dimensions of the problem situation. The primary difficulty in practice is that the greater the level of information quality specified by the decision-maker, the greater the cost of producing it is likely to be. When it comes to justifying this high level of cost, it will be recognized that it is difficult to assess the potential benefits of the additional information. Decision-makers commonly make subjective approximations, asserting that the additional information may be useful. But it will usually be impossible to quantify this value or usefulness in advance, and it may not even be possible to do so after receiving the information. The reason for this difficulty is that additional information will probably only have a marginal effect, often doing no more than providing confirmation of the decision already taken. So, while it may be argued that decision-makers ought to continue to collect and analyse additional information until the marginal benefit derived from the last item of information received equates to the cost of providing that information, decision-makers are in practice unable to achieve this through their inability to quantify the marginal costs and benefits.

Decision taking

At some stage in this process, the decision-maker will proceed to the *decision-taking* stage. Arrival at this moment may be at the natural conclusion of an exhaustive analytical process, or it may be more premature. Decisions are often hurried because:

- a deadline has been set, or the decision-maker is reacting to other less formal time pressures which make it expedient to produce a solution, even though it is known to be less than perfect
- there may be no further information or analytical methods easily available
- the decision-maker may be too tired to continue
- more pressing problems may require attention.

Sadly, in these more competitive times, the premature rather than the exhaustive response is likely to be the norm in practical business. The concluding decisions are taken because it is considered inexpedient and uneconomic to take no decision. They may be a positive response, in terms of a particular action proposed, or a more negative or passive response, by deciding not to take any action.

In summary, information contributes to the decision-making process as:

- a trigger to initiate the process
- a resource to facilitate the definition and structuring of the problem situation
- a resource to aid the evaluation of the proposed decision
- a vehicle to communicate the decision to others and to provide a basis for implementing the decision
- a basis for feeding back the results of a decision to facilitate performance monitoring and control during the implementation and subsequent running of the planned responses.

Programmable and non-programmable decisions

A further distinction has important implications for an organization's information requirements. Decisions may be classified as either **programmable**, highly structured decisions, or **non-programmable**, highly unstructured decisions. In the case of programmable decisions, the problem situations are generally predictable and so the decision-making activities of problem definition, structuring, analysis and resolution may be specified or programmed in advance. The solution will normally depend on the application of **algorithms**.

Programmable decisions are usually those which:

- occur relatively frequently
- require the consideration of only a few factors which may be incorporated in a predetermined structure
- display relatively simple interrelationships between the various factors
- have a limited and predictable range of possible solutions
- have decision criteria that may be explicitly stated and easily applied to selecting the most appropriate solution from the limited range.

Examples of programmable decisions include:

- the credit rating of new customers
- quality control inspection
- equipment maintenance
- delivery scheduling.

If the organization is able to develop suitable algorithms (i.e. formalistic rules) for each general decision-making situation, the information requirements will be readily identifiable in advance and, given the frequency with which such decisions are likely to occur, the organization would probably incorporate the collection of the necessary information as part of the routine transaction information system outlined earlier in this chapter. An alternative term for programmable decisions is routine decisions.

Non-programmable decisions are usually less routine and less predictable in at least one of the stages of the decision process. They may, for example, require novel approaches to defining, structuring or analysing the problem situation, and require the decision-maker to develop and formulate the criteria to be used in selecting the best solution strategy. This involves the application of heuristics (a system of making choices using non-linear methods). Examples of such decisions include:

- fixing the pricing policy for a new product
- selecting the best location for a new warehouse and distribution outlet
- evaluating a proposal to acquire another organization to provide the capacity to expand market share and production capacity.

Each of these decisions will have one or more unique features: for example, the prospective sites for creating a new warehouse will all have different attributes, some of which, on investigation, will prove to be advantageous, others disadvantageous. Although it would be possible to lay down general information requirement guidelines in advance, the decision-makers are only able to specify the actual information requirements for each decision when the preliminary problem analysis has taken place. This means that the information system must have a degree of flexibility in its design and operation to enable it to respond to the variable information demands of the non-programmable decisions. An alternative term for non-programmable decisions is **non-routine decisions**.

This distinction between programmable and non-programmable decisions and their information requirements will be developed in Chapter 3.

Planning and implementation

Having selected what appears to be the appropriate solution strategy for the particular problem situation, we approach the next stage in the decision process: planning and implementing the necessary steps to make the decision effective. Figure 2.6 illustrates the main stages in this planning and implementation phase.

Planning involves:

- determining the sequence (logical or otherwise) of action and/or inaction which will be required
- establishing the dates or times required for the completion of each step in the plan
- estimating the resources which will be required for, and the durations of, the individual steps
- scheduling the programme of necessary activities.

Although planning and implementation are concerned with the detail of putting a decision into practice, the process itself incorporates a series of second-order decisions involving, for example, establishing priorities of resource usage within the organization as a whole and making commercial judgements as to the timing of the implementation. A more detailed treatment of the issues and methods involved is provided in a later discussion of project management.

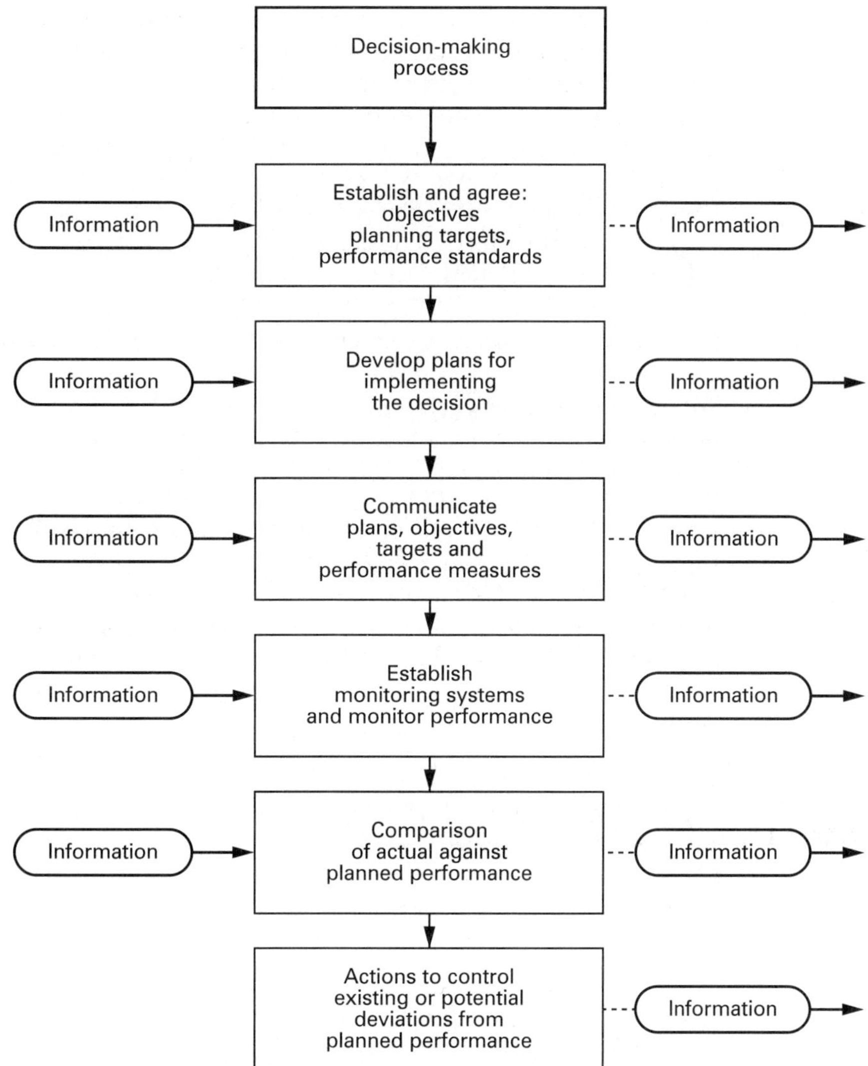

Figure 2.6 Stages in planning, implementation and control.

Performance measurement, evaluation, monitoring and control

The final stage in the decision-making process, as illustrated in Figure 2.6, involves measuring the levels of performance achieved against those set as the justification for the project in the decision-making and planning stages. The measurement of actual performance against planned or budgeted performance is a fairly common technique which is used in most of the standard planning approaches. Performance measures may include timescales, target completion dates, resource usage, costs incurred, or other similar measures of efficiency and effectiveness. The original decision-maker, or those subsequently responsible and accountable for implementing the decision, will continuously monitor the performance levels achieved both during the implementation phase and in its initial and subsequent operation. For these purposes, the monitoring may be directed towards the assessment of both effectiveness and efficiency. Since commercial organizations depend on the efficiency of their systems to maintain or enhance profitability, a considerable proportion of any organization's information processing activities is necessarily devoted to supporting performance measurement and monitoring. These activities may be related either to specific projects or to the ongoing operations of the primary and support activities.

Performance monitoring

In a number of areas, the organization will incorporate a continuous process of performance monitoring as a part of the transaction processing system. This may involve the regular recording of costs, revenues, time spent, resources used, and so on, in its operations. A prerequisite of performance measurement is the establishment of clearly defined objectives or targets which can be related to the desired performance levels as the key parameters (for example, profit levels, budgets or standard costs). These may be established follows:

1 the actual levels of performance required will be explicitly stated
2 some minimum acceptable levels of performance may be indicated
3 the targets may be implicit rather than explicitly stated.

Irrespective of the method adopted for setting performance requirements, the information received will be used to indicate whether performance is adhering to planned targets or deviating from those targets. The scale of any deviation detected will influence both the degree of urgency perceived necessary and the scope of any corrective action to keep the operation under control – that is, within the planned performance parameters.

Control

The control process is a consequence of performance monitoring and involves taking actions either to prevent anticipated deviations from planned performance or to correct deviations after they have occurred. Control will encompass decision-making elements together with planning elements, and may involve:

- applying corrective action to existing operations or to stages in the planned implementation
- modifying future plans to reflect changes in present circumstances or current performance levels
- re-appraising objectives and performance targets in the light of current performance.

Reactive and proactive approaches

It is important to recognize the distinction between the **reactive** and the **proactive** approaches to control, as these have differing implications for the organization's information system.

In the former approach, the organization's management responds to existing deviations from the planned activities or performance levels. Managers will act to correct the deviations, or to prevent those deviations from damaging the future interests of the organization.

In the proactive approach, management consciously explores the potential sources of future deviations with a view to instituting the necessary avoidance or damage limitation measures in advance. The implications for the information system of a proactive approach are that the information requirements will be oriented more to future events, and the decision support tools and software will be directed more towards forecasting, model building and sensitivity analysis, providing the management with assessments which will help to answer the *what if?* type of question.

Reactive approaches will rely more heavily on historical data, although, again, the management will require decision support tools to underpin the analysis of alternative solutions and their implications.

It is likely that both approaches will co-exist in most organizations. This reflects the fact that the development of paranoia in management is not a viable strategy: if an organization continually plans on the basis of the worst possible case and seeks to predict every potential deviation in advance, a substantial amount of redundant activity and expenditure will be achieved. Responsible management acknowledges that the organization must be able to respond flexibly to existing, realistically predictable and unpredicted problems. The result is that the emphasis in management development and training is moving strongly towards the need to adopt a more proactive approach, and this trend is being increasingly supported and facilitated by developments in information technologies.

The ability to control a situation depends largely on the receipt of timely and good-quality performance information. Should symptoms of the deviation from planned or anticipated performance targets not be clearly signalled in time, the necessary trigger to initiate the decision-making activities within the control process will not arise. One of the difficulties in designing an effective control system is the potential volume of information which may be generated on the organization's activities. The greater the volume, the greater the level of resources that must be devoted to analysing and reviewing it. An important principle adopted by many organizations is therefore that of exception reporting or 'management by exception'. This operates on the presumption that actual performance levels either matching or closely matching the planned levels are under control and do not require special attention. Thus, management requires information only on those areas of performance that are failing to meet the planned levels by a significant margin, as these may be considered to be out of control and to require attention. This principle has important implications for the design and operation of management information systems.

Communications

The communications system in any organization is essentially concerned with the movement of data between one area or element and another. It should be considered as the system of veins and arteries which carries the life blood of data to all parts of the organization. In the strategic brain of the organization, decisions are made which must be circulated to all sections and units. But to function efficiently, the brain must be refreshed by the 'oxygen' of data drawn from the external and internal monitoring senses. To that extent, the communications system is the heart of the organization's information system, providing channels for the effective and efficient transfer of data to the right person in the right place, so that quality information may be transmitted. The communication of information in an organization may be classified into two broad forms:

1 **Hard communications**, where there is some physical, tangible or hard copy of the information being transmitted – a written memorandum or letter, minutes of a meeting, a tape recording of a telephone conversation, or an electronic recording on a computer's magnetic disk. In each of these cases there is a tangible record of the information which may be passed to the receiver and, if required, provide a permanent record of that information.
2 **Soft communications**, where the information is transmitted in a less tangible form: the tone of voice, the facial expression or other mannerisms used while orally transmitting the information, or the general atmosphere in which the communication takes place. These less tangible features may be particularly important for the correct interpretation of the information. They may equally be responsible for incorrect interpretation of the information by the receiver, by giving undue weight to certain dimensions or elements.

Both types of communication co-exist in almost every organization. From the information systems development and design point of view, however, the emphasis tends to centre on mechanisms for delivering the hard forms of the organization's information. This is mainly because economical methods have been developed to capture, store, process and transmit this type of information by using the electronic media. The development of cost-effective processing methods for the soft elements is less readily available. This would take the form of teleconferencing systems incorporating live CCTV links, and electronic messaging systems that convert video images into electronic media prior to storage and re-convert then when they are required. There is little doubt that the handling of these soft elements is technically feasible, and that they are likely to become increasingly cost-effective (and hence useful) in the future.

Summary

In this chapter we have examined the key components of information technology and the constituent elements of information systems. We have focused on the following points:

- Information technology is essentially a convergence of technological developments in computer hardware, software and communications which constructively interrelate and interact with potential information users in the organization.
- Effective information systems are user-orientated rather than technology-orientated in their operations.
- Information is recorded data which may be used in organizations to support the planning function in particular, and decision making in general. Information of a variety of types allows the organization the opportunity to monitor and control every aspect of its operation.
- When problem situations have been structured, it is possible to identify the information required to resolve them.
- A key function of management is to ensure that data flows support good communication links between the different parts of the organization.

Self-test questions

1 Identify four benefits that may be derived from the increased use of information technologies.
2 List the features that you would expect to find in an effectively integrated organization.
3 Distinguish between the terms *programmable decision* and *non-programmable decision,* and give an example of each.
4 Provide some examples of data items that would typically be recorded in the sales transaction processing system in an organization.
5 Identify five dangers inherent in the increasing use of information technologies.

Exam-style questions

1 The entire decision-making process can be viewed as the acquisition and processing of information.
   List and briefly describe the stages in the decision-making process.
2 The continuing development of technologies is increasingly revolutionizing both the data processing and management information system.
   Discuss the potential benefits and dangers of the increasing use of information technologies.

(*All answers on pages 547–549*)

CHAPTER 3

Information, decision making and the organization structure

Decision making is an important element in the successful functioning of any organization. This chapter undertakes a detailed analysis of the information required to support decision making at different levels in the organization. Here we evaluate the implications for both the type and the quality of the information required to support decision making at these different levels. Attention is then given to the influence that the organization's structure and culture have in dictating the nature, quantity and quality of the information resource and its usage.

We identify the qualitative dimensions of information and examine the differences in the quality of information required at each level of decision making. We then consider the different ways in which organizations may be structured. Our emphasis is on understanding the factors that influence organization structure rather than on providing exhaustive examples of different structures. The two common generic models, the functional model and the matrix model, are examined in some detail the purpose being to establish the influence that organizational structure has on the nature and structure of the information system. We then develop the distinction between the formal and the informal organizational structure with a view to establishing the possible implications for information systems.

We shall look at the issues associated with organizational structure and the impact of structure on information systems in subsequent chapters, as this represents a key element in the formulation and development of information systems.

The nature and levels of decision making

The activities of decision making, planning, communicating, performance monitoring and control occur extensively and continuously in almost every organization. We can differentiate these activities in a number of ways, most commonly by reference to:

- the functions involved, for example marketing or financing
- the aspects of the operations to which the decisions relate, such as pricing or employee remuneration
- the time period concerned: short, medium or long term.

A further generally accepted division of the range of decision-making activities in an organization is illustrated in Figure 3.1.

Decision-making levels

The three levels of decision making illustrated here reflect essential differences in the nature of the decisions being taken. Consequently the position of the potential decision-maker in the hierarchy gives rise to different information requirements to support the decisions. The differences in the type and quality of the information required for each of these levels are explained in more detail later in this chapter.

We can consider these decisions quantitatively – in terms or their volume or frequency – or qualitatively – in terms of their significance or consequences for the organization. The **operational** decisions are the most prevalent in an organization and the **strategic** decisions the least prevalent. Conversely, strategic decisions are potentially the most significant, while operational decisions have little potential impact on the organization as a whole.

We may not assume that the clear distinction between the three levels represented in Figure 3.1 is reflected in practical terms in organizations. The distinction between decisions at the **operational** and **tactical** levels on the one hand, and those at the tactical and strategic levels on the other, is often a matter of interpretation within a specific situation: it usually reflects the nature of the particular processes employed in managing the organization. The distinction between operational-level and strategic-level decisions is usually more clearly observable in practice. Let us now look at the nature of these three levels of decision making and provide some examples of the types of decisions involved in each of the groups. We shall keep discussion of the tactical level to the end, because it interacts significantly with the other two levels.

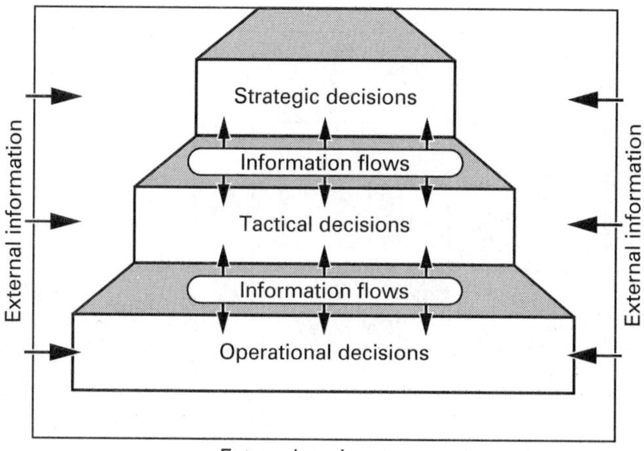

Figure 3.1 Levels of organization decision making.

Operational decisions

Operational decisions are concerned with the ongoing daily or routine operations of the organization, relating mainly to its primary activities. Figure 3.2 illustrates the main groups of primary activities and shows a few examples of the decisions associated with each of them. Our list of examples is not exhaustive and relates to a manufacturing organization, although some features would also be found in the operations of a service-sector organization, such as the sales ledger system.

Each of these groups represents a major sub-system in the organization's overall information system. The sequence of activities and decisions indicated in Figure 3.2 is not necessarily the order in which they would occur in practice. Indeed, many of the activities shown will take place simultaneously. Another important feature highlighted in the figure is the linkages between each of these primary sub-systems. They usually reflect some flow of data between them. The figure also indicates the two-way flow of data between the operational sub-systems and corresponding elements at the management level.

Operational decisions are concerned primarily with:

1 **Short timescale and routine programmes** to promote the effectiveness and efficiency of daily operations: sales and customer order taking, the acquisition and stocking of raw materials, production operations, delivery and installation of goods and services, and the subsequent invoicing and collection of payment for the goods and services.

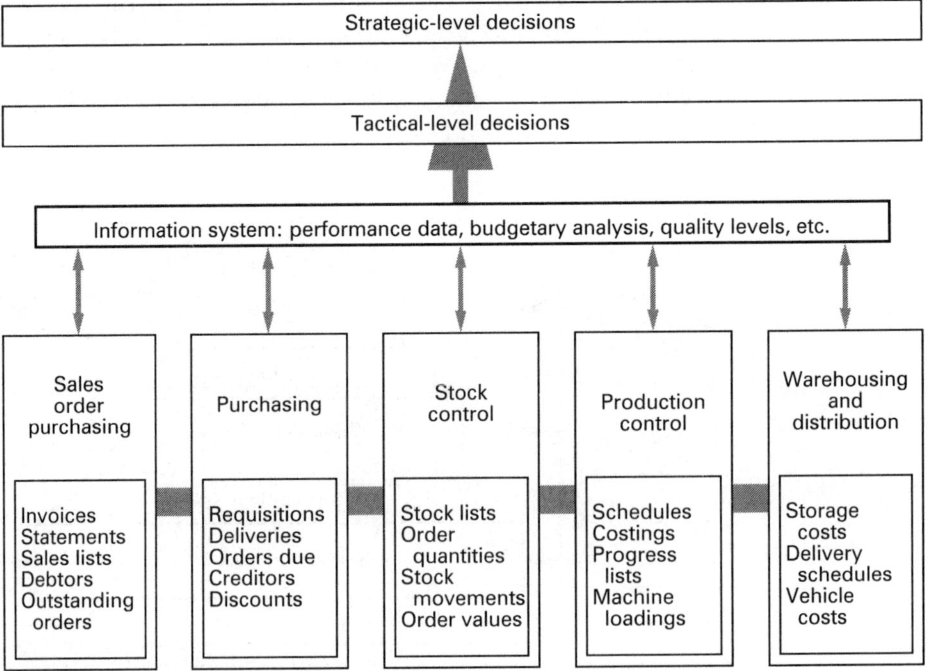

Figure 3.2 Operational decisions in an organization.

2 **Explicit and specific performance objectives** facilitating direct and often very objective measurement of efficiency and effectiveness: for example, the number of items manufactured in a particular day, or the number of transactions processed by the sales order staff in a day.
3 **Highly programmable and well-documented decision-making procedures,** which are frequently encapsulated in operating procedures, operations manuals and where specific instructions are given.
4 **Decisions where there are relatively low levels of uncertainty and risk** and where decision-makers mainly use objective analysis methods and simplified selection criteria in making their decisions.
5 **Highly predictable information demands** in terms of the information required to make the decision and to monitor its consequences.

Strategic decisions

Strategic decisions are concerned with long-term development and planning for the whole organization, as opposed to specific functional areas or individual operations. The major groups of decision activity within this level are shown in Figure 3.3.

Strategic decisions can be characterized as follows:

1 They concern the long-term development of the organization in terms of the nature of its business, the markets it should serve, its range of products or services and the nature of its competitive position in the market. As we noted in Chapter 1, the precise definition of 'long term' depends on the nature of the markets serviced by the organization.
2 They involve the selection, development and articulation of organizational objectives from a range of potential objectives, against a background of constraints imposed by the external environment and by the organization's internal structure and operations.

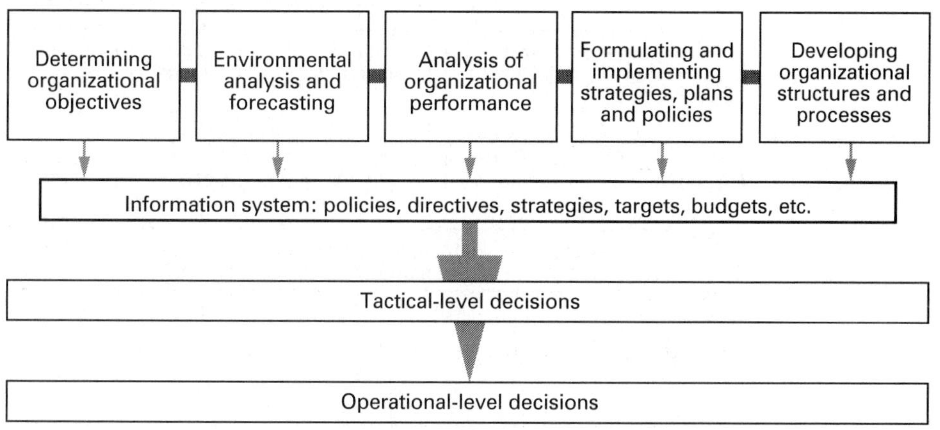

Figure 3.3 Strategic decisions in an organization.

3 They tend to be highly unstructured or non-programmable, and are often novel to the organization and its decision-makers, with no guarantee that they will recur in a similar context.
4 They involve high levels of uncertainty and risk, requiring significant levels of personal and subjective analysis, appraisal and choice within the decisions.
5 The kinds of information needed to support them are not generally predictable, although certain types of external and internal information will be regularly processed for the decision-making group as a general part of the organization's need to develop good sources of intelligence and broad performance indicators.

Tactical decisions

Tactical decision making may be considered as filling the centre spread in the spectrum of decision types between 'operational' at one extreme and 'strategic' at the other. This level shares a number of features with both the operational and strategic levels, and is considered last for this reason. Figure 3.4 indicates the broad areas of decision handled at this level.

The role of individual managers in this section of the decision hierarchy also needs to be recognized: in addition to decision making, this level of management also has the task of integrating and co-ordinating activity and communication between the strategic and operational levels. The function of these managers is to interpret, implement, monitor and control the strategic objectives, plans and

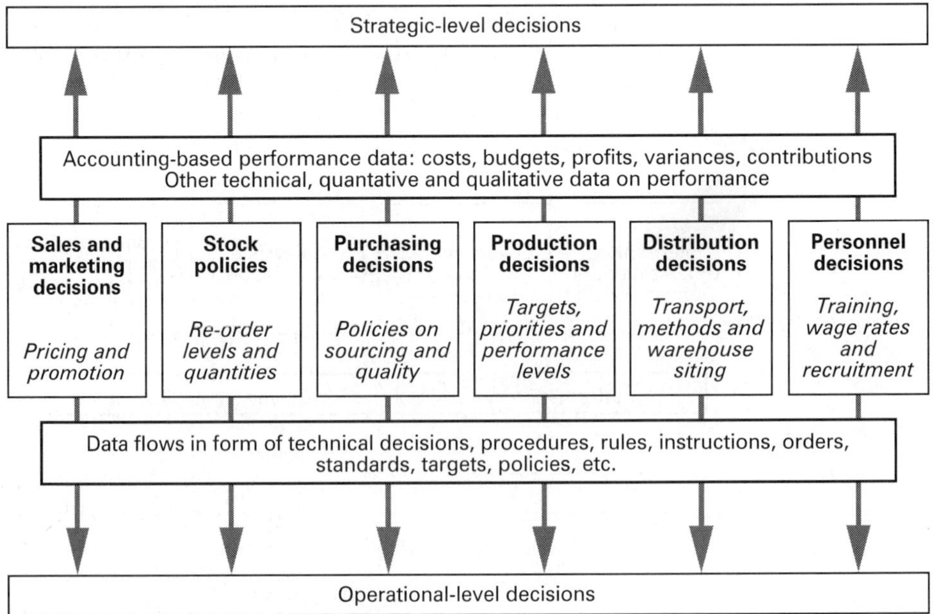

Figure 3.4 Tactical decisions in an organization.

policies established by the organization. This may involve developing plans, performance levels, guidelines, procedures and operating instructions for the operational levels in the organization.

In addition to this enabling link from the strategic to the operational levels for implementation purposes, the tactical level also has a responsibility to monitor the operations of the organization and to feed back summarized performance data to the strategic level. This management role is arguably the most crucial element in the organization's operation, as it provides a vital interface between the long-term plans of the organization and their more immediate implementation and control.

Tactical level decisions may be characterized in terms of:

1. A practical concern with the short-, medium- and long-term perspectives of organizational performance, although the main emphasis will tend to be medium term.
2. The need to relate primarily to the functional elements in the organization while recognizing the overall strategic objectives, strategies and development proposals.
3. The involvement of moderate degrees of uncertainty and risk in appraising the decision options and the alternative solutions available.
4. The semi-structured nature of the problems encountered, since there will be some elements in each problem which may be relatively common, while other elements are novel both to the decision-maker and to the organization. (A core of standard analytical techniques has been developed to provide some basic tools to tackle different problem situations. Examples include operational research methods such as linear programming or queuing algorithms, statistical methods, variance analysis methods in budgetary control, and spreadsheet software packages. The real skill at this level of decision making is the ability to structure the problem encountered into an appropriate form and to select the correct decision tools to assist in the analysis and selection of the best solution strategy.)
5. Information requirements which are only partially predictable, such as the regular performance monitoring requirements and reports. (The unpredictable elements reflect the need for management to focus on particular novel issues and problems as they arise, and to use standard-purpose analytical tools to evaluate the alternatives and to take decisions.)

Types and quality of information

Our discussion of the levels of decision making in the organization indicated that the nature of the decisions taken at each level varies significantly. We suggested that the type and quality of the information required to support the three levels of decision making would also vary. The effective specification, design and operation of an organization's information system require a clear recognition and understanding of these differences, both in terms of the types and the qualitative dimensions of the information that will be required.

Information classification by type

Several dimensions may be used as the basis on which to classify information. These include:

- **source** – internally- or externally-generated information
- **time frame** – information relating to the historical, current or future situation
- **communication media** – presentation of information in either written or oral form
- **functional orientation** – relating the information to the primary functional area or activity affected – for example raw material costs and the purchasing function, or statistics on employee absenteeism and the personnel function
- **decision level** – relating information to its primary use at one or more of the operational, management or strategic levels.

These classifications are not mutually exclusive; a particular item of information may be classified using each of these dimensions. For example, information on the sales achieved by a particular product in a given month may be classified as internally generated, historical, written and appropriate to management level decisions in the sales function – whereas forecasts of market demand for the product may be externally generated, futuristic, written and primarily for use in strategic-level decisions in the marketing function.

Qualitative dimensions of information

In addition to classifying by type, we can also differentiate categories of information on the basis of quality. The term quality in this context refers to the dimensions which enhance the value of the information to the user. Figure 3.5 illustrates a number of the more important qualitative dimensions of information.

Four key points need to be stressed in relation to these quality dimensions:

- not all the dimensions will be relevant in any given decision situation
- each dimension may be represented by a range of potential levels of quality
- even where there are several relevant dimensions, certain dimensions may be more important than others. In the case of financial accounting information, for example, a high degree of accuracy may be more important than the timeliness or currency of the information received
- the importance of a particular dimension in a given decision situation is a reflection of the decision situation, the nature of the problem faced, and the skills of individual decision-makers. In the case of a decision-maker with strong analytical abilities, the provision of detailed and comprehensive information as opposed to summarized and partial information may enhance the decision taken. However, if the decision-maker's analytical abilities are less well developed, a more summarized version of the information may yield higher value.

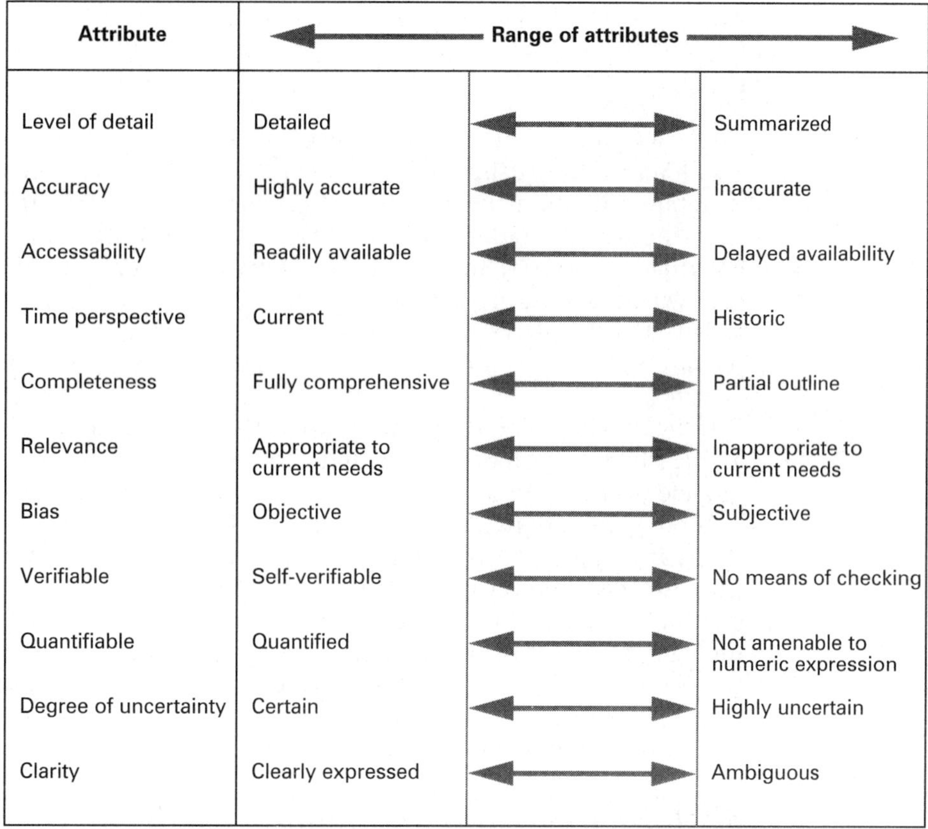

Attribute	Range of attributes		
Level of detail	Detailed	⟷	Summarized
Accuracy	Highly accurate	⟷	Inaccurate
Accessability	Readily available	⟷	Delayed availability
Time perspective	Current	⟷	Historic
Completeness	Fully comprehensive	⟷	Partial outline
Relevance	Appropriate to current needs	⟷	Inappropriate to current needs
Bias	Objective	⟷	Subjective
Verifiable	Self-verifiable	⟷	No means of checking
Quantifiable	Quantified	⟷	Not amenable to numeric expression
Degree of uncertainty	Certain	⟷	Highly uncertain
Clarity	Clearly expressed	⟷	Ambiguous

Figure 3.5 Qualitative dimensions of information.

Costs

The improvement of quality or the enhancement of the value received by the user from the information will normally necessitate additional information processing costs. Each of the qualitative dimensions listed has a cost associated with the improvement of the quality of the information in that particular dimension. Thus, if a production planning and control department operates on the basis of reports received at the end of each day, the proposal might be made to improve the timeliness of the information received by providing information on a real-time or 'immediate response' basis throughout the day. This will involve considerable investment in:

- the computer hardware and communications equipment needed to capture and transmit the data from the shopfloor
- the development or acquisition of appropriate software to process the information
- increased staff time, both in capturing the primary data and in accessing the resulting information

Systems designers therefore need to understand the needs of the user and to translate these into the appropriate levels of information quality provision.

Limitations

While we can accept that additional expenditure on information processing may improve the quality of the information provided, we should recognize that there are limitations on the degree to which quality may be improved, apart from the cost limitations. The quality of the source data used will dictate the potential to improve the qualitative dimensions. For example, market survey data which failed to record the ages of respondents could not have this detail added later. Similarly, costing information recorded in units of hundreds of pounds could not be provided in greater accuracy – say, in terms of pounds and pence.

Technical limitations may also restrict the potential improvements in quality, as the ability to capture, store and process the volume of data necessary to provide a comprehensive statement of the organization's markets may be limited.

Another important restricting factor is the cognitive capacity of the users. While it may be possible to improve the detail and comprehensiveness of the data provided, the capacity of the overworked user to use it effectively may be constrained by the sheer volume of information provided. So, enhancing the inherent quality of the information does not necessarily add value to the user in the decision-making or control activities. Alternatively, no matter how much time is available, good-quality information on its own does not convert a bad decision-maker into a good decision-maker.

Decision levels and information needs

Differences in the nature of the decisions at various levels in the organization will be an important determinant of both the type of information required and its quality. Figure 3.6 illustrates the differential nature of type and quality for the three broad levels of decision making outlined earlier.

Strategic decisions are concerned primarily with positioning the organization in the environment to meet its targets and objectives most effectively, while planning to allow the organization to develop dynamically in response to changes in that environment. Such decisions typically involve a higher proportion of externally generated data, often presented in a summarized form and relating more to future potential than to historical or current developments. The information required will also generally be less accurate, in the pedantic sense, and incorporate more subjective valuations of future trends and developments. This will tend to make the contents less predictable, as the information needs will be largely dictated by developments in the external environment which, by definition, are largely outside the organization's control.

Operational decisions tend to be based on information originating primarily within the organization and relating to either historical or current activities. The conduct of the decision making at this level will also require detailed and accurate information, which is often predetermined by both the content and quality necessary to be incorporated into highly structured decisions.

Information attributes	Operational	Tactical	Strategic
Orientation	Primarily internal	Internal and external data utilized	Greater orientation to external data
Planning horizon	Immediate to next few days	Short to medium term (weeks and months)	Medium to long term (months and years)
Performance focus	Focus on current activities	Historic and current activities	Focus on predictive rather than historic performance
Coverage	Relates to specific activities	Relates to groups of activities within department/function	Coverage of total organization
Level of detail presented	Highly detailed	Mixture of detailed and summarized reports	Data typically in highly summarized form
Uncertainty levels	Low uncertainty levels	Moderate levels of uncertainty	High levels of uncertainty as focusing on longer term
Degree of objectivity	Objectively measured data normally	Combination of objective and subjective data	Data incorporate higher proportion of subjective valuations
Level of accuracy	High levels of accuracy usually required	Moderate accuracy levels	Accuracy less critical of decisions at this level

Figure 3.6 Decision levels and information type and quality.

Tactical decisions are concerned with the tactical planning and control of the organization. A significant proportion of the information inputs to this level will comprise summaries of the operational performance of the organization's primary activities, usually on a periodic basis. In such cases, the information inputs will be highly structured and predictable in terms of the required content, detail and accuracy.

The summaries given above are intended to illustrate general distinctions in the type and quality of information at each of the three levels. In any organization, the differentiation between the three levels is often blurred and consequently differentiation in the type and quality of information used may similarly be imprecise.

Organization structure and information requirements

All organizations are built up from standard resource-based components, but the individual motives, pressures and constraints which operate at the time of construction tend to produce strongly differentiated organizational structures, even where the organizations to be compared seek to serve the same market. However, there are a number of 'common denominator' themes which emerge in the structuring period, regardless of whether the organization is taking decisions explicitly or implicitly. At a 'macro' level, the organization will seek to structure its human resources and operations in the most effective and efficient manner to achieve its objectives. To make these objectives operational, the organization must:

- formally identify and structure the available resources
- establish efficient information and communication systems
- create processes for effective decision making, planning and control.

Primary issues

The strength of any organization ultimately lies in its human resources. But if the best possible use of these resources is to be achieved, the organization must take key decisions to allocate authority and responsibility. Without properly defined roles and a career structure which is likely to develop and maintain staff morale, it will be difficult to make effective use of the other resources – no matter how easy it may actually be to exploit them – and management skills will fade. This depends, in turn, on the development and communication of a personnel policy which can be perceived as co-ordinated with the more general policies of the organization. So training must be planned to introduce new skills and enhance the old, and a pathway of promotion must be set in place to allow each manager to gain experience and insight into the aims and methods of the organization.

Motivation and responsibility

The ways in which an organization may be controlled vary from the autocratic excesses of an aggressive entrepreneur to an open and democratic system of decision making. The power structures which will develop will come to represent the culture of the organization and will be a vital factor in setting the tone and feel of employment. Key factors in maintaining motivation are the extent to which each manager is allowed to participate in significant decision making and the degree of authority delegation. If a manager is trusted with specific responsibility and found to be competent, this reinforces the mutual confidence between manager and organization and should lead to better performance.

Power and political structure

But no organization can afford to accept success uncritically. The predicted outcomes may have arisen through circumstances entirely outside the control of the organization – such as blind luck – and survival depends on recognizing that the current organizational structure is not necessarily the most effective or efficient. Thus, structural appraisal and evaluation may lead the organization to propose changes to allow greater control or better decision making. But all change is a threat to established power structures, and where individuals have had responsibility and authority it can be difficult to make the change effective.

To that extent, all managements need to be aware of the *political* structure within the organization, so that the process of change can be steered through the matrix of entrenched self-interest. The political structure may map directly on to the formal decision-making structure, with power and influence controlled by the largest, the most productive or the most profitable departments. Sometimes the survival of power is an anachronism: the original managers of the first form of the organization retain influence, even though new parts of the business have long since outstripped them in performance terms. This inevitably means addressing the issues of the size of organization and its component elements. Empire building by one or two ambitious individuals can be a way of promoting rapid growth, but it does not necessarily lead to better management or to the right balance of activities.

Factors influencing organization structure

Reflecting on the primary issues discussed in the previous paragraphs, we can identify a range of factors that will influence the structure of any organization. These include:

- **the size of the organization:** smaller organizations tend to have a less rigidly defined structure and fewer specialist functional units, and work on the basis that individuals or units may undertake a number of different functions or operations
- **the nature of the product or service** package provided, the methods used in its manufacture or provision and the means used to deliver, support and service the final consumers' needs
- **the type of market** in which the organization operates, the nature of consumer needs, and the types of competitive pressures encountered
- **the strategy pursued**, which will often determine the most appropriate structure for the organization. Growth through product or geographic diversification will usually require a structure based on common products and/or geographic areas, for example a European sales division or a special products division
- **the nature of the environment** and the rate at which key elements change, which may have to be reflected in the corporate structure: an organization faced with rapid change in its markets will need to develop systems which are equally responsive to changes in consumer preferences or in competitor strategies
- **technological change** will also influence the form of structure as the organization seeks to adapt to new products and/or manufacturing technologies and processes
- **the history, background and previous developments in the organization,** which will all influence the management's preference for a particular structure
- **the style of management** preferred, reflecting (for example) the degree of decentralization of authority and responsibility for decision making
- **the power structure within the senior management**, which will often provide an important barrier or stimulus to organizational change

- **the culture of the organization**: the organization's culture and structure are essentially interrelated, though the processes through which one influences the other are outside the scope of this present discussion.

It should be fairly evident from the nature of these factors that the range and relative importance of each will vary from organization to organization. Indeed, each organization has a unique structure which may be said to reflect the unique set of influencing factors facing it. The management literature broadly accepts that there is no 'best structure' for all organizations and argues that a *contingency approach* is more appropriate for organizational design. At its simplest level, the contingency approach suggests that the appropriate design or structure for a particular organization should emerge as a response to the particular factors or issues facing the organization among those outlined in the previous paragraphs.

Formal and informal organization structure

Understanding the distinction between the formal and the informal organizational structure is essential, because it may have significant implications for the organization's information and communications systems.

The *formal* structure represents the agreed grouping and allocation of resources, activities, responsibilities and authority. In many respects, this structure will accommodate all the normal routine activities, linkages and processes in the organization outlined in Chapter 1.

The *informal* structure represents a series of linkages or relationships between individuals or groups in the organization. The informal structure is unlikely to mirror the formal structure and evolves through workplace or social relationships and friendships, or through political associations within the organization.

A debate on the reasons for the development of informal structures and their implication for the organization is outside the scope of our present objectives. However, the informal organizational structure may represent an important element of the organization's total information and communications systems. One frequently hears reference to the speed or efficiency of the 'grapevine' in communicating information within an organization. Difficulties arise in incorporating this element of the information system into any planned systems development, because the informal system is:

1. difficult to identify, as few members would admit to being part of an informal structure
2. transient and likely to change as members of the organization and their personal relationships change
3. only a partial system, catering primarily for the more sensational items of information as opposed to processing the more routine data
4. often inefficient in terms of the quality of the information communicated, as members in the communication channel may modify the basic data to suit their particular purposes
5. unpredictable in terms of when and how effectively it will operate in each situation – the absence of a particular member for a brief period may result in the total collapse of the system.

There are several reasons for not incorporating the informal organization structure and its associated information system within the formal processes of information systems development. However, the fact that such systems exist in all organizations must be recognized and any implications should be reflected in the formal systems development process. Indeed, knowledge of the informal information system may aid the process by identifying possible problems or inefficiencies in the formal organization structure or information systems. Once the problems are identified, countermeasures may be devised which will lead to successful outcomes following implementation of the system.

Organizational structure and information systems

Earlier in this and previous chapters we referred to the type and structure of the operations and activities undertaken within an organization. We distinguished between:

- different types of primary activities, for example inbound logistics or purchasing and marketing and sales activities
- these primary activities and the other commonly found support activities, such as management of human resources
- different levels of management activities: operational, tactical and strategic
- different types of management tasks within each of these broad activities (i.e. primary and support activities) and the different levels (i.e. operational, tactical and strategic). These include the planning, decision-making, monitoring, evaluation and control tasks.

The generic models used in the earlier chapters were designed to illustrate these features and to show their implications for organizational information systems in general. However, each organization will develop a unique structure to undertake these activities and management tasks; the factors leading to this unique structure were outlined in the previous paragraphs.

There are a number of general principles or models which organizations use to guide the development of their particular organization structure. The following paragraphs outline two of these major models: the *functional* or *line and staff* model, and the *matrix* model. These two should suffice to illustrate the major implications for the organization's information systems.

Functional structure

A simple model of a functionally structured organization is shown in Figure 3.7. Key features of this form of structure include the following:

- The functional line activities and responsibilities are those directly associated with the manufacture of the product or the delivery of the service: handling receipt of raw materials, production operations, warehousing and distribution.
- The functional staff activities and responsibilities provide the specialist support to the line activities, such as financial services and human resource

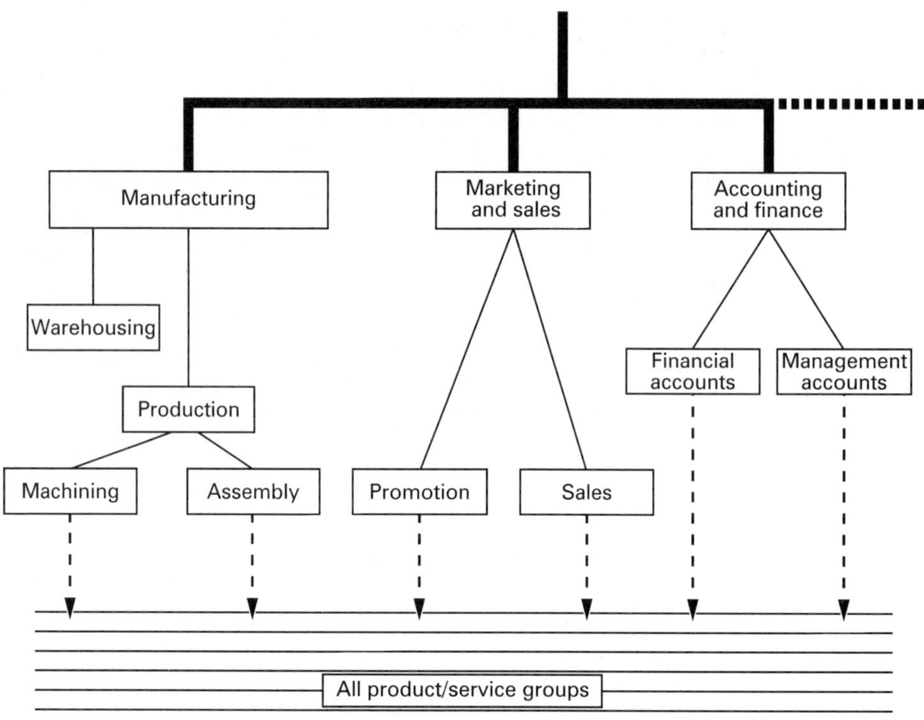

Figure 3.7 Functional organization structure.

management services. These functions provide a service to the line functions, enabling them to conduct their operations effectively and efficiently. Some of these activities will be directed towards the customer (e.g. marketing), while others provide services to the organization as a whole (e.g. strategic planning).

- Implicit within this structure are the principles of hierarchy and division of responsibility. The chain of command or authority rises vertically through successively higher levels within particular functions. Decisions of a particular scale or disagreements between functions on particular decisions at lower levels in the structure are resolved by referring the problem up the hierarchy of command to the appropriate level at which this may be resolved between the two functions.
- The division of responsibility means that a particular function has the responsibility and authority to decide factors only within its sphere of responsibility. The marketing function may decide the appropriate means to promote the product but, in general, it would have no influence over the manufacturing methods used. In practice, this division of responsibility may not always be as evident as this might suggest, as the development of personal relationships, working practices and the general culture of the organization may modify the outcome.

Matrix organization structure

The matrix type of organization structure provides an alternative form to the functional structure. A number of features are associated with the matrix form of structure:

- The organization is divided on two bases, as illustrated in Figure 3.8: a functional basis (e.g. marketing and manufacturing) and a product/service basis (where the components are often identified as separate business units or profit centres).
- Product/service units have responsibility for the total business operations, management and development of the specific range of products or services (including, for example, research and development, marketing, sales, manufacture, distribution and financial systems).
- The functional units contribute their specialist knowledge, skills and expertise to each of the business units as required. However, the functional resources are not owned by the product/service units but are in most cases hired by those units. The functional units have their own management structure with responsibilities for the management of all the staff and the services offered by the function.

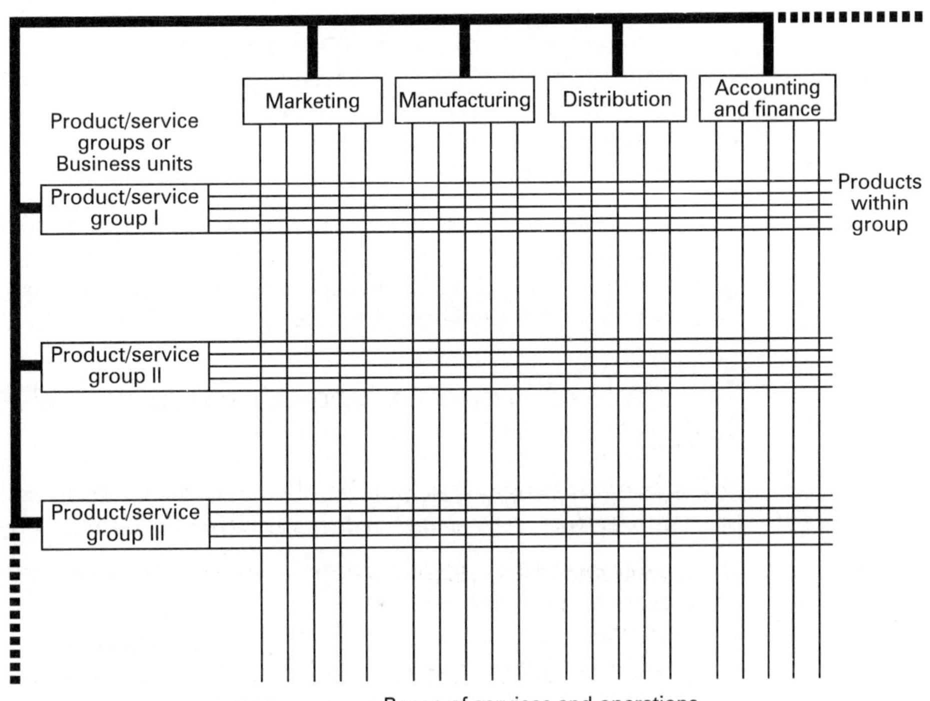

Figure 3.8 Matrix organization structure.

- The operation of a product/service unit involves a team of functional specialists, brought together to manage or develop the particular product or project. The composition of these teams may vary over time as the product passes through different stages in its life cycle, each one requiring different specialist inputs. Each functional unit will be involved simultaneously in a number of different products or projects and some individual members may also be involved in more than one project simultaneously.

The key advantage of this form of structure is that it can readily adapt to new demands, i.e. the development of new products or technologies, or the changing needs of existing products.

Other advantages claimed for the matrix structure are these:

- it is more efficient in allowing the exploitation of specialist functional resources
- employees have a more direct involvement and interest in particular products and hence are more motivated to achieve success
- it encourages a more market-oriented approach within each product/service unit
- it improves communication and co-ordination between functions.

The matrix structure is also said to have a number of disadvantages, the more significant of which include the following:

- individuals experience personal problems, as they must often report to more than one manager, say, a functional manager and one or more product/service managers
- co-ordination and communications across the total organization rather than within the particular product/service group may be less effective because of the complex interrelationships of functions and product/service groups
- tensions may arise between the objectives and plans pursued by the product/service units and those pursued by the functional units.

We are not concerned here with an exhaustive evaluation of the alternative organization structures. Our aim is to use this discussion of the two alternatives to clarify the structural issues that relate to planning improvements to information systems within the given structure.

The effect of organizational structure on the information system

The primary objective of any information system must be to provide an effective and efficient support service to all its users. To achieve this, the system should be:

- capable of acting independently of the specific organizational structure at any particular point in time
- adaptable to the changing structure of the organization
- flexible enough to meet the changing needs of the organization
- independent of the organization's power structure.

Let us consider these four desirable attributes in more detail.

Independent operation

If the information system is tied too closely to the structure, local needs may be satisfied but organization-wide demands may be met less effectively. For example, the information system that is tailored to meet the structure and needs of the marketing function may prove less effective in providing the same data to other users elsewhere in the organization. On the other hand, there is considerable evidence to show that uncontrolled systems development often results in fragmented systems provision for each element in the organization, involving considerable duplication of effort and resources. So the development of an effective system for the total organization's needs may require compromises in terms of meeting the needs of specific functions or users.

Adaptability to change

Our earlier discussion of the functional and matrix organization structures highlighted the need for greater responsiveness from the information system in a matrix organization as new products/services emerge, the composition of existing teams alters or their information requirements change.

Flexibility

In the matrix structure, different business units may have differing information needs, reflecting the problems faced by the particular business at its stage of development. Thus, the provision of a standardized system to all product or service groups may prove totally inappropriate.

Independence from the power structure

The power structure may seek to influence the information system structure on the basis that exclusive knowledge of certain types of information provides the possessor with a degree of power. If the information system is used in this way, it will lose credibility with the other users or suppliers of data to the system.

Changes in strategy and, hence, in information needs may occur in advance of any significant changes in the structure of the organization. Research studies have established that changes in the strategy of an organization usually take place before any change in the organizational structure. Indeed, organizations may seek to maintain their present structure for a number of years following a significant change in strategy, before being compelled to change the structure to ensure the effective management of the new strategy. The information system needs to adapt to the changing needs of the management as strategies change and the information to monitor and control these new strategies changes. Tying the information system too closely to the structure rather than to the needs of different levels of management would result in a failure to meet the objectives of the information system in any organization.

The information required

Up to this point, we have assumed that the primary information requirements are to permit the organization to monitor and control the way in which its processing systems work together to meet the demands of the external environment. Thus, production must supply sufficient stock so that the sales force can confidently locate buyers and thereby generate revenue. The data required to build up a picture of these processes are limited in their potential information content. So when the production department supplies data on the number of units manufactured in each time period, the following data from a series of key questions would also be desirable:

1 **Costing data**. What volume of raw materials and consumables was used and what was the level of wastage? How many effort-hours were required to produce the given level of output? What is the value of capital resource tied up in the plant and equipment used for this output?
2 **Scheduling and production data**. What is the percentage of productive capacity utilization, i.e. what is the level of plant and equipment reliability? How frequently does it break down? How long does it take to restore production? How long does it take to retool between different production runs? What are the shift arrangements? What is the accident record? Is there any record of sabotage?
3 **Personnel data**. What is the absenteeism record? In comparing the different manufacturing processes, where the equipment is comparable, are there significant differences in the output performance per man-hour? Are the staff prepared to work overtime? Are the staff prepared to engage in further training?
4 **Predictive data** based on *what if?* questions. If particular work practices were modified, what would output be? If the scheduling was changed, would retooling times be reduced? If parts of the equipment were upgraded, what would output be?

Analysing these data would make it possible to draw a variety of conclusions. Thus, it might appear that there is a high absenteeism rate in certain areas of production. The plant may be old and temperamental, the wastage rates high and staff morale low. Improving the production environment and upgrading the equipment may provide an opportunity to improve performance. Should the plant be new, it is obvious that there may be a problem in training, or that the design of the human–machine interface is defective. If it appears that either situation has been going on for some time, why have none of the operational or managerial level staff pressed for change?

Thus, the data may supply hard information in terms of real numbers which can be processed or analysed. The data may also permit soft information to be inferred or deduced. This latter category is all the more important when a self-critical appraisal of organizational structure is called for. Power brokers who play the political game will not freely give information showing managerial inadequacy. The information requirement should therefore be specified to extract information which is either:

- **evidential** – positive data on actual performance; or
- **inferential** – data allowing the organization to appraise performance indirectly, for example through failure to supply evidence of performance or to take action, and so on.

By using both sets of data together, an information picture of the organizational structure can be built up which should reveal those issues which justify further examination by more direct methods of investigation.

Summary

The decision-making process in an organization may be divided into three levels – strategic, tactical or operational – depending on the timescales involved and the nature of the decision to be taken.

Each of these different classes of decision requires different types and quality of information. The information system needs to provide the appropriate type and quality of information for each level.

Organizational structure is a major influence on the information system in any organization. This will affect not only the structure of the information system but also its operation. Different approaches to structuring the organization – for example, functional or matrix – will impose different demands on the information system. (Subsequent chapters will consider other organizational structure issues that influence the nature and operation of the information system.)

Information systems need to be flexible and adaptable to respond to the new and developing needs of the organization. In this respect, the information system needs to be independent of the organizational structure at any particular time to enable it to respond effectively. Changes in business strategies and in management/user needs for information are likely to happen rapidly and often significantly in advance of any change in the structure of the organization.

Self-test questions

1 List the factors that are likely to hinder or prevent the incorporation of the informal organization structure within an organization's systems development process.
2 List the key features of organizational structure and information requirements.
3 List the main desirable attributes relating to the quality of information.
4 Distinguish between tactical and strategic decisions within an organization, listing their characteristics and giving examples of each type.

Exam-style questions

1 A matrix structure is likely to place significant demands on an organization's information system. Explain the nature of a matrix structure and the reasons why the related information system would be different from that in a more conventional, functionally structured organization.
2 A commonly accepted model of organizational decision making has three levels.

Briefly describe the three levels of decision making, indicating the characteristics of the decisions made at each level and using examples where appropriate.

3 Woodline plc manufactures and retails a range of high-quality wooden furniture products. The organization's information system provides data to all users at all levels to support their decision-making and control activities. The quality of data required by users at different levels will vary. Identify the main qualitative dimensions of accounting information that would be required to support users making decisions at the different levels in the organization.

(*All answers on pages 549–551*)

CHAPTER 4

Systems theory and information systems

Information systems are only one of an almost infinite variety of systems which may operate within an organization. An important prerequisite to understanding the specific role and operation of information systems in an organization is therefore an appreciation of the significance of the term *system* and of the major components of any system, irrespective of whether the system relates to information or some other resource in the organization. The main purpose of this chapter is to introduce the major concepts involved in **systems theory** – the general theory which applies to systems of all types. These concepts will then be related and applied specifically to information systems within organizations.

Initially, the chapter provides a general outline and explanation of the primary principles and concepts underlying general systems theory. It goes on to highlight some key issues faced in dealing with systems, including the definition of system boundaries, the systems hierarchy, the required level of system definition and the interaction and integration of systems and sub-systems. Some particularly significant issues are communications, feedback and control, which we examine here in relation to general systems.

We then relate the concepts, principles and findings from general systems theory to the area of organizational information systems, identifying and evaluating the contribution of certain generic system components in organizational information systems, including text processing, spreadsheets, databases and expert system shells.

Finally, we introduce the different areas in the organizational information system, outlining the key sources of interaction and integration between them.

Systems theory and concepts

In general terms, **systems theory** or the **systems approach** is a structured method for developing a model or a conceptual framework used to assist in the analysis and exploration of a given situation. The method can be applied in many fields, including:

- manufacturing systems
- telecommunications systems
- central heating systems
- traffic systems
- human behaviour systems

- waste disposal systems
- information systems
- accounting systems
- education systems.

Basically, any situation which involves the handling or manipulation of materials or resources of any kind, whether human, financial or informative, may be structured and represented in the form of a system. This is basically achieved by logically classifying elements and components in relation to particular situational needs. This approach is not dependent on the application of computer or information technology: indeed, the development of systems theory predates the extensive use of computer technology in business and commerce. Moreover, this approach can be applied equally effectively to both manual and computer-based information or other systems within an organization. However, in order to ensure the effective and efficient application of computer technology to commercial or other organizational situations, a *logical* approach to the modelling of the situation, as incorporated in what we term the *systems approach,* is essential.

The usual purpose behind the development of a system model is to improve the level of efficiency and effectiveness in a given situation or set of operations. The systems approach recognizes that no organization can permit activities, processes, decisions and resources to exist completely independently of each other. The analysis is therefore aimed at producing a pictorial representation of the relationship between each of the important components which comprise the organization. It attempts to map even the most inaccessible regions of the organization. The resulting charts should therefore allow observers to:

- gain an improved understanding of the situation by using a structured approach to the analysis
- identify and classify the important elements or components
- more effectively disclose the mutual interaction of these system components within the part of the system being studied
- analyse the interaction and integration of the system components with elements of other systems or sub-systems.

This last point is one which is particularly highlighted through the systems approach, as opposed to other forms of structured analysis.

The elements of a system

The first step in the systems approach involves a functional decomposition of the given situation or activity into the four basic elements shown in Figure 4.1.

The four main elements may be defined as:

1. **inputs**
2. **process**
3. **outputs**
4. **environment**.

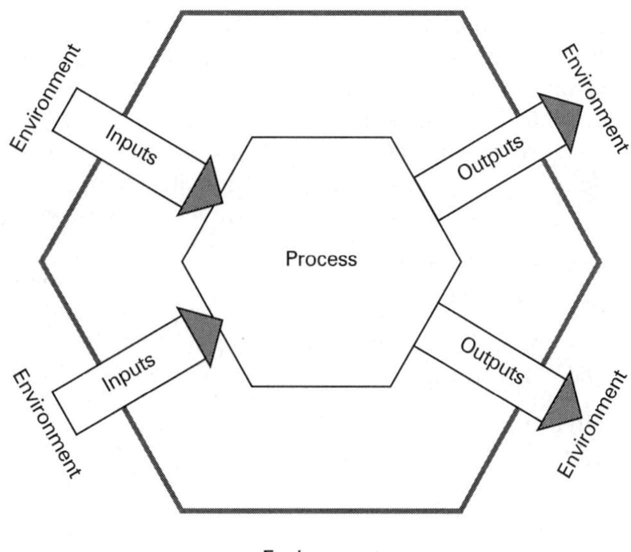

Figure 4.1 Elements of a system.

Inputs

Here the part of the system under study receives some form of resource material which might take the form of people, finance, energy or information. These resources may be received either individually or in combination, and they may also originate from a number of different sources. Further, they may occur as discrete and sometimes infrequent events or as a continuous and regular flow.

Process

Some form of activity takes place as a response to the inputs received which typically, though not exclusively, enhances the value of those resource inputs. These activities may include:

- recording
- storing
- machining
- heating
- transmitting
- calculating
- assembling.

Outputs

Once the process is complete, the (perhaps) modified resources will be output into the organizational environment. This may involve the return of the resources to their original source (where, for example, the data elements are returned to a central database), or their transmission to a new system or sub-system (e.g. where sales data items are transmitted to the marketing department for consolidation and analysis). At some point, the resources may leave the organization and reach the consumers of the product or service. Typically, the value of the output resources will be greater than that of the input resources, as a result of processing within the system: in the more usual sense, the system is seen to **add value** to the resources used. Some care needs to be exercised in defining the precise nature of the value which is added, as the term *value* may mistakenly be understood as confined to the needs of particular output recipients and not applied to all recipients. For example, a new motorway system may provide considerable added value to car users able to use the new roads, but the roads provide no added value – indeed, they may provide *negative* value – to the local residents in terms of increased noise and pollution. Hence, a system may add value to only part of the total environment to which it relates.

Environment

The environment represents the context or framework of organizations, institutions, structures, procedures and constraints within which a system operates. In essence, the system will receive and respond to various inputs from the environment and will provide outputs and responses to the environment. This dimension and the system's interaction within it are discussed in more detail later in this chapter.

To illustrate the first three of these system elements in a more general context before specifically applying them to the information system, let us consider three different examples:

- a domestic heating system
- a telephone system
- the human response system.

A domestic heating system

A typical domestic heating system may be decomposed into three basic elements:

1. **Inputs** – energy in the form of fuel such as coal, oil, electricity and/or gas. For installation or implementation purposes, there must also be conductor, carrier or distributor elements to deliver the heat created to the users. This may take the form of the boiler and associated system of pipework and radiators, and water as the circulating medium.
2. **Process** – conversion of the fuel inputs into energy, usually by a process of burning, to release energy in the form of heat, and then pumping the heat through the distribution system to heat the house.
3. **Outputs** – these may be *direct* – in the form of heat within each room of the house, hot water for washing, waste products from the fuel combustion processes involved, and so on – or *indirect* in the form of waste-water products after use for washing, etc.

A telephone system

A public telephone system may be modelled in terms of:

1. **Input** – the message spoken into the telephone handset.

2 **Process** – the conversion of the spoken message into a series of electrical pulses which are transmitted through the telephone cables and exchanges to the receiving handset. Upon receipt, the electrical pulses are converted back into sound waves to recreate the original spoken message in the receiver's handset.
3 **Output** – the spoken message transmitted by the sender.

The human response system

Apart from these examples of physical or tangible systems, it is possible to construct models of systems which are less tangible – or, indeed, intangible. These systems are only detectable by observing the externally manifested processes or activities that take place as a result of hidden operations within the system. An example of this type of system is the operation of the human brain in responding to a particular stimulus. Such a system may comprise the following elements:

1 **Inputs** – the messages received from the various senses of sight, hearing, smell and touch. This will tend to stimulate recall of previous comparable experiences which are stored in the brain's memory banks.
2 **Process** – the conversion of the messages received from the senses into a form convenient for evaluation and then comparison with the recalled experiences, to create images or perceptions of the situation immediately faced. This should generate appropriate signals to other components of the body which are designed to make the necessary responses.
3 **Outputs** – a set of views, opinions, perceptions and conclusions which relate to the situation faced, with decisions to act or not to act based on those conclusions as to the necessary responses required.

As an example of the operation of this system, consider a driver who approaches a traffic light at red. The visual message of the red light is transmitted to the brain. This is matched against previous knowledge and experiences stored in the brain, which suggest that the red light means danger and that the law requires the driver to stop the vehicle (even a fire engine on the way to a major disaster will technically be breaking the law if the instruction of the red light is ignored). Following this processing, a series of output commands is transmitted, resulting in the necessary actions of the driver's limbs to halt or not to halt the vehicle.

System environment

Our examples focused on the input, process and output elements of systems. The fourth element in the modelling of a system is the environment. In fact, every system must operate within a context or environment and, if it is to function effectively, it will interact with this environment by receiving inputs and delivering outputs. But the parts of the environment from which the system receives its inputs are not necessarily the same as those to which it delivers its outputs. Hence, a retail food shop as a system will receive its primary inputs from food manufacturers or suppliers in the environment, and the outputs will be collected by, or delivered to, its customers in the environment. Similarly, in the domestic heating example the fuel input will be received from the energy suppliers, but it produces an output for the customer and not the supplier.

The other components of the environment with which the system interacts may themselves be classified as systems. Figure 4.2 provides a schematic view of the interdependence of a system with other systems in its environment.

In conceptual terms, the environment may be viewed as a series of levels or layers of systems which surrounds and supports the primary system under consideration. The innermost layer represents those elements or systems within the environment which have the most direct and positive effect on the system. Other systems or elements in the outer layers have progressively less direct interaction with (and therefore less effect on) the system at the centre. Indeed, the more remote the systems in the outer layers, the less likely it is that their influence will be felt in the inner layers. Thus, when a systems analyst is called on to map a system's environment, only those systems in the innermost layer would normally be considered, although in planning damage limitation strategies the analyst needs to recognize that systems in the outer layers may, by a form of 'domino effect', occasionally produce a significant and unexpected impact on the centre system. Consider, for example, the unexpected rejection by consumers of the Coca-Cola Company's 'New Coke' brand in 1985 and the effect it had on the manufacturer's marketing information system, forcing it to reinstate its old product.

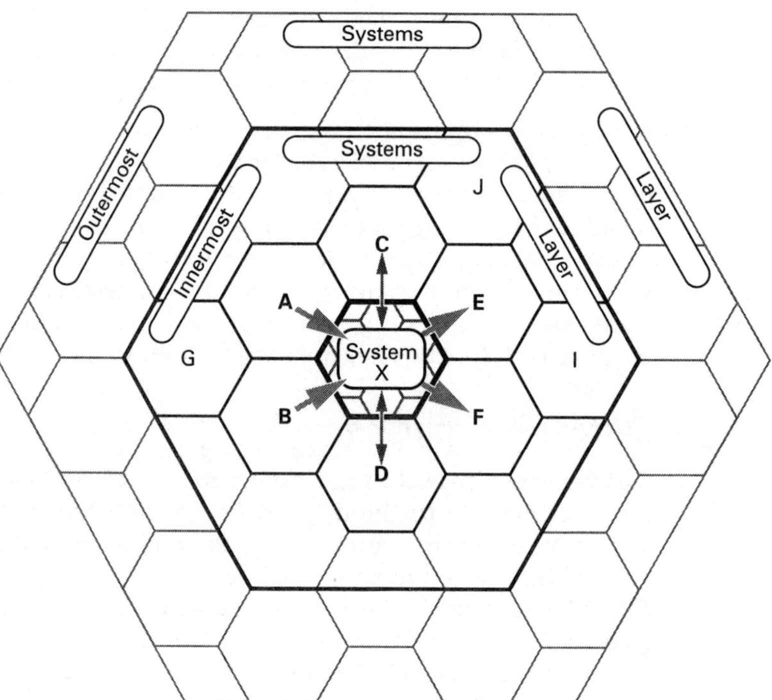

Figure 4.2 Layers of interacting systems in the system's environment.

System X (not to be confused with the telephone system) in Figure 4.2 may interact directly with each of the other six systems shown in the inner layer of its environment. In a practical situation, the degree of interaction or the nature of the interdependence is likely to vary in each of the relationships between the various systems. For example, Systems A and B may only provide inputs to System X and receive no outputs, while Systems E and F may only receive outputs from System X without contributing any inputs. Systems C and D provide a model of the third possibility in that they provide inputs to, and receive outputs from, System X, following processing. In our earlier example of the domestic heating system, the systems would match up as follows:

(A and B) = the fuel supply system which provides the basic inputs
(C and D) = the system of pipework and radiators which receives heated water for distribution and returns the water to System X for further processing or reheating
(E and F) = the flue system designed to extract the waste and often harmful products from the fuel combustion process and to dispose of these safely into the atmosphere
(G, I and J) = systems which do not interact directly with System X but may have an indirect impact on its inputs, processes or outputs through the other systems. (This may be represented by dislocations in the primary processing or distribution of the fuel used, for example a power cut, or the enactment of legislation to control the emission of harmful waste products into the atmosphere, such as carbon monoxide or smoke.)

This schematic view of the interaction of systems grossly understates the complexity of such interactions in practice, as:

- Each individual system may interact with a very large number of other systems over a period of time. Taking an organization as a total system, it would be quite possible to identify an extensive range of interactions with other organizations and systems. This would also be true of smaller-scale systems. The problem from the systems analysis and design viewpoint is to decide which of these interactions should be included in the model of the system.
- Some interactions may occur on a continuous or regular basis, while others may be either infrequent or one-off events. It may be necessary to construct different models which represent varying timescales of interaction, so that relevant events are clustered together.
- The importance of certain interactions (as distinct from their *regularity)* is also likely to vary between systems. Any failure to incorporate details of an irregular, although significant, system interaction may invalidate the effectiveness of the analysis and design of a system.
- The nature of the interactions themselves may be complex and not always predictable or amenable to 'straight line' representation. The interaction of humans as part of a system and their differing behaviour patterns serve to illustrate the difficulty. Approaches that may be adopted to represent these less tangible elements include, notably, Checkland's 'soft system

methodology', which focuses on the analysis, design and development of the 'soft' elements of a system – the human, behavioural and process components – and differentiates them from the 'hard' elements such as physical equipment and 'hardware'.

- The nature and pattern of system interactions is likely to be dynamic. There may be either slow incremental changes or more rapid and radical changes, depending on the general stability of the total environment within which the systems are to operate. Hence a model representing the current system and its pattern of interactions may offer an inappropriate representation of the future situation. This factor of 'continuity of change' in the system's environment is important in determining the length of the system's life cycle. (See Chapter 8 for a fuller treatment of the system's life-cycle concept.)

Systems, sub-systems and the system hierarchy

Another approach to describing the situation shown in Figure 4.2 is to use the terms **system** and **sub-system**. By using these terms, it is usually possible to develop a **systems hierarchy** for any given situation: any system can be seen to be made up of several sub-systems, each of which in turn may comprise further sets of sub-systems. Further, the immediate system may be viewed as a sub-system of a larger system. In Figure 4.2, all the systems lettered A to E and X may be classified as sub-systems of the larger system, a possibility represented by the dotted line embracing them. In turn, each of these sub-systems may be represented by a number of further sub-systems. Thus, in the domestic heating example, System X in the figure may represent the energy conversion process and may itself comprise the following sub-systems:

- the ignition system
- the temperature control system
- the timing system
- the safety cut-out system.

Each of these sub-systems could potentially be further decomposed into sub-systems which would more particularly relate to their constituent parts or activities in undertaking their function. The energy conversion process of which they are part is itself only a sub-system of the total domestic heating system.

Thus, because it is almost impossible to conceive of the nature of the last or highest element in the hierarchy of systems, every system is almost inevitably a sub-system of a larger system. The actual decisions in the modelling process to select elements for inclusion, as being either a system in its own right or as part of a larger system, will depend on the purpose behind developing the model of that system, and generally relate to the level of detailed analysis and investigation that can be cost-justified. Progressing down the system hierarchy, the level of detail successively increases, allowing more detailed analysis and design to be undertaken of the various sub-systems. Conversely, progressing up the system hierarchy provides a broader view of the systems and the sub-systems operating within them. We shall illustrate the advantages of viewing the system hierarchy at differing levels by considering an organization's system hierarchy.

The organization as an example of a system hierarchy

Any organization ought to be viewed as part of an overall system operating within an environment comprising a number of other systems. For example, a commercial manufacturing organization may be viewed as operating within an overall system of business and interfacing with other systems, including the prevailing:

- economic system(s)
- political system(s)
- government policy-making or legislative system(s)
- financial system(s)
- social system(s)
- technology system(s)
- market system(s)
- competitive system.

At a 'macro' level, the organization may interact with each of these broad systems at a number of different levels, including local, national and international. At a 'micro' level, the organization itself may be viewed as a system comprising a number of levels of sub-systems, as shown in Figure 4.3.

The five levels of the system hierarchy identified in the diagram may be summarized as:

1 **Corporate/strategic**. These are systems concerned with supporting the direction, co-ordination and management of the organization as a corporate unit in terms of its objectives, policies, strategies and relationships with the key systems in the external environment. Systems at this level are often termed **strategic support**:
   - business/economic/market forecasting
   - corporate budgets and performance analysis
   - financial planning and modelling.

2 **Business unit**. Many larger organizations comprise a number of distinct units which operate within different areas of technology, offering different product lines or serving different markets or elements of the environment. These units may either be identified as divisions within the organization or will operate as subsidiary companies within a holding company arrangement. The systems which are designed to support this level are also primarily related to the strategic management issues although, in this context, the focus of attention may tend to be the specific product rather than the technology or market aspects of the unit itself. Such systems are also likely to be termed strategic **DSS** (decision support systems), even though their content will differ in some respects from the corporate-level systems. Examples of the type of system at this level would be:
   - market research and forecasting for specific products and markets
   - competitor intelligence and performance
   - performance analysis of particular product lines.

3 **Function**. Systems at this level will be designed to support the management of the primary functions of the organization and to incorporate systems

concerned with aspects of strategic and medium-term planning in addition to co-ordination, performance monitoring, evaluation and control. The more general term for this type of system is a DSS. Systems at this level may incorporate:

- financial planning and budgeting
- manufacturing performance analysis
- profit/volume/pricing analysis.

4 **Departmental**. The primary issues at the departmental level are related to the implementation of strategic plans and the management of the resources and operations within the department. Typically the time horizon is short to medium term, and the systems used are often similar to the DSS, although the term applied to these is often **operational control systems**, as they focus more on the planning and control of operational activities than on the analysis, planning and control of tactical or strategic issues. Typical examples of these systems are:
   - credit management and control
   - stock control
   - quality control.

5 **Operational**. The operational level systems are designed to support the individual day-to-day operations of the organization, and they appear in a wide variety of forms depending on the nature of the operations or transactions concerned (for an example, see the sales order processing system described later in this chapter). The terms **operational support systems** or **transaction processing systems** are frequently used to refer to systems at this level. Examples of this level of system include:
   - sales order processing
   - stock requisitioning
   - production progress chasing.

Indistinct aspects

Although a number of terms have been developed to assist in distinguishing between the systems which appear at different levels in the hierarchy, in practice the degree of distinction is less obvious because of the following factors:

- **common data** – systems at different levels frequently use the same data sources, and the processing of the data relevant to each level is undertaken simultaneously. This follows from the fact that the information used at a higher level is often little more than a summarized form of the same information used for activities at the lower levels
- **decision interdependence** – the nature of the activities between the levels is often interlocking, as it is rarely possible, say, to make strategic decisions without also considering the management or operational implications. Moreover, the analysis of strategic alternatives may often require detailed investigations of certain dimensions of the operations to test the feasibility of each possible alternative
- **common decision-makers** – in smaller organizations, many of the levels of decision-making and control which are differentiated in Figure 4.3 are

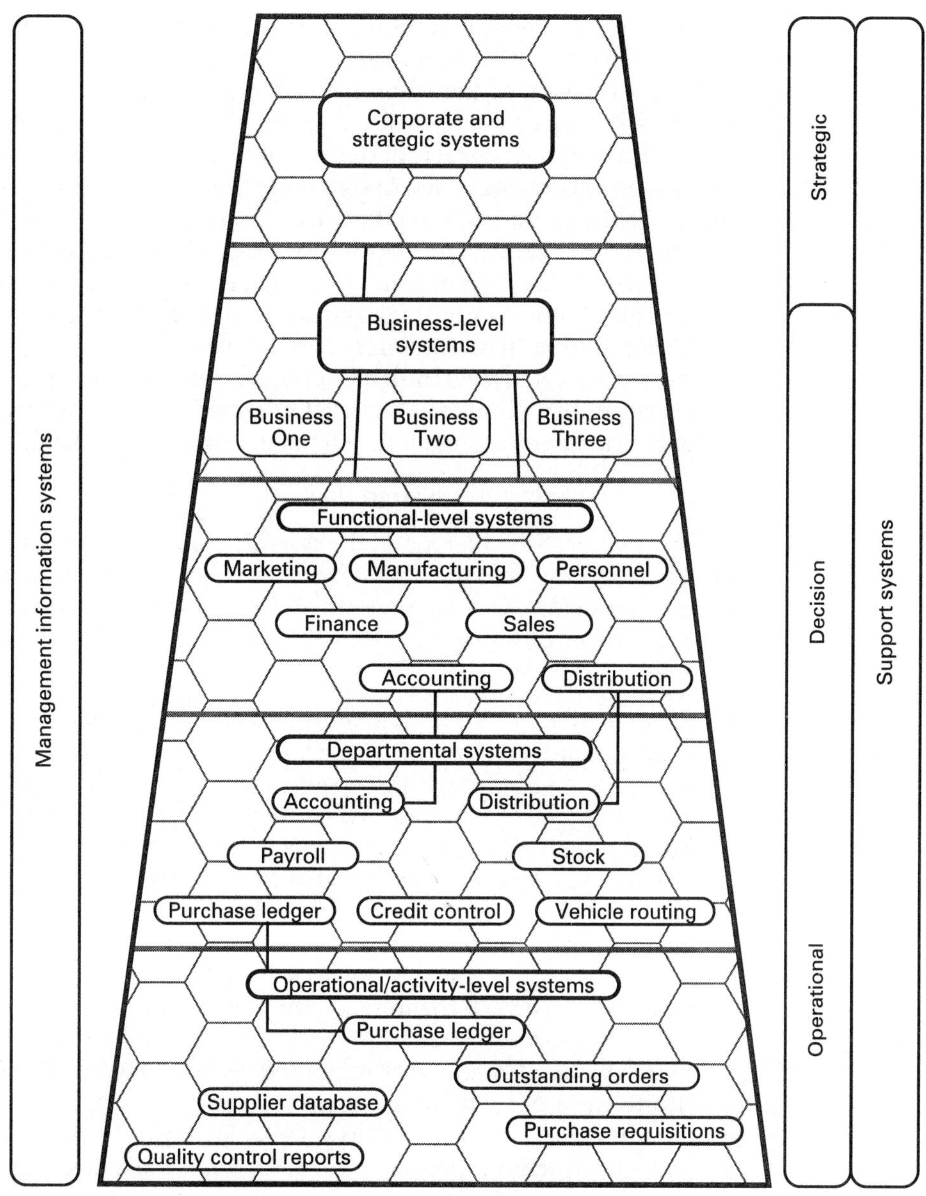

Figure 4.3 Hierarchy of systems in an organization.

undertaken by the same person, who may be simultaneously responsible for strategic, management and operational control in a certain functional area of the organization.

A broad term used to define all the systems designed to support the management and control of the organization at all levels is **management information systems (MIS)**, which generally encompasses strategic support systems, DSS and some elements of the operational support systems concerned with the monitoring and control of departmental operations.

While a number of these sub-systems may operate within clearly identified functional or departmental boundaries, there are also sub-systems which necessarily operate across several functions or departments within the organization. To simplify management's decision-making task by reducing the number of variables to be considered, the various internal sub-systems in the organization will usually be organized so that they interact with only a limited number of the other systems in the organization's external environment, and often with only a part or sub-system of the total system in the environment. For example, the payroll sub-system in an organization may have links with the income tax sub-system in the overall government legislative system and with the local banking sub-system within the overall financial system, but may have few or no links with any of the other environmental systems that we identified earlier.

Benefits of studying the system hierarchy

Recognition of this hierarchy of systems and sub-systems is of particular importance to the activities of analysis, evaluation, development and design as applied to systems. Viewing a system and its component sub-systems at different levels provides differing and valuable perspectives for these activities. For example:

- the total system level provides an overview of the entire system, indicating the major interactions with other systems in the environment, the overall balance and structure of the system and the major component sub-systems. The systems analyst or designer needs this view, as it provides the perspective within which the overall or strategic development of the system may be viewed, and it also assists in locating, or putting into context, the specific sub-systems which are of more immediate or tactical concern
- the functional/departmental sub-systems level provides an understanding of the major sub-systems within a particular function or department, and the nature and extent of the interactions between each of these sub-systems. The tactical (or short- to medium-term) system development activities need to be aware of these interfaces and should seek to maximize the efficiency and effectiveness of these interactions
- the individual operational sub-systems level within functions, departments or areas of activity provides the basis for the detailed analysis and design activities concerning the operation of the system and its effective interaction or interface with humans, whether inputting resources, controlling the processing or receiving the resource output.

System boundaries

While the analyst may be able to separate systems and sub-systems on a conceptual basis, either in terms of their different levels in the hierarchy or of some functional division between those operating at the same level, the task of differentiation in practice is far more difficult. The primary difficulty lies in identifying where one system or sub-system ends, in terms of its outputs, and where the next system begins. This applies equally at both the horizontal and vertical levels of system interfaces, and it is evident in the physical processing systems as well as the information systems. This problem of *boundary definition* is typically seen in the context of information systems where two sub-systems require the same basic input data but process these data in different ways to produce different outputs.

Consider a manufacturing organization which creates a manufacturing reporting system for recording, collecting and processing the production output levels achieved by individual employees. It is likely to function as a sub-system of the performance monitoring process for employees as productive workers, and for operations in general. The wages system may equally use these data as the basis on which to calculate the wages due to each employee, say, on a piece work rate. The data as used are the same for both systems, but the nature of the processing and the outputs may differ. The issue is whether, in analysing or constructing a model of the wages system, the analyst should incorporate the activities of recording and processing the basic data currently undertaken within the manufacturing reporting system. In practice, this involves fairly pragmatic decisions by the systems analyst, based on:

- the nature and scope of the analysis and design task in terms of the detail required
- the relevant stage in the overall systems development process
- the importance of data input or output quality and the need to exercise control over assuring this quality
- the degree of integration proposed between the appropriate sub-systems and the importance of ensuring effective interaction.

System interfaces

The essential feature inherent in the interface between the various sub-systems, both internal and external to the organization, is that there is some form of *resource exchange*. This exchange is normally in the form of an input–output relationship and, in the business and commercial context, it will be a reciprocal exchange. Thus, the provision of raw materials by a supplier usually involves the reciprocal supply of money or equivalent value to pay for those materials. Similarly, the delivery of processed outputs to another system, for example to the wholesale distributor, will usually be reciprocated by payment for the goods or services delivered.

The overall objective of the business or commercial system, as outlined in Chapter 1, is to undertake each system represented by the input–process–output cycle of operations at a level which yields an economic reward or profit. In the not-for-profit organization, the incidence of financial compensation in return for resources received or delivered is likely to be less evident, although there will still often be a reciprocal exchange of other resources or services to assist in meeting variable costs. In a number of general situations, the financial compensation provided will be less than the value of the resources exchanged, as in the present structure of public benefit provision in the UK through local education or the health services.

Other systems also involve the exchange of resources or value between the various sub-systems. The domestic heating example, outlined earlier, involves an exchange between the unprocessed fuels, heated water and waste products. In this system there is less evidence of the exchange of financial compensation other than to the supplier of the unprocessed fuel and, if it is efficient, the ability to avoid other payments to create or run an alternative or supplementary heating system. Similarly, the telephone system involves the exchange of resources between the various sub-systems, although the level of reciprocity between the sub-systems is less evident. Thus, financial compensation is usually paid to the supplier of the telephone system which makes the communication possible or, if different, to the company which supplies the telephone-based service – for instance, a chat-line service which provides friendly conversation to relieve boredom or loneliness for a fee. In our third example, the human brain system, there is an exchange of resources between the various human sub-systems, though no evidence of financial compensation for the supply of the resources other than payment to the present holder of the brain if the output is marketable!

Communications

The reliability of the interface between systems depends on the effectiveness and robustness of the communications. The quality of integration and interaction achievable between the various systems will largely be determined by the following four factors:

- the quality of the original data
- the quality of the transmitter and receiver
- the quality of the channel
- the effectiveness of the feedback loops employed.

The main elements which comprise the communications system are shown in Figure 4.4, and the analysis of the figure is followed by three illustrative examples relating to voice, written and electronic communications.

1 Quality of original data

The quality of the data available will be judged either by the content or by reference to the other qualitative dimensions outlined in Chapter 2. There is a direct relationship between the initial data quality and the maximum quality level of data that may be produced by a system. The commonly used expression for this situation:

Rubbish in = rubbish out

discussed in Chapter 1, indicates this connection. In one sense, there is no doubt that if the initial data item is corrupted, little can be made of it. But if the information is merely inadequate to support decision making in its initial form, processing may enhance its quality. The question is as to the degree of

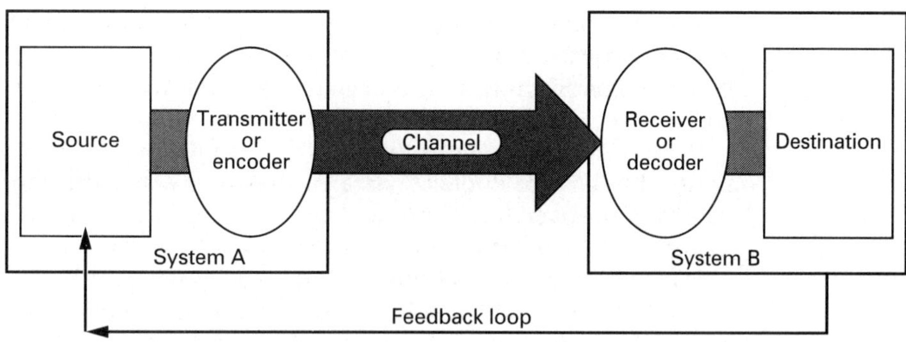

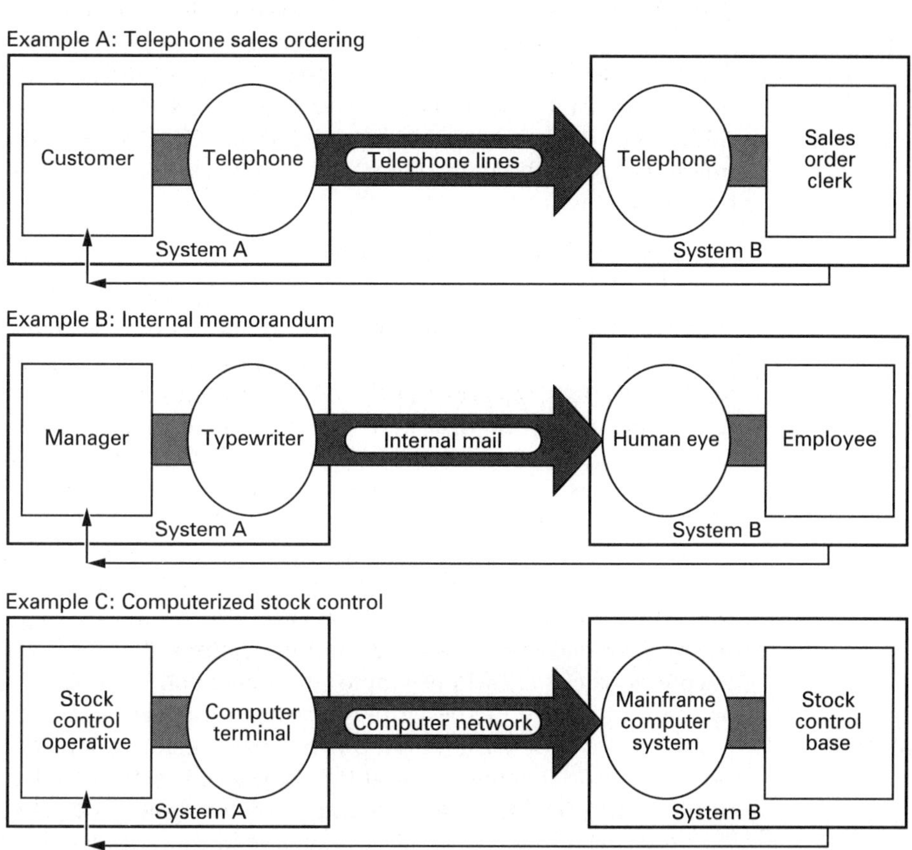

Figure 4.4 System communications.

improvement achievable. This will always be limited by the quality and detail of the input data as obtained and recorded.

Issues related to quality are those of **data redundancy** and **data reduction**. Data redundancy implies that parts of the data collected and input are unnecessary for the processing required to produce the desired outputs.

Generally, this would suggest inefficiency as additional units of unwanted data are being collected, stored, transmitted, sorted out and, possibly, discarded. This may add considerably to the overall communication, handling and processing costs.

There are some situations in which data redundancy is deliberately introduced. Here, additional or duplicate data elements are created to assist in assuring the quality of the overall communication process. (See later in this sub-section under *feedback loops systems*.)

Data reduction, on the other hand, usually represents a deliberate policy of reducing these costs by only transmitting a summarized or truncated version of the complete data. The use of abbreviated words in telex transmissions is an example of data reduction. While this technique may improve the speed of data transfer and reduce the cost because of the lower volume of data, an obvious danger is the greater potential impact that interference or noise may have on the quality of the data received. In the worst case, the transmission of only key characters or data elements may result in either unintelligible or misleading data being received, depending on the nature and severity of interference or noise in the communications system. (See the paragraph below on channel quality.)

2 Transmission or receiver quality

The quality of the devices used to transmit and receive the data at either end of the communications channel will also influence the effectiveness of communications. The transmitting or encoding systems largely involve some form of human interface, such as the use of a telephone, transcription by typewriter to hard copy, or the use of a keyboard by stock control operatives to input data. Such human interfaces are frequently the source of the greatest loss of data quality and, as a result, considerable research and development has been undertaken to improve or often eliminate this interface. The use of bar coding on products and EPOS tills with their electronic sensors at the supermarket, instead of relying on the checkout assistant to accurately key in the identity and price of every item sold, is an example of such a development. A similar problem exists at the receiver/decoder end of the communications channel, as in the cases of the telephone sales clerk who is employed to hear and then record the data received, or the human eye of the employee who must read a memorandum from the manager. Technological developments have made a larger impact here. The primary reason for this is that, if the data have been transmitted in an electronic form, it may be input directly into the electronic processing system without further human involvement. The example of a network of terminals linked to a mainframe computer system, as in the stock control example in Figure 4.4, is illustrative of this.

3 Channel quality

The type and quality of the media used to channel the data from the transmitting system to the receiving system will influence the quality of the communications. To adopt engineering terminology, the channel may be affected by interference, distortion and noise.

Interference is often associated with some form of technical difficulty, for example inadequate shielding in the cabling used.

Distortion is where a material change occurs in the form of the data during transmission. Any reduction in the volume of a telephone message during transmission would be a form of distortion. The term often refers to changes which have qualities of predictability and uniformity of effect, so that the data can be restored by an inverse operation at the receiving end; for example, by increasing the volume on a telephone receiver.

Noise, as distinct from distortion, represents a more random and unpredictable form of interference or change in the message transmitted. In the case of noise, any part of the message as transmitted may be altered, corrupted or misinterpreted by the receiving system. The term may also apply to superfluous data content in the message transmitted which obscures the intended meaning, or to the use of language or a writing style in a document which may be misunderstood by the recipient.

4 Feedback loops

A fairly common method of ensuring the integrity of any communication between two systems is to institute some form of feedback loop so that the received message, or parts of it, may be transmitted in the reverse direction and checked by the originator. A telephone sales order clerk may, for instance, repeat the full details of an order to the customer prior to completing the transaction, the employee may telephone the manager to verify the intended interpretation of the instructions in the memorandum, and the mainframe computer may retransmit the message received to the computer terminal screen for final validation by the stock control clerk.

Another method of improving the integrity of communications is to incorporate extra elements of data which may be used to verify specific dimensions of the data transmitted. Thus batch totals provide a check that all the items transmitted have been received, while column and hash totals provide some check on the integrity of the data within the records. The incorporation of check digits or other coding systems may also be used to improve the quality and accuracy of the communication process. Each of these methods invariably increases the amount of data to be handled and transmitted and therefore adds to data redundancy. The irony is that the more data requiring transmission, the greater the potential incidence of interference, distortion and noise, thus counteracting some of the benefits to data integrity achieved through their use.

While feedback loops and other methods of verifying the integrity of the data will probably improve the quality of communications and reduce the problems associated with transmission, receiver and channel quality, they are not infallible. Equally, they will not be capable of improving the quality of the original data prior to transmission, given that they can at best only produce a perfect reproduction of the original data. It should also be recognized that each of these mechanisms involves additional costs, both in the initial design and to operate, and may also reduce the *efficiency* of the communications system even while improving its effectiveness.

Delays in the system

A feature of system operation associated with that of the communications system is the efficiency or speed with which the feedback loop operates and, consequently, the system itself responds to changes in its environment. Delays in the system may occur for a number of reasons, some of which are planned, while others are unintentional:

- Failure arising from faulty or inadequate sensors to detect data which would indicate a change in the environment. A faulty fire detector, or one requiring significant changes in temperature before operating, will result in a delay before the alarm is raised.
- Delays in transmitting the data received from the environment may be caused by the data recorder deliberately delaying transmission while awaiting further confirmation. Thus, a quality inspector in a car factory may delay reporting a particular fault on one vehicle and wait for confirmation through further examples of the fault on other vehicles before initiating the feedback process.
- A fault or failure in the communication itself will result in unplanned delays: a fault on the telephone line, for instance, may interrupt transmission and cause delays in the system.
- People operating the system may deliberately cause delays in the system to cause maximum disruption or damage. For example, to create a bigger and more profitable job, a maintenance engineer may deliberately delay reporting the first signs of pipework corrosion. This could have disastrous consequences for, say, a chemical plant
- The nature of the data and the method used to process them may result in deliberate delays being introduced into the system. Thus, it may prove more economic to collect the data into large batches before processing it rather than to process each item as it is received. This distinction between 'batch' and 'real-time' processing is developed later in this chapter.

The needs of the system or its users are an important factor in determining the degree of responsiveness required from the system. If the system is not required to respond to every minor change in its environment, it may be perfectly acceptable to examine the environment periodically rather than continuously. Thus, the sales data for an organization will be collected continuously, but the managers might decide that it is acceptable to delay the analysis and review of this data until the end of the monthly accounting period.

Delays may also result from the decision-making process following feedback. Managers may hesitate before taking action for a variety of reasons:

- they fail to understand the new situation
- because of lack of experience, they are unable to decide what to do
- there is a dispute as to the best course of action
- the resources are inadequate for an effective response to be made
- they are afraid that their proposed action may upset other people who work in the organization or disrupt other systems within the organization.

It is important to realize that people can have complicated motives for their actions, so delays may be both intentional and unintentional to different people within the system. You should therefore be aware that delays are not necessarily a sign of any inefficiency or inadequacy in the system itself. Indeed, many system delays are planned to improve the efficiency and effectiveness of the system.

System control

A feature of many systems is the incorporation of some form of regulatory or control mechanism which monitors and corrects any deviations in the desired performance of the system. This may either be *internal* to the system, so that the system is self-correcting, or it may be *external* to the system and require action by another system to provide the necessary corrective action. In addition to correcting any detected deviations in the internal processing elements, a system may also have to respond to changes in the environment, both in terms of inputs received and outputs required. Most naturally occurring systems have in-built control systems which take corrective action, either for changes in the environment or for deviations in the normal system processes. In the case of human-generated systems, these control features need to be designed into the system itself. Hence, excessive increases in the temperature of the fuel core in a nuclear power station ought to result in a sequence of activities to control the deviation, although the nature of these activities and their effectiveness will depend on the quality of the design process.

The basic issue from the systems design point of view is the degree to which potential changes in the environment and the difficulties which may be encountered in the processing and communications systems may be accurately predicted or foreseen. The designer also needs to establish the extent to which the system should be capable of responding to changes in the environment. Because of the additional capacities, the design of systems which are highly responsive or flexible often incurs significantly higher design and operating costs than those designed to meet only the more obvious demands of the environment. Failure to predict certain situations, inadequate detection systems, ineffective feedback systems, or poorly designed features to respond to the situation could have serious consequences for the overall system's effectiveness and efficiency. The organization must therefore make design decisions based on accurate cost–benefit analysis.

The term **closed system** refers to those systems which are not responsive to changes in the environment. Such a system has a one-way relationship with its environment, having no mechanisms to monitor the effect of its outputs on the environment and hence no means of adapting to changes in this environment. If the environment is relatively stable then such systems may operate effectively for long periods of time. In more dynamic environments, such systems will rapidly disintegrate or become obsolete relative to the requirements of their environment. Systems which are completely immune to the needs of their environment are increasingly rare – particularly in the field of information systems, where changes in the technological and the general organizational operating environments are becoming increasingly rapid and dramatic.

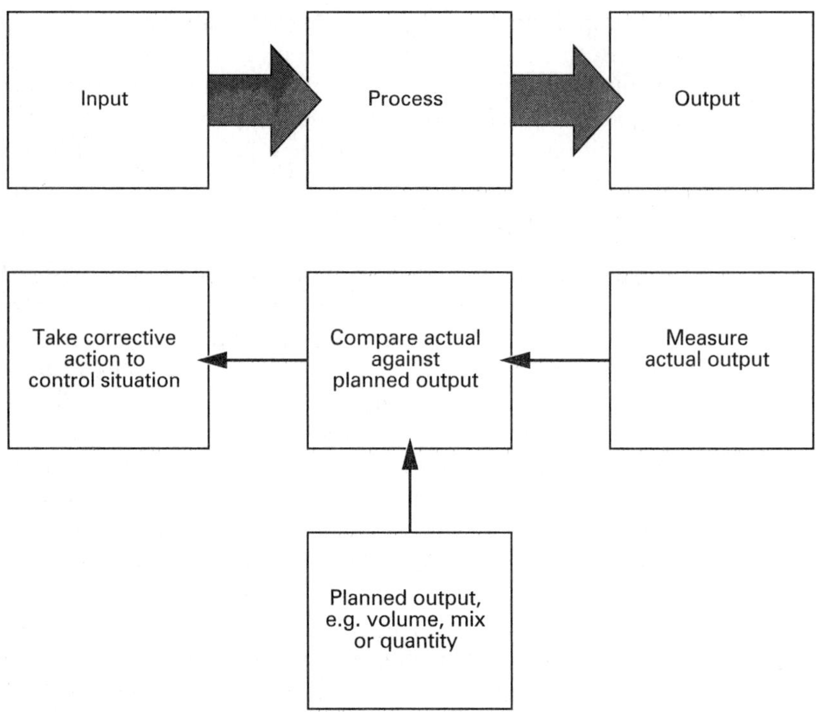

Figure 4.5 Control and feedback systems.

A **open system** is the term applied to systems which are responsive or adaptive to the environment within which the system operates. Usually the system would incorporate desired or planned performance parameters, which may be specified in terms of the different anticipated environmental situations that may be encountered. Figure 4.5 provides a schematic outline of the main components of the control system. Few human-generated systems are completely responsive to changes in the environment: systems will differ in their degree of responsiveness, a factor often determined by the effectiveness and quality of the control system in operation. In reality most systems are on the continuum between an open and a closed system, i.e. a semi-closed system. The system may be permitted to respond to environmental needs within certain predetermined parameters or rules.

Positive and negative feedback and exception reporting

The signals received by the system from the environment and transmitted through the feedback loop may be classified as either positive or negative. Whether the classification is positive or negative will depend on a comparison between the *expected* and the *actual* situation.

Positive feedback

If the input received by the system from the environment matches what is expected, this is a *positive feedback:* that is, it will affirm that the relationship between the organization and its environment is normal, and no corrective response is required. Thus, the presence of a green light on the railway signalling system provides a positive feedback to the train driver: it indicates that the next set of track is clear and that the signalling system is working properly (as a design, the default signal is always red). Similarly, the monthly financial statement indicating no significant overspends on any of the budget headings provides a positive feedback that no corrective action is required by the accounting or management systems.

Negative feedback

Data inputs from the environment which do not match the expected level or type of input are termed *negative feedback*. This will always require some form of corrective action by the system. The presence of a red light on the railway track would signal another train on the track ahead or indicate that the signalling system had failed. In either eventuality, safety requires the driver to stop the train. Similarly, the reporting of a significant overspend on the capital budget in the monthly financial statement would indicate a problem for the accounting or management system to address.

Exception reporting

A modified version of negative feedback is the process of *exception reporting*. In situations where the systems only need to respond if the variation in expectation is significantly different from that expected, only those variations which exceed the threshold value need to be fed back through the system. The variation threshold may be determined by reference to:

- **frequency** – for example the system would only respond if the number of customer complaints exceeds 20 in any given day
- **scale** – for example only budgets overspending by more than 10% of the monthly budget level should be reported
- **source** – for example requests from particular customers demand an immediate response.

The justification for exception reporting is that it reduces the volume and cost of data processed by the system which does not require responsive or corrective action. Equally, the reduction in the volume of data processed and fed back will assist in directing the attention of the system and its users to the more important decisions and action required.

Organizational information systems

The development of the concepts and approaches of the systems theory may be applied to any system which deals with resources, including the information resource.

Functions of an information system

An information system in an organization may be represented by one or all three of the following functions:

- recording transactions between particular systems and sub-systems in terms of the inputs and outputs. This may be between the organization and other external systems, or internally between the organization's various sub-systems
- recording or monitoring the processing activities within a system or sub-system with a view to providing information on the efficiency and effectiveness of the operations or activities involved
- processing the information itself as the basic resource. Examples of this would include market research and intelligence systems, library catalogue systems and teletext services.

In the two latter functions the information system is operating in parallel to the other operational systems within the organization and is providing information on the activities involved. In a sense, the information system and its sub-systems are essentially 'shadow' systems designed to monitor the performance of the other (productive) systems. This would be true even in the first function, where the primary resource being processed is information itself. The situation is complicated further by the existence of information sub-systems which are designed to monitor the development and operational performance of the organization's information systems themselves. These latter information systems will be explained later.

Elements of an information system

A model of an information system can be produced by applying the elements from the general systems approach. From a functional point of view, an information system is a system primarily concerned with the conversion of data into information, as discussed in Chapter 1. The contribution that such a systems model makes to the analysis and design process is outlined below in relation to each of the major system elements discussed earlier. Only a broad view of the contribution of the systems approach is provided at this stage, as a more detailed view is provided in later chapters dealing specifically with the development, analysis and design of information systems.

The contribution of the general systems approach to the analysis and design of information systems may be summarized as follows:

Inputs

- identification both of the data available in other sub-systems and of the data that may have to be originated by the system itself

- evaluation of the potential to interface with other sub-systems, either in the technological/technical sense of compatibility of the systems or in the commercial sense of feasibility and costs
- assessment of both the content and quality of the information available and the degree to which this matches the needs of the information system's users.

Process

- analysis of the processing activities required to convert the input received into the outputs required, which may include a selection from:
  – recording
  – conversion into other units or media storage
  – calculation
  – summarization
  – retrieval
  – communication
- assessment of the quality standards required in processing to maintain the content and quality of the data input
- evaluation of the potential effectiveness and efficiency of the processing activities involved
- an investigation of the interaction between the various sub-systems involved in processing the data.

Output

- analysis and evaluation of the potential users of the information and their requirements in terms of content and quality
- an investigation of the alternative means of communicating to the users in terms of media use, frequency, content and style
- an examination of the nature of the interaction between the system, its users and other sub-systems in terms of regular communications or *ad hoc* enquiries.

Environment

- identification and assessment of the interaction between the system, as both currently and potentially constituted, and other external systems or sub-systems. This aspect is becoming increasingly important as developments in technology facilitate rapid and cost-effective communications through the networking of information systems
- evaluation of the appropriate methods for assessing the quality of the output from the system.

Communication channels

- recognition of the potential communication channels and alternative media and selection of the most appropriate for the given situation in terms of volume and quality of data transmission required.
- the identification of likely sources of interference, distortion and noise on the channels used and an evaluation of the possible means of overcoming these difficulties.

Feedback and control systems

- the analysis and development of appropriate feedback systems which will record the quality, effectiveness and efficiency of the input and processing stages in the system and monitor the environmental responses to outputs
- an appraisal of the likely situations requiring control actions, and the development and evaluation of automatic control routines or the provision of information to facilitate effective human control.

Major components in the organization's information system

The major components in a typical business or commercial organization are shown in Figure 4.6. Not-for-profit organizations will have a number of similar components, although the terminology used and the nature of their functions may vary from the model shown.

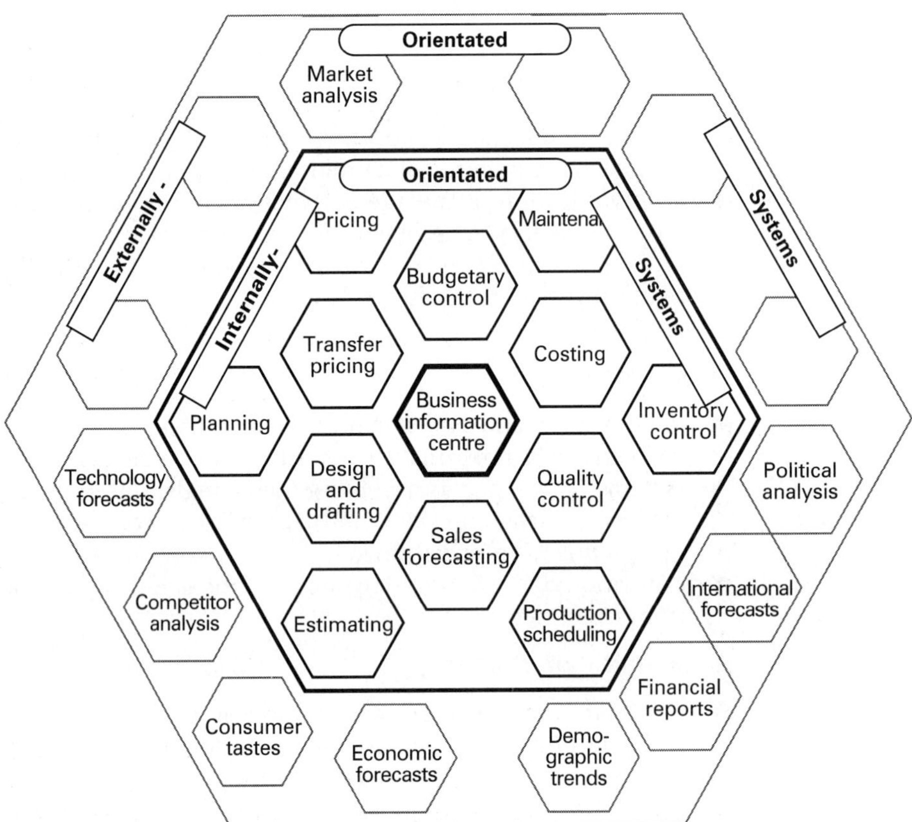

Figure 4.6 Components of a business organization's information system.

The sub-systems in the overall information system have been divided into two groups according to the degree with which they interact with the external environment and its sub-systems.

Externally-orientated sub-systems

These sub-systems record the transactions between the organization and the systems within its environment in terms of suppliers, customers and other agencies, incorporating:

- purchasing
- goods received
- purchase payments ledger
- marketing
- sales
- distribution
- sales invoicing
- sales receipts
- personnel
- wages and salaries
- research and development.

Many of these sub-systems reflect the primary activities of the organization. As such, there is likely to be interaction, both internally and externally, as data are transferred between each sub-system to facilitate co-ordinated actions relating to the suppliers, customers or other agencies in the environment. For example, the transfer of customer order and credit details from the sales sub-system is essential for the preparation of sales invoices and the subsequent collection of monies owing.

Internally-orientated sub-systems

The internally-orientated sub-systems are primarily concerned with supporting the operations, decision making, control and management of the organization at the operational, managerial and strategic levels. Such sub-systems include:

- cost accounting
- budgetary control
- inventory
- production scheduling and control
- quality control
- forecasting
- planning
- product design and drawing
- transfer pricing.

Typically, these sub-systems will not only interact with each other but will also draw on the externally-orientated sub-systems to provide some of the data for their processing and output. At the centre of this group of interlocking and interacting systems and sub-systems is the **information centre**. This represents a location (although not necessarily a physical location) from which either all or part of the data in these systems may be accessed. A more detailed treatment of information centres is provided in Chapter 8.

Generic system components

The typical organizational sub-systems outlined above frequently contain one of four generic components in their processing activities:

- text or word processing
- spreadsheet manipulation
- database storage and retrieval
- expert system operations.

These activities are equally likely to be found in either the externally-orientated or the internally-orientated sub-systems. A number of the applications are also likely to be met in systems which rely more on the manual processing of data than on electronic technology. This should not conceal the fact that the advent of powerful and rapid data processing technology has considerably enhanced the power and potential contribution of each of these components. The basic elements of each of these will be introduced in the following paragraphs, with more detailed treatment of generic components in Chapters 6, 7 and 9.

Word processing

Text or word processing concerns the manipulation of data in the form of text by the processes of creation, storage and modification. The efficient application of these processes does require appropriate computer or word-processing technology, although systems of standard format letters and correspondence have permitted the modest application of such processes in manual systems. Such processes may prove efficient in situations where:

- the original data or text entered may require significant modification prior to final output and distribution
- the bulk of the data or text remains the same for a large volume of potential recipients, with only minor modifications required: for example, changes in name, address and title for the recipients of a standard letter.

Different documents may be created for communication (whether electronic or manual) by selecting from a series of standard paragraphs or blocks of text. Thus, different combinations or sequences are prepared to meet the particular needs of a given situation, such as the compilation of contractual agreements and conditions of employment for differing groups of employees in an organization by abstracting, and perhaps modifying, appropriate clauses from a databank of precedents.

The applications associated with or developing from word-processing include:

1. **Desk-top publishing (DTP)**, which provides a range of specialist facilities to design and modify the layout of the text to improve its appearance and communications effectiveness.

2 **Mailing list applications**, which provide a constructive link between word-processing facilities and databases. The best results are achieved when powerful facilities are created to tailor the contents and layout of correspondence to the needs of particular recipients.
3 **Business graphics**, representing a link between the text processing and spreadsheet components and allowing sometimes complex information to be displayed in a more easily understood form. This may be screen-based or modern printers may reproduce the output in a form which can be incorporated into reports and other textual material, thereby enhancing the effectiveness of the communication. DTP software facilities now provide sophisticated packages to manipulate the presentation of text and graphics on the printed page.

Common examples of PC-based word processing packages include WordPerfect and Microsoft Word. More sophisticated DTP packages include Ventura and Adobe Pagemaker. An example of a popular business graphics package is Harvard Graphics. The majority of the more sophisticated packages require a high-specification PC and monitor.

Spreadsheets

Spreadsheet processing primarily concerns the manipulation of numeric data, although textual data may be incorporated to facilitate titling and other forms of brief commentary relating to the data. The layout of a spreadsheet is in the form of a matrix with a series of rows and columns, as shown in Figure 4.7.

The operation of a spreadsheet simulates the sequence of manual processes or calculations that may be performed on a set of data. The application of spreadsheet processing is particularly appropriate in cases where:

- A set of identical or standard calculations or manipulations needs to be repeated several times for different sets of data, for example technical calculations in the engineering design department to establish the precise composition and tolerances required in the manufacture of a particular component to meet differing customer requirements.
- The data item is to be processed using a continuous sequence of calculations, such that the output from one calculation represents the input to the next calculation in the sequence. The calculation of profit within an income statement represents this type of application, or the preparation of monthly budget forecasts, as shown in Figure 4.7.
- The use of spreadsheets to support forecasting is significant. This may be achieved either by analysing the effect of changes in a single variable in a given situation or by simulating the effects of changes in a variety of the parameters. This is normally termed sensitivity analysis. Its utility lies in the scientific testing of the robustness of the predicted model. Measuring the effect on the profitability of a capital investment under differing assumptions of rates of interest, market growth rates or inflation rates is typical of the type of application involved.

	Sales forecasts/income and expenditure budgets						
	January	February	March	April	May	June	Total
Sales revenue forecasts							
Product A							
Units	1200	1253	1246	1368	1413	1395	7875
Price (£)	20	20	20	20	22	24	
Revenue (£)	24000	25060	24920	27360	31086	33480	165906
Product B							
Units	960	950	1005	1010	1020	1100	6045
Price (£)	35	35	35	35	35	35	
Revenue (£)	57600	58310	60095	62710	66786	71980	
Total revenue (£)	57600	58310	60095	62710	66786	71980	377481
Expenditure forecasts							
Wages and salaries	27000	27000	28600	28750	28900	29000	169250
Materials	12000	12400	12560	12760	12850	13505	76075
Direct overheads	4000	4500	4500	4600	4200	4300	26100
Indirect overheads	7000	7500	7500	8000	8500	9000	47500
Total expenditure (£)	50000	51400	53160	54110	54450	55805	318925
Profit forecast (£)	7600	6910	6395	8600	12336	16175	58556
If sales volume and price increase by 10% (costs remaining constant)							
Profit forecast (£)	18096	17465	17849	20033	24656	29510	127609
If sales volume and price decrease by 10% (costs remaining constant)							
Profit forecast (£)	-1744	-2479	-2777	-1579	1352	4279	-2948

Figure 4.7 Spreadsheet application.

Although the spreadsheet approach may be applied in manual systems, the true power of this system tool may be realized only in conjunction with a computer system which facilitates the rapid calculation of the many formulae incorporated in the construction of such models. Manual calculation often proves too time-consuming to enable more than a few modifications to the model parameters to be considered effectively. The trend for PC-based packages was set by Computer Associates' Visicalc. Packages introduced since have tended to concentrate on the following enhancements to the original concept:

- increasing the maximum size of the matrix which can be manipulated
- producing more attractive graphical displays from the results of the calculations
- exchanging data with stand-alone database and word-processing packages
- producing more user-friendly interfaces
- providing availability for mini and mainframe computer platforms.

Examples of popular spreadsheet packages include Lotus 123 which became very popular on the IBM PC, and Microsoft Excel which proved equally popular with Apple Macintosh users. Borland QuattroPro is another package which contains many advanced features. An example of a spreadsheet package for mini or mainframe computers is Oracle SQL*Calc, which interfaces with the Oracle relational database and fourth-generation language (4GL).

Databases

The database component essentially collects data together into convenient groupings and provides a facility to achieve rapid access to retrieve data elements which are required for processing by other system components. These sets of data or records may be classified by contents as the customer database, the product database, the employee database, etc. In the manual system such databases would normally be housed in filing cabinets, whereas in computer-based systems the larger databases will be stored on disk packs. In addition to providing storage for the data records, the database system typically incorporates facilities for adding to or maintaining the existing records, and a facility for retrieving the particular data required. It is the speed of response and the sophistication of the retrieval through the use of **Boolean connectors** which make the computer-based system significantly more powerful than the equivalent manual systems.

PC databases share the same type of user-friendly interface as the spreadsheet and word-processing packages. Although obviously not able to hold as many data items as a large mini or mainframe database, a PC package such as dBase IV or Foxbase will allow the user to carry out the basic operations of data insertion, amendment, review and deletion, and allow simple tabular reports to be produced. Examples of mini or mainframe databases which could supply the information needs of a large organization include Oracle and Relational Technology's Ingres.

Expert systems

Expert system components essentially comprise *routines* or sets of instructions relating to the data processing and analysis tools and techniques available for supporting the organization's decision making. Typically, such systems are designed to emulate the analytical and choice processes undertaken by human decision-makers and to incorporate some of the knowledge elements and choice criteria that would be applied in specified decision situations. These systems may be either allowed the responsibility of taking the complete decision (electronic share-dealing systems, for example, buy and sell on world markets without immediate human supervision) or used to screen or filter out the unacceptable decision alternatives on given criteria before the human decision-maker makes the final judgement, based on a wider set of less predictable or quantifiable criteria.

Development issues in expert systems

The development of expert systems is becoming an increasingly important issue for larger corporations. One of the first questions to answer is whether there is any role for the enthusiastic amateur to capture the expertise which is already held by the organization. No matter what the nature of the information system, whether centralized or decentralized, or the form of the organizational management structure, all organizations are little more than small pockets of expertise which are harnessed for the common good. To achieve the requisite level of co-ordination, departments are being created to manage the formally acknowledged human resources and knowledge engineering skills are being developed in the area known as **artificial intelligence (AI)** to help capture and support human expertise. Efforts in this direction have become more positive, not only because the technology has improved but because the increasingly competitive climate makes it essential on two quite different but equally important fronts that the organization makes the most effective use of all the resources available to it. So an organization can typically take one of two attitudes to the harnessing of expertise for the corporate good:

- it can view it as part of the human resource management side, ensuring that people who have expertise should be exploited to the best advantage of the existing organization; or
- it can see it as a way in which the best possible automated systems to support the organization can be built, by eliciting and incorporating available knowledge or expertise into decision support systems and expert systems on which the organization can rely for many years to come – and, of course, long after the human experts involved may have left the organization. This approach also makes that expertise available to a much wider range of managers and professional staff.

Knowledge engineering may therefore be seen as an increasingly important but difficult and specialized function.

The construction of expert systems

One of the mistakes most easily made is to believe that computers can be expert in the human sense. In fact, a so-called expert system is nothing more than a computer system which possesses a set of facts about a particular area of human knowledge and, by manipulating those facts in line with the programming, can make useful inferences for the end user. The concept of intelligence has different dimensions but, at the end of the day, the computer cannot be intelligent until it develops sufficient semantic understanding to be able to convert its own data into knowledge. Until then, it can only be made to mimic intelligence by performing tasks which humans *think of* as intelligent. Sometimes, the programming can achieve this by elegant means: thus, simple exhaustive searching, if sufficiently fast, could produce results which might be taken as evidencing intelligence. But it might be considered more intelligent to avoid the search altogether, or to delimit it by prior enquiries.

The way humans think of intelligence will also be determined by the use to which the computer is put. The usual point of distinction is that an intelligent system is one capable of solving problems which cannot be resolved by using crude computational methods – that is to say, there is a distinction between standard data processing techniques and the genuinely expert system. The point made by those who market expert systems is that they will exhibit expert behaviour. In practice, the power of any truly expert system is that some representation of the knowledge used by a human has been achieved in a preprogrammed form which can be used as a basis for computation.

The computer system depends for its effectiveness on the facts which have been elicited from human experts. These facts, which are often expressed as rules, then form a conceptual representation of the relevant expertise. There are two levels of difference between a human expert and a beginner:

- a human expert knows more
- a human expert is likely to use the knowledge more effectively.

Eliciting human knowledge

In the first instance, the actual content of the knowledge base will be unique to each individual who supplies the data, and the explanation of the content will be a personal process. But in learning how to capture and write down exactly what the expertise is, the notional system of concepts which emerges can be applied to other experts' knowledge. Knowledge acquisition (the extraction of the knowledge which forms the underlying base of the expertise from the human expert), or knowledge identification by the expert for entry into a shell are the most difficult aspects of developing an expert system of any size. In some domains where the procedures involved are simple and algorithmic, the knowledge can be made explicit fairly easily. A preliminary survey through basic textbooks, followed by confirmatory interviews or discussions with colleagues, will usually be sufficient to permit the creation of a prototype conceptual model which can then be tested.

Generally, the most effective ways for a knowledge (or software) engineer to acquire information from experts are by observation in the field or in-depth interviewing. These methods are inherently slow – a major problem, given that experts' time tends to be limited. It can also be difficult to represent the rules which are obtained in this way, because an observational data item is often incomplete and inconsistent, and the observer must continually refer back to the experts for clarification. This substantially increases the amount of time involved, and tests the patience of all involved. The most usual approach is to rely on informal interviews to elicit information, which is then converted into empirical rules (usually in a form laid down by the target shell). However, not all expertise is capable of being represented as a rule system: for example, areas of medical diagnosis may depend on extensive practical experience and strategic knowledge which is difficult to verbalize, and the informality of the interview may enhance the incompleteness and inexact nature of the information that is acquired.

Any expert knowledge is likely to be of different types. It is difficult, if not impossible, to classify knowledge but we can suggest the following broad categories:

- **overview knowledge**, i.e. knowledge of concepts and the relationships between different parts of the domain
- **knowledge of the routine procedures**, backed up by knowledge of key facts which are particular to certain areas of the expertise and of the heuristics, i.e. the rules of thumb for choosing how to solve a problem
- **classificatory knowledge**, i.e. the ability to make fine distinctions between a number of similar items.

One way for the expert to gain an insight into knowledge held is to write information down. For the objective outsider, an interview of the expert with these classifications in mind can be helpful. This can quickly generate a lot of information that indicates the terminology and the main components of the intellectual domain in question, and is thus a good starting procedure to establish a basic framework. It is also useful to ask the expert to give a one-hour lecture which can be followed by later systematic probing interviews where depth is added. But, as indicated above, all interviews have limitations. Although experts have the knowledge, it may not be easily communicated in the course of interviews.

It is possible to combine knowledge extracted from several different experts and thereby to overcome the problem of incompleteness, but this may cause severe problems if the experts approach the resolution of problems with different methods. The ideal solution would be to produce systems which could induce rules from all the examples given by the contributing experts. However, the danger with such systems is that there may be a large number of rules generated, or that the one or two rules induced work well with the particular examples given but do not work well outside the particular data set.

A recent development, **protocol analysis**, records the behaviour (verbal or otherwise) of the expert and shows how a problem is addressed and solved. The protocol is then converted into a set of productions that moves sequentially through the solution methodology. Its merit is that it goes beyond what the expert can actually tell the knowledge engineer, and permits detailed inference as to what knowledge the expert must be using but either cannot verbalize or may not even be aware of. By reconstructing the solution using the inferred production rules, the expert's knowledge can be modelled. Protocol analysis is preceded by **task analysis**, i.e. the constraints imposed by the nature of the task are determined. By taping the expert at work, additional or incidental protocols may be elicited: informal remarks may provide key insights into the expert's thinking which might not have emerged during a formal interview. The problem is that this approach is labour-intensive, requiring the transcription and analysis of significant quantities of data and reducing the useful amount of end-product material. A number of multidimensional scaling techniques have been used in psychology to show how a particular set of concepts are structured: for example repertory grids can elicit finer grain criteria than formal interviews. By identifying clustering on the dimensions, the system designer can give a structure which more clearly differentiates the domain objects. This can also lead to the development of *meta-knowledge,* an overview understanding which provides a conceptual framework for structuring individual elements or concepts. However, such techniques are extremely specialized and demanding.

Expert system shells

The answer to such questions for the administrative and commercial sectors lies in the expert system shell. There is an increasing range of expert system shells now available on the commercial market. Most are supplied in two versions: a larger mainframe system, more suitable for complex tasks, and a smaller version suitable for use on a PC, e.g. SAVOIR™ and Micro Expert™. Although the ideal system for the creation of software would be subject-led and not software-led – because that would permit the human expert to structure the information in the most internally consistent and intellectually satisfying way – this presupposes that the experts actually understand their subjects in a way which is suitable for conversion into a knowledge base. It was this problem which could be reduced by allocating a specialist knowledge engineer to each expert, and giving that engineer the task of both representing a form of external objectivity to the creative process involved and tailoring the software to the knowledge.

Without this outside assistance, the expert needs a series of prompts from the software itself to indicate the format requirements of the particular system. The danger in this is, of course, that the software will then represent a form of intellectual strait-jacket, restricting the structure of the knowledge and the computational range of the processes that are to be performed. Thus, if the domain expert, when asked, clearly stated that the method adopted to solve a particular problem was a given series of procedures, a knowledge engineer could either select an appropriate piece of software off the shelf or create routines which would perform those procedures in their proper context. But if the expert is told from the outset that only a limited number of software procedures are available in the particular shell supplied, it is entirely possible that none of these procedures will match those required within the domain expertise. In such a case, the expert either will be deterred from attempting to create the system or will distort the real-world expertise to meet the constraints of the shell. Neither result is satisfactory, but perhaps some effort is better than none. Even if the expert is unhappy with the result, it may still be better than nothing and offer some assistance to the organization.

Because the concept of the shell has been elaborated to allow newcomers to develop their own expert systems without the need for specialist knowledge engineering skills, the standard shell will provide a means for encoding the domain knowledge and inferencing mechanisms to make use of the encoded knowledge. Most fact-seeking expert systems elicit findings by interviewing the user in an inflexible way. The user has no control over the course of the interaction, which tends to be lengthy and tiring. This pattern may be acceptable for interviewing clients in a professional context, but it is not completely acceptable for the busy professional. However, whether through interview or through self-generated input, the knowledge database can be constructed.

Because some shells make it relatively easy to adjust the knowledge modelled, it is even sometimes better for the knowledge engineer to prototype by using a shell before building a bigger system from scratch. However, if a shell is used without expert assistance, there are still problems:

- a shell is not self-critical and cannot iterate towards an optimum solution
- shells cannot be trained to think, so if the user does not know the answer to a given question, the shell cannot rephrase it and will fail to elicit the information
- the correction facilities must be good, so that if the user realizes that a mistake has been made, it should not be necessary to scrap the program and to start again. It should be a simple matter of going back to the relevant point in the program and changing the wording of the material displayed or amending the switching commands.

There are also fundamental difficulties in basing detailed evidential evaluation on the **Bayesian odds** approach, which is quite common in shell designs.

In the future, knowledge engineers and information scientists will be providing software and data systems which allow an organization to meet the needs of the market place more effectively. The more completely the organization captures an individual's expertise which is making money or adding value today, the longer the period over which that person's expertise can benefit the organization. In general, selecting which skills to capture is a strategic management decision. The difficulty is that if a computer-orientated person looks at another's expertise and skills, the perspective selected may be the immediate feasibility of automating the whole or a part of that skill, or something may be discarded as unimportant because, from the DP person's point of view, it is not a necessary skill – whereas organizationally it might be considerably more important. The decision should be taken by the human resource managers; it will then feed down to the knowledge engineers who will appraise the feasibility of actually capturing the identified skills.

Integrated packages

One can buy packages which integrate the features of a word processor, a spreadsheet and a small database. An example of such a package is Lotus Symphony. The **advantages** which are claimed for such a package, as against separate packages, include the following:

- the user has only one interface or set of commands to learn. The overall time taken to make use of all three components is thereby reduced
- the problems of exchanging data between three separate packages are eliminated. Adding spreadsheet results to reports (such as a cash budget proposal) or merging a report from the database into a word-processed letter (such as an 'overdue' letter sent to a defaulting debtor) would be much easier
- an integrated package may be cheaper than three separate packages. This is because the marketing and support costs will not be tripled and the amount of programming involved in producing the package is generally less
- the user has to deal with only one supplier for maintenance and support.

All of these features would appear to make a strong case for the integrated PC package. However, the following **disadvantages** should be borne in mind before selecting such a package:

- the separate package approach may be more flexible. A single package may be upgraded if a new version is released or even changed if another package is later found preferable, whereas an integrated package may be upgraded less frequently and component packages cannot easily be replaced by packages from other manufacturers
- an integrated package usually only proves useful to someone whose job includes data storage, manipulation and calculation. While this rules out many managerial and clerical workers, it describes an accountant's role quite accurately!
- there may have to be design compromises in terms of the features or performance of one of the components of the integrated package, striking a balance between the size of the package itself and its data handling capacities. The word-processing component of an integrated package is the one most usually sacrificed by the manufacturer, and it will rarely be as powerful as a specialist word processor. This may be of importance if the intention is to produce significant amounts of text or to perform a general secretarial function
- separate packages may be more flexible. The user can tailor a mixture of separate packages to his or her own requirements: for example, an accountant may place less importance on the word processor and therefore require fewer features in this component.

A formal method of carrying out a comparison to determine the merits of an integrated package as against separate packages would be to use the 'weighted ranking' technique (see Chapter 7).

Components of a typical business information sub-system

The scale and complexity of the total information system within even small organizations makes a detailed description impossible in this text. However, we have selected a particular sub-system of the total information system, which itself comprises a number of identifiable sub-systems, to illustrate and consolidate a number of the concepts and issues relating to the systems approach developed in this chapter, including:

- **data inputs**: distinguishing between those that are internally generated and those that are externally generated
- **processes**: illustrating a number of the typical data processing activities, and showing how they combine within an information system
- **outputs**: identifying those that are directed towards users outside of the environment, those that are used internally, and those that essentially provide an input into another processing sub-system
- **communications** and the nature of the channels used

- **interaction** between a particular sub-system and other sub-systems
- **hierarchy of levels** within the organization's decision-making system and the way in which the same data may be successively reprocessed to meet the needs of users at each different level.

The system used to illustrate these points is the sales order processing system which, in its general operation and components, is fairly common to most types of business and commercial organizations. A schematic representation of this type of system is provided in Figure 4.8.

Operational level

The function of the system at the operational level is to facilitate and support:

- the effective processing of each sales order transaction and to produce the necessary outputs for both internal and external users to facilitate the completion of the sales transaction
- the monitoring and control of the transaction operations on an ongoing basis.

Inputs

In addition to the receipt of the customer's order, the system requires inputs from internal sources identifying, say, the customer's address, any special delivery instructions or discount arrangements (held in the *customer database*); the product descriptions, specifications and prices (held in the *product database*); details of the amount already owed by the customer and of the credit limits allowed (held in the *sales ledger*); and the availability of the items ordered (held in the *stock database*).

Process

Typical activities involved in processing the order as received are the preparation of the necessary instructions to fulfil the order, requesting payment from the customer, recording the transaction details and updating its effects on the other activities in the business. It should be recognized that these broad processing activities in themselves comprise a number of individual activities, each using parts of the data inputs.

Outputs

At this level, the primary outputs are internal instructions (or inputs) to other systems in the organization (not shown in Figure 4.8) to undertake the prescribed processing or activities required to fulfil the customer's order. The input resources used in processing the sales transaction are also updated with a record of the transaction prior to being used on subsequent transactions, either for the same or different customers. These outputs will remain within the overall organizational system, although the delivery note and invoice will be despatched outside the organization.

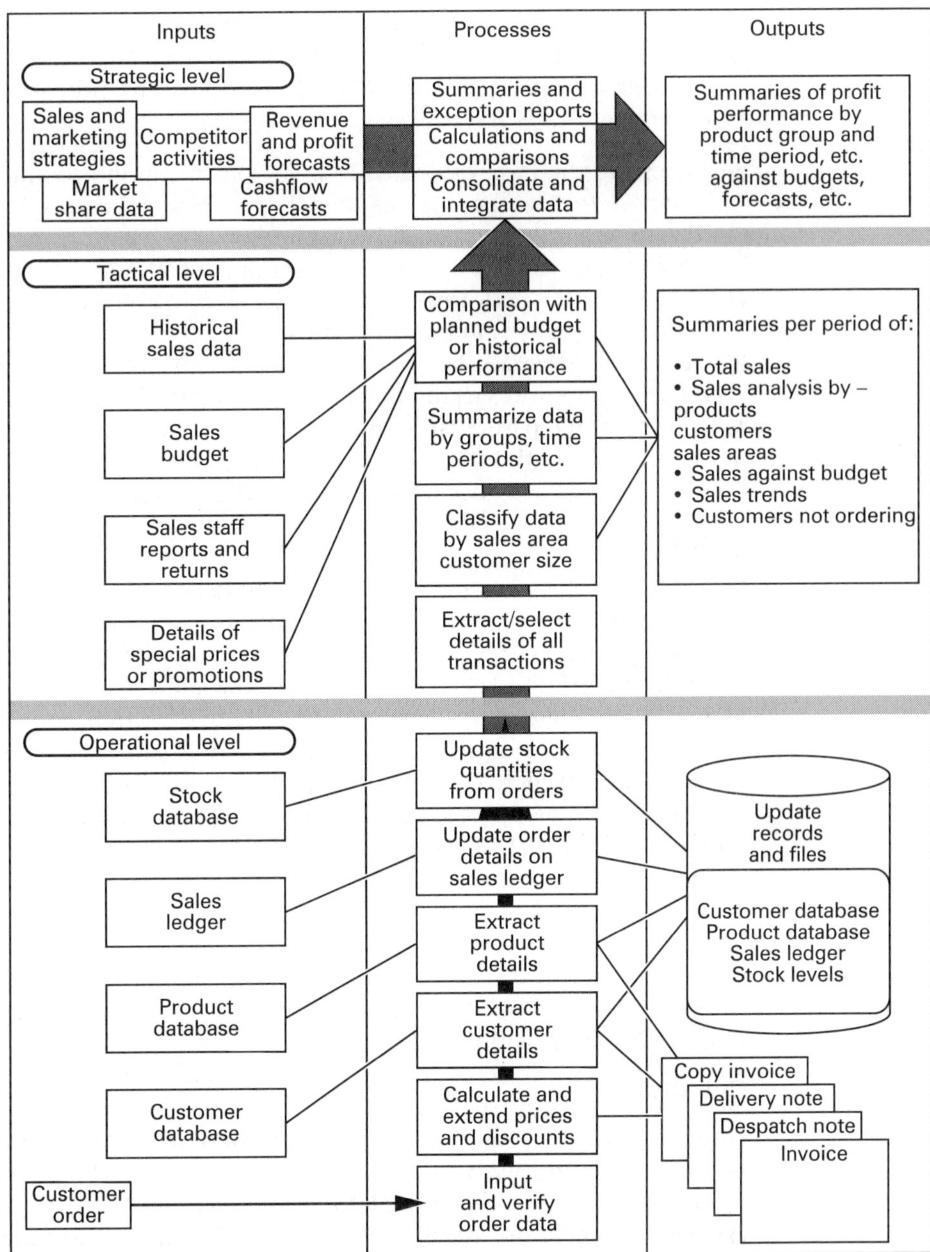

Figure 4.8 Sales order processing system.

Tactical level

The function of the system at this level is concerned less with the processing of individual customer sales transactions but more with extracting significant elements of the data from every transaction. The intention is to produce guidelines, measures or indicators of the performance levels of the various dimensions of the organization's sales activities. The primary concerns of the management at this level are:

- Assessing the level of demand for the organization's products or services in relation to forecasts or planned levels. If expectations are not fulfilled, decisions must be made either to improve the methods of forecasting or to identify and correct defects in the selling operation.
- Evaluating the performance of the sales staff in exercising their functions and identifying potential improvements.
- Identifying particular products which are failing to achieve market expectations and seeking possible explanations for this deficiency.
- Highlighting particular customer accounts which have low or declining levels of activity in terms of either the frequency or the size of orders, and directing the attention of sales staff to these levels.

Inputs

In addition to the extracted and summarized data elements from the transactions processed at the operational level, a number of other inputs will be required to provide the necessary coverage and detail to support the above functions. For example, historical sales records or budgets would be required as a comparative base to assess the current level of sales activities; written or verbal reports from sales staff may be required to supplement this quantitative data; and details on special factors likely to cause temporary distortions (such as price promotions on a particular product or geographical area) would provide some explanation for observed deviations from plans or expectations.

Process

The processing activities illustrated in Figure 4.8 are typical of those found in many management level systems, involving selection/extraction, classifying/sorting, summarizing/collating, and comparing with some benchmark such as previous levels or planned levels.

Outputs

Outputs from the system at this level are primarily, though not always exclusively, destined for use within the organization itself. Thus, summaries of total activity levels may be provided to trade federations, governmental statistical agencies or similar organizations concerned with monitoring aggregate sales and activity levels in markets or industries. But the processed and summarized data will usually continue its upward path to the strategic level, although this migration will often be enhanced by the addition of the analysis, evaluation, commentary, explanation, potential implications and proposed corrective actions produced as a result of information supplied to management for performance monitoring, control and decision making. The transfer of this information to the next level will typically be in report form, often more selective and summarized than at the management level.

Strategic level

Systems at the strategic level are primarily concerned with providing an overview of the performance of the total organization, highlighting any potential deficiencies, and providing information to guide and support the strategic development, planning and overall control.

Inputs

The data captured in the sales order processing system at the operational level, and subsequently aggregated and summarized at the management level, make an important contribution towards this strategic analysis and development by providing data on the performance of the company in the market. The sales revenue data items are also consolidated and integrated with cost and expenditure data generated from other operational information systems to provide assessments of profit performance and the cashflow implications. In addition to the use of internally generated information, the strategic appraisal process utilizes a significant volume of externally generated data, as illustrated in Figure 4.8, to facilitate comparative analysis of the organization's performance with its competitors in terms of sales growth trends, market shares, profitability and other performance criteria. The strategic level is typified not only by the increased reliance on externally-generated data, but also on the diversity of data sources used internally.

Process

The data processing activities at this level are primarily concerned with integrating performance data from the different functions and operations in the business to provide a consolidated view of overall performance, for example consolidation of revenue and cost data to provide a monthly income statement or budget summary. Other typical processing activities are summarization of the data, identification of exceptional elements and the comparison of actual performance against plans or targets.

Outputs

The format and content of the outputs from this processing stage will invariably be more summarized, more integrated across all the operations or functions of the business, and concerned more with the implications of the observed trends for the future of the organization. In the context of the sales order processing system, the output would identify the broad pattern of sales trends for each product, comparing these with the sales forecast and the planned levels or competitors' sales, and extrapolating these trends into the future.

Communications within the system

A feature of most systems which operate in a hierarchical organizational system is the successive filtering of the data as they progress up the hierarchy. The key implication of this data reduction is the loss of detail. The greater the degree of abstraction from the source data, the more likely is the loss of accuracy. Counteracting this, however, is the potential reduction in the incidence of interference, distortion or noise as the volume of data being transmitted reduces as it progresses upwards. In this context, the impact of information technologies is greater at the operational levels than at the tactical or strategic levels. Hence, there is likely to be greater use of electronic capture, processing, communications and output at the operational level than at the higher levels of the system.

For example, in many sales order processing systems the first task is capturing and converting the data into an electronic format via electronic tills, keyboards or electronic scanners. Once converted into the electronic form, all the subsequent processing at the operational level may take place without further manual manipulation, thereby reducing the labour content (which is revenue-expensive) and minimizing the chances of error. Subsequent processing at the tactical or strategic levels may involve manually-orientated processes of selection, integration and analysis. The results may appear in the form of written reports, and the preparation will be demanding where the format and content is to vary each period. If the content and format are relatively static, the automatic production of these outputs by utilizing the electronically stored data becomes technically and economically viable.

Summary

This chapter has demonstrated that any operation or activity, whether it be in a commercial, public or private situation, may be expressed in the form of a system. Each system may be decomposed into the key elements of inputs, processes and outputs. Such a decomposition aids the analysis, design and developments of the systems in question. A key feature in practice is the degree to which a system interacts with other systems in its environment. Recognition of the level and nature of such interactions provides the basis of the systems approach to analysing and designing systems. Each system may be further broken down into sub-systems, each of which interacts with others to perform the functions of the total system. These concepts are fundamental to understanding the functioning of the various elements within an organization and the organization's interaction with its environment.

An important element of any system is the quality of its communications and linkages with other systems. This directly influences the quality of the information system and hence the quality of the information provided to users in the organization. Effective communications should be designed to minimize interference, distortion and noise. Control systems may be developed within a system to test both the appropriateness of the system's outputs in relation to the environment's needs and the effectiveness and efficiency of the communications channels.

Systems which have the facility to monitor and feed back responses from the environment, and to modify their operations to meet the changing situation, are termed **open** systems, as opposed to **closed** systems which do not interact with their environment.

Information systems contain a number of generic components: word processing, spreadsheet, databases and expert systems. These are frequently combined to facilitate specific types of data processing. The components of the information system are required to meet the needs of users at all levels in the business, operational, tactical and strategic. The data generated at one level will typically provide the data for further processing to provide information to another level.

Self-test questions

1 Describe the main elements of a system and explain their operation.
2 Write brief notes on system boundaries and provide examples to explain this concept.
3 List and briefly describe the five levels of the system hierarchy which may be found in a large commercial organization.
4 Explain the difference between externally-oriented sub-systems and internally-oriented sub-systems.
5 Distinguish between 'open loop' and 'closed loop' control systems.

Exam-style questions

1 'The reliability of the interface between systems depends on the effectiveness and robustness of the communications.' Explain what is meant by this statement and discuss the factors which largely determine the quality of integration and interaction between systems.
2 A model of an organization's information systems can be produced by applying the elements from the 'general systems' approach. Identify the major components of an information system and explain how the general systems approach may be applied to them.
3 Perco plc distributes its products through a network of wholesale organizations and direct to independent retailers in the High Street. This approach typically requires Perco plc to offer extensive trade credit, almost 70% of sales revenue, and involving average credit periods of 70 days to trade customers. The company has decided to exert greater control on its credit policy to improve its financial position. Using the principles of systems theory and the associated control systems, outline an approach that Perco plc might use to develop a system to handle this problem.

(*All answers on pages 551–553*)

CHAPTER 5

Financial and related information systems

In this chapter we set out to identify different forms of organizational structure and to assess their effect on the kinds of information system that can most successfully meet corporate needs. In particular, we examine the characteristics of organizational types that affect management needs and their implications for the use of information resources. Our discussion distinguishes data structure from organizational structure and examines the formal and informal elements of information systems.

Next, we look at the ways in which information systems can grow and evolve within organizations, identifying key phases within development frameworks. We then relate various system types – ranging from specialized data processing systems through decision support systems to the more complex management applications of expert systems – to levels of decision making, planning and control priorities, and information sources and destinations, identifying specific management requirements and related system features. These relationships are depicted in an information systems model.

We finally give attention to the use of information systems to support corporate strategic management and to improve or defend the competitive position of organizations in the market place.

Organizational structures and information systems

You should bear in mind that the structure of any organization is not just a geographical concept. It has important implications for the management process and the flows of information within organizations. Therefore, different types of organization will require different information systems. An important factor in information systems design or selection is to understand the organization in question and its processes – specifically the following:

- the extent to which the business unit is self-contained in decision-making terms
- the amount of information that is exchanged with other parts of the organization
- whether the information systems which exist within the organization are formal or informal in nature
- the historical development of the organization and the nature of the emerging culture in its different parts
- the management style of the organization.

We discuss and illustrate the impact of these factors in the following paragraphs.

Types of organizational structure

First of all, let us consider some examples of the different types of organizational structure and their characteristics which affect management and information systems.

1 A major retail chain will usually have a number of similar stores with a national or regional distribution – usually a single unit in each major town or city. These stores will be responsible for their own low-level information processing, such as internal stock control, and will have a management structure with limited autonomy, within guidelines set by 'head office'. The head office will contain the major functions of the business, such as purchasing, marketing and accounting, and will contain managers who are responsible for making strategic decisions – on new markets, products and price increases, for instance – and who set the guidelines within which each store must stay. A decision to start a marketing campaign or to hold a sale will be made at this level. In some city-centre stores even decisions on the layout of the store and the amount of stock that may be displayed are taken at head office, by people who may rarely visit the stores they control!

   This situation is complicated by the fact that items for sale may arrive at the regional stores directly from suppliers, in response to orders placed by head office. The information system needs to provide continuous information flows and processing between head office, suppliers and stores to monitor and control deliveries.

2 A financial services company may be organized in divisions, each of which offers a separate service. Considerable autonomy will be given to each division in decision-making terms and their exchange of information may be at best periodic (for example the end of an accounting period) or even non-existent. Often the main board will not operate from a separate headquarters location but will be made up of the heads of the separate divisions. In our example these may be insurance, brokerage and pensions.

   In this case, the organization has chosen to specialize at the expense of duplicating some of its major functions. There will be a personnel department and an accounts department in the insurance division, for instance. Our divisionalized organization may choose to locate at sites which are appropriate to its businesses. The brokerage department may be sited in the capital city's financial quarter, for instance. Often organizations which have this structure have grown by acquisition – through mergers or take-overs – and may have radically different information systems and management styles.

3 A manufacturing company which makes a single type of product may choose to operate on a single site so that it can concentrate its technology. In this case the major business functions – design, operations and sales, for instance – will be closely articulated by a shared information system. The management of

such a company will be in close touch with the functional areas and will be in direct receipt of 'control' information resulting from transactions carried out at an operational level.

Factors affecting information system design

Clearly, the information systems required by each of these types of company must match the organizational structure if they are to be successful. Factors which may influence this matching of system to organization include:

- The importance of a dynamic environmental response to the organization. (Obviously, the ability to react to changes in the environment is important to all organizations, but some firms are in business areas where, for instance, adaptation to economic or market conditions makes a dynamic ability particularly crucial to their existence.)
- The management style of the firm, as seen in the formality or informality of its information systems and in whether the information processes are centralized or decentralized.
- The structure of the organization. (An organization may be 'tall' in that it has many layers of management with relatively narrow spans of control – the number of persons who report to each supervisor – or 'flat' in that the span of control is broad with few layers of management.)
- The information intensity of the operation of the business. (This is a measure of the extent to which the organization relies on information to carry out its everyday activities. A bank, in processing its account transactions, is far more reliant on 'low-level' information than a general engineering company would be.)

Implications of organizational types

The 'height' or 'width' of an organizational type has further implications for the way in which the organization uses its information resources. Look at the organizational types in Figure 5.1. It is possible to draw some conclusions:

- A hierarchical organization will be relatively slow to respond to strategic opportunities, such as new products or market changes. There are many layers of management through which decisions will have to be 'filtered'.
- A 'flat' organization will respond more quickly to information which is passed down from the top management or which is gathered at the bottom level. Some authors see the 'flat' organization as representative of a more modern type.
- 'Flat' organizations may be prone to 'information overload' where managers need to pay attention to information from all their subordinates in the organization. The ways in which this disadvantage may be overcome are discussed elsewhere.
- In a 'flat' organization, 'islands' may develop as the greater autonomy in decision making which may be apparent (one way to overcome 'information

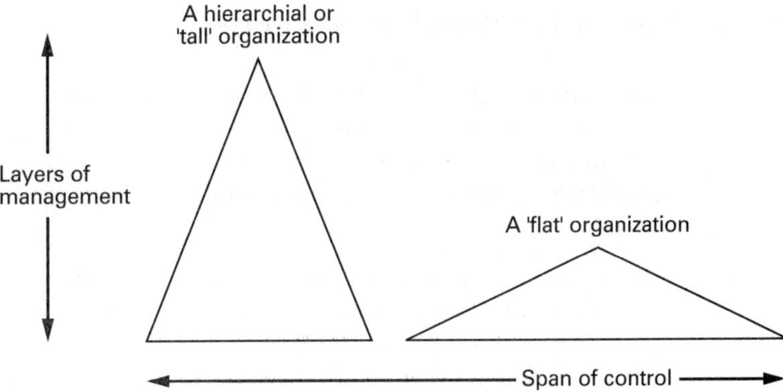

Figure 5.1 Organizational types.

overload') may also cause the functional areas to act separately from one another. The term used where computer-based systems are concerned is 'islands of automation' the piecemeal development of incompatible systems.

Mechanistic and organic organizations

Burns and Stalker (Burns, 1961) identified two forms of organizational design which effectively summarize the different features that we have discussed so far. At one end of the spectrum, a mechanistic organization may have a centralized decision-making function with a hierarchical management structure and rigid procedures and methods of work (e.g. division of labour). The management style will be *directive*. At the other end, an organic organization will be decentralized and flat, with flexible methods of work and a *participative* style of leadership.

Neither organizational form is necessarily better than the other, but one may be more appropriate than the other for certain environmental conditions. A mechanistic form of organization may be more efficient in a stable environment but unable to react to rapid change. An organic form may better support a strategy of growth rather than stability and may offer advantages where many high-level decisions have to be enacted quickly. Similarly, an organic organization may be superior at providing technical innovations. A summary of the characteristics of the two forms is given in Figure 5.2.

Feature	Mechanistic	Organic
Environmental factors	Stable	Dynamic
Decision making	Centralized	Decentralized
Rules and procedures	Rigid	Flexible
Management style	Directive	Participative
Strategy	Stability	Growth
Innovation needs	Low	High

Figure 5.2 Mechanistic and organic organizations.

Structures of information systems

The characteristics of an organization will therefore determine the structure of its information system. Looking at the different types of organizational structures and drawing on the several examples of organizations which we have examined, a number of generalizations about the structure of information systems can be made:

1. A centralized organization with numerous identical outlets (the example of the chain store group) will tend to develop an information system which includes the following features:
   - it will be formal in the way in which the head office deals with the branches. (The branches themselves may develop informal information systems for internal use)
   - the development of the information system and its management will be centrally controlled
   - all the identical business units (branches) will be expected to adopt standard operations and information structures
   - results will be gathered from the branches by the information system on a regular basis
   - control information will pass from head office to the branches.
2. A divisional organization will tend to develop a number of discrete information systems which may have relatively little interaction. In addition, the following characteristics will apply:
   - planning information (regarding major strategic decisions) will be passed from the main board (executive body) to the divisional boards
   - control and result information (e.g. a budgetary process) will stay within each division
   - the development and management of the information systems will tend to be autonomous within each division. Where the information system is computerized (as most are) this could result in incompatible systems or 'islands of automation'.
3. A distributed organization will share some features of the company which has divisions, but with the following differences:
   - there will be much closer coupling between the systems. The units are in the same business and will therefore tend to have more interaction at the system level than do the functional divisions
   - there will be a decentralized approach to information systems development and management
   - communication between the business units will be informed by and will tend to rely on an appropriate infrastructure (e.g. compatible communications links) rather than a formal reporting structure.

Many people regard a distributed organization with a decentralized management approach and a 'flat' structure as the most modern type of organization.

Data independence

It is important to note that the structure of the data which the organization owns and uses should be isolated or separated from the organizational structure. This data structure (sometimes called the 'information architecture') defines the *logical* system, whereas the organization structure is part of the *physical* system. The differences between the two concepts are as follows:

- the logical system deals with the 'what and when' aspects of the system: that is, what is done (e.g. updating a ledger or creating a customer record) and when it takes place (e.g. at the end of a financial period)
- the physical system deals with the 'how and who' aspects: in other words, the mechanism of how tasks are carried out and who is responsible for carrying them out.

Many people hold that to analyse a system in logical terms gives a stable view of what the relevant organization is about. The data, and the operations which are carried out on it, are permanent. How the information is manipulated and who does the manipulation are both liable to change (for instance, where a computer-based system is introduced) but a retail company will always process product, supplier and customer information.

The advantage of data independence is that it allows changes to take place to the physical system – for instance, a more modern computer network – without having to carry out a major re-analysis or redesign of the users' needs.

Formal and informal information systems

All organizational information systems are a mixture of formal and informal elements. The differences are as follows:

- Formal information systems use reports, meetings and pre-defined data to process data around the organization. Much of what goes on in a formal information system will be well structured, routine and capable of being defined with precision. For this reason formal systems are sometimes called 'hard' systems and are relatively easy to computerize.
- Informal information systems consist of less well-defined exchanges of information, using less structured channels of communication. Telephone conversations, memos and discussions over lunch are all informal. Most managers rely far more on informally obtained information than they do on formally produced reports. Opinions, feeling and 'hunches' are all important factors in decision making and are central to an approach to information analysis called 'soft systems' which has links with operations research and general systems theory.

It is impossible to state whether one type of information system is more important to an organization than another. A good system will take both elements into account and will seek to allow the users some flexibility in how they use the information.

How different types of system develop

In order to understand the nature of the different types of information system which may be found in an organization, we need to understand the ways in which such systems can develop.

Stages of information system growth

The process by which information systems develop within organizations was first placed within a formal framework by Richard Nolan (1979). In proposing a six-stage theory of development, Nolan stated that 'There is now a . . . descriptive theory of the evolution of a DP activity – the stage theory. One can use this theory to understand where the company has come from; which problems were a result of weak management and which problems arose from natural growth. More important, one can gain some insight into what the future may hold and then can try to develop appropriate management strategies that will accomplish corporate purposes' (p. 125).

Although later authors have proposed alternative frameworks which may now be more widely accepted, Nolan's model has had a considerable influence on management thought. The six stages of growth are given below.

1 **Initiation**. This denotes the first attempt at computerization by the organization. In Nolan's day, this interest came from the technologists in the organization with little involvement of strategic managers. The focus is now on operational (i.e. data processing) systems which are intended to reduce costs by automating clerical operations.
2 **Contagion**. This occurs as demand from users for information system development exceeds the capacity of the original system. This usually occurs because users have become convinced of the benefits which such systems can offer. There is probably little control at this stage, with piecemeal development (in response to user requests) due to political pressures on the central DP department. It is during this stage that a steering committee may be formed. Senior management may also become aware of (and alarmed by) the increasing level of DP expenditure.
3 **Control**. This occurs when senior management acts in response to the pattern of user demands, increasing costs and failed or unsatisfactory system development. Control will be exerted by imposing the necessary structures on the organization (for example an information manager, steering committee, and so on) and by introducing processes (for example information strategy, systems analysis, and design methods and standards). Sometimes this action may result in a backlog of undeveloped applications and more dissatisfied users.
4 **Integration**. This takes place when control begins to be effective. Senior management gives full support to the structures and processes which are in place, and the stabilizing effect of an information strategy results in systems which exploit opportunities rather than react to problems. 'Islands of automation' are broken down and a database and network will be set up.

5 **Data administration**. This is necessary when information becomes a shared corporate resource. The information systems division (under the control of a board-level information manager) will concentrate on managing data, allowing users to develop their own applications using customized packages and fourth-generation languages. End-user computing and information centres are a feature of this stage.
6 **Maturity**. This arises when the information strategy and the business strategy are closely matched.

We can conveniently regroup Nolan's six stages into three stages, as follows:

1 **innovation** – a period of introduction and experimentation with the technology
2 **incorporation** – during which great efforts are made to control the effects of the technology and to make systems a part of the organization
3 **exploitation** – when the company is comfortable with the technology and is able to use its systems to further its business aims.

An explanation of some of the objectives and actions which typify each phase is shown in Figure 5.3.

Most organizations will have passed through Phase 1 and are involved in overcoming resistance during Phase 2. Reasons for the resistance to the development into the 'exploitation' phase may include:

- a discovery that the technology is inappropriate or too difficult to learn, perhaps due to poor user involvement or inadequate support by the vendor for training
- limited acceptance of the technology, perhaps due to inadequate consultation with the users or 'internal politics' in the organization

Phase	Objectives	Strategies
1 Innovation	■ Introduce technology and explore its potential ■ Institute 'organizational learning'	■ Develop small 'pilot' computer-based systems ■ Help users to learn about the technology
2 Incorporation	■ Gain management control over the technology ■ Technology transfer	■ Introduce controls and planning procedures ■ Help users to identify opportunities to use the technology
3 Exploitation	■ Use technology as a strategic weapon ■ Support the management decision process	■ Develop systems to give competitive advantage ■ Introduce support technology

Figure 5.3 Phases in technology assimilation (after Zwass, 1992).

- artificially restricting the spread of technology in the organization by applying too rigorous management controls over its use or by making it too expensive by internal transfer pricing.

Another view of the ways in which development of systems may be managed is that which was first put forward by Cash of the Harvard Business School (Cash, 1988). In Cash's view there have been three 'eras' in the development of information systems. These eras may be represented by

- the objective that management has for the system – what the developers of the system set out to achieve
- the justification for introducing the system to the organization
- the 'clients' for whom the system is developed and who benefit from its operation
- the 'source' of the system – the part of the organization that is responsible for acquiring the technology and developing the systems.

The importance of Cash's view is that the eras represent not only periods of time but also modes of information system development. Therefore (unlike Nolan's model) an organization can have systems which represent all three modes (or eras) functioning at the same time. The eras/modes are given below.

1 **Data processing** or **'DP-centred' systems organization**. Originally this was the only way in which organizations could organize their information resource. 'DP-centred' companies had a single DP or MIS department which had considerable discretion over which systems were developed, how and when.

   Professional computer expertise was needed to operate the computer technology and to develop new systems. The 'applications backlog' (systems awaiting analysis and design) was controlled by the DP department and therefore opportunities for technology assimilation were limited.

   The aim of DP-centred systems was (and is) to a large extent the support of operational activities. Cutting costs and increasing efficiency are the performance measures for DP systems. Most organizations have a DP department to process their everyday transactions.

2 **Management support** or the **MIS-driven organization** arose to take advantage of a valuable by-product of the DP system: information to support the decision-making process. At first such systems relied on a MIS department to provide reports, but later the rise of end-user computing (personal computers, applications packages and database management systems) led to the technology 'moving out' of the MIS department. Users were able to develop their own systems and the information systems management response was to provide advice and help rather than skill (e.g. advising on the choice of a spreadsheet package rather than writing a computer program to manipulate the data). During this era, information systems became regarded as a corporate resource, often within the responsibility of a management services department. Control of the MIS was the responsibility of a information manager or chief information officer (CIO), with a data or database administrator and information centres to give end-user support. The policy was one

Mode	Obtective	Justification	Client	Source
1 Data processing	Operational support	Increasing efficiency	Departments DP/MIS	Single centre
2 Management support	Decision support	Increasing competitiveness	Individual managers	Mgt services End users
3 Competitive strategy	Enhanced competitive position	Profitability Market share	Strategic business unit (SBU)	Top managers Mgt services End users

Figure 5.4 Modes of information system development (after Gallagher, 1988).

of encouraging development by end users under the benign control of management; the watchword was – and is – 'informate'.

3 **Competitive strategy** marked a new way of regarding information systems. In this mode the information system is a vital competitive tool. The links between the business strategy and the information systems strategy are very close and top managers are directly concerned with development and operation of systems within their organization. The division between system developers and end users may practically disappear. The watchword for this mode is to 'empower' managers to use IT to increase corporate and personal effectiveness.

Almost all organizations that use computer-based systems have a 'Mode 1' DP centre. Often this will handle the 'big engine' work – the repetitive transaction processing which needs the power of a mainframe computer. The DP centre may also be responsible for running the machines which support the corporate database. Often the DP centre is at a remote, well-guarded physical location. Many organizations also operate in Mode 2, using information systems for management support. Far fewer (and usually large) organizations are organized to manage information systems at boardroom level – for instance, having an IT director reporting directly to the chief executive. Figure 5.4 illustrates the principles of Cash's model.

System types and characteristics

The above framework is a convenient one for explaining the types of system that will be found in a typical organization. The nature and application of the system are affected by:

- the level of decision (operational, tactical and strategic)
- the use of the information (planning or control)
- the source and destination of the information (internal or external).

Therefore we can talk of a *strategic planning* system or of an *internal operational control* system.

Organizational information systems can conveniently be placed into the following categories:

- data processing (or internal reporting) systems
- management information systems
- executive information systems
- decision support systems
- expert systems
- strategic information systems.

All these systems have both technical and organizational dimensions.

Data processing systems

In the beginning, computers were all rather limited, highly specialized machines which required a dedicated environment and specialist personnel to make them function correctly. Such machines were called 'mainframes' and the organization needed a computer department to provide the necessary data processing services or to produce reports. The systems which these computer installations supported were called *data processing* (DP) or *transaction processing* systems. Some examples of DP systems in a typical organization are:

- a payroll system
- a stock control system
- an order entry system.

All these system types have one thing in common. They involve repetitive tasks using well-defined information which is easy to capture and to store. In a word, they are *operational* systems. While they may have helped the business to run efficiently, they probably did little to support the decision-making process or to help manage the business more effectively. Some other features of DP systems include the following:

- the computer programs are written in a third-generation language (3GL) and are capable only of carrying out the task for which they are designed
- the data storage files are structured to suit one particular application (e.g. payroll) and are not easily changed to cater for new requirements
- there is an identifiable gap (organizational and cultural) between the specialist data processors and the users.

These factors led to a lot of frustration between the users (accountants, production and sales people) and the computing specialists. Typical reasons for such frustration include:

- the fact that the DP department seemed to have different objectives from the user departments. There were frequent arguments over who 'owned' the data and complaints that 'the DP department only wants to develop systems which are technically interesting'
- the limitations of the technology. Until the 1970s many DP systems were still running important applications in batch mode (the 'overnight run') and simple requests for changes to programs could take months to achieve

- the computer specialists' lack of understanding of the users' problems. Information systems seemed to take years to develop and, when completed, often did not do what the users wanted.

Clearly, there was a need for systems which were more flexible, which could put information into the hands of the user and which could support the processes of tactical (or even strategic) management.

Management information systems (MISs)

If the first phase of business computing was to automate the manual and clerical processes of business with the aim of increasing efficiency, the second phase was to emphasize the role of information.

Early management information systems sought to use the output from existing DP systems (and the DP department) in some form which made it more suitable for middle management to understand. Here are two examples:

- a stock control system used to automate the capture, verification, collation and storage of information about goods may produce potential information about purchasing patterns, stock replenishment and the profitability of certain product lines or outlets
- airline booking systems may provide 'spin-off' information to management about customer preferences, route patterns and reactions to world events.

It soon became apparent that MISs had considerable potential for the firms that were prepared to develop them. Forecasting, reporting and budgeting/control systems were developed and for the first time managers began to be affected (sometimes positively, sometimes negatively) by computerization projects. It also became apparent that MISs would require major technological and organization changes.

- The 'corporate database' containing all the information that a company owned about its products, customers, suppliers, and so on, could be accessed in a number of different ways and could be changed in format without requiring major programming effort.
- The MIS function was seen as part of a service to management. Hence the profile of computing tended to be raised within the organization and often the DP department became part of a management services department. Other, complementary functions such as operations research were therefore to be found alongside the information systems specialists.
- Much new technology (or 'old' technology which previously existed only in an academic or scientific environment) came to be offered for commercial use.

The objective of an MIS is to provide the operational and tactical (lower and middle) managers of an organization with the information which they need to carry out their function. MISs are based on report-producing software which draw data from the same source as the data processing system – usually the corporate database. If the DP system is said to carry out the company's day-to-day business processes, then the MIS is the 'feedback loop' which monitors the system. It is possible to form some generalized facts about MISs:

- MIS reporting structures are relatively rigid (the software and procedures are not flexible) and therefore MISs are more suitable for monitoring a stable environment
- the analytical powers of a MIS are limited. MISs tend to rely on information being extracted in a routine way and presented in a form (usually management reports) that makes it more meaningful than 'raw data'
- MISs cope best with well-structured decision situations, such as ratio analysis or stock control calculations. As such they do not directly support the decision-making process, but make available information on which a decision may be based
- the information which MISs produce is usually internally gathered and deals with the reporting of past performance rather than projecting the future
- there are frequent time delays in MISs between an event occurring and it being reported.

Computer-generated reports are clearly a very important part of a MIS. The designers of MISs often go to great lengths to limit the amount of information to which managers are subjected. The principle of *responsibility reporting* applies: managers are informed only about things which are under their direct control. Specific types of report include the following:

- **Exception reports**, which are another method of preventing information overload by causing the software to produce a report only when a significant event occurs – for instance, when specific control conditions are broken. An example would be a report which listed only the customer orders which had not been delivered within five days. If no orders were overdue by this length of time, no report would be produced.
- **On-demand reports**, which enable managers to request reports on a particular fact or part of the organization on an 'as and when' basis. Such a reporting system requires flexible technology, such as a relational database and 4GL system.
- **Scheduled reports** are produced automatically on a daily, weekly or monthly basis, usually to a fixed format. Experience shows that such reports may lose their news value and may be ignored as, unless they are presented in minimal summary form, they contain much information which requires no management action.

Executive information systems (EISs)

In spite of (or perhaps because of) the success of MISs at the tactical level of management, it became apparent that IT had not produced any significant benefits for top-level executives. The strategic decision-making processes (e.g. new product development, changes in market position, growth by acquisition) were often noticeably ill informed. Many chief executives in the late 1980s had not used any form of computer system at all. Because of this, it was apparent that new developments such as Windows™ technology and recent developments in human–computer interaction (HCI) such as buttons and touch-sensitive screens would form the basis of EISs.

The basic features of an EIS are as follows:

- It contains powerful software for supporting the types of risky, unstructured decision which are found in strategic management. Decision support systems (DSSs) which contain complete statistical or financial models of a firm and its market (or even a national economy) allow executives to make 'what if?' projections by altering sensitive variables. Expert systems software contains the rules which a human expert would use to come to a conclusion about facts which are entered into the system. Executives therefore have access to tireless, reliable expertise to support their decision making in specialist areas.
- It will use sophisticated graphics displays, both to output information in an understandable form and to allow executives to interact with the system. As well as using the normal graphics such as histograms, charts and trend graphs, a typical EIS will allow summary text or numbers (e.g. balance sheet items) to be 'hot spots' which, when touched with a finger or mouse pointer, will display the detailed data. Some companies have 'war room' displays using multimedia projection facilities and high-powered workstations.
- It will allow flexible data manipulation and presentation. The ability to 'move around' between different sets of data in the corporate database is called 'navigation'.

It will allow users to use the system in a way which gives access to different levels of detail. For instance, an executive may view the sales figures for all the divisions of the company. Under normal circumstances this level of detail may be sufficient – but if the figures for one division are abnormally low, the executive can easily access more detailed figures, month by month or area by area, until the cause of the fall in sales is identified. This may involve 'drilling down' through a number of levels of increasingly detailed data.

It is possible for the management services function and the data processing function to combine in the creation of an EIS using conventional 'analysis and programming' development techniques. It is more than likely, however, that an off-the-shelf EIS package will be acquired. Examples of such system are Comshare Corporations Commander EIS and RESOLVE by Metaproxis.

Decision support systems (DSSs)

Decision support systems were developed to overcome the rigidity of MIS-type reporting structures and the limitations of spreadsheets. In addition, there were advances in corporate database technology and EIS-type interfaces on which to draw.

The main difference between a DSS and any of the previously mentioned information systems is that it contains complex mathematical models to simulate the behaviour of an organizational component in an unpredictable situation or an ill-structured problem area. Such problems are often a feature of the task of middle- and top-level managers in dynamic, 'organic' companies. In a rapid-response environment there will rarely be time to explore all the possible solutions to a complex, ill-structured problem. Therefore a DSS needs to be able to carry out the following functions:

- To produce results rapidly by allowing a model to be built which represents the relationships between objects or variables in a given system. A budgetary model may therefore contain data which model the spending patterns of budget holders in relation to the level of budget and the activity of the firm.
- To be flexible in use by allowing various models to be built and modified to suit a range of business decisions. A DSS is a generalized rather than a specific decision aid.
- To allow the generation of alternative solutions to a given problem, enabling managers to carry out creative problem solving through the use of 'what if?' scenarios. It should be stressed that the DSS does not make the decision. It provides information on which the manager may make a decision.

In addition, the DSS will have a user interface which makes it attractive to use. Some DSSs allow a group of users to interact with the system to bring their individual expertise to bear in building the model, changing variables and interpreting the results.

A DSS will typically have three components: a **data management module, a local management module** and the **user interface.**

The data management software is needed to extract the necessary data from the corporate database or from external data sources. The model management module contains the algorithms and procedures which allow users to build models and to modify them to represent different scenarios. The user interface is the means by which the user manipulates the model and retrieves the data. It will usually be intuitive and graphical in style. Figure 5.5 shows the components of a typical DSS.

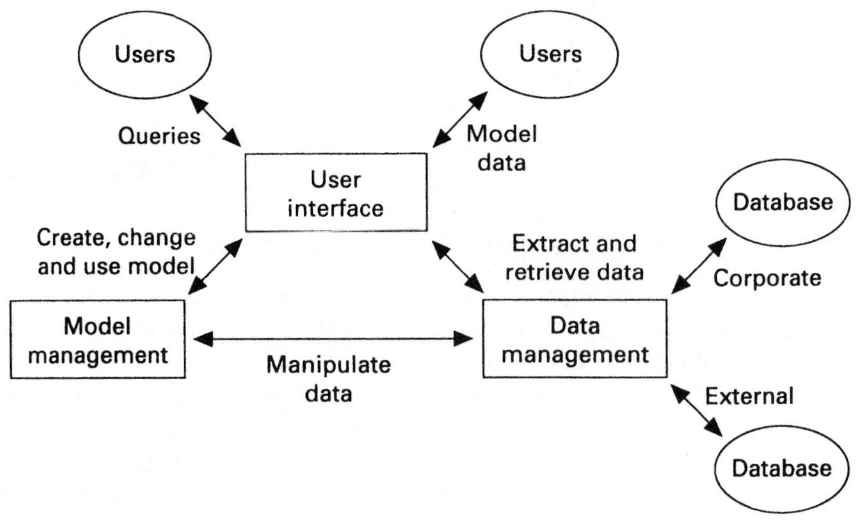

Figure 5.5 A DSS architecture.

Models which may be part of a DSS include the following types:

- **Data analysis models** contain generalized statistical formulae to allow the user to identify causal relationships, extrapolate results and to carry out sensitivity analysis by observing the effects of changing variables.
- **Simulation or response-prediction models** show the relationship between changing variables and allow the user to model queuing or waiting situations by generating random data to influence the model.
- **Optimization models** deal with resource allocation problems, using techniques originally developed in the field of operations research and management science, such as linear programming or inventory optimization.

It is possible to obtain specialized 'libraries' of model data which apply to marketing, production or financial modelling. An example of a financial DSS which is capable of modelling the financial behaviour of a complex organization is FINAR. Such a package will require a powerful minicomputer to run successfully. Also, due to the intensity of the processing, the use of a large DSS on a multi-user system may degrade the performance of the system where the other users are concerned.

In theory, a DSS may be sufficiently flexible to allow its application to a wide range of problem situations, depending on the models which are in place. Some examples of DSS applications include:

- share dealing and investment or unit trust management, where decisions need to be taken on the scale, risk and timing of investments and disposals. Since many of these types of decisions are at best heuristic, the fund managers need to use their experience to vary the data on which the model is based to observe the effect
- market analysis – for instance, the modelling of the complete national market for a product with information on competitive brands, output volumes and sales estimates. The effect of the introduction of a new product to the market may be observed and a competitive strategy may be devised.
- 'one-off' projects (such as construction or civil engineering projects) where the risks of failure must be computed and the effect of delays on scheduled costs must be predicted
- budgeting exercises, such as the linking of sales and production budgets and the modelling of the effect on short-term cash flow and long-term profitability. Using a financial DSS such as FINESSE or FINAR will provide decision support which goes far beyond the use of spreadsheets, pro-forma accounts and cash budgets.

Expert systems (ESs)

Whereas a DSS is capable of modelling a given situation and making available information on which a decision may be made, an expert system (ES) is capable of arriving at a decision when certain facts are made available to it.

An ES, as its name suggests, is intended to offer a consultancy service and to give similar advice to that given by qualified experts about problems in their domain of expertise.

As a piece of software, the ES has a number of advantages when compared to a human expert:

- it can be replicated. Where a human expert may be unique or in short supply (there may be only one management accountant in a firm), an ES may be put into every office
- it is more reliable. A human may suffer illness or accident and may need time off work. Within the normal limits of hardware/software reliability, the ES is tireless and will be available at any time
- it is more cost-effective, since human experts are usually paid high salaries and require regular payment. An ES is usually a one-off investment.

On the adverse side, it must be said that no ES can offer the complete flexibility and capacity to learn which a human has, and that an ES is capable of coming to the wrong conclusion (or not performing at all) when confronted by data outside its normal range. An ES cannot use common sense or apply a 'hunch'. Also, some people would rather consult a human than a computer-based system.

An ES is in some ways similar to the architecture of a DSS, except that instead of a database it has a *knowledge base* and in place of a model management facility it will have an *inference engine* (see Figure 5.6). An additional facility in most ES is an explanation facility.

The knowledge base contains information that describes the associations and actions which a human expert would apply to a particular situation. In most ESs this is in the form of production rules – a conclusion or action which will result from a particular condition. The rule-base for a credit control ES may contain the following rules:

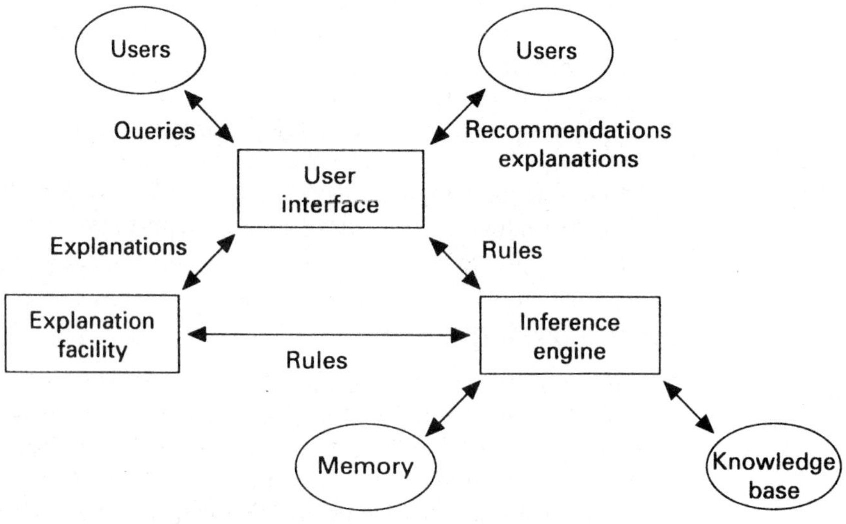

Figure 5.6 An ES architecture.

Rule 1	**IF customer = new** **or order-value > £1,000** **THEN ask for reference**
Rule 2	**IF customer @ credit-limit** **and order placed** **THEN reject order**

These rules are mechanistic – they do not take into account the 'hunches' or rule-of-thumb judgements which form a large part of human expert knowledge. Such heuristic rules may be expressed in production rule form, such as:

Rule 3	**IF customer @ credit-limit** **and order placed** **and customer-contact = qualified accountant** **THEN accept order**

There may be 50 to 200 production rules in a rule-based ES.

The inference engine provides the 'reasoning' facility by controlling the order in which the production rules are applied to select the most appropriate rule should a clash occur. The inference engine works backward and forward in the rule base, entering the current state of knowledge about a case into the working memo (confusingly often called the 'database'). The inference processes for most rule-based ESs rely on one of two logical forms:

- **forward chaining logic**, which moves from the facts as they are accumulated to a conclusion. This is called 'goal-seeking'
- **backward chaining logic**, which makes an assumption and then attempts to identify the facts which would prove it. This is called 'goal-proving'.

Both strategies will produce the same results (an opinion or recommendation) where the facts which are input are the same.

The explanation facility allows the user to query the ES to find out why it (the ES) is applying certain rules or has come to a particular conclusion. Thus, the explanation of Rule 3 in the example above may be:

Rule 3 because qualified accountant = trustworthy payer

Such feedback marks the interaction between the user and the system.

There are two basic types of ESs, those which are *domain-specific* and those which are called 'shells':

- domain-specific ESs are designed for use in a particular domain or problem area (such as credit control). The ES package comes with the rule base already loaded with the knowledge of an expert or group of experts
- ES shells are, as the name implies, 'empty' of rules and may be tailored to work in any application. The purchaser must obtain the necessary rules. In a simple system this may be straightforward (the similarity of production rules

and decision tables will be noticed) but a complex domain will require knowledge engineering to be applied.

Knowledge engineering is a variety of systems analysis in which the 'analyst' – the knowledge engineer – uses recognized techniques to elicit the needs of the user (what facts are likely to be needed) and to structure the knowledge of the expert (the rules which explain the facts).

Typical applications for ESs include:

- credit control systems, so that clerks may have access to the knowledge of an expert credit controller
- auditing, to allow part-qualified staff to call upon the expertise of an experienced auditor
- investment appraisal, to allow experience and expertise in the area to be spread throughout those in a position to make decisions.

The important differences between an ES and a DSS are summed up in Figure 5.7. Although ESs have been used by top-level managers to reach judgement on specialist matters (often in conjunction with the use of a DSS) it is worth pointing out that the process of management itself is so complex and broad that it is rarely suitable for the use of an ES.

A model of ISs

In summary, it is possible to arrive at a model of the information systems which an organization may use, based on the type of decision making and on the information needs of its management. This model builds on the three-layer model of management which was given in a previous chapter.

Figure 5.8 shows that:

- the transaction processing/data processing (TP/DP) systems cover the information needs at an operational level
- the MIS uses information gained from TP/DP to provide tactical management reports
- the needs of top management are met with an executive information system (EIS).

In addition, expert systems (ESs) cover both the operational and tactical levels and decision support systems may supply decision-making information at the strategic and tactical management levels.

Item	DSS	ES
Organization level	Management	All levels
Objective	Decision aid	Spread expertise
Domain	Narrow, simple	Broad, complex
Interface	User queries system	System queries user
Explanation	Limited	Considerable

Figure 5.7 Comparison of DSS and ES.

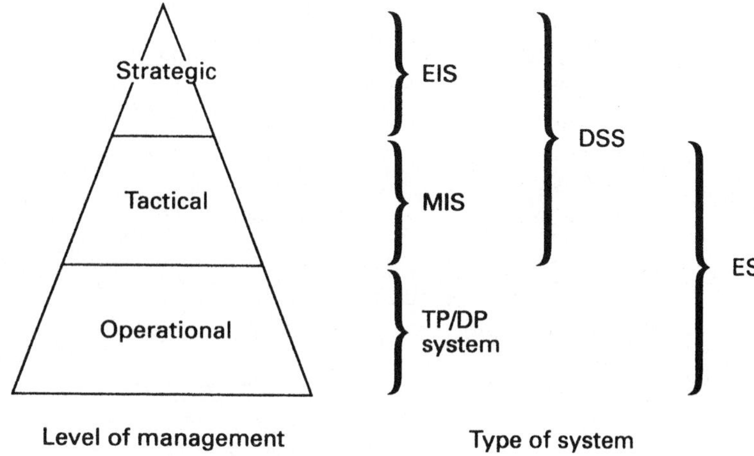

Figure 5.8 Coverage of an organization's IS.

Strategic information systems (SISs)

Strategic information systems (SIS) may be said to sit outside the framework described in Figure 5.8. This is because of a lack of agreement on what an SIS is. Some definitions are as follows:

- A system which gives competitive advantage to the company that operates it. Such systems are often designed to exploit marketing opportunities and to give an advantage (which may be temporary at best) to the first company to develop the system.
- A system which allows the organization to affect the industry in which it operates, usually by 'locking in' customers or suppliers or by preventing potential rivals from entering the industry.
- A system which supports the strategic management process (i.e. a DSS or EIS).

The last definition is clearly the least satisfactory, since it appears to cover what has already been described in EIS and DSS definitions. Clearly, such systems are for strategic purposes. The other definitions are more useful.

An example of a competitive SIS would be a bank's ATM (automatic teller machine) system or cash dispenser. The first bank to introduce an ATM had a clear advantage over its rivals and did considerable out-of-hours business. Soon, however, the providers of ATM technology had supplied it to other banks and the first user lost the advantage. Faced by increasing expenditure with no prospect of an individual advantage, the banks decided to pool their resources and share ATMs with a wide-area network system (i.e. LINK or MATRIX). This gives rise to the idea of 'collaborative necessity': organizations are tied into the use of expensive systems which give no clear advantage, but which none dare give up.

An industry-affecting SIS can be explained by using Porter's model of the five forces of industry competition. This model explains the forces with which an organization has to deal in order to maintain stability in a given industry. Figure 5.9 depicts the model.

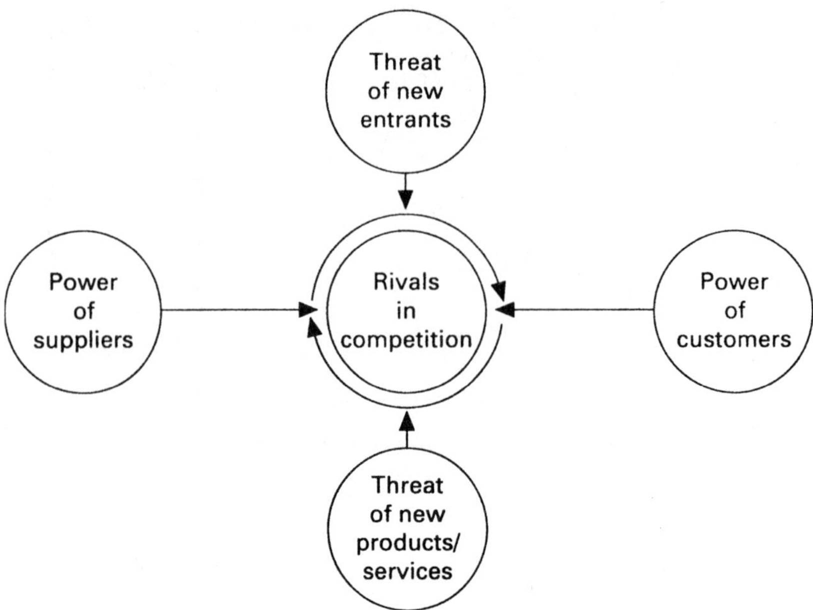

Figure 5.9 Industry competition model (after Porter, 1985).

The use of information systems as strategic tools in this model may be summarized as follows:

- New entrants to a market may be deterred by one or more companies which are already in the market using an information system as a barrier to entry. The enormous cost of developing an holiday booking system from scratch and the length of time that it would take to develop the IT infrastructure to support such a system allow the current leader in the UK holiday and tour business to defend its position against would-be rivals.
- Rivals in competition may use information systems to change the basis of competition, either by one of them gaining market leadership through innovative first use of a system, or by both agreeing to collaborate for their mutual good, as has happened with banks' ATM networks. Equally, improvements in one aspect of a product or service which are enabled by an information system, such as speedier delivery or the ability to track an order, may differentiate the product or service from that of a competitor.
- Supplier bargaining power may be controlled by the use of systems which link suppliers to customers, as in the case of 'just-in-time' (JIT) systems in manufacturing. A customer sharing its stock control and ordering system with a supplier creates the potential of considerable switching costs should the supplier seek to change its major customer: it may have to develop its own replacement information system.
- Customer bargaining power may be reduced by the use of systems to 'lock in' the customer to a particular supplier. Major firms in the pharmaceutical and travel industries have supplied free hardware and software to customers in

order to secure their business and to make it easier to order from them than from their rivals.

- Substitute products or services may be developed through the innovative use of IT public information systems and the use by banks of ATMs in airports, supermarkets and other non-banking public places are examples of the strategic use of information systems in this area.

Transaction processing and strategic systems

The view that data processing or transaction processing systems (i.e. systems developed at the operational level of the organization) may have a strategic value is best explained by using the value chain model (also developed by Porter). Figure 5.10 depicts the value chain and the type of system which may occur at various points within the chain.

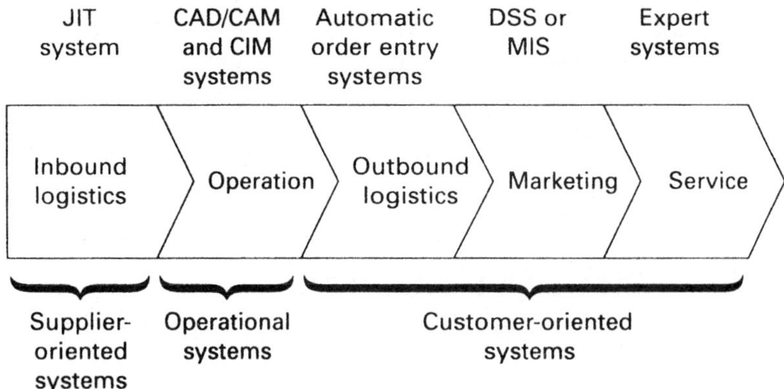

Figure 5.10 Information systems and the value chain (after Zwass, 1992).

Summary

- The form and structure of an organization – in particular, the 'height' or 'breadth' of its spans of control and its 'mechanistic' or 'organic' character – significantly affect the decisions that are made on the structure of its information system. A number of non-technical' factors, such as the organization's management style and culture, may make some types of information system (which variously combine formal and informal elements) more appropriate to its needs than others.
- Observers – notably, Cash and Nolan – have identified discrete stages or phases in the introduction and development of information system cultures within organizations. These stages can be represented in a model which can be used to view the evolution of systems in a given organization.
- Different types of information system (for data processing, management information, decision support, executive information and decision-making expertise) are appropriate to the different levels of management – strategic, tactical and

operational – within an organization. These system types have different technologies, objectives and information needs: DP systems involve repetitive tasks using easily captured data, for example, while expert systems require the integration of knowledge bases with facilities for making inferences and offering explanations of choices. An additional category, strategic information systems, can serve organizations as a strategic tool, typically for aggressive or defensive action in the market place.

- Porter's value chain model shows that systems developed for data or transaction processing at the operational level of the organization may serve a strategic purpose.

Self-test questions

1 Identify the six stages in Nolan's framework for IS growth.
2 List the types of decisions you would expect a strategic information system to support.
3 Identify the major factors that influence the structure of an information system providing brief examples of each.
4 Distinguish between the roles of decision support systems and expert information systems.

Exam-style questions

1 Describe the three 'eras' of information systems development which are generally recognized and explain the links between this and the types of information system which may be found in a typical modern organization.
2 Identify and describe briefly an application (taken from a manufacturing company) for each of the following:
   (a) a management information system (MIS)
   (b) a decision support system (DSS)
   (c) an expert system (ES)
   (d) a strategic information system (SIS).
3 Bison Tools plc manufacture a wide range of tools for the professional in the construction industry and the Do-It-Yourself enthusiast. The company has suffered intense competition in its major markets, suffering loss of market share and substantial financial losses in its aggregate performance. The directors have been advised to undertake a formal process of strategic management to resolve its long-term future. As a first stage in the process, the directors have decided to establish a strategic information system. Outline the elements you would expect to find in this system using Porter's model of the five forces of industry competition.

(All answers on pages 553–555)

CHAPTER 6

Organizational information systems – a case study

In previous chapters we have used examples to illustrate the various terms, concepts or models associated with information systems and their development. These examples have necessarily focused on different elements of organizational information systems and therefore could not reflect the overall complexity of practical system structure. In this chapter we shall use a comprehensive case study of an organization to explore the practical applications of the concepts we have discussed and to provide some insight into the complex and interactive nature of information systems.

The case study will provide a practical illustration of the kinds of information system to be found in most organizations, developing the schematic model presented earlier by describing the main elements of a practical system. We shall confine our attention to the more significant features of an information system rather than attempt to give an exhaustive analysis of all elements and subsystems. Our aim will be to demonstrate the operational contribution of such a system to tactical and strategic decision making, identifying the roles of manual and computer-based systems elements and the areas in which they can be most appropriately used. We shall outline the function of a database (in preparation for more detailed treatment of this concept in later chapters) and suggest ways in which more recent technological developments can be used to benefit organizations.

Two themes or issues that we address here are central to the successful operation of most business organizations: **profit performance** and **quality management**.

These themes are not only important as key business objectives but also demonstrate the different nature of the data and systems required to support decisions that will promote each corporate objective. While profit performance relies heavily on financial and numeric data typically derived from standard systems, quality management requires an increasing proportion of non-numeric or textual data derived from less structured information systems.

We shall examine these two main themes at each organizational level of decision making – the short-term (operational), medium-term (tactical) and long-term (strategic) – to highlight the range of problems, issues and decisions that are likely to be encountered in the organization and the information required to analyse and take decisions at each level. The case study will also consider the interaction required between four key functional activities or operations if effective information provision is to support decision making:

- purchasing – inbound logistics
- production/operations
- warehousing/despatch – outbound logistics
- sales/marketing.

To avoid the duplication of material, we shall address only the relevant areas of each function's information system. Strategic decisions, by their nature, involve decisions that span the total organization and its constituent functions and so will be treated separately at the end of the chapter.

The background of Scribe plc

Scribe plc manufactures and sells a range of office furniture products, including desks, chairs, tables and specialist computer furniture. The company has been in the business for some 35 years and employs 260 people with a sales turnover in the last year of £5.4 million. The products may be constructed from wood, metals or plastics (or a combination of materials) and are finished to a high standard of quality. The company's operations involve the purchase of raw materials such as sheet steel, wood, plastics, fabrics, fasteners and other fittings. The production operations essentially involve the preliminary processing of the raw materials and components, assembly of these into the end products and, finally, finishing, painting, polishing and inspection.

The total product range is quite extensive, with 16 product groups (group classifications are normally set by function – for example, typist/secretarial desks) and a total of 285 individual product items. In order to meet immediate delivery requirements, the company has a policy of maintaining stocks of those product lines which typically have a regular and substantial demand pattern. Delivery of such products is normally guaranteed within seven days of receipt of order, should the customer require it. The initial delivery quotation on other product lines will be on a six- to eight-week timescale, subject to some flexibility to meet the needs of important customers.

The company uses a variety of selling approaches. These involve:

- dealing with independent office equipment suppliers
- making direct contact with the new office contract market through architects and the building trade
- directly mailing catalogues to business and commercial organizations
- placing direct advertising in the trade press and professional magazines.

Profit performance

The overriding objective in most business organizations is to attain profitability. Scribe plc has suffered a deterioration in profitability in recent years, from a 12 per cent return on capital employed (ROCE) three years ago to a seven per cent ROCE in the latest full trading year. The target originally established by the management team was to increase the ROCE to a rate of 15 per cent by the end of the present trading period. In general, the implementation of strategies to achieve profit performance objectives requires an organization simultaneously to manage sales revenues and costs to ensure that the maximum profit is generated in both the short run and the longer run. The deterioration of Scribe plc's profit performance has been due to a combination of reduced sales revenues and poor cost controls. This has greatly reduced profit margins. Clearly, every organizational function has a contribution to make towards achieving the profit objective. Let us consider the ways in which the information systems in each major function may potentially contribute towards improving the control of revenues and costs at both the operational and the management levels.

The purchasing function

This function has a particularly significant role in the profit performance of commercially-orientated organizations. Indeed, in the typical organization, over 50 per cent of the resource inputs are likely to be handled by this function. Scribe plc is no exception, with 54 per cent of the cost of finished products being represented by the goods and services acquired by the purchasing department. Improving the profit performance requires seeking the most competitive prices, as well as ensuring appropriate standards of quality, reliability of delivery and security of the supply sources. At the same time, accurate and sufficiently detailed information must be made available to facilitate the effective planning of subsequent business operations.

Operational decisions

Operational decisions and activities within the purchasing function involve the acquisition of a variety of inputs, from raw materials to packaging and services. As in most companies, the buyers are required to maintain a list of suppliers for each major input, showing delivery times, prices, technical specifications and target quality standards. This information needs to be updated regularly and to be readily available to the buyers when required. Although it may be possible to compile lists of the main suppliers, the products supplied and credit terms, and to store such data on a computer using a database application, other types of data would prove more expensive and less effective to store on computer – for example, glossy catalogues or product samples. This collection of information, whether stored manually in a set of filing cabinets or within a computer system (say, using a computer output microform system or optical disk system), would be described as a purchasing **database**.

In operating this form of database, the user seeks access to individual supplier details, as and when they are required. The normally expected result, when an entirely manual database is used, will be the storage of a more comprehensive and detailed set of information, but it may take longer to identify the physical location of the data set and it may not be in a conveniently pre-digested form to allow rapid comparisons to be made between different suppliers. Computer-based systems provide more rapid access to the data and, because the typical database system stores less detailed and more structured information and reports, it is easier to make comparisons between different suppliers. If the system is only partially automated, the buyer may need to access not only the computer-stored information on a possible supplier but also the other data sources. This points to a need for compatibility between the computer-based and the manual database storage and for ensuring that good cross-referencing is used.

Scribe plc has retained a manual system for storing the product details and price lists of its suppliers. It is referenced alphabetically by supplier name. This has caused frequent problems when it comes to locating alternative suppliers for a given input, as there is no cross-referencing by inputs or services provided. In the past, this information has been retained in the memory of the individual buyers as the product of each person's direct experience. The problem implicit in this approach is that the information is not readily available to the other buyers and the departure of a particular employee from the organization also results in the departure of this element of the organization's database. A simple computerized database could be established to generate a list of all the suppliers for each type of input or service, simply by listing each product or service and locating against this a supplier code or reference number. The manual database could then be used to retrieve the more detailed information required.

The primary financial information within the purchasing department comprises records of each transaction between the organization and the given supplier. This provides details of the value of the transaction and shows the timing and the relevant stage of completion of the transaction between the two parties. The primary focus of operational decisions based on this information is related to the control of the costs and of the quality of materials and service inputs. Hence, at various stages in the ordering cycle, the need may arise to corroborate different financial elements – for example, the unit price, quantity and discount terms from:

- the supplier's original quote
- the subsequent purchase order raised by Scribe plc
- the delivery note from the supplier
- the goods received documentation
- the final invoice submitted by the supplier

should all be consistent in terms of these details. The purchasing function needs to monitor the accuracy of the data at each of these stages on each order. At present, Scribe plc operates a manual system for raising purchase orders and checking subsequent deliveries prior to the payment of suppliers' invoices.

Persistent and frequently significant problems arise because of changes to the original purchase orders. Such changes may have been initiated by Scribe plc itself or may be the result of unexpected shortages in the supplier's stocks. There may have been an accident or an instance of incompetence in the supplier's despatch department, or the goods sent may be a deliberate substitution of replacement items by the supplier at the time of delivery. In each of these circumstances, the reconciliation of the supplier's invoice with the original purchase order invariably requires time-consuming research, both to establish the reasons for the variations and to take appropriate remedial action if necessary. This process would prove more cost-effective and efficient if the data were provided through a centralized computer system. This would mean that any changes arising in the various stages of handling the purchase orders could be amended against a central data source. This **purchase order system** interfaces not only with the purchasing department but also the accounting and financial control departments and the goods receiving and warehousing departments. Each of the departments involved would be able both to access the purchase order data for a specific order at any time and to input the necessary confirmation or amendment data at the various stages in the purchase order processing.

More recent developments in this field concern the automatic transmission of data from the buying organization's computer system to the supplier's computer system. For example, Scribe plc can raise an order for the purchase of fittings (drawer handles, say,) from a particular supplier. Once the order has been entered on Scribe plc's computer system, the computer automatically locates the instructions for communicating directly with the supplier's computer (a set of dialling instructions) through a communications network. When the link with the supplier's computer has been established, the order can be transmitted automatically and entered into the supplier's sales order system for processing and delivery. Confirmation of order details, delivery dates and possible stock-outs may be transmitted back to Scribe plc's computer for the attention of the purchasing clerks. This process of **electronic data interchange** (EDI) is already being used in many industry sectors and, in some cases, is being further developed to include the automatic transfer of funds from the buyer's bank account to the seller's bank account on the successful completion of the order.

This is known as **electronic funds transfer** (EFT). For Scribe plc, developing such a system would require significant preliminary investment in the analysis and design of a computerized purchase-ordering system. Further investment by the organization and its suppliers in communications and networking systems and agreement on standard formats for order documentation would also be necessary to ensure the effective use of EDI developments.

Tactical decisions

These decisions are concerned with assessing the efficiency and effectiveness of the purchasing function over the medium-term period. This assessment would be made not only on the basis of the function's capacity to reduce, maintain or control input costs per unit but also in terms of its ability to ensure appropriate delivery times, while maintaining the quality of the inputs delivered and ensuring the accuracy of the supporting accounting and information systems.

The management and control of the financial position regarding purchases depends on access to appropriate information. The financial data necessary to support and control these operations are derived from:

- specific quotations from the suppliers
- previous correspondence with the suppliers on prices and discounts
- supplier price lists
- credit arrangements and limits agreed
- the current level of credit owing to the supplier.

The management in Scribe plc, for example, receives monthly statements of

- the total expenditure on goods purchased classified by different categories
- the total credit outstanding to suppliers
- the incidence of late deliveries
- production problems or returned goods resulting from inferior quality inputs.

This information originates from a variety of sources, including the accounting systems relating to accounts payable, the costing systems and budgetary control systems and the less formal reports of the purchasing department staff.

The information used to manage the purchasing function comprises both *quantitative* and *qualitative* data. The former originates from summaries derived from the purchase order system. The qualitative data originates from the reports and views of the staff involved in the purchasing process, and requires more effective communications systems to capture, record and transmit the information to the management. The majority of computer systems and applications software packages are designed to handle quantitative (i.e. numeric) data rather than qualitative (i.e. textual) data. The major exception to this is the word-processing application. But although such applications are designed to manipulate textual data, the capacity of systems to retrieve specific parts of the stored text quickly and to communicate their substance to readers is less efficient than the equivalent systems for handling numerical data.

However, the power of text processing software is increasing significantly and, while it will never match that of numerical processing systems, it will provide sufficient scope for many routine information retrieval applications. The use of the electronic mail application throughout the organization also provides a valuable communication channel for distributing memoranda and instructions requiring a wide circulation. Further developments of this basic data of message transmission system through a network involve (for example) the storage of diaries designed to fix meetings with colleagues when they are not available for telephone arrangements to be made. Additionally, standard reference materials may be stored and accessed as and when required by employees: for example, instructions and procedures on sickness, maternity leave, or travel and subsistence rates.

Production operations

The production operations at Scribe plc are sub-divided into a number of different departments, each carrying out such specialist operations as upholstery or steel cutting and shaping. The major department is the assembly department, which undertakes the assembly of the processed parts and bought-in parts to form desks, tables and chairs. Following assembly, the products enter the finishing department which applies paint or polishes to produce the finished product. The assembly department comprises some 65 employees, most of whom are engaged in general assembly operations. A minority are engaged in more specialized assembly operations relating to lower-volume items.

Operational decisions

These decisions within the production operations context focus on ensuring that the profit performance objectives are related to the productivity of the operational resources being employed. It is quite usual in batch processing systems, such as those used in Scribe plc, to establish standard costs in terms of the materials and the machine and labour time requirements for a particular item. Performance may then be measured against these standards and any significant deviations assessed.

Scribe plc operates a computerized manufacturing recording system. The essence of the system is that each type of product is estimated prior to production in terms of the materials and the machine and labour inputs, expressed as standard costs. The overheads relating to the batches or individual units are then apportioned. At each stage of the manufacturing process, the production operatives are responsible for the input, via a terminal, of:

- the works order number
- the materials used
- the time spent processing the job or batch (including the time taken to set up the particular machine(s) for the job).

These data items are collated and accumulated against the particular job, which may be for a single item or for a batch of similar items. It is then employed by the cost accountant to evaluate the profitability of each order in relation to the standard data. While the cost accountant may access a summary of the cost statements for a particular order or for a particular period in time, the normal procedure in Scribe plc is to produce a print-out of all the orders completed at the end of each month. This represents the aggregate performance data for the period. The system is being used to record data on the operational performance of the production department on a real-time basis (i.e. as it happens), but the only use being made of this information is the analysis of general performance in production during the period of a month. Scribe plc is clearly not utilizing this valuable data resource fully, given that it is capable of continuously monitoring the production system and indicating whether it is functioning effectively. Further development of the system should therefore enable this same data to be transmitted to the supervisors and production management, to enable them to undertake such monitoring and to detect potential sources of sub-standard performance or other problems as and when they arise. Inefficiencies detected at an early stage may be corrected before significant deviations occur. Under the present system, the data can normally only be analysed and the problems identified at the end of each month, when corrective action may prove less effective or more costly.

Tactical decisions

These decisions in production operations concern not only day-to-day activities but, more importantly, the evaluation and control of the effectiveness and efficiency of the entire production function over a period of time. For these purposes, the cost and, hence, the profit performance may be assessed by type of product and by size of batch. Such assessments may lead to major improvements in production planning and scheduling. In addition, details of plant and individual operative efficiency can be helpful in taking decisions to upgrade the plant or in producing shift rosters to allocate operatives to particular tasks or working groups. At present, Scribe plc's manufacturing recording system concentrates on providing a more generalized financial appraisal of the operations. Yet, as indicated, the data items are available within the system to provide other forms of analysis to support the management of the operations, and the whole system clearly contains the key information required to support management decisions in terms of the efficiency of the operations, machine utilization and capacity usage.

A typical tool used in the analysis of both the financial and non-financial information is the *spreadsheet* application. This facilitates the manipulation of data and the comparison of actual performance against budgeted performance. For example, a typical spreadsheet for Scribe plc could have the following structure:

- **spreadsheet rows**: elements of the cost structure for a particular product, such as material cost, direct labour and overheads
- **spreadsheet columns**: various products produced by the company: chairs, desks, filing cabinets, and so on.

Further (and perhaps more importantly), use of a spreadsheet will permit the consequences of current performance to be extrapolated to indicate its effects on future periods of production and on profitability in general. While many spreadsheets are viewed as two-dimensional, it is becoming increasingly common to consider such tools as providing three-dimensional data and, hence, analytical power in three dimensions. This is not essentially a new development, but rather a recognition that data may be structured and analysed in a number of different ways simultaneously. Often this **third dimension** relates to analysing blocks of data for different time periods.

Another development that may enhance the use of spreadsheets is the automatic transfer or capture of data from the organization's existing information systems. For example, Scribe plc could transfer the necessary data from its manufacturing recording system to a spreadsheet, which would enable management to undertake the immediate analysis of the performance rather than the more tedious task of manually inputting all the required data from the computer listings.

Warehousing and distribution

The post-production activities of warehousing and distribution have often been viewed as contributing less to the cost and profit performance of the business. However, closer analysis of such activities indicates that they are equally important in ensuring both the effectiveness and the efficiency of the total business.

Operational decisions

These decisions must be based on accurate and detailed records of the stocks available. This concern interfaces both with the production department (for planning the future production of buffer stocks) and with the sales department (in providing an improved service to customers through shorter delivery times). Scribe plc currently operates a manual system for finished goods stocks by using a series of stock cards for each item. Receipts from production and deliveries from stock are manually recorded. This results in frequent inaccuracies in the stock recording system. If the system were to be computerized, quite apart from enhancing the accuracy of data, it would also provide information on excess stocks, slow-moving items and redundant items, all of which could be used by the sales and marketing functions to promote particular products or to reduce prices to remove such items.

Tactical decisions

These decisions relating to the outbound logistics are directed primarily towards managing the resources effectively and providing a high level of service to the organization's customers. The planning, monitoring and control of finished goods stocks is a key element in this process, as excessive stocks incur costs for the business in terms of storage space, insurance and financing charges. Insufficient stocks, on the other hand, may be reflected in a poorer quality of service to the customer, particularly in terms of delay in delivery. Irrespective of the stock level policy in operation, the system of assembling, despatching and delivering orders must operate efficiently if costs are to be minimized and if the loss of revenues from poor service is to be eliminated. The required efficiency level should therefore be identified and adopted as a specific target by the organization.

Marketing and sales

In many respects, this function may be considered as the most crucial for any organization in terms of profit performance, as it provides the primary interface between the market, the customers and the organization.

Operational decisions

These decisions are supported by the sales order processing system. Currently the sales orders from customers, coming either directly from the customer via the tele-sales ordering service or via the sales force, are passed to the sales order clerks who enter the relevant details into the sales order processing system. This system employs two databases: a *customer database* containing details of each customer and accessed by a unique customer number for each customer, and a *product database* containing details of each product, prices and specifications, accessed by a unique product code for each product. The sales order clerk only requires to enter the customer code followed by the appropriate product codes and quantities requested to produce the appropriate invoice, despatch notes and entries on the sales ledger for the particular customer.

Scribe plc have been evaluating a **portable direct entry** (PDE) system for use by their field sales force in completing orders. This essentially involves providing each salesperson with a portable computer system (typically, a laptop) with keyboard, screen and printer. The portable system contains the customer and product databases. The salesperson enters the order from the customer directly into the computer at the customer's premises by using a series of menus to guide the input of data – the customer's code, the product codes and the quantities. The system will advise immediately on the availability and the expected delivery times for each item, and produce a full invoice listing extended in terms of quantities, prices and totals. The customer checks the details of the order and signs one copy. Details of the customer's credit levels and unpaid invoices may also be displayed if required, permitting the salesperson to remind the customer of any outstanding balances or, if necessary, to indicate that no further orders may be accepted until the outstanding balances have been cleared.

At the end of each day, the portable computer system is connected via the telephone lines using a modem to the central computer, and all the details of the orders for that day are transferred to the central computer, automatically updating customer records, sales and stock records, and producing despatch notes for the warehouse to fill on the following day. The main computer will also update the portable system in terms of both the availability of stock items, delivery times on non-stock items and changes in prices, as well as changes in the balances owing and the credit limits for all customers within the salesperson's territory.

A key requirement is that the finished goods stock and the production control system are fully integrated to permit the generation of the necessary data for the product database. For example, the sales staff should be in a position to advise the customer at the time of ordering on the availability of items in stock or the likely delivery time from the production schedule.

Tactical decisions

Tactical decisions in relation to the sales force are primarily concerned with ensuring the effective and efficient use of their time and effort. The geographic distribution of the sales force and the differing nature of the territories, in terms of both geographic spread and the size of potential customers, makes direct comparisons between individuals problematic. The more usual approach is to measure performance against sales targets, in terms of either the number of new contacts made or the value of orders taken.

In supporting management decisions, the PDE system potentially provides valuable information to aid the management of the sales force and also to establish sales trends and patterns by customers and by products. For example, data relating to the number of visits undertaken and the sales generated per visit may be used to evaluate the effectiveness of the sales force in general and of individual staff. Similarly, the study of information on sales generated from particular customers or by groups of similar customers may indicate potential improvements in either sales or marketing approaches to enhance effectiveness and the volume of sales. Additionally, if any changes to marketing and sales promotions are instituted, this system may be used to assist measurement and evaluation to determine their effectiveness. Moreover, the analysis of sales patterns by type of product may be used to enhance the short-term forecasting of the organization and, hence, the production scheduling, but equally to provide valuable information for the development and analysis of all marketing plans and activities.

Quality management

The management and assurance of quality is arguably the function and responsibility of everyone within the organization, although certain functions such as purchasing and operations will often have a more significant impact on the overall level of quality by virtue of their role in the overall process.

Purchasing

In relation to the operations function, buyers need to have access to quality and performance data concerning the material and service inputs, as this may influence purchasing decisions, for example whether to buy from the same source or from an alternative source if quality is inadequate. Similarly, information on faulty inputs is required not only to seek credit or the replacement of faulty inputs but equally to alert buyers to the nature and scale of the problems encountered. There is a requirement to establish quality standards for the general performance of suppliers and their relationship to the organization and also standards relating to specific material or service inputs. This may be produced in the form of a standards manual, which may also specify the precise standards relating to each type of input. There is clearly a potential need to store such data on the computer, as this would provide a manageable means of updating and retrieving it.

Managing quality within the purchasing function ultimately relies on establishing strong initial standards, followed by effective monitoring and control of quality assurance procedures and standards. The achievement of quality standards data derives from a number of sources within the organization:

- goods inwards inspection
- production departments during processing, assembly and finishing operations
- quality inspection at completion of production
- customer support services, including delivery, installation and after-sales support
- the sales department, which will report complaints or commendations made directly to the sales office or to sales personnel in the field.

Production or operations

The management and control of quality is practised most regularly in the production stages. However, evidence suggests that many systems that have been developed to maintain quality have become ineffective.

An essential prerequisite for effective quality control at the operational level is the establishment of the necessary standards and procedures to ensure that appropriate quality levels are attained in the end product. Scribe plc, like many other manufacturing companies, has a set of operational procedures and a quality standards manual, copies of which are intended to be available to all staff in the various production departments. In essence, this document represents a database of common procedures and quality standards, together with detailed instructions on how to handle a range of variations from the normal procedures.

Despite efforts by the management to maintain this paper-based system by issuing amendments to the manual at regular intervals, a recent survey of the manuals and their usage indicated that most of the manuals were outdated and contained very few of the most recent updates. Further, few of the staff were prepared to refer to the manuals unless there was a dispute about a specific procedure. Of even greater concern was the finding that the general practice and manufacturing approach adopted in the production departments was substantially different from that suggested in the manuals, with operatives modifying official procedures and tests to suit the circumstances of particular jobs or the equipment being used.

The solution proposed to this problem was the computerization of the system, such that each section within the production department would be able to access the procedures and standards manual through their own workstations. Since all employees would be using the same central data source, this would simplify the communication problem when it came to updates and would help to ensure that all staff were utilizing the same procedures and observing the same work practices. But despite a significant investment in extending the computer network, providing workstations in each section and establishing the central database system, the desired benefits have not materialized. It now appears that the issue that those recommending the computer-based system have failed to address (as had those who implemented the paper-based system) is the reluctance of the staff to use the system. The longer-term employees prefer to rely upon their own experience and will not willingly adhere to the supposedly agreed procedures and standards. The solution really lies in managing and training the staff in the correct procedures rather than in the development of an effective information system.

From the tactical perspective, the control of quality in the production stages is essentially one of setting the necessary standards and then of monitoring production activity to see whether the standards are being achieved and to ensure that the necessary quality of outputs is being provided. The two keys to effective monitoring are:

- the detection of sub-standard outputs at an early stage
- the ability to trace these problems back to their cause – this allows the necessary corrective actions to be taken.

For this purpose, an on-line production monitoring system may provide rapid feedback of potential problems in quality. But this is never enough on its own. Management must consider the nature of the work to be done and modify their expectations accordingly. Thus, it is often the case that inferior quality materials or components will require more time and effort in the machining and assembly processes than normal quality standards. So if it is known that one batch of in-house produced components is of marginal quality, appropriate instructions must be given to the operatives affected in the assembly and finishing sections before work is commenced, to minimize wastage.

The management of quality in the production operations is thus not simply concerned with monitoring the quality inspection reports, which are essentially a record of quality achieved after the event. It is far more important to ensure that quality standards are being achieved *continuously*. This is likely to involve information flows that are concerned less with numerical data and more with oral and written reports of a textual nature. For example, feedback on problems experienced in machining the initial pieces in a particular batch of prefabricated metal parts may require changes to normal procedures or the reworking of those items to ensure that appropriate quality standards are maintained in the finished product. There should also be a review of the source of the parts. If they have been bought in, the manufacturer should be alerted to the defects so that future batches may be corrected. The goods received department should also be notified, so that a more detailed inspection of the next batch can be undertaken when the goods come into the factory. If the batch was produced in-house, production records should be reviewed to determine the cause of the loss in quality.

Marketing and sales

The operational links between the marketing function and the objective of ensuring market effectiveness may be addressed at two levels.

First, the purchasing function needs **to ensure that sufficient materials will be available** to meet the forecast demand and schedule of deliveries to customers. This requires the presence of an effective channel of communication between the marketing/sales function and other functions. Within Scribe plc, this system involves the development of a spreadsheet by the marketing and sales departments to generate sales forecasts. The forecasts are presented as monthly forecasts for the next 12 months and quarterly forecasts for the following year.

Secondly, the marketing function within Scribe plc has recognized that the purchasing function is often the first to be approached in respect of such issues as new materials, new processes or changes in the design and colour of fabrics available. There is therefore a strong need **to improve the channels of communication** between the marketing function, which is monitoring and evaluating the needs of the consumers; the design department; and the purchasing department, responsible for ensuring the availability of inputs which may be used to satisfy market opportunities. The company is developing a product-profiling database and news-sheet to overcome some of these problems. The system involves the purchasing department inputting a summary of any new products encountered in their dealings with existing and potential suppliers. These summaries, which are restricted to about 30 lines of text, are stored in a simple database which contains five different product classifications. The marketing and design staff (or other purchasing department staff) can access this database and, by using a simple menu, study short reports on the latest developments in the relevant field, such as the types of finish that may be applied to desk furniture or the quality and range of colours.

Strategic management issues

The strategic management of profit performance and quality requires an overview of the organization and its relationship to the market opportunities that it seeks to exploit. The management team has been considering the concept of **total quality management (TQM)**. For these purposes, 'quality' means *meeting the customer's requirements at the lowest cost,* first time every time:

- **customers** are all those to whom the organization supplies products, services or information
- **requirements** are measurable specifications covering such factors as durability, reliability, accuracy, speed, method of delivery or price
- **'at the lowest cost'** means that no time, effort or materials are lost or wasted in the delivery of the product or service, so that profitability is maximized.

It is recognized that the primary methodology for achieving quality is to improve the service to customers, both internal and external. This means that (for example) advice from the marketing function to the production function should be treated as a service in the same way that the sales department deals with external customers. Communication has therefore to be considered both internally and externally, with training given to all those who must deal with customers. Accountability has also to be properly established and proper lines of control drawn up to maintain quality of service.

The organization must therefore set the corporate mission, determining the appropriate business objectives and goals and developing strategies to align departmental and functional objectives to those of the corporation. The information necessary to support these processes comprises both externally- and internally-derived material. Scribe plc, like many other organizations of this size, has failed to develop the externally-derived information systems needed to support the strategic management process. While many governmental and private sector publications provide data on general economic trends, market trends and technological developments – all of them available at relatively low cost – there is little awareness of these data sources and where they may be accessed. The company's senior managers have tended to rely heavily on their personal perceptions of the external environment without the necessary information to support or validate such judgements.

The internal information used in the current strategic management process is derived from the existing functional sub-systems in the form of regular summarized reports – for example, monthly financial statements. But the unique nature of many of the problems encountered at the strategic level usually requires *ad hoc* reports researching and analysing the particular problem and its potential solutions. Usually, this calls for the analysis of both quantitative and qualitative data. The differing problems, data and analytical techniques required and the lack of predictability of these requirements usually mean that such analysis cannot be handled in the existing information system.

The development of decision support systems and executive support systems would result in a computerized toolkit of analytical techniques that could be used to support strategic management. These toolkits would provide software tools to enable decision-makers to structure the problem, develop financial or other quantitative models of the organization, access data from internal and external databases, and perform analytical manipulations on the data, using spreadsheets and other techniques. Scribe plc would need to make a significant investment, not only in the hardware, software and information systems to provide these tools but, more particularly, in the education and training of senior management to provide the necessary skills to use these systems effectively.

In relation to the strategic decision making within Scribe plc, two problems currently facing the company emphasize the nature of the information required to undertake such decisions.

The first of these concerns the strategic development of relationships with the organization's suppliers. These relationships depend on:

- general appraisal of the effectiveness and efficiency of the existing relationships
- detailed records of delivery, cost and quality over a period of time.

Much of the data may originate from a further summarized form produced at a management level. If the database showed a record of production dislocation or increasing customer complaints due to poor quality of inputs, then the organization might need to address this issue strategically to resolve the problems.

Scribe plc has for some considerable time experienced problems with the supply of the upholstery fabrics and materials required for its chairs. Despite changing suppliers more than three times during the last two years, it is still experiencing extensive delays, erratic deliveries and inferior quality from UK suppliers. The costs of these problems in terms of production dislocation and delayed deliveries to Scribe plc's customers has necessitated the strategic reappraisal of the company's supply chain. The organization is considering either purchasing the upholstery materials from overseas suppliers or acquiring one of its existing suppliers and installing its own management to improve the quality and delivery schedules. The data to support the analysis of this latter move would be derived from the quantitative reports accumulated regularly within the management level of the purchasing function. It would also require more qualitative data and assessments concerning the prospective acquisition, including details of the quality of its promotional materials, its pricing policies and the effectiveness of the sales staff. Much of these data may be available within the purchasing department (because it results from the dealings of Scribe plc's staff with the supplier), but it is unlikely to be formally recorded until requested for this specific purpose.

The second problem identified by the directors of Scribe plc is the need to improve the efficiency and effectiveness of the production operations, while seeking to minimize the costs involved in holding stocks of raw materials. They would like to adopt a form of the just-in-time (JIT) system, although they recognize that the diversity and low volume of some of the inputs required may make this total approach unfeasible. A systems consultancy has quoted a figure of £1.2 million for a comprehensive computer system which would:

- provide automatic scheduling of orders as they are received
- develop forecasts for finished goods stock items

- initiate the acquisition and ordering of raw materials and components required and provide a schedule of the delivery dates
- produce the necessary paperwork, drawings and schedules for each item or batch prior to production
- provide monitoring and evaluation data on an enquiry basis.

Although Scribe plc has recognized the potential benefits that such a system could provide, the company has also been advised by an independent consultant that before a commitment is made to any system of this type, the management should formulate and develop their strategies in relation not only to their production operations but also to their customers and suppliers. For example, the company needs to develop a strategic relationship with its major suppliers, such that the interests of all the companies involved are fully recognized within each relationship. This would permit a more effective form of supply in which both companies were protected and developed. The company ought also to review its strategy in relation to its markets and customers. The strategy which seeks to focus on larger customers, guaranteeing larger volumes of particular products rather than one-off orders from smaller customers, may provide scope for the development of JIT systems because it provides greater levels of predictability in supply. However, it should also be recognized that the profit margins on such high-volume business are likely to be smaller than those available in the supply of specialized products to a more limited niche market. Scribe plc would also have to assess the potential risks involved in adopting a JIT system which effectively reduces the stocks held by the manufacturer to a minimum – possibly one or two days' supply – while placing heavier reliance on both the supplier and the transport systems to deliver the right quantities on time and to the correct quality specification.

A summary of the issues in the case study

This case shows that development of the information system is an integral part of the strategic development of Scribe plc, and the decision-making processes within it. But irrespective of the quality or sophistication of a particular computer-based information system, unless it is consistent with the overall strategies and profiles of both the company's operations and its external relations, it will be doomed to failure from the outset. The logic of any planning method demands a clear statement of the mission which the plan intends to achieve. The mission is the embodiment of all corporate purposes and intentions. For this purpose, the company should conduct an audit of all its resources, strengths and weaknesses so that it can better identify its future objectives and match these with its resources. This will then enable the company to consider how its competitive advantages can be brought to bear on market opportunities. In evaluating competitive advantage, the managers must inevitably consider quality and the cost advantages that enable the company to extract higher margins than its competitors and to maintain profitability in the face of price turbulence. Note that it is not the sum of resources which determines a company's competitive position; it is the way resources are matched and deployed to exploit the company's competitive advantages.

The key resource issue facing Scribe plc is the need to adopt an integrated approach to developing the information system across the whole organization. The process of computerizing the organization's information system highlights the interactive nature of the various elements or sub-systems operating in the various functions. The primary danger faced by organizations like Scribe plc is that the piecemeal development of individual elements in isolation will at best prove significantly more expensive (and at worst be counter-productive) in achieving the eventual objectives of effectiveness and efficiency.

The first task facing Scribe plc is therefore the generation of an IT strategy. This strategy must span the next three to five years and should clearly articulate the major developments envisaged in the information system and the sequence in which the component elements are to be developed.

What approach should the company adopt, therefore, both at the strategic level and at that of the individual system?

Many of the proposed developments under consideration by Scribe plc seek to make more effective use of data already available in the organization and are essentially concerned with providing wider and more ready access to such data. It is often found, as in the case of Scribe plc, that fuller utilization of information resources already available can produce significant benefits at relatively low levels of cost or investment. However, other developments are likely to require more extensive investment in the processes of analysis and design to support the development of software, and in the acquisition of hardware if the full range of benefits from the information system is to be achieved.

All decision-makers have to recognize that computerization is not a panacea. Indeed, the solution to many organizations' information needs is often not best served by a policy of computerizing *all* systems. Even in these technological days, there will always be a number of information systems that can operate more efficiently and effectively as manual systems – for instance, the detailed supplier database in the purchasing department. The important factor, however, is to ensure both the compatibility and the effective integration of manual and computer-based systems, aiming to achieve a high level of mutual support between the two facets of the overall system.

The final issue which influences the success of both manual and computer-based systems is the *effective use of those systems* by the staff involved. The experiences of Scribe plc mirror those of most organizations, in that effectiveness of use depends on the quality of the users, both as suppliers of data to, and as receivers of data from, the system. The system must be designed to support both types of user and the organization must be prepared to invest heavily in education and training so that the maximum benefit from the information resource can be achieved, both for individuals and (ultimately) for the organization. This is particularly the case if TQM is to succeed. Total quality means that everyone is involved, at all levels and across all functions, in ensuring quality in everything they do. The ethos in which the information system is implemented must incorporate participation. Everyone must feel that they have a share in the solution of the problems, with education and training designed to develop awareness and understanding from the top management down to the lowest employee.

Summary

The key points of this case study may be applied to all areas of business. The information resource and the complex system providing the information are seen as significant elements in helping an organization to achieve its corporate objectives. Elements of the information system interact across functional boundaries and different levels of decision making, as well as with external systems. The case study also underscores the importance of some basic principles of information system design and development:

- information itself is a potential source of competitive advantage to an organization, but the realization of this potential requires careful planning and management
- the development of an organization's information system requires strategic planning in addition to medium- and short-term planning and control
- most organizations can gain significant benefits simply from the more effective use of information already available
- manual and computer-based elements of the information system should be viewed as compatible parts of the same system, with each providing appropriate solutions in different situations. The key to effective and efficient business information systems lies in the ability of the organization to manage change in its human resources as data providers, processors and users.

Exam-style questions

A case study of this size and scope will not normally be a feature of examinations in this field. However, you will probably find it helpful to consolidate your learning by giving attention to the following questions on Scribe plc.

1 Explain the potential sources of competitive advantage available to Scribe through the use of its information system.
2 How should Scribe plc seek to encourage a positive attitude in its employees to the application of computer technology in the organization?

(*All answers on pages 555–556*)

CHAPTER 7

The characteristics of information technology

An understanding of how information systems operate in practice requires some understanding and knowledge of the information technologies used. In this chapter we shall introduce the main elements of computer hardware, software and communications, and explain the characteristics of their overall role in information systems. The reader should not aim to develop an in-depth or detailed understanding of the operation of the IT elements covered in this chapter, but rather to gain a basic working knowledge to assist in following our discussion of these elements in subsequent chapters.

This chapter indicates the basis on which selections between the different systems types should be made and we give attention to the configuration of new systems. This should help you to appreciate the capacities of hardware in relation to the range of software which is available, both as operating systems and as business applications. We then evaluate the options available for developing communications systems. The primary forms of technology that can support office automation exercises, introduce the concept of the 'knowledge worker' and evaluate the developments in office automation necessary to support such new organizational roles are also considered.

System types

Central processing

Originally all computer systems were centralized in the sense that they used large mainframe computers to carry out the processing with remote terminals (VDUs and printers) which communicated only with the central machine. This type of system required specialist skills (programmers and operators) to maintain the computer and a special environment in which to operate it. These large mainframe systems usually processed the bulk of an organization's business transactions and were often called **data processing** (DP) systems or **transaction processing** (TP) systems. The management of such systems was usually centralized in the DP or computer department and the technologists often had a considerable say in how and when new systems (or applications) were developed. Such systems tended to involve large-scale projects with complex data analysis exercises being undertaken and much documentation being involved. Systems analysis and design methods such as SSADM were introduced to control such system developments.

The advantages of these central mainframe-based DP systems included the following:

- the technology became comparatively reliable due to the expert operation and controlled environment in which the hardware and software operated
- the processing of an individual transaction was very cost-effective due to the economies of scale that could be achieved
- the mainframe systems had the speed and capacity to cope with large applications such as corporate databases
- the routine processing which forms an important part of many 'back-office' systems was ideally suited for the type of software which these systems used.

It would be wrong to assume that these systems are now to be considered obsolete. Many organizations, particularly banks and airlines, would be lost without their 'big machine' system, but there are some disadvantages including the following:

- they encourage the emergence of *islands of automation* rather than integrated systems which would follow from developments using a 'total systems' approach
- they can be inflexible – changes to the software, say as a result of data users' requirements, can take a long time to implement and an *applications backlog* may form
- they can become obsolete in terms of the technology which supports them and it can be difficult to replace these *legacy systems* with more modern technology if the organization relies on them for too long a time.

Distributed processing

This implies the sharing of computer resources across potentially or actually independent systems. In other words, although an on-line processing system may have terminals that are geographically remote from the central processor, these are no more than slave terminals that do not act independently of the processor and remain part of a single system. Similarly, an on-line system that uses multi-processing (i.e. two or more processors sharing the jobs of a set of terminals) is a computer configuration and may be considered a single system. The basis of a distributed system is that it uses a data communications system to create and maintain a network of computers or computer systems, which are equally capable of independent operation and of resource sharing as required. This sharing may range from the simple access of data on a remote file or the transmission of a message or image, through to the ability to transfer whole files, programs and processing jobs across systems in a way that is virtually *transparent* to the user; in other words, the user does not have to be aware that several different systems have been involved in performing the given task.

The implications of this trend for information systems development are considerable. The distribution of processing in this way is a logical extension of a trend which has come to be known as *end-user computing* (EUC), meaning that responsibility for acquiring IT resources has been delegated to the individual users. This implies not only a possible proliferation of computerized business functions but a decentralization of control over their processing. This trend can be traced through four stages:

1. the development of systems capable of supporting non-DP computing activities for a wide range of users, for example CAD/CAM and process control systems
2. the proliferation of user-friendly hardware and software (in the first instance, usually microcomputers with single-user operating systems) which allow a *one-per-desk* approach to computing in appropriate organizations
3. large-scale database systems capable of treating information as a corporate resource to be accessed and used across an organization's functional boundaries (for instance, finance and production departments both accessing the same data)
4. distributed computing, in which the application of data communications technology to the three stages above allows the development of flexible, independent and yet integrated information systems.

In this cycle, the more unfortunate characteristics of systems development during the first two stages are overcome. Specialization and lack of integration (*'islands of automation'*) were often associated with system developments which simply automated the existing manual systems, and which continued to permit each office to have the exclusive use of its own data files. Moreover, the idea of the information system as an image of the real-world system which it serves may be reinforced. Hence, the people responsible for carrying out a given function within an organization – in finance or sales, for example – may now be seen as responsible for creating, storing and processing the data used to support that function, while at the same time (and subject to adequate security measures) making it available to other users across the network.

The factors that have influenced the growth of distributed systems include the following:

- economies of scale do not necessarily apply to processors. Large single processor systems incur huge overheads in the form of system servicing and operations costs
- diminishing returns tend to apply in the equation of processing power versus cost. Thus, spending ten times an amount on a single processor will not necessarily increase processor speed and capacity by a factor of ten. Buying ten smaller computers is likely to be more cost-effective
- users are more ready to accept systems over which they have more control. Distributed computing suits the line management view of systems in organizations, and the practicality of involvement and responsibility tends to encourage greater enthusiasm and commitment on the part of the staff
- reliability and robustness may be provided more cheaply by distributing the processing rather than taking other measures such as the development of a special computer configuration, and communications costs may be reduced because data can be moved in its most cost-effective form.

- organizational information needs to be allowed to grow and change organically in a way which most directly benefits the organization which it is to serve. It is difficult for a centralized processing system to mirror the diverse needs of the different classes of user. Hence, the concept of the distributed system tends to fit in well with *systems theory*.

In fact, many organization-wide information systems still contain a considerable data processing element (for example batch processing with a major printed-output component) – with payroll, invoicing and many statistical or reporting applications being the most common. A distributed system of microcomputers may not be the most appropriate or the most efficient way of processing these tasks. Many systems therefore combine a distributed set of small computer systems with a centralized large-scale processing facility (often termed the host computer). The remote processors may be general-purpose micros or workstations with additional features to enhance their performance in a particular environment, such as business graphics or CAD/CAM. This type of *system architecture*, which separates the systems which store and manage the data from the systems which handle the applications, is called the *'client–server'* approach.

It is not only the hardware that may be geographically dispersed in a distributed system, but the data itself may also be shared among the computer systems on a network. This is different from a set of stand-alone computers, each possessing its own files, because the user is able to access data across the systems, without needing to know where the data items are stored. Such a data organization, called a *distributed database*, is intended to combine the cheapness, speed and ease of access to local files with the 'information sharing' advantages of an organization-wide network. The system design usually calls for each item of data to be stored at its most frequently used location, with *'gateways'* making it available to other users. Although these systems may bring significant improvements in the quality of organizational decision making through improved access to relevant information, they can prove to be more expensive to implement and operate than a centralized database and can suffer from increased vulnerability to breaches of security. In spite of these problems client–server architectures are being promoted by software developers and *IT service providers* because of their relative flexibility and high performance. Major changes in the business operations and organization do not cause catastrophic changes in the IT infrastructure, which sometimes used to occur with large-scale centralized computer-based systems.

Office automation

The concept of the office as a place where people gather to undertake a certain type of work (information processing) is as old as commerce itself. Offices have been subject to technological developments which have affected their working practices on an increasing scale. Meyer traces the history of office automation through the evolution and development of technological products and techniques, which may be summarized as follows:

1870s: The development of the typewriter allows speedier communication and limited copying.

1920s: The invention of the telephone enables both wide-area and local communication in real time. This is the beginning of telecommunications.

1930s: The use of scientific management (Gilbreth) is available to analyse and rationalize office practices. This represents the direct ancestor of systems analysis.

1940s: The mathematical techniques developed in World War II (operations research) are applied to the decision-making process.

1950s: The introduction of photocopying facilitates cheap and rapid document production, and the (limited) introduction of EDP speeds up large-scale transaction processing.

1960s: The emergence of management information systems (MISs) provides the background within which office automation can develop.

1970s: The setting up of telecommunications networks allows distant communication between computer systems; the widespread use of word processors speeds up text editing and enables personalized document production, and the emergence of the personal computer starts the trend toward user computing and forms the enabling technology for office automation.

1980s: The development of office automation systems which combine data, voice, text and image and the advent of processing hardware with multipurpose software packages (graphics, spreadsheets, and so on) exploit full telecommunications services. Further, the development of decision support systems (DSSs) and fourth-generation languages (4GLs) which are capable of operation in a distributed computing environment extends user computing into the areas of decision making and code generation.

1990s: Further development of multimedia systems and improvements in user-friendly operating systems such as MS Windows and IBM's OS/2 coupled to greater networking power and compatibility such as Novell Netware.

2000s: Practical development of the concept of *computer-supported collaborative work* (CSCW) and *groupware* such as Lotus Notes.

Despite all these changes, however, the basic tasks which take place in office environments remain fundamentally unchanged: offices receive, store, process and communicate business information. In a conventional office, much of this will be in the form of documents, telephone calls and mailed letters, with all the slowness, expense and inefficiencies of duplication and manual filing. Much of the work involved in carrying out these operations is of a routine nature and therefore very amenable to automation. Yet the balance of the work involves non-routine, personal activities and complex social interactions. Office automation should therefore be seen as a merging of the products of technological science with aspects of social science in support of, rather than replacing, normal commercial activities.

Office automation implies the use of computers, office products and communications technology in managing an organization's information resource. This view of information as a corporate resource suggests the integration of the four means of communication: data, text, image and voice into office-oriented multimedia systems. CSCW is a way of allowing people to share the development and subsequent management of on-line documents, processes and data in a 'real-time' collaboration. As well as shared applications such as multi-user spreadsheets and word-processing packages, groupware systems will include methods of virtual communication such as on-line bulletin boards and electronic mail. This reflects a move towards a new, high-powered way of accessing and processing information which is known as *knowledge work*.

The information explosion

One of the most observable features of the macroeconomic scene in recent years has been the general decline and retrenchment in manufacturing industry which has taken place in many of the so-called industrialized nations. As a form of compensation, the service sector has increased in importance, with the production and dissemination of information growing to a position of clear dominance during the last 30 years. Most of this information is textual or narrative in form. It is usually printed and the larger part of the bulk will pass through offices at some time in its life cycle. There is therefore a widening gap between the total amount of information stored in offices and the information which is stored as part of conventional computerized DP systems. Office automation systems have been developed to handle more efficiently the information that constitutes this gap.

Office automation and productivity

One of the main reasons for the application of IT to the office environment is to increase the productivity of office workers. Studies in the mid-1970s appeared to show that improvement in 'white collar' productivity was lagging seriously behind that of industrial and manufacturing workers.

A study of companies in the USA over a ten-year period in the late 1980s showed that industrial performance had risen by almost 90 per cent, compared to an approximate four per cent increase in office productivity. During this period, companies reported that corporate expenditure on office functions had increased from 20–30 per cent to 40–50 per cent of total budgets. One of the conclusions which could be drawn from the study was that the office environment had been consistently undercapitalized, and that the technology which had been applied to the problem area was less effective than that which had been applied in other environments. Estimates suggested that factory investment had been largely on computer-controlled plant and equipment and had exceeded white-collar investment by a factor of ten. The obvious conclusion was that increased investment in the office version of 'productive plant' – that is, automation technology – would result in a comparable increase in office productivity. Hirschheim suggests caution in accepting this conclusion, for a number of reasons:

- it is difficult to measure productivity in an office environment, and to compare industrial and office-based findings

- the link between productivity and capital expenditure may not be consistent. The influence of personal factors in the office environment means that, sometimes, the introduction of new technology may result in unrest, industrial action and lower productivity
- the relative levels of productivity at the beginning of the study were undefined. It may be that office workers were already more efficient, and therefore improvements through changes in working methods were less likely to be achieved.

Productivity improvements from office automation, where they occur, are likely to affect organizations in the following ways:

- better utilization of the workforce by a reduction in staff numbers or by a greater output per person
- improved utilization of time due to greater efficiency
- improved quality of management through better decision making
- increased output through better individual performance
- greater effectiveness through the use of information found to be available in the environment.

The knowledge worker

Current thinking identifies a particularly important role in the modern office for knowledge work. The primary activities of knowledge work, as opposed to physical work, are diagnosis (of a problem area or a potential opportunity), decision making, monitoring and scheduling. A knowledge worker is therefore someone involved in analysing situations, evaluating alternative courses of action, making decisions or recommending procedures based on the use of information. This information may come from internal data sources (such as a corporate or distributed database), from the environment (such as the World Wide Web (WWW) or an on-line database) or from the knowledge worker's own experience.

In order to combine this creative aspect of problem solving with the routine activities of the workplace, the knowledge worker must be provided with a support system having the following features:

- an information management function which is capable of handling the collection, storage and retrieval of the appropriate information in a speedy manner, for example, in a *database management system* (DBMS)
- interactive processing functions to perform calculations and to generate alternative solutions, such as *a DSS*
- communication facilities to carry the knowledge worker's output to the right place at the right time, as in an *electronic mail system* (EMS).

The benefits of office automation

By providing a suitable support environment, office automation systems are intended to benefit the knowledge worker in two ways:

1 **Direct benefits** involve an increase in output or a saving, usually in time or labour. Such benefits are usually measurable and may have a direct, and therefore short-term, effect on cash flow. These benefits can include:
   - better control over work, due to less division of labour
   - fewer conversions from one form of information to another – such as dictation on tape followed by typing on paper
   - fewer non-productive activities such as filing, record keeping and updating
   - better personal organization due to reduced travel and gathering for meetings by the use of teleconferencing facilities.

2 **Indirect benefits** are less quantifiable, and may enrich the organization through longer-term profitability and growth. These benefits can include:
   - less dependency on other departments for support with copying, printing and similiar activities
   - less need for procedures and controls to monitor work flow between departments
   - increased individual job satisfaction, due to greater personal effectiveness in carrying out a range of tasks
   - greater customer satisfaction, due to better information production and a more timely service
   - increased competitiveness of an organizations through the improved use of its information resource and its ability to respond to business pressures an opportunities.

One of the most important implications of shift to 'knowledge work' and particularly to CSCW is that the individual and the group does not need to be located physically in the same area or even on the company's premises. Therefore, through the use of IT, the ultimate implication of 'office automation' may be that offices as we know them have the potential to become a thing of the past.

Teleworking

Perhaps the greatest effect from an organizational point of view is the growing phenomenon of *telecommuting* or working from home using office automation technology for communication with customers, suppliers or the workplace. This trend, if continued, is likely to make the office a logical rather than a geographical concept. Some people see this as the natural phasing-out of a mode of working introduced by the Industrial Revolution and its replacement with one from the 'Information Revolution'.

The knowledge worker is likely to find the following advantages under the new system:

- there is a complete saving of commuting time or time spent travelling to meetings and conferences
- there is greater flexibility in working hours. This has been particularly supported by the growth of asynchronous message systems, where both

parties do not have to be on-line at the same time, as with telephone messages. This facilitates the staggering of work patterns

- a significant reduction in the number of interruptions should lead to greater productivity in some tasks
- reduced reliance on personal contact for communication purposes can benefit the smaller organization (as, for example, a self-employed accountant or consultant).

The advantages for employers are based on a reduction in operating costs, including:

- rental of office space (which, especially in large cities, greatly exceeds telecommunications costs)
- welfare support facilities, which are less of a priorty in the case of homeworkers
- travelling expenses.

A number of major organizations (significantly, ICL and Rank Xerox, two leaders in the office automation products market) are using networks of *teleworkers* to integrate specialist skills.

Electronic data interchange

Another example of the use of IT in support of innovative business processes is electronic commerce or 'paperless trading' which uses *electonic data interchange (EDI)* systems in a variety of applications. EDI is intended to replace conventional business documents, such as invoices and delivery notes, with structured data transmitted electronically over networks. The data must be structured – presented in a common form – so that the documents are standardized at both ends of the transmission. Such structured data have a long history. Military dispatches were presented in a standard form – for ease and accuracy of reading under difficult conditions – as long ago as the 18th century. Money transfers by telegram used a standard format in the 19th century and weather reports followed in World War II. Indeed, the fact that German weather reports were always in the same format enabled Allied intelligence to break the Enigma code.

The benefits of 'paperless trading' are obvious. Surveys have shown that paper documentation accounts for 3.5–7 per cent of total transport costs and up to ten per cent of finished goods costs. Also, it is estimated that around 70 per cent of the output from computer systems becomes the input to other computer systems by transcription, and some 40 per cent of all transcriptions involve some form of error. The estimated savings which EDI can achieve are 20 per cent of the cost of 'trading with paper' or some £200 *billion* pounds world-wide!

EDI services tend to be offered by service providers and are 'single sector' (i.e. specific to one industry) such as the banking systems SWIFT/BACS and the retail TRADACOMS system or 'multisector'. Attempts at EDI standards began in 1985 with the ISO 95 standard and ANSI X12, followed in 1987 by EDIFACT (EDI for administration, commerce and transport) which is becoming the multisector standard world-wide.

Office automation technology

The basic functions which may be required in an automated office can be supplied by the installation of a number of basic systems. Each of these may have a different *system architecture* (the devices and software which they use) but the functions or features will be broadly similar. The main categories of office automation systems (otherwise known as 'office IT') are set out below.

Electronic mail

Electronic mail systems (e-mail or EMS) are intended to replace the movement of paper messages (internal and external to the organization) with the electronic transmission of coded graphic or textual information. Such a system should provide the user with:

- **text manipulation facilities** to allow the composing, editing and storing of messages
- **a variety of message formats** – for instance, formal letters, notepad memos or financial statements
- **communication over long or short distances** (the communications technology that makes this possible is discussed later in this chapter)
- **the ability to receive messages in real time or asynchronously** – in other words, when both sender and receiver are at their terminals – or to store them in a mailbox for later reading, as in asynchronous messaging systems
- **the ability to route messages** to a single address, a range of specified addresses or to all the users of a local system and to forward messages to other users.

Electronic mail is said to offer the advantages of speed and versatility over its conventional rivals and to combine the best features of telephone and paper communication. However, more extended use and greater knowledge of the costs involved will be needed before the true impact of electronic mail can be judged. Since e-mail often exists within other computer-based systems the cost may be hard to assess as it consists mainly of software packages which may be bundled together as a single cost item when purchased. It is possible to send e-mail messages across the world for a subscription fee plus a nominal charge per message. Subscribers to the Usenet service may participate in *news groups* which allow them to 'post' questions and answers onto computer-based *bulletin boards* and to exchange e-mail messages directly.

Facsimile

Facsimile transmission facilities (or fax) are being used increasingly in business. Fax allows the sending of an exact copy of an original (using, for instance, radio transmission or the telephone network) to be recomposed by the receiver's equipment. This is of obvious use with diagrams and pictures, but may also be used with documents – for example, to verify signatures. Facsimile systems work by scanning a document and digitally coding the contents which are then transmitted and recoded at the receiving end. There are 750,000 code bits in an A4 sheet, which tends to make fax conversion a slow process, and inconvenient where a single telephone line may be engaged in fax transmissions for long periods.

Other major fax problems involve incompatibility and lack of standardization between manufacturers of equipment. CCITT recommendations have been agreed within the industry and Group 3 systems, which will transmit an A4 sheet in less than one minute, have been accepted as the standard and it is consequently in these systems that most development is taking place including the development of portable fax machines. Further, many fax devices are capable of sharing a telephone number which can be 'switched' automatically.

Computer output microfilm (COM)

Essentially, such systems involve the decoding in a COM recorder of computer-generated magnetic media (usually tape) into human-readable images which are then photographed on microfilm or fiches. Such media are easily stored and retrieved. Some systems use software for fully automated retrieval from a VDU – called *computer-assisted retrieval* (CAR) – and may be read or hard-copied from a reader/printer device. The importance of COM in an office environment lies in its ability to store and retrieve large volumes of data easily and cheaply. An obvious application is the storing of invoice copies and purchase orders, which are often held for up to seven years and can create considerable cost and nuisance if stored on paper, and the storing of records which may include hand-written documents.

Teleconferencing

The advantages to an organization of being able to conduct presentations, meetings and negotiations without the attendant difficulties of travel and accommodation are obvious. It is reported that over 80 per cent of the Fortune 500 companies have, or are planning to install, teleconferencing facilities. Users of such systems report the following benefits:

- meetings can be arranged at shorter notice
- personnel report less disruption to everyday activities
- individuals do not feel at a disadvantage on other people's territory.

The first generation of teleconferencing technology was audioconferencing, which was inexpensive and has been available for some time, but poses some operational problems (for instance, lack of visible presence and identification of speakers). Videoconferencing overcomes these problems but it is far more expensive and, given present levels of technology, potentially requires specialist studio equipment. Teleconferencing allows the linking of two or more locations (using a choice of transmission media including satellites) and is likely to become an increasingly important aspect of office automation once technical problems such as the *bandwidth* or amount and speed of the transmission of the data can be overcome. Indeed, teleconferencing and telecommuting are part of a mode of working called telework which uses IT as a substitute for physical presence and is thought to have considerable potential for the future.

Voice mail

Sometimes called 'voice store-and-forward', voice mail systems (VMS) are the asynchronous counterpart of telephone calls. Such systems allow the sender to record and store a voicegram in digital form, which is stored (usually on a dedicated disk drive or server) for delivery the next time the addressee uses his or her telephone. IBM, one of the first in this field with audio distribution systems (ADSs), is claiming the following advantages for VMSs in general:

- less wasted telephone time, as voicegrams tend to have the same precise qualities as a memo
- fewer interruptions, as the messages are stored until it is convenient for the user to receive them
- rapid response time, as dictation and typing are eliminated.

Despite adverse features such as the one-way nature of a voicegram, the absence of social discourse and the high installation costs, the integration of voice mail into office automation systems seems inevitable.

Videotext

Videotext (or Videotex) is a generic term for systems which use the concept of data transmission in the form of text and limited graphics, from databases to remote terminals which are usually adapted domestic television sets. Originally intended as a public service extension to public broadcasting, Videotext services are now developing features which may have important applications in the automated office. All Videotext systems fall into two groups which are distinguished by their transmission media: *Viewdata*, which uses the public telephone or cable TV network, and *Teletext* which uses normal TV channels. The information is actually transmitted in the interval between the conventional television picture lines. While Viewdata allows limited interaction between user and computer (via a keyboard or small keypad), Teletext allows only one-way communication. Ceefax is a commonly-used teletext service in the UK.

Public databases

Both Viewdata and Teletext exist to make factual information available to users. However, because of their limited powers of interaction, the usefulness of both systems is bound to be restricted in a commercial environment. It is not possible to match the complex searches or data manipulation facilities available on the standard database system. Thus, while information on all the shares in the Financial Times Stock Exchange 100 index is made available, a user who wanted to compile a list of those shares with a current dividend yield greater than five per cent would be obliged to resort to pen, paper and patience. Such a task would need more detailed information and a special method of access called a *query language*. Such a service is offered by international government bodies and commercial organizations in the form of public databases, which are large bodies of information capable of being accessed on-line via wide area networks or by off-line batch searches. It is estimated that there are more than 2000 commercial databases. The most common types are:

- **legal**, containing an index and the full text details of both national and supranational statute law (including EU laws) and case law, which is either classified by subject or held in general files
- **econometric databases**, containing national and regional financial and demographic data, usually indicating trends and, possibly, forecasts
- **commercial**, which may be industry-wide, by product or market, or for individual companies, showing the financial structure, business activities and management banking details
- **scientific databases**, holding technical information or reference tables on a wide range of subjects, including patents.

These databases are likely to have considerable commercial impact because of their obvious applications in product development, marketing, credit control and consumer affairs. Public databases involve the activities of *information providers* (IPs) who collect and supply the data, the operator or host who creates or maintains the database, and the transmitter who provides the telecommunications network. These participants may be a single organization or separate organizations acting collaboratively. It is customary for the operator to provide the necessary software package containing the query language and having the correct protocols for compatibility with the host system.

World Wide Web (WWW)

The WWW is a source of information which is increasingly used for academic and commercial purposes. The WWW exists on the Internet (the virtual network which links computers all over the world) and consists of *pages* of information at *sites* which are accessed by a unique address called a *universal remote locator* (URL). WWW sites may be accessed and viewed through a *web browser* such as Netscape Navigator and can be addressed directly or through a *search engine* such as Lycos which can be used to search the WWW by topic or keyword. WWW pages are set up by using a relatively simple programming language called *hypertext mark-up language* (HTML), which allows hypertext links to other sites and pages of information to be formed. This makes the WWW a powerful and flexible source of business information. There were an estimated 12.8 million users of the WWW in 1996 and an increasing number of businesses are choosing to have 'an Internet presence' in this way. Much useful information about potential customers and suppliers and their products and services can be accessed in this way.

Input devices

The peripherals which may be used to control and communicate with a computer system, or to enter data for processing or storage (called *data capture*), are particularly important factors in the choice of hardware. Input devices form a major part of the *human–computer interface (HCI)* and therefore represent much of the user's view of the system. The choice of input device, and any medium which it uses, must suit the characteristics of the system and the purpose for which the system is intended.

As with computers themselves, input peripherals may be broadly categorized into special-purpose (or dedicated) and general-purpose devices. Special-purpose devices are characteristically used for the routine capture of large amounts of data. It commonly happens that the capture process will not be immediately acknowledged by an output or detailed response from the system. General-purpose devices typically offer a wide range of features and may be in physical proximity to an output device. The resulting two-way communication between computer system and human user is called a *dialogue*. The design of this dialogue, which is an important part of the design of an effective computer-based information system, should ensure that a constructive and positive attitude is created in the human user. An exception to this rule is the case of service points (such as ATMs or cash dispensers and EPOS terminals) which are designed for a special purpose, yet offer a limited dialogue and range of features. The main types of input device which are likely to be incorporated into an information system or commercial application are decribed below.

Visual display unit (VDU)

This device combines a display monitor with one or more control devices to allow both input and output; in other words, the screen allows the user to monitor the input of data from the keyboard or other source, and the screen can also display machine-generated output. It is necessary to specify the type of monitor and control devices in accordance with the use to which the system will be put. Most DP system applications usually require only alphanumeric display – the lowest-cost option. Most office IT applications run software which require a higher degree of resolution than such basic VDUs allow. Many business graphics or CAD/CAM systems use larger 'screens' with a higher resolution such as are found on high-powered *workstations*.

In spite of this move to better definition, workers who use VDUs for long periods of time are alleged to show symptoms of medical disorder. Following a European directive which took effect in December 1992, employers must adopt reasonable measures to protect employees when they are using video display terminals (VDTs) or workstations. This involves:

- providing proper lighting in the rooms where VDTs are to be used
- ensuring that the screens, keyboards and seating arrangements are ergonomically sound
- avoiding screen glare and maintaining the stability of the screen image

- scheduling rest periods
- providing regular eye tests.

There are only two categories which are exempted from the operation of the directive, namely the self-employed and students!

Some MISs require a high-resolution graphics display capability, for which these high-definition colour monitors are required. These monitors are most costly because higher specification hardware is needed to support them. In addition, some or all of the following control or input devices should be incorporated.

- **Mouse or trackball devices**. These use the rolling motion of a ball (a mouse is rolled on a flat surface, a trackball is moved manually) to act as a cursor control or to move data about the screen quickly, as with a WIMP (windows, icons, mouse, pull-down menus) interface.
- **Voice data entry (VDE)** systems employ a modified VDU and microphone to accept vocal input. The simplest speech recognition systems may be programmed to recognize a limited number of keywords. The natural language capacities of computers are still very restricted, but some of the more advanced speech-understanding systems are now able to extract a more complex input of combinations of words and numbers from normal speech patterns. The applications for these systems are limited but include *high-responsibility systems*, such as those which help to regulate and control air traffic and some aspects of financial trading. The advantages claimed for VDE are:
  - operator training can be reduced
  - the potential information transfer rate is significant (normal speech conveys between 150 and 220 words per minute)
  - the ergonomics of operator activity can be improved, because the operator is not restricted to the use of a keyboard terminal for control and input purposes.

  For such systems to become truly practicable, however, the inaccuracies of interpretation produced by individual speech characteristics and environmental sounds must be overcome.
- **Light-pen and touch-screen inputs** use the VDU screen as part of the input medium. A light-pen connected to the terminal is placed against the screen, and a light-sensitive device recognizes the position by X and Y co-ordinates. A touch-screen uses an inlaid screen to accept input through the act of physically touching the screen. Obvious applications in an information systems context include menu-driven programs, where a chosen item is touched, and dialogues involving a hierarchy of multiple-choice records, as with the part numbering systems in some inventory control systems.

Data capture devices

These devices are intended to allow the input of routine data, often in large amounts, and usually with as little human intervention as possible. Some of these devices use input from a sensor – an electronic eye or transducer – to measure or count data items, as on a production line. These are termed 'direct input' devices as they create input directly from the object. Other devices derive information from some form of coded data-carrying medium, either printed on the item or attached to it. The medium and the sensor, together with the attendant software, make up a data capture system, a classification which includes two broad divisions:

1 document readers and 'scanners'
2 point-of-sale terminals.

Document readers

These readers have a wide range of applications in business and commerce. In the context of information systems, they are often used for providing input where the data and its source are of a uniform nature and in quantities that make keyboard input impractical. The two methods of document reading in common use are *optical* and *magnetic recognition*, and the following systems are found in practice:

- **Optical readers** are usually free-standing peripherals not dissimilar to photocopiers or fax machines. It is quite common to find collating or sorting hoppers included on the output side, and a feed hopper sited on the input. *Optical character recognition* (OCR) documents are printed in a special stylized form using standard type fonts. The most common fonts (there is as yet no universally agreed standard) are OCR-A and OCR-B. OCR-A, standard in the USA, is used in four sizes. OCR-B, a European standard, comes in three sizes of character. Most OCR readers can recognize both the specialized fonts and some will also recognize conventional fonts. Further developments in this area may lead to a more general capacity to accept direct document input in word processing systems. OCR documents may be pre-printed, typed or produced on suitably equipped computer printers. OCR is currently used for Giro credit transfer forms and for turnaround documents, such as remittance advice notes and sales order forms.
- **Optical mark recognition** (OMR) systems involve the use of documents which are designed so that a mark or perforation, made in a particular position, represents data. Typically, each possible position is a box in a type of multiple-choice array. The box which is applicable is then marked manually or with a special printer. In this way, numbers and dates may be built up or coded with a series of boxes – for units, tens, hundreds, and so on, although some practice is necessary to enable a human to make sense of these codes directly from the document. OMR readers must work in conjunction with special software, written to read a particular document, and they are therefore less flexible than OCR systems. OMR is typically used to extract data from survey and questionnaire forms, sales order forms, stocktaking and medical records. One interesting application is employed by one manufacturer of office equipment, whose forms have an exploded view of a machine, each part having a marking box. This provides direct input to the ordering system and avoids the problems and delays which may result from ambiguous descriptions and incorrect part numbers.

- **Magnetic ink character recognition** (MICR) systems use human-readable characters which are pre-printed in a special ink impregnated with iron oxide. Before being read, the documents are passed through a magnetic field which is picked up by the printed characters. The machine reader recognizes the character by its magnetic field pattern, codes it and provides input to the computer. Most models of MICR reader offer programmed sorting facilities, but they are of limited flexibility because of the need to have the characters to be read in the same position on the document, although the documents may vary in size (as with cheques). A further limitation is that most systems will read only a single line of data. Two fonts are in common use: E13B, which is used mainly on cheques in the USA and the UK, and CMC7, which is used on European cheques and UK postal orders. Because of the need for pre-printing to high-quality standards, the use of MICR is largely limited to banking operations and as input to EFT systems, where the high-speed capability of MICR readers (over 2000 documents per hour) is important.
- **Scanners** are similar devices to optical readers but are more flexible and powerful and are physically smaller, making them very suitable for the office environment. They do not need to have documents presented in any particular format (for example OCR) or type (for example MICR) but can read or 'scan' text and pictures from 'normal' documents. Scanning can be used to insert images into documents created by *desk-top publishing* (DTP) software or into WWW pages.

Point-of-sale (POS) systems

POS systems combine the features of a sophisticated cash register (itemized receipts, coupon refunds, and so on) with data capture for an information system. Initially, POS systems were to be found as a part of major applications, as in supermarket chains and department stores, but the technology is now being implemented in smaller shops as system prices come down. The design of each system, and particularily its data-carrying media, will vary according to both the nature of the goods being handled and the size of the organization and its information needs.

Typically, a supermarket will use POS terminals at each service or outlet point, each incorporating a laser scanner (a static barcode reader), a keyboard with special function keys, a tally-roll printer and an LCD display for customer information. The keyboard is provided both for use with *commodity codes* – abbreviated codes which, when input, will identify items such as fruit and vegetables (which cannot have a bar code) or deal with those situations where the scanner cannot get a clean image from a barcode – and to permit the general housekeeping tasks to be performed, such as operator verification and log-on, session and daily totals. Otherwise the check-out operator will simply pass the bar-coded package over the scanner. The unique barcode will identify the item, enabling the description, price and VAT rating to be looked up and the stock record to be updated.

There are two European standard barcode formats: European Article Number 11 digit code (EAN11) a similar eight-digit code (EAN8) which is intended for use on smaller items and labels. The US format Uniform Product Code (UPC) uses ten digits and has been in use for a longer period of time. In all cases, a human-readable equivalent of the data (in OCR-B) is printed below the barcode. In EAN8, the first two digits identify the country of origin, the UK being 50; the next five are exclusive to the manufacturer; the following five identify the product/package combination; and the final digit is a check digit. Thus, each manufacturer may register up to 99 999 codable items. The bars may be in various sizes, although larger codes tend to be read more accurately. Similar systems (although the structure of the codes will vary and hand-held wands may be used instead of a scanner) are used as part of the circulating system in libraries, to identify books and borrowers, and in other stock control applications. An alternative to barcoding which is often used in clothing stores is the coded swing tag or *Kimball tag*, which can be read on a punched-card reader, usually at a centralized DP location.

Output devices

The most common methods of supplying output information from a computer are:

- visual display
- hard-copy production
- computer output to microfilm (COM)
- audio output.

Visual display

This has already been described in general terms earlier in this chapter as part of an input–output terminal – a VDU or multifunction workstation. In an information systems context, the importance of a visual display is its ability to represent *transient information* – that is, information which is frequently updated or need not be saved, or complex information such as may be represented by business graphics. Displays may be *alphanumeric* – showing only the standard range of digital and alphabetic characters (although simple graphics may be produced using such characters) – or *graphical*, for more sophisticated graphics applications. The difference between the two types lies in the issue of cost versus performance. Most personal computers now have monitors which will perform either function well. Indeed, current developments in liquid crystal displays and 'flat screen' technology are being used in 'laptop' and 'palmtop' miniature computers. many of which are capable of running the same Windows and graphics applications as desktop Pentium PCs.

Hard-copy devices

These devices include printers and plotters, which may be used for a variety of purposes and applications, and they are still widely used in the information systems area – even in so-called 'paperless' offices. The features offered by hard-copy output devices, their operational performance and, above all, their cost, vary more from type to type than for any other form of peripheral. The range of different types available is equally great. The choice of device for a particular application must therefore be made with care. The most common types of printer and plotter, together with their salient features, can by described under four headings:

- character printers
- line printers
- page printers
- plotters.

Character printers

These printers, also known as *serial printers*, are the basic type of device associated with personal computer systems. The method of operation is similar to a conventional manual typewriter, except that the paper, often sprocket-fed, stays put and the print head moves. Two types of printer are in common use: *impact* and *non-impact*. Non-impact printers usually produce better-quality output; the relevant terms are *letter quality (LQ)* and *near-letter quality (NLQ)*. Impact printers are required where multipart output is to be produced, such as for invoices and delivery notes. These systems will use either carbon interleaved or *no carbon required (NCR)* stationery. The standard forms of printer are as follows:

- **Dot matrix printers** are the most basic form of impact printer, in which the print head consists of a matrix of tiny tubes containing needles. The needles are fired on to the printer ribbon by solenoids in a pattern corresponding to the shape of the character required. Quality of output can be improved to NLQ standards by using high-density matrices, several print heads or multiple print passes. The latter method tends to compromise the dot matrix printer's greatest advantage, which is speed of output where cost is a more important factor than print quality.
- **Ink jet and bubble-jet printers** were developed to combine the speed and flexibility of dot matrix printers with an added quietness of operation. The dots which form the characters are formed by tiny jets of ink shot at the paper under electronic control. Although ultimately limited in terms of speed by single character operation and their inability to produce multipart documents, ink jet printers dominate one important application – business graphics. Some models can print graphs, bar and pie charts in up to eight colours, but at considerable expense as special paper must be used.

Line printers

Line printers are able to produce a complete line of text in a single printing operation, giving the operational speeds necessary for the bulk printing requirements of a DP system – for purchase orders, say, or invoicing runs. The two common types of line printer, *drum printers* and *train printers*, are impact types using carbon ribbons and NCR stationery for multiple copies. The other type, the *electrostatic printer*, is less common. It also prints one line at a time, and uses wires to electrically charge the paper before passing it through an ink solution to form the characters.

Drum or barrel printers employ columns of complete character sets, embossed around the circumference of a rapidly rotating drum. Thus, every print position is capable of being occupied by any given character. A print hammer situated at each print position forces the paper against the drum, through the ribbon, when the appropriate character is in position. As the drum never stops moving (a process called *fly printing*) the results are often somewhat blurred and irregular. Also, the character set cannot easily be changed. Drum printers have therefore largely been replaced by train printers, the principle of operation of which consists of a set of characters or type slugs mounted on a chain or flexible band rotates continuously in a horizontal plane across the paper. Hammers at all the print positions 'fly print' through a ribbon as the correct slug passes. The print quality is better than that achievable by drum printers and the character sets are easily changed. In addition, train printers are cheaper.

Page printers

Page printers are unequalled in their print quality and speed. Their features may include double-sided printing, collating and copy multiples greater than seven (the effective limit in impact printers using NCR stationery). Although page printers produce an image one line at a time, their speed of operation is such that the full effect is that of creating a complete page instantaneously. The devices vary from small desk-top laser printers such as the HP Laserjet used with PCs or in office automation systems, to large machines resembling printing presses, such as the IBM 3800 laser printer which is capable of producing sufficient output to supply the needs of the largest DP system. Whatever the form of the printer, the paper feed may be by a single-sheet hopper system, fan-folded as with normal computer stationery or on large reels.

- **Laser printers** form their characters by flashing a low-powered laser beam on to a rotating drum, somewhat in the manner of a photocopier. The photoconductive drum surface stores the resulting images, which are transferred on to paper with the use of a dry toner. An almost infinite variety of character fonts may be used, and even mixed in the same line. Logos, tone-block illustrations and graphics may be printed in black and white or colour, giving laser printers an important role in many IT applications.
- **Xerographic printers** use photocopier technology capable of accepting computer output and offer many features common in office copiers.

The factors which will most influence the choice of printer will tend to be the following:

- **the nature of the document** to be printed, for example multipart invoice set, personalized mail shot letter, and so on
- **the volume of output** – high volumes usually imply a need for high printing speeds and volume stationery feed
- **the environment** in which the printer will operate. (An office-type environ-

ment would suggest the use of a quiet, versatile printer capable of several character fonts. A centralized DP department might suggest a large, high-output line printer)

- **the costs involved**, both initial costs and cost per copy. (A single, high-output printer may actually be less expensive than a small impact printer dedicated to each workstation in an office.)

Plotters

These have been used in CAD systems where diagrams and working drawings of considerable complexity are produced. The general trend towards cheaper, smaller and faster hardware and the development of business graphics software packages has made applications in this area possible. Pen plotters come in drum and flatbed types, both of which are capable of producing high-quality graphics output by using multiple-colour stylus pens. Some plotter systems will produce output in up to six colours, although output is very slow because a separate pass must be carried out for each colour. The inclusion of a digital plotter in the standard information system would be unusual, because the precision of which such a plotter is capable is usually of less importance than speed, so colour ink jet printers are a more frequent choice.

Storage devices

Most types of computer system will have three forms of storage facility:

1. buffers
2. main memory
3. backing store.

Although the first form is transparent to the user, it is important to the operation of both input and output devices. The latter two types of storage are very significant in the specification process to fit a particular software application to a given computer system.

Buffers

These are temporary storage devices which allow the speed of input and output devices to be matched to the speed of a *central processing unit* (CPU). Input buffering is essential on most data capture devices (including VDUs) and serves two purposes:

- the characters typed from the keyboard are accumulated in the buffer to form data blocks. A block is then transferred to the processor at a transfer rate far in excess of that of the terminal or its user
- a CRT screen must be refreshed periodically by retransmitting the screen image contents. This is done from the buffer.

Output buffers are used with all printers and plotters and operate like input buffers in reverse. In large-scale computer installations, the data buffers will be separate components and will have a significant effect in increasing the input–output capacity of the system.

Main memory

This is an extension of the CPU and is directly accessible to it. For this reason, it is often called *immediate access storage* (IAS). Main memory holds three types of content:

- the program instructions which are to be executed
- the data which is to be processed
- the results of processing awaiting output.

The first form of content is permanent and will be held in *read only memory* (ROM), even when the power is turned off. The latter two types are volatile and are stored in *random access memory* (RAM) as they move in and out of the main memory storage. RAM represents the largest part of main memory and is often used as a measure of the power of a computer, especially with personal computers.

Main memory is composed of uniquely addressable storage locations, each of which can be accessed by a control unit. The capacity of these storage locations varies from one machine to another. Until recently, most microcomputers had locations holding eight binary digits and were therefore said to have an eight-bit word. Minicomputers often had 16-bit storage locations and mainframes tended to be 32-bit machines. Now these factors no longer apply; there are even 32-bit microcomputers.

The number of storage locations in main memory (particularly the RAM) dictates the storage capacity of the computer. This figure, quoted in megabytes (Mb) is important in choosing a computer for a particular application. Many current micro-based software packages, particularly those offering spreadsheet or business graphics facilities, will occupy 4 Mb or more of RAM. Many recent personal computers have now been designed to provide at least twice this level of RAM or to permit 'memory expansion'. The trend in microcomputer design in recent years has been towards producing greater main store capacity (greater word size for more processing power) and faster data manipulation by using a larger bus and a more sophisticated microprocessor. Intel's famous chip, the 80486 runs at over four million instructions per second (4 MIPS), a rate which compares with many mainframe computers of several years ago, and the later 80856 chip used in the Pentium PC has considerably more processing power and speed than this.

Backing store

This is also known as *secondary storage* and is a necessary part of all general-purpose and most special-purpose computer systems, because no matter how large the main storage of a computer, its RAM is volatile. Therefore, losing power, whether deliberately or accidentally, would mean the loss of the RAM-stored memory contents. Also, even with recent advances in semiconductor production technology, main storage is still relatively expensive. Therefore backing store is used to hold program and data files ready for transfer to main memory. The trade-off is speed versus cost, as access to read data from even the fastest backing store will be slow compared to IAS.

To overcome this problem, some special purpose systems use *electronically programmable ROM* (EPROM), which may have semipermanent data burned into it. Such an application might be the prices of those goods in a supermarket POS system which are relatively infrequently updated. Price look-up would then be faster than from secondary storage and would not be affected by the number of users requiring access at any one time. Attempts have also been made to produce storage devices that are midway between RAM and backing store, in that they have few moving parts, giving improved access speed and reliability. Devices in this category include RAM disks (actually plug-in auxiliary chips); bubble memory, which uses magnetized crystal wafers; and *charge couple devices* (CCDs), consisting of arrays of electrically charged metal squares. All of these devices seem to offer considerable potential but are yet to be accepted in common use. One reason may be cost. Also, CCD and RAM disks lose their contents when power is lost.

For a practical data storage device to gain general acceptance under a variety of operational conditions, a compromise must be reached between the following design characteristics:

- **cost** – the initial cost and running costs must be acceptable to the user. It is possible to derive a cost per item of stored data for a given application. This will vary from one type of storage device to another
- **reliability** is important in two ways:
  - the device should have an acceptable mean time between failure (MTBF) rating
  - it should hold data without undue risk of loss or corruption

  Obviously, the way in which the device is used will have a radical effect in both these areas
- **capacity** – the estimation of the number of data items (records) which will be necessary to support a particular application should include provision for future growth. Also, the number of devices must allow for sorting operations (normally, a minimum of two devices are required)
- **speed** – two factors are open to consideration in this area:
  - access time, i.e. the average time taken to find a particular record. This should be suitable for the given application. Normally on-line systems will place a premium on access time
  - data transfer rate, the speed at which data may be read from, or written to, the storage media on the device. This is obviously important in a batch-mode system.

Devices in which these features are balanced will vary from one system to another, according to the category of computer (micro or mini), the system type (DP or real-time) and the processing mode (on-line or batch). A range of typical backing store devices includes the following.

- **Floppy disk** drives are incorporated into all PCs and they have enough speed for most business applications. Since the mid-1980s, 3.5-inch diskettes of various capacities have been adopted as the industry standard. The disks are contained in a plastic envelope, with the access port covered by a retractable plate. They are therefore reliable in ordinary 'office use'.

- **Hard disk** drives are robust machines built into many personal computers or, more rarely, available as stand-alone devices. Hard disk drives were developed by IBM to overcome the problems of limited storage and reliability to which many small-system drives were felt to be prone. Using an air-tight enclosure containing a permanently fixed hard disk with lubricated surfaces allows the read/write heads to move closer to the disk – they touch when the drive stops rotating. This produces greater storage capacity, faster data transfer and improved reliability. Typical hard disk drives may contain disks of 160 (or more) Mb capacity, and several drives may be linked to one computer via a disk control unit. One disadvantage of using a hard disk for the storage of permanent data (customer records, general ledger, and so on) is the need for more careful security procedures. Whereas a floppy disk may be removed and locked away for security, a hard disk must be backed up regularly – usually to a streamer-tape cassette.
- **Magnetic disk-packs.** This form of storage uses changeable disk packs and has become the most popular type of backing storage for large-scale DP systems, with the ability to give direct access to any record by specifying its address outweighing the superior robustness of tape storage. A disk pack unit into which the disk pack or cartridge is loaded will consist of a control unit and a drive assembly which will rotate the disks continuously when in operation. A disk pack will be loaded by the system operator according to processing requirements and will usually contain several master files or a whole database. Replacement of one cartridge by another takes about one minute. It is usual to have a number of identical drives to allow files to be moved between processors in a multiprocessor system. An installation with three disk drives may have 10–12 packs containing active data in the form of master files, program files, and so on, with those not immediately required being stored off-line.

  A single disk pack can have a storage capacity of over 100 million characters and a data transfer rate of 300,000 characters per second, depending on the head movements required to produce random and direct access. The speed and capacity of changeable disk pack storage tends to outweigh the fact that the very fine tolerances involved in the read/write operation necessitate a 'super-clean' environment if reliability is to be maintained.
- **CD-ROM drives.** These devices use a variant of the technology employed in video disks in the entertainment industry and may, in time, supplant the magnetic disk-pack. A single 'optical disk' (CD-ROM) may have a storage capacity of three to four gigabytes (15–20 times that of an average magnetic disk) and access times are much faster because the system relies on a smaller number of simpler moving parts. As a result, the achievable data transfer rate of over three megabytes per second is an attractive proposition. However, the long-term attraction of CD-ROMs is the promise of increased reliability, due both to the simplicity of the read/write operation (which uses a low-power laser and photocell) and to the robustness of the disk itself. There is the

further advantage that the gap of 2 mm between laser unit and disk surface means that air filtration or air tight sealing is not required to prevent head crashes.

But there is a material limitation. Optical disks cannot be erased or overwritten, so updates have to be written to another part of the disk or to a completely new disk. The relevant term is *write once, read many times* (WORM). This drawback has restricted the use of optical disks in business information systems to a few specialist applications where updating is required only infrequently. An example of this is the Ordnance Survey Map database of the UK, which is used by motoring organizations to locate and assist the drivers of vehicles which have broken down. A particularly attractive commercial market lies in the exploitation of *interactive video* (IV) in which a video disk player is controlled by a microcomputer to give varied visual stimulus materials according to the user's responses to a computer-driven dialogue. The main market for IV is in vocationally-oriented *computer-based training* (CBT) packages and educational encyclopaedia packages such as Microsoft Encarta.

Software and programming

Many of the decisions which must be made in the specification and design of an information system are inevitably rooted in the computer hardware – in particular, in its response and output speed, storage capacity and the likely costs of processing or maintenance. But machines are nothing in themselves. Thus, the ultimate characteristics of the system when installed, and its success in maximizing the opportunities offered if the above physical design issues have been properly addressed, will depend to a great extent on the choices which have been made about the software. Software may be classified by function as either the computer *system software*, which allows the system to provide services to the user, or the *applications software* which carries out the user's more detailed requirements.

All the primary functions (i.e. storing, accessing, retrieving and modifying all the data in the system, whether persistent or transient) are carried out by programs. Program development should be the subject of a design process exactly comparable to that necessary to design the hardware configuration, that is, the program development cycle. The aim should be to produce a system which most closely meets the end users' needs. To that extent, the design process ultimately begins and ends with the user. For this reason, a basic knowledge of software characteristics, alternatives and trends is necessary for a complete appreciation of information systems development.

Systems software

This software comprises programs or routines which are largely hidden from the user – in other words, they are transparent – yet which help in the process of writing, testing, modifying or running an applications program. Most of the software residing in computer memory is in this category and is termed the computer's operating system. The more sophisticated the computer system, the more powerful and complex the operating system required to manage its resources. In general an operating system could be expected to perform the following functions:

- memory allocation and management
- multi-user scheduling
- access control
- input–output control
- job scheduling
- providing utilities and user services
- interfacing with other systems and devices.

An operating system will contain programs designed to carry out four separate, but fundamental functions, namely:

1. control
2. utility
3. translation
4. communications.

Control programs

These programs are designed to manage the general functioning of the processor, memory and terminal interface. As in human organizations, these programs are arranged in a hierarchy. At the top of the system, the *supervisor* or *executive program* controls the running of the other programs in the operating system. Most monitor-equipped microcomputers hold the supervisor in ROM. The result is that the system is ready to accept commands from the keyboard or elsewhere as soon as the computer is switched on. Other small computers are made operational by the loading of a system disk containing the program. On larger systems with fixed disks, the machine must be booted up by commands from the control console which cause the supervisor to be loaded into main memory from the backing store. Only when the supervisor is in position and the machine has self-tested can the rest of the system be offered to users.

Within the broad control of the supervisor, a variety of tasks are to be undertaken. Thus, the part of the operating system known as the *job scheduler* will queue and sequence the jobs which demand the use of the processor and main memory. Similarly, it is the responsibility of the *file manager* to achieve the interleaving effect of multi-programming (see the explanation earlier in this chapter). Further, the interface with terminals and with the backing store in response to the requirements of any applications program which is being executed is handled by the *input–output manager*. Obviously, the greater the sophistication of use that is intended for the computer system, the more complex the suite of control programs must be to control the more modern system features such as multiprogramming, timesharing and virtual memory. Yet, no matter what the level of sophistication actually achieved, it is generally the case that the detailed functioning of the control programs is not even considered by the naive user – it is invisible or transparent.

Utility programs

Such programs (also known as *service programs*) are designed into the operating system by the manufacturer or software house, primarily as a support to programmers and, to a lesser extent, to help users when writing, storing and running their programs. The functions most usually provided are:

- **loaders** or programs responsible for loading programs into main memory
- **linkers** or programs designed to link program modules together
- **editors** or programs which permit the modification of program code
- all those routines which sort, merge and otherwise manipulate the data.

Translation programs

This software converts source programs from a high-level language into machine-executable code. There are two types of translator:

1. **A compiler** requires the programmer to finish coding the entire program or a freestanding module which is then translated completely into machine code for execution. If the program is error free, it remains in this compiled form, and therefore runs more quickly than programs which have to be interpreted during each run.
2. **An interpreter** converts and attempts to execute a program one statement at a time. Although the program can be tested as it is being coded, the run time of the completed program will be slower, because the translation into machine code has to be undertaken line by line for each run.

Communications programs

This form of software has become increasingly important as the technology to support network computer systems has developed. Many systems now exist, exploiting a variety of techniques, to link different hardware and software into local or wide area networks (LANs and WANs). The result is that many system designers now want the modern types of microcomputer, minicomputer and mainframe computer to communicate with each other. Software is necessary to execute the mere physical linkages and to make the connections that will allow meaningful communications to take place. The communications programs may be required to help select the best transmission medium for a given message, coding and sending the data, and then waiting for, receiving and storing a reply. The control of this interface between two otherwise separate computer systems is governed by a protocol – a pre-defined procedure indicating the message format and the agreed data transfer rate. Sometimes communications software can enable two different types of equipment to assume the same characteristics for the purpose of communication – for example, a stand-alone microcomputer can be programmed to act as a terminal to another computer system. This process is known as *emulation*.

Operating systems

All the main utility and applications programs will be individually identified and stored in the computer's program library. The users can obtain the details of this library through a program directory. In addition to this straightforward function, access to certain programs will probably be security-restricted by a piece of software called the *library manager*, which also inserts and retrieves programs and maintains the directory. This form of overview function is a part of the operating system.

Operating systems may be *proprietary*, i.e. specific to a certain manufacturer or computer, and probably protected by copyright, or *portable*. The choice of operating system is critical for the system user as it may dictate the availability of applications software packages and manufacturer support. The current industry trend is towards hardware-independent portable operating systems – particularly in the field of personal computers, where mutual compatibility between an operating system and a market leader's software applications products is a strong selling feature. A truly portable operating system will usually consist of four modules:

1. **The nucleus**. This acts as job scheduler and controls both the filing system and the main memory. The design trend is to make it dedicated to a particular microprocessor, but independent of the remaining system hardware.
2. **The storage I/O module**. This handles all access to the backing storage.
3. **The terminal I/O module**. This recognizes and holds the characteristics of input and output terminals.
4. **The user interface**. This module offers a generalized set of commands which can be exploited by the user, together with the appropriate responses, including error messages. This should not be confused with the dialogue, which is the process of interaction between the user and an applications program.

Leading PC operating systems

The leading operating systems for personal computers are MS-DOS (the proprietary **d**isk **o**perating **s**ystem produced by Microsoft), IBM's OS/2 and the Apple Macintosh operating system. IBM originally pioneered the adoption of its own variant of DOS (disk operating system) in its PC machines. The development of PC compatibles or 'clones' led to DOS coming close to being a *de facto* standard for small computers, but the market began to be disputed by Apple Computers' Macintosh machine which had a WIMP interface which was more user-friendly and powerful than DOS's command-based interface.

Developments which sought to equalize this situation (and which later became competitors in their own right) were Microsoft's Windows environment (which runs on the DOS operating system 'platform') and IBM's OS/2, which was intended to make DOS obsolete. At the moment, the market dominance of Microsoft (in terms of both operating systems and applications software) implies that MS-DOS and MS-Windows will be common for the foreseeable future, with the latest version, Windows '95, fast becoming the new standard for office IT systems.

Unix

The other main contender for operating system domination in the personal computer market has migrated down from minicomputer systems, where it has been popular since the late 1960s. This is Unix, which was developed by AT&T's Bell Laboratories for general purpose multiprogramming systems using DEC's PDP/11 minicomputer. Unix, which has become widely available on microcomputers, claims superiority over the other systems because:

- it offers better resource sharing and also concurrent processing features. Hence, a user may run a program, edit a file and print another file simultaneously, a feature with obvious attractions in a busy commercial environment. The user interface, called the *shell*, operates on the interpreter principle but has particularly rapid response
- it offers a powerful range of utility programs as standard for a range of high-level languages including C, Java, BASIC, Pascal and COBOL
- it is particularly suitable for the modern generation of *object-oriented languages* such as Smalltalk and Eifel, which have important links with the development of the multifunction workstation in the context of office automation.

The problem is that the industry cannot agree a common standard, despite the efforts of the Open Software Foundation (OSF) to promote a peaceful resolution of the conflicting interests of manufacturers. Unix tends to be associated with the multi-purpose 'high-and-low level', 'systems and applications' programming language 'C' which some experts say will replace COBOL as the business applications language of the future, particularly as Internet-based applications become more important in business. The 'C'-like language Java by Sun Systems may become the standard for writing applications which run on the Internet.

Selection criteria for operating systems

The selection of an operating system is crucial because the applications software which the user may want to use may not all be compatible with the same operating system. Further, most hardware manufacturers make design decisions which limit the availability of operating systems so that the choice of a particular computer is often really a choice of operating system. It is this control software that gives a computer system its identity and individuality of characteristics. Thus, even when planning the acquisition of a small-scale system consisting of a personal computer with applications packages, considerable thought in the choice of operating system is justified. The decision must be seen in the light of the fact that the immediate cost of the software for a automated office application, for example an accounts package such as Sage, together with an integrated IT package such as Microsoft Office and a small-scale database package such as MS-Access – might equal or exceed the cost of the hardware on which it runs.

A further factor to consider is that the hardware is more prone to obsolescence, yet any change to a computer of a higher specification might make applications software of considerable value redundant if the operating system of the new machine is not compatible. It is important for both manufacturers and users to try to achieve a smooth migration from one generation of technology to another.

This would not be so important if the IT industry could agree on standards which would ease the problems of portability, but opinion is divided on what is likely to come closest to an industry standard operating system for microcomputers. Some experts favour Unix or one of its derivatives, such as Xenix, while others await the industry's final response to IBM's OS/2 system or the next Windows offering from Microsoft.

With minicomputer and mainframe systems, the choice of operating system is more specialized, yet no less important. A key factor in the decision to purchase will be the degree of manufacturer support for a particular system in the form of new releases, that is, updates which generally improve performance levels. When surveying the market for software, it is vital to remember that the applications software is likely to be written specifically for a particular generation of operating system and may need modification, or even rewriting, if the operating system has been upgraded. Finally, consider that the choice on acquiring a new minicomputer system may be between a new, relatively untried operating system with the potential of a long life, and an older, well-tried system which may well soon lose its viability. Thus, either there may be work to be done to fit existing applications software to the new system, or existing applications packages may soon be amended to run on the new systems and the user will be forced to stay with the less effective older packages.

Applications software

This has been likened to the tip of an iceberg: it is the part of the software most visible to the user, while the operating system (which may be many times larger) is hidden and therefore not appreciated. Applications software performs the functions which the user requires from the system, such as data processing or process control. For the computer user, the range of options involved in choosing application programs exceeds even that of operating systems, and the effects of an incorrect choice are, if anything, more difficult to live with. For this reason, applications program selection and development is a particularly important part of the overall process from the inception to the operation of a system, which is known as the systems life cycle.

Criteria for software effectiveness

Although applications software effectiveness may be measured in a number of ways, an effective program will exhibit three main characteristics:

1. accuracy
2. flexibility
3. performance.

In addition, information systems software will require explicit documentation and a workable human–computer interaction (HCI).

Accuracy

This means that the software must be free from errors or 'bugs'. The two common forms of error are *syntax errors,* such as wrongly spelled command words, and *logic errors* which arise from the way the program has been constructed. The first category is usually easy to deal with, as the interpreter or compiler in the operating system will pick out the more obvious errors and prevent the program from running. A program with logic errors may appear to run successfully but will give inaccurate or unpredictable output. It may be very difficult to put such errors right, as correcting one part of the program may introduce errors into other parts. Therefore, software errors may persist for years, or even appear to surface in programs which were thought to be error free. Attempts to provide accurate software therefore centre on program design methods.

Flexibility

This means that the software must be capable of handling a range of transactions and of accepting a variety of input enquiries, while remaining robust under changing operating conditions. The inherent flexibility of a program, together with the quality of its HCI, contributes to the quality of user-friendliness and therefore to the system's popularity with users. One way of ensuring flexibility is *programming modularity* – the separation of program code into discrete sections, each having a special purpose. Modularity is an important aspect of structured programming, as it controls the interaction between program sections and therefore limits the impact of changes in code on other parts of the program. Modular programs are capable of being more easily modified to suit new business requirements and encourage 're-use' – the principal that software applications may be 'built up' from standard modules.

Performance

This is usually taken to be the efficiency with which the software responds to user enquiries (the response time) and its ability to execute a particular task quickly (the 'run time'). The performance characteristics of each applications package not only depend on good program design – typically through the elimination of time-wasting loops from the code – but also the ability of the program to optimally exploit the good features of the system's software and hardware. An important factor in this context is the choice of programming language. Most operating systems, including those for personal computers, will support a variety of languages and packages, some of which have a higher performance capacity than others, depending on the application.

Software engineering

Accuracy, flexibility and performance are ensured in large-scale applications by the use of the discipline of *software engineering,* a relatively recent concept (the term was first used in 1968) which developed in an attempt to control a perceived software crisis. This situation occurred as newly enthusiastic users and naive programmers jointly attempted to plan and produce increasingly complex applications for their computers to perform, and the level of complexity overwhelmed the capabilities of the processes by which programs were developed. Such processes in the 1960s were based on the assumption that programming was a *creative* process, generally lacking in methods or principles. The resulting software was often found to have the following drawbacks:

- it failed to meet the user's real requirements
- its completion was often delayed
- it became usual to run over budget because of poor time estimation
- the software designers failed to take proper account of the users' lack of expertise and so the software was generally difficult to use
- control over the software design was poor. It was therefore hard to identify programming errors and the software was often difficult to maintain
- a large proportion of the software was unreliable.

Software engineering attempts to use similar principles to those used in other engineering disciplines to overcome equivalent drawbacks and to impose quality and usability on software generally. Thus, there was a trend to construct a program product out of proven, re-usable modular components. Work was done to ensure that the performance of the product was formally (i.e. mathematically) specified and tested. But the key step was to recognize that quality cannot be introduced to a system after the event. It must be designed in from the outset.

The sources of software

Applications software may be obtained from three sources:

1. off-the-shelf
2. from a contractor
3. in-house.

Off-the-shelf software

Buying software packages is a common approach for well-established applications such as financial accounting, or small databases. Since the package is designed to perform a specific set of tasks, the potential user's detailed requirements for the application must be carefully mapped on to the features offered by the package. The closer the match, the more successful the package is likely to be in meeting the organization's needs. Some applications packages are *generic* in nature: in other words, they are intended for a broad area of use and come close to having some of the features of a programming language. Examples of this package approach are MS Excel and FoxPro, which enhance the standard features of the package (spreadsheet and database respectively) by using special language commands or 'macros'. The 'package approach' is almost always the cheapest method of software acquisition, especially if the developer can spread the costs over thousands of installations. There is also the advantage of continuing vendor enhancement and support for all the better packages. Off-the-shelf software packages may be integrated into application suites (e.g. MS Office) or separate (i.e. stand-alone) although it can be argued that multipurpose 'desktop' environments such as MS-Windows '95 make such distinctions less important as applications can be 'bundled' within the same interface.

Software from a contractor

Where no package is suitable for a particular application and the necessary skill is not available for in-house development, software production may be *contracted out*. There are several possible drawbacks to this approach:

- the contractor may not have sufficient experience of the application to produce a satisfactory specification
- an extended period may have to be spent in gaining sufficient familiarity with the user's problems to produce good solutions, which can make this approach prohibitively expensive
- there may be exclusion clauses in the contract which affect future maintenance and support, or the contractor may cease trading, leaving the user without any help, whether practical or documentary, in the event of difficulty.

It is almost implicit that if an organization cannot develop its own software, it will not be able to maintain it. Contract programming is therefore perhaps used most successfully as a 'threshold resource' to smooth out the workload on an existing programming team, rather than as a primary programming resource.

In-house software

In-house software development implies the existence of a programming team, with one or more systems analysts to examine the user's requirements and to produce a programmable specification. The approach has the advantage that this specification, if arrived at correctly, will be precise and specific to the application. For in-house software development to be significantly more successful than other methods, an organization must have high-calibre, reliable and trained staff, and the necessary procedures, tools and documentation, not only to create the programs but also to maintain them.

In many organizations, it is likely that a mixture of all three approaches will be used. It is possible to obtain off-the-shelf packages which may be modified or tailored to make them more suitable for a particular application. The software engineering concept of reusability encourages users to create or acquire so-called *library routines* which are, in effect, package modules that may be linked together to form coherent programs. This is a central feature of some recent programming languages, such as Ada and Modula 2. A variation on the theme of in-house development dispenses with the use of a conventional programming team, allowing the users themselves to write programs, using an easily learned user-oriented language called a *4GL*. Such languages are a step beyond 'programmer-oriented' languages and allow new methods of program development, called 'prototyping' and 'report generation'. 4GLs will be described in more detail later in this chapter.

Program development

Conventional programs – those using third-generation languages – are developed according to what is known as the *software life cycle*. Although the actual constraints of this cycle may vary from one organization to another, a typical version would include four discrete tasks.

1 **Program design**, which attempts to ensure that the logic and structure of a program are sound and that the program will perform as required. A common design method is Jackson Structured Programming (JSP). The output from the JSP technique will be a design specification using structure diagrams and a text part way between natural language and program code, called *structure text*. In this way, the coding requirements are communicated unambiguously (see below in this chapter).
2 **Coding**, which converts the specification into a programming language. The details of the coding process will vary according to the programming language being used, and the choice of language can affect the performance of the system.
3 **Documentation**, which serves the dual purposes of communication and recording the details of both design and coding stages. Documentation is particularly important for maintenance purposes and where a piece of code may become a reusable module. Its precise functionality must be documented if it is to be used effectively. Ideally, documentation should be produced at each stage of the development cycle and should be updated in line with program maintenance. Often these tasks are neglected, so when the persons who designed and coded the program move on it is not easy to see how the program works, or even what it is trying to achieve.
4 **Testing**. The testing of software forms a part of a wider testing procedure, and will involve extracting test data from existing files or creating it artificially, to test each program module for errors of syntax and logic. The whole program will then be similarly tested. Ideally, the test results will be included in the documentation for the software.

Programming languages

Next to the choice of operating system, the most important tactical decision which a system developer has to make is programming language selection. An organization may choose to standardize and use a single language, or it may reserve different languages for different purposes – for example, one language may be used on the DP system minicomputer and another on the individual mangers' personal computers. Special purpose applications, such as process control systems, will tend to use different language types from those for general-purpose MIS and DP applications. The programming languages which are available fall into the following categories or levels of coding:

- high-level languages or third-generation languages (3GLs)
- 4GLs.

High-level languages

High-level languages or 3GLs were developed to provide independence from specific computers by including features that are relatively abstract and not limited to one processor design or even to a particular machine.

Effectively, the program specifies what the computer is to do, not how it is to do it. The source program is translated into machine code by the compiler or interpreter, which is dedicated to the particular type of machine on which the program is to run. Such languages are often termed *procedural languages* and are relatively easy to use. Programs can be designed correctly since many procedural languages (Pascal is a good example) have strong features which encourage structured, well-designed code. Also, a particular application may be coded more easily, because high-level languages have features more like human languages, and the abstraction means that the programmer can concentrate on writing a problem-oriented rather than machine-oriented code.

4GLs

These languages were developed to follow the trend towards user computing which began in the middle 1970s and is still continuing. These languages, which have a very high level of abstraction, are often termed *non-procedural* and they are designed to be easy to use. Some 4GLs are close to natural language in terms of the syntax of individual commands. A further advantage is that the languages themselves tend to provide features which are difficult to achieve in a procedural language. The combination of these factors has led to the possibility of non-trivial applications software being developed without the need for conventional programming and, hence, programmers. The implication of this is that end users can design their own systems and produce the necessary software. The features which make this revolution possible include:

1. **Prototyping**. This is a systems development technique that uses software in a package of forms, programs and screen painters, to allow the user to produce quickly a simulation of the output required from the finished system. This prototype has the appearance of a completed working system, and it may be tested and subjected to experimentation by the user in a way quite different from that achievable when evaluating a conventional paper-based systems specification. Users are therefore better able to clarify their requirements which may be refined through the subsequent evolution of the prototype. The system will undergo a number of iterations as the user, with probable advice from a systems analyst, finalizes the model.
2. **Query languages**. These are 4GL tools which may be used in conjunction with a DBMS to enter, update and retrieve information, without having to use conventional programs. It is therefore possible to achieve significantly greater flexibility and speed of use for non-routine applications. Hence, a single question in almost human-language format can produce an answer which would require 50 or 100 lines of code in a procedural 3GL such as COBOL. Examples of query languages include Informix-SQL and Oracle-SQL. Both can provide useful information from an existing relational database after a few hours' practice on the part of the user.
3. **Report generators**. These augment the features of a query language with the ability to format a management report with headings, sections and totals. The user specifies the report requirements in simple statements, and the software performs the necessary retrieval manipulation and controls the formatting of the output.

4 **Applications generators**. These go beyond the answering of questions and the production of reports to allow the creation of complete application programs in a 4GL. The degree of sophistication of these programs may vary from an end user setting up a program to accept data and produce business graphics, to a more experienced 4GL programmer creating software capable of sophisticated file management and transaction processing. Oracle SQL-Forms is an example of a package providing many such features through the design of screens or 'forms'.

Choosing an applications development language or package

The choice of a language in which to program a newly developed application can be bewildering as there are so many different languages, each offering certain distinctive capabilities. Yet the choice of language may have an effect on systems development throughout the organization for the duration of the systems life cycle. In a large-scale DP system or MIS, this may be years. To resolve the difficulty, software engineers have developed empirically derived sets of features or benchmarks against which the strengths or weaknesses of a program may be evaluated.

While the features of the language or package are an important factor in making a choice, it is necessary to examine the potential application and the resources which are likely to be available for the implementation. Factors which will influence this aspect of the selection process are:

- the performance characteristics of the system
- the future policy on systems development
- the system development budget.

Performance characteristics

This element refers to the response time, file-handling requirements and operational environment. This requires the programmer to have a thorough knowledge of the features of the languages involved to obtain a good match with the application. COBOL, for instance, has good file-handling capability, is efficient when processing large volumes of data and is self-documenting. Although COBOL would be ideal for a banking system, it could be inappropriate for use in an airline reservation system. Such a quick-response multi-user application would probably require a more efficient language, such as C or MC Visual Basic.

Systems development policy

This would appear to dictate that a commonly used language should be chosen. This approach can lead to stagnation, as many of the most popular high-level languages are also among the oldest. COBOL was developed in 1959 and is still the main language in more than 50 per cent of the large computer centres. It is important to appreciate that even as the technology is changing rapidly with time, so are the requirements of many specifications. ATMs are now a commmon feature of banking systems, but in terms of language requirements, they would have little in common with existing banking applications such as 'back office' transaction processing or 'front office' customer enquiry systems.

Systems development budgets

Organizations must, at an early stage of their development, make a policy decision as to the percentage of fixed and circulating capital that can be diverted to the IT budget. This budget must cover the initial cost of the hardware acquisition, the development of suitable systems and long-term maintenance. One of the many problems is that when organizations are taking their first major decisions in this area the knowledge and experience of the management team as a whole is at its most limited. Those later responsible for implementing the plans by selecting suitable software can therefore find their budgets artificially limited or unrealistically generous. Proper standards of critical self-awareness must be maintained to ensure that inadequate budgets are aligned to real needs and that expenditure does not simply fill money available.

Fourth-generation languages will need to be evaluated by reference to different criteria from those that will apply to high-level procedural languages. Typically, a 4GL user will look for the features which the language offers, such as *ad hoc* reports, queries or spreadsheet work and a short learning curve. Less apparent features which may be sought when assessing a 4GL include the following:

- **user help** from an on-line help facility, which should be comprehensive yet easy to understand
- **different user levels**, appropriate to the experience of the user and the nature of the application – the same 4GL could offer features which are of use to both a computing professional and a naive user
- **result orientation**, which enables the user to specify the details required from the program (the 'what') while leaving the 4GL to translate the request into a procedure (the 'how') to produce the report
- **user-machine independence**, enabling the user to operate the language with a minimum knowledge of hardware and software commands, e.g. those from the operating system.

Weighted ranking

In order to evaluate and compare alternative pieces of software, whether bespoke programs or applications packages, the National Computing Centre (NCC) has adopted an approach known as *weighted ranking.*

In this approach, an expert user will review the features such as those listed in Figure 7.1 which a piece of software ought to have if it is to perform successfully in a given application. The features are given a weighting (for example 9 = very important, 1 = not important) and the programs or packages are given a score for the way in which their features meet this standard. A total score for each piece of software may then be produced. The technique should prove to be reliable providing that the estimates are reasonably accurate and that the comparisons are conducted properly (for example by using benchmark testing).

Weighted ranking table for software packages A & B

Feature of package	Weighting (out of 10)	Package A score/10	A total	Package B score/10	B total	Note
Processing speed	5	8	40	5	25	
Storage capacity	7	5	35	6	42	
Ease of use	9	6	63	8	72	
Quality of documentation	4	7	28	4	16	
Compatibility with system	6	8	48	9	54	
Cost effectiveness	8	6	48	3	24	
		Total	262	Total	233	

Package A total 262 ranking 1
Package B total 233 ranking 2

Figure 7.1 Weighted ranking table.

Networking

Data communication or *telecommunication* systems are vital to a number of modern computing applications, including MISs and office automation systems. The term *networking* refers to communication between individual computer systems which otherwise maintain a degree of autonomy. Networks may link computer systems in different organizations (just as the telephone network does) and may involve widely separated sites – in the case of a 'long haul' or *wide area network (WAN)* – or systems within the same site – a *local area network (LAN)*. Where the WAN uses dedicated links it is called a *physical network* and where a combination of links which is used, which are 'transparent' to the user, the network is called a *virtual network*. The Internet is an example of such a network. Messages and data can be routed across the world by using telephone lines, satellite and microwave communications, and the communicating computer systems may range from PCs to mainframe systems.

Networking a computer system allows many of the functions of the automated office to be carried out, such as teleconferencing and electronic mail, and also supports many types of MIS. Expensive computer resources may be shared between the users of a network. This may apply to a large-scale computer system being timeshared or to the infrastructure of the network itself. Such an application, where a network operator or carrier allows many users to share the network's facilities on a local or global basis, is called a *value-added network* or VAN. Value is added by managing the apportionment of costs among the users, with the network owner or 'service provider' making a profit. Such services are common on the Internet. With AOL, Compuserve and Demon being among the main examples in the UK.

Many organizations are adapting Internet technology for internal use. These *Intranets* offer the usual Internet features, such as web-sites and -pages, but are separated from the WWW by *firewalls* – software which is intended to keep out unauthorized browsers – and contain internal corporate data which are of use to a range of users. Product catalogues, quality standards, operating procedures and organizational responsibilities are examples of suitable subjects for Intranet web-pages for the following reasons:

- they are not subject to processing or data extraction in a way which would modify their content, as would a conventional database
- they need to presented in a clear, attractive manner, possibly with photographs or diagrams which cannot be included in a conventional database
- they often involve 'links' with other sources of similar data and involve a certain degree of interaction on the part of the user.

Network topology

The principal design features of a network are its topology – the way in which the network is configured – and the way in which data items are directed through the network, called its *switching mode*. A network may be seen as a number of nodes joined by possible communications or linkages. Where a completely separate physical linkage does not exist between all the nodes, it is necessary to connect communicating nodes by setting up circuits. This is achieved by switches, which may be at the nodes themselves or at separate exchanges, forming paths of linkages on demand between nodes. When the communication period is over, the circuit is dissolved.

Circuit switching

This is the most basic transmission technique. It is used for public switched telephone network (PSTN) services world-wide, and can carry digital data communications. The drawbacks to its use for computer networks are the quality of the lines (narrow bandwidth and slow data transfer) and the general inefficiency of use. For instance, a connection must be made at the start of a session and disconnected afterwards. This can take longer than the data message takes to transmit. The alternative is to leave the circuit open for long periods of time, with costly idle periods between message bursts. No attempt is made within the system itself to optimize the use of the line. Further, the communicating nodes must have completely compatible equipment using identical data transfer rates. Finally, the circuit switching systems lack any method of detecting and retransmitting messages containing errors. Data communication users can attempt to minimize these difficulties by leasing private circuits between sites with regular message traffic: an example would be a chain of supermarkets linked to a DP centre, or remote manufacturing depots, each wishing to update each other's stock records. Apart from cost–benefit considerations, the choice between private circuit leasing and the use of public circuits is one of traffic volume.

Message switching

Message switching, or the 'store-and-forward' technique, hands over the task of switching management to the network itself. The user's item of data is given the address of the destination node and is accepted for transmission, even when that destination is not immediately available to receive. The message will be stored at each switching node between the sender and the destination and forwarded as the next node becomes ready. Each node must therefore have enough memory to store a number of messages. The slight delay which may be involved can make message switching unsuitable for distributed real-time processing, but the method is very efficient for most DP or MIS applications.

Packet switching

Packet switching is the most common transmission technique for both LAN and WAN use. It exploits the fact that much of the system-to-system communication which goes on takes place in short, high-speed bursts. It also takes account of the fact that distributed computing implies a number of concurrent processing activities, all of which may require simultaneous connections. The first of these features is achieved by splitting a message into short data packets, each with a destination address. The packets (also called *datagrams*) may be routed differently by the network management system and may be received in a different order from that in which they were transmitted. Concurrent transmission is achieved by the setting up of *virtual circuits* through the network. A virtual circuit is established by sending the first header packet of a message, which is used to create a route through the system (taking into account usage and cost) which subsequent packets to the same destination will follow. The technique arranges the correct sequence for the delivery of a message in a way that optimizes the resource efficiency of the network as a whole. Reliability and availability are assured by the fact that a *packet switched network (PSN)* can route messages around faulty nodes or links. Moreover, because of the flexibility achieved by the use of small packets of data, less buffer memory is required at each node than with message switching.

Protocols

In order to ensure compatibility and to synchronize data exchange throughout the network, it is necessary to impose common conventions or protocols on those who wish to communicate. Protocols must define the format of the datagram and also the functions which are involved in sending and receiving data. These functions, which are carried out using protocols, are conventionally modelled in layers which are often explained by using as an example the protocols of international diplomacy – where the use of the word began.

In the model of diplomatic convention shown in Figure 7.2, the individuals on each layer converse according to the conventions of their level. These communications between peers are, for the most part, indirect, the two sides only communicating directly at the lowest layer. An exchange between the two top layers (other than at a summit conference) involves passing messages down through the layers on one side, changing in form at each layer, until direct communication at the lowest levels can be achieved. The message is then passed up the opposite layers. The exchanges at layers 2 and 3 are virtual; they are observable only as functions, and each function cannot take place until the function below it has been concluded.

Ironically, this metaphor is particularly apt, as governments were the major players in WAN technology in the early days of its development, particularly through the medium of national telecommunications utilities. Theirs has been a history of strong control, which has now become modified to stress regulation, rather than ownership. New players in the WAN market are from unexpected areas; in France the national railway company SNCF has expanded its own

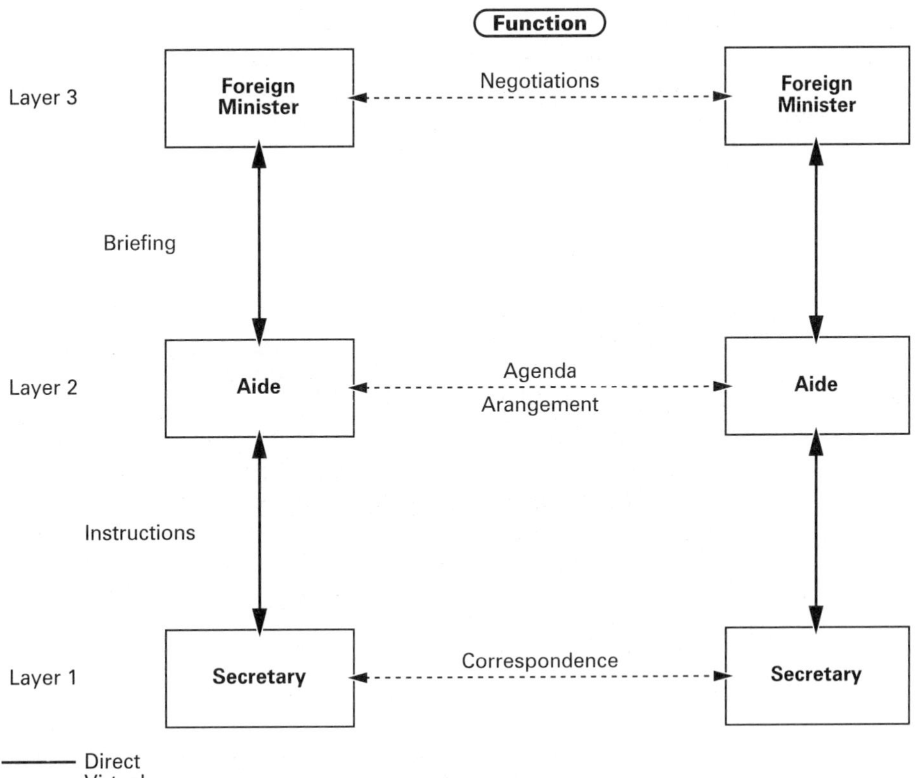

Figure 7.2 Diplomatic protocol numbers.

communications network to become a major service provider. In the UK Energis – a coalition of the electricity providers – has taken up a similar role in the business.

The early development of networks was marked by incompatibility, as the grouping of functions into layers tended to be arbitrary. Standardization was sought by the International Standards Organization (ISO), which as produced a reference model for Open Systems Interconnection (OSI) as shown in Figure 7.3. The model used seven layers of functions, arranged as described below.

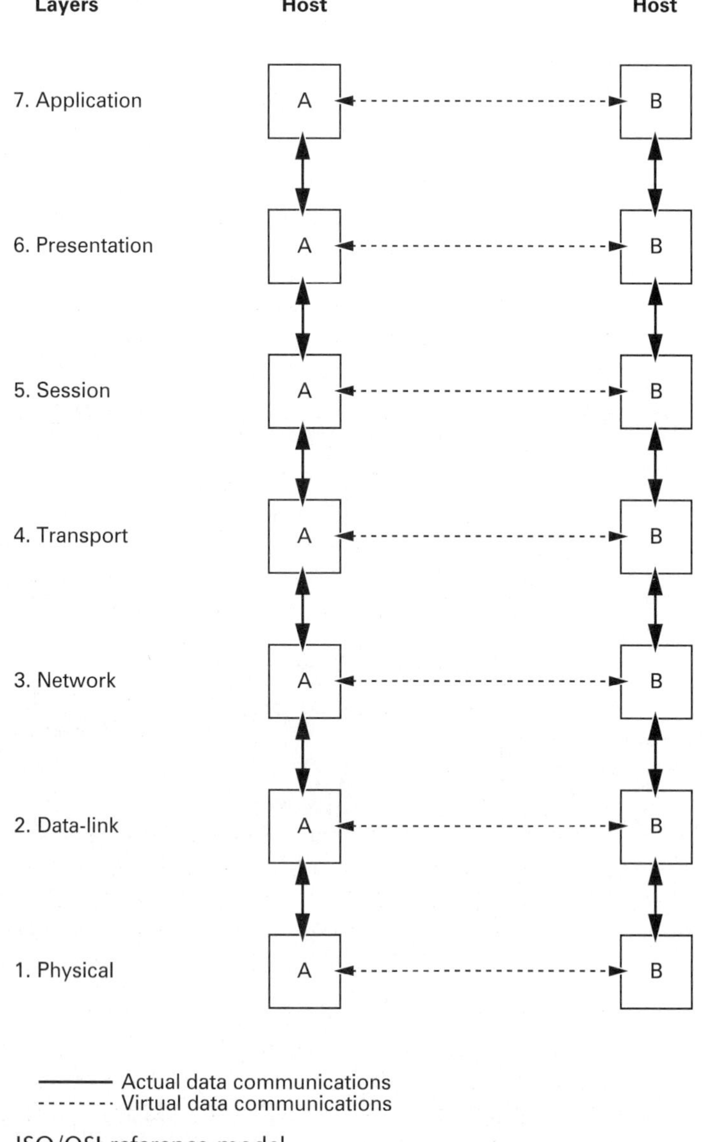

Figure 7.3 ISO/OSI reference model.

1 **The physical layer**. This handles the transmission of raw data over the chosen communications medium.
2 **The data-link layer**. The produces reliable communications by handling error detection and transmission speed conversion.
3 **The network layer**. This is concerned with the routing of messages and the setting up of circuits by switching.
4 **The transport layer**. This layer handles addressing and flow control functions, ensuring that data packets arrive in the correct order.
5 **The session layer**. This is the lowest layer which is perceptible to the user. The setting-up and termination of communications between a sender and an addressed destination is termed a 'session'. The layer also handles security.
6 **The presentation layer**. This layer handles the format in which the data items are sent to and from the session layer. This could involve test compression for shorter messages, data encryption for security, and file format conversion for the transfer of large blocks of data between systems.
7 **The application layer**. This layer deals with the functions defined by the user, including input and output, processing and storage. There is obviously a great variety of hardware and software configurations which must be able to communicate with each other.

The protocol which is standard for use on the Internet is called TCP/IP (transmission control protocol/Internet protocol) which offers networking services in four forms:

- **Connection-oriented** which involves the establishment of a direct connection between two or more network 'nodes' – called a 'network session' or 'virtual circuit' – and is often used for 'real-time' applications involving the transfer of large amounts of data, such as teleconferencing.
- **Connectionless** or packet switching which involves no direct connection between nodes and which uses addressed data packets of a standard length which may find the addressed node by different routes through the network. When the packets arrive at their destination they are recomposed into a message in the form in which it was sent. The public standard for packet-switching networks (PSNs) is called X25, and is noted as being relatively slow (in modern terms) but reliable enough for e-mail
- **Frame-relay** uses fewer checks than PSNs and has variable length data packets which usually reach their destination more quickly than X25 systems, but which are still rather slow for voice transmission
- **Cell-relay** is a compromise between the connection-oriented and connectionless modes and has very high bandwidth and is likely to become the standard for the broad band integrated services digital network (B-ISDN) which is the Internet standard of the future for sound and vision transmission.

The network requirements of a system which is to support sound and vision applications (such as video conferencing and multimedia) are high bandwidth – the ability to route large amounts of data in a short time period – and a high degree of symmetry – the ability to transmit data equally in both directions. Without these properties the metaphor of the 'information superhighway' can tend to be modified to a motorway – which can allow several hundred vehicles per minute – leading onto to a house driveway – which can only hold one stationary car! This latter part of the network is under the organization's direct control and is called the local area network (LAN).

Local area networks

Good LAN designs tend to have the following features:

- **great bandwidth**, allowing high data transmission rates which readily support distributed processing, including file transfer and some real-time applications
- **low error rates**, because of the compatibility between devices and the relatively simple transmission system and
- **low-cost** installation and operation, as the complex digital–analogue conversion equipment of a public media network is not needed.

There are a confusing number of LAN types and structures, developed by both manufacturers of office automation equipment, such as Xerox and Wang, and academic bodies such as Cambridge University. The three important variables in LAN specification are:

1. topology
2. access control
3. transmission medium.

Topology

Topology refers to the physical arrangement of nodes and links which make up a particular network. The simplest is a *non-switched network (NSN)*, in which all nodes are connected by dedicated links. Such a network may be *fully connected* or *hierarchical* using 'store-and-forward' messaging at the intermediate nodes (see Figure 7.4).

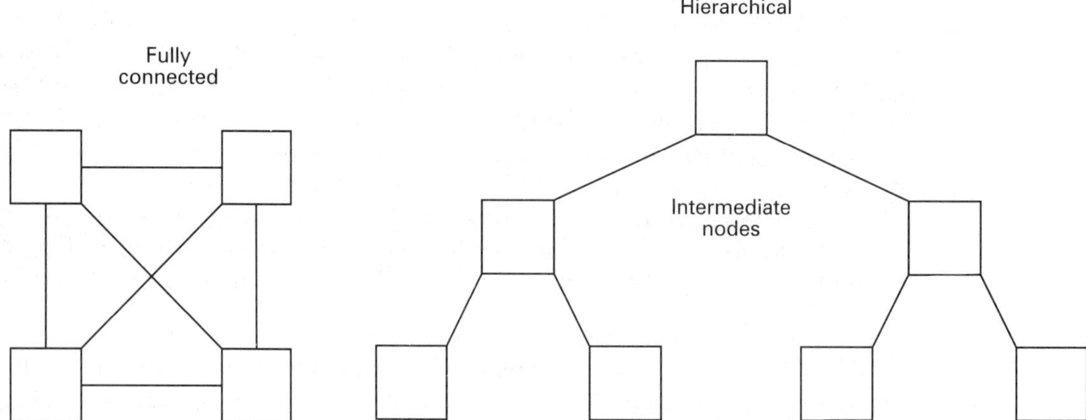

Figure 7.4 Types of non-switched network.

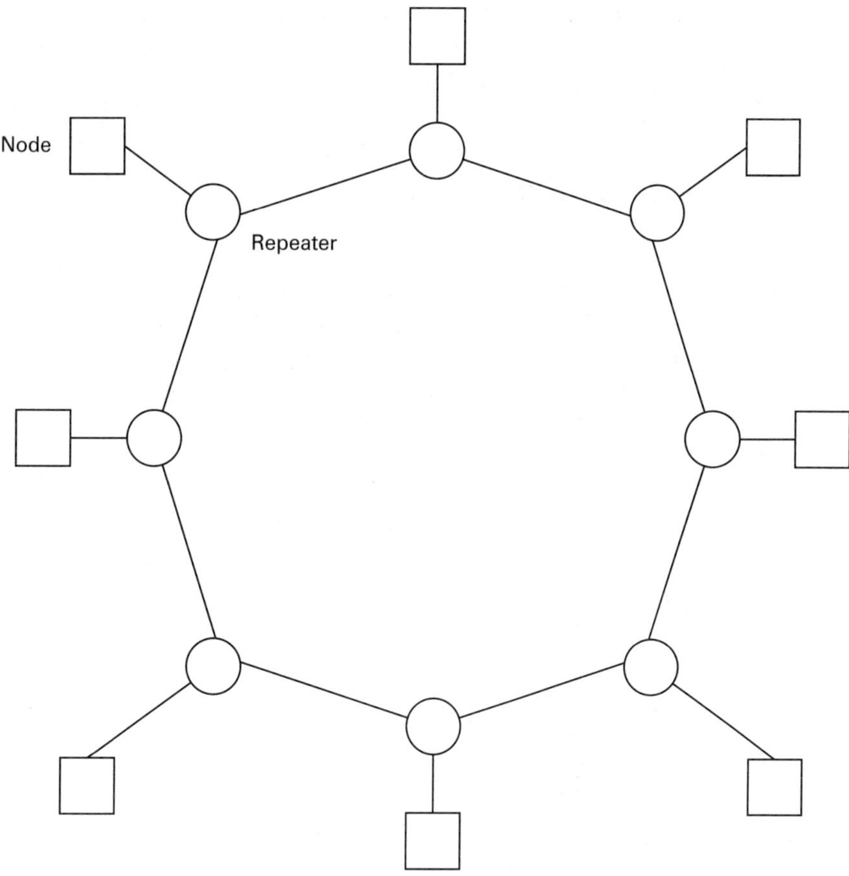

Figure 7.5 Ring network.

Ring network

The ring network, also called a loop, consists of a number of nodes with receiver devices attached to a continuous medium. Data packets containing a destination address are circulated around the ring. Each receiver examines the message and re-transmits those which are intended for nodes other than its own (see Figure 7.5).

Bus networks

The bus network, also known as spines, is similar to the ring system in that receivers and nodes are connected to a single medium, and messages are broadcast with addresses. The major physical difference is that the medium is not a continuous loop (see Figure 7.6).

Star networks

The star network, as its name suggests, consists of 'branches' radiating out from a central node, usually a *server* – a computer dedicated to controlling the network traffic.

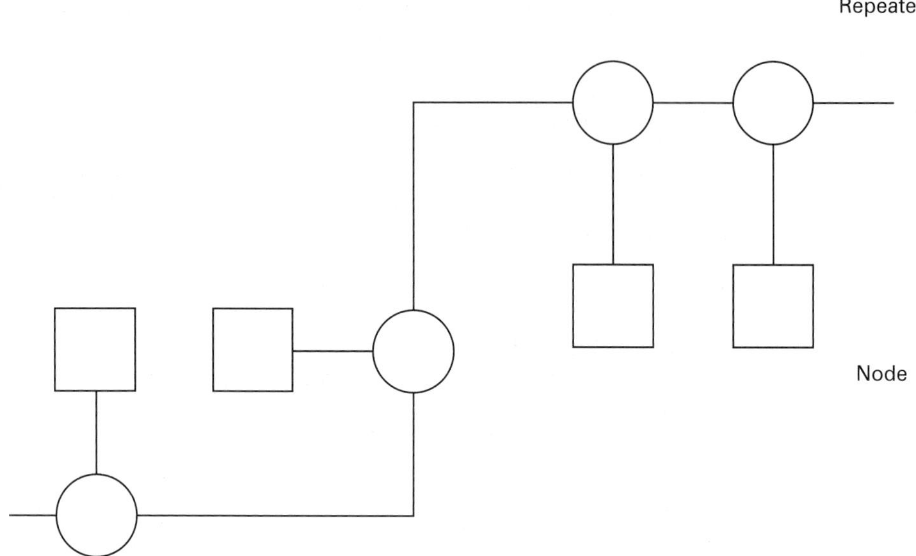

Figure 7.6 Bus network.

Access control methods

These methods govern the ability of a particular node on a bus or ring network to broadcast its message in competition with other nodes which desire the use of the medium. The two main strategies are *contention-oriented and non-contention-oriented* control. The first category allows nodes to transmit simultaneously. Such transmissions may collide and, as a result, they may be garbled. The system then makes efforts to retransmit the lost messages. When traffic volume is low, such collisions will be within tolerable limits, but as traffic increases, network performance degrades sharply. The most common contention-oriented strategy is *carrier-sensed multiple access/collision detection (CSMA/CD),* which is used on Ethernet systems. Each node listens for other messages during its own transmission and shuts down if a collision is detected. The nodes involved wait for a random time period and then attempt retransmission.

Non-contention-oriented methods are most often found on ring networks and aim to avoid retransmissions. The most common methods are as follows:

- **Polling systems**, where nodes are sequentially sampled to see if they have a message to transmit and are given sole use of the medium.
- **Token systems** are popular, circulating a special message which enables the holding node only to transmit – therefore, each node has equal priority in a 'round robin' manner.
- **Slotted systems** work like token control except that, instead of a single token, a number of slots circulate into which packets of data may be inserted by transmitting nodes. The destination node reads its message, but leaves it in its slot for the sender to remove as it recirculates. The transmitting node

therefore receives acknowledgement that its message has been received. This method is used by the Cambridge ring systems.

Transmission media

The choice of a transmission medium for a LAN system is largely a matter of balancing installation costs against the required levels of performance in terms of bandwidth and error rates.

- **Twisted-pair cable** is likely to be the cheapest medium. It also has the advantage of wide availability, as it is widely used in telephone systems. The disadvantages include a relatively high error rate, due to poor anti-interference screening, and moderate data transmission rates. Despite these drawbacks, twisted-pair cabling is a popular option for small-scale LANs.
- **Coaxial cable** is a medium which is also widely used in telecommunications for multiplexed trunk channels and the growth area of cable TV. Increased use has brought down cabling costs and coaxial cable has considerably better performance than that of twisted-pair cable. This is due to superior screening and a high bandwidth which gives very high data transmission rates. Additionally, the heavier grades of coaxial cable allow broad band transmission which involves many signals being carried simultaneously. This feature, which is of less use in LANs than in some other applications, may be outweighed by the higher costs and more difficult installation of the thicker cable.
- **Fibre optic cable** is not so easy to 'tap into' – that is, to add on a repeater and node – an important factor in LAN applications. Otherwise fibre optic cable has a very low error rate and extremely high bandwidth. Although fibre optics are becoming more popular in WAN applications, their relatively high costs and practical problems limit their use in LANs. The tapping problem makes their use with ring-type LANs problematical, and the essentially one-way transmission of fibre optics inhibits their use in bus-type LANs.

Summary

Earlier chapters mentioned the idea of converging technologies and the impact that these would have, not only on the efficiency and effectiveness of the information systems but equally on an organization's capacity for gaining competitive advantage in the market. This chapter has illustrated the developments that have arisen from technology convergence and the ways in which these are being applied, focusing on several key points.

- Centralized mainframe systems (or DP systems) are an important part of most organizations' information provision.
- Office automation has taken place against the background of an information explosion which has posed real problems of productivity for manual systems and has led to the creation of the knowledge worker and the 'information super-highway'.

- If knowledge workers are to be effective, office automation systems such as electronic mail and DSSs must be properly tailored to their working practices.
- Input, output and storage devices appropriate to the automation system must be selected to be compatible with one another and with the operating software.
- Networking, both local and wide area, is achieving fundamental importance in supporting the growth of automated systems. The development of adequate standards and protocols must therefore be a high priority.

Self-test questions

1 Describe the two types of software which you would expect to find in a typical company.
2 Identify and describe briefly the criteria which may be used when assessing the effectiveness of software for a given application.
3 Describe some of the uses to which a fourth-generation language (4GL) may be put by a typical end user.
4 Identify the main factors which should influence the choice of an applications programming language.
5 Identify the main criteria which a local area network (LAN) design should meet

Exam-style questions

1 'Decision support', in an automated office environment, refers to the application of IT to the problems met by decision-makers and in particular to problem analysis and evaluation.

Discuss the typical requirements for a decision support system (DSS) and the factors involved in the choice of DSS software.

2 Applications package evaluation and selection is a particularly important part of the systems life cycle.

(a) Briefly describe how you would use the technique called 'weighted ranking' to compare two applications packages.

(b) Discuss the advantages of integrated applications packages.

3 ABCO Ltd has decided to replace its existing sales order processing and accounting system. The company's existing software development team have identified the requirements of the system, the performance levels required and necessary user interfaces. The decision facing the company is how to source this applications software. Identify the three main sources of applications software and evaluate the appropriateness of each source in relation to ABCO Ltd's situation.

(*All answers on pages 556–558*)

CHAPTER 8

Systems development strategies

In the first stage of the process of developing an information system, an organization must establish an information strategy. In this chapter we look first at the issues which ought to be considered in designing such a strategy before giving attention to the various stages in the process known as the systems development life cycle, which converts the more abstract strategic aims into implemented reality.

Within any information strategy there will typically be a choice of potential system development projects. We examine here the approaches available to the organization to evaluate, select and then justify particular automation projects – in particular, approaches such as cost–benefit analysis and the standard investment appraisal methods.

Strategic issues in systems development

All commercial organizations must have some sort of long-term plan to guide their operations. This plan may be arrived at formally (in some multinational companies, a department may be dedicated to the activity) or the process may be carried out informally by the senior managers. In any case, a **business plan** for the next five to ten years will be produced. This plan will contain details of:

- the markets in which the company expects to operate, and all the steps necessary to enter those markets
- the range of products and services which the company plans to offer
- the projected size and shape of the company during the projected period.

These plans will have an appreciable effect across the range of business functions from the obvious – training and recruitment, product design, finance and marketing – to the less obvious, but no less important, computing and telecommunications. Information systems and information technology have a radical effect on the business plan (and vice versa) for a number of reasons:

- some organizations spend more than ten per cent of their annual budget on IT. In many cases, this is more than the advertising or the raw materials budget
- many of the strategic opportunities that companies seek to pursue depend largely or entirely on IT for their success (home banking, for example)

- information systems are endemic to modern organizations. Although there is evidence that around half of the small businesses in the UK do not use computers, in most medium-size and large-scale companies IT is used to support all operations and functions
- information systems, although intangible, are vital to modern business. The managing director of a large UK tour operator is quoted as saying 'apart from our information systems . . . (our company) owns very little'.

Establishing an information strategy

It is therefore important that there should be a strategy for information systems and technology within the organization and that it should be matched to the business plan. The strategy for information is conveniently called the **strategic information plan** in many companies. It is capable of being broken down into two tactical plans; one for the **information** (the subject of **information management**) and the other for the **technology** (sometimes referred to as the **infrastructure**). Information management seeks to optimize the capture, storage and output of information, while the infrastructure defines the hardware, software and communications links. A little consideration of a typical application (such as the establishment and operation of a corporate database) will show that these two sub-plans are also closely related. One is necessary to support the other. The outcome of the whole process is a range of possible information systems developments and uses for IT, often called the **applications portfolio**. It contains plans for new applications which are:

- in support of opportunities that have been identified in the business plan
- technically within the scope of the plan for the infrastructure
- consistent with the availability of data, as defined in the information plan or data architecture (to be discussed later this chapter).

The way in which this portfolio is implemented may be in line with a **systems architecture** – the way in which the information manager wants systems in the company to develop. The overall process is shown in Figure 8.1.

User participation in design

It is most commonly found that the most effective design is deduced from accurately stated users' requirements. This means that to get the greatest appreciation and utility from the design, the users should be consulted – and it is especially important to consult with the users who will be most involved in operating the implemented version of the system. The difficulty in discussing needs with a group of lay users is that they will often find it difficult to visualize and evaluate ideas without some points of reference. Abstract discussions are helped by having access to simulations and prototypes, or by visiting other organizations where solutions to problems can be studied. In this way, workers who have not previously been exposed to automated systems can make a real contribution to the debate. But when managers are approaching staff for their views, morale must be maintained. If any jobs are to be lost as a result of the

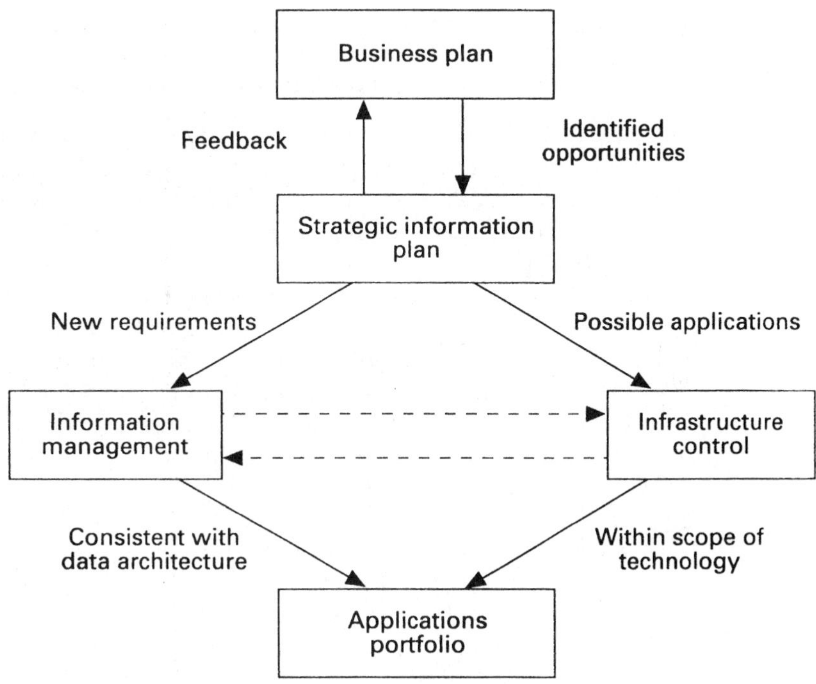

Figure 8.1 The strategic information planning process.

proposed computerization, the identity of those who are to stay should be known at the earliest possible time, and those who are to be relocated or made redundant should receive proper counselling. This means that the designers must have social skills. They are the catalyst for change and must act responsibly in their role.

For these immediate purposes, it is necessary to propose a more practical definition of an information system. An information system is a mixture of methods of work in a structured work place environment. That environment depends on a reporting structure for monitoring and controlling its operations. Information system and organization system design are therefore inextricably linked. It is the task of the designer to identify the organization's objectives and the roles of individuals and groups in both their internal and external relationships. This information can be elicited through the use of the following techniques.

- **Questionnaires**. These are limited in terms of what can be asked and, to ensure the consistency of stimulus materials for evaluation purposes and to save time, no discussion of the questions is possible; but they are an efficient data-gathering mechanism.
- **Interviewing**. This represents a strong opportunity for discussion of all key issues, but it is a very inefficient way of using staff time – unless only a few senior managers are to be questioned.

- **Group discussions**. These are aimed at achieving a consensus view, but their value may be limited if not everyone contributes; and they are not necessarily efficient, because there can only be one speaker at a time.

With this collected information, the designer can propose formal changes to functions and roles. If these proposals are to have substance within the political framework of organizational debate, they must have the support of the senior managers. The designer should then debate the proposals within the most used participation arena. It is not possible to talk to everyone within a large organization, so the discussions should take place in the most representative forum. This should not exclude the real users in favour of the managers who may lack the necessary level of detailed operational experience. At this point, the organization must decide the emphasis of the movement for change – that is to say, it should consider whether participation and direction should be 'from the top down' or 'from the bottom up'. Perhaps, as a compromise, the designer should aim for a consensus among the affected managers and good representative consultation with users.

To determine the feasibility of a full information system planning and development exercise, it is helpful to determine the degree of organization maturity. This will help to prevent the organization attempting something too ambitious, given its level of experience and expertise. At a simple level, the content of the exercise contains the following stages of system development (although the precise order may vary from one organization to another):

- **conceptual design**
- **prototyping**, which breaks down into:
  - **screen**, i.e. a 'shell' to give the users a feel for what the system could look like
  - **application**, i.e. different versions of the possible end product are produced for evaluation
- **programming**, which must always be done sooner or later
- **database design and data architecture**, which considers:
  - the **conceptual layout of data model** which is later adapted to
  - the **actual system** – ideally, the designs will be normative so that the data items are transportable from one application to the next
- **organizational design** – the information system must be integrated into the organization. Because IT is a catalyst for change (it reallocates resources and therefore tends to redistribute power), the implications of IT implementation for the organization must be worked out
- **objectives analysis** – good IT design considers the system from the users' point of view and tries to take account of their needs and objectives.

The design will specify the information system boundaries and the interfaces between the different systems. Each system will perform various processes to achieve identified objects. The best way to identify all the processes is through the technique of *decomposition* or 'top-down design'. A **process** is a group of logically related decisions and activities required to manage the resources of the organization. The whole of a system and its component parts must be given a priority and a place in the proposed sequence of development. All planning decisions should be taken at a strategic level, because the issues involved can only be resolved at an overview level: for example, decisions about costs, efficiencies and human resource utilization.

The first or study phase

In the study phase, those who are proposing and sponsoring the project seek to justify the proposals, and the aims and motives of those involved are made more explicit. If the project is accepted, the study team will begin detailing the data flow within each of the process sequences, the team thinking about the shape and form of the organization following the proposed changes. The team should also identify the current objectives of the organization and the facilities and people involved in achieving those objects. Some features of the organization will be identified as representing vulnerable points, where there will be a risk of loss if the tasks are not properly carried out. Such features should be under the control of the more senior managers, but the degree of control imposed will depend on the frequency of occurrence and the extent to which that feature is organizationally desirable. Some of these features will relate to existing objects; others will allow the organization the opportunity to aspire towards objects. In each of the processes that are involved, there is a life cycle in operation:

1 the organization must draw up forecasts and plans
2 it must then implement the plan, say, by developing products or services, or by acquiring raw materials or staff
3 it then engages in the processes of production, supply and maintenance – in other words, it must keep the planned output and services going and must sustain the environment by providing adequate buildings and staff
4 if the organization is commercially orientated, it must convert production or service provision into income; otherwise, it must meet the performance criteria laid down by management
5 it must circulate equipment and staff. The organization will depreciate plant and equipment and replace it when necessary; it will also promote and retire staff as competence and age respectively increase
6 it will reappraise the plan in the light of actual (rather than forecast) performance and decide whether to retain or modify the given processes.

Once the life cycle of each process has been assessed, the organization should identify the factors in each process which are critical to the success of the process. Self-evidently, greater supervisory management time should be devoted to those factors. It is helpful, in planning the ultimate form of the information system, to discuss each process with representatives of the staff who actually do the work. This will allow a vital comparison to be made between senior management's more abstract perceptions of the process and the practical working view. Those who undertake this work should be trained in interview techniques so that the maximum of relevant and useful information can be extracted in the minimum time. Those who are consulted should feel free to criticize the processes actively (and constructively) or to make suggestions, either for changes to those processes or for new processes. This will allow the study team to address such issues as whether the information arrives where it is supposed to arrive and, if it does, whether it is useful. The interviewees should be asked to identify what information they need to make the process work efficiently.

Following this consultation process, it should be possible to make a preliminary judgement about the quality of the data available to staff at all the points which are considered significant in the information system. It should certainly be possible to identify those parts of the system which do not work at all, or which work too slowly to provide the up-to-date data required for effective decision making. A further outcome should be the ability to construct a series of **network diagrams** by clustering the data-dependent processes into systems. These are organizational decisions which could significantly affect the existing power structures and therefore require careful handling. Sometimes existing departmental or other power centres have to be disturbed in order to break down process isolation and to achieve proper data flows and process coupling.

Systems architecture

These are the first steps towards the creation of a systems architecture, in which the relationships between the different processes or systems of processes will be ranked according to:

- the **logic of their position** in the decision process
- their **level of criticality** to the success of the organization
- the **risk factor** – so the more critical to the organization and the greater the risk if anything goes wrong, the more senior the management supervisory role must be. (Risks may arise during development, implementation or operation and, at each phase, the level of risk should be quantified.)

At this point, sometimes difficult design decisions have to be taken. Some processes which depend on data supplied by other systems may have been directly shaped by the form of the data as supplied. This may have led to distortions and inadequacies in the dependent processes' performance. But the optimization process may involve a considerable number of knock-on amendments being made to the supplying systems. The cost-effectiveness of these consequential amendments will have to be carefully appraised.

Data architecture

At this point, the processes can be placed within a detailed information systems architecture and the primary data flows – both real and ideal – will have been identified. It should then be possible to begin work on creating the data architecture. Databases are collections of related data which are stored together for convenience and which can represent a resource for one or more applications. The different applications may simply present different views of the data through processing. This can be achieved so long as each database has a common structure or a common system of definition. The purpose of this architecture, which should be developed alongside the information system architecture to ensure maximum compatibility, is to allow users to gain an insight into the different data needs and forms within the organization and to allow useful relationships to be established between the different data files. If too much information is mixed together in a single database, there may be security problems over access, the attribution of costs on a departmental basis may become difficult and the quality of the data may become too abstract because of the mixture of non-specialized subject matter. Large databases can also be slow to respond and may become too big for the hardware.

The most effective designs call for a clustering of the most used interdependent data files. This produces the most efficient use of computer resources by having the most used data readily available, while leaving the less commonly used data for batch run access or for access at predetermined times when the given database is loaded up. This model should be fleshed out by considering the organization model. To what extent should the responsibilities for data control and data processing be centralized or decentralized? Should responsibilities be consolidated for some of the processing by specialists, or should functionally differentiated processing be allowed to take place in parallel in several locations? This must depend on the extent to which the tasks are independent, how easily controlled they are and the extent to which the resources will be economically used instead of standing idle for some of the time. This is a problem of economics and logistics which can only be decided at the strategic, tactical and operational levels, given the availability of hardware and personnel and the market needs to be serviced. The organization will therefore have to consider the costs, revenues and payback periods in the light of:

- the more detailed budgets and ratios
- the hardware and software available
- the degree of market share achievable in the commercial sense (if appropriate)
- the skills and morale of the staff to be involved.

Centralization and power structures

If the system is centralized, it will result in increased data communication and no splitting of data, whereas decentralization means that both the incidence and the data view is split and data communication is minimal. The problem arises when the wishes of the three levels of choice are different. At a tactical level, it may be preferable to relate the data closely to the operational area, whereas the strategic level leavens operational data with both external and historical data to produce a more distanced view. Thus, operational data processing will require highly formalized data, but tactical decision making requires data in a form to allow control and analysis of the operational activities. The strategic requirements are to allow modelling and extrapolation techniques to plan for the future.

The design decisions will be based on an attribution of responsibility for decision making and an analysis of the data required to give effective support to each level of decision making. This will also allow the organization to decide whether the responsibility and authority structures match. The initial justification for centralization was the cost of the hardware: all processing had to be centralized to achieve economies of scale. To persist in this view is to concentrate on the cost element rather than the benefit to be derived by the individual user. Now organizations can afford to aim for the most effective structures of distribution within a data architecture that will permit the interchange of data for those purposes and processes foreseeable in the immediate future. The solution may be that some parts of the information system must be decentralized, while others should be paralleled or integrated. The emerging pattern will be substantially determined by the degree to which organizational responsibilities are differentiated and specialized.

For each data block, the planners need to decide the pattern of distribution:

- at which locations is data to be stored and processed?
- who is to be responsible for updating data, who should be notified of the update, and who should have access to the updated data?
- given that the central data core is not distributed but represents a resource accessed from different locations, each user will potentially generate a separate data view given local processing: thus, who will be allowed access to the split data views?

At this stage of the planning exercise, the study team should be in a position to offer decisions as to the level of new computerization appropriate to improve the organization's information systems. Amending the bureaucracy affects the culture of organizations and potentially shifts power. The critical factors, the risks and the priorities will have been identified in this initial planning phase and should allow suggestions to be made as to how improvements can be made with the least risk both from an economic and a sociopolitical point of view. This may include making parts of the organization more autonomous, but will certainly involve the improvement of vertical information routes and of horizontal resource sharing to give more employees access to the best tools for resolving local difficulties. The organization could develop by:

- buying off-the-shelf packages
- paying a software house to customize existing packages
- in-house programming, whether by the users themselves (with central support) or by a special unit which positively consults with the users that need to be supported.

Information centres

The availability of cheap microcomputer technology and powerful applications software such as 'off-the-shelf' business packages and 4GLs has led to the rise of 'end-user computing' where users are able to develop their own systems.

Many companies promoted 'end-user computing' as a way of overcoming the 'applications backlog' of systems projects in the development queue. They were quick to recognize the potential benefits of more 'IT literate' workers and flexible office technology. It soon became apparent, however, that end users could not be left completely to their own devices with regards to IT. The more the technology proliferated, the more problems users had in terms of choosing the correct hardware or software, learning to use a package or language, or achieving compatibility between machines or systems.

Some organizations sought to solve this problem by setting up 'information centres' in the company, which help and provide users with support in the choice and use of IT. The IBM definition of an information centre (IC) is '... a dedicated resource established to promote and support the use of personal computing to assure optimal utilization of IT throughout the enterprise'.

A typical IC will be staffed by people who are 'hybrids' – they have a mix of technical and applications skills – who can act as the interface between the users and the providers of the technology, which may be the organization's own DP department or outside vendors or consultants.

The basis for preliminary planning decisions

The organization must start by clearly identifying its **objectives** and the **processes** by which it attempts to achieve them. The problem with using a life cycle approach is that it tends to be a top-down technique and untrained users may be uncomfortable if they cannot relate the study to the level of the organization with which they are most familiar. Similarly, techniques of functional decomposition may be too limited because they focus on the components rather than the system within which they operate. The best techniques require planners to think at a level of abstraction and to model the top of the organization. But no matter where the model starts, there are a considerable number of entities and information sets to be reflected in a complete model, and complexity is a constant problem.

The answer therefore lies in separating out the objectives and identifying and grouping the processes which support them. Although this will be a simplified (and, some might say, superficial) model, it will avoid the problems of the signal-to-noise ratio if too many variables are included (it is doubtful that the quality of decisions is improved through the mere addition of more data) so long as each item actually included has been verified for relevance. The designers can then consult more accurately with senior management as to the level of information required to support each group of processes effectively. This is achieved because users can more easily understand issues in a model form, and so better consultation arises to set guidelines and strategies for overall system development.

Implementation planning

As a precondition of implementation, the affected users must have endorsed the declared objectives of the proposed changes. This validation exercise should have been used to produce models of the tasks, processes and resources which are to be created. By doing this, the planners and prospective users are evaluating the change constructively and identifying the most important intended results. If conflicts emerge, it is better to confront them at this stage and to redefine task boundaries and responsibilities on paper instead of leaving it to politically entrenched attitudes when work has progressed to the point where investment in implementation represents a direct threat to existing responsibility on the ground. If the organizational and administrative disputes cannot be solved through arbitration and compromise, senior management should be involved to make decisions before too many resources have been committed to a contentious project.

This stage of the planning process involves a redefinition of perception. The initial plan, now approved, must be seen as a 'metaplan' to be broken down into its functional components, each of which must be grouped according to the objectives to be supported and given a priority. The priority is likely to be based on the criticality of the given component as a factor in the success of the organization. This should allow the planners to gain a sense of the coherence of the different changes to be made and to produce a framework within which the changes can be most efficiently introduced into operation. It may be useful to group organizational objectives by reference to the five basic categories suggested by Land:

- **economic** – the organization hopes to exploit the changes to derive financial benefits
- **organizational** – the organization hopes to achieve practical improvement in its management
- **staffing** – the economic and organizational benefits can only be achieved through changes in the practices and attitudes of the staff involved
- **third party** – the organization must be seen as a node in a framework of interactive relations with other parties and organizations, and all internal changes must be monitored by reference to the effect on existing and future relationships
- **public policy** – to a greater or lesser extent, all change is aimed at meeting the constraints of the sociopolitical environment in which the organization wishes to operate. Commercial organizations must, for example, organize their information systems to comply with legislation requiring the submission of annual accounts and all must consider data security for the purposes of the Data Protection Act.

Once the basic grouping has been achieved, the plan should be rechecked against the organization structure to make sure that the implications of the changes remain consistent with the long-term objectives of the organization. If compatibility is maintained, the planners continue the decomposition and should cluster the component processes into applications: the designers should identify those processes which can conveniently be undertaken as a single step (the formation of process flow diagrams will be useful here). In turn, this will permit greater definition of the data architecture and of the data views, because it will be possible to see greater logic in the emerging sub-systems and to specify the likely form of the data before and after each grouped processing activity. The end product should be a good basis from which to take strategic decisions of feasibility. The test of feasibility is based on three interdependent issues:

1. will the staff be willing and able to turn the paper proposals into a working reality?

2 is it technically possible to make the design operate efficiently?
3 will implementation represent a good economic return on investment?

The systems development life cycle

The background to systems development

Initially, early computer-based systems tended to be associated with scientific applications. This arose because such systems were relatively straightforward to design, as the application (which was often highly mathematical) was usually capable of being exactly defined and expressed in formal terms. The complexity and difficulty lay in the production of the software to make the system operational.

In the 1950s, those responsible for selecting projects for automation began to develop more commercial applications for the computer-based systems. These applications were inevitably centred around the data processing functions appropriate to batch processing systems with their somewhat crude data capture facilities – the emergent mainframe computer technology of the time. But because of the limits of this technology, their impact was usually felt at the operational level of information preparation and decision making. This trend was reinforced because the prime justification for computerization during this period was cost saving, and so the areas which were most usually selected for automation were those which made intensive use of clerical labour, or which offered scope for direct financial benefits. The result in organizational planning terms was that these computerization projects were often viewed as piecemeal, one-off solutions to current problems rather than long-term strategies in line with an orderly scheme of organizational development.

The difficulty of design and implementation was further exaggerated because the systems had to be developed without the benefit of previous experience or a formal development methodology. The result was that many of the early commercial systems were notoriously unsuccessful as development projects. The symptoms were commonplace: the software product was often delivered late, the programmers underestimated the time required and overran their budgets and, faced with intractable problems and looming deadlines, the eventual botched-together system failed to meet the user's objectives. But as computer technology improved and the range of applications to which it was applied grew more complex, three factors became apparent to systems developers:

1 the piecemeal development of systems (or single programs) in response to individual problems should be supplanted by an **integrated systems approach**
2 systems development tended to follow a recognized pattern, called the **systems development life cycle**, which included the same stages irrespective of the application
3 the characteristics of the life cycle could be exploited by using a systems development methodology to plan and control the project through all its stages.

Such thinking led the United Kingdom's National Computing Centre (NCC) to put forward a seminal systems development approach based on the version of the life cycle which had emerged from their research. This approach, first introduced in 1968, is based on the following stages:

- feasibility study
- systems analysis
- systems design
- implementation
- review and maintenance.

The approach can be viewed as a serial process in which each phase produces an output in a deliverable form which, in turn, becomes the input to the next phase (the *waterfall model*), or as a series of iterative cycles in which prior phases can be modified by the results of subsequent phases. In practice, the latter view is probably nearer to the truth.

Let us look at the individual stages of this approach in detail.

The feasibility study

In the traditional systems development life cycle, it is the function of the feasibility study to undertake a shallow investigation of the current system and to evaluate its potential for partial or total computerization. This will involve a **problem analysis** and the production of several outline systems designs or possible alternative solutions to current problems. These outline plans might include various methods of computerization or a mixture of manual and computer-based systems.

The alternatives are then compared in terms of their technical, economic and operational costs and benefits, the aim being to produce a recommended solution. This will be the system which has the greatest apparent benefit value. The results of the study are compiled into a formal **feasibility report** to user management, which will then decide whether or not to accept the recommendations contained in it. This is sometimes termed the **'go/no-go decision'**. A positive outcome will lead to the setting of terms of reference, indicating the scope and constraints for the next phase of the system life cycle.

Systems analysis

This is a detailed fact-finding exercise about the applications area or areas recommended in the feasibility study. This will require the systems analyst to spend a considerable amount of time with the users at various levels of the organization while building up a file of data on the current situation. Among the techniques which the analyst may use are:

- **Interviewing** the users and their managers to obtain a detailed account of the functions which the relevant people carry out, the information which they need to do their jobs, and how they use and update the most common records. This is the most common fact-finding technique in the majority of systems analysis projects. It also represents the greatest area of interaction between analyst and user. The advantage of the technique is that it is flexible and direct and encourages the user to feel involved in the system project. In deciding the scale of any interviewing, it should be recognized that interviewing as part of a large project is very resource-hungry. All interviews should therefore be carefully planned to derive the maximum benefit in the time available, the overall process taking the following form:

  - **preparation**, in which the analysis team will select the users who are to be interviewed, examine the facts which are already available and prepare a list of areas for examination
  - **conducting** the interview by asking open-ended questions, listening carefully and taking structured notes
  - **following up** after the interview by transcribing the notes, comparing notes with others in the team who may be interviewing users in similar areas of the organization, and producing a summary of the interview. This may be checked with the user.

- **Observing** the people at work to establish their movements and the number of times they need to access records, to communicate with one another, or to obtain new work. The technique is sometimes the only one that can be used (e.g. for industrial processes) but it is very time-consuming. The notorious 'Hawthorne effect', which predicts changes in behaviour when users are observed, may also be a problem.
- **Questionnaires** perform a similar function to interviews (both are effectively question-and-answer sessions) but they are usually aimed at fact-gathering from people outside the organization (typically from suppliers or customers) or where the interview population would be too large. Well-structured and properly designed questionnaires which exploit optical mark recognition (OMR) (see Chapter 7) may be directly input for computer analysis. But systems analysis using questionnaires often suffers from a low rate of returns. This can be partially overcome by making the questionnaire easy to answer. Three common types of question may be used:
  (a) **yes/no questions** are easy to answer and to analyse, but offer no real opportunity for shades of meaning
  (b) **multiple-choice questions** have the capacity to produce answers which contain more information, but the question setter requires more skill in drafting the questions to avoid forcing the answers through lack of real choice
  (c) **open-ended questions** remove the element of suggestion and allow almost infinite shades of meaning. They are the most difficult questions to set, and the answers are equally difficult to analyse.

  A well-designed questionnaire may contain an appropriate mixture of all of these types of question.
- **Record sampling** involves the examination of files and documents to find out their contents, their use and their source and destination. Existing computer files may be examined by producing a print-out through the use of a special extract program.

Interviewing and record sampling, used in conjunction, can identify the data that an organization stores, the information that moves around the organization and how that information is produced, used and modified. Sometimes the same applications are analysed by different fact-finding techniques to produce a cross-reference check on accuracy.

The results of these activities are recorded using a variety of documents and charts. The systems team then carry out a **problem analysis** exercise based on the data gathered. The issues covered may include:

- why current methods and working practices are used
- what alternative methods are available that will achieve the same, or better, results
- what problems are restricting the effectiveness of the current system, and the reasons for their existence
- what volumes of transactions and data exist, and what rates of increase are likely to apply to them
- what performance criteria are required from the system and how they can be measured.

The emphasis of the detailed investigation and problem analysis phases is on what is to be done to solve the users' problems.

Systems design

The results of the systems analysis stage of the life cycle, modified by the output from the problem analysis exercise, provide the basis for the design of the new system. This phase is both the most creative and the most technical of the whole life cycle. Design will address both computerized and manual procedures in the following areas:

- data capture methods, source documents and data inputs
- program design and specification
- output design in terms of screen and print layouts
- file design of computer and manual file records and data items
- security and back-up provisions.

The aim of the systems design phase is to arrive at a detailed statement of how the system is to be made operational. The final steps of the phase are to decide on the hardware and software specification and to put out a tender to suppliers for the necessary items.

Implementation

The implementation phase is concerned with putting the systems design into practice. The tasks which must be carried out will include the following software-orientated tasks:

- program coding in an appropriate language
- testing the individual programs, suites of programs and the whole system – this will involve the use of packages of test data
- file set-up and conversion of manual files.

Possibly at the same time as the above, the suppliers' bids in response to the tender specification will be examined. The bid which most closely matches the specification on the most favourable terms will be turned into a recommendation to user management. The hardware (and its environment) will then be selected, ordered and installed.

Implementation goes beyond the physical environment and includes the intellectual. The management must therefore plan for user and operator training and for the creation of documentation, such as user manuals. The implementation strategy – the way in which the system goes live – must also be devised. The standard methods are as follows:

- **direct changeover** from the old to the new system, with the manual functions being dropped in favour of computerized processes, and manual files being directly converted. This method is comparatively cheap but carries a high degree of risk, so it is rarely used for critical or strategic systems
- **phased changeover** involves the conversion of manual to computer-based functions in a gradual manner throughout the whole system. This may be done on a file-by-file or department-by-department basis. The disruption and level of risk is therefore more controlled, and the change may be effected reasonably cheaply, as there will be little, if any, increase in staff. There is no reason in principle why a complete organization cannot be computerized in this way
- **parallel running** is used on strategic systems where the risks and consequences of failure are great. It means that the present system continues to run normally, while the new system functions fully alongside it. Only when a satisfactory performance has been established from the computerized system will the old system be curtailed. This period may vary from weeks to months, depending on the application. The general effect is to minimize the risk of failure at the expense of considerable cost. Thus, it may be necessary to pay overtime premiums for existing staff, or even to take on temporary staff to cover both systems.

Review and maintenance

The degree of success achieved through the use of an implemented computer-based information system will depend on the cumulative success of all the previous stages in the systems development life cycle. Such success can be measured in four ways.

1. The extent to which the features of the system are accepted by the users. Some programs and reports tend not to be used because they are difficult to operate or to understand. This could be a symptom of inadequate work during the systems design phase.
2. Whether the functioning system meets the objectives set for it during the feasibility study phase. This may occur if the running costs of the new system are higher than expected, or if the actual direct benefits are lower than was intended.
3. Whether the performance of the new system is adequate for the users' needs, for instance in terms of response time, the number of users who may log-on simultaneously or the degree of reliability.

4 The operational integrity of the system. This typically requires a measurement of the correctness of processing or the accuracy in the functioning of the procedures for setting up batch runs, etc., and of the ease with which users can recover from crashes and losses of data. This would include an examination of security and back-up facilities.

These factors are assessed by a major review activity, usually involving all the people involved in the systems project. This review, often called a **post-audit review**, is intended to correct any shortcomings which may be identified under operational conditions and to provide data for subsequent enhancements. All the data arising from such an exercise can and should be recycled to improve the system team's competence in all phases of future projects.

Project selection and justification

The decision to commit resources to transforming all or part of an organization's operations from a manual or primitive computer-based system to a more efficient computer-based system is termed a **systems project**. The project will follow through the stages of the SDLC and will probably be carried out using a systems development methodology with attendant project management techniques. Before this process can be undertaken, however, the need for such a project must be identified, the project must be defined as a solution to this need, and the project must be tested for feasibility within the constraints imposed on it by the organization. This **project selection process** is applied to both piecemeal and total system development. However, although the process is the same, the way selection is applied differs radically between the two approaches.

The **piecemeal** approach will tend to place the project selection process in the form of a feasibility study at the beginning of the SDLC (see Figure 8.2). This is a feature of the traditional methodologies (see Chapter 9) which originated at the time when a test of technical feasibility was of utmost importance. Since individual systems become obsolete and require replacement in turn, the period of time during which the complete system will be functioning optimally will be short.

The **total system approach** as typified by several of the newer database methodologies places the feasibility later in the life cycle. At this stage, much more is known about the type and size of system which is likely to be implemented. This is important, given the number of alternative technical solutions which are available to the modern systems designer.

The project selection process in a total system environment serves to match the implementation of a complete system with the resources of money, manpower and time which may be devoted to that implementation. Only if such resources are not sufficiently available (for instance, owing to **capital rationing** or a **skill shortage**), would projects A, B and C in Figure 8.3 not proceed simultaneously. Their partition is for the convenience of the project management.

It is important for information system developers to appreciate that system development projects are often in competition with other income-generating

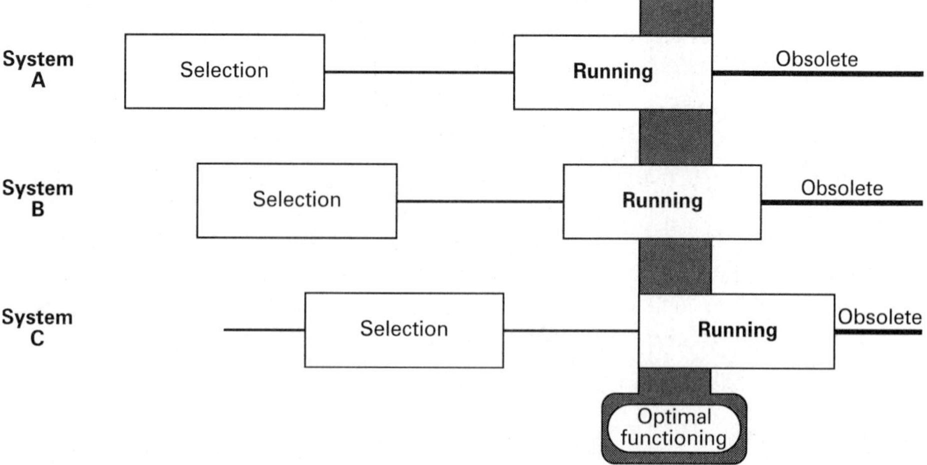

Figure 8.2 Project development in a piecemeal environment.

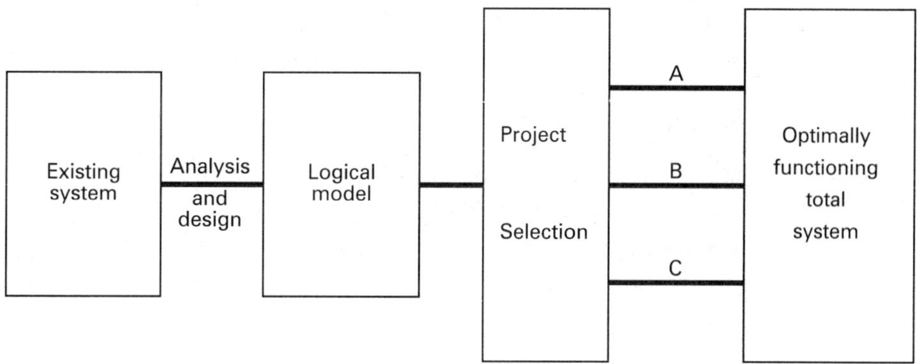

Figure 8.3 Project development in a total system environment.

projects such as improved production machinery or extra retail outlets. When carrying out major investment appraisal exercises, we should recognize that top financial managers may not be predisposed to favour computerization against apparently less risky areas of return.

The placement of the project selection process in the two approaches (piecemeal and total system) creates a trade-off between minimizing the **sunk costs**, if a project should fail an early feasibility test, and acquiring more information through the systems analysis phase.

In Figure 8.4, a project abandoned at A is liable to incur a small cost penalty. A project that reaches point B will incur a heavy penalty if called off, but will benefit in the following ways:

- there will be more information about the existing system, for instance size of file storage and processing requirements

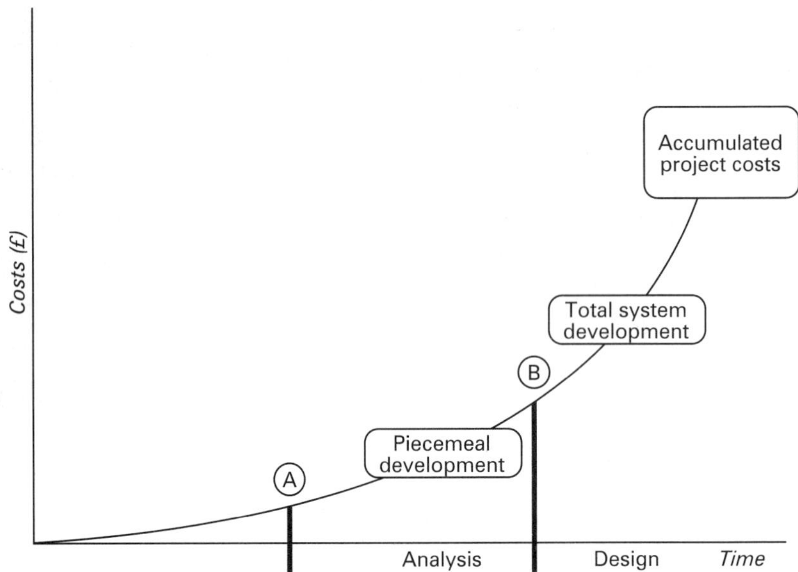

Figure 8.4 Alternative placements of project selection.

- the planners will have more detailed knowledge of the resources that will be required to carry out the project
- there will be a greater likelihood of the project meeting its objectives, as these are set closer to actual implementation.

If the project is not likely to be abandoned or heavily modified, it can therefore pay to delay the project selection process, as in the CACI methodology (see Chapter 9).

Project generation

Under the piecemeal approach, **candidate projects** – those which will be submitted for selection – will be generated from a number of sources, typically including:

- requests from user departments for help in overcoming operational problems in an existing system
- the reports from a steering committee which, at the behest of senior management, has been considering ways of improving operational efficiency
- input from a formal policy on systems development
- voluntary suggestions made by the computing or systems development group itself.

The effect of collecting possible projects from such sources is that an organization will have a portfolio of candidate projects which will be continuously tested for selection. Under the total system approach, the initiation of the project will come from strategic management or a steering committee.

The selection process

The process of project selection has been likened to a funnel containing a number of sieves of differing coarseness. They represent the three tests which make up the feasibility study, that is technical, operational and economic feasibility.

1. **Technical feasibility**. This is concerned with matching the system requirements to the performance which could be achieved from available hardware and software. This factor is changing rapidly with technological progress. The technical needs of a system might include:
   - the ability to support a certain number of users
   - a certain response time under certain operating conditions
   - the ability to process a certain number of transactions within a certain time
   - the capacity to hold a certain number of records on-line
   - networking with distant locations.
2. **Operational feasibility**. The issues are those concerning organizational and human factors and matters of policy. Operational questions might include:
   - the effect of the proposed system on departmental boundaries; for instance, will a new credit control system overlap into traditional sales and accounting areas?
   - changes to manning levels and working practices and how these changes may be managed and absorbed (this will involve predicting the reaction of the people affected both inside and outside the organization)
   - the effect of the system on the organization's image: for instance, should a building society with a reputation for friendly personal service replace counter staff with ATMs?

   In reaching decisions, due weight should be given to custom and practice within the organization, to local and national trade union agreements and to any relevant legislation.
3. **Economic feasibility**. This recognizes that most business projects, computing or otherwise, must show positive financial returns. For this reason, the economic performance of proposed system projects is regarded as very important by senior management with one important exception. That is when a project is seen as being part of a technological advance within an organization that will provide a return in the very long term, a so-called **loss-leader project**.

The generic term for this part of the project selection process is a **cost–benefit analysis**. It will usually be carried out with the expert advice of an accountant, who may be drafted into the project team specifically for this purpose. The items which are likely to be encountered during a cost–benefit analysis fall into the categories given below.

- **Direct benefits** having an immediate effect on cashflow, including:
  - reduced operations costs, such as a reduction in clerical staff or overtime payments
  - reduced systems costs, such as replacing a primitive computer-based system with a more modern one

  - greater turnover due to increased sales (perhaps as a result of an on-line ordering system) or increased output due to automated production capacity.
- **Indirect benefits** having an effect on long-term profitability. These could include:
  - better decision making, due to better use of information
  - greater control over operational processes such as stock control and credit control
  - more freedom to innovate, as much of the routine work is automated.
- **Development costs** involve the problems of measuring the costs of the existing system and estimating the proposed system costs. This will include the costs of:
  - users' time while involved in the fact-finding exercise (this may be considerable for a senior manager)
  - systems analysts' and other systems designers' time
  - hardware specification and tendering.
- **Implementation costs** are those related to setting up the new system, including:
  - hardware and software package acquisition (note that cost patterns can be changed by changing the method of acquisition)
  - commissioning and installation, including services
  - staff recruitment and training
  - in-house program design and coding
  - file and database creation.
- **Running costs** are those which will continue for the life of the system. They usually make up the greater part of a system's cost (estimates of as high as 70 per cent have been made). Such costs will include:
  - maintenance of hardware, software and services (air conditioning, power supplies, and so on)
  - financing charges, such as loan repayments
  - staff wages
  - stationery and sundries
  - security and back-up.

Cost–benefit can be applied in several ways. It can measure the benefits of a proposed computer-based system as compared to an existing manual system, or it can be used to select the apparently most beneficial from a number of proposed systems (for instance, credit control versus stock control versus sales order entry) where capital rationing applies.

Intangible costs

As well as the costs which are measurable and which are directly attributable to the new system, there may be considerable, long-term hidden costs:

- **switching costs**, which relate to the investment that has been made in the system to be replaced. It is unrealistic to think that all systems development is of a 'green field' nature – that is, the simple computerization of existing manual systems. The rapid pace of technological change means that computer-based systems which have been installed relatively recently may be replaced with more up-to-date hardware and software. The cost of making the switch from one technology to another will include intangibles such as training, reduced efficiency and, perhaps, initial user discontent

- **locking-in costs** are incurred when an organization makes a strategic choice of technology, for instance a preferred hardware manufacturer, operating system or software house. Once locked in by this major choice, the organization may be making a commitment which incurs a cost, since other suppliers might be able to provide parts of the system in a more cost-effective way. Dedication to a particular type of system – locking in to a generation or type of technology – is therefore a cost
- **opportunity costs** are created when any investment choice is made. Since information systems and technology form a large part of the budget of many organizations, the choice is obviously to forego investment in other resources with the potential to give a greater return.

It is therefore important when considering long-term system development to plan an 'update' path from one generation of hardware and software to another. This process, known as **migration**, is a critical factor in information systems development. Over time, migration has tended to become more straightforward owing to the adoption of standards and the dominance of certain manufacturers (such as the open systems standards, Microsoft MS-DOS and IBM-PC compatibility) and yet it is complicated by the increasing pace of technological change.

It is important that the development of a replacement information system is under way before the current system ceases to perform effectively. The aim of a migration plan should be to have a mature system permanently in place. The effect is shown in Figure 8.5 overleaf. In order for this process to work effectively, it is necessary to have a strategic information systems plan and a means of evaluating the performance of an operational information system. Managers should also be able to predict the end of the current information system's useful life, as well as having a thorough knowledge of new technological developments.

Techniques of cost–benefit analysis

The techniques used in the economic evaluation of computer-based information systems are the same as those used for investment appraisal in other areas of the commercial world. These techniques tend to produce contradictory results, and none of them is universally accepted. Briefly, the techniques are based either on *marginal costing* methods, which deal with a snapshot of a system's performance at a given moment in time, or *life cycle costing* methods which, more realistically, attempt to measure a system's performance over its working life. Commonly used techniques include the following.

- Breakeven analysis can be usefully applied when a proposed system is likely to achieve a direct benefit such as an increase in turnover or production output. The method recognizes that computerization can produce a change in cost pattern. For instance, the cost of processing a customer order

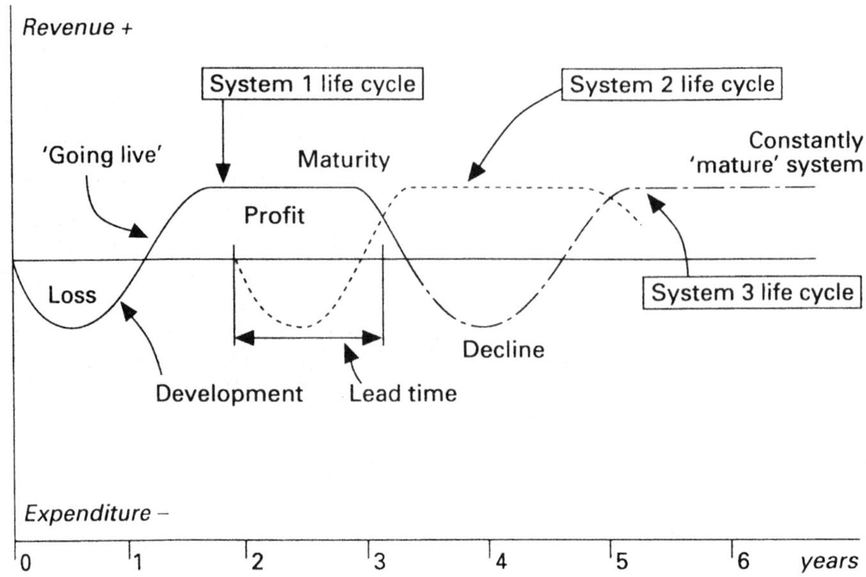

Figure 8.5 Migration or upgrade path.

(a variable cost) may be less than with a manual system, but the system running costs (fixed costs) may in fact be greater. This is familiar to management accountants as **volume/cost/profit analysis (VCP)**.

In Figure 8.6, outputs to the left of point C do not justify the use of the proposed system (profit area A), while for outputs above point C (profit area B) the system would be justified. Point C is therefore the **breakeven point**. If the expected average output from the proposed system was indicated by point D, the difference in between C and D would be called the system's **margin of safety**.

- **Payback period** attempts to measure the time in which the benefits from a proposed system will recoup the initial investment in the system. An organization which uses this method may have a policy that investments of all kinds must pay back within, say, five years. There are three major drawbacks to the payback method. First, it stresses liquidity at the expense of profitability, and may therefore favour safe, short-term projects (often not a feature of information technology). Secondly, the method fails to take into account the **time value** of money – that is, revenues that accrue in the near future are worth most. Thirdly, the payback method is extremely coarse: it is possible to have two projects with completely different cashflow patterns and sizes of initial investment, both giving a payback period of, say, three years.
- **Net present value (NPV)** method discounts future cashflows in line with a present value factor to give all projects, irrespective of their cashflow pattern, a common benchmark of today's value by which they can be judged. The method takes profitability into account by examining revenues for the whole

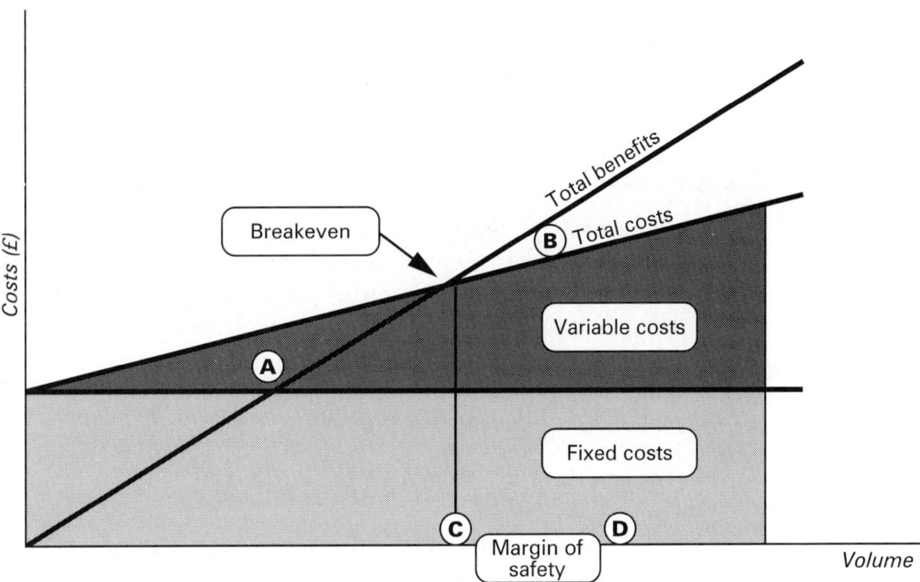

Figure 8.6 Breakeven graph for a proposed system.

of the project's working life and is less prone to favour short-term views. A development of the net present value method is the internal rate of return (IRR) method, which produces an estimated percentage return that is claimed to be more closely comparable with other forms of investment.

The biggest problem to be overcome in all three tests of feasibility is that of predicting the future performance of the system before its design is finalized. This applies as much to the technical aspects (such as response time) as to the economic aspects, such as the generation of a certain cashflow in a ten-year time span.

Functions of project selection

The project selection process has two functions:

1. rejecting proposed systems which do not pass the three tests of feasibility
2. ranking the remaining projects in order of priority for implementation. What this order is may be a matter for the body in charge of systems policy (the steering committee, say) to decide. Often the proposed system which addresses the most pressing functional problems or performs best in the cost–benefit analysis will be ranked highest. The NCC has developed a method of comparing the non-quantifiable system features, such as user interface, called **weighted ranking**.

Summary

The information strategy of an organization is an important component of its overall corporate strategy. The information strategy needs to be consistent with the other components and must contribute to the achievement of the organization's objectives.

- At the strategic level, the organization must identify its level of maturity in IT terms, and assess the criticality of each of the major processes which it undertakes. In other words, the organization will determine the extent to which it is dependent on automated systems and the desirability of that dependence. To get the best out of its information system, the organization must properly plan the systems and data architecture and make decisions on whether to produce a centralized or decentralized system.
- The systems development life cycle is normally broken down into five stages: feasibility, systems analysis, systems design, implementation, and review and maintenance.
- Care must be taken to select the automation projects which will most effectively promote the organization's objectives at a cost which is economically justifiable. The standard method applied to the selection of projects is cost–benefit analysis. This relies on identifying all the benefits, both tangible and intangible, and weighing them against the costs (which include the cost of not automating). The standard techniques are breakeven analysis, payback period and net present value.
- The design process will always be strengthened by the addition of good user participation at all stages of the development life cycle.

Self-test questions

1. Identify and describe briefly the stages in the systems development life cycle (SDLC).
2. Distinguish between technical, operational and economic feasibility studies.
3. Describe the more common fact-finding techniques and explain their advantages.
4. Identify the methods that may be applied in the economic evaluation of system projects and comment on the contribution they make to project selection.

Exam-style question

1. The senior managers within Betta Products are about to consider whether the proposed redesign of their existing IT system will be economically feasible. This will be the first time that all the managers have been involved in this process and many have little knowledge or experience of detailed IT issues.

   Write a report which explains how the managers should make this assessment.

(*All answers on pages 558–559*)

CHAPTER 9

Systems analysis and design

In the previous chapter, we outlined the need for an information strategy and described the various stages in the systems development life cycle. The processes of systems analysis and design were introduced within this model. In this chapter we examine the primary system design methodologies, incorporating process-driven, data-driven and user-driven development elements, and evaluate the more modern structured methodologies, which include process-driven and data-driven approaches. Next, alternative data file structures are identified and explored, plus the factors controlling the choice of file organization are considered. We look at the nature of databases and assess their possible benefits to an organization. Finally, the distinction between logical and physical concepts in constructing a model of an organization's information needs are considered.

Design methodologies

The National Computer Centre (NCC) approach and other similarly idealized versions of the life cycle provided a general framework within which systems designers could use procedures, rules and guidelines more effectively. This, in turn, developed into sets of guidelines and standards for systems development which are now termed **methodologies**. A methodology consists of an underlying framework based on a particular approach or philosophy. This theoretical framework will be applied by using a range of practical techniques supported by a set of tools contained within the methodology.

Ideally, a methodology should cover all phases of the life cycle but, inevitably, some methodologies are biased towards certain phases or may omit other phases altogether. As a generalization, methodologies which concentrate on the first two phases identified by the NCC tend to be called **systems analysis** methodologies, while those focusing on phases 3 and 4 are often termed **software engineering** methodologies. The difference is mainly one of emphasis and approach. The choice of an appropriate methodology for an organization has come to be associated with the degree of success experienced in previous software development projects. Those organizations with a need to develop large information systems have therefore developed or adopted a proven in-house methodology. Indeed, the development or adoption of a workable systems development methodology has become a major strategic decision in many organizations.

Categories of systems development

Broadly, the range of established systems development methodologies can be separated into three main categories:

1. **process-driven** development
2. **data-driven** development
3. **user-driven** development based on **human activity systems (HAS)**.

A further category called 'event-driven' development applies largely to real-time and process control systems. An emergent approach called 'object-oriented' development is considered to have a great deal of potential for the future.

Let us examine these three development approaches in detail.

Process-driven development

This is the approach taken by a number of so-called traditional methodologies, of which the NCC approach is typical. The term **process-driven** refers to an emphasis on the **activities** or functions which are carried out in the system. The philosophy behind such a methodology is that an improvement in the way things are done – by computerizing a manual process, for instance – will produce a better, more efficient system. The techniques contained in such a methodology tend to concentrate on describing processes and their input–output flows in increasing levels of detail. This is called **functional decomposition** and should result in an understanding of every process at a level of detail sufficient to allow a computer program specification to be written for it.

The approach is represented in Figure 9.1.

Critics of process-driven systems development point out that such techniques, used in isolation, can result in a system that concentrates on the routine, mechanistic activities of transaction processing at the operational level of the organization. It has also been said that decomposition leads to piecemeal or fragmented systems development, with a lack of **enhancement** by the new systems over the old ones.

Data-driven development

The proponents of data-driven development claim that to concentrate on modelling detailed activities or processes is bound to create an unstable system. They argue that operational details will be more liable to frequent modification and, therefore, the system will be costly to maintain. This is because the methods by which business activities are carried out are transient and likely to change as the business itself changes.

The philosophy behind data-driven development is that the data which a system uses are more constant and will be consistent, irrespective of *how* they are processed (see Figure 9.2). A data model is therefore inherently more stable. The theory then states that a system which is developed by concentrating on the storage and manipulation of data will be more flexible and robust. At its heart,

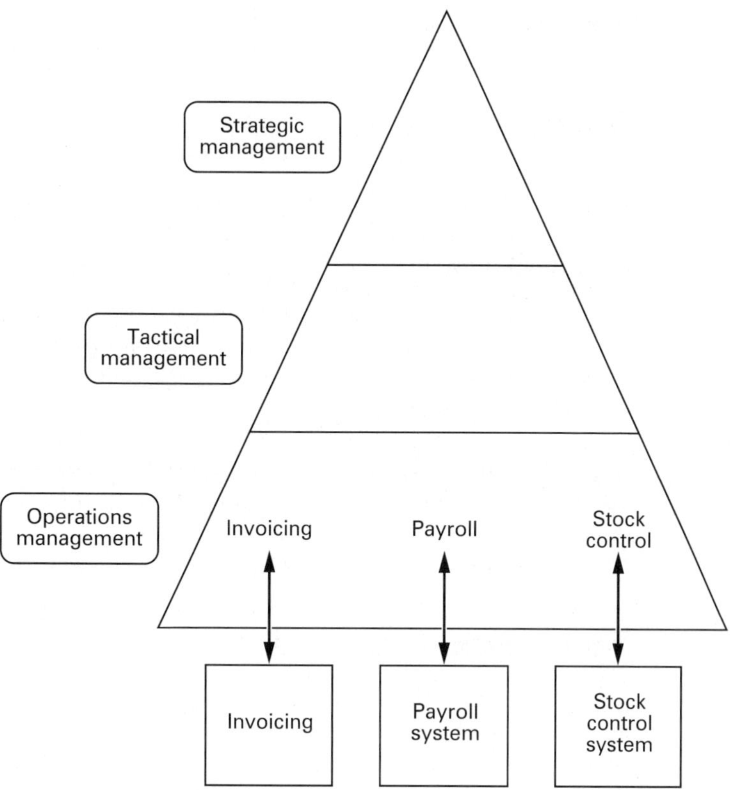

Figure 9.1 A process-driven system.

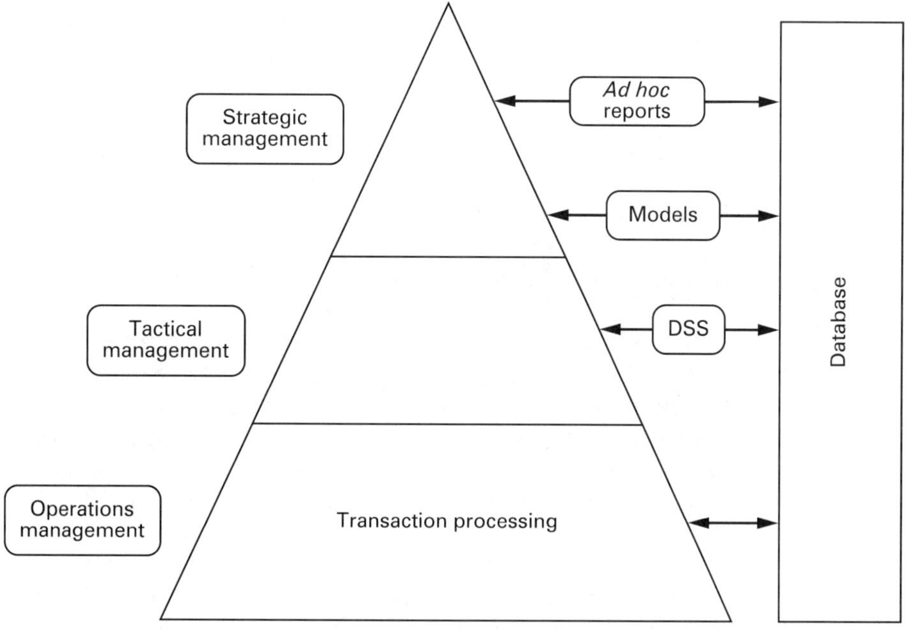

Figure 9.2 A data-driven system.

data-driven development is based on techniques that are intended to model the things which are most important to the system:

- **the entities**, or things which are most important to the system
- **the attributes**, or what the system needs to know about the entities
- **the relationships**, or the ways in which the entities fit together to make up the system.

Such techniques are typified by the **entity-relationship models (ERMs)**, used in the **data analysis** approach developed by Chen in 1976 and in a number of more modern methodologies.

Data-driven development is frequently associated with the development of large-scale relational database systems with a DBMS, using a non-procedural query language. Information systems having these features are capable of addressing the needs of non-routine decision-making activity at the tactical and strategic levels of business, through the use of *ad hoc* reports, DSSs and user-created models.

User-driven development

User-driven development concentrates on the behavioural aspects of information systems design. Technical methodologies which are either process-driven or data-driven have the computer specialist, usually the systems analyst, as the development driver. The user supplies facts and may be involved quite closely with the project at some stages, but it is the analyst who makes most of the important systems decisions. User-driven systems development seeks to overcome apparent user dissatisfaction with technically developed systems by recognizing the importance of user involvement and encouraging active participation in the analysis and design process.

The emphasis during a project is on the **system team** approach, with users and analysts working in equal partnership. The role of the analyst then becomes that of a technological facilitator, giving advice on a range of design possibilities. The decisions and choices are then made by the user. The philosophy behind such development is that systems only address the users' needs by incorporating those users into the development process. This approach is said to produce systems which are less technologically complex and less reliant on experts. Therefore, they are more likely to be well accepted, flexible and capable of being adapted to meet changing organizational needs.

The techniques employed in user-driven development are typified by the **soft systems methodology (SSM)**, developed by Checkland, which applies systems theory to address the type of fuzzy, poorly structured or ill-defined problems which are often met in systems analysis. It is argued that modelling processes or data are deceptively convenient, but that to understand an organization, the objectives, attitudes and perceptions of the stakeholders must be understood. This is difficult because of the non-linear unpredictability of human activity systems. SSM attempts to address this problem by using a pictorial representation of the system, called a **rich picture**, and a textual description called a **root definition**. The aim is to construct a series of conceptual models of the system, identifying the users' ideas, problems and behaviour.

The design phase of a user-driven development project lends itself well to the use of prototyping techniques or **rapid applications development**, where the user can employ 4GL tools experimentally to produce a system which has the appearance of a functioning system (screen dialogue, print-outs, and so on) without the internal functionality (file accesses, program executions, etc.). Such a prototype may be produced in a fraction of the time a real system would take. When the prototype is pronounced to be satisfactory to the user, the technologists add the necessary functions to make the system operational. An extension of the prototyping approach is **evolutionary systems development**, which attempts to recognize that systems change is inevitable (even desirable) and therefore should be exploited. The systems design phase is seen as being a continuous process. Effectively the system is never finished. Obviously, the approach requires the long-term involvement of system users.

Alternative development life cycles

Examples of methodologies from the categories given above involve life cycles which may be radically different from the traditional example previously used. Also, there is some cross-fertilization between categories. Hence, a process-driven methodology may include a phase in which data analysis is carried out. Similarly, a methodology based on data-driven philosophies can sometimes contain large elements in which processes or functions are examined. But, most modern methodologies now recognize the importance of user participation as a common denominator in the design process.

Process-driven methodology

Most process-driven methodologies are related to the American Yourdon consultancy house. This includes methodologies published by DeMarco (1978) and Constantine (1978), and one called STRADIS by Gane and Sarson (1979). These approaches are sometimes called the **structured school** and the methodologies are often referred to as *structured systems analysis and design methodologies*. The example chosen to illustrate the life cycle of a structured methodology is, however, one developed in the UK by BIS Applied Systems and known as MODUS.

MODUS, as described by Collins and Blaye, is a structured framework for information systems planning, development and management. The methodology is conveniently broken down into six phases.

1. **IS strategy creation**. A strategy for information systems development may already exist within an organization, or it may be carried out specially at the start of a systems project. In any case, four categories of strategic planning are envisaged:
   (a) broad analysis of information needs in functional areas of the organization
   (b) outline of system type and processing facilities for the proposed new system

   (c) identification of projects and of broad implementation plans
   (d) rough forecasts of resource and manpower levels.
2 **Feasibility study**. The first major project phase looks at the technical and economic feasibility of developing the information system(s) identified in phase 1. The approach is to include the following steps:
   (a) broad identification of organizational objectives and performance targets, using **key performance factor (KPF)** analysis
   (b) identification of system requirements in terms of speed, controls and security
   (c) generation of alternative outline systems which would meet the organization's requirements
   (d) selection of the system which best matches the technical framework, and is most feasible economically. (Typical cost–benefit analysis tools, e.g. payback or net present value (NPV), would be used at this phase)
   (e) recommendations to user management and the development of detailed plans.
3 **Systems analysis**. The objective of this phase is to produce a detailed specification for the new system in organizational rather than technical terms. MODUS operates in three areas:
   (a) Functional analysis, using structured techniques (i.e. functional decomposition) to describe first the existing system and then the new system in increasing levels of detail. The tools used in this area are **activity diagrams** and **activity summaries**.
   (b) Data analysis, in which data items (e.g. purchase orders and stock items) are defined and their relationships examined. MODUS allows the use of two alternative tools at this stage: **logical data association (LDA)** or **relational data analysis (RDA)**. The former is less detailed, while the latter is of particular use when a large-scale DBMS is planned. Both result in **data structures** for use in phases 4 and 5.
   (c) Requirements analysis, where the new system requirements are compared to the features offered by the existing system to indicate the need for change. The tool used for this is a **function/activity matrix (FAN)** which is based on the results of the KPF analysis.
4 **System design**. The activity diagrams and data structures from the systems analysis phase are used to produce program specifications and file/database specifications. Tools used to do this include structured English, decision tables and decision trees. Attendant documents produced at this stage will include output layouts, security requirements and back-up plans.
5 **Program development**. Program development in MODUS follows a common pattern: design, coding and testing. The tools recommended are typically flow-charts and data structures as used in **Jackson Structured Programming (JSP)**. Testing at this stage is applied to individual programs or program modules.
6 **System testing**. System testing is intended to prove the reliability of the whole system. MODUS recommends testing for processing accuracy, communications between systems, and security and recovery procedures. The final stage of testing is user acceptance testing under realistic operating conditions.

Not included as separate phases in MODUS, but implicit in the structured approach, are reviews at important project milestones. The recommended review method is a **structured walkthrough** – a non-critical team review of progress during or after a phase. There is also provision for a post-audit review of both project success and system effectiveness. The most significant aspects of MODUS as a structured methodology are:

- the placement of the feasibility study and chosen outline solution *before* the detailed fact-finding exercise
- the use of functional decomposition as a major analysis tool, concentrating on processes or activities at increasing levels of detail
- a comprehensive set of techniques, procedures and documentation standards. (MODUS is less rigid than some structured methodologies in that some alternatives are allowed, for instance RDA or LDA)
- intended applicability to be applicable to a wide range of systems types and processing modes. (The methodology includes a section on design for real-time systems.)

MODUS became available as a computer-aided systems engineering (CASE) tool in the form of BIS Applied Systems' IPSE (Integrated Project Support Environment). This computer-based system allows all the guidelines, techniques and document standards of MODUS to be accessed and used by a range of project staff. Their efforts are then integrated into the final systems specification.

The phases of the MODUS methodology are shown in Figure 9.3.

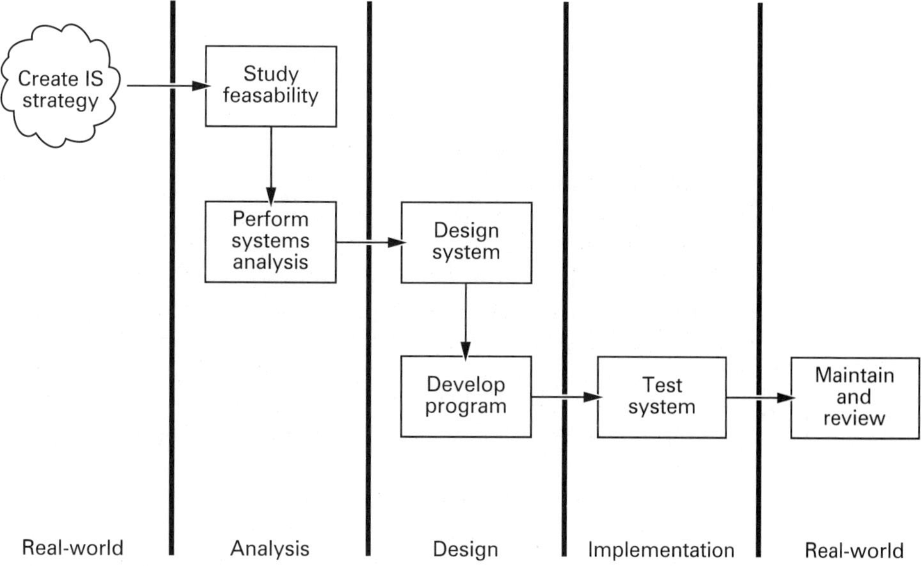

Figure 9.3 MODUS structured methodology phases.

Data-driven methodology

Just as the development of process-driven methodologies may be related to one school of thought, so the same names tend to appear throughout the complex and confusing evolution of data-oriented development methods. The two main types of data-driven methodologies are **information engineering**, introduced by Martin and Finkelstein in 1981 and subsequently developed into several different versions by subsidiary companies throughout the world, and **systems development in a shared data environment (D2S2)** developed by Palmer and Rock-Evans in (1981) working for the CACI consultancy company. Early versions were more simply termed the **CACI methodology** and this title is still used by many people. Both Palmer and Rock-Evans later joined James Martin Associates to add many of their data analysis ideas to the information engineering methodology. But the CACI methodology is still used in its own right, and it is chosen as an example to illustrate data-driven methodology in the form in which it was published in 1981 – the form which, incidentally, is often used for relational database design.

CACI methodology features five main phases which, unlike those of structured methodologies, may be undertaken concurrently rather than sequentially, or even in a different order (see Figure 9.4). The broad phases are as follows.

- **Entity analysis**. This phase concentrates on identifying the entities or things that are important to the organization, the way in which those entities relate to one another, and the facts or attributes that are held about them. The resulting ERM provides both an understanding of the organization's

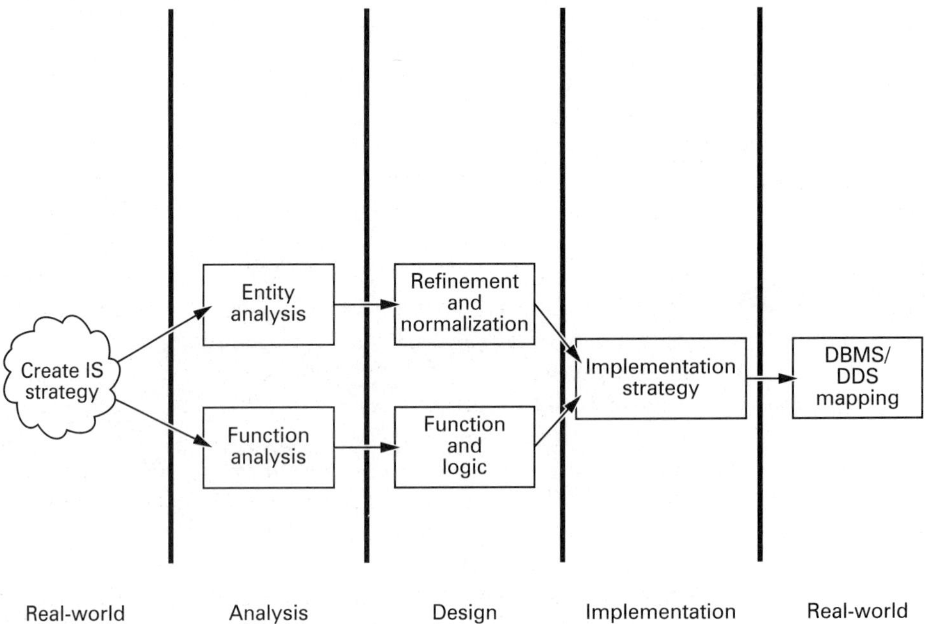

Figure 9.4 CACI data analysis methodology.

objectives and activities for planning purposes, and a basis for database design (for more details, see Chapter 10). The documents which are produced to support the model and to provide input to the **data dictionary** include entity, relationship and attribute forms. In making this analysis it is important that the organization is analysed and modelled as a whole rather than as separate functions or departments.

- **Function analysis**. This phase examines the processes or activities which occur within the system. These functions act on or change the state of entities. The phase begins with the drawing of a **function hierarchy** – a functional decomposition chart. This identifies the make-up of tasks within the system and is used as a test of completeness. The completed hierarchy can be used to identify common functions – those tasks that take place in different areas of the organization, but that are basically identical in operation, such as looking up records, changing to the new day's date, and so on. A hierarchy modified to take this into account is termed a **function network**. The common functions which are identified may then be eliminated during the implementation phase to reduce the overall amount of duplication. The function hierarchy has no time or sequence precedence, and so in order to record when functions take place and in what order, a set of function dependency diagrams is produced from the elementary or bottom level of the hierarchy. A function data flow dependency diagram is somewhat similar to a **data flow diagram (DFD)** in some other methodologies, except that events which trigger or mark the end of functions are included.
- **Normalization**. This technique structures data into ordered groups such that attributes occur with a minimum of repetition and the correct relationships between sets of attributes exist. The result is a set of tables or **relations** that represents a refined ERM, in that the data held are accurate and stable, permitting access by unique **keys**. The usual standard is normalization to **third normal form (TNF)**, which means that the reorganization has gone through three stages of normalization.
- **Function logic description**. This phase of the CACI methodology serves to describe in detail the operation of all or part of the function dependency diagrams produced during function analysis. The descriptions are usually of actions which take place in relation to entity types, for example 'create', 'update', 'modify' and 'delete'. These actions are described in **structured English**, **decision tables** or **decision trees**. A second exercise called **function logic quantification** examines the frequency with which such actions are likely to be taken in the implemented system (for example, one thousand accesses of a given record per hour). This can form the material for a **sizing** operation to find out how powerful the hardware and software of the implemented system will need to be. Function logic description and quantification documents are used for program design, database design and the specification of manual procedures. They correspond to program specifications in other methodologies.
- **Implementation strategy**. The most significant difference between the CACI methodology and the traditional or structured methodologies is the placing of the implementation strategy (corresponding to a feasibility study) at a late

stage of the development cycle. The rationale behind this late placement consists of two main points:

(a) Previous (older) methodologies stressed the technical aspects of feasibility studies to reject systems unsuitable for computerization at an early stage, that is before an accumulation of development costs. Technical developments of late have reduced the importance of this factor, as most applications have become amenable to automation.
(b) It is held to be unwise to decide implementation issues (that is, what is to be computerized and how) before a sufficient amount of detail is known about the data and functions used and performed in the existing system. Later decisions are felt to be better decisions.

The implementation issues addressed in the CACI methodology involve decisions, based on technical, operational and economic criteria, on the drawing-up of two system boundaries:

1 **the domain of change** contains sets of functions which are carried out differently, but not necessarily through the use of a computer. The reasons for not changing a manual function might be that its current method is satisfactory or that political reasons for not changing it exist (e.g. trade union agreements)
2 **the boundary of automation** exists within the domain of change and contains sets of functions which are to be computerized.

Both these systems boundaries can be physically drawn or mapped on to a collection of all the function dependency diagrams for the whole system. The entity types within the boundary of automation are then mapped on to application files or tables in a database and their attributes written to the data dictionary, which may contain specifications for data validation, security and audit.

As well as the development of large-scale software and database projects, the CACI methodology has been used in situations such as the following:

- business analysis, policy study and strategy planning
- computer package evaluation, based on a comparison between the business entities and functions and those supported by the package
- establishing security and audit procedures by analysis of the data model
- organization and method studies.

What makes data analysis so universal is that it takes the **total system** approach and so produces a multipurpose model of the whole organization.

General-purpose methodology

The UK's Central Computing and Telecommunications Agency, which was set up to provide information systems services to the Civil Service and Government departments, identified the problem of diverging approaches to system development in the late 1970s. The result was an attempt to produce a standard, general-purpose methodology which could be used by a variety of organizations to develop systems serving a wide range of applications. Such a methodology would give the advantages of standardization of techniques and documentation, with consequent possibilities of improved training and provable quality standards. The methodology which was finally developed was called **structured systems analysis and design method (SSADM)**.

In spite of its name, the methodology is a hybrid, claiming to combine features from three approaches:

1. the process-driven approach to model processes, documented in SSADM by the use of dataflow diagrams (DFDs) and functional decomposition
2. the data-driven approach to model the entities, relationships and attributes of data items, documented by the use of logical data structures (LDSs) which are a variety of entity-relationship model
3. the event-driven approach to represent the changes to which entities are subjected by modelling events and states. The resulting document is called an **entity life history**.

The philosophy behind SSADM is that a true picture of the system under study may be obtained by viewing it from three perspectives: processes, data and events. The analogy which is often used is that of an architect's drawing. From three drawings, a plan view (from above), an end elevation and a side elevation, the eye can create an idea of what the finished building will be like.

SSADM, which is in its fourth version (SSADM V4), is a very complex method, with precisely defined methods and exhaustive documentation. Briefly stated, the methodology has five modules which provide full or partial support to the development process over the whole of the system development life cycle (SDLC). The stages are in turn broken down into a number of steps which are decomposed into further tasks. The aim of the methodology may be summarized as follows:

- to represent the various aspects of the system (i.e. data, processes and events). It should be noted that the developers of SSADM describe it as data-driven
- to provide a means of controlling and managing large-scale information systems projects. This is the reason for the size of SSADM (there are 50 steps and over 200 tasks) and makes the application of the methodology rather prescriptive. A task covers a precisely defined area of work in considerable detail
- to be a framework to guide system developers and to be flexible in approach. SSADM avoids being over-prescriptive by allowing some choice in the way in which the guidelines are to be followed. The feasibility study stage is often regarded as being optional and there are versions of SSADM for small-scale projects (called 'micro SSADM') and for system maintenance. In addition, extra modules may be added to SSADM (such as strategic planning and socio-technical design techniques). Finally, the method is committed to change. SSADM is currently up to Version 4.0. Future developments would involve the merging of SSADM with other methodologies to produce a Euromethod which would be an EU standard.

The latest version of SSADM (Version 4) contains four types of components:

1 the **structure**, which describes the framework of the methodology in terms of its modules, stages and steps
2 the **techniques**, which define how the steps are to be carried out
3 the **procedures**, which are the project management activities (see Chapter 12) which are 'outside' of the SSADM methodology, but which are associated with its use
4 the **dictionary**, which contains the data about the data and the documentation produced by using SSADM.

The structure of SSADM V4 is shown in Figure 9.5 and is described briefly below.

- *Stage 0: The feasibility study module.* This is to evaluate the potential of a system development project to be a success before major expenditure of time or money is undertaken. It is also when the objectives of the proposed system, the criteria for success, and the 'boundary' of the system are decided. The use of critical success factor (CSF) analysis and cost–benefit analysis techniques are appropriate at this stage (see Chapter 13).

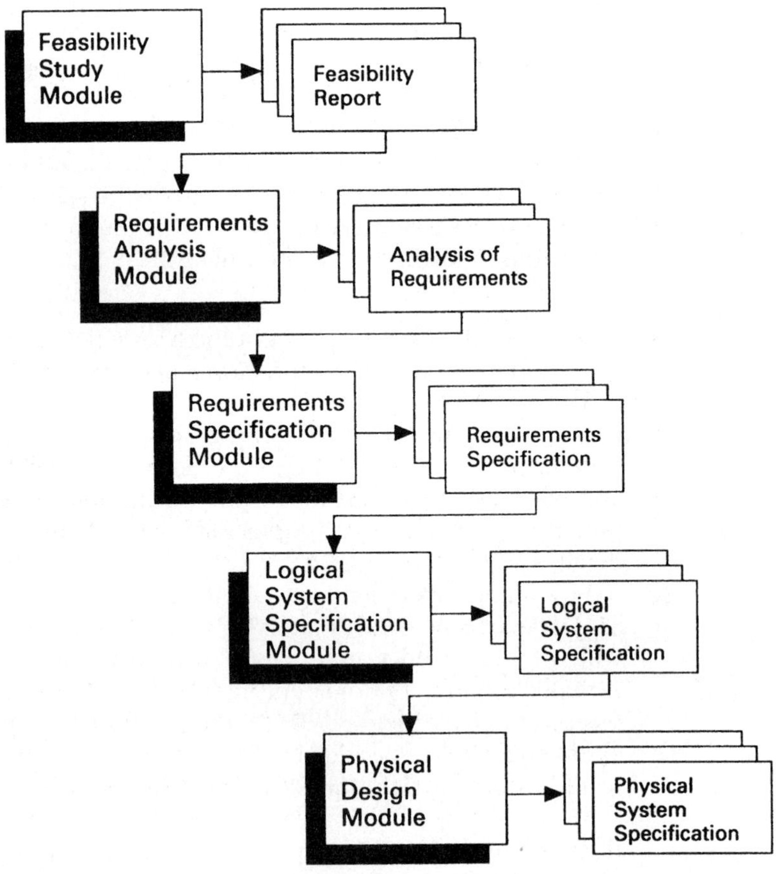

Figure 9.5 Modules and deliverables from SSADM V4 (after Ashworth and Slater, 1993, McGraw-Hill).

- *Stage 1: The requirements analysis module.* This is to investigate the current system in terms of its data, functions and events and to produce requirements for the proposed system by eliciting the users' needs. The stages are completed when the 'overview' specification of several system options is produced.
- *Stage 2: The requirements specification module.* The purpose of this module is to carry out a detailed analysis of the requirements for the new system based on the 'overview' produced in the previous module. The data, function and event modules are produced in detail at this stage and the objectives of the proposed system are made more explicit. Prototyping techniques (see Chapter 10) may be used at this stage to specify the human–computer interface.
- *Stage 3: The logical system specification module.* In this module the detailed specification of the processing and human–computer interface requirements of the proposed system are produced and the technical environment (the hardware and software) for the new system is described in 'overview' form.
- *Stage 4: The physical design module.* The purpose of this module is to turn the logical specification into a physical (i.e. real) design for the programs and data storage requirements which will make up the chosen system.

The following points are important in understanding SSADM:

- the current system is useful for understanding the scope and the environment of the new system
- there is a progressive expansion of detail throughout the various stages
- there is a separation of logical and physical systems; the new system is not constrained by the old system
- logical design always precedes implementation issues.

Database design issues

Any computerization project will involve the specification and design of data storage. The choice of storage media (disk or tape) is of less importance than the way the stored data items are to be organized and structured. The two storage design issues are whether to use *application-specific* files or a *database.*

Application-specific files

The traditional method of storing computerized data on large-scale systems, and the most common storage method for microcomputer systems, is on application-specific files. These are files (on any media) in which records are grouped according to a common purpose or dedicated to a single application. There will therefore tend to be a set of files dedicated to each of the major functions of business, for instance:

- **sales files**, usually a customer file and a sales order file
- **purchase files**, often consisting of a supplier file and a purchase order file

- **accounts files**, equivalent to the sales ledger, purchase ledger and general ledger
- **stock files**, also containing product details.

File security is maintained by the fact that these files are read from and updated by specific programs, to which access is limited, usually by a password, the programs being in a user account or accessible area.

Four types of file are commonly used for storage and data manipulation in an application-specific environment:

1. **masterfiles** contain permanent data for use in an application such as sales, purchasing or accounts. Some of the fields on such files will contain virtually static data (names and addresses, say) or data subject to update (for example sales to date, account balance, etc.). The latter will be updated either directly (on-line) or from a transaction file
2. **transaction files** contain temporary records of values and amounts input from a batch of source documents, such as invoices or customer orders. After updating the masterfile(s), the contents of the transaction file are overwritten by the next input batch
3. **look-up files** contain data which may be used for reference purposes, for instance price lists and mailing lists
4. **archive files** contain historical data which must be kept for legal or organizational reasons but which will not be referred to regularly.

Application-specific files tend to be associated with piecemeal systems development – a direct conversion of a department's existing manual to a computerized system, or a traditional approach which regards data as being owned by a particular department or function. Such file design can lead to the following problems:

- data may be duplicated on several masterfiles, for example the part/number/description may appear on purchasing, stock control and sales files. This is wasteful of storage space and gives problems with integrity and consistency between files
- other applications may be allowed intermittent access to a department's specific file, therefore avoiding duplication of processing or manipulation, but this can involve clashes when accesses are tried and lead to increasingly sluggish response times
- different applications may have different access or processing requirements, which may not be compatible. For instance, an invoicing program may access a stock file in sequential batch mode overnight, and a stock control program may access the same file on-line. The two types of application would suggest different types of storage media and organization. Care must be taken, because a choice of the wrong medium may lead to an inferior performance in one of the applications.

A system which is completely application-specific will appear to be a number of piecemeal systems, each having its own programs and files, each of which is owned by a single group of users. There will also tend to be massive duplication of data holdings and problems with data integrity and consistency between files, as the data items change due to processing.

Database management systems

Since piecemeal systems development and fully application-specific files were the order of the day, the DP and MIS environment has changed radically. Two major changes have affected file design: the trend towards *on-line systems* and the development of *database* systems.

- **On-line systems** require quick response times and necessitate a high degree of security and data integrity. The database approach implies that data items may be accessed in a number of different ways by different users. To this extent, the database approach goes beyond the use of commonly accessed masterfiles. The major difference is in the attitude towards data. The database approach implies that information (and therefore data) is regarded by the organization as a corporate resource. (The analogy which is sometimes applied is that of finance: it is used by many different people for different purposes, but it is owned and controlled by the organization as a whole.) In spite of this centralized control of the database, the use of the data is devolved. Individual departments may be responsible for providing, and in some cases, maintaining the accuracy of the data, but access to the database will be more free and flexible in the user's terms.
- A **database** is a collection of data organized in such a way that it can be regarded as a single unit. Important aspects of database use include the following:
  - **data independence** means that the item of data is stored for its own sake, and not for any specific use. An employee record, for instance, may be needed for production control, payroll, and health and safety purposes. These purposes may be specific, but the use of the data item is generalized and not optimized for one particular purpose at the expense of others
  - **controlled redundancy** implies that duplication of data within the database is kept to an acceptable level. The description of a stock item would therefore not appear separately on the purchasing, production and sales system files, nor would there be a need to access application files across system boundaries
  - **data integrity** means that when the facts about a data item change (for instance, a stock balance is increased), only one update needs to be made. The possibility of inaccuracies in the same data item on different files is therefore eliminated
  - **flexibility of use** of data is achieved by allowing the data to be accessed in many different ways. Generally, these can be categorized as routine accesses or *ad hoc* (one-off) queries.

All of these features are generated by the use of a DBMS, a complex suite of software by which the database is maintained and controlled. Most database applications will use a proprietary DBMS package, because the cost of producing such a system in-house with acceptable security provision would be prohibitive for most organizations. The features offered by a typical DBMS package may include:

- **record control**, which involves creating, amending and deleting records, the basic functions of file maintenance in a traditional system
- **access control**, which allows the processing of a complete file, or the retrieval either of individual records by direct access or of all the required records by selective sequential searching
- **security control**, which protects against unauthorized access and data corruption, and provides recovery and restart mechanisms after processing interruptions.

The implications of the use of a DBMS are that while security and control of data are centrally maintained, the use of the data is made more flexible, with the facility to enable user-determined access by query languages, and so on, as well as the routine applications programs, such as batch-run programs in a language such as COBOL (see Figure 9.6).

Advantages of a database

Experience of large-scale database use in a variety of organizations during the 1970s pointed out operational problems in the following areas:

- systems development projects in a complex environment were difficult to implement. Later systems methodologies, particularly those based on data analysis techniques, were introduced to help overcome this problem
- the performance of such systems often proved disappointing, as the technology was new and not well understood

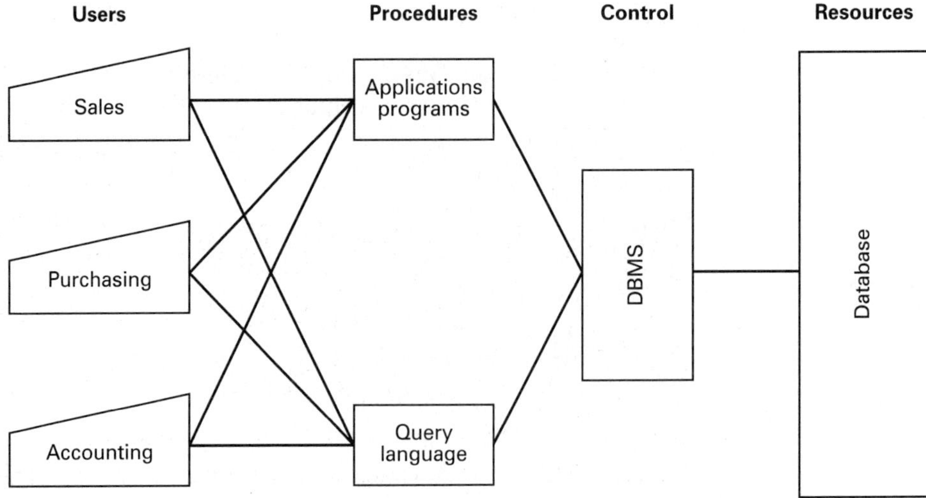

Figure 9.6 Use of a DBMS.

- high overheads, particularly fixed costs, were needed to support the database environment. The nature of a database implies large backing storage, much of it used relatively infrequently, and expensive security, back-up and recovery procedures due to the increasing dependence of most organizations on their databases.

In general, technological development and experience have mitigated these problems. The advantages which DBMS suppliers now claim for the user include the following:

- the view which is achievable through the use of the database reflects the corporate view which managers take of their organization. This view takes in data from a number of divisions, departments and sections. This enables the use of expert systems and DSSs to augment the query languages in supplying the strategic decision-making needs
- improved standards due to improved data integrity and better system project implementation. These are afforded by the ability to impose procedures and standards more easily in a single-project environment than in several piecemeal projects
- faster system development, due to the fact that, as organizations grow, more and more functions tend to be subject to computerization. If the database is set up at an early stage in a series of system projects, subsequent work may concentrate on computerizing tasks and functions as the developer is assured that the information is already available
- migration from one technology to another is easier, as the database is isolated from the applications (it is *application-independent*). This means that changes in the hardware or operating system will not cause major reanalysis and reprogramming, as would be the case with changing a system with application-specific files from, say, COBOL to Pascal.

Features of a DBMS

Most database systems will tend to include some or all of the following features:

- A **database administrator** (**DBA**), a management post with special responsibility for relating an organization to its database. The DBA must have a working knowledge of both the DBMS and the organization. The DBA will supervise the addition of new data items, ensure that the security and back-up procedures are being carried out, create user manuals and documentation, and supervise the data dictionary.
- A **data description language** (**DDL**) in the DBMS which will uniquely describe each data item in the database. This is necessary for standardization.
- A **data manipulation language** (**DML**) which will access and manipulate the data items for output.
- A **data dictionary**, which is a directory or catalogue of the data within the database. This is often called **data about data**. It will cover the data item description, how it is validated, who is allowed to access it and which programs may use it. A data dictionary may stand alone outside the DBMS in

some very large-scale systems, in which case it will be called a **data dictionary system (DDS)**. Examples are ICL DDS and IBM DD/D. DDSs can supply useful management information such as costs and statistics about data use, but may themselves incur considerable overheads.

Some DBMSs are dedicated to a particular physical system; others will support a number of alternative file organization methods. The method chosen, often the choice being made by the DBA, should relate to the type of system and the use to which it will be put. A batch-mode system using a very large-scale database could have a hierarchical structure at the logical level and an indexed sequential structure on magnetic tape at the physical level. A system requiring direct access to individual records within a database (i.e. a system expecting a low hit rate), such as an on-line enquiry service using a query language, may use a relational logical structure and a random physical structure, obviously on magnetic disk. Mass storage systems, which are suited to database use by virtue of their capacity, are not suitable for responsive on-line enquiries. The potential within these applications for the use of high-capacity laser disk storage would seem to be enormous, as the technical problems of applying normal file processes to this medium are being overcome.

Object-oriented systems

An alternative environment to the conventional database, which contains data relevant to the enterprise but is separated from the programs which process it, is the object-oriented environment.

In an object-oriented environment system objects are stored which are analogous to 'entities' in a relational database design, but which contain *both* data and instructions. Rather than the instructions being applied from 'outside' the environment (through the access or query language) the objects contain their own instructions or programs (called 'methods') which control their use and which indicate with which other objects they can communicate. This is termed 'encapsulation' and means that, as objects are self-contained, object-oriented systems are very flexible. Objects can be added, modified or removed from the system without the unwanted side effects which can occur with conventional file or database structures.

From the design point of view, object-oriented systems have something in common with relational databases, as some of the design techniques are similar to data analysis (see Chapter 10). The greatest difference is that object-oriented systems depend on a class hierarchy, and properties of one class are 'inherited' by its sub-class. The creation of a new class of 'Employee' called 'Accountant' would automatically inherit some of the properties of 'Employee' such as name, age, address and payroll number. Other properties which are specific to 'Accountant' would be added at design time. Object-oriented languages – such as Eifel and Smalltalk – are sometimes said to be suitable for prototyping or rapid applications development for this reason. Having said this, however, most of the current object-oriented systems represent a radical departure from the sort of technology which most organizations use and they have, therefore, yet to gain widespread acceptance.

Summary

This chapter has focused on the conceptual or theoretical framework for the design and development of information systems. This framework and the related methodological approaches are important for an understanding of the more practical or operational-level aspects of systems analysis and design which we shall address in the following chapters.

Key points to be remembered include the following:

- the development methodologies are an attempt to model scientifically the things that are most important to the systems which the organization uses, and to show the relationships between each of those things. This modelling is likely to be most informative when there is a high degree of user participation
- the more refined the methodology, the more likely it is to become structured – in the sense that it identifies separate steps and places them in a coherent framework. The focus of the methodology may be on the processes and activities of the organization or it may be information engineering, i.e. data-driven
- files may be application-specific, but care should be taken to avoid piecemeal development and to develop systems as a part of a properly developed information strategy instead of simply converting each department's manual system into an automated system. Database systems may help an organization to centralize its data resources, thereby gaining significant advantages in achieving a strategic view of the organization's activities and improving standards of data integrity.

Self-test questions

1 Explain the term 'user-driven development'.
2 Distinguish between *entity* analysis and *function* analysis, providing an example of each to illustrate.

Exam-style questions

1 You are advising a medium-sized manufacturing company, which has decided to adopt a systems analysis and design method, on approaches to selection. As a preliminary, you have decided to list the available methods (e.g. SSADM, SADT) as major schools of thought or categories. Identify and describe two such categories.
2 The Managing Director of your company has asked you to produce a report on the way in which an information system (IS) development project would be carried out. You are required to draft a report describing the phases which make up the life cycle of an IS project based on an actual method (e.g. SSADM) or on a generalized life cycle.

(*All answers on pages 559–560*)

CHAPTER 10

Analysis and design: tools and techniques

The last two chapters explored the strategic framework within which system development takes place and the broad methodologies which guide the analysis and design process. We shall now examine the detail of the tools and techniques that are available to support the practical process of implementation.

We look at the basic tools used to capture the strategic intentions of the organization and to enable the programmers to produce functional software employing the SSADM approach. The design techniques employed to facilitate interaction between the automated system and its users by producing quality output or friendly dialogue are then reviewed.

We go on to consider in detail the primary procedure specification techniques (both graphical and narrative) that are used to define the operations which the system must carry out. The chapter concludes with a look to the future and discusses the extent to which these detailed design and analysis processes can be automated.

Tools and techniques

The tools and techniques used by systems analysts have been developed over the years to assist in addressing two basic problems:

1. describing and summarizing a mass of highly detailed information, such as the results of a fact-finding interview or a set of instructions on how to write a computer program
2. communicating and documenting a description or a design to others who may have different skills or levels of knowledge, such as a user who is a member of a project team or a systems analyst who may become involved in designing a replacement system in ten years' time.

Such tools may be said to make up a basic **toolkit** which has evolved through improvement in use. The result is that broadly similar tools appear in slightly different forms in many of the common systems development methodologies. But by examining the detailed content of each methodology, it is possible to categorize methodologies and their tools into traditional process-driven or data-driven. This arises because systems development tools generally fall into three categories of use:

1 Describing the **current physical system**, for instance the formal organization, the flow of documents between departments and the things that people do to the documents.
2 Describing or designing the **logical system**, whether for the existing system or for the one undergoing development. The logical system is the fundamental set of tasks that exist independently of the administrative conventions of an organization. For instance, it does not matter whether credit checking is carried out by someone from the sales department or someone from credit control. The important things, if a converted system of limited scope is to be avoided, are the data and the processes which act on it. A logical system is therefore a system in its raw state.
3 Designing and describing the **new physical system** and forming the working drawings for the new system, the detailed specification, and the documentation which will describe the system's workings as it becomes invisible in use. This will cover the areas of program specification, data storage design and the human computer interface (HCI). A variant of the latter is prototyping.

SSADM differs from some other system development methods in that the same set of tools is used for both logical and physical analysis and design. These tools are diagrammatic and tend to be used whatever 'template' of SSADM (e.g. microsystems or maintenance) is being applied. The basic tools are:

- data flow diagrams (DFDs)
- logical data structures (LDSs) also known as entity-relationship models
- entity life histories (ELHs).

There are other tools which may be used within SSADM, for example data normalization and project management techniques. The point about a system development method is that clear guidelines should be given to the analyst and user as to when and how to apply the tools. SSADM provides support with documentation, standards and periodic review meetings.

The context diagram

DFDs form the basis of the decomposition techniques which are used in most structured methodologies. While the conventions and symbols may vary between methodologies, the basic purpose is the same: the description of the flow of data between entities, processes and data stores. The highest level DFD (that which shows the overall system as a process) is called the **context diagram** or Level 0 DFD. The context diagram defines the system boundary and shows how information enters and leaves the system. It also shows with what external entities (things outside the system) the system has transactions. The symbols of a context diagram are shown in Figure 10.1.

A context diagram (Level 0 DFD) for a college system is shown in Figure 10.2.

The decomposition process begins by defining the major processes (probably the business functions) within the system. This is done by using data flow diagrams.

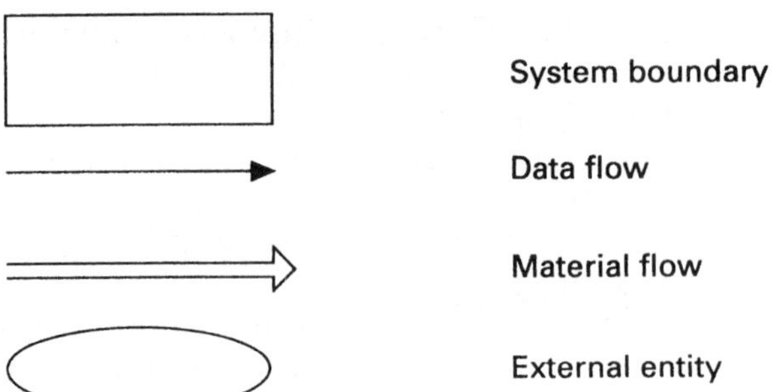

Figure 10.1 Context diagram symbols.

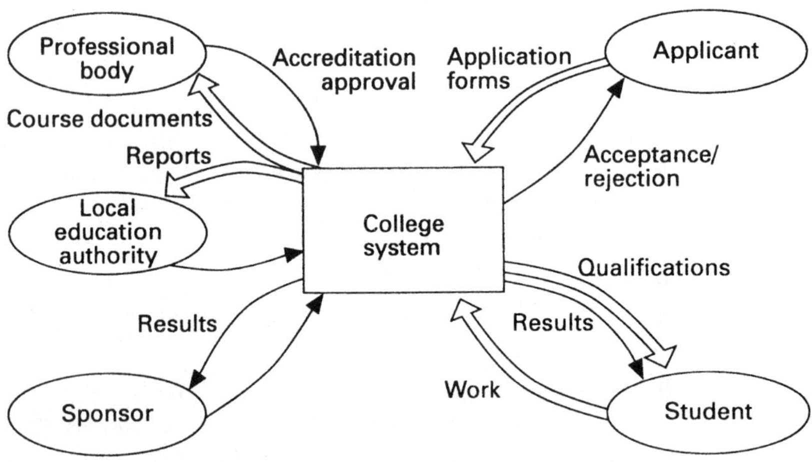

Figure 10.2 Context diagram.

Data flow diagrams (DFDs)

The decomposed DFDs enlarge on the information which is contained within the context diagram. They have the following purposes:

- showing where data items are stored
- defining what changes information
- making sure that analysis is thorough and complete
- providing a basis for software specification.

The symbols for decomposed DFDs are the same as those for the context diagram, with the additions shown in Figure 10.3.

A process is a task, activity or operation which changes or manipulates data. For this reason, the names which describe processes are always active verbs. They are never a physical location (a department, say) or a responsibility (a clerk, for

Figure 10.3 Data flow diagram symbols.

example), although some analysts may include this information in the top right-hand corner of the process box when detailing the **physical system**.

A datastore is where data items are held within the system. Obviously, at a higher level, the major datastores will be *aggregated* (as in the case of student records) and *persistent* (a record will last as long as a person is a student). At lower levels of decomposition, the data will be *detailed* (for example, examination results) and may be *temporary*. A physical datastore may be a card index or a computer database. Logical datastores are **abstract**: it is the content of the data which is important, rather than their form or how they are stored.

Each DFD will take one of the processes from within the higher-level DFD and draw a further DFD of its internal processes. Subsequent levels repeat this process until a level is reached at which the process can be described in sufficient detail to design and code a computer program from the description. DFDs are therefore used at various levels:

- **top-level DFDs** show a broad view of the system with very little detail to confuse the issue. This helps in the objective setting process and in communications between management and the analysis team
- **low-level DFDs** allow each sub-system to be examined in isolation from the rest of the system, aiding project management and communication between the users, analysts and software engineers.

Figure 10.4 shows an example of a high-level DFD relating to the college system.

When a process is decomposed, the numbers which are used to identify the sub-processes use the identifier of the higher level process as a prefix. If process 1 (at Level 1) is decomposed, the lower level processes would be 1.1,1.2, and so on, and the Level 2 processes would have the identifiers 1.1.1, 1.1.2, etc. This is shown in Figure 10.5.

It is customary to decompose processes to an elementary level. This will vary according to the application being studied but relates to the level of detail which is required and the clarity with which the process can be described in structured English or pseudocode (known in SSADM as **elementary function descriptions**).

Logical data structure (LDS)

Logical data structuring (or entity-relationship modelling) is the most important tool within the technique known as **data analysis**. This can be used as the

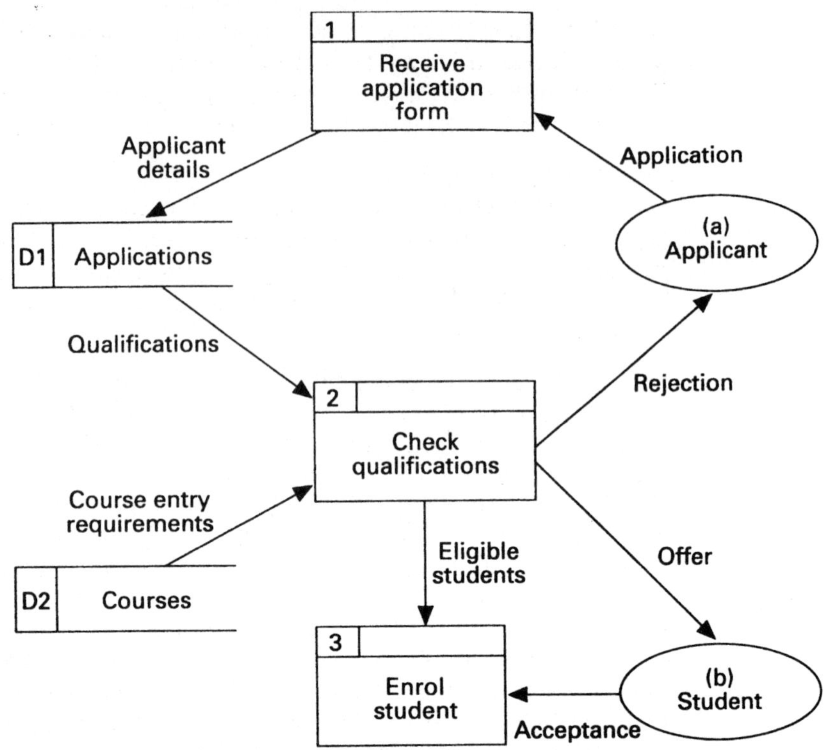

Figure 10.4 DFD for college enrolment system.

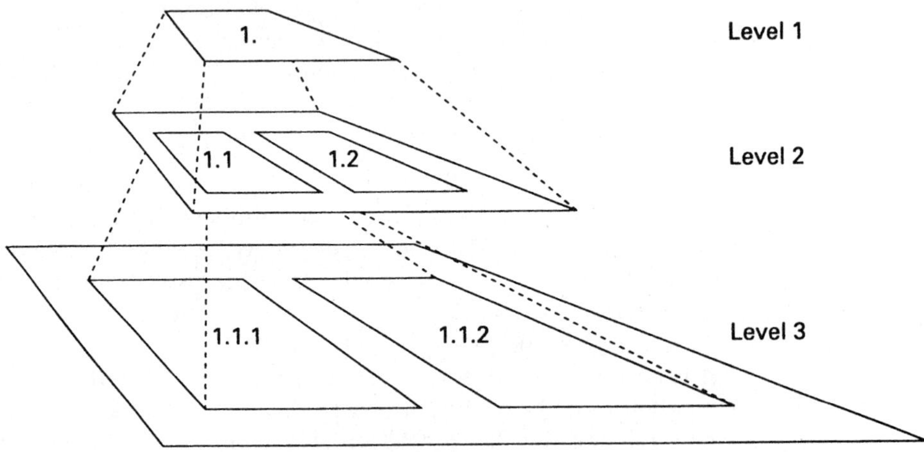

Figure 10.5 Decomposition of DFDs.

mainstay of a methodology, as with CACI or Information Engineering, or as one of a number of tools in a methodology such as SSADM. LDS use three basic concepts:

1 **entity types** or things which are of importance to the organization
2 **attributes**, which are facts or data about entities
3 **relationships**, which are the logical links between entities. In the physical model, these will form the access paths between data items.

An entity type is a generic or classification term, such as 'student'. The individual, 'J. Smith', is an entity *occurrence* which will need to be uniquely identified by one of its attributes, called the **identifier** or key, for example a customer account number. It is possible to describe the logical data system in some detail: for instance, the degree a relationship between entity types may be of three orders, as shown in Figure 10.6:

1 **one-to-one** (1:1) means that an entity occurrence, relates to only one other entity occurrence, as in the statement 'student IS ON course'
2 **one-to-many** (1:n) means that an entity occurrence may relate to one or more occurrences as in the statement 'course CONTAINS subject(s)'. (This is the commonest degree of relationship)
3 **many-to-many** (m:n) means that a number of entity occurrences may relate to one or more entity occurrences, as in the statement 'subject(s) HAVE lecturer(s)'.

The degree of relationships is important for later systems design, as incorrect physical constraints can be imposed by incorrect analysis. For instance, if 'customer PLACES order' were to be recorded as 1:1 instead of 1:n, the system might be designed to allow each customer to place only one order at a time – obviously not what the sales department would want. Also, relationships may be expressed in

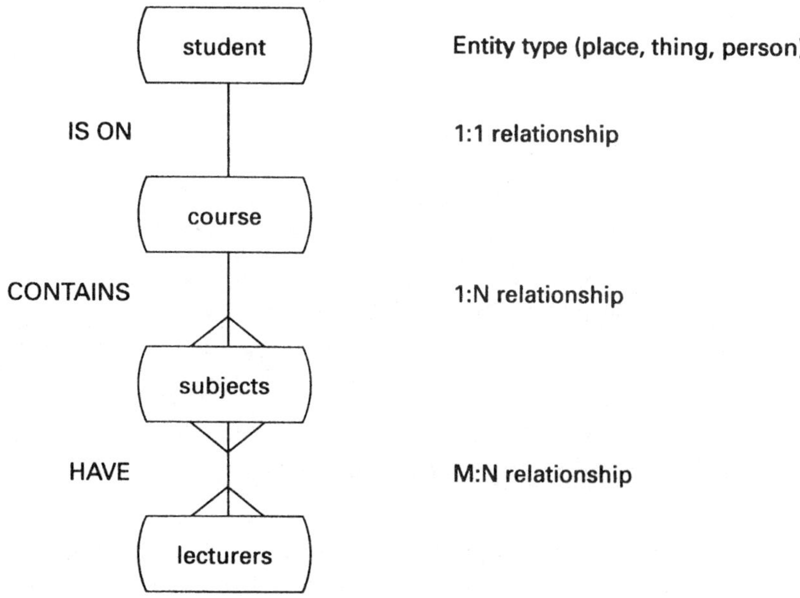

Figure 10.6 Degree in relationships.

terms of their **optionality** – whether or not all occurrences of an entity type may take part in a relationship. A relationship may therefore be:

- **mandatory**, where all occurrences of an entity type must take part in a relationship with another entity type – as in the statement, 'course (must) HAVE student'
- **contingent**, where some occurrences of one entity type may take part in a relationship with another entity type, as in 'student (may) ATTEND interview'
- **fully optional**, where some occurrences of both entity types may take part in a joint relationship, as in 'interview (may) LEAD TO job offer'. (Students may attend interviews which do not lead to job offers, or get a job offer without having to attend an interview.)

Optionality has important effects on the design of the system, as it can indicate the number of accesses for read or update which may occur between two data items (see Figure 10.7).

Logical data structuring is a process of refinement during which the analysts' and the users' understanding of the logical system may be improved. It is not unusual for a model to go through four or five phases of refinement before being declared satisfactory.

The process will include both removing redundant entity and relationship types and adding **intersection entity types** to overcome the fact that many DBMSs will not cater for m:n relationships. The entity type 'course-module' has been created in the 'college system' model as an **intersection** entity type shown

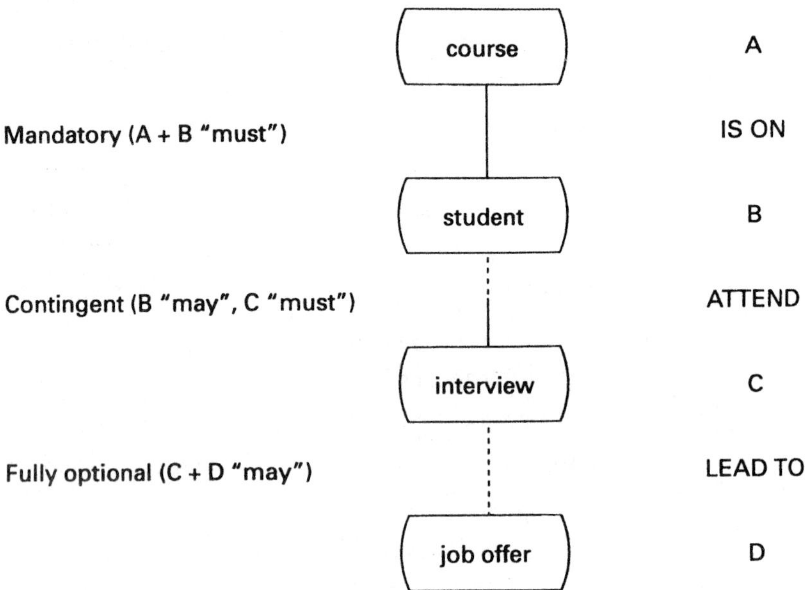

Figure 10.7 Optionality in relationships.

by two bars across the relationship line. This could be prompted by the analyst's experience or by the normalization process. The finished model has attributes assigned to it (later **normalized** into tables) and is then documented into the data dictionary. The LDS conventions which are used in SSADM are as shown in Figures 10.8 and 10.9.

The attributes which will be assigned to the entity types in the form of tables may be derived from the entity-relationship model (the top-down method) or from the more detailed data flow diagram (the bottom-up method). Either will produce a table of attributes.

Relation data analysis (RDA)

Relational data analysis or *data normalization* is used to divide raw data up into tables which contain a minimum of redundant data and which have a measure of independence – they are linked only by shared **identifiers**. The advantages of normalization are claimed to be:

- there are reduced data storage requirements in the final physical system
- access paths in the logical system are rationalized, with possible improvements in response times
- processing (writing, updating and deleting) of data items should have minimum disruption.

The technique is common in many methodologies (i.e. structured, process and data-driven) and may be carried out in its own right in setting up a **data**

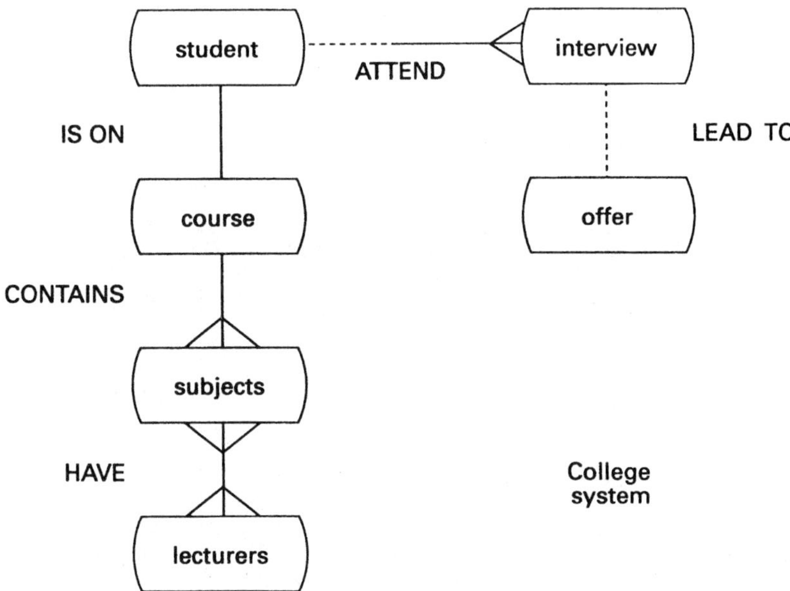

Figure 10.8 Entity-relationship model before refinement.

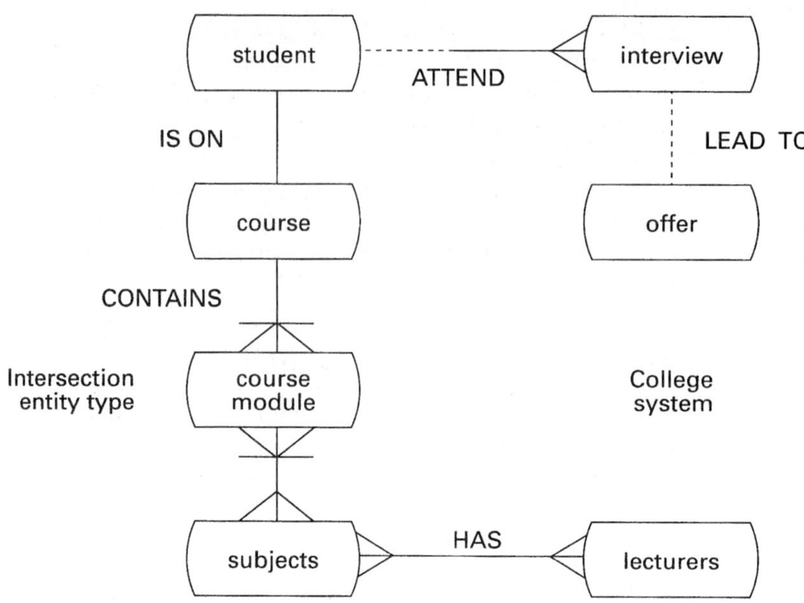

Figure 10.9 Entity-relationship model after refinement.

dictionary system (DDS). Normalization is particularly suitable where a **relational database** schema is to be used.

Normalization produces sets of tables called **relations**. Each column in the table is called an **attribute**, and each row is called a **tuple**. For instance, the items in the attribute columns for Business Studies in COURSE table (see Figures 10.10–10.13), are called *attribute values*. Usually the features desired from normalization can be attained by three manipulation steps. These are transformation into first, second and third normal form:

Course code	Course name	Level	M. code	Subject name	Year	Max. mark
BS10	Business Studies	B.Sc.	BS101 B5102 BS103	Accounting 1 Accounting 2 Marketing	1 2 3	50 100 150
LA10	Law	B.Sc.	LA101 LA102 LA103	Statute 1 Statute 2 Contract	1 2 3	50 100 150
CO20	Computing	M.Sc.	CO201 CO202	Programming 1 Programming 2	1 2	50 100

Figure 10.10 COURSE table in un-normalized form.

Course code	Course name	Level	M. code	Subject name	Year	Max. mark
BS10	Business Studies	B.Sc.	BS101	Accounting 1	1	50
BS10	Business Studies	B.Sc.	B5102	Accounting 2	2	100
BS10	Business Studies	B.Sc.	BS103	Marketing	3	150
LA10	Law	B.Sc.	LA101	Statute 1	1	50
LA10	Law	B.Sc.	LA102	Statute 2	2	100
LA10	Law	B.Sc.	LA103	Contract	3	150
CO20	Computing	M.Sc.	CO201	Programming 1	1	50
CO20	Computing	M.Sc.	CO202	Programming 2	2	100

Figure 10.11 COURSE table in first normal form.

Course table

Course code	Course name	Level
BS10	Business Studies	B.Sc.
LA10	Law	B.Sc.
CO20	Computing	M.Sc.

Course module table

Course code	Module code
BS10	BS101
BS10	BS102
BS10	BS103
LA10	LA101
LA10	LA102
LA10	LA103
CO20	CO201
CO20	CO202

Subject table

Module code	Subject name	Year	Max. mark
BS101	Accounting 1	1	50
BS102	Accounting 2	2	100
BS103	Marketing	3	150
LA101	Statute 1	1	50
LA102	Statute 2	2	100
LA103	Contract	3	150
CO201	Programming 1	1	50
CO202	Programming 2	2	100

Figure 10.12 Tables arranged into second normal form.

1 **First normal form (1NF)** ensures that all the attributes are discrete – in other words, they may stand alone. This is achieved by the removal of repeating groups such as subject details in COURSE table. Ostensibly, this is done by filling in the gaps, but effectively it means that the tuples may be rearranged without losing their meaning (Figure 10.11).
2 **Second normal form (2NF)** involves splitting off into separate tables any attributes that do not depend wholly on the identifier. Thus, by referring to the COURSE table in 1NF, it will be seen that the attributes Subject-Name, Year and Max-Mark depend on the identifier M-Code, not on Course Code, so a new table SUBJECT is formed. Likewise for the COURSE-MODULE table (Figure 10.12).
3 **Third normal form (TNF)** extends 2NF by making sure that all attributes which are not themselves identifiers (non-key attributes) are independent of one another. Again, this involves splitting off into new tables, as is done with the attribute 'year' on which Max-Mark depends (Figure 10.13).

Course table (course – 3)

Course code	Course name	Level
BS10	Business Studies	B.Sc.
LA10	Law	B.Sc.
CO20	Computing	M.Sc.

Course module table

Course code	Module code
BS10	BS101
BS10	BS102
BS10	BS103
LA10	LA101
LA10	LA102
LA10	LA103
CO20	CO201
CO20	CO202

Subject table

Module code	Subject name	Year
BS101	Accounting 1	1
BS102	Accounting 2	2
BS103	Marketing	3
LA101	Statute 1	1
LA102	Statute 2	2
LA103	Contract	3
CO201	Programming 1	1
CO202	Programming 2	2

Figure 10.13 Tables arranged into third normal form.

Data dictionary

Data dictionaries are closely linked to DBMSs and 4GLs and, as such, are part of the movement called **user computing**. In this context, it means handing over the use of data to the functional departments (accounts, sales, and so on) while the DP or systems department assumes responsibility for its control. This control is effected, usually by the **database administrator (DBA)**, through the use of data about data – this is what the data dictionary contains.

The data dictionary may be a piece of software or may be maintained manually but, in either case, it will usually contain at least the following information (see Figure 10.14):

- entity, relationship and attribute descriptions with cross references to functions
- process descriptions (events and functions) with details of frequency and timing and cross reference with entity types
- programs which may write, update or delete a data item
- data structure, the format (numeric or alphabetic) and length of the data item
- ownership of the data item (for instance, security and privacy constraints).

Most commercial DDSs offer considerably more sophisticated features than this, such as operational statistics on the use of access paths and processing activity on data items.

A data dictionary is central to the concept of the management of data as a corporate resource. The use of a data dictionary underpins the setting-up and

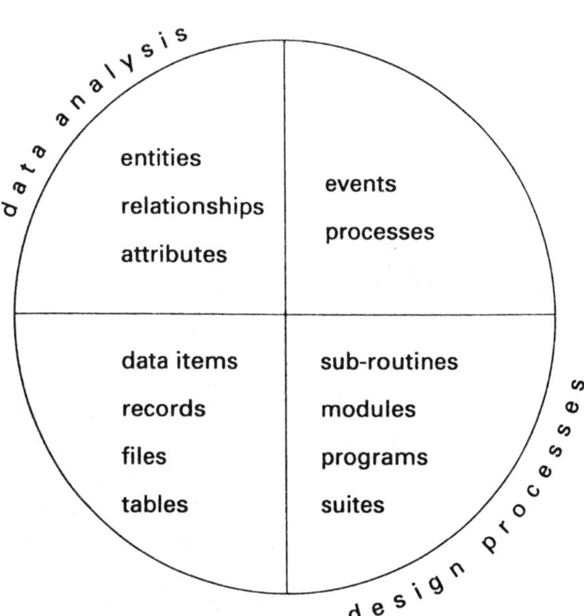

Figure 10.14 Elements of the data dictionary system.

maintenance of most of the analysis and design tools mentioned in this chapter. Since by definition a data dictionary is relatively easy to automate, it is now common to find one at the heart of computer-based systems development tools such as **analyst workbenches** and **integrated project support environments (IPSEs)**.

Entity life history (ELH)

The previous techniques are intended to model the following aspects of the system under study:

- the ways in which information flows around the system (DFDs)
- the information that is held within the system (LDS)
- how the information is structured (RDA).

SSADM caters for one further viewpoint of the system: the way in which information is changed over time. The technique employed to do this is the application of entity life histories (ELHs). An ELH is a diagram showing the changes to an entity which can take place between its creation and its deletion. This 'life' is represented as a series of events which cause the entity to change through a series of permitted states. The ELH therefore links with the DFD (it is the processes which change the entity) and the LDS which records the entities. As the changes of state are recorded as attributes, there is also a link with the RDA technique. A simple example of an ELH relating to the entity Student is shown in Figure 10.15. The basic notation of an ELH models the three types of process logic – *sequence, iteration* and *selection* – as described below.

1 **Sequence**. The boxes at each level of the ELH read from left to right. In the Student example, an instance of the entity (for example, Jane Smith) enrols

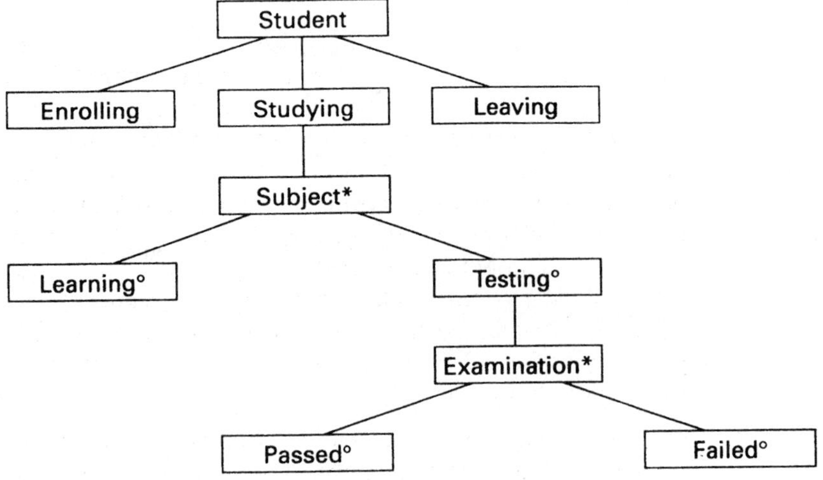

Figure 10.15 Entity life history for entity 'Student'.

(her record is set up), then studies (for a period of time) and then leaves (her record is deleted).

2 **Iteration** (or **repetition**). The box 'Subject' with an asterisk (*) in the top right-hand corner shows that the student can study a number of subjects between enrolment and leaving. Similarly, the tests for each subject will consist of a number of examinations.
3 **Selection**. The boxes with circles in the top right-hand corner show that for each subject, a student may be either learning or testing but not both at the same time. Similarly, for each examination, the student may either pass or fail (but not both).

When the four techniques have been applied, the 'three views' of the system have been modelled and the diagrams can be checked with each other to give a 'perspective view' of the system. Examples of the checks could include the following:

- check between DFDs and ELHs: the DFD for the student enrolment system in Figure 10.4 should be checked against the LDS in Figure 10.9. For example, the existence of the process 'enrol student' and the external entity 'Student' implies that there must be an entity 'Student' on the LDS. Without this, the DFD is incorrect
- check between the LDSs and ELHs: there must be an ELH for all the major entities on the LDS. The ELH for 'Student' in Figure 10.15 relates to the entity of the same name on the LDS in Figure 10.9
- check between ELHs and DFDs: the events in the ELH act as triggers to the processes in the DFDs. For instance, 'enrolling' on the ELH in Figure 10.15 starts the process 'enrol student' on the DFD in Figure 10.4.

This process is an important control during the systems analysis and design phases as the consistency and completeness of the models can be checked.

Case tools

It has long been something of a joke in industry that the last department to be 'computerized' in many organizations is the computing or IT department. In a famous case study an international credit card company installed more than 10,000 PCs in user departments as an aid to efficiency and productivity but had just three PCs in all of its IS offices – which were used for word-processing program documentation! Clearly, if computer technology can aid productivity in the functional areas, it might have a role in the IT development process.

This thinking led to the development of the first computer-aided software (or systems) engineering (CASE) tools. The aim of such tools is to produce cost-effective software in a carefully controlled project management environment – a part of what has been called 'the information systems factory' idea.

The commonly accepted categories of CASE software tools are:

- **integrated project support environments (IPSE)** which link project management and system methodology tools to provide support for project workers (analysts and programmers) over the whole of the ISD life cycle

- **redevelopment tools** which include software to support the restructuring of program code as a part of the maintenance programme, *reverse engineering tools*, which generate design documentation from existing code from one application language to another
- **workbenches** which are derived from the working tools of structured systems development methodologies and project management.

Usually the term 'workbench' is taken to mean a workstation and a set of software tools. Workbenches tend to be of two kinds: **analysts' workbenches**, which support the earlier stages of the development cycle, and **programmers' workbenches**, which generally support program design, coding and testing. The former are known as 'upper CASE' and the latter as 'lower CASE' tools.

Analysts' workbenches may offer generalized features, or may be dedicated to the techniques of one particular methodology. A typical system would allow the automatic construction of ERMs, the production of function models or data flow diagrams, and the normalization of data, and many systems contain report and dialogue design facilities. The most well-known analysts' workbenches are probably Excelerator by Index Technologies and Automate Plus by LBMS.

A programmer's workbench will typically offer features such as a code library and code generator. A **code library** will contain modules of pre-written, pre-tested code which may be re-used and combined in a variety of ways. A **code generator** is capable of producing programs in a high-level language from program specifications (probably in the form of decision tables or pseudocode – a variety of structured English). Most programmers' workbenches contain diagnostic aids and fault-tracing tools to reduce non-productive time spent on program testing and maintenance. The most widely used system is possibly PDF (Program Development Facility), which will produce source code capable of being compiled in a variety of high-level languages including COBOL, Pascal and C.

Prototyping tools

The alternative to systems development methods which follow the conventional systems development lifecycle (SDLC) is to involve the users in the design process to a greater extent. A variety of this approach is **prototyping**, which combines the user-driven approach with the use of 4GL tools.

Tools which are used for system prototyping (or, more simply, prototyping the human–computer dialogue) must be user-friendly and capable of producing rapid results. Report generators, application generators or screen painters and even the basic query language are often used as prototyping tools.

Report generators

A report generator (or writer) is a piece of software which uses a 4GL or form-based screens to design the heading and contents of a report. The program is capable of retrieving the necessary data from the database carrying out the processing (i.e. calculations) on it and structuring the layout of the report according to the user's needs. Obviously, the layout and contents of the report may be altered until the user is completely satisfied. The 'SQL*forms' feature of Oracle is a powerful report generator. Most small database packages (such as Ashton Tate's dBase IV) now contain useful report generators.

Screen painters

A screen painter is a more flexible tool than a report generator, allowing the designer to create the screens which make up an application by 'painting' the required layout on to the screen. The painter can create windows, menu bars, icons, 'buttons' and graphics, and text can be built in. The prototype of the application is only 'finished' when the user is happy with it. Some application generators may then be compiled to produce 3GL code.

Query languages

Most computer-based systems now support the use of a query language or 4GL. Such implementations lend themselves to prototyping because they are **non-procedural**: the designer states what the output from the program needs to be rather than how the program should work. This approach to prototyping may be seen as less specialized than the use of a report generator but may still produce successful prototype applications. Some ingenuity has been shown in the use of applications packages (particularly spreadsheets) for prototyping, although there are obvious limits to what can be achieved by using this approach.

Advantages of prototyping tools

In some ways, prototyping as a systems development method may be regarded as a separate issue from the use of the tools. The advantages of the use of the tools centre around their ease of use. This has several implications:

- prototypes may be created quickly and 'scrapped' just as quickly. Therefore, system developers are encouraged to experiment and not to feel constrained by technical details
- the experimental nature of prototyping tools means that they can be used for clarifying the system requirements where they are not well defined. This is particularly useful where a new application is being developed (i.e. there is no existing manual or computer-based system)
- users may become involved in system development to a far greater extent than is usually the case with structured development methods and 3GLs. In theory, this should cut out a whole area of possible misunderstandings between users and programmers, and radically change the role of the data processing or systems department. In practice, relatively few organizations have handed over responsibility for systems development to the users and

their prototyping tools. What has tended to happen is that applications are developed by the analyst and user using the tools in partnership, with the user providing the design input and the analyst/programmer providing the technical expertise in the use of the tools.

Automated development tools

One of the problems of applying a structured methodology to a typical business situation is the number of steps, techniques and diagrams, the complexity of the cross-checking procedure and the amount of documents. The purpose behind the introduction of structured methodologies was the control of complexity in system development, yet they introduced a new variety of complexity – that of the methodology itself. One of the ways in which developers have sought to control this complexity is by providing automated support for the development process. This is called **computer-aided systems** (or **software**) **engineering (CASE)** and the software tools are called **CASE tools**.

It is convenient to categorize CASE tools by their coverage of the system development life cycle (SDLC). Tools which address the whole of the SDLC tend to be called **integrated project support environments (IPSEs)**. Tools which address the first part of the SDLC (requirement analysis and data modelling) are called '**upper case**' tools. Tools which concentrate on the latter part of the SDLC (design and implementation) are called '**lower case**' tools.

Integrated project support environment (IPSE)

An IPSE, by definition, attempts to provide a set of techniques and the software tools which follow a set methodology (such as SSADM). The Alvey Foundation, which was formed to examine the role of the UK in IT development, recognized the importance of IPSEs as a central component of a future concept of the 'information systems factory' – an automated process for the rapid development of high-quality computer-based systems. Most current IPSEs (for instance, Philips' MAESTRO) are multi-user systems and contain at least the following features:

- **Graphics tools** which will allow the system designer to produce the diagrams (e.g. DFD, LDS and ELH) that are contained within the development methodology.
- **A help facility** or some sort of guidance in following the stages of the methodology. For this reason, CASE tools tend to be dedicated to and support a particular methodology.
- **A forms generator**, which will allow the system designer to produce the necessary documents and forms. As with the diagrams, these will tend to conform to the standards of the chosen methodology.
- **A system model** or **designer's data dictionary**, which will contain a 'picture' of the system as it is built up. The model contains data about the data which make up the system. This will describe the entities, attributes, data flows, processes, events and states.

It is possible that future developments in IPSEs will include some form of artificial intelligence (possibly an expert system) which will partially automate the systems analysis and design process.

Output and dialogue design

The aspect of the physical system design with which the user is likely to become most involved is the design of *hard copy output* – that is, computer-generated documents such as invoices and reports – and *user–computer dialogue*, the combination of input and output which enables the user to interact with the computer.

The design of output must begin with a choice of medium; basically the choice will be between printed hard copy and screen 'soft copy'. The next choice should then be the selection of suitable output hardware. Finally, the physical design of the output of dialogue can take place. The choice of the medium will involve the following factors:

- how the information will be used, whether as a formal contract document such as a purchase order, or as a desk report which may be filed and compared with other reports, for example, an end-of-month cost-centre analysis.
- the complexity of the information contained in the report. Physical constraints such as the size of the CRT screen (80 columns × 24 rows of characters) may dictate a larger medium
- the period of usage of the report – whether the information will be used for a brief period, or will be referred to over a long time. Since backing carries operational overheads, long-term storage on paper at the user's site may be more attractive
- other outputs from the system. A suite of programs will usually contain a number of reports which will use different media. These reports should have regard for and complement each other, taking into account the other factors.

The matter is slightly complicated by the use of computer output microform (COM), which is becoming increasingly common, particularly where documents must be stored long term for legal reasons.

Printed output design

The user may become involved in the design of two types of printed output: *pre-printed forms* and *computer-generated reports*.

Pre-printed forms

Examples of such forms include purchase orders, invoices and statements. Their design might begin as draft copies (usually a collaboration by the user and the analyst) which are passed on to a specialist graphic design company to create the necessary artwork. This will then be printed on to continuous stationery. The programmer will then write a program which will control a specified type of printer in the filling in of the variable data on the document.

Reports

These are free-format, but often must comply with organizational standards. It is important at an early stage in output design that the user sees what the finished report will look like. There are two ways to do this: the use of print layouts or prototyping. A **print layout** corresponds in terms of rows and columns with the finished report. Many organizations and all the major vendors have their own layout stationery. If the user does not like a particular report layout, it can be changed at this stage more cheaply and easily than when it has been programmed. A typical report design which aims to combine clarity with visual appeal will adopt the following standards:

- line 1 contains the run date and time of the report, the sender's name and the page number
- line 2 contains the report number and name
- line 3 states the time period which the report covers. This is particularly important in the case of accounting reports, and should clearly indicate whether the dates are inclusive ('For month ending...') or exclusive ('Up to ...')
- lines 7 and 8 contain **literals** (column headings) which should be centred and spaced clearly. Abbreviations are almost always needed, and effort should be made to ensure that these are understandable to anyone who may receive the report
- line 10 (and onwards) gives the information detail in brief form. The character 'x' is used to represent alphabetic characters, and '9' to represent numeric characters. The purpose of the fields of the characters is to indicate the totals which may be needed (perhaps up to £9999 for an invoice total) and the format required (such as part numbers). Often only the user will know these facts
- lines from 20 onwards include column totals which should be clearly indicated, for example by double spacing or underlining. It should be remembered that totals need more character spaces than individual lines.

A progressive approach to report design is to include a separate summary report containing all the totals. This is intended for routine despatch to the user, who may then request a detailed (full) report should more information be required. This is a variety of exception reporting.

Screen dialogue design

A well-presented printed report can ensure that the user gets maximum benefit from the information produced by a system. Screen dialogue, or the **user interface**, is possibly more important since it involves the user's direct interaction with the system. The user's perception of the system's success is highly coloured by the effectiveness of the dialogue design, so it is important that the knowledgeable user participates as fully as possible in the design process. In order to produce an effective screen dialogue, several factors must be considered:

- **The hardware** on which the interface is to be implemented. The ability to use graphics, colours and touch-sensitive screens is largely dependent on the choice of hardware. Also, a large memory allows more comprehensive help and error handling facilities to be built in.

- **The software** – specifically, the operating system which will be used. This will govern the facilities which can be built into the screen dialogue, from simple features like paging and flashing highlights to complex WIMP (windows, icons, mouse, pull-down menus) interfaces.
- **The application** for which the system is designed. A sales order entry system which involves capturing data from customer orders needs a different type of interface from a credit control system, which involves accessing detailed customer records.

Interface techniques

Possibly the most important factor when designing the dialogue for a particular application is the characteristics of the future users of the system. The system designer should consider such factors as the following:

- The frequency with which the user is likely to use the system. A 'casual' user will almost certainly require greater guidance and considerable prompting, since he or she will tend to 'forget' the dialogue.
- The user's familiarity with the application. For instance, an experienced bookkeeper will only have to learn the dialogue; a trainee will have to learn the application and the implementation.
- The familiarity of the user with similar technology. Having good keyboard skills can help someone to use a 'long-winded' dialogue which requires the input of many commands. For this reason, the interfaces to some executive information systems (EISs) are very simple, using on-screen 'buttons' and even touch-sensitive screens to keep keyboard use to a minimum.

This last point is important. Experience suggests that the general intelligence of the user is less important than might be expected. A less well-educated user may take longer to ascend the 'learning curve' and perhaps require more training but, once that individual is trained, frequency of use and familiarity with the system become the critical factors. To maintain this familiarity between application packages (often from different suppliers), the large computer manufacturers and software houses have tended to adopt interfaces which have the same appearance, no matter what package is being used. This 'standard interface' approach was pioneered by Apple Computers with the Macintosh interface and is typified by the Microsoft Windows graphical user interface and the IBM OS/2 operating system.

Some of the main points which should be considered when choosing a dialogue design include the following:

- there should be sufficient guidance from the dialogue itself, from an on-screen help facility and from printed manuals (if necessary). The dialogue should be free from jargon and doubtful abbreviations and should make clear what response is required in answer to a question

- the appearance and content of the dialogue should be consistent. Fields of data (such as dates, title of programs) should appear in the same places and the terminology should be standardized
- commands from the keyboard or mouse should be acknowledged on the screen. The user should know that instructions are being carried out
- verification and validity checks should be carried out on all input data and clear error messages should be shown to the user.

Having established these features, a modern screen dialogue design will tend to use a mixture of three interface techniques: form filling, menu selection or a WIMP interface. We shall look at these individually.

Form filling

This is an effective interface method where the application involves a lot of data capture – names, transaction values, stock items, and so on – and the hardware/software environment is unsophisticated. The user is shown an input screen consisting of a number of prompts and blank fields. A **prompt** will instruct the user to input data into the associated field. To accept this input, the cursor will be programmed to move from field to field (called *cursor addressing*). Usually a new field will be selected when the carriage return key is pressed. Often the user is not allowed to manipulate the cursor – all fields must be covered as part of the validation process. This is called **field protection** (see Figure 10.16).

The bottom of the screen is usually reserved for help messages and error messages. The former will attempt to provide an explanation of the input requirement for the field at which the cursor is positioned: for example, an instruction may be given to enter the date in dd/mm/yy format. Often the completed soft copy form will only be input to the file or database after the user has confirmed the contents as correct. A system with buffer storage and page-mode operation is therefore desirable.

Menu selection

This works well with more complex applications, such as systems which integrate the purchasing, stock control, sales and accounting functions. These are made more manageable by the hierarchical nature of menu selection; the user is allowed to select increasingly detailed option choices, each menu screen covering a different function (see Figure 10.16).

The option choices are represented by discrete program sub-routines, capable of independent operation. The individual screens within a menu module may operate in the form filling mode. It is necessary to have help functions, error messages and a 'return to main menu' feature available on screen at all times to allow mistake correction and log-out provision. Menu selection can be made clearer and more effective by the use of colour screens and a WIMP interface.

WIMP interfaces

WIMP (windows/icons/mouse/pull-down menus) interfaces are a feature of microcomputer systems, multifunction workstations and 4GLs. The WIMP interface is not created by the systems team but is an environment that allows the user to

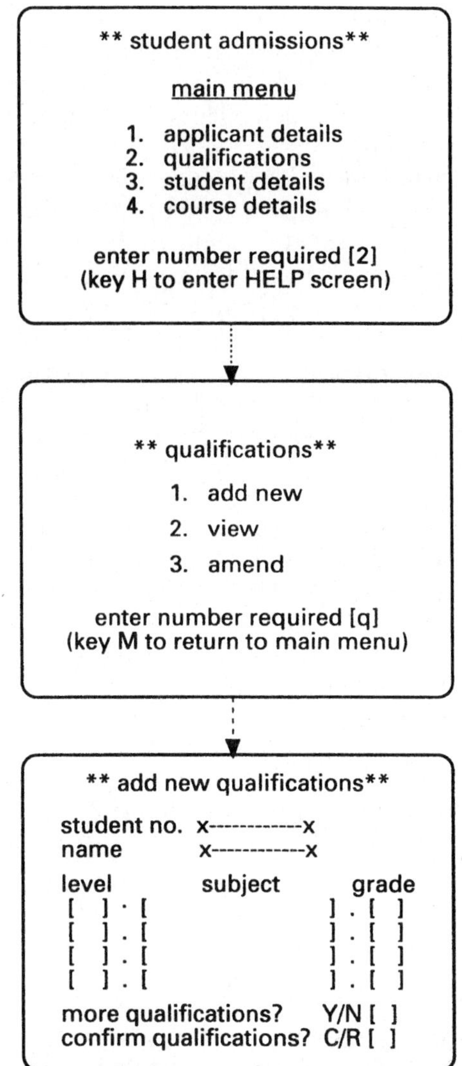

Figure 10.16 Menu selection interface.

manipulate the operating system as well as an applications program. One of the reasons for the increase in popularity of the Unix operating system in office applications is that WIMP interfaces have replaced the difficult commands on which Unix used to rely. A WIMP interface removes the need for the user to remember commands and file names, and largely removes the need for advanced keyboard skills.

- **Windows** are frames or screen compartments which can be dedicated to different applications and can be moved around the screen and changed in size by the use of the mouse and pointer. The user can therefore have several documents on screen at once and can bring into the foreground the one which is being worked on. It is possible to move from one document to another on screen, just as one could on a real desk-top. The user can file away non-current documents and even dispose of unwanted documents by the use of icons.

- **Icons** are small graphical symbols representing features of the system which can also be selected by the use of the mouse and pointer. For instance, a file is represented by a filing cabinet icon, a word-processing facility by a paper pad icon, and an electronic mail facility by an envelope or an in-tray/out-tray icon. An attempt has been made to simulate the everyday office functions with which the average business user will be familiar – including a waste-paper basket for permanent disposal.
- The **mouse** is a device which, when rolled around a desk, will move a pointer or cursor about the screen. According to which icon or menu item is selected (by clicking a button on the mouse) the pointer will accept text, open a window or produce line drawings. A **trackball** performs a similar function but does not require the user to find clear desk space.
- **Pull-down** (or **pop-up**) **menus** allow a complete change of function – for instance from word processing to spreadsheet to project management – without apparently leaving the program. The menus for each function are stored in bars (usually at the top of the screen) which, when selected by means of the mouse, expand to show all the processes that can be carried out on that function. Again, these can be selected by using the mouse, pointer and click button.

The first commercially viable WIMP interfaces were introduced by Apple Computers with their Lisa, and later Macintosh, microcomputers. These tended to be aimed at the desk-top publishing market. The advantages of WIMP interfaces in general, helping users who are not computer-literate to produce quality documents and screen designs, have led to a move towards this type of interface. The main industry standard WIMP front-ends are the Macintosh interface and Microsoft's Windows system, which is available for IBM PCs and compatible machines. IBM's new standard operating system OS/2 includes a WIMP interface using a **Presentation Manager** which resembles Windows.

Although WIMP interfaces tend to be more prevalent in PCs and multi-function workstations than in larger computer systems, they are a feature of many of the 4GLs which allow the user to produce screen dialogue by prototyping. The advantage of producing interface prototypes is that they can overcome one of the major problems of systems design – the inability of users to imagine what the interface will look like in operation. Even when users are encouraged to take part in dialogue design by producing their own screen layout sheets, there can be disappointment with the finished interface. Prototyping not only allows the user to see the interface on screen, but can simulate the operation of menus, cursor movement and screen changes in form-filling dialogue.

Procedure specification

The main tools of systems analysis and design, DFDs, LDSs and ELHs, are central to understanding, describing and documenting a system. However, in common with all the tools and techniques reviewed so far, they are insufficient for specifying the way in which a computer program should be written. Program specifications, also known as **minispecs** or **function logic descriptions**, are created by systems analysts and passed on to the software engineer or programmer along with the system documentation, particularly the screen and print layouts. From this document set, a program or programs can be designed and coded. A specification must therefore contain the following:

- sufficient detail to describe the operations which must be carried out – which records are to be addressed, what the identifier is to be, which fields are to be read or updated
- the order in which such operations are to be carried out and when they are to start and terminate
- actions which result from decisions or tests and are mutually exclusive; these are called **cases** or policies.

It should not be assumed that the programmer has any familiarity with the application. A programmer who has considerable experience of working on financial ledger systems may be able to produce correctly functioning code from a slack or vague specification, but successful programmers often move on, and the code may have to be maintained by a novice. The three main strands of system specification are as follows:

1. mathematical or formal methods, which are capable of extreme precision but are difficult for non-experts to understand and therefore to approve. (Formal methods tend to be used for specifying real-time systems with high-risk profiles; they may also be used for the rigorous testing of completed programs, called *program proving*)
2. graphical techniques, which represent the basic structure of logic
3. narrative techniques, which may involve the use of a variety of high-level computer language (a specification language), a variety of natural language, or something in between called **pseudocode**. Specification languages may form the input to application generators, thereby almost completely automating the programming process.

Since formal methods of specification and specification languages are not yet widely used, they are not described in detail in this section. The tools that are included are those that a user involved in information systems development is likely to encounter. Sometimes a specification will contain a mixture of some or all of these tools, as they all have different strengths and uses.

Graphical techniques

Graphical specification techniques are particularly suitable for indicating under what circumstances a task is to be carried out. They tend to be less useful for describing precisely *how*, as descriptive detail is lacking from all the tools in this category. The main graphical tools are decision tables, decision trees and program flowcharts.

Decision tables

These are often used for systems with complex logic, where many decisions and alternative cases might apply. They are relatively easy to construct and may have a built-in validation process that can check the consistency of the logic with which the table is constructed. Further, some programming languages may be coded directly in the form of decision tables linked by GOTOs or macros. Some code generation software will accept input from decision tables converted to computer-readable format. The commonest form of decision table is the **limited entry table**. It has a standard format and is constructed as follows:

- the conditions that can apply within the process logic are listed in any order in the condition stub
- the actions which the program must carry out in response to the conditions are listed below in the action stub, again in any order
- the remaining empty part of the table is divided into vertical strips, called **rules**, which are usually numbered. It is possible to calculate in advance the maximum number of rules which will apply; a table with three conditions will have 2 to the power 3 = 8 rules, four conditions will have 2 to the power 4 = 16 rules. If the actual number of rules exceeds this number, there is a logic fault. It is possible to fill in the condition entry by careful consideration of the logic, adding Y (yes) or N (no) as applicable. A simple, effective alternative is to begin by filling in half of the rule spaces in the top row with Y and the other half with N. The next row is split into two sections, and again half of each section is filled in with Y and the other half with N. The bottom condition row will therefore have alternating Y and N entries
- the action entry is filled in, with X being entered in a rule space if an action would result from the value(s) in the condition entry. An action can result from any number of rules from one up to the total.

The limited entry decision table in course administration (Figure 10.17) describes the policy for course admission at a college. The key points which can be gleaned from the table are:

- five GCSEs will qualify an applicant for the HND course
- two A Levels will qualify an applicant for both the degree and the HND courses
- a part-qualified applicant will be offered a place on a professional course, in addition to any other course(s) for which they may be qualified.

Note that the table is concise and unambiguous, but somehow lacking in information.

An **extended entry** table is an attempt to include more detailed information. Rules are replaced with conditions, which are often quantified. There are several forms of extended entry table of which one, concerned with examination results, is shown in Figure 10.18. Note that in this example, an [X] effectively means

Stubs	**Entries**							
Condition	**Rule**							
	1	2	3	4	5	6	7	8
Has 5 GCSEs	Y	Y	Y	Y	N	N	N	N
Has 2 A Levels	Y	Y	N	N	Y	Y	N	N
Part-qualified	Y	N	Y	N	Y	N	Y	N
Action								
Make HND offer	X	X	X	X	X	X		
Make degree offer	X	X			X	X		
Offer professional course	X		X		X		X	
Send rejection letter								X

Figure 10.17 Limited entry decision table.

'yes', and a [–] means 'no'. Extended entry tables have advantages where the conditions are related to one another, as their basic layout is more simple.

Decision trees

These are most often used in preference to decision tables where a system does not have too many decision points and each action tends to apply to only one case. In this respect, if not in its complexity, the course admission example used previously would lend itself best to a decision table. Decision trees can be formed from very complex process logic, but this is difficult as their construction tends to be less structured than that of decision tables. Normally, the tree is written (and read) from left to right, with a list of actions being recorded at the extreme right of the tree. It is conventional to structure the decisions so that each only has two outcomes. This can lead to several problems. The program itself may be inefficient if designed in the same way as the tree, and an action may relate to more conditions than the tree can show. This is the case with the example shown in Figure 10.19, which describes the course admission procedure.

Actions	**Exam marks**			
	<35	<40	40–69	=>70
Record exam failure and notify student	X	X	–	–
Arrange exam resit and notify student	–	X	–	–
Award exam pass and print certificate	–	–	X	X
Enter student for annual college prize	–	–	–	X

Figure 10.18 Extended-entry decision table.

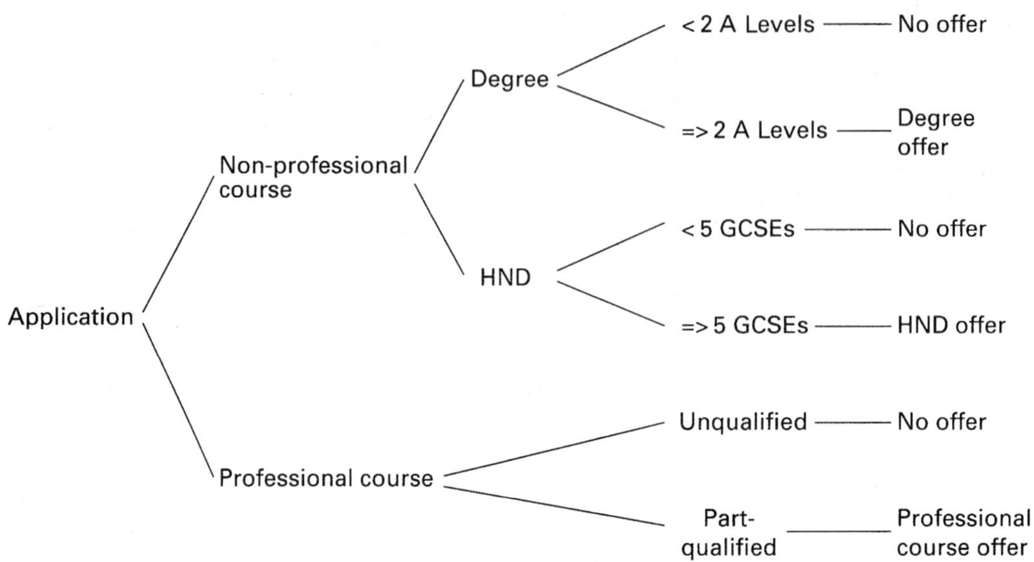

Figure 10.19 Decision tree for course admission.

Notice that, in the decision tree, to properly represent an applicant receiving offers for more than one course would require either more than one pass through the tree, for which there is no provision, or a much more complicated tree structure.

Narrative techniques

It is possible to write procedure specifications in natural languages such as English. It is possible to include great detail in such specifications – for instance, what input is to be used – but they tend to be ambiguous and to lack the logical structure of a flowchart, and therefore may be difficult specifications from which to write a program. At the other end of the scale, the use of a specialist specification language or pseudocode (structure text in JSP) makes for extreme clarity and programming ease but may be beyond the understanding of the average user. This is one of the most important aspects of system specification. as it may be the last opportunity to check the working of the new system before commitment to programming. Significantly, this event is often called **user sign-off**.

The most common narrative technique is called **structured English**. This is a sub-set of natural language which attempts to combine the narrative scope of English with the structure and specific nature of a graphical technique. Being fairly close to English, it is relatively understandable to the user. The technique is based on the use of keywords and logic structures. **Keywords** are words or phrases which have a consistent or reserved meaning, as in a high-level programming language. Typical keywords (dialects of structured English vary) are as follows:

- DOWHILE
- ENDDO
- IF ___ THEN ___ ELSE
- REPEAT ___ UNTIL
- ENDIF
- CASE (1,2, etc.).

Such keywords usually describe actions on data items which should be correctly specified within the data dictionary. The words are used to define the logical structure of a narrative. The actions which are carried out, for instance read/write and mathematical operations, are usually described in a terse form of English which allows the user some understanding. The basic logic structures which may be described are sequencing, selection and repetition (Figure 10.20).

- **Sequencing** implies that different (perhaps unrelated) processes occur one after another in a particular order.
- **Selection** describes a situation where a condition will cause a choice between alternative courses of action. This is called a **conditional statement**. Where one of a number of mutually exclusive actions may be chosen, **case statements** are used.

```
Sequencing:
COURSE ADMISSION
    Get student application
        Check academic references
        Check student qualification
    Send acknowledgement letter
    Add to application list

Selection:
    a)  Conditional statement
        IF student qualification = part qualified
            THEN offer place on professional course
        ELSE refer to Degree/HND course tutor
        ENDIF
    b)  Case statement
        IF course has vacancy
            CASE student qualification inadequate
                Reject application
            CASE student qualification adequate
            Make definite offer
        ENDIF

Repetition:
DOWHILE student application
    Check course offered
    Send offer letter
    Add to course list
ENDDO
```

Figure 10.20 Examples of logic structures.

```
EXAMINATION AWARD
DOWHILE student record
    Get examination details
        IF overall performance = pass
            IF average mark > 70
                THEN award distinction
            ELSE (average mark < 70)
                IF average mark > 50
                    THEN award credit
                ELSE (average mark < 50)
                    THEN award ordinary
                ENDIF
            ENDIF
        ELSE (overall performance = fail)
            IF average mark > 35
                IF attendance percent > 80
                    THEN record resit
                ELSE (attendance percent < 80)
                    THEN record fail
                ENDIF
            ENDIF
        ENDIF
ENDDO
```

Figure 10.21 Structured English specification for examination award function.

- **Repetition** means that an action will be carried out repeatedly as long as a condition exists or until a new condition applies.

The basic features of one variety of structured English are as follows:

- keywords are stated in capitals
- logic blocks can be named for reference or used elsewhere – again, capitals are used
- data elements as defined in the data dictionary are underlined
- indentation of text (or *nesting*) is used to show which sub-processes relate to a higher-level process.

In spite of these constraints, structured English should be written in a way which is understandable to users (Figure 10.21). DeMarco believes that many users are misled by structured English specifications, as the syntax is subtly different from natural language.

Summary

This chapter has focused on the tools and techniques available to aid the practical development of information systems. A range of systems analysis and design techniques is used within the common system development methodologies. A complete 'view' of a system may be derived from three models which are produced by using the common tools called data flow diagrams (DFDs), logical data structures (LDSs) and entity life histories (ELHs).

- Data normalization is fundamental to database design in allowing designers to show the relationships between data items.
- The development of comprehensive data dictionaries is necessary to provide a central record of the data elements used by an organization and of their role and characteristics.
- No matter how effective the computerized system may be in objective terms, the system will fail in human terms if care is not taken to design the output in the most user-friendly form. This applies whether the output is in hard or soft form.
- The programmer or software engineer requires precise instructions in the form of procedure specifications and system documentation if the best quality of system is to emerge. Graphical techniques are good at showing the order in which operations are to be performed; narrative techniques may include greater detail. The use of prototyping tools may promote a new way of involving users in the system development process and of clarifying user requirements which are not precisely defined.

Self-test questions

1. Describe what is meant by the term 'WIMP interface'.
2. Explain the contribution made by computer-aided system engineering (CASE) tools to resolving the problem of complexity in system development.
3. Identify the key factors involved in computer dialogue design.
4. Describe the role and characteristics of graphical specification techniques.

Exam-style question

1. Your company is planning to adopt a structured systems analysis and design method. The Managing Director has asked you to research and to report on two of the main analysis and specification techniques:
   - entity-relationship models or logical data structures (LDS); and
   - decision tables.

   Produce a brief report, using diagrams where appropriate, to describe these techniques.

(*All answers on pages 561–562*)

CHAPTER 11

System implementation and maintenance

The completion of the system design phase leads naturally to the phase of system implementation. The first part of this chapter deals with approaches to the effective implementation of systems and the issues that they raise. Subsequent sections consider the equally important activities involved in maintaining the system once it has been implemented. The processes of planning and managing the implementation and maintenance are discussed in the following chapter.

The system implementation phase involves a number of elements, including the acquisition of IT resources, the training of staff, the preparation of documentation and the validation of the new system itself. In our initial discussion we evaluate the alternative implementation strategies that are available to secure a smooth transition from the old to the new systems. We look at the options available to an organization for acquiring the necessary hardware and software, including purchase, rental and leasing. The factors and potential problems associated with the licensing of software for use in the system are also evaluated.

We go on to consider approaches to testing the system, both during the implementation phase and for the purposes of acceptance testing. The training needs of users and the factors involved in preparing effective documentation are examined. We finally give attention to the services required to support and maintain the new system once it is operational.

System implementation strategies

The term 'changeover' can cover a range of situations.

- Changing from a manual system to a computer-based system. This involves a considerable amount of disruption, with a major training effort and potentially significant changes to working practices. Nowadays such a change is quite rare in a medium-sized or large organization – most have some degree of computerization. With small businesses, it is a different matter. Recent studies show that more than half the respondents in an IBM/MORI survey in the UK had no form of computer-based system.
- Moving or 'migrating' from one computer implementation of the system to another. This type of change is a fact of life, as one generation of technology is replaced by another or as the system outgrows its current implementation.

- Enhancing an existing system (manual or computer-based) by adding extra features to it in response to changes in business requirements. A company may enhance its sales office system by adding a direct-line telephone sales operation. Considerable efforts are put into system designs to achieve **flexibility** in the form of systems that will cope with change.

A completely new system is quite rare, except where a new business is being set up.

Reasons for change

Organizations usually change their systems as a result of external pressure (reaction) and to exploit opportunities as part of the systems planning process (proaction). Given that all business systems have a finite life cycle of development – growth, maturity and decline – an enlightened organization will have some method of monitoring the effectiveness of its current systems, with a view to initiating their replacement in advance of their decline. This is necessary because, in spite of the use of CASE tools and rapid applications development (RAD) techniques (mainly prototyping, applications packages and 4GLs) there is still a lag between the identification of the need for a system and that system being designed, tested, converted and being made ready to 'go live'.

Figure 11.1 shows that, owing to this lag, it is necessary to start new system development (i.e. to begin the SDLC) during the mature period of old system use.

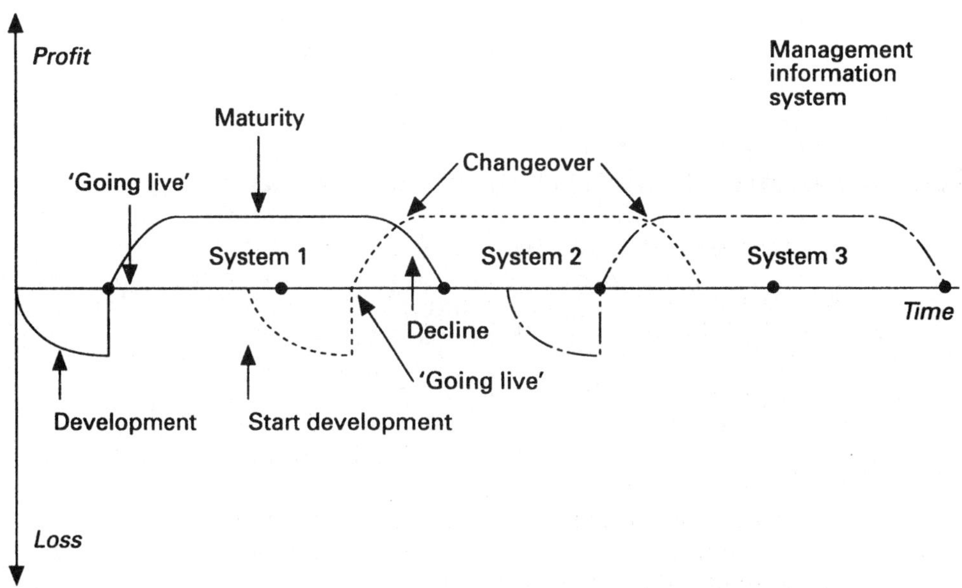

Figure 11.1 A life cycle of life cycles.

Triggers of changeover and decline

Migration or evolution from one system to another (for example, from a multi-user mainframe to a LAN with workstations) may occur naturally as part of the strategic information systems planning process. Alternatively, and more problematically, the changeover may be forced on to an organization by factors which are likely to precipitate a decline in the effectiveness of the existing system. Such factors may include the following.

- Changes in the operational environment, such as new legislation or changes in marketing opportunity. As well as creating the demand for new systems, such opportunities can render old systems obsolete almost overnight.
- Cost reduction programmes, brought about by efficiency drives or by poor company performance. On the whole, this is a poor reason to develop new systems and it can be the result of a knee-jerk reaction. Such exercises, with fewer staff working harder with more automated systems, are often referred to as 'downsizing' programmes.
- Response to competitive pressures (and possible business opportunities) arising from the actions of competitors in the business environment. Companies seek to survive or to grow by changing, and the systems development process is affected directly by such changes.

Prolonging the effectiveness of systems

It is important that the organization keeps a given application (such as the management information system in Figure 11.1) in the mature phase for as long as the application is of use to the company. There are several ways in which this may be achieved.

- **Flexibility** should be a design objective so that the implementation (particularly the software and data) can cope with changes in the application. A flexible system will therefore have a longer mature phase and will require fewer changes in the form of 'perfective' maintenance (see later in this chapter). In general, systems which use a relational database, applications packages and 4GLs are more flexible than systems which are implemented in 3GL with application-specific files.
- **Rapid applications development (RAD)**, using prototyping methods and tools in order to short-cut the systems development life cycle (SDLC). The effect is to shorten the elapsed time between 'start development' and 'changeover' in Figure 11.1. The response to the 'trigger for change' may come later in the system life cycle.

It is important to maintain quality during this process. Endless maintenance of a deteriorating system and hastily developed implementations are symptoms of an application which is unlikely to prove effective in the long term.

The first issue to consider is how to make the changeover from the existing set of organizational practices and methods to the new system. This is a question of planning. There are three possible routes for changeover.

- **Direct changeover** or 'cold turkey' (as it is known in the USA). Here the organization displays such confidence in the new system that the old may be immediately discarded in favour of the new. This is the strategy of greatest risk, as the new system may not perform satisfactorily.
- **Phased changeover** or **pilot running**. In this approach, the new system is tested in one department or area of operations. If the test proves successful, the system is introduced to the rest of the organization.
- **Parallel running**. In this approach, the new system is run alongside the old until it has proved itself reliable. The old system is then phased out. This method is the most expensive in both systems and staffing terms, but it is the most secure.

These routes are illustrated in Figure 11.2.

The method selected in part depends on the **risk profile** that attaches to the particular project. If it is a small, low-risk system – for example, the introduction of a word-processing system in a conventional, non-sensitive office environment – the organization might opt for a direct changeover. But if it is something like the organization's equivalent of the installation of a distant early warning system for a nation's defence, the managers will opt for some form of parallel running until it is clear that the new system can safely be left to run on its own. This raises the question as to what criteria to apply to quantify the level of risk. There are various factors:

- the size of the system
- the complexity of the system
- the newness of the technology
- the experience and skills of the users
- the percentage of the total budget for IT development that is involved in the implementation of that one system.

Thus, in financial terms, if there are ten projects with one tenth of the budget involved in each project, the level of risk involved in the implementation process is inherently less than having one project with one hundred per cent of one

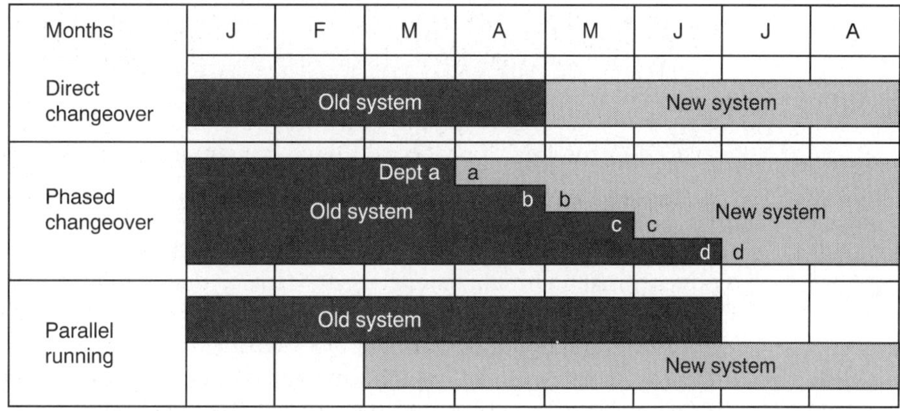

Figure 11.2 Changeover routes.

year's budget involved. But, in making the choice, it must be recognized that not all systems can be implemented by using parallel running. Hence, if the organization is not replacing an old system, the option is to create a back-up system to run alongside the new system – a modified form of parallel running.

Risk considerations

The task of producing the risk profile usually falls to whoever is sponsoring the project. This might be one of the senior managers, the steering committee or the benefiting user department. But, in practice, many less thoughtful organizations tend to have fixed policies on this issue. Some organizations may always adopt the practice of parallel running, regardless of whether it is justified in each case. This amounts to mechanical decision making and it will only be the successful strategy when the actual circumstances happen to fit the rule. In all other cases, the organization may be acting quite unreasonably. If the organization is going to take more objectively justifiable decisions, the question arises as to whether there is a cost–benefit surplus attaching to the changeover options.

In first considering the planning of the implementation, it should be recognized that the greater the apparent benefit which is to be derived from the new system, the greater the pressure which will be experienced by the management to implement that system. Managers must not allow themselves to rush the process because the level of risk will rise if standard safeguards are not applied. In deciding which strategy to adopt, the key factor is the predicted **cost of loss**. The managers must attempt to quantify the costs of failure. This will include development, implementation and maintenance costs on the one hand if the system has to be written off, and the cost of failure on the other through lost orders, lost production, and the possible need to recreate the system itself and/or the data.

The rule is that the greater the cost of loss inherent in the prospective system, the more significant the contribution to the risk profile. A system with a high cost of loss will have a high-risk profile. Each organization must establish the level of criticality in the use of the system and the potential cost of recovering from each disaster (for more detail, see later chapters). In assessing the level of criticality, time is one of the most important factors. Some parts of the system may be less critical than others, and a greater time may be allowed to pass before they are restored. But other parts may make such a vital contribution to the well-being of the organization that their restoration must be given a high priority. In this evaluation exercise, it must be acknowledged that all information has an intrinsic value. For example, a mailing list may be lost; such a resource will have to be replaced or the loss of orders will have to be made up from another source.

Staffing the system

The management must also consider the *human aspect*. To a certain extent, if a conventional manual system is to be partly or wholly automated by using a 'parallel run' approach, the problem is that the organization will be required to continue the employment of the staff who are ultimately to be replaced by the machine. This gives rise to real problems of security and motivation. Alternatively, if there is no existing system, the organization will have to recruit and train the relevant staff. This might be on a temporary basis to run a manual back-up system during the period of testing, or it may be intended as a permanent addition to the staffing. The training issue becomes far more severe if the organization intends direct implementation rather than parallel running because, in the latter case, there is time to phase in the system and to train the staff. Parallel running also enables the organization to monitor the performance of the new system more effectively and to produce more relevant data about the comparative benefits of the system.

What happens at the planning stage?

The management team will discuss the possible strategies and pick the change-over options which most closely fit in with the organization's needs. In taking decisions about the larger systems, the organization will probably have to attribute a priority to each of the component elements of the implementation, because some aspects of the system may be more important in fulfilling corporate objectives than others. It may be useful to create a data model of the organization so that, in line with the cost–benefit analysis, more informed choices can be made about the order in which the different parts of the system should be made operational. Self-evidently, the things which are of most benefit to the organization should be installed first. But it must be recognized that there may be difficulty in attempting whole-system development as opposed to piecemeal development. On paper, it is relatively easy to complete an idealized and ambitious analysis exercise, to document it by producing a data model, and to arrive at a system which cannot be implemented in cost terms because the budget is not big enough. So, if the organization is to aim at the ideal, it has to impose capital rationing, given that computer systems are in competition with other departments for funding.

Ranking

The probable result is that only a part of the system can be installed at any one time. Those parts of the system which are deferred must then be ranked. The NCC have developed a system which is called **weighted ranking** (see Chapter 7). This is simultaneously the most easy and the most difficult of concepts. All the affected user departments are contacted and are asked to review the list of those elements left to be installed. Each group of users will then give marks out of ten for each part of the residue and for the desired quality of the system at each stage in the implementation process, in terms of speed of response, size of storage and the extent to which it achieves the users' objectives. The trouble with the weighted ranking system is that it is pseudo-scientific: it seeks to give objectivity to a choosing process based on a series of self-interested opinions. The result is a set of numbers given by a computer following detailed calculations which mere humans might be tempted to take as an authoritative and absolute representation of what is otherwise mere prejudice and opinion.

The decision-makers then move on to the more detailed planning. There are two elements which tend to run together:

1 testing
2 training.

Testing

Testing may apply both to the program and to the system. It may also be the formal process of acceptance testing. The former is a part of the systems development life cycle. It first looks for syntax and logic errors in the programs, and then moves on to a second stage which is designed to establish the performance characteristics of the system in terms of:

- the response time and similar practical matters
- the robustness of the system (the testers will try to break the system)
- the ease with which the system can be reactivated following failure.

The link between acceptance testing and training is that of the chicken and the egg. Hence, it is the responsibility of the users to undertake the acceptance testing, but if they cannot make the system work, they cannot test it effectively. So, before any major computing system is installed, a core of the users must gain a basic understanding of the system's intentions.

Training

The cost of training offered by many manufacturers and suppliers is high and the training itself is often not done well. Part of the reason for this is that some suppliers, in order to make the sale, cut their margin on the system, or the initial margin is not generous. The cost of the training cannot be subsidized out of the sale and is therefore offered at the economic price; but many purchasers are not prepared to pay this price. The result is that much of the training which is thrown in with both hardware and software acquisition tends to be minimal. Generally, it will be unusual for the training to include background information, and refresher courses (which can be so vital to consolidate and extend understanding) will always have to be paid for separately. Moreover, those who market the products need not be the best trainers. The system developers may be too close to their product and may not realize what the users will find difficult. The sales staff who demonstrate equipment may not be able to modify their sometimes aggressive selling style to become good teachers. In an attempt to meet the gap in the market, specialist organizations now offer training courses at conference centres or in-house. But courses where the trainees do a lot of work under supervision are labour-intensive and therefore tend to be expensive.

Acceptance testing

If the staff already have the expertise, or training has given sufficient insight to allow work to begin, acceptance testing may be undertaken. Presumably, in their initial requirements specification, the users have laid down minimum performance standards. If they also provided the designers with test data packs, it would be possible for the design team to test each part of the package thoroughly before it was allowed to go live in the system, although final acceptance testing must always be by the end users in the 'real-world' situation. The underlying truth is that no system can be properly judged purely by looking at the results. The literal correctness of the processing or manipulation functions undertaken by the system is only a part of the standards to be applied. The key factor in acceptance testing is the way in which the system works – it is *how the system achieves the results* which makes it acceptable or not. Any mechanical approach intended simply to determine whether the system achieves the results in the way indicated in the requirements specification, and not to take account of the users' response to the system, is potentially doomed to fail.

A computerized control system was introduced at one of the Royal Dutch Steel's strip-rolling plant at Hoogeveen in Holland, but production fell disastrously because, although the system produced excellent results in dry testing, the operators failed to communicate successfully with the system in the real-world situation. Similar problems have been reported in respect of air traffic control systems, and were identified by the Kemeny Commission into the Three Mile Island nuclear plant accident as one of the factors contributing to the accident. There is only one way in which problems with the human interface will be identified: when real-life operators (as opposed to computer designers and programmers) are told to make it work. This can be one of the advantages of prototyping, because the users can be given an early insight into the look and feel of the future system.

Documentation

The organization must not only co-ordinate the functions of testing and training, but also must parallel those activities by the creation of documentation. Documentation is used for a variety of purposes.

- It is a useful reference point for training purposes. In many ways, the ideal systems would always have comprehensive help facilities, so making detailed documentation unnecessary, but few products genuinely aspire to this ideal. Whoever is to operate the system will have to develop routines and habit patterns which are efficient, and documentation which supports the acquisition of efficient day-to-day skills is desirable.
- Once installed, the detailed operation of the system must be described in clearly worded user manuals. This descriptive material will perform two functions:
  (a) It will act as a form of reference manual and describe what the system is. This account is likely to be very detailed, and will provide detailed technical explanations of the less commonly used aspects of the system and of the more advanced uses and facilities.
  (b) It will act as an aid to immediate problem solving by telling the users, both experienced and inexperienced, how the system is supposed to work. For this purpose, the results of the testing and the detail of the test packs used in dry testing should be included in the system documentation.

Interim summary

The co-ordination of all the tasks of training, testing and the creation of documentation is a part of the overall project management (see Chapter 12). As a necessary precondition to the implementation of each phase of the project, the appropriate environment must be created and the necessary hardware installed.

The precise sequence of events is likely to vary in each project, but the necessary constituent elements are:

- to acquire
  - the hardware
  - the software
  - the appropriate level of staff competence
- to install
  - the hardware
  - the software (which may also be seen as an aspect of staff training)
- to negotiate or arrange
  - maintenance;
  - services, which, in the case of a large system, involves the creation of a protected environment including air conditioning and uninterruptable power supplies (see later). Specialist services include consultancy, time sharing and bureaux facilities.

Hardware and software acquisition

The hardware is comparatively limited in function as compared to the software, which can be designed to achieve great flexibility. The total package required is:

- the computer hardware itself and appropriate peripherals
- the software, both operating system and applications packages
- documentation
- maintenance/support.

Acquisition procedure

Following the design phase, the organization must specify its requirements in terms of hardware (together with a suitable support environment) and of software. This is best achieved by identifying the existing data flows and showing how the new system should work. In one sense, the decisions should be taken by those users who will have to make the resultant system work (obviously with guidance from those with technical expertise). But there are dangers.

- The choices made may not be compatible with those made by other departments and a piecemeal system may come into being.
- Through inexperience, the managers may select a package which is less than ideal, or may negotiate terms for supply which are disadvantageous to the organization.
- Each department may be struggling to reinvent the square wheel, whereas centralization of decision making and the pooling of experience can reduce the chances of repeating the mistakes of the past.

The organization's ultimate decision-makers are actually going to answer four deceptively simple questions:

1 what is going to be required?
2 why is the suggested degree of automation appropriate?
3 when should the new system be installed?
4 does the organization have enough competent staff to make it work?

Tendering

Given that the organization has identified and justified what it needs in the design phase (to reduce costs, to improve the quality of data available to support decision making, to improve profitability, etc.) and has fixed the timescale, it may then issue an invitation to tender (ITT), which is known as a 'request for proposal' (RFP) in the USA. This document should be sent to as wide a range of possible suppliers as is sensible, given the scope of the overall project. It will normally describe:

- the context in which the new system is to operate
- the functions which it is to perform
- the proposed timescale of implementation
- the performance criteria that will have to be met in terms of volumes, of transactions, data handling facilities, output required, etc.
- the target price
- whom to contact within the organization for further details.

The potential suppliers will also need to know what criteria will be applied to evaluate the proposals and what the proposal deadline is. The serious contenders will exercise their right to ask for more details of the system requirements or to suggest modifications so that their products might be more acceptable.

In due course, assuming that the market is responsive, a number of tenders will be received. These should be analysed for the features most useful to the organization's needs. But many suppliers are not that helpful. There is a tendency to send out standardized product information rather than to make a specific response to the immediate invitation. In such cases, the organization should seek to identify those products worthy of further investigation for inclusion in a short-list. It may be possible to arrange for the selected suppliers to attend to give a detailed demonstration of their products, or some form of trial might be arranged. This is increasingly necessary because most acquisitions are software-led rather than hardware-led, that is they are based on the ultimate capacities of the system rather than the hardware on which the applications will be stored and run. Program testing should be run using packs of test data simulating average and worst-case conditions. Such testing, alongside discussions with other users, should allow an informed decision to be made on whether the package should be adopted for trial use and acceptance testing.

Involvement of users

The use of the package by those who are ultimately to be responsible for making it work is essential if a detailed understanding of the product is to be achieved. Simply seeing test results produced in a one-off test is not a reliable basis for taking a final decision. Those involved in this last stage must be committed to the process. There must be real effort to make the package work. If the staff are unmotivated, either a decision will have to be made because the deadline has arrived rather than because detailed results are available for evaluation, or the trial will fail. Engaging in the trial must involve the same level of energy as installing and using the package productively. Ironically, the right attitude is frequently induced because many suppliers charge for the use of their products during this phase. This addition to cost overheads does focus the mind of the commercial organization, even though the charges can usually be set against the ultimate purchase sums or rental charges payable.

The decision to purchase or lease

Organizations may acquire the hardware by one of the following methods.

- **Buying**. This may take the form of outright purchase – where title is immediately vested in the purchaser – or the time of the transfer of ownership may be delayed, say until payment has been made. One of the main problems in buying the hardware is that the new owner assumes all the risks of ownership (so maintenance agreements should be made), and the terms of any agreement should be carefully studied to see when the risk of loss is transferred, so that a decision can be taken as to whether to insure. The primary advantage of buying is that because the system is owned, the operator has significant freedom to modify the system to meet the requirements of the organization.
- **Renting**, sometimes known as *direct hire*. Here legal title in the hardware remains in the manufacturer or supplier during the term of the agreement. Historically, many mainframe computers were only available on a direct rental basis from the manufacturer, the philosophy being that manufacturers needed protection from financially unreliable customers. Today, the direct rental customer has to ensure that an adequate environment is provided for the equipment and, when the system is installed, will pay a charge which is divided between the cost of hire and the cost of maintenance. The hire charge will be fixed for a minimum period and will thereafter be subject to review. The service charge is reviewable at any time, subject to notice being given. This reflects the fact that maintenance is labour-intensive and reasonable increases will always be allowed. If the manufacturer defaults and fails to provide the hirer with the level of availability required, notice to terminate the agreement can be given. The period of notice is to allow the hirer an opportunity to plan the replacement of the service. The other form of rental agreement is for short-term or intermittent use – typically where the user wants to try out a system or to cover during a breakdown or similar emergency. It is common to find rental agreements for smaller pieces of equipment.
- **Leasing** (usually termed an *operating lease*). In principle, legal title remains in the supplier, but the lessee may be given an option to purchase during the term of the lease or at some predetermined time. This is a long-term commitment to the supplier, but it has the advantage that the longer-term risk of obsolescence is assumed by the lessor. Further, one of the biggest advantages from the point of view of the lessees is that, because the acquisition is done through the leasing organizations as third parties, the

purchasing tends to be done by one or two very big purchasers. They have commercial 'muscle' and can therefore get the best terms, the benefit of which may be passed on to the lessees.

Given the change in the ratio of cost as between hardware and software (decreased cost of hardware, and increased cost and availability of software) the direct rental of the hardware is not as attractive an option as it used to be. The increase in the number of leasing companies has also reduced the attractiveness of the direct rental agreement, and flexible leasing (where the lessee is offered the option to upgrade the system at regular intervals) is becoming the more common form in the commercial world.

If the organization decides to buy the package, the initial investment costs are high. Thus, either the capital sum paid out must be replaced out of future revenue, or the loan to the organization must be financed. This cashflow effect must be set against the fact that if the package is kept operational after the end of the payback period, there is a long-term saving as against the continued payment of a rental or hire charge. Whether this is achievable will depend on the degree of obsolescence in the package. Such is the rate of change in the world of high technology that some aspects of the system may be considered out of date within months of acquisition. Moreover, all the risks of ownership and upkeep have to be borne by the organization so that, even if the organization immediately pays for the package out of capital, there will still be an increase in overheads through operational, maintenance and insurance costs.

The standard lease runs for between three and five years, with some suppliers offering an option to purchase at the end of the specified period. To the extent that no initial capital outlay is required to lease equipment, this option makes automation a more accessible proposition. It also has the advantage that the revenue implications are more regular and predictable, with most rental and leasing agreements including the cost of maintenance in the sum payable. In general, leases are written so that the longer the period of hire, the lower the rental payable. Alternatively, the amount of the rental can be varied during the period of the lease. Thus, the sum payable might be reviewable after a specified period of time, or specific sums might be included for identified periods. It is relatively common to find a higher charge in the initial years while the package is most use, and a lower sum as the package moves towards obsolescence. But whatever the sums payable, as a part of the organization's running costs, the rental or leasing charges are tax deductible.

Balancing options

There are several problems in adopting the leasing option, and care must be taken during the period of negotiation with the lessor organization to ensure either that the best terms are achieved, or that planning can begin at an early stage to avoid the worst effects of the agreement actually made. At a strategy level, there are balancing decisions to be made between the three options of buying, renting and leasing. Organizations do not have to buy, rent or lease the whole system. The management must look at the speed at which the technology is likely to go out of date. For the equipment which is most volatile and tends most rapidly towards obsolescence, it is probably better to rent. Data capture terminals, for example, are liable to rapid obsolescence – so it is better to rent the terminals, even if the organization buys the central processors. But this may be offset by the ability to upgrade systems within leasing agreements. In the more flexible operating leases, the lessor initially puts out new equipment at a full rental. As and when upgrades take place, the lessor seeks to find a new lessee for the old equipment at a reduced rental. The organization ought to develop a plan and discuss it with the leasing organization before signing. Otherwise it may be difficult to achieve a properly phased development of the affected systems and it will certainly be difficult to get accurate cash flow planning.

Upgrades

If an organization buys or rents from the manufacturer, it is normal to receive regular system upgrades. This will produce incremental improvements in the quality of service supported by the system, and will go some way towards reducing the damage inflicted by the tendency towards obsolescence. Because the majority of leasing organizations are independent of the manufacturers, they will not necessarily have the technical expertise to upgrade all the systems leased. For example, a number of merchant banks offer this leasing facility to their customers, but are unable to offer any technical back-up or support. Alternatively, if the expertise is available, there may be charges made for the upgrading which make the economics of the improvement marginal. The result in both cases is that the lessee has to operate an increasingly obsolescent system over the period of the lease. Financially, the organization could be badly placed with high overheads but reducing revenue realized through the use of the system. However, as indicated, many modern leasing agreements allow the lessor to update the equipment, usually through replacement.

Terms of warranty

If there are technical problems with the package, a whole series of difficulties may be faced by the lessee. Because the lessee is not the purchaser from the manufacturer, none of the standard guarantees and warranties included in the contract of sale are enforceable. The general rule of privity of contract states that only the immediate parties to a contract can enforce its terms. Similarly, statutory remedies which might otherwise be available under the Sale of Goods Act 1979 are not available as of right. Some protection may arise by virtue of the Supply of Goods and Services Act 1982, but all prospective hirers of hardware and software should carefully consider their legal position before entering into the agreement. It is therefore important to examine the terms of the lease on package reliability to see whether there are express terms which deal with the rights of the lessees. Moreover, the lessee may well have assumed the responsibility of maintenance during the period of the lease. The result is that there may be an enforceable duty to continue to pay the rental, while perhaps paying out substantial sums to repair the equipment. If the lessee tries to opt out of the agreement by seeking to exercise the right of termination, there are often very high (but not penal) sums payable to compensate the lessor for the loss of expected income from the residue of the period under the lease.

Acceptance testing

The tests have to be designed to show:

- **functionality**: does the package actually meet the performance criteria set out in the requirements specification?
- the appropriate **response times** and throughput in volume terms achievable with reasonable user friendliness
- system **compatibility** with the existing installation
- sufficient **robustness** and **reliability**, with a reasonable ease of service and maintenance if there has been the opportunity to acquire this information – quite often trial periods are not long enough
- a satisfactory modularity and facility for future expansion or modification
- an **acceptable level of cost** in terms of both acquisition and operation.

Many organizations find themselves under pressure to get the system operational. Implementation plans can always look good on paper, but even with the help and support of the suppliers, there can often be a significant shortfall in the amount of time available for acceptance testing. Sometimes, organizations take the decision to omit the testing procedures and fail to detect errors which would have been easy to put right at that stage, but will prove difficult to put right once the system is live.

Software acquisition

The software may be purchased separately, or it may be bundled with the hardware as part of the package. In either eventuality, the organization must address the issue of licensing. A licence is a permission given by the licensor to the licensee to do something which the licensor has the power to prevent or regulate. Licences are either:

- express or
- implied.

Under normal circumstances, if an organization buys software, it is buying only the medium on which the software is stored, and it is not buying any other rights. Naturally, if there is no express agreement to allow the use of the software, one will be implied to make commercial sense of the contract which has been made – it would be nonsensical to buy the software product without also having the right to use it. Why, then, should organizations only get a licence to use the software? The legal problem is that all intellectual property rights – copyright, patents, registered designs, and so on – are formal legal rights which are capable of ownership independently of the physical means of representing them. Such rights have been designed to give some protection to the creative and innovative members of society. The holder of, say, a copyright has a form of legal monopoly in the exploitation of that right. This allows the creative designers and programmers a reasonable return on their inventiveness during the period of protection. But no particular legal formalities are necessary to transfer these intangible rights and so the problem confronting the owners of the copyright in computer software is to exclude the possibility that the sale of the program also transfers ownership of the copyright. A failure to reserve the copyright in the owner would lead to the loss of the right to continue exploiting that copyrighted material.

The rights of the respective parties

The simplest way to ensure this protection is through an express term, or set of terms, which clarifies the respective rights of the parties. This is easily organized where large software packages are to be dealt with, but the situation has become more complex in those smaller, high-volume packages which are sold in retail outlets not controlled by the copyright owners. The way of attempting to deal with the problem is through the use of the so-called **shrink-wrap licence**. Thus, the software is supplied in a clear plastic package through which can be seen the terms of the software licence. It is customary for the document to have a warning in large letters to the effect that opening the package is acceptance of the terms which are visible. By this agreement, the software copyright holder attempts to make a contract quite independently of the purchase transaction. Because of the terms most usually included in these documents, it is unlikely that they could be construed as a unilateral contract, and there are difficulties in arguing the case that they could be a binding bilateral contract.

In the case of a formal licence, the licensee must take care to observe the terms of the permission. The standard clauses cover issues relating to:

- delivery and acceptance
- the use to which the software can be put
- confidentiality
- the documentation
- restrictions on copying (including archiving)
- warranties
- maintenance and support
- training
- termination.

A breach of the terms will entitle the licensor to terminate the licence and to claim damages for any losses sustained as a result of the breach. If the software as supplied causes loss or damage to the purchasing organization, the potential liability of the software producers for the economic loss is slightly unclear.

The financial implications of acquisition

A cost–benefit analysis of the project can be a way of seeking to justify the acquisition of the package. As to the costs, those who respond to the ITT will supply a part of the costing data. Other costs, such as the salaries of the staff who will install and operate the package, should also be ascertainable. At an early stage, maintenance costs should be quantifiable as either the suppliers or independents bid for the contract(s) on larger systems. It is more difficult to quantify the running costs. The basic site costs of space, staff and consumables are likely to remain reasonably stable. The possibility that the same work can be achieved in a reduced proportion of the site is irrelevant, unless the now empty space can be used for some other productive purpose. Indeed, there may be a slight loss unless the costs of physically reorganizing the use of the space can be recovered. Increases in the overheads are likely to result from:

- structural alterations to house the hardware or to relocate some of the affected staff
- installation or enhancement of the building's service infrastructure: of the wiring, cabling, air conditioning, etc.
- additional furniture to house the hardware and appropriate storage facilities
- additional security costs, which may include additional insurance premiums
- the need for specially qualified staff – which may lead to increases in staffing costs, as there is increasing competition in the market place for competent employees
- the training costs, which are likely to be substantial.

Phasing costs and assessing benefits

The **costs of financing** will depend on the method of acquisition selected, but the figures should be reasonably quantifiable. One of the possible areas of difficulty may arise if the package has spare capacity with a phase 2 expansion planned. Thus, if a two-stage project will call for a total of 150 gigabytes of storage, it may be convenient to acquire all the necessary hardware in one package. But if the first part of the project only uses 40 per cent of that capacity, should the whole cost be apportioned in some way, or should the whole cost be written off as phase 1 expenditure? It may be convenient to write off all the expenditure against the first project, but in some cases the more precise allocation of costs may be appropriate. In any event, if the decision is taken to purchase the whole or part of the package, the initial capital requirements may be specified. This is likely to be acceptable for small systems, or where the organization does not want to go through the process of justifying the project to a bank or another source of finance. But, in the case of the larger packages, the organization is almost certain to require some form of loan financing. This will allow the organization to spread the costs over a period, usually of from two to five years, but will involve an addition to the overheads in the form of arrangement fees, interest payments, and so on.

If capital rationing affects a number of projects over a given period of operation, it is possible to implement more projects if the organization opts for leasing. With such a strategy, there is a lower initial outlay – but it treats everything as an increase in the organization's overheads. This is a short-term view to get the most powerful or useful system installed for the least immediate drain on resources; and, in the longer term, it may be problematical, because a high proportion of leasing introduces a significant element of fixed costs in the future. To some extent, a middle line may be taken by acquiring second-hand equipment and software. Here a substantial package may be put together for a more modest outlay. But such has been the rate of technological development that this may be a strategy of some risk: depending on the age of the equipment, it may not be reliable, and it may be difficult to find good maintenance cover (in particular, spares may be hard to find). Given that the outlay on an integrated information system will involve the installation of plant and equipment, capital allowances will be available to cover expenditure. Organizations must appraise each option in the light of the current tax regime.

Benefits can be either tangible or intangible. Direct savings can be measured in terms of staff time and other consumables. If the manual system has been reasonably efficient, direct savings will tend to be modest. Indirect benefits include factors such as increased cashflow through the more efficient processing of invoices and account statements, the better management of stock and other circulating assets, and the better processing of data. These savings are one step removed from the actual benefit. Thus, if responses to mailing lists are kept up to date so that mail shots are targeted on those most likely to respond, more trade may be generated from a lower outlay on stamps. Intangible benefits are more difficult to quantify. The difficulty lies in putting a value on, say, improved access to information or better-quality information. If managers spend less time on finding the relevant data to support their decision making, will the additional time they can devote to the taking of the decisions lead to better decisions? It is obvious that little will improve the decision making of the bad manager, and that the good manager will only have more time if the use of the new system is properly learned and practised. What is not clear is whether giving a person more time leads to better decisions. All that can be said is that it *might* do so.

The issue often arises as an abstract question as to what percentage of capital or revenue an organization should devote to the development of an IT strategy. It is easy to pull figures out of the air and to quote innumerable examples of expenditure to show that, say, between 10 and 15 per cent might be something of a norm. The problem with such approximations is that every organization's needs are the product of the immediate environmental pressures which have promoted its growth, and figures from one organization might be completely misleading for another, even though both organizations might be in the same market sector. Thus, some organizations might defer expenditure and therefore require a substantial investment for an initial installation. Others might have invested little, but often, and therefore appear to spend comparatively little in each trading period. The scale of investment will always depend on the potentially unique nature of the organization.

Quantifying expenditure

An additional complication is that, with the growth of user computing, it is becoming increasingly difficult to quantify the precise level of expenditure. When the work was all undertaken by a single DP department, it was quite easy to quantify expenditure. If a value has to be put on every individual's use of IT facilities within an organization where a distributed system has been installed, the costing becomes more nebulous. Equally, not all the work undertaken by a systems analyst must result in a computerized system. Sometimes, the work will be partly to improve the management environment, to enable it to better exploit the proposed automated system. So unless the staff complete detailed time sheets, allocating their time between computer and non-computer tasks, it will be difficult to get a precise figure.

The actual system

Once the physical hardware and the appropriate services have been installed, the steering committee can proceed to the next step. The hardware must first be tested and the operating system installed. If the new system is compatible with the old, the set of files and programs can simply be copied from one set of hardware to the other. This must be subject to a proper security audit to ensure that data integrity is maintained during the transfer. However, most new systems have different characteristics and require the user to engage in *file conversion*. The users must compare the old with the new and determine the precise way in which to reformat the data records to make them compatible with the new system. This is a convenient time for the organization to review its data holdings. It may well be found that some holdings are redundant and that it is not economical to convert and transfer them. The interest and commitment of the users is of vital importance in this task. Again, proper security auditing procedures are required, firstly to test the conversion process and secondly to check for data integrity after conversion. An unscrupulous employee could enter new data or modify the old data for the purposes of private gain during the conversion process.

Once the data and software have been installed and all the necessary database creation or modification work has been done, the organization should produce the final versions of all necessary documentation. The staff should already be partly trained and ready to commence work on the new system. It is now appropriate for the new system to go live for the purposes of acceptance testing. During this period staff training is completed on the full system.

Database creation

The largest, most difficult and most time-consuming part of the changeover of most systems is conversion from the old form of data storage to the new. This is particularly true where disparate records stored on various media are being input into a central database. The setting up of a 'product' database may involve such records as:

- specification details from the design department
- stock movement details from production control or remote depots
- cost and supplier information from the accounting and purchasing sections
- price and customer information from the sales function.

All these sets of data (which may hitherto have been jealously guarded) will probably be in different formats, on different media (including human minds) and to different degrees of accuracy! With a single database, a phased changeover route is not usually practical and the direct route is dangerous for a repository of all the organization's data, so parallel running is often used for such conversions. Where information is being captured from the 'live' system (ledger postings, stock transactions, etc.) it is usually possible to 'freeze' the files during a non-working period (a holiday or week-end) and to 'bring up' the database with the start of work.

Who manages the change and reviews the effect?

It is likely that there will be a formal project team or steering committee to manage the larger exercises. Contributions can also be expected from the system auditor, security advisor and IT manager. But whether the exercise is large or small, it is customary to designate one individual as the **project manager** and to make that person accountable to the overall IT manager for the success or otherwise of the project (see Chapter 12). Quite often this task will fall to someone in the management services department rather than to someone in the computing/DP department, but because much system development is undertaken on a piecemeal basis, each project tends to be controlled by the department which is going to derive the greatest benefit. So if a credit control system is going to be installed, the credit controller will either directly manage the transition or be closely involved in monitoring the process. In this respect, the direct responsibility of the DP department has given way to the user department. This is almost inevitably the case for the detailed work of acceptance testing, but it is becoming more common for the whole process.

The post-implementation audit

When the system has been live for a specified period of time, a post-implementation audit can be arranged to conduct an evaluation and review of performance (see Chapter 12). This sees the system in the context of the organization, whether merely in a part of the organization or as a whole, depending on the degree of integration. It seeks to answer the following questions:

- has the attitude of the staff changed?
- has the manner of the work changed?
- what informational contribution does the system make to the organization?
- has the new system changed the level of the organization's costs?
- to what extent does it facilitate an optimization of decision making within the organization?

The general process of acceptance testing will be measured against the criteria laid down in the requirements specification. The post-implementation audit goes beyond those technical objectives: it looks at the broader objectives which either explicitly or implicitly caused the organization to authorize the project. The difficulty confronted in this auditing process is whether the observer is measuring the success of the system or measuring some other form of success which just happens to show up at the same time. At all times, the management must allow for the so-called **Hawthorne effect**. This effect is an improvement in performance resulting from increased morale. Such an improvement is more likely to be caused by the enthusiasm of the researcher or the sense that the management is constructively interested in the workforce, rather than by the actual changes made to the working practices or environment.

Key performance factors

Various methodologies have been developed to attempt to quantify the success or otherwise of system implementations. **Key performance factor analysis** is one of the techniques whereby the auditor attempts to identify and set the standards required from the system, but the end product is usually an organizational standard. In general, if the organization installs a stock control system, one of the key performance factors would be either in the savings made through making staff obsolete or in the increased stock turnover. The difficulty is in being able to recognize whether the right facts are being reported to allow the success of the system to be measured. It may be that the management is able to measure an increased stock turnover, but to what is this improvement attributable? Many people will be encouraging activity within that part of the organization through a process of appraisal and attempted measurement. If stock controllers are encouraged to use a new system – and this might be simply because of its novelty or because supervisors are more in evidence – there may be significant short-term improvements. But as the staff become more complacent through familiarity with the new system, bad habits from the manual system days may reassert themselves. If this can happen, it may point to design defects in the automated system – the system design ought perhaps to have allowed for human frailty and should, say, have been based on exception reporting rather than on a simple replication of a card-based system which requires human monitoring. In short, the auditing function attempts to measure, in organizational terms, whether the investment has produced beneficial results.

Maintenance: the practicalities

To be accounted a success, the information system must enable the organization to make a profit or to meet its performance criteria. This can only be achieved if the system is reasonably reliable. Maintenance agreements may offer immediate response and an around-the-clock service. In its simplest form, this may be a help-line – a telephone service where a sympathetic expert offers advice to clear up a user's misunderstanding. This form of service is not necessarily helpful. The user may not be able to identify the problem with sufficient certainty to allow the expert to answer the question, or the question may be outside the expertise of the particular telephone operator. Further, because questioning the user, giving detailed answers and providing comfort all take time, it can be an expensive service to offer to a large number of users. In such circumstances, it may be more cost-effective for the suppliers to offer training courses.

If the extent of the problem goes beyond the help-line's capacity, formal maintenance is required, because there are positive faults to be corrected. But what happens if no-one turns up for hours and then the person who attends is too poorly trained to offer satisfactory repairs? A maintenance agreement is not an insurance policy against loss. The essence of a maintenance contract is that the service provider will maintain the system and remedy defects. That is distinguishable from an insurance policy, where the insurer agrees to compensate the insured if some specified event causes loss.

Identifying the maintenance provider

Originally maintenance was supplied only by the manufacturers. This was logical. Computers were unreliable and needed regular attention. The manufacturers were more knowledgeable about their own machines and, with the experience which they obtained on all their users' sites, they were best placed to provide the service. The contracts were somewhat unfavourable to the customer, because once the capital had been invested in the hardware, the customer was trapped into accepting whatever the manufacturer offered. Now that hardware has become more reliable, independent companies offer maintenance and the market has hence become more competitive. Some manufacturers have responded by cutting their own prices and improving the service which is offered. Others adopt the strategy of not releasing technical information about their machines and therefore making it more difficult for an independent to maintain them.

The first decision to be made by a computer user is the identity of the service maintenance provider. Small independent companies can provide a highly professional, very efficient service on a local basis. Such firms are much more willing to consider tailoring the service to the user's needs and may offer impartial advice on the equipment generally available on the market. They will also be more likely to offer a total service. Many manufacturers only service their own equipment. In these more modern days of networking, the smaller independent may be prepared to service and maintain all the different hardware on the site. This will cut the administration overheads of the user who, for example, will need to make only one telephone call, no matter which manufacturer's equipment needs attention. Because of their size, the price for the service offered is likely to be less than that available from the large manufacturer.

Maintenance back-up provision

However, just because the service may be cheaper it is not necessarily the best value. As organizations become more technology-dependent, they need to guarantee the availability of the service. To rely on a single service provider may be dangerous, as financial margins may be cut down in these competitive times and bankruptcy comes unannounced. It may make more sense for the large user with high criticality of use to employ a back-up firm to provide maintenance. Further, whereas all manufacturers must maintain reasonable standards of care if their overall reputation is not to suffer, there are several 'cowboy' firms in the market place who do not provide the service promised. A part of the difficulty is the cost of maintaining buffer stocks of all the main components. Whereas manufacturers originally would have had no difficulty, small independents may not be able to afford any stocks other than of the most commonly unreliable components. Even the larger companies may now have some problems, either because they are reliant on other manufacturers to supply components for assembly or because they have developed the policy of high stock turnover, with the minimum of capital tied up in a buffer stock. Before entering into any maintenance agreement, it is therefore sensible to discuss the service provided with the tendering organization's existing customers.

There is, however, one factor which may favour the manufacturers. The manufacturers may offer upgrades during the lifetime of the hardware. If these are not undertaken, the resale value of the hardware may be significantly reduced. Because many manufacturers do not release this technical information to the independents, many of them cannot undertake this upgrading work, thereby reducing the capital worth of the equipment. It should also be noted that if a problem emerges which the independent cannot solve, some manufacturers insist on carrying out all the missing upgradings before solving the immediate problem. This can make the call-out very expensive.

Preventive maintenance

In theory, it is better to engage in prevention and to solve problems before they occur. This would mean that preventive or planned maintenance should be a standard part of the contract, including the planned replacement of components and diagnostic testing of critical systems at regular intervals. Indeed, it may be required by a third party:

- by the manufacturer, as a precondition of a guarantee or warranty
- by the manufacturer, as a precondition of issuing a certification of maintenance for the purposes of boosting the price on resale or trade-in
- by the lessor, as a term of a lease
- by the insurance company, as a precondition to offering cover against loss.

The problem with this system is that it may disrupt the operation of the machine while it is being maintained and repaired. The organization should therefore consider whether to attempt to negotiate for work to be performed outside the normal office hours. Although this may cost more, it may be better than the disruption. The cost–benefit analysis and risk profile should give the answer as to whether the expenditure is worthwhile. In the long term, the user should have fewer problems: for instance, by regularly checking and adjusting the tracking on the head alignment on disk drives, organizations should avoid misregistration problems. It will also get much better information on levels of wear and can make earlier plans for repair or replacement, rather than having to react to an emergency. It should also be recognized that this form of service is relatively costly, because service engineering time is paid for regardless of whether any fault is detected in the equipment. As manufacturers produce more reliable equipment, the case in favour of preventive maintenance may weaken and apply only to the peripherals with major moving parts.

Response times

If maintenance is on a call-out basis, negotiating the response times is of vital importance. The shorter the response time, the more expensive the service is likely to be, so cost–benefit analysis is essential to justify the level of expenditure. It is also advisable to check where the service engineers are based and to calculate whether that firm can supply the quality of responsiveness required. In taking the decision, it should be remembered that, from their nature within the organization's information system, batch-run systems may tolerate more delays. On-line systems usually require faster response times and deal with more immediate data needs. The essence of the task is therefore to specify the criticality of each data resource and the level of service which the equipment must maintain if losses are to be kept to a minimum.

This leaves the question of what should happen if the maintenance contractor is in default and fails to provide the specified service with due diligence. In principle, the answer is straightforward. There should be a right to call in new contractors and to pass on the cost of the work to the contractors in default. There should also be a right of termination built into the agreement in the event of a serious breach. A period of notice for the termination to be effective may be required.

Types of software maintenance

Some studies in the USA in the 1980s showed that over 70 per cent of the total cost of some systems over their lifetime is tied up in software maintenance. It is generally accepted that there are three categories:

1 **Corrective maintenance** covers maintenance which is needed to put right coding errors and other faults which may be introduced into the software. It includes the routine 'debugging' of newly produced or recently amended code and emergency error correction in response to reported faults (often by the users).
2 **Adaptive maintenance** covers the changes which are made to the software to meet new or changed circumstances, such as the restructuring of a database, alterations in operating procedures and changes to hardware or software versions.
3 **Perfective maintenance** covers attempts to make the software perform more effectively. It may include user requests for enhancements, improvements due to experience, changes to make the software more easy to use and rewriting the code to make the programs run more quickly.

It may be said that the last category (and some instances of the second) are not maintenance at all but arise from the analysis team's failure to predict what the file requirements might be – or even their failure to capture the user requirements correctly in the first place.

Outsourcing

So far, this chapter has assumed that the organization will want to continue the evolution of its in-house information systems. Such an assumption might have been justified in the immediate period following the end of World War II and for so long as the world economy appeared to provide continued opportunities for commercial growth. But two problems have emerged:

- recession and economic stagnation throughout all the major economies, particularly following the end of the communist regimes in the East
- increasing pressure for improved performance both to meet the threat from more effective competitors and to pacify more demanding investors.

So management teams have been forced into a critical reappraisal of their costs and an evaluation of the rates of return on the capital employed in all aspects of the organization's activities. The consequence has been the growth in the practice of **outsourcing** and **facilities management (FM)** arrangements. The main stimulus for this growth in the UK has come from the twin Government policies of privatizing much of its own work and of requiring local government to use competitive tendering. Hence, there are now FM specialists able to service most of the tasks needed to run any organization and, increasingly, a range of companies including ICL, Rank Xerox, Mowlem, Tarmac and Pitney Bowes is becoming as well-known for their FM subsidiaries as for their traditional strengths. The specialist IT provision builds on the services traditionally offered by commercial computer bureaux. Since the 1960s, these bureaux have acted as time brokers, i.e. they have made time available on their systems to perform routine batch operations such as the weekly/monthly payroll for client organizations.

It has always been open to managers to consider whether it is more cost-effective to develop in-house resources or to buy in goods and services. But history shows that many managers simply opted for empire building and developed large DP departments. There have been a number of difficulties with this strategy:

- the organization's capital expenditure for equipment and overheads for staff are likely to increase substantially
- even though the organization may develop significant processing power, there is no guarantee that resources will be used more effectively or that better decisions will be taken
- developing traditional centralized resources often leads to a lack of user-involvement, poor lines of communication and possible user alienation
- demand may fluctuate, leaving the resources under-utilized for significant periods of time
- specialist IT staff, whose focus of interest is the maintenance and enhancement of their DP functions, are not necessarily the best people to advise the organization on its long-term IT strategies
- changing market conditions may make it hard to recruit and retain skilled staff.

The senior managers may therefore consider buying-in IT services and skills from outside the organization. This may range from contracting out a part of the DP department's existing services such as programming or maintenance, to entering into a full FM arrangement where the whole of an organization's IT operation is to be provided by an external organization. The expression, 'outsourcing a department' usually describes a situation in which all the services provided by the in-house department are transferred to an outside FM provider/supplier.

Outsourcing may be either partial or full. The decision to opt for partial outsourcing depends on identifying operational packages that may safely and economically be contracted out. Thus, for example, outsourcing the large batch operations such as the payroll may allow the organization to make a more effective use of its existing resources to support core business processes. Full outsourcing involves the organization in making the more dramatic decision to transfer responsibility for all major IT functions to the FM provider. This represents a major strategic decision because it involves the organization in the surrender of a degree of control over processes critical to the survival of the organization. As an example, British Aerospace (BAe) recently contracted out the management of the computer networks in its aerospace business to Computer Sciences Corp (CSC). BAe paid £900 million over ten years for an FM contract. In return, CSC paid £75 million in cash for BAe's hardware, software and a number of building leases. CSC also took a transfer of 1250 IT staff who were then employed by BAe. Similarly, the Inland Revenue has begun to discuss outsourcing its entire IT operation. To a greater or lesser extent, outsourcing may have the following advantages:

- there may be a reduction in the cost overheads – some FM users have reported savings in the order of 15 to 20 per cent, which may arise because an outsider supplier may be able to achieve significantly greater economies of scale in its provision to many client organizations than could be achieved by any one organization in its own operations
- it may be better to replace more unpredictable in-house costs with fees set by a fixed-term contract over, say, a three- or five-year period
- the outsourcing arrangement may act as a form of buffer against fluctuations in demand for the services of an in-house DP department
- the arrangement may be a form of insurance against shortages of skilled labour which may hamper the implementation of an organization's IT development strategy
- because of the better career prospects in large specialized organizations, the FM provider may be able to recruit, train and retain more skilled staff, and so offer a much wider and more consistent range of services to client organizations, i.e. the outsourcer may get the benefit of quality human resources for just as long as they are needed (also remember that, in Europe, part-time workers now have the same employment law protections as full-time workers which makes outsourcing even more attractive)
- once the FM arrangement is made, the outsourcer may be able to achieve a better match between its existing skill profile and the core tasks and processes to be undertaken.

This last point raises a significant possible shift of emphasis. At a general level of activity, most organizations spend substantial sums on non-core support activities such as cleaning, catering and security. When BP were looking for an FM company to assume responsibility for £24 million worth of non-core activities on its Sunbury site, the search was for a 'service partner' and not a 'service provider'. The intention was to find an organization that would be able to enter into a long-term relationship of mutual benefit. In this, 'cultural fit' was considered a key requirement, i.e. that both organizations should have highly compatible management styles and decision-making processes so that they could work together successfully. One element in this strategy was to ensure that the outsourcer would get the benefit of staff who became familiar with the buildings and their roles within them. Better long-term working relationships could then be established which should reduce staff turnover. If this type of closer relationship became the norm, it would mean that the outsourcer is not so much engaging in a selection process but engaging in a courtship exercise to find a partner that can be trusted and relied on over significant periods of time. This would have the added advantage of eliminating the costs and stresses of regular retendering by the service provider. Hence, the outsourcing organization ought to consider the following factors carefully before entering into an IT-orientated FM arrangement:

- the outsourcer should be not be looking for simple cost savings, but for improved value for money – this will require a full analysis of organizational needs rather than a statement of short-term management desires
- although short-term economies may be achieved, all contracts come up for renewal and, at that time, the FM provider may seek significant increases in the fees to be charged – the problem which the outsourcer may have in resisting this claim is that the costs of reinstating the IT facilities in-house may be high (to assist in negotiating or renewing contracts, a growing number of databases of comparative costs are being made available to provide more objective data about the level of expense organizations should expect to incur when engaging in a range of business activities)
- the FM contract will establish a fee base for a defined level of service and this fee will be payable whether the service is used or not
- the FM contract will establish maximum levels of service availability and, if the outsourcer wishes to exceed those levels, significant extra costs may be incurred, assuming that the additional resources can be made available to meet this unexpected demand
- many FM arrangements involve the redundancy or transfer of staff which may be demotivating both to the staff who are to be lost or transferred as well as to those who remain unless this change is carefully managed – there may also be costs involved if staff have to be compensated for physically relocating or it is decided that premises have to be upgraded to make the move more attractive. A further problem is the continuing reinterpretation of TUPE (the European directive dealing with the Transfer of Undertakings, Protection of Employees) which was designed to protect the rights of employees when companies change hands, but which is now being applied in some contracting out situations. Until the resulting uncertainty is resolved, it may be prudent to assume that TUPE will apply to all transfers of staff between European undertakings. This will mean that all staff should be transferred on the same terms and conditions
- there may be significant time and cost implications in deciding to go through the process of exploring outsourcing (the more the outsourcer decides to move in the direction of partnership, the greater the likely costs) – detailed information must be prepared for tenders and contracts, the bids must be

evaluated and the FM suppliers compared, detailed contractual negotiations may be involved, etc. (do not forget that this may be a recurrent item of expenditure every time the contract(s) come up for renewal)
- although the FM provider will always have some degree of commercial imperative to reflect the interests and needs of the customer, the provider will have its own strategic goals and objectives to meet – this may create a tension between the needs of the two parties and system developments may be driven by what is most convenient to the FM provider rather than by what is most useful to the individual FM user
- once the arrangement is in place, the FM user must establish careful monitoring and reporting procedures on the level and quality of service provision – remember that this activity may not be a part of the existing in-house functions so staff may have to be redeployed and trained (new systems of benchmarking the standards of service to be expected are now being developed and staff should keep up-to-date in both the national and international discussions on standards)
- if the FM provider proves less efficient than expected, frustration may arise if the outsourcer is contractually bound to the provider by a fixed term contract, say of five years
- expenditure on arbitration and legal dispute resolution systems may significantly increase
- even if efficient, the FM user should seek to ensure that the FM provider continuously improves the quality of the service, adopting the most commonly accepted standards and 'open systems' principles when designing new applications
- there may be significant security implications if commercially sensitive data may come under the control of an outside provider.

From this, it should be apparent that all decisions in this area should be taken at a strategic level within the organization. This recognizes that organizations may achieve significant advantages through partial or full outsourcing, but care is needed to ensure that all the required changes achieve the desired results.

Summary

Starting from a consideration of system implementation strategies, this chapter has examined the acquisition of system resources and the factors to be considered in the efficient and effective operation and maintenance of a system. You should keep the following key points in mind:

- The organization must select an appropriate system changeover strategy by considering the risk profile of each project. The organization must be accurate in specifying its hardware and software needs, and should take care in communicating those needs to potential suppliers through the tendering process.
- The training of the staff and the testing of the new system tend to run together. Both depend on the availability of good system documentation.

- In taking the decision to buy, rent or lease the hardware and software, the organization must balance the costs of acquisition against the benefits of possession. Acceptance testing and post-implementation auditing are vital steps for measuring the degree of benefit accruing to the organization from the system changes.
- Unless adequate maintenance arrangements are made, the organization may be without critical systems for an unacceptable period of time.

Self-test questions

1 Evaluate the possible routes for system changeover.
2 Explain what is meant by an 'invitation to tender', commenting on its content and distribution.
3 Describe the purposes of a post-implementation audit, identifying the aspects of system operation on which it will focus.
4 Which factors lead an organization to consider changing its information system?

Exam-style questions

1 The chief executive of BC plc has heard that over 70 per cent of the development and running costs of some computer-based systems are committed to software maintenance.

You are required to draft a report to the chief executive describing the three types of software maintenance which are commonly encountered in computer-based systems.

From CIMA Information Technology Management paper, November 1992

2 Cardweld Packaging is reviewing the operation and management of its information and data processing services. One option being considered is to sub-contract this work to an external agency.

Discuss the ways in which partial facilities management and full facilities management could be adopted in a company and evaluate the impact their introduction would have on the company and on its information technology services.

(*All answers on pages 562–564*)

CHAPTER 12

Project management

The overall process of system development, covering the phases of analysis, design, implementation and maintenance, is typically a complex process requiring effective management. Many of the principles and practices that we describe in this chapter can be applied equally effectively to small or to large-scale developments. The chapter considers the management of projects from a number of perspectives, seeking to highlight potential key issues, the sources of common problems and possible approaches to their solution.

We begin by looking at the overall sequence and pattern of activities involved in project management and reviewing the primary issues encountered in the process of managing an information system development project. We then discuss approaches to resolving these issues, including the types of structural arrangements within organizations that are needed to support an effective project management process.

The next part of the chapter investigates project management processes and the role, responsibilities and authority of the project manager. Apart from considering the structural issues, our discussion makes an appraisal of the major tools and techniques that may be used to support project management. Particular emphasis is placed on the importance of human resource management and the role of project teams.

In addressing and developing these themes, our emphasis will be directed towards the means for improving effectiveness and efficiency in the project management of an information system's development.

Project management: an overview

Being able to create an effective specification, supported by the analysis, design and implementation stages of the software development life cycle, and to deliver a system to the required standards and within the time and cost constraints imposed depends on the effective management of the entire development process. A common experience of those organizations that develop their own information systems is that while the system may perform to the required standards, the delivery is often considerably later than the target date and the final costs greatly exceed those included in the budget. Examples of systems taking twice as long to complete and costing twice as much as budgeted are not uncommon. Alternatively, it may happen that the system is completed within the allotted time and financial constraints but is inadequate in terms of its quality and its ability to meet user needs. The major cause of such outcomes is poor project management.

Effectiveness and efficiency

The primary objectives underlying any process of project management – whether related to investments in information systems or to some other capital expenditure project – may be encapsulated under two headings.

1 **Effectiveness**: ensuring that the project (in this case, the system):
   - meets the required needs of the users or the other objectives that have been established
   - produced to specified quality standards to satisfy user needs
   - can be integrated within existing organizational information systems, structures and processes
   - is sufficiently flexible to respond to changes in the environment in which the system will operate, or to the changing requirements of users – which may only become articulated and refined during the development process itself
   - provides appropriate support to decision-makers at all levels: operational, tactical and strategic.
2 **Efficiency**: ensuring that the system development project – including development, delivery, installation and final implementation – is:
   - undertaken within the manpower resources, costs and time targets or constraints specified at the outset
   - efficient in exploiting the resources of the project team members' and the users' time as fully as possible, avoiding unnecessary idle time, delays or time wasted in undertaking unnecessary tasks or activities
   - effective in integrating the activities of those within the project team, and also those interactions and dependencies with other parties outside the project team, including users, suppliers, consultants or managers
   - capable of delivering the resources (including hardware, software, services and training) on time – neither too late nor too early to cause problems of storage, loss of value due to deterioration, unexpected fluctuations in planned cashflows or loss of benefits from training due to excessive time required for the user to apply the knowledge or skills acquired.

In practice, the project management process may involve the management of *either* a small team of one or two internal systems staff, to cover all aspects of the systems development, *or*, at the other extreme, a large group of both internal and external staff, many of whom will be specialists in limited features of the system during its development. Irrespective of the scale or complexity of the project, the issues concerned are broadly similar and the practices used to ensure improved effectiveness and efficiency may be applied equally well in all situations.

Project management elements

The terms **effectiveness** and **efficiency**, as defined above, may be expressed in terms of the key elements of any project, namely:

- time
- resources
- costs
- quality.

The term 'efficiency' relates primarily to the elements of time, resource utilization and costs (measuring the value of the output produced against the costs and time taken to produce the system). 'Effectiveness' is concerned more with the quality of the system in terms of the required performance standards and objectives.

Let us look at these project elements in detail.

Time

The time factor represents a key parameter in the project management process. Typically, the objectives of the project will stipulate either a target time for completing the development of the system, or the date by which the system should be fully operational. Other intermediate dates or targets may also be specified for completing particular component elements or phases in the development process. Failure to meet these prescribed target completion dates may have both direct and indirect consequences for the organization, some of which may be highly significant. For example:

- losses of potential financial returns, reduced operational efficiency and lost competitive advantage from the system operation itself
- reduced benefits and potential opportunities if other organizational developments are tied to the project, for example the launch of a new product involving an expensive promotional campaign
- resources remaining idle: specific staff recruited and not utilized, or hardware, software and environment facilities all arriving ahead of requirement and increasing the organization's risk of loss, damage or deterioration
- delays that may require either the extension of contracts negotiated with specific programmers or analysts hired only for the duration of the project (possibly at increased rates), or the use of overtime working to recover lost time (at higher rates)
- the retention of existing computing equipment beyond the anticipated time, necessitating the extension of maintenance contracts and often incurring higher maintenance costs than the new equipment. This may also apply to staffing costs, particularly if significant reductions are anticipated as a result of the developments
- unplanned cashflow effects from either early or delayed purchasing and delivery
- the impact on other system development projects, either concurrent with the delayed project or utilizing part of the current system project or the staff employed in its development.

Details of the planning approaches and tools needed to control the time element, resources and costs are given later in this chapter.

Resources

For these purposes, the term **resources** relates to both material and human resources. Material resources will include the hardware, software, consumable materials and support services. Although the acquisition and management of material resources may prove demanding, the management of human resources is usually the key element. The staff involved are likely to differ in terms of their specialisms, skills and experience. There will also be differences in personality and attitudes. Generally, the management of resources involves:

- evaluating alternative suppliers of hardware, software and services; negotiating prices, quality standards and delivery times; and progressing orders placed
- recruiting and training the staff for the project
- planning workloads for individual staff, scheduling and co-ordinating the work of the project team, establishing performance targets, and regular monitoring and appraisal of individual staff performance.

Costs

Management priorities for both the time and resource elements will be reflected in the project costs. A key performance indicator used by senior management to assess the project during its development phase is the level of expenditure incurred relative to the budgeted expenditure. Managing the costs of a project involves the following:

- Forecasting and estimating the costs of the project in total so that the level of anticipated expenditure can be established for each month or quarter. These costs will normally be subdivided into a variety of sub-headings relating to capital and revenue expenditures, and costs associated with staff, materials and overheads.
- Monitoring the actual expenditure in total and under each of the sub-headings within the budget. This will allow the project team to assess the degree to which actual expenditure matches budgeted expenditure. In cases where there are significant variances, the project team will be required to establish the cause and the consequences for the total project costs.
- Significant overspending on a project may require the project manager and the organization to review either the subsequent stages of the development process or the initial system objectives and performance standards, with the intention of modifying the more expendable elements to meet budget limits.

Quality

The task of managing quality differs from that of managing the elements of time, resources and costs, which are concerned primarily with the inputs, processes and activities involved in developing a system. Quality management is primarily focused on the output of the development process as an operational system. It may be more difficult to measure quality than the three other elements, because it may be assessed against more subjective criteria. Thus, the perception of quality may differ, depending on the position or role of the individual in relation to the information system. For example, a system designer may perceive a particular system as being of inferior quality in a technical sense, as it fails to use the file space on a disk file efficiently. However, a user of the same system may perceive it as a high-quality system, as it employs simple and easy-to-use human–machine interfaces to search for the data required. While different perceptions of quality exist, the important assessment of quality relates to the system's ability to meet the users' requirements. Generally, the management of quality incorporates:

- establishing quality and performance standards for the system at the outset and developing methods for measuring these less tangible elements
- establishing procedures and methods of working which will assist in assuring the achievement of the standards in the final system
- monitoring the system regularly against the desired standards and ensuring that the necessary procedures are being observed.

Managing interaction

Managing each of these elements of time, resources, cost and quality in isolation would impose demands on the project manager. However, in practice all four elements must be managed simultaneously, and not only do they interact with each other but they are continuously changing. Further, the four elements may often appear to be pulling in different directions, so that the project's objectives are continually under threat, as illustrated in Figure 12.1.

In managing the project, the manager is continuously making judgements and decisions on the influence of these elements and seeking to guide and control the development to achieve the objectives. Examples of the type of interaction and decisions required include the following.

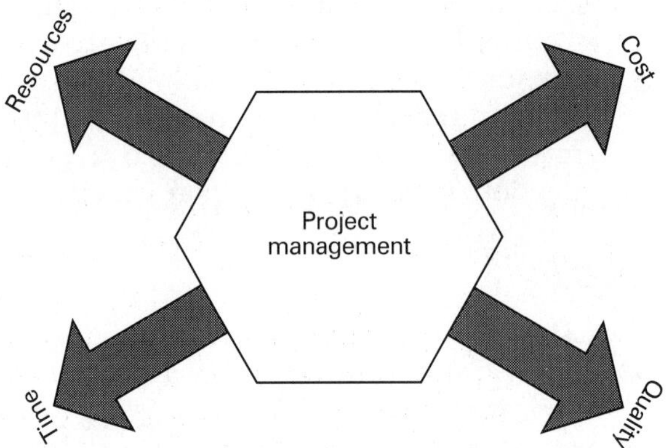

Figure 12.1 Key issues in project management.

Managing time

If the project is behind schedule and there is serious doubt over achieving the target completion date, the manager may resolve this by:

- acquiring extra resources to speed up the completion of the work, or asking existing staff to work additional hours – both of which may intensify resource management problems and will certainly increase costs
- either reducing or eliminating particular inspection and testing procedures and checks, which may reduce the time required but at the expense of quality and (possibly) user confidence in the system.

Managing quality

The decision to establish and maintain high quality standards in terms of system performance and user interface will usually enhance the resources, but the time required to assure this quality level will almost invariably prove more expensive. Some managers would suggest that quality does not necessarily require additional time, resources or cost. They would argue that, providing that the staff involved are properly trained and motivated, maintaining high quality standards would be a normal feature of systems development operations.

Managing resources

Given the opportunity, most project managers would probably prefer to extend the timescale of the project rather than manage periods of peak demand for skilled resources which are beyond the existing complement of the systems team. The hiring of additional temporary staff to cope with the peak workload may not only increase the costs of the project but result in a reduction in quality and generate new problems involving human resource management.

Managing costs

Costs (as can be seen from the previous examples) are inextricably woven into the management of the other three elements. Managing a project by reference to the cost element would involve seeking to reduce or minimize the costs incurred by:

- extending the time required – and therefore avoiding the hiring of extra staff or working extra hours
- utilizing less expensive resources, where possible
- decreasing the minimum acceptable quality standards.

The integrated management of these four elements does require the project manager to strike an appropriate balance between them in the ongoing decision making and control activities. The project manager will usually be held responsible for the project's performance across these four dimensions and will usually be required to report the decisions taken and their effects on these elements to senior management. Often the difficulty facing the project manager is the variation in the perceived importance of these four elements in different areas of the organization. For example, the management in the potential user department may be particularly concerned with the time element, while the operational users in the same department may be more interested in the quality of the system. The finance director may only be interested in keeping costs within the agreed budget. The project manager therefore requires skills not only in decision making but also in judging the relative importance of these differing perceptions and the extent to which any one of them may be safely ignored. The key danger from the project manager's perspective and, more particularly, from the organization's point of view is that concentration on only one or two of these elements at the expense of the other elements may result in significant under-achievement in promoting the total objectives of the system.

Project management activities

The management of these four elements within an information systems development project involves a number of major activities, which are shown in Figure 12.2.

The project manager will not undertake all of these activities personally. Some require a strategic input and will be undertaken by superior bodies within the organization, while others will be delegated to team leaders or other subordinates. (A treatment of the relationship between organizational structures and the project management process is provided later in this chapter.) For these immediate purposes, the project manager is likely to be involved to some extent in most of the activities described below.

Planning

The planning process comprises a number of interrelated activities, encompassing:

- translating the broad objectives into more specific and measurable targets, timescales and performance standards
- developing the logical sequence of activities required to complete the project, estimating the time, resources and costs properly attributable to each of these activities
- establishing the necessary structures, procedures and information systems to support the planning process by feeding back data on the progress of the project in terms of time, resource usage, costs and quality.

Continuity

Planning is not a single event that occurs once only at the outset of the project; it is a continuous activity, involving the reformulation of previous plans to accommodate changes in the situation as a result of:

- delays in completing internal activities (this may be due to variables such as staff illness or over-optimistic estimates of the time required)

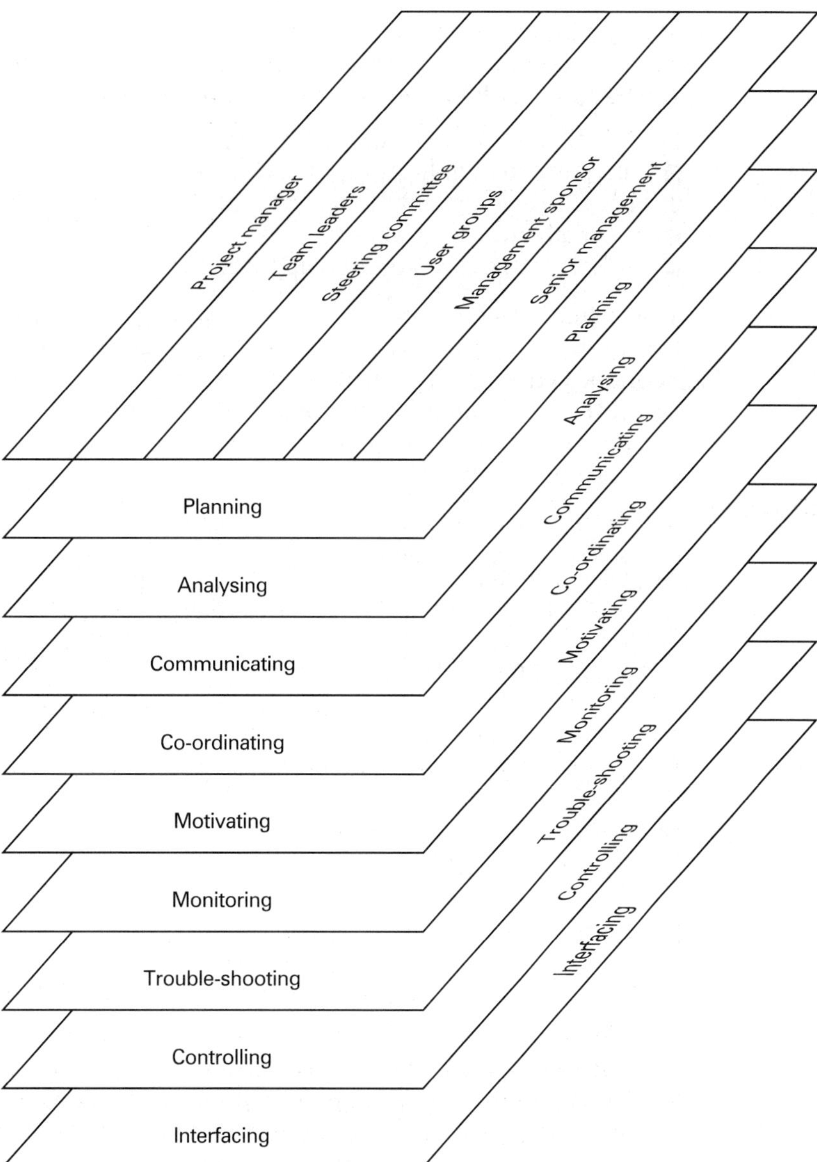

Figure 12.2 Major elements of project management.

- delays in performance by external agencies, such as late delivery or inadequate quality of supplies of computer equipment, software or support services
- unanticipated problems encountered in the development of the system
- changes in users' requirements as these become more explicit during the analysis and design process
- changes in the organizational environment in which the system is required to operate – for example, a change in the allocation of staff and management responsibilities.

Analysis

This is a general term for a range of activities which includes:

- identifying the cause of a problem
- assessing the implications of each problem
- searching for possible solutions
- evaluating each possibility
- selecting the most appropriate for the given situation.

This definition of analysis is somewhat wider than that used previously in this text in discussing decision making. The change arises because it is necessary to decompose the activity functionally into the next layer of component parts. At this level, the analytical methods used are both quantitative and qualitative. Ensuring the efficient and effective use of resources and adherence to timescales involves the analysis of:

- the primary logical sequence of activities to be conducted and the alternative or contingent sequences that may be adopted, either to achieve quicker responses or to deal with foreseen difficulties
- the effect that any changes in the existing patterns of resource utilization within the organization may have on completion time
- the degree to which modifications to the scheduling of activity and resource utilization change the cost profile of the project
- the level of quality that can be maintained in the system if faster target completion dates are adopted.

Communication

A key feature of the project management process, and one that is frequently conducted inadequately, is that of communication. Communication is inextricably linked to the planning and control process and requires effective relationships between:

- members of the project team itself, between the members of the team and the project's sponsoring department or manager, and between the project manager and project team members
- members of the project team and the affected users, to build a degree of mutual collaboration and constructive interaction
- the project management and the management of the organization, to report and review the progress of the project and to indicate any changes in policy or objectives that may influence the development work
- the project management and external suppliers of equipment, software or specialist support services, to ensure clear understanding of requirements and priorities.

The issue of communication is further developed later in the chapter, where we consider the structures and processes required to facilitate effective communications and control within the overall project management.

Co-ordination, integration and co-operation

Planning and managing the co-ordination and integration of the activities and staff of the project, both:

- **internally** within the project team and with other staff in the organization and
- **externally** with outside suppliers and service support agencies,

is a continuing feature of the management process throughout the project. While effective communication contributes to this process, often more positive actions are required to ensure effective co-ordination and integration. The larger the project team involved and the more external suppliers and services are used, the greater the issues of co-ordination and integration become. The term 'co-operation' also relates to the nature of the interrelationship and integration between staff, although it usually relies more on the inherent culture and personality of those involved rather than on the quality of the planning approach. Most development projects rely heavily on the co-operation of other people, particularly the users involved, and will frequently fail to achieve their desired objectives under all four of the elements (time, resources, costs and quality) if this co-operation is totally absent. Co-ordination and integration involve:

- the detailed planning of the contributions to be made by each participant in the process and the dovetailing of their contributions
- regular monitoring of progress in each area or activity and taking the necessary actions to ensure that each component element is progressing in reasonable harmony with affected elements within the structure of the plan
- arranging regular meetings of the staff involved, to appraise and review progress and to identify the implications of problems or delays encountered in specific areas of development work.

Monitoring, evaluation and control

This group of activities is of considerable importance and will involve all the staff working on the project or associated with the development of the system. Irrespective of the quality of the initial planning and scheduling activities, or of the quality of the staff and management responsible for undertaking the scheduled activities, it will be necessary to monitor the progress of the development programme continuously and to identify areas where actual performance is deviating from that planned in terms of time, resource usage, quality and cost. In addition to identifying such deviations or variances, the project management also must undertake an evaluation of:

- the causes of each deviation
- the consequences if no corrective action is taken
- the alternative solutions available and their potential effects on the four key elements
- the suggested ways of implementing the selected solution.

In many respects, the key to effective management of the information systems development process itself is the development of an effective and efficient management information system. The manager requires the appropriate quality of data feedback on the progress of the development in terms of detail, accuracy and timeliness. More importantly, the quality of the initial planning process and the use of appropriate methods or tools will facilitate effective monitoring and evaluation of performance in a structured way, and may often provide a vehicle for evaluating alternative actions to resolve or control the situation. Indeed, if the control system is to operate effectively, the whole monitoring, evaluation and control process should be made explicit or obvious to those involved in the development operations. Even if the development work is on schedule or even ahead of schedule, the manager should convey knowledge of the project status and the status of individual contributions to the members of the team on a regular basis. This latter point would also be valuable in regard to the issue of leadership and motivation, to be discussed later.

Trouble-shooting

One of the more onerous and regular tasks encountered in the project management process is that of resolving problems as they arise. This trouble-shooting activity is arguably part of the monitoring, evaluation and control group of activities discussed above, but it has been highlighted separately as it represents a less regulated and more dynamic form of these activities. Because a more immediate response is often required, decision making will primarily involve the project manager and team leaders rather than the committee structure supervising the project. Indeed, the project management team's ability to respond effectively to problems as they arise may be important for determining the eventual success of the project in meeting the stipulated performance objectives and targets.

Associated with trouble-shooting is the need to consider the delegation of authority and responsibility for managing the various areas of the project. The project manager ought to develop a degree of management decentralization and encourage the team leaders or development staff to tackle an increasing proportion of problems. In delegating this responsibility, the manager also needs to delegate explicitly the authority to make decisions, carefully identifying the limits of each individual's authority. A part of this process of delegation involves the project manager, and indeed other levels of management in the organization, in identifying key or critical issues and problems, and retaining responsibility and authority for their management. If some degree of decentralization is encouraged in non-critical areas, it increases the importance of developing and maintaining a good feedback system on problems that have arisen and the solutions adopted, so that current levels of criticality throughout the project can be monitored.

Quality assurance

An issue that has acquired significant importance in the last few years is that of enhancing and ensuring the quality of the system delivered to the users. The first step should be taken during the specification phase of the systems development life cycle, when the quality standards or objectives in terms of system performance are established. These quality standards are to be made operational by the activities of the systems design, development and programming staff involved in the project. The initial planning of the project should therefore have incorporated the quality dimension into the plans by specifying:

- the timescales allowed
- the level of resources to be allocated to specific activities
- the performance targets or standards to be achieved.

It is crucial that the staff should not only know the specified standards but be able to measure them throughout the entire process, with control actions taken as appropriate to correct deviations. It is often too late to correct deficiencies in the quality of the system once it has been delivered because, although it may be possible in principle to correct operating deficiencies, the cost of doing so and the possible knock-on effects to other elements of the system are too high.

The confidence of the user may also be seriously eroded if poor-quality interfaces or software performance have been encountered at any early stage, even though the problems are subsequently corrected. This would apply particularly where the information system being developed requires significant changes in staffing, working practices and methods. Human resistance to change is a common feature of many situations but appears to be more prevalent and vociferous in cases where IT is the source of such changes. Inferior quality systems development or implementation provides a golden opportunity to criticize IT in general, and the organization's systems development team in particular.

Leadership and motivation

Irrespective of the project manager's planning, analytical and co-ordinating abilities, there will usually be a requirement to display effective leadership skills and abilities. A team of systems analysts, designers or programmers will require a manager to lead the team and to identify sources of personal conflict, to motivate the team during periods when there appears to be a continuous stream of problems, and to provide support when the team are under criticism.

In essence this highlights a key feature of effective project management that is frequently ignored, as the emphasis is usually placed on technical expertise and on ability to utilize analytical or quantitative approaches to management. While these attributes of project management are self-evidently essential, they cannot alone ensure effective management. Qualities such as: good interpersonal skills; the ability to understand different personal perspectives and needs; adaptability in approach to motivating, encourage or censuring different individuals, and the potential to generate enthusiasm, interest or passion in the task facing the individual or project team are essential to the effective management of a project. It is not sufficient for the project manager alone to be imbued with such qualities; the other management or supervisory levels in the project team also need to display similar attributes to provide a consistent and reinforcing environment and culture.

Managing interfaces

Given the complexity of many organizations in which systems development and implementation take place and the more integrative nature of the systems themselves, project managers are increasingly concerned with managing internal and external interfaces. If a system spans several departments of functions (a not untypical situation), the system interfaces between the departments should be managed:

- To ensure that departments recognize the total benefits arising from the system, and not just those relating to a particular department. The fact that the workload placed on a particular department has increased as a result of the system – a requirement, say, to input additional data items as information for other areas of the organization – is frequently a source of contention, and requires effective management if the interfaces are to be maintained on a reasonably stress-free basis.
- To prevent departments from seeking to frustrate the development of the project on the basis that it erodes their historical power base in the organization as the only source of given information.
- To avoid situations where certain users may seek to dictate system parameters, operations and outputs to an extent greater than their role as users, providers or processors within the system itself.

The organizational information systems which are being currently developed are increasingly incorporating external organizations – suppliers, agents and distribution channels – in an attempt to achieve increased competitive advantage through greater collaboration and integration of systems. The 'external' role of the system manager is often more demanding than in the internal context where, arguably, a formal structure of authority may be used to enforce a certain degree of compliance. How much authority or control the organization may exercise over external suppliers or distributors may vary considerably, but it will usually be less than absolute.

Stages and levels in project management

The process of project management is a progression through a number of identifiable stages. In addition to this time dimension, it may also be viewed in terms of a series of *levels*. These levels will operate within each of the stages, performing different roles and having different responsibilities. Figure 12.3 highlights the six main stages or phases of project management and shows examples of the different levels.

The nine broad management activities outlined in the previous sub-section will operate throughout each of the phases and to differing extents at each of the levels in the project management structure.

The outline planning phase

This phase covers the period from the initial generation of the system proposal and incorporates:

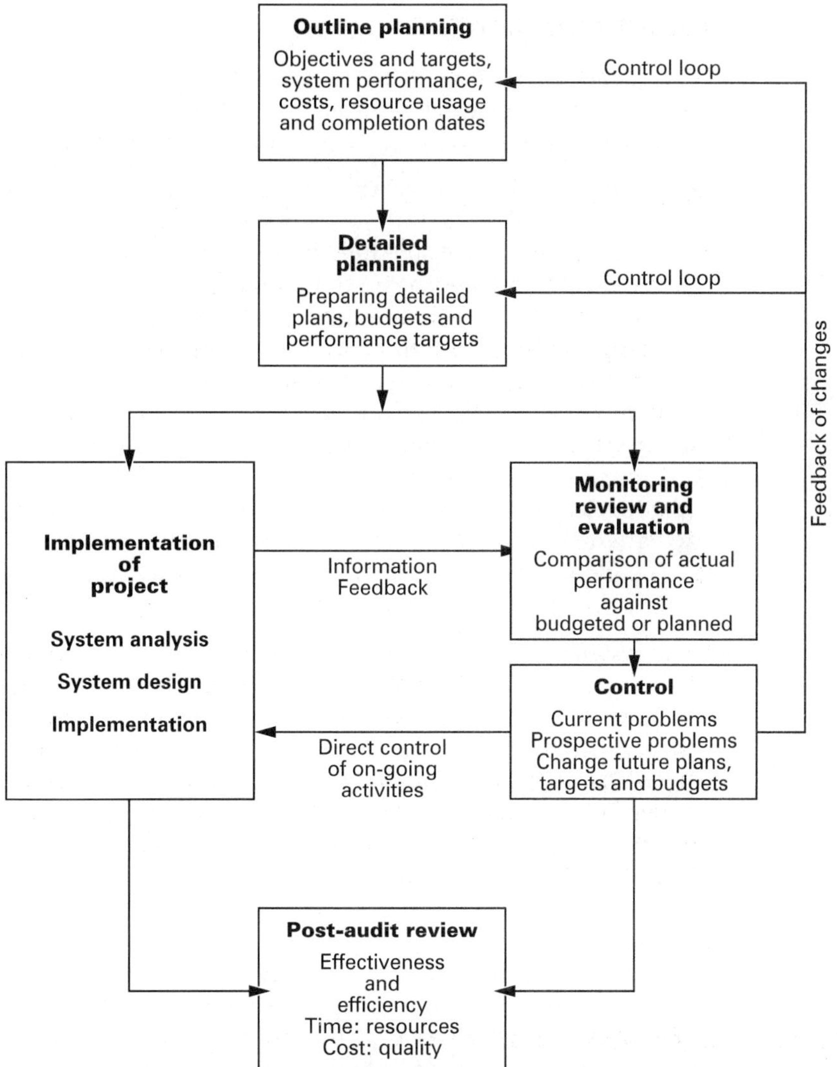

Figure 12.3 Stages in the project management.

- establishing objectives and targets for the system in quality terms
- setting targets for the completion of particular phases
- estimating development expenditures and formulating budgets
- preparing an outline plan of the major development stages, estimating the likely time required for each and identifying the resources required.

The nature of this process is essentially iterative, as a number of proposed plans, objectives, targets and budgets will be prepared and subsequently modified in the light of discussions at differing levels of the project management hierarchy. Following these discussions, agreement will normally be reached on the outline plans and approval given to undertake the next phase.

The detailed planning phase

The detailed planning of the project will primarily involve the project manager and members of the project team. Their task will be to convert the broad outline plan into a feasible action plan for developing the project, incorporating:

- a detailed schedule of the activities or tasks to be undertaken, the logical sequence in which these may be performed, and the identification of potentially critical activities or sequences of activities within the overall plan
- an assessment of the resources available and the allocation of particular resources to the activities identified in the schedule and the identification of associated staff recruitment and training needs to provide appropriate skills to undertake the project (for example, staff may be required to attend courses on new computer systems, operating systems or applications packages)
- a schedule of external purchases of equipment, software or other services required for the system
- detailed budgets covering both internal and external expenditures
- a system for monitoring and controlling the progress of the system development activities in terms of time, resource utilization, costs and quality standards.

The system as developed will itself incorporate an information system to report on progress, but it will also include guidelines on the processes to be used in monitoring, reviewing and controlling performance, for example the establishment of steering groups, user groups or meetings of the project team itself would represent differing processes for monitoring and controlling the project, and would require the formulation of terms of reference, membership, frequency of meetings and the administrative structure to support them.

It would be a mistake to assume that the team must complete all the detailed planning before proceeding to implement or commence work on the project, as many parts of the detailed planning may require further information which is either not readily available or may materialize only as the project proceeds. However, the organization should ensure that the detailed planning has adequately addressed each of the issues itemized above. The conclusion of the detailed planning phase should typically result in the submission of the detailed plans to the management (in the form of the sponsoring department or manager) and to the steering committee (if this has already been formed). These detailed plans require consideration, modification and authorization prior to implementation.

Implementation

The implementation phase of project management refers to the complete cycle of stages incorporating analysis, design and implementation of the information system. The content of each of these stages has been discussed in detail in Chapters 8–11. In most respects the implementation phase in project management represents the operational activities required to produce the system, and project management is concerned with measuring both the effectiveness and the efficiency of these activities, both individually and in aggregate. Figure 12.3 shows the implementation phase paralleled by the phases of monitoring, reviewing and controlling.

Progress monitoring and review

The monitoring and reviewing process may take place at a number of different levels and consequently at different time intervals. Irrespective of the level or the frequency of the process, the essential element that these have in common is the measurement of *actual* performance against *planned* performance. Although this measurement could take account of a variety of criteria, it is customary to limit the scope of the exercise to the four elements – time, resources, costs and quality – identified earlier in this chapter. Examples of the performance measurement approaches to these elements are given in the following paragraphs.

Monitoring time performance

The main test is a comparison of actual completion dates against the planned completion dates, with management requiring progress reports on current activities to determine whether each element of the project is on or behind schedule. Tools to aid this monitoring process (such as PERT or Gantt charts) are discussed later in this chapter.

Monitoring resource performance

It would be common to measure performance under three headings:

- the extent to which resources have been made available to the project
- the percentage utilization of those resources in promoting the plan
- the extent to which the resources are being used efficiently and effectively.

The term *resources*, in this context, refers not only to the human resources working on the project but also to the computer resources, accommodation and other supporting services. However, because humans are more prone to error than machines, attention will usually be focused on measuring the performance and effectiveness of the human resources.

Monitoring cost performance

The usual source of information for monitoring the cost performance of the project will be the organization's costing and budgetary control system. If the project has been established as an identifiable cost centre within the budgetary system, all the directly identifiable or attributable costs incurred by the project will be collected and reported against the project. The costing system may also incorporate the allocation or apportionment of indirect or overhead costs to the project. The monitoring and review process will again involve comparisons of actual expenditure against planned expenditure, although the level of detail in terms of types of costs will depend on the detailed breakdown available within the budget reports. To produce a comprehensive evaluation of performance, it may often be necessary to collect and report other cost data or more detailed data than are available through the standard reports, including the range of quotations received for particular items of expenditure.

Monitoring quality performances

The regular assessment of quality is often a more complex task than the other measurements of performance, particularly in information systems development. In the more usual situations where a product is to be manufactured, quality can be measured in terms of the number of units that either fail intermediate or final quality inspection and testing, or are returned as faulty by customers within the given period. The measurement of quality in organizations providing services rather than manufactured products is more difficult, because it inevitably relies on a more subjective evaluation of performance against the desired standards.

The nature of the interdependent functions of systems analysis, design and implementation is that of a continuous development process with the eventual product or services, represented by the final operating information system, not available until the completion of the project. In this respect, performance measurement needs to relate more to the degree of conformity between the initially agreed standards of quality and the standards actually achieved during the intermediate stages. For example, it can be instructive to monitor the quality of the interviews conducted with users and the resulting reports (see Chapter 8), the user's views on the quality of the training courses (see Chapter 11) or the degree to which the documentation conforms to agreed standards (see Chapter 11). As in the provision of most services, many of the quality performance measures in this area are less objective, because they rely on opinion which may be coloured by self-interest. However, this possible lack of objectivity should not be regarded as an excuse for ignoring the measurement of quality. It is a key element which requires continuous monitoring throughout the entire systems development project, although the nature of the measurement process will vary, both in the level of detail and in the form of the output produced.

Evaluation

An important activity that occurs within the monitoring and review phase, and is implicit in the above discussion, is evaluation. The evaluation process involves:

- measuring the progress made during the current reporting period and the cumulative progress to date in meeting the time, cost, resource and quality targets
- assessing the implications of lack of progress or of current difficulties for the work scheduled to be undertaken in the following reporting period, and for the total project (again in terms of the four elements)
- generating a range of alternative actions that may be undertaken to resolve specific problems or delays which have been, or which are likely to be, encountered
- analysing the potential effects of these alternative actions in terms of the four elements, often using differing assumptions concerning the future situation or environment in which the project will develop. (This **what if?** type of

analysis, or **sensitivity analysis**, is a common feature of the evaluation process. It may use computer modelling techniques for the more quantitative dimensions, and the human mind is available (with DSS or expert system help) to handle the more qualitative or subjective dimensions.)

Control activities

Control, like the monitoring and review phase, is an ongoing activity throughout the entire system development and implementation phases. It refers to actions which are designed:

- to prevent deviations from arising while planned activities are taking place (this is achieved through a continuous process of monitoring and supervising)
- to correct those deviations from the plan which have been observed in previous reporting periods
- to prevent any future deviations from planned activities or performance standards by instituting revisions to future plans, performance standards, targets and monitoring systems
- to implement any other findings from the monitoring, review and evaluation processes.

It should be recognized that control is not merely *reactive* – a series of actions that respond to problems once they have occurred – but is equally important in controlling current and future activities. Arguably, control is more effective in the *proactive* role of seeking to predict potential problems and taking the necessary precautions or actions either to avoid their occurrence or to minimize their effect on the project should they occur. Figure 12.3 illustrates the **closed loop control system** (see Chapter 4) as it applies to the project management process. Control activities may influence the previous phases in the process in the following ways. They can:

- make changes in current operations or activities (for instance, the reallocation of an additional member of the project team to a particular activity that is behind schedule, or to cover for the illness of another member)
- implement changes to the detailed plans for future activities in the project, for example reorganizing the sequence of activities to be undertaken as a result of the anticipated delay in the delivery and installation of a key component in the equipment ordered
- revise the original outline plans, targets, objectives or budgets to reflect significant changes in the project requirements or environment. An increase in the number of workstations that is deemed necessary to support the users in a particular department will increase the budgeted costs for equipment and training, and may require revisions to the timescales or the performance standards of the eventual system – say, in terms of the average response time to users, which may deteriorate with more workstations on the system.

Each of these control activities or decisions will require some form of discussion and agreement, depending on the scale of its impact. Control activities concerning current operations will typically involve the project manager and members of the project team, while changes to the future detailed plans or the project's objectives, targets or budgets will usually require authorization at more senior levels of the organization's management hierarchy. These levels and their role in the project management process are discussed later in this chapter.

The audit and the post-audit review

The final phase of the project management process which is conducted after the completion of development and implementation is an audit of the complete development process. This audit, which addresses both the information system itself and the process of developing the system, ought to assess:

- the effectiveness of the completed system in relation to user requirements and the standards of performance, as either initially specified or subsequently modified – in other words, the achievement of the required quality
- the efficiency of the system during operation against the agreed performance standards
- the cost of the development in relation to the budgeted expenditure and the reasons for over- or under-expenditure
- the time taken to develop the system in relation to the target completion date, and the reasons contributing to completion before or after schedule
- the effectiveness of the management processes and structures in managing the project
- the significance of the problems that have been encountered and the effectiveness of the solutions produced to deal with them.

The primary purpose behind the post-audit analysis is not the generation of excuses for the poor performance of the delivered system, nor the criticism of the inadequate performance of either the project management process itself or of the members of the project team who were supposed to make it work. The real value to the organization from conducting this appraisal is to improve the organization's experience and learning, so that it may:

- enhance the organization's planning and forecasting abilities
- identify problems or issues that may arise in future development projects, and make appropriate adjustments or allowances
- develop the monitoring, control and management processes to achieve greater management effectiveness in future projects
- document the experiences gained to enable future staff not involved in the project to build on previous experiences.

These benefits may prove significant to the organization in the future, but their achievement will usually require an open style of debate or a supportive culture in the organization. Otherwise those directly involved in, or responsible for, the project will react defensively. Those under attack will therefore seek to draw attention away from their own inadequacies or mistakes by attributing the source of the problems to another point in the project development or management system or by blaming external factors such as late deliveries by suppliers. If the post-audit review is conducted in such a negative fashion, the social and political costs will significantly outweigh any potential benefits. Indeed, the outcome which emerges may prove more harmful to future projects than if no review had been undertaken at all.

Levels of managing the project

Each of the above phases needs to be managed at different levels which match the need to manage the total organization at a strategic, tactical and operational level.

1 **Strategic**. This level involves taking a broad view of the total project and of all the major stages involved. The aim is to integrate and co-ordinate the contributions, both direct and indirect, from each area of the organization and from outside it. While the decision making is inevitably concerned with the issues of time, resources, costs and quality, the perspective adopted is to view these issues in aggregate terms – say, the total capital expenditure or staffing costs incurred on the project to date in relation to the budgeted levels. Reporting at this level will generally be directed towards the organization's senior management, and in addition to being in a summarized form, it is also likely to be on a monthly or quarterly timescale to allow the planning, monitoring and control activities to focus on broad issues of performance, timescales or costs.
2 **Tactical**. This level is concerned with viewing and managing the project on a short- to medium-term timescale. The actual time horizon of planning, decision making and control will depend on the total scale of the project in terms of resources and time, but it would be usual to review both the work in hand and the work to be undertaken in each of the main activity areas of the project over the coming one or two months. In larger projects, separate teams of development staff may be given specific responsibility for monitoring and controlling the main activity areas. While still concerned with the four basic elements of time, resources, costs and quality, the information used for this purpose is likely to be more detailed and the reporting period will probably be shorter. For example, the performance of a particular team of staff during the previous week may be evaluated to measure the progress made and to identify any problems and the appropriate corrective action.
3 **Operational**. Management activities at this level are concerned with the more detailed aspect of supervising and controlling the ongoing operations of the development. This will tend to focus on the problems associated with a particular activity and on the direct supervision of staff. The main tasks are resolving any specific technical difficulties encountered, ensuring the maintenance of appropriate standards, motivating the staff and trouble-shooting. While the priority remains the maintenance of effectiveness and efficiency, this is now directly related to specific activities and to individual members of the project team. One of the more important consequences is that the management process at this level will involve less formalized reporting systems; the style usually depends on a more direct and frequent

method of monitoring performance and greater emphasis on interpersonal relationships. An example of an operational management issue would be a debate on the most appropriate method of structuring the organization's customer database to ensure effectiveness and efficiency, both in responding to users' requests and in the utilization of the disk file space available.

Structures for managing the project

As you may conclude from the above examples, the nature and composition of the management process will be dictated largely by the particular level at which the project is being viewed. There are also a number of differing structures used to perform these management activities at the different levels. A typical structure for the management of the systems development process is shown in Figure 12.4.

We outline the primary role and responsibilities of each of the major components of this management structure in the following sub-sections, indicating the level at which they operate.

Project teams

The key feature of the systems development process is the project team – a group of people brought together specifically to undertake the development of a particular project. Since the scale and duration of projects will vary, the size of individual teams and their period of activity will also vary. In many organizations, there will be an almost continuous process of creating and dismantling project teams as new projects appear and existing projects are completed.

Project team membership

The composition of a particular project team will be determined by the nature of the system development and the type of expertise, skills and experience required to undertake the work. Membership will usually be drawn from the following groups:

- specialist IT staff – systems analysts, programmers or computer operations staff
- specialist functional staff, providing technical expertise in the business area concerned (management accountants, for instance, may be required to advise on the product costing system)
- representatives from the users of the system within the organization. (The term 'user' may apply equally to staff involved in inputting or processing data in some way – for example sales order processing staff – as to those using the outputs from the system. In large-scale developments, the user representatives on the team may be required to represent users from other functions as well as their own)
- specialists in training and human resource development, to facilitate implementation of the project proposals
- external specialists or consultants, providing particular expertise not present in the organization (this could relate to IT, functional and training expertise).

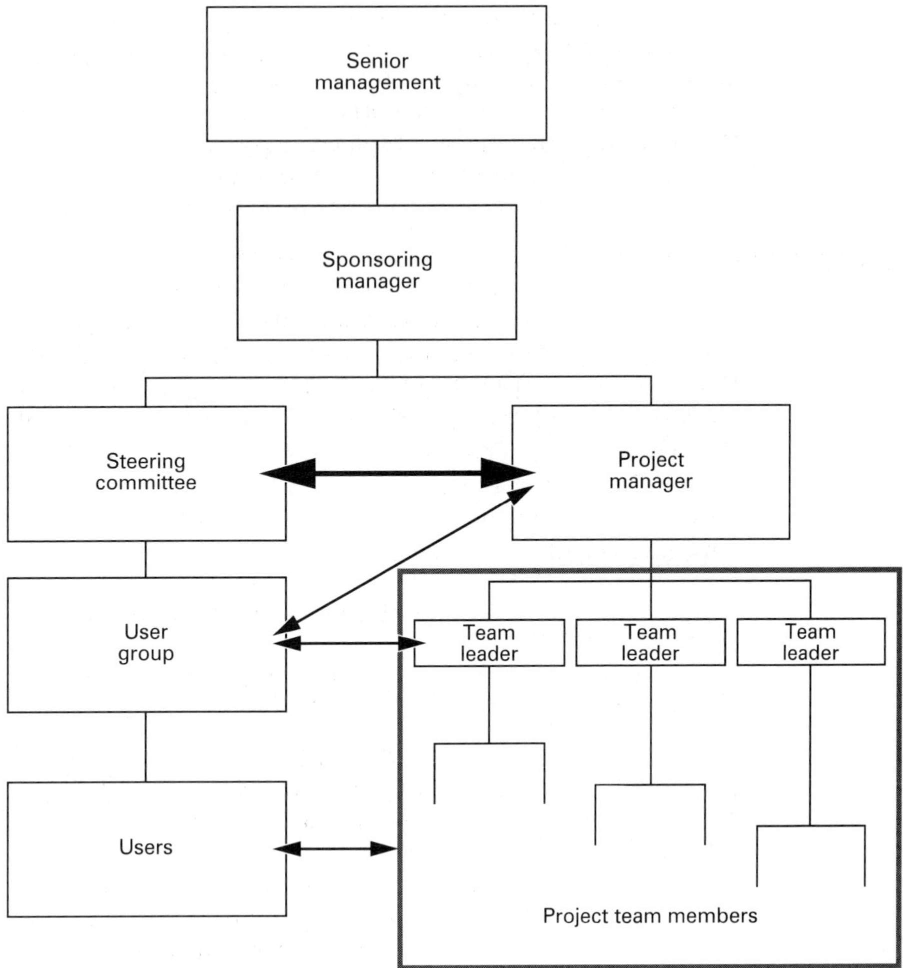

Figure 12.4 Project management infrastructure.

The members of each particular project team may also be members of other project teams, and many organizations have developed matrix organization structures (see Chapter 3) to facilitate the effective operation of team-based working arrangements.

Principles of effective teams

The structure, membership and operation of teams within a specific organization will reflect the specific situation within the organization: the staff available, size of organization, management style, and so on. However, a number of principles and practices are considered to make an important contribution to effective team operation, including:

- developing a shared perception and commitment to achieving team goals and objectives

- encouraging a mutually supportive environment between team members, so that members will share workloads, discuss problems and provide advice
- generating a high degree of confidence within the team (this will be based on members' respect for each other's professional skills and abilities)
- building on acceptance of shared responsibility for the work of the team and respect for the authority of the team leader
- developing sound interpersonal relationships between all members of the group.

Organizations have devised a variety of approaches in their attempts to achieve these attributes of effective team working, but they are outside the scope of this discussion. Organizations that require a large number of project development teams (or where membership of these teams will involve a considerable number of staff from different functions working together) may find it beneficial to develop a team-building strategy across the whole organization, rather than just for IT project developments.

Team leaders

It is usually necessary to appoint a team leader whose main responsibilities will be:

- planning and organizing the work of the members of the particular team on a daily or weekly basis
- continuously supervising the activities of each team member
- providing advice or taking decisions on technical difficulties
- co-ordinating and supervising interaction with user departments and other project teams
- reporting progress to the project manager or user group, and providing advice on possible solutions to problems that have been encountered
- providing feedback to team members on any changes in the project that have resulted from decisions at a more senior level
- implementing any changes to the planned activities and schedules as a result of control decisions.

In larger development projects there may be several project leaders. The project manager should establish a regular pattern of joint meetings between the leaders to assist in the co-ordination of the development work as a whole.

The user group

The user group provides a forum for the joint review and appraisal of developments within the project. Ideally, at least one representative from each of the main departments affected by the systems targeted by the current projects should attend this group, together with the project leaders and the project manager. This is frequently a valuable vehicle for exploring issues and concerns raised by the users, gauging the strength of user opinion and discussing the possible solutions to any problems identified. However, the user group is primarily an advisory body, designed to highlight and discuss the problems that affect users as the system develops. Consequently, although it does not have any executive authority, there must be some degree of responsiveness from the executive management to the issues raised if it is to maintain the support of the users and to provide a useful function in the management process. In relation to minor problems, the project leaders or the project manager may be able to agree a course of remedial action to resolve the issue without further authorization. More substantial issues which may significantly influence the nature of each project, its objectives, budget or targeted completion date will require discussion and agreement at more senior levels in the management structure. This could be facilitated by reports or recommendations from the user group meetings that are transmitted up to the project steering committee.

The project steering committee

The steering committee membership should comprise representatives from the user departments who are also members of the user group, some or all of the project team leaders, the project manager and members of the senior management who are either responsible for the system's development staff or the functional areas primarily affected by the developments in progress. The steering committee performs a key role in:

- providing a forum for the discussion of user concerns, where alternative solutions may be discussed at a more senior level with a view to providing recommended courses of action
- reviewing the current status of the project by reference to the dimensions of time, resources, costs and quality
- analysing the cause and effect of any deviations from the plan and evaluating alternative corrective action
- recommending changes to the project, either to correct current or anticipated deviations, or to reflect developments in the users' requirements from the system
- providing advice on policy formulation for the operation of the information system within the organization at the strategic, management and operational levels.

Although the steering committee's function is nominally to provide advice, it may have real power and be able to persuade the executive arm of management to adopt its recommendations. This will be particularly true if the senior managers responsible for taking the ultimate decisions participate fully in the work and meetings of the committee. Thus, even though the committee may not have either the responsibility or the authority to make decisions, it will often exert power indirectly, through the power of its individual members to impose decisions. To that extent, any failure on the part of senior management to participate in the steering committee will usually relegate its role to that of a mere 'talking shop', making no valuable contribution to the effective development and management of the information system.

The management sponsor

Senior management must show commitment and involvement in the user group and the project steering committee. Mere participation in these bodies is not enough. They must give tangible evidence of their commitment to the development of improved information systems by:

- formally recognizing the potential value that the improved systems will provide to the organization
- displaying a real interest not only in the technical aspects of the development but equally in its impact on user departments
- supporting and encouraging both the project manager and the development team in their work.

The development of information systems, whether for manual or computer-based solutions, will usually involve change. Most organizations and their employees have degrees of resistance to change. If the management of change within an organization is to be successful and effective, it therefore requires the explicit support of the senior management. One solution is to appoint a member of the senior management, preferably at board level, with responsibility for the development of the organization's information system, a role which is termed the **sponsoring manager** in Figure 12.4. In larger organizations, one individual may be the IT manager with sole responsibility for overseeing development, while in smaller operations this role may be combined with other functional responsibilities. An obvious danger in the latter situation is that the systems development role is either relegated to a subsidiary level, because of demands from other functions, or is totally ignored. In fact, the importance of information as a corporate resource and its potential to provide significant competitive advantage to the organization ought generally to justify the post as a separate functional responsibility.

The other important feature of the sponsoring manager's role is to provide a channel of communication, either between the project manager and the senior management or between the users and the senior management, to report on progress and potential future developments.

The project manager

The project manager may be required to interface with all three levels (strategic, tactical and operational) at different times, although, in the larger projects, the team or group leaders would be responsible for the operational level management of the activities and personnel within their team. The project manager's primary responsibility is to ensure effectiveness and efficiency across the complete project, which involves the following action at each level.

1 **Strategic**. At this level, the manager should:
   - evaluate and analyse the strategic impact of each proposed system on the organization's operations, in promoting competitive advantage, and on the other existing or proposed information systems within the organization

- report to senior management on the results of the strategic evaluation and quantify the potential costs and benefits that may be derived from each system development
- contribute to the strategic decision-making process of the organization in terms of the information resource
- review and evaluate the strategic consequences of the progress achieved in developing the system at regular intervals.

2 **Tactical**. At this level, the manager's responsibility is to:
   - convert the objectives, targets and performance standards agreed for the project into operational plans
   - develop the outline and detailed plans for the project, identifying the time, resource and cost parameters, and producing a schedule of activities for the project staff
   - monitor the performance of the project against the agreed plans, budgets and quality performance standards, and report progress to both the steering committee and the management sponsor
   - liaise with management and staff in the user departments, to ensure an effective interface in terms of integration and co-operation between the users and the project development staff
   - facilitate a similar level of co-operation with project staff and outside agencies – either with suppliers or distributors for the company's main business, or with the specialist agencies supporting the system development project itself
   - analyse deviations from planned performance, evaluating alternative solutions and recommending appropriate control changes to future plans or targets
   - develop appropriate information systems to provide the necessary information to monitor and control the project.

3 **Operational**. At this level, the manager should:
   - manage and control the daily activities of the project team members, either directly or through the project team leaders
   - conduct regular progress meetings with the project staff and team leaders to identify and resolve existing and potential difficulties
   - appraise the performance of individual members of the project development staff and seek to assure the achievement of the required quality standards throughout the project development.

The project manager plays a key role in the effective management of system development and (although other participants may contribute significantly to this process) fulfils the major role of integrating all the various contributions.

Tools and techniques

Various tools and techniques are used in the planning and control of investment projects in other areas of management and may be equally effective when applied to information systems development. These tools and techniques are primarily concerned with three of the key elements discussed earlier in this chapter – time, resources and costs – but it is important to recognize that they are designed merely to *support* management. No single tool or technique can be an effective *substitute* for good management.

Critical path analysis (CPA)

The CPA approach to planning and controlling projects is often referred to under other titles, the more common of which are the **program evaluation and review technique** (**PERT**) or the **critical path method** (**CPM**). Although there are some variations in the detailed approach of each of these methods, the basic assumptions are the same. The stages involved in the CPA approach are as follows.

Programming

For these purposes, the term 'programming' refers to the following tasks:

- The identification and listing all of the major tasks or activities that are to be undertaken in the project. In the initial stages it is often easier to identify only the broad activities rather than to break each of them down into very detailed activities. Figure 12.5 illustrates a **network diagram**. At the initial level, it provides an overview of the total project development process. Subsequently, each of the activities which are shown as arrows in the diagram will be developed into increasingly more detailed network diagrams. The following stages relate to the development of these more detailed diagrams.
- The construction of a network diagram shows the logical sequence of each of the activities listed. The symbols used are an *arrow* (which represents a task or activity, with the arrowhead indicating the direction of the logical flow) and *circles* which represent events. An event is essentially a logical device to connect up the activities and to indicate the point at which an activity starts and finishes. It also ties together all of those preliminary activities which must be completed before the particular activity may commence. For these purposes, activities have durations associated with them, while events are seen as a point in time with no duration. Structuring the logical sequence is often a difficult and time-consuming process. It is dependent on receiving accurate additional information from the key people involved in the project,

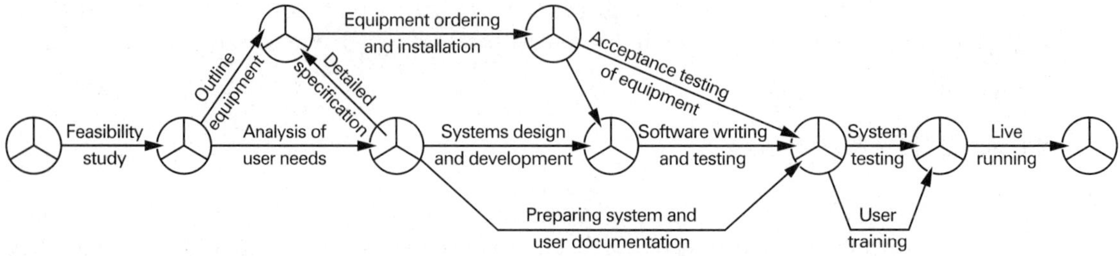

Figure 12.5 Outline network diagram of the systems development.

and relies on the judgement of which activities are to be completed before the next activity may commence. In practical terms, it is often possible to start a subsequent activity prior to the full completion of a preceding activity. The requirement to allow this to happen is that the interdependent proportion of the work is completed before the subsequent activity can commence. This change in the logical relationship between activities may be represented in the diagram by dividing the earlier activity into two parts (see the subsection on Evaluation later in this chapter).

Figure 12.6 illustrates a simple network diagram. The structure of the diagram suggests that activity 4-6 cannot commence until both activities 2-4 and 3-4 have been completed. Even though activity 3-4 may be completed before the other activity, the subsequent activity may still not commence. There are other methods of designing the diagram to show the logic that activity 4-6 may start after a certain proportion of 2-4 has been completed, but this is outside the scope of the present treatment. The correctness of the initial logical representation in the diagram will be examined at later stages in the planning process, when attention is focused on specific areas of the plan.

- The estimation of the time which will be required to undertake each of the activities in the diagram. In the normal project development process these estimates would either be expressed in days or weeks. Certain approaches such as PERT employ a system of estimation based on three time classifications for each activity, i.e. pessimistic, most likely and optimistic.

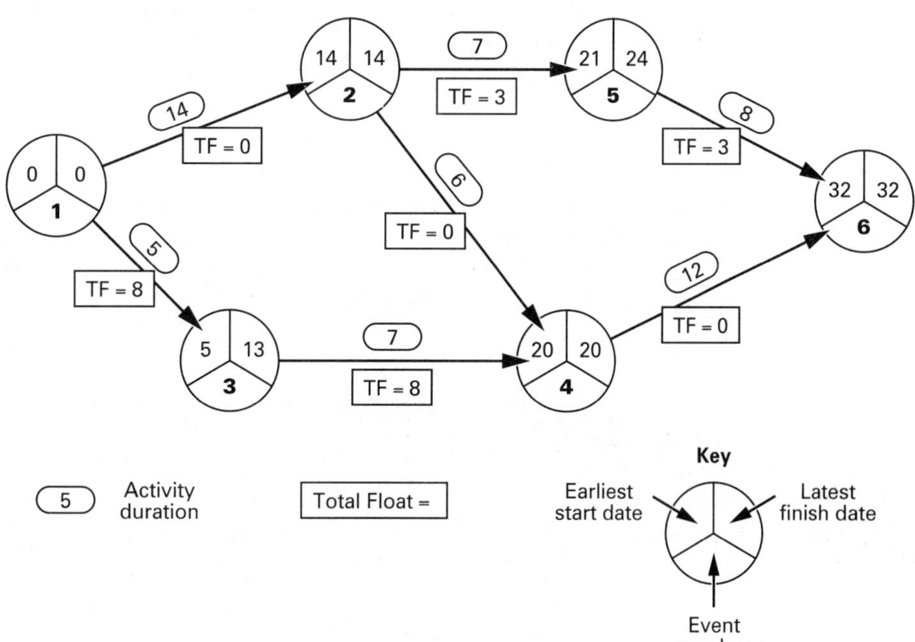

Figure 12.6 Critical path diagram.

The three estimates are then aggregated into a single estimate for the *expected duration* of the activity by using a weighting formula of the type:

Optimistic + 4 × Most likely + Pessimistic.

The expected duration calculated by this process is then applied to the network calculations, as illustrated in Figure 12.7. The use of the three estimates will provide some additional data to aid the planning and analysis of the project, although the difficulties in capturing these estimates, the costs of doing so and the degree of accuracy of the data may suggest that this added value may be significantly outweighed by the costs.

- The use of the network diagram and the estimated durations for each of the activities to calculate the *earliest start* and *earliest finish* times for each of the activities thus:

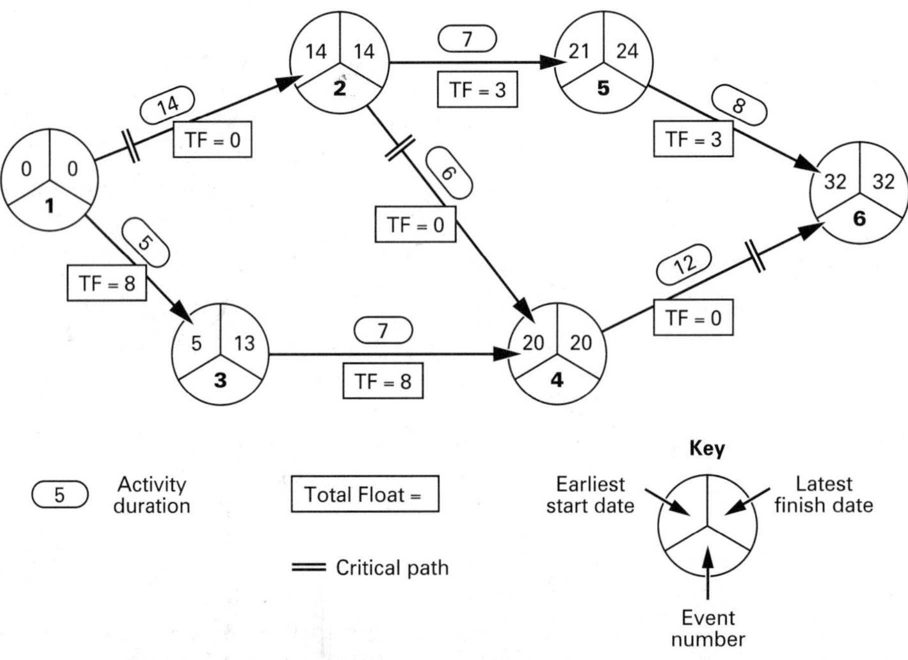

Activity numbers Start	Event End	Duration	Earliest Start		Latest Start		Total
1	2	14	0	14	0	14	0
1	3	5	0	5	8	13	8
3	4	7	5	12	13	20	8
2	4	6	14	20	14	20	0
2	5	7	14	21	17	24	3
4	6	12	20	32	20	32	0
5	6	8	21	29	24	32	3

Figure 12.7 Critical path diagram with activity schedules.

(a) Starting at the beginning of the network and setting the initial time to zero, progress along each of the paths of activities in the diagram, adding the duration to the earliest finish date of each activity. For example, activity 12 may start at time 0, and requires 14 weeks to complete; hence the earliest finish date would be week 14. Activities 2-5 and 2-4 may commence as soon as this activity is completed and will result in the estimated earliest finish times of these activities, as shown in Figure 12.7.
(b) In situations where more than one activity **enters** an event, then the later of the finish dates of the activities entering is taken as the earliest start date of all the activities coming out of the event. For example, the earliest time that activity 4-6 can start is week 20. Although activity 3-4 is completed by week 12, activity 4-6 cannot start until activity 2-4 is completed at the earliest time of week 20.

- The calculation of the *latest start* and *latest finish* times by reversing the above process for calculating the earliest times, that is:
  (a) Set the latest finish time for the project equal to the earliest finish time calculated, week 32 in the example.
  (b) Deduct the duration from this latest finish time for the activity to calculate the latest start time for the activity. In the case of activity 5-6, the latest finish of week 32, less the duration of eight weeks, would require the activity to start by week 24 at the latest to ensure the completion of the total project by week 32.
  (c) Repeat the process for all activities, working backwards throughout the network. In situations where more than one activity **leaves** an event, the latest finish time for the activities preceding the event is the earlier of the latest start times calculated. The latest start of activity 2-5 is week 17, and for activity 2-4 is week 14, hence the latest finish of activity 1-2 is week 14, the earlier of the two times.

  A complete schedule of the earliest and latest start and finish times is shown in Figure 12.7.
- The calculation of the *total float* for each activity which allows the determination of the critical path for the project is as follows.
  (a) Calculate the time available to do the project

Latest finish time – Earliest start time.

Deduct from this time available the time required to do the activity, i.e. the duration. The resulting figure is termed the *total float* for the activity.

Total float = (Latest finish – Earliest start) – Duration.

The total float for activity 2-4 would be calculated as

TF = (20 – 14) – 6 = 0 weeks.

The total float values for the remaining activities are shown in the table in Figure 12.7.

(b) The sequence of activities from the start of the project to the end which has the lowest total float, a value of zero in our example, is termed the *critical path*. This is the longest logical sequence of activities within the project and dictates the overall length of time required to complete the project.

(c) Although the total float in the example used is a value of zero, this is due to setting the latest finish time of the final activities equal to their earliest finish times. However, if a target completion date were used as the latest finish time for the project, positive or negative values of total float would ensue. For example, a completion date of week 30 would result in a negative value of minus two for the total float on the critical path activities, whereas a completion date of week 38 would result in a positive total float value of six weeks on the critical path.

(d) The interpretation of the total float value indicates the degree to which particular activities may be delayed in starting, or extended in terms of their duration, without affecting the completion date of the project. Activities 1-3 and 3-4 have a total float of eight weeks, which means that either the start of these activities may be delayed to week 8 or week 13 respectively, or the total duration of the activities may be increased by a further eight weeks before the project completion time of week 32 is jeopardized. It is important to recognize that the total float relates to a sequence of activities and not to the individual activities. Thus, if activity 1-3 is delayed by six weeks, the total float on the subsequent activity 3-4 would reduce to two weeks.

Evaluation

Following the completion of the network diagram and the calculation of both the activity and project completion dates and the total float values, it is usual to evaluate the plan against the target completion dates for the project. In most situations, the initial plan will fail to meet the required completion date and it will be necessary to engage in a process to evaluate alternative strategies for the reduction of the time required. CPA is a powerful tool in supporting this evaluation of possible changes to the plan, and it provides a rapid means of assessing the effect of changes in one part of the plan or network on all the other activities and the completion date. It also assists in refocusing the attention of the management on new areas of the plan which may become critical as a result of changes or delays. Two examples of changes to the simplified network illustrate the power of this technique in aiding management decisions.

1 **Reducing activity durations.** One approach to speeding up the completion of a project is to reduce the duration of particular activities. Initially, this process should concentrate only on those activities on the critical path, as savings in time on these activities will directly influence the project completion date. If activity 4-6 could be reduced from the initial time required of 12 weeks to five weeks, this might suggest that the project would be completed five weeks earlier than planned, as this activity is on the critical path. The revised schedule in Figure 12.8 indicates that the

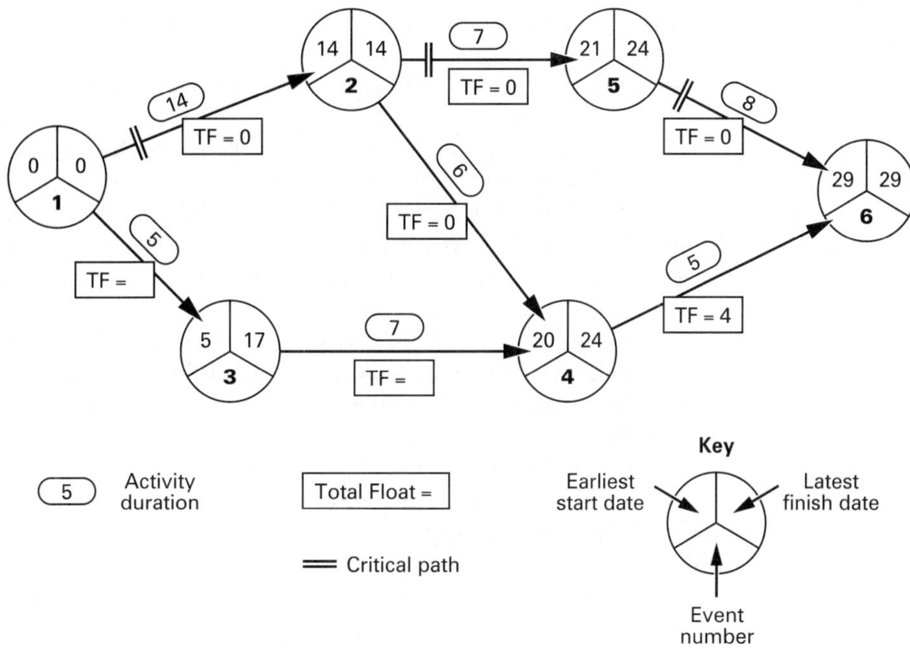

Activity numbers Start Event	End	Duration	Earliest Start		Latest Start		Total
1	2	14	0	14	0	14	0
1	3	5	0	5	12	17	12
3	4	7	5	12	17	24	12
2	4	6	14	20	18	24	4
2	5	7	14	21	14	21	0
4	6	5	20	25	24	29	4
5	6	8	21	29	21	29	0

Figure 12.8 Critical path diagram – changing activity.

completion date is reduced by only three weeks. The reason for this should be evident from the reduction in the total float on activities 2-5 and 5-6 which now have zero total float and represent the new critical path. Any further reduction in the project completion date would now require a reduction in the durations of either of these activities or the earlier activities on the critical path, as activities 2-5 and 5-6 have a positive total float value of four weeks. The reduction in activity durations below the normally anticipated time will usually imply an increase in the costs of the activity itself. This dimension of the planning process is developed more fully in the sub-section on PERT/cost later in this chapter.

2 **Changing the logical sequence of activities**. Another approach to reducing the overall time required to complete a project is to review the logical sequence of activities in the initial plan. The purpose is to identify those activities which may be:

- undertaken in parallel with other activities that are currently shown as following
- commenced when only part of the logically preceding activities has been completed
- not fully dependent on the completion of all of the preceding activities currently shown in the network.

Again, attention in analysing these possibilities should be focused on those activities on the critical path. In our example, if it were established that activity 1-2 comprised two basic stages, and that activity 2-4 could be started after the completion of this first stage rather than the completion of the entire activity, then the network could be redrawn as indicated in Figure 12.9. The second stage of the original activity 1-2 is now shown as activity 2-7 and is being conducted in parallel with activity 2-5, which also depends only on the first stage of activity 1-2 being completed. The overall effect of this change in the logic would be a reduction of six weeks in the project completion time and the detailed effects on the individual activities are shown in the table in Figure 12.9.

Review

The final stage in the application of the CPA approach to project management is the monitoring and review of progress as the plan is implemented. The basic stages of this process involve the following:

- periodic reports, either weekly or monthly, indicating those activities that have been completed and the date on which they were completed; those activities which are currently in progress, the extent to which they are completed and any revised changes to the time required for the activity; and identifying any changes in the estimates of future activities on the basis of improved information or experiences in conducting the initial activities in the project
- the incorporation of these actual completion times or revised estimates into the network diagram and the assessment of their effect on the project completion date and the critical path
- the evaluation of alternative approaches to the resolution of delays in the project completion time, as indicated in the earlier 'Evaluation' sub-section, and any necessary attempts to secure agreement to any changes which may be required to activity durations, the sequence of activities, or extensions to the total project completion date
- the provision of revised schedules of activities which incorporate new start and finish dates for all the future activities in the project.

An example of the revised schedule on our simplified project is provided in Figure 12.10. The graphical presentation in the figure is termed a **Gantt chart**, and its purpose is to indicate all of the activities in the project. Managers use shading highlights to indicate the extent to which each of the activities is either on, behind or in advance of the schedule. Consequently, Gantt charts are a useful method of displaying the current state of a project and they are frequently placed on the project manager's wall. They are, however, only really suitable either for the display of relatively small projects with limited activities, or for summarizing the activities of a larger project. The major problem associated with the use of this type of chart is that the logical interrelationships between the component activities or tasks are more difficult to deduce from a chart than from a network diagram. The main advantage lies in the chart's capacity to represent the current state of the project clearly. This latter point is essentially true of all control methods.

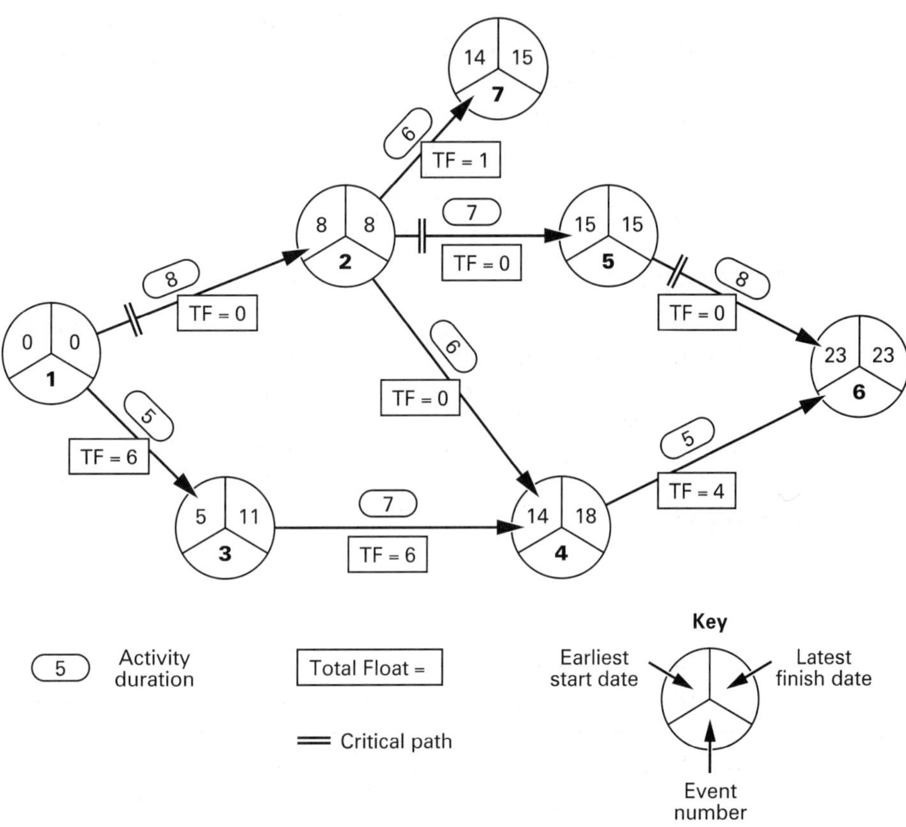

Activity numbers Start Event	End	Duration	Earliest Start		Latest Start		Total
1	2	8	0	8	0	8	0
1	3	5	0	5	6	11	6
3	4	7	5	12	11	18	6
2	4	6	8	14	12	18	4
2	5	7	8	15	8	15	0
4	6	5	14	19	18	23	4
5	6	8	15	23	15	23	0
2	7	6	8	14	9	15	1
7	5	0	14	14	15	15	1

Figure 12.9 Critical path diagram – changing network logic.

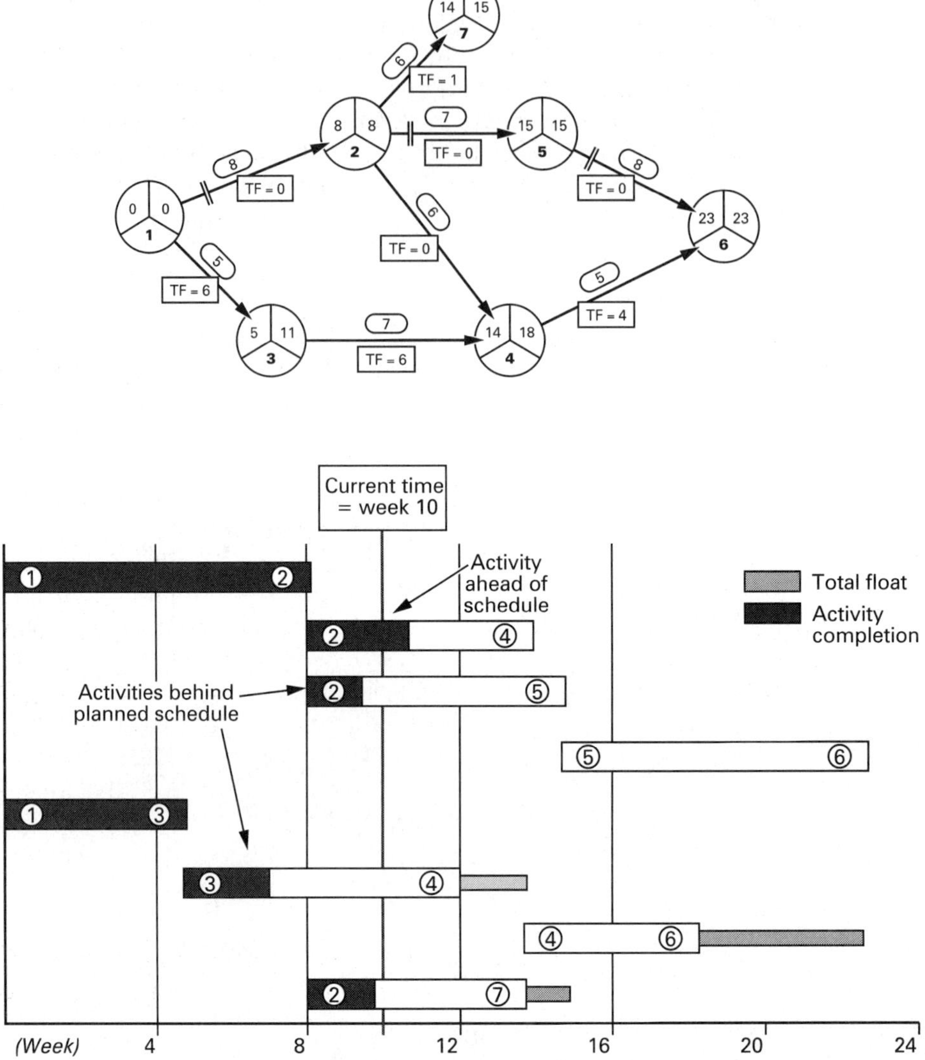

Figure 12.10 Gantt chart.

PERT/cost

Our discussion so far has concentrated on the time dimension of the project, although some reference was made earlier to the increased costs which might result from changes in the durations of activities. PERT/cost is a further development of the CPA approach which deals with the influence of changes in time on the cost of a project. In summary, the approach involves four key activities.

- Estimating the normal duration for an activity and the normal cost associated with this time period.
- Estimating the extent to which this normal duration may be reduced and the additional costs of doing so. The additional costs may arise from the hiring of additional systems staff or the overtime worked by existing staff. However, the additional costs do not always relate to human resources and may, for example, involve additional payments to secure faster methods of delivering the supplies required. Further, not all activities are capable of being reduced in terms of time, and for those where reductions may be achieved, the costs may rise more steeply as successively more time is saved on the activity. In this, the reductions usually plateau at a lower limit in terms of duration and it proves impossible to secure further reductions.
- Addressing those activities on the critical path, so that each activity is ranked in terms of the cost of saving one week of time. Starting with the activity that costs least to save a week, and moving down the list in terms of the ranking, produces an assessment of the time that it is possible to save on the total project time and the consequent increase in total costs for each incremental week saved. The process is complicated by the fact that initial changes in the duration of activities on the critical path may result in a change in the direction of the critical path (as seen in the example illustrated earlier in Figure 12.9) requiring the consideration of the time–cost trade-off of other activities.
- The project managers assessing the potential benefits of saving time on the project against the incremental costs of doing so. The application of the time–cost trade-off is not only useful before the start of a project, but can become a useful aid to the project manager in controlling the project, as it will indicate the costs associated with proposed changes in future activities and the time that may be saved.

Resource analysis

The third key element to consider in the management of the project is that of resource utilization. The network plan may also be used as a basis for aggregating and allocating the resources within the project:

- The resources required in undertaking each activity are estimated. This may often include a variety of resources, for example employees with different skills.
- It is necessary to monitor, and to progress through each week of the project duration, the value of each particular type of resource that is required during that week. This is achieved by adding across all the activities planned for that week.
- A histogram may be produced that shows the overall pattern of demand for each particular resource throughout the project. An illustration of the histogram is provided in Figure 12.11 for the sample project. The assumption is made that all activities start at their calculated start times.
- Analysis of the resource demand pattern indicates a peak demand for eight programmer/analysts during the period from week 8 to week 14 inclusive. If

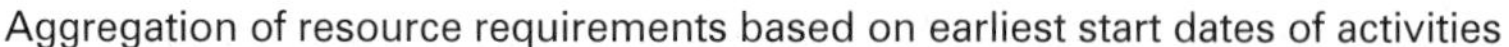

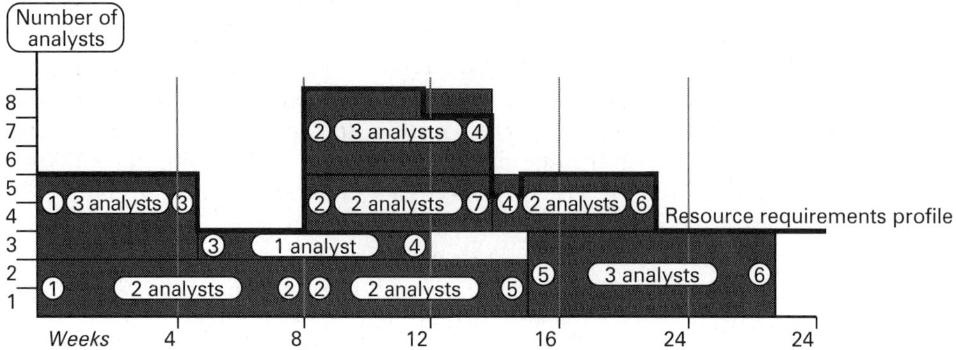

Smoothing the resource requirements by delaying activities within their total float

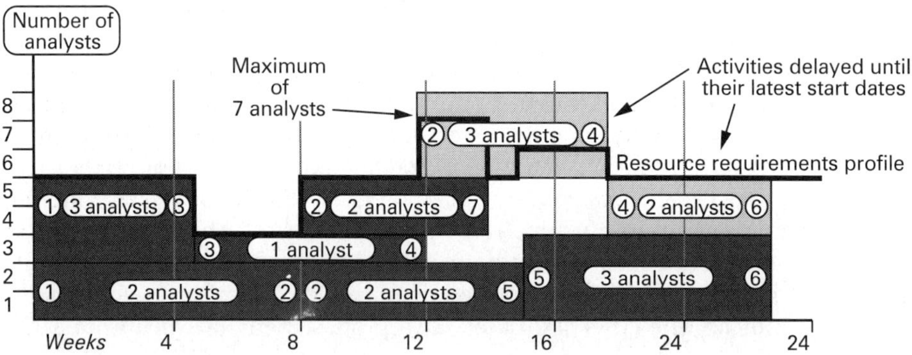

Further smoothing the resource requirements by extending the project completion time

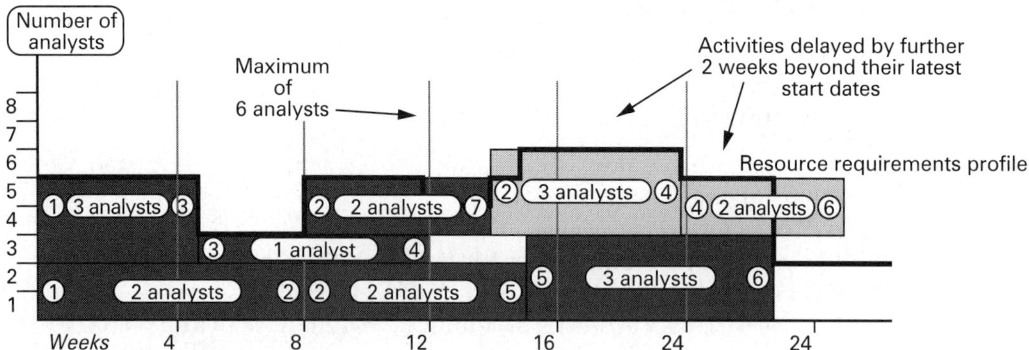

Figure 12.11 Resources analysis and scheduling.

there were only six such staff available, the implied schedule of activities would be difficult to complete on time without the recruitment of an additional programmer/analyst.

- A reallocation of the activities may assist in smoothing out the demand for the particular resource without incurring any delay on the project as a whole. If the start of activities 2-4 and 4-6 is delayed by four weeks (i.e. by the length of the total float on the activity), a more even demand for the resource is produced, as shown in Figure 12.11, with no consequent delay in the subsequent activities or the total project time.

A number of algorithms may be used to reschedule activities within a project to achieve a more balanced use of the resources available. Such algorithms are primarily based on the rescheduling of activities within their total float time, and the process is generally termed **resource smoothing**. Although these algorithms may be applied manually, the effort required in applying them to even a small number of activities is usually very high. Fortunately, there are a variety of software packages available on the market which will facilitate:

- the input of the network logic, activity durations, cost and resource estimates
- the calculation of the start and finish times and total float for each activity, and a highlighting of the critical path
- the analysis of time–cost trade-off, resource aggregation and allocation
- the provision of schedules of activities to be undertaken by different groups of staff, indicating the target start and finish dates, and the resources and costs to be incurred
- the input of data on the progress of the project at periodic intervals and the reproduction of the processes and output referred to above, which incorporate the revised estimates and plans.

Management of the project, in terms of planning, evaluating and controlling, therefore involves an integrated and simultaneous treatment of the time, resource and cost elements, as stressed earlier in this chapter. Changes in one of these elements of a project will invariably have some effect on either one or both of the other elements. The task of the project manager is to balance these elements, and the tools and techniques described in this section are an essential requirement to support this management function.

Quality

The remaining key element identified earlier in the chapter (but not referred to in the previous discussion of support tools and techniques) is that of quality. Although quality has always been an element in system development, it is only in recent years that it has been recognized as an important element requiring effective management in planning and control terms. Quality control in the manufacturing areas of the commercial sector has developed a range of support tools to aid the planning, measurement and control of quality. Such tools are less evident in the area of systems development, although increased attention is being given by many organizations to improving performance. Examples of approaches to the management of quality include the those given below.

- Identifying particular indicators of quality in each area of a project and developing methods of measuring them. Examples might include: the types and number of faults in the coding produced for a program; the response rate in answering users' queries or problems; users' assessment of a training programme; or the number of errors detected in setting up system database files.

- Reaching agreement with the staff involved on the objectives to be achieved by producing quality in a given indicator and on the stages through which the project must pass to achieve the final objective.
- Developing methods of improving quality – usually by the involvement of those directly concerned, through quality circles, suggestion schemes or some other appropriate means.
- Recording data on each indicator and monitoring the quality level achieved at regular intervals, reporting back to the staff involved, and discussing and initiating further proposals to improve performance levels.

Managers should recognize that improvements in quality performance will not be achieved solely by the use of charts but will require the exercise of considerable skills by the project manager and the team leaders in motivating the staff. In the final analysis, organizations may be forced to introduce a system of financial rewards linked to the achievement of quality performance targets.

Summary

- The ultimate effectiveness and efficiency of an information system will be significantly influenced by the quality of the project management: the control and balancing of the interdependent elements of time, resources, costs and quality, given that improvement in one may result in the deterioration in some or all of the other elements.
- The management process involves a variety of activities, each of which should be conducted effectively and efficiently: planning, analysing, communicating, co-ordinating, motivating, monitoring, trouble-shooting, controlling, interfacing. Project management also involves a variety of different individuals and groups, each of whom is required to make an effective contribution if the project is to achieve its objectives. These include the project manager, the team leaders in the project, users, the user group, the steering committee, the management sponsor and the senior management in the organizations.
- Information is an organizational resource and the development of systems to apply it more effectively to solving the organization's problems and to developing its added value requires a commitment and contribution from all areas, including senior management.
- The project manager plays a key role in planning, integrating and controlling the contributions from the various internal and external contributors and he or she is increasingly involved in managing the interfaces between the organization and its external suppliers or distributors. Various tools and techniques can support the management of a project, but these are only support tools and they will not replace effective management.

Self-test questions

1. Summarize the objectives of the project management process under the two relevant key headings.
2. List the nine project management activities.
3. Describe briefly the stages in project management.
4. List the levels of project management and summarize the key concerns of each.
5. List the tactical actions that you would expect a project manager to undertake.

Exam-style questions

1. In practice, a project manager needs to manage simultaneously the elements of time, resources, cost and quality. These elements not only interact with each other but are continuously changing.
   (a) Briefly explain the role of each of these elements in the project management process.
   (b) Give examples of the type of judgements and decisions which the project manager may be required to make.
2. 'The efficient operation of project teams is critical to the process of systems development.'

   Write a report for the project leader, identifying the main factors contributing to effective team working.

(*All answers on pages 564–565*)

CHAPTER 13

Systems evaluation

A system's performance is evaluated at a number of different stages in its life cycle by a variety of people in the organization using a range of different performance measures. An important feature of this activity is that it is (or ought to be) seen as a continuous process of measuring performance against the ever-changing needs of the organization and its users. Systems evaluation is therefore a wide-ranging, multifaceted, continuous and dynamic process of performance measurement.

In previous chapters we referred to many of these dimensions of systems evaluation. In this chapter we shall attempt to provide an integrated view of the process, identifying the different management levels at which evaluation may be conducted within the organization, together with the different performance criteria and measures that may be used at each of these levels. We note the fact that different people in the organization who interface with the system in various ways (for example, users or data providers) may view the system's performance from different perspectives. We also give attention to the assessment of the concept of an optimum system and to the practical issues and problems inherent in the process of systems evaluation.

Evaluation in the management process

In the previous chapter we outlined a structure for the management of projects within the information systems development field. This structure is applicable not only to individual projects but to the overall management of systems development – and, indeed, the management of other types of project or the organization as a whole. Evaluation was identified as part of the monitoring, review and control process. However, the evaluation process is wider than this in practice, involving the earlier stages of objective setting and planning, as explained below. A generic model of the main stages of the evaluation process is presented in Figure 13.1.

The key elements in the process of evaluation are:

1 **Determining the objectives and performance criteria**. To 'evaluate' is to compare the acceptability of particular outcomes against those that might have been expected or desired. For this to be meaningful, it is necessary to establish in advance what levels of performance are expected or which objectives are significant. But this is not straightforward. In any situation, there is a wide range of criteria that can be applied to measure the performance of a system; and each criterion may vary in importance, depending on

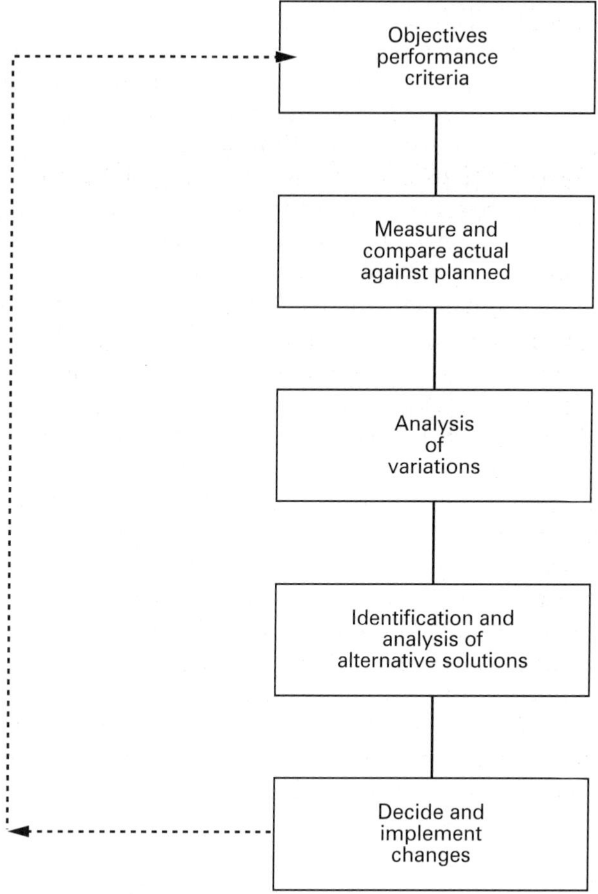

Figure 13.1 Systems evaluation process.

the type of system and the management level at which the evaluation is being conducted. The best that can be done, therefore, is to outline these criteria in the generic system evaluation framework and to examine them in some detail later in the chapter. However, for these purposes, the organization must specify its objectives and lay down performance criteria to be met.

2 **Measuring performance**. The second data input required by the evaluation process is the measurement of the actual performance of the system. While this may be a relatively straightforward exercise in most operational systems, it may prove more problematic at a tactical level and almost impossible at a strategic level. So, for example, it ought to be relatively easy to count the number of units produced by a factory in a particular period, but it is not so easy to measure the customers' opinions on the quality of the products produced. Some of these problems are addressed in a later section of this chapter which examines the practical issues in systems evaluation.

3 **Comparison of actual performance against the planned performance.** Once the measurement data have been collected, the next step is a comparison of the performance data against the performance criteria and objectives previously established. Two issues should be mentioned at this stage. First, this comparison process does not need to be on a continuous or even a regular basis. Although it will be convenient to accumulate and compare some performance data on a regular and periodic basis (for example, financial expenditures can be matched to budgets at the end of each month – see Chapter 4 on system delays), in many cases, the comparison will be on an irregular or infrequent basis (for example, through internal audits of a system or random testing by external regulatory bodies).

   Second, the process of comparison may only be triggered by certain unusual or exceptional events. A major leakage of chemical pollutants into the local environment, for instance, will typically initiate a series of comparative studies on the environmental consequences. This generally accepted management principle of **exception reporting** is equally applicable to the process of system evaluation. (See Chapter 4 for further discussion of this principle in relation to systems theory.)

4 **Analysis of the nature and scale of the differences.** By and large, organizations that aim to learn from their experience are more successful. So a key feature of the evaluation process involves analysing data to see whether it is possible to explain any of the differences which emerge from the comparisons. Of course, it would not be economic to investigate every deviation of actual from planned performance. We have just noted that the process of exception reporting only triggers evaluation and control where the scale of the performance deviation is significant enough to warrant further investigation. So if further analysis is justified, this stage breaks down into the following activities:
   - identifying and investigating potential reasons for the deviation from planned performance
   - forecasting whether the effects of the deviation will have a real effect on future performance
   - assessing whether corrective action is required – obviously, if the causes appear to be outside the control of the organization (changes in the external environment, for example) or possibly the result of certain freak events which are unlikely to recur, no response is required.

5 **Identification of potential alternative actions to resolve the deviation and achieve the necessary performance criteria.** At its best the management process is creative and judgemental. While frequently under pressure, senior managers need to be able to analyse the costs and the likely benefits of potential alternative strategies to resolve the problem and to assess their impact on the range of performance criteria. The decision will often be demanding because there is likely to be more than one possible strategy, and each strategy may involve different costs and, given the multiple range of criteria involved, may also produce different consequences. For example, the cause of falling sales may be attributed to deteriorating levels of product quality. But if the proposed strategy is to increase the levels of quality

inspection, this may in turn cause reductions in productivity levels and increases in delivery lead times – both of which may be other important performance criteria and may also affect the ability of the organization to maintain customer goodwill.

6. **Decision and implementation of the appropriate solution strategy**. The final stage in the process is for the managers to take the decision and to move towards implementation. As Figure 13.1 indicates, this will result in a further loop of the evaluation process. The solution strategy proposed may involve changes to the expected performance criteria and objectives. Before confirming implementation, the managers should repeat the process to evaluate the changes undertaken against the new performance objectives.

These elements in the process of evaluation are common to all three levels of general organizational management: operational, tactical and strategic.

The differences between the evaluation process at each of these levels will be evident in:

- the nature of the issues addressed
- the performance criteria and measures applied
- the type of data used
- the scale of the problems
- the potential impact of the possible solutions.

Relating this process of evaluation to the field of information systems will equally involve differences in the nature of the evaluation at the operational, tactical and strategic levels. We shall examine the nature of these differences in the remainder of this chapter.

Systems evaluation: a framework

In practice the process of systems evaluation is complex, not only because it comprises a number of stages (as described in the previous section), but also because it involves a variety of different people in the organization, each of whom will be evaluating the system from a different perspective and for different purposes. Figure 13.2 identifies two important dimensions of the systems evaluation process:

- **Differing management levels**. The three primary levels are shown in the diagram. The distinction between these management levels in the organization was discussed in Chapter 1. We shall now relate this more general discussion more specifically to information systems evaluation.
- **Performance criteria**. The other dimension in the diagram relates to the range of performance criteria against which the information system may be evaluated. We shall discuss these criteria in the next part of this chapter.

There is a third dimension. It is not shown explicitly in the diagram, but it is equally important to the overall process of systems evaluation and underpins the other two dimensions, namely:

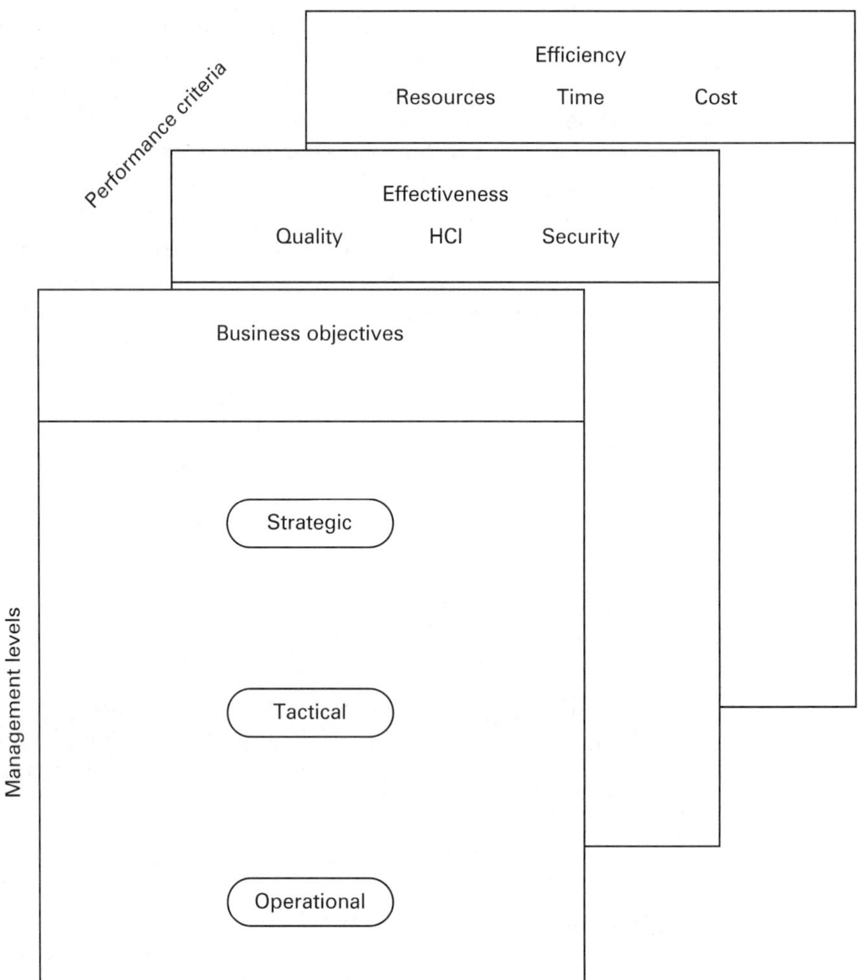

Figure 13.2 Systems evaluation: a framework.

- **Differing user perspectives**. In the opening paragraph to this section, we indicated that different people would be involved in the evaluation process. But not all those people will be users in the strict sense (for example, some of the senior directors may have no direct experience as users). The term 'user' is intended to include only those people who are:
  - required to rely on output provided by the system
  - involved in the activity of providing or inputting data to the system
  - concerned directly with the operation and development of the information system.

  The basis on which the evaluation is conducted will clearly be determined by the perspective from which it is viewed. Although a common set of criteria may have been accepted by the users, the relative importance of each criterion may vary according to the perspective and management level from which the system is viewed and the degree to which the system is 'used'.

The three dimensions of systems performance criteria, management level and user perspective provide the broad structure for the remainder of this chapter. Each of these dimensions will be examined separately in the following sections, but you should recognize that they are all essentially interrelated.

Systems performance criteria

In this context, the term 'systems performance' is applied to the performance of the total information system and not just to those elements that have been automated or are computer related. If we are to arrive at a fair assessment of the total information system's performance, then every aspect of the information handling and the people involved should be considered equally relevant. The criteria for assessing systems performance have been grouped into three broad headings:

- business objectives
- systems effectiveness
- system efficiency.

Although each of these headings will have some relevance in every situation, the degree of relevance and appropriateness is likely to vary depending on the level of management under consideration. You should already be aware of the general nature of business objectives, and of the concepts of effectiveness and efficiency in the context of the organization from the discussion in the earlier chapters. From this you will have recognized that terms in this area do not have exclusive meanings. Thus, it would be perfectly acceptable to read the first criterion, business objectives, as including the goals of efficiency and effectiveness. But, this separate treatment of effectiveness and efficiency is a constructive step in identifying and developing the range of factors that contribute towards the performance of a system.

Performance criteria: business objectives

Of the three sets of criteria this is the broadest – in the sense that it seeks to evaluate the contribution that the system or system component makes towards the objectives of the organization or business as a whole. The early chapters provided a number of examples of how information systems can provide advantages for an organization. Their contribution towards organizational objectives may also be reflected at the three general levels, namely strategic, tactical and operational. Let us examine these three levels in turn.

The strategic level

At this level, the total information system will be expected to make a positive contribution towards meeting objectives in more abstract terms. For example, the organization may look for evidence that there has been an improvement in the degree of competitive advantage or added value either directly by the system itself or through the use of the system in support of particular activities. This evidence might take the form of monitoring data said to demonstrate that the business can respond more rapidly to customer orders following the connection of the organization and its customers through an EDI network (see Chapter 7 for details of EDI). Such claims are rarely uncontroversial. We start with the fact that major IT developments make substantial capital demands and organizations frequently find it necessary to assert that these developments have delivered real strategic and corporate benefits (say, to keep institutional and private shareholders happy). But because of the broadness of strategic objectives, it is always going to be difficult to quantify system performance criteria with any confidence. There are also considerable problems in distinguishing between the contribution made by the information system and the contributions made by any of the other factors that could have supported the achievement of the objectives. Who is to say whether any particular corporate benefit resulted more from the quality of the management team and its ability to use the information rather than from the quality of the information system supporting it?

A further difficulty is the time horizon associated with strategic management and planning. Many of the strategic objectives are set and pursued over periods varying between five and ten years. Given the pace at which technology is developing, the life cycle of a typical information system may be significantly shorter. This often means that the total information system is continuously evolving, making it difficult to give credit to any one version of the system in contributing towards an organization's strategic objectives.

The type of criteria that may be used in assessing the contribution of the system at the strategic level could include whether:

- the system is able to provide timely information about the present and future external environment
- the information flows provide quality lines of communication and support the day-to-day operation of the organization
- the system provides analytical models and techniques which the decision-makers actually use to support their analytical needs
- the use of information provided by the system actually presents opportunities to gain competitive advantage.

The tactical level

At this level, the business objectives will tend to be more focused – requiring managers to achieve clear performance targets for a particular function within a defined time. For example, the board of directors may set month-by-month targets for improvements in the productivity of shopfloor personnel. The system performance criteria used to measure success or failure at the tactical level will examine the extent to which the information system supports the middle managers as they attempt to achieve this. Some of the criteria which may be relevant are:

- how long it takes to collate the monthly performance data

- whether the data output is accurate
- whether the output communicates real information to the relevant managers
- the extent to which this information actually helps the managers to encourage the workers to improve their productivity.

As with measurement at the strategic level, the problem would be how to disaggregate the contribution made by the information system to improving performance from (say) the quality of the management involved or other factors influencing performance. The closer we get to operational matters, for example, the more likely it is that staff training has improved skills or that changes in working practices will contribute as much towards improved productivity as the information system supporting the function.

The following generally stated criteria are typical of those that could be used to assess the contribution of the system at this level:

- effectiveness in monitoring the organization's existing operations
- whether the system feeds back to the right individuals
- the quality and timeliness of the feedback provided
- whether the system provides information which clearly highlights the problems to be addressed
- the degree to which the system supports the decision-makers if they wish to analyse the problems
- whether the system enables the decision-makers to model potential solution strategies
- the degree to which the system supports lines of communication
- whether the system supports the implementation of the decisions taken, say, by providing effective monitoring of the implemented solution.

The operational level

At this level, the organization-related objectives will be expressed in more precise terms. For example, individual operations such as the speed of preparing invoices may be nominated and targets for direct improvements in productivity will be set. Similarly, the contribution of improved working practices for the employees involved can be monitored, say by measuring response times before and after a migration from manual searching through large volumes of paper records stored in filing cabinets to a database system. Targets for improvements in the quality of the outputs can also be set, say, by a group monitoring the output of newly acquired desk-top publishing software to assess the design of brochures and price lists resulting from the application.

At this level, it may be possible to achieve more precision in the measurement of the system's performance, given that:

- the objectives are directly related to specific and identifiable operations or activities
- the information system itself will be required to perform a more mechanistic role in the operation either by providing users directly with the data necessary to conduct the operation, or by providing the basic tools with which the operation is conducted

- the measurement of performance will usually relate to a short time horizon, possibly limited to randomly selected hours of performance within a particular day (remember that the ability of the computer to monitor users directly, say by counting the number of keystrokes per minute achieved by a typist, makes them potentially unpopular)
- there are usually fewer other factors contributing towards performance and so the system's contribution may be more readily identified
- the performance criteria are generally stated in more objectively measurable terms; for instance, by counting the number of 'widgets' produced in a period and not making more qualitative judgements.

But do not fall into the trap of believing that it is always possible to identify and quantify the contribution made by the information system to operational-level objectives. More realistic conclusions from this discussion of the three levels would be that:

- as you proceed from operational through tactical to strategic levels, the criteria used to evaluate system performance become more complex and more subjective as we assess outcomes less directly attributable to the information system itself
- the relevant objectives are of an integrative nature in practice. Although managers may state these objectives differently at each of the three levels, we should expect complimentary outcomes, namely that the achievement of the operational objectives ought to contribute to the achievement of the tactical objectives, which in turn should facilitate the achievement of the strategic objectives.

As the organization tries to evaluate the contribution of the information system to the achievement of business objectives, management at each level will need to pose a variety of questions and to consider a variety of possible answers. For example:

- Does the business display any aggregate benefits which may be attributed to the use of its information system?
  - tangible benefits may be achieved through cost reduction, improved efficiency and a quicker response to customer queries at the operational level
  - less tangible benefits may be gained if it can be shown that better-quality information leads to better decisions
  - improvements generated by the system may enhance the capacity of the organization to add value to its customers through a more reliable and efficient service.
- Does the system assist the organization to achieve specified objectives?
  - improvements in profit performance can result from the use of the information system
  - enhanced quality standards may be achieved in the products or services provided by the organization
  - sales growth targets may be met as a result of using the information system.

- Does the system itself provide the organization with a competitive advantage?
  - having a better-quality system than competitors can give management an opportunity to gain competitive advantage
  - direct advantages may be gained through quicker contacts with customers and suppliers
  - more effective warehousing systems may improve delivery times and customer service levels.

Performance criteria: effectiveness

The term 'effectiveness' is used to express the extent to which a particular activity, process, system or organization achieves the objectives set. This measure of performance is important not only for the information systems, but in all aspects of an organization's activities. For example, the marketing function may be interested in assessing the effectiveness of the latest television advertising campaign by asking, say, what increase in sales (if any) has followed the campaign. The accounting function may wish to measure the effectiveness of revised customer credit policies by establishing, say, whether the customers are paying more rapidly on average and whether the organization has reduced the level of bad debt. For these purposes, the use of effectiveness as a measure of performance begins with the managers setting the objectives or performance criteria. But, cause and effect may become confused because many organizations drift into the simultaneous pursuit of multiple objectives, and a particular activity may appear to be highly effective in relation to one objective but less effective in relation to another. In these situations, the problem is rather more than a simple matter of definition. For example, a decision to reduce stock levels in a warehouse from an average of three weeks' supply of finished goods to only one week's supply may prove effective in reducing working capital requirements but it may be far less effective in enhancing the service levels offered to customers. So unless and until the organization reconciles the relationships between its objectives and establishes clear priorities, it is not possible to measure effectiveness.

The problem is compounded because the effectiveness of an information system may be measured in a variety of ways and at different levels within the organization. The more commonly applied criteria include:

- value for money
- decision support effectiveness
- quality
- human–computer interaction
- security
- reliability.

Let us consider each of these in more detail.

Value for money

Because money is conveniently divided into units, it is tempting to use it as means of expressing the idea of effectiveness. Most commonly, organizations claim that the installation of an information system provides benefits at least equivalent to the total capital invested in the system. Although this may appear an appealing principle, it is particularly difficult to apply in many business situations, not least that of information systems evaluation. Some of the problems of determining the benefits and costs associated with information systems have been addressed in our previous discussion of business objectives. Other associated issues and problems are developed in the final paragraphs of this chapter.

Decision support effectiveness

This also sounds an attractive measure of system performance – how effectively does the information system support the various users at different levels in the organization? But, as with other criteria, the problem is that the type and extent of support required by users and decision-makers varies, not only according to the level in the management system, but also with each person's competence in undertaking each task. For example, at the strategic level, the marketing function may be interested in the system's ability to provide external information on markets, competitors and customers. The financial function may be more interested in using the system's analytical and model-building functions to plan and develop alternative capital structures and funding arrangements. At the operational level, the type of support required from the system by those processing purchase invoices will differ from that required by staff in the drawing office. This is not intended to imply that the information needs of one user are more or less important than any other, but rather that the types of information required and the tools necessary to support the processing will differ from one functional area to another. Moreover, by virtue of functional training and general expertise, what one user may consider obvious may require the most careful explanation before another can understand it.

Quality

The effectiveness of the system in producing the necessary quality of information is a factor on which each user will have an opinion but unthinkingly reacting to individual's subjective responses may not be a sound basis on which to evaluate the system. This reflects a number of factors, including the quality of the original data entering the system, the design of the system used to process the data, the operation of the system itself and the competence (and mood) of the users when interfacing the system. (Remember that we discussed the different quality requirements for information in each level in the management hierarchy in Chapter 3.)

Human–computer interaction

Information quality is directly related to the effectiveness of the interaction between the system components and the user and, yet again, every user will have an opinion on the quality of the interface. For measurement purposes, managers should start by compiling an inventory of the type and quality of the hardware peripherals that have been provided for the users. It would then be useful to parallel the use of questionnaires and interviews with more formal tests to determine:

- how easy it is to use the hardware – in part this is a test of ergonomics, but the care with which the hardware is configured and maintained has a real effect on user attitudes
- whether the system design makes it easy to enter data into the system
- what software is in use and whether it is equally friendly to both novice and experienced users
- system reliability – if the hardware and software are robust, this will build the users' confidence when they use the system
- the ease with which the technical and support staff can use the system. (For example, if it proves easy to manage and maintain a database or programming staff prove adept at accessing, modifying and testing the software, this will greatly encourage the lay users in using the various parts of the system.)

Security

A less obvious measure of the effectiveness of a system is the level of security provided for the data in the system. The issues associated with the security of information and the approaches to ensuring it are addressed in later chapters. However, we can summarize some of the measures that might be used in relation to assessing the total information system's effectiveness as follows:

- **The integrity of the data needs to be protected** from the time it enters the system, through storage and processing until such time as it is no longer required by the system's users. This means verifying the new data before they are allowed to mix into the master files and reducing the risk of subsequent loss from accidental or deliberate activities (fraud and crime are major problems for the modern organization). Even the disposal of sensitive data may need to be undertaken effectively to prevent it from falling into the hands of unauthorized users. All these elements can be monitored through the auditing function.
- **Critical functions of the system should be available** at all times and the organization should have effective plans to make a rapid recovery from disasters.
- **The level of protection** afforded to users of the system should match the sensitivity of the data. In the best systems, the users are able to retrieve, analyse and process data to which they have a legitimate right of access without the intrusion of other users into their files.

Reliability

Because it is relatively easy to monitor, this criterion is commonly used to measure the effectiveness of automated systems. Reliability may be measured in a number of ways, including:

- the regular availability of the system without loss of service due to breakdowns
- the ability of the system to handle the data in a regular and predictable manner
- the ability of the system to produce the necessary reports as and when required.

To some extent, these factors overlap which makes it difficult to use them in a measurement system. This is reflected in the everyday reality that although it is possible to produce statistics showing the availability and performance of each component of the system, users tend to take a composite view of the system's effectiveness. For these purposes, therefore, more qualitative measures of effectiveness are preferred, including:

- the nature and quality of the data provided and the ability of users to apply that data in meeting their own decision-making needs
- the level of help (both human and automated) available to decision-makers at each level in the organization
- whether the decision-makers are able to use system to obtain timely monitoring information on the performance of the organization's critical functions
- whether the decision-makers are able to obtain quality feedback as decisions are implemented so that effective control action can be maintained.

It will be obvious that this form of assessment aims to measure not only the effectiveness of the technological elements of the system, but also the ability of the human elements involved in the design and daily use of the system.

Performance criteria: efficiency

This third performance criterion, efficiency, is concerned with the relationship between resource inputs and outputs from a system or activity. The greater the quantity of outputs produced from a given quantity of inputs, the more efficient the system or activity is said to be. Thus, the assembly line that produces 100 widgets at a total cost of £800 (inclusive of materials, labour and overhead costs) will be seen as more cost-efficient than one which produces the same number of widgets at a cost of £900. But it would be a serious error to characterize efficiency as purely a financial dimension. Any factor may be the basis of a test of efficiency. For example, let us return to the second assembly line mentioned above. Suppose that although it may appear less efficient in cost terms, it is more efficient in time, producing the 100 widgets in eight hours as against ten hours for the more cost-efficient line. That two hours 'free' production time may then be used for the manufacture of other higher profit products. This leads us to the proposition that, in this context, efficiency may be assessed against three broad parameters, namely:

- use of resources
- time
- costs.

As with previous lists of points, we must start with the semantic point that there may be conceptual overlaps to resolve – so it could be said that cost efficiency is essentially the same as resource efficiency. This is not necessarily true because many costing systems are relatively arbitrary when allocating some costs. So if the organization has achieved efficiency in the use of a particular resource, say, a general overhead resource such as office floor space, this may not always be reflected in the cost-efficiency performance measures.

Resource usage

The resources employed within an information system may be sub-divided into:

- human resources
- equipment resources
- data resources
- technical support resources.

Human resources. The test of whether human resources are being exploited efficiently is a particularly broad and imprecise topic because we are concerned not only with the human resources directly engaged in operating and managing the information system itself, but also with the suppliers of data (some of whom may be external to the organization) and people who have yet to use the system.

All organizations employ people to develop, operate and manage their information systems. The first part of the evaluation exercise requires an analysis of each person's job specification to determine the contribution that each person is expected to make to the functioning of the organization's information system. Once the benchmark of paper expectations has been set, we can move to an appraisal of the actual role and functions of each individual. This is a direct comparison between the activities of individual employees and the needs of the organization and its information system – the intention being to produce a measure of the value actually provided to systems operation. Let us start with the assertion that, if it is going to be meaningful, this measurement needs to be conducted on a regular and continuing basis. At its simplest level, this reflects the survival strategy that financial budgets for the operation of the information systems must be monitored to ensure that total expenditure stays within agreed budget limits. But this would miss the true issue wrapped up in the word 'value' used above. The real need is to ensure that each employee's abilities are being exploited in a way that creates the greatest efficiencies for the organization. This is not an easy thing to measure. The total information system will be comprised of many functional sub-systems, each of which may have different costs and may add value to the organization's products and services in different ways. Many of the employees will contribute to a number of these sub-systems. It will therefore be difficult to segregate their particular contribution to each sub-system and equally to apportion their costs against various sub-systems.

If we accept that it is difficult to measure the contribution of those more directly and continuously associated with the system, it becomes even more problematic when we begin to consider whether the organization is making an efficient use of data providers and users. How can we begin to measure whether a data provider is being used efficiently when this individual may only provide data very infrequently (for example, customers may be asked to complete a questionnaire once per year or even less frequently)? Similarly, there may be dramatic differences in the level of system use. Some operational staff like the sales order processing staff may use their sub-system regularly, while others use it much less frequently – a sales manager, for instance, may only log on to analyse the sales statistics at the end of each month. In some organizations, it is the role of those involved in the ongoing maintenance and system development to monitor and evaluate the extent to which the system uses these human resources efficiently. Other organizations put the test the other way round and investigate whether employees can carry out their functions efficiently through their interaction with the system. A significant source of human resource inefficiency may be the time taken for users to gain access to the system owing to technical barriers, the location of the entry peripherals or the lack of user knowledge. Further sources of inefficiency may become evident after users have gained access to the system. Once these sources of inefficiency have been identified, managers can respond by targeted training or installing better help facilities on the system. (In one sense, these are aspects of systems analysis and design and you will find a discussion of efficiency in this respect in Chapters 9 and 10.)

Equipment resources (in this case including both hardware and software). Measuring the efficiency of the automated or computerized elements of the information system would represent an expected test of efficiency. The major hardware elements would include:

- the communications network
- input peripherals (e.g. keyboards)
- data processing equipment
- data storage/retrieval equipment
- output peripherals (e.g. printers).

The software elements associated with the hardware include:

- communications software
- operating system software
- database software
- applications software.

The technical performance of each of these hardware and software elements could be measured individually, for example it would be easy to monitor the number of characters printed per second or the time taken to retrieve records from a database. The approach to measuring efficiency would be to compare actual performance against the performance benchmarks established by the manufacturer of the particular hardware or software element. We should remember that these benchmarks may have been stipulated by the organization at the time of the system specification and so may be of direct interest to those managers concerned with the technical operation and performance of the system.

System performance. Although it may be interesting to discover how well the components function, the true test of efficiency is the extent to which all the different elements can be integrated and operated as a single system. Systems are not transparent to lay users. In other words, users tend to see as much of the system as they need and do not think of the system as being made up of separate elements. A total systems approach is therefore to be preferred.

Capacity utilization. This aims to measure the extent to which the available capacity is used, the variation of this utilization over time and whether there are any significant peaks or troughs in demand. In this, the utilization of available disk space, the frequency with which particular lines in the network are used and the demand for printed output will all be potential measures of the efficiency of capacity utilization. It will also provide useful data for the disaster planning process (see Chapters 14 and 19).

Data resources. One of the fundamental objectives underlying the analysis, design and development of information systems is the need to achieve the efficient use of the data resources available to or within the organization. The capture, processing, storage and communication of data within the system are all activities which consume resources. The more efficiently the system uses the data resources available, the more efficiently it may be able to use the other resources involved. For example, if the sales department and the accounts department both require access to data recording customer orders, it would be more efficient to give both users access to the same database rather than create and maintain two separate databases for each user. The ability to develop information systems that cater for the needs of the maximum number of users from the same data sources is a key determinant of efficiency in the organization's data resources.

Technical support resources. The other integral element in the system is the human contribution to the development, implementation, maintenance, support, operations and management of the system. The measurement of efficiency will broadly reflect the measures employed in other organizational activities. This may involve the assessment of the number of system development days required to develop a particular system, or the speed with which the system is repaired following a breakdown.

This particular element of the system's efficiency is becoming increasingly important in many organizations, as it represents a significant and generally rising proportion of the total system costs. Developments in technology have resulted in significant cost economies and efficiency improvements in the hardware and software elements employed in information systems. These efficiency improvements have not generally been matched in the human resource inputs. Although some of the developments in structured methodologies and automated design tools offer opportunities to improve the productivity of these technical support resources, these benefits may be outweighed by the increased costs of recruiting personnel with the appropriate knowledge and skills to use these new developments. The fact that outsourcing has become an increasingly popular option suggests that organizations have found significant inefficiencies in their own resource utilization.

Time efficiency

The use of time as a measure of the efficiency of information systems involves considering factors such as:

- the length of time it takes either to gain access to the system or to move from one part of the system to another
- the response time – this is the time taken for the system to respond to user requests or instructions – research shows that users are increasingly annoyed by slow response times and that some may even physically abuse slow machines
- the processing or computing time taken up in the various stages of processing the data – some processes such as sorting, or complex calculations can tie up a computer for significant periods of time.

These factors can be assessed against both the automated components and the information system as a whole. The production director who requests a statement of the budget deviations in the last month is primarily interested in the time taken from initiating the request to receiving the information, that is the total system response time including the activities of people. The deputy who is given the task of producing the report will be more interested in the performance of the report-generating components of the system. It is unlikely that either of them will be interested in the speed of the computer system, say as expressed in MIPS, but this will be important to the operations staff who must maintain general system availability while special applications are running.

Cost efficiency

Cost is the most usual basis for measuring the efficiency of any activity or system because it appears to provide a convenient and commonly understood unit of measurement for all the input resources used and the outputs generated. With particular reference to information systems, the major elements of costs involve:

- **Development costs**. These are the costs associated with the development of the total information system or sub-systems and include hardware, software, development team costs, training, implementation costs, and so on.
- **Direct running costs**. Once operational, the system will incur a variety of costs, including the salaries of operations and maintenance staff, media costs (such as disks and paper) and software licence payments. These costs will all be directly attributable to the provision of the information system.
- **Indirect or overhead costs**. The expenditures within the organization which may result from the operation of the information system (but are less easy to charge directly to its operation) include lighting and heating costs, the provision of personnel services for the data processing staff and property insurance costs.
- **User costs**. Less evident from the perspective of the data processing function which provides the information services are the costs incurred by users in using the system and the information provided. Such costs may be evident in the form of user training requirements, the time required to access the data from the system or the additional costs incurred in further processing the information received from the system in an inappropriate format.

The cost efficiency of the system may be measured in terms of one, several or all of these elements, depending on the performance measurement that is considered most important.

Alternative evaluation perspectives

As we have seen, determining the performance criteria under the headings of business objectives, effectiveness and efficiency provides a reliable framework within which to conduct the evaluation process. But no framework can be enough in itself to ensure an effective evaluation process. The success of any evaluation of a system's performance will always depend on a range of more human factors, such as:

- the identity and roles of the people undertaking the evaluation
- the purposes of the evaluation
- the objectives they expected the information system to achieve
- the level of achievement they believe the system reached in each of these objectives.

There is no universal set of objectives or achievement levels which can be applied to all organizations. Each organization will have its own management agenda.

Consider the case of a national hotel chain which operates a centralized room reservation system for each of its 20 hotels located in the major cities in the UK. Each hotel is connected via a network to the central booking service computer. Room reservation requests may be received either locally through the individual hotel receptions, or through the central reservation service. Additionally, reservations for any hotel in the group may be made at any of the other hotels, a service designed to encourage existing clients to use other hotels in the chain. The evaluation of the system may be viewed from a number of alternative perspectives. A sample of the possible perspectives would include the following.

Providers of data

If consulted directly, the hotel reception staff at each of the hotels and the specialist staff responsible for handling telephone reservations would probably apply the following parameters in their evaluation of the system:

- the effectiveness of the system in supporting them in their operational tasks
- the response time – how quickly the system responds to instructions may directly affect them in their dealings with customers
- the reliability of the system and frequency with which service is lost which may also affect customer goodwill
- the ease of using the system and the quality of the screen dialogue
- the level and quality of the technical support available if problems arise
- their ability to verify data input and to modify data.

Technical system support staff

The staff responsible for the development, operation, support and management of the system will probably apply the following parameters in their evaluation of the system:

- the effectiveness of the system in supporting them in their particular tasks
- the response time – how quickly the system responds to instructions
- the reliability of the system and the frequency with which service is lost
- the ease of identifying and correcting problems
- the level and quality of external technical support services
- the capacity of the system to monitor its own performance and to undertake appropriate self-corrective actions

- the quality of the housekeeping procedures and systems associated with the computer facilities
- the speed and accuracy of fault diagnosis and clearance.

Users of information from the system

The staff involved in using the system at different levels and in various functions within the organization will probably apply the following parameters in their evaluation:

- the effectiveness of the system in supporting them in their particular tasks, say in the analytical tools provided for management use
- the response time – how quickly the system responds to instructions
- the reliability of the system and the frequency with which service is lost
- the ease of using the system and the quality of the menus
- the quality and accuracy of the data provided.

The reception staff in this system will be both data providers and users of the system. The perspectives they apply may vary according to the particular mode in which they are interfacing with the system. The managers of the hotel are more likely to be net users of the system, as opposed to providers of information. Each group will start with the entirely human and selfish desire to judge how well the system supports them as individuals, but only those in the more senior positions will have a sufficient overview of the organization to begin making more objective judgements. Whether or not more objective judgements are ultimately made will depend on the political situation within the organization and the competence of those involved.

Tools for system evaluation

The discussion so far in this section should highlight that the measures of effectiveness and efficiency may be both diverse and interrelated. For example, senior booking operations managers might specify a performance objective as the improvement of data reliability within the system. It is well known that greater effectiveness in quality terms may be achieved by increasing expenditure on data verification, but this frequently makes the response times slower (which would be unpopular with the reception staff and customers) and produces inefficiency by increasing processing costs (which would not appeal to the finance director). Given this diversity and complexity in performance measures, a range of tools has been developed to measure and evaluate particular aspects of system performance. In this respect, the evaluation of an information system is no different from the evaluation of any other system in the organization (the production system, for instance) and it is possible to apply common techniques to the evaluation of such systems. Examples of these tools and techniques include:

- **Budgetary control systems**. The cost efficiency of a system may be monitored and controlled through the organization's budgetary control system. Budgets should be established both for the various phases in the development process, as well as for the costs associated with operating and maintaining the information system.

- **Post-implementation audits.** As we have seen in earlier chapters, it is standard to review system performance immediately following changeover. This auditing of a system once it is in operation provides a useful basis for all future evaluation. In the first instance, the measurement will focus on the performance criteria that were specified during the design phase of the system development. But it is important that this audit should not be viewed as a single exercise limited to the period immediately after the system becomes fully operational. The performance of a system will usually change over time, not only in terms of its efficiency but more often in terms of the effectiveness with which it meets the changing needs of users. This process of user adaptation and system evolution should be monitored carefully using a variety of tools to test and evaluate the different measures of performance:
  - moving from the dry statistics of the frequency of system failure
  - through the monitoring of maintenance and operational costs
  - to the more subjective user satisfaction levels and tests of user habits by establishing the frequency, skill and intensity with which particular elements of the system are used.
- **User questionnaires.** One of the more common approaches to the assessment of the quality of any service that an information system provides is to ask the users to give their opinions, whether orally or in writing. The use of structured questionnaires to elicit evidence about the perceived effectiveness of the system can provide valuable information. But considerable care has to be taken both in the structuring of the questionnaire and in the analysis of the responses, given that the quantification of subjective user assessments can be difficult, particularly because users are not always truthful in what they say.
- **Benchmarking.** Another approach to assessing system performance is to use a benchmarking approach. The system's current performance is measured and compared against certain desired or agreed standards (i.e. the benchmarks). These performance standards may have been established during the system development phase, may be based on a comparison with other systems in operation, or may possibly have been derived from some theoretical assessment of optimum performance. For example, the time taken to retrieve a record at random from the database may be compared against:
  - the performance standards established for the system at the outset
  - the performance of the system in another environment, or the previous version of the system
  - the optimum retrieval time for the size of file and the hardware/software systems in use.

Each of these comparisons may provide valuable information on the efficiency of the system. Benchmarking may also be used to evaluate effectiveness, say, by measuring the number of times the users fail to access the appropriate data.

The optimum system

In discussing the evaluation of systems performance, it is useful and interesting to consider the idea of an optimum system. A system may be said to have reached optimum performance levels when it achieves the maximum level of performance whether in relation to all the pre-implementation criteria or in relation to a particular performance criterion of significance. These performance criteria will be contained within the framework of the business objectives and the factors of effectiveness and efficiency outlined earlier in this chapter. The system which minimizes response time may be considered optimally efficient in this measure of performance. The optimum system in financial efficiency terms will be the system which produces the necessary level of service at the minimum cost. Optimum effectiveness may be produced by the system which maximizes the level of decision support to the senior management users. These examples have all been related to single performance factors or criteria. Although the concept of optimality is interesting, there have been a number of difficulties in defining and evaluating the optimal system in practice:

- if multiple performance criteria are used in assessing a system's performance, say under the headings of business objectives, effectiveness and efficiency, the basis of measurement is likely to be uncertain
- the achievement of higher levels of performance in one factor may often be to the detriment of the performance in another
- many of the performance parameters or criteria involve qualitative (as against quantitative) measurement
- the perceptions of different users as to which are the important criteria and levels of achievement will vary, as we saw earlier.

The concept of an optimal system may be useful for a technical evaluation of the automated system functions (in relation, say, to the speed of retrieval of records within the database, or the speed of undertaking particular calculations). But widening this concept to the total information system and its performance is unlikely to be successful in practice.

Issues and problems in systems evaluation

The preceding discussion of the role and meaning of the term 'systems evaluation' should have alerted you to the fact that performance measurement and analysis is a multidimensional process, operating at different levels in the organization. We conclude this section with the proposition that, although it may be difficult, it should always be possible to apply a diverse set of criteria to evaluate an information system, even though the ranking of the criteria may vary between different groups or individuals within the organization. The following section therefore highlights some of the key issues and problems likely to be encountered in evaluating an information system in practice.

Defining terms

The first and most obvious problem is that not everyone will agree on a definition of 'information system'. Some users will perceive it as only those parts of the system with which they particularly interact (the sales office staff, for example, may view the system as the sales order processing system). Other members of the organization will perceive the system as those elements that are computerized or automated in some way. Only a few members of an organization will understand that the information system in a corporate context includes both the automated and manual elements of data processing, information usage and decision making.

Differences in criteria

Even if common definitions prevail, the same problem affects the performance criteria – for example, the speed at which the system responds to requests or the reliability of the system – and even if a list of common criteria can be agreed, the relative importance or the ranking may vary between different users or participants in the system. For example, an order processing clerk may rank the speed of response time as top priority, whereas a user making less frequent enquiries may consider this less important, preferring a system that is more user-friendly.

Differences in perception

Even if users agree on a list of performance criteria and their relative importance, it may still prove difficult to achieve similar judgements as to whether any particular criterion is satisfied. For example, the way in which people perceive response times may vary considerably, depending on each person's previous experience, expectations and, even, their patience threshold.

The users

These differences in perception and the ability of the users to make an effective contribution to the evaluation process will be strongly affected by the knowledge, competence, training and experience of those users. So novice or inexperienced users will tend to work from a more limited range of performance criteria and may expect lower levels of performance than the more experienced users. For example, help-lines and user support systems may be important performance factors for the new user but may be significantly less important for more experienced users.

System quality

User perceptions may also be skewed by the quality of the design, development, implementation and maintenance of the system as it affects each user. Systems which have been successful in meeting the needs of the users and satisfying their organizational requirements are likely to be more highly rated than those which fail to do so. This success will also represent a benefit to the organization as a whole.

Cost–benefit evaluation

The evaluation of a system in cost–benefit analysis terms poses a number of problems. Although many of the costs involved in the provision of an information system may be readily identifiable and directly attributable, a significant proportion of the costs may be less easily attributable (including shared staffing overhead costs such as personnel services or the cost of electricity used in running the system). The latter costs are becoming increasingly difficult to determine as networking becomes more common and a significant proportion of the power is supplied to local workstations rather than a centralized facility. Similarly, although some benefits may be tangible and directly measurable in financial terms, many benefits are less tangible – for example, improvements either in general staff morale and job satisfaction or in the quality of the decisions taken by managers at different levels in the organization – both resulting from the use of the system – are difficult to quantify in financial terms.

Optimality

The development of any system must be driven by realistic targets, but the concept of an optimal system is difficult to sustain in any practical organizational environment. The problem is that although a system may be viewed as optimal on one performance criterion, say the efficient use of memory capacity, it may equally be viewed as sub-optimal on another criterion, say, the quality of the human–computer interfaces. The achievement of an optimal total system is probably an unrealistic development target.

The evaluation process

The process of conducting the system evaluation itself may encounter a number of difficulties. For example:

- Identifying the cause of a particular deviation from performance expectations may be frustrated by lack of data, lack of knowledge or difficulty in analysing the data that are available.
- Poor performance may result from a variety of interdependent factors and there may be problems in disaggregating the effects of each of these factors. For example, slow response times on the system may result from inadequate hardware specifications, software or file design deficiencies or incorrect user operation. Each of these causes may contribute to some degree but the extent to which each does (and whether work intended to remedy one of the problem will improve the situation) is difficult to predict.
- The underlying problem is that evaluation is both a subjective and an objective process. Although there may be some factual data available to underpin the process, whether those data will be brought to the attention of the decision-makers and, if they are, how they are interpreted are matters likely to be affected by motivational and political forces – many of which will be outside the control of the organization. The acceptance of this limitation is the most important and constructive step that any manager can take towards making good decisions. Managers who assume blindly that both all available data have been made available to them and that they are accurate, are unlikely to make good decisions.

Summary

This chapter set out to provide an understanding of the framework for evaluation and the key issues involved. The evaluation processes applied to the management of organizations in general may be applied equally to the evaluation of information systems. The tools, techniques and analytical methods used in evaluation have been considered in the earlier chapters.

- Systems evaluation may be conducted at different levels (i.e. the operational, tactical and strategic). The performance criteria for a system may be sub-divided into business objectives, effectiveness and efficiency, although criteria within each of these are not mutually exclusive. The effectiveness of a system may be measured in a variety of ways by different users of the system.
- System efficiency may be viewed from such perspectives as the use of resources, time and cost–benefit factors. The perspective of the evaluator will determine the type of criteria used and their relative importance. The optimal system can usually only be measured on a single or limited range of performance criteria.

Self-test questions

1. Identify and briefly explain the main stages in the system evaluation process.
2. Discuss, with examples, the type of criteria that may be used to measure system performance at the strategic level in the organization.
3. Identify the criteria that may be used to identify the effectiveness of an information system.
4. List and explain the main elements of cost involved in measuring the efficiency of a system.
5. Describe, with the use of an appropriate example, how the providers of data may assess the performance of an information system with which they interact.

Exam-style questions

1. During a recent management seminar, an outside consultant stressed the importance of the organization achieving an optimum system. A colleague has asked you to explain this term and to show how the organization might measure this.
2. 'System effectiveness means different things to different people.' Evaluate this statement with reference to an information system.

(All answers on pages 566–567)

CHAPTER 14

Control and security issues

Computerization, often thought of as providing comprehensive solutions to problems of data storage and access, seems to have raised as many difficulties as it has solved. Press and media reports often focus on the activities of brilliant, but dangerous, 'hackers' who manage to break into the supposedly secure databases of government departments, international corporations and university research projects. You may well have read articles in computer journals highlighting the threat to corporate resources presented by software viruses and describing the methods that can be used to combat them. And all computer users need to guard their hardware and software against the dangers of extreme temperatures, unauthorized or inexpert access and accidental data corruption or loss.

In this chapter we set out to introduce the concepts of security and privacy and to address the background issues which are fundamental to an understanding of the function of security in modern organizations. First of all, we introduce and explain the role of security systems in present-day society. Next we present a series of definitions of key terms and concerns which should help you to understand the more detailed discussion of corporate security issues later in the chapter. Following an analysis of risk and uncertainty, and their implications for security management and systems, we consider how organizations can approach the formulation of a security strategy and the task of risk management.

Our discussion then moves to the detail of the security planning process. We examine the problem of avoiding or minimizing complexity in systems design, looking at the priorities and critical issues involved. Next we give attention to the scope and impact of current data protection legislation, focusing on the provisions of the UK's Data Protection Act 1984, surveying similar EU legislation and noting some important transborder concerns. The last part of the chapter deals with the intellectual property rights inherent in software, summarizing key legal debates and regulations on copyright infringement and issues of clarity.

Security in contemporary society

When offices depended on paper systems, all that security required was that the sensitive documents were locked away in filing cabinets and safes. Now that more organizations have automated, the nature of the security process has had to change to match the new technologies. Instead of having to read through heavy files of documents, new machines allow faster access to information, potentially from anywhere in the world. This apparent advantage arises both from the array of word and text processing facilities and from the extensive data retrieval and manipulation facilities that are often made user friendly through Operating Systems and decision support systems (DSSs). One result of this ease of access has been that the old functional departmental barriers have been broken down. Workstations and personal computers can now be sited anywhere whether in a conventional office, or in a home worker's sitting room, or in a sales representative's car using a modem or cellular radio. Thus, problems of security can no longer be solved simply by placing good locks on the office doors.

Indeed, the very idea of organizations being tied to one or more office sites with centralized facilities is being challenged by the development of networks and other communication facilities between machines which potentially allows remote access to all centrally provided facilities. The opportunities for error or fraud are therefore multiplied by the number of machines that are linked together and by the number of people who can gain physical access to those machines. If data are incorrectly entered or corrupted, the effects of the inaccuracy may be spread throughout the computer system within a fraction of a second. It is true that most data errors will be corrected eventually but, depending on the volume of the data, this can often lead to an organization having to run fast to stay well behind the true facts. This can be critical because the information itself is now recognized as an important and valuable resource in its own right, with data either sensitive or worth millions of pounds (whether as information or as electronic funds transfers).

The blight of data corruption most usually arises through the natural cause of human error and there are many data validation checks which can reduce the effects of these unintentional errors. But wilful tampering with either the data or with the control software can have a fundamental effect on the integrity of the data and, therefore, on the reliability of the organization's decision making. As more of the data are held centrally but remain accessible from remote terminals, the organization becomes increasingly vulnerable to loss or damage. In practice, computers may have one or more of the following roles in criminal or fraudulent activity:

- The hardware itself may be the target, i.e. it may be stolen or damaged.
- The information system may be the means whereby the crime or fraud is carried out.
- The wrongdoer may hope to conceal the crime or fraud by using the information system itself.

People have the capacity to make terrible mistakes but some are highly ingenious in making frauds *seem* like mistakes. Since the beginning of record keeping, no one has managed to devise a security system which can wholly control what people may do, nor prevent all the information corruptions and the consequential losses which can occur. This leads us to make three general interconnected propositions:

1. Security should never be introduced for its own sake – it must always be provided because it is seen to be for the good of the organization, e.g. through the application of cost–benefit analysis.
2. Good security is a matter of awareness and commitment, i.e. senior managers must be aware of the problems and have a commitment to providing and enforcing the most appropriate countermeasures.

3 It is sensible to start with the assumption that any item of data may be recorded inaccurately so validation techniques must be applied to reduce the risk of consequential losses.

Basic definitions

The main issues in this chapter are security and privacy. Taking security first, it may be defined literally as 'a means of providing protection against anticipated attack'. But, in this context, it is generally taken to refer to a general protection system which parallels the ordinary commercial systems of the organization. The aim of this secondary system is to minimize or eliminate the risk of loss and its implementation signals to the world that the organization intends to survive and to maintain the safe and continuous operation of its systems under the control of an authorized and well-trained staff. These definitional themes have remained constant as technology has developed through the following progression:

- from simple **data security** in a paper-based system and, subsequently, a single mainframe computer
- through to **information security** which needs to be more comprehensive to protect the information wherever and however it may be stored, e.g. on a database held on a distributed system
- and leading to the modern need to **protect sensitive knowledge** (which can even require employers to consider how to secure the knowledge inside someone's head, e.g. by including a confidentiality clause in that person's contract of employment).

Until recently, IT systems have been centralized. This has promoted reasonably high levels of security because physical access by a limited number of staff was fairly easy to manage and the technology of mainframe systems has been developing for nearly 40 years which, in turn, allowed security skills to emerge. But the use of distributed knowledge-based systems is becoming increasingly common and this creates real risks. Most modern organizations make the issue of information security their main focus because it is reasonably practical, being based on the following three constants:

1 the weather and other natural acts of god as a source of danger to the buildings and the physical form of the data
2 people as a threat both to the hardware and to the integrity of the data
3 the information that may be lost or damaged.

Accordingly, all security systems are intended to perform the following functions:

- to avoid or prevent naturally occurring loss or damage
- to deter as many people-based threats as possible
- to promote a quick recovery once losses are sustained
- to identify the cause(s) of those losses
- to correct the known vulnerabilities to reduce the risk of repeat losses.

All five functions must be subject to security in their own right. Thus, one of the concerns of the security department (if any) will be how to ensure that staff do not discuss security systems with outsiders, say, at conferences or in the local pub.

So far, we have been considering general security issues. Within this broad ambit, we may identify three concerns which are particular to computers:

1. maintaining the availability of the information system itself
2. maintaining the integrity of the data which it processes and stores
3. maintaining the confidentiality of the data before, during and after processing and distribution.

The first two concerns are common to all information systems, but confidentiality may not affect all organizations and their systems to the same extent. The concept of availability tests whether the information system is working adequately. Managers will have to consider whether their computer systems are available for sufficient periods of time during the working day, and ensure that the response times are acceptable both where services are provided in real-time and in batch-mode.

The concept of integrity applies at two different levels within the organization. It will be said that true data integrity has been achieved if all the data are error-free and have not been accidentally or intentionally altered, disclosed or destroyed. It is extremely unlikely that perfect integrity will ever be achieved in the larger organizations, but it is always desirable to have it as a corporate goal. The concept of integrity may also be applied to information systems generally. The test for this purpose will be whether those systems continue to conform to their design specifications, i.e. the systems must be robust and resist any attempts (whether out of curiosity or for fraudulent purposes) that may have been made to make them behave differently. To that extent, the concepts of availability and integrity together form the necessary guarantee that the data supporting the operation of the organization and its decision making is accurate, complete and reliable.

The scope of the concept of confidentially refers to the need to ensure that sensitive data are not disclosed to unauthorized persons. Large organizations will store large quantities of data, but only a relatively small proportion of that information will be so commercially sensitive that it has to be kept secret from all but a small number of employees. It is up to each organization to decide who should be allowed access and who should be denied access to each element of data and these decisions will tend to vary depending on the nature of each organization and its culture.

Key concepts and issues

The following must also be considered and defined.

Organization

We use this word to include all bodies or groups (whether commercially oriented or not) which aim to provide a service for clients or consumers.

Disaster

A disaster is any form of security contingency in any part of the organization which materially interferes with the ability of the organization to provide the given service.

Fraud

A simple definition of fraud is, 'any deviant behaviour which is intended to gain a dishonest advantage at the expense of the victim', and the usual outcome is a reduction in the victim's net worth. Various factors are common to all fraud situations. Thus, we may start with the proposition that greed is the usual motive for theft but, whereas some more bold criminals engage in mugging and other physical activities, the instinct for self-preservation usually prompts fraudsters to try to conceal their guilt. Their usual strategy is to alter the relevant records. The intention is either to prevent the loss from being immediately apparent or to conceal the identity of the taker. Altering the records is therefore not an end in itself. The real object of the exercise remains depriving the victim of physical assets or money. Because of the security systems, many frauds have to be conspiracies between several individuals. This may be so that they can pool their access resources, or so that specialist skills may be acquired, or because pursuit will be restricted if the fraud is institutionalized. We will return to the question of fraud in greater detail later on.

Privacy

The concept of privacy runs parallel to confidentiality. Information is confidential if the holder or the law designates it as such. The modern context for privacy lies with individual rights and civil liberties. At its simplest level, privacy may be seen as 'the right of each person to have some say in which data about him or her shall be collected and made available to others'. We shall return to this issue at length when we consider the UK's Data Protection Act later in this chapter.

Vulnerability

The process of identifying vulnerabilities is focused on those weak points in the various systems which might allow the system or the related data to be abused. The following factors increase vulnerability:

- The development of distributed processing means that it is often possible for the staff from many departments within the organization physically to access the computer hardware, i.e. it is easier to steal or tamper with the hardware and the communications media.
- The development of networks means that an increasingly large body of people (including those outside the immediate organization) may be able to gain logical access to more of the applications and data.
- Manual systems used to divide the work between many people – increasing the centralization or the networking of both computer hardware and data

holdings makes it easier for one person to gain access to all the system facilities and so to commit fraud, industrial espionage or extortion.

- Increasing centralization means that more hardware may be lost in a single fire or other disaster (good security practice requires that back-up copies of software and data should be kept off-site) – this may become less of a threat as more organizations move on to distributed configurations.
- Increasing system reliability means that users will become more confident about the accuracy of computer output and even accept it as correct without question. This change in user psychology makes it easier to conceal a fraud.
- Whereas altering paper records is likely to leave a trace which may be noticed as pages are turned, altering electronic records leaves no trace and automated systems do not encourage browsing through the data holdings.

Threats

These weak and vulnerable points can only be identified by classifying all the potential threats, i.e. demonstrating the ways in which damage may be caused to the function or purpose of the system. The undesirable consequence of a threat is loss or damage to the organization, say through the loss of business and/or the opportunity cost of resources used in recovery. The purpose of threat analysis is therefore to assess and/or quantify the risk of loss.

Risk

In simple formula terms:

$$\text{Risk} = \text{probability} + \text{criticality.}$$

In other words, there is some measure of how often the event might occur plus some evaluation of how great the damage will be if the event occurs. The concepts of risk and uncertainty are inseparable. The problem for management is therefore to balance the projected cost of avoiding foreseen harm against the loss estimated when neither set of figures can be calculated with certainty. The first step in the process requires managers to make a value judgement on the importance of the threat to the particular system under consideration. Thus, it will not be unusual for organizations to suffer short disruptions to the availability of some systems. The significance of each disruption will vary with each organization's dependence on the particular system. A few hours might be no more than a nuisance to some organizations but, to a commodities broker, a few minutes could represent a severe loss. One way of assessing the degree of criticality is to use the historical evidence available, i.e.:

- some situations of loss will already have arisen in-house
- some situations may be known to have arisen in similar organizations
- threats to paper-based systems may translate into machine-based threats.

Unfortunately, although this evidence may be helpful, any form of risk assessment is nothing more than educated guesswork because it is impossible to achieve accuracy in predictions. To claim that techniques may be devised, whether computerized or not, which give precise quantifications is misleading. Although insurance companies have access to substantial bodies of statistical information, say, on the likelihood of damage to motor vehicles, and the risk quantification based on this information will be moderately reliable, the security risks run by an individual organization are much more difficult to evaluate. What makes the process more uncertain is that while some risks may be obvious, many are not obvious at all or their existence may be suppressed by the victim. Much electronic crime falls into this less obvious class. A further problem is that the risks to be considered may be spread over a wide range of business activities. A different way of approaching the problem may therefore be to classify risks as **acceptable**, **controllable**, **transferable** and **critical**.

Acceptable risks

Some risks may be acceptable to the organization. This may be because:

- the chances of any loss occurring are so remote that they may be ignored
- even if losses may be sustained, the amount lost is likely to be small
- the cost of the controls which would be required to prevent loss may be more than the amount of loss at risk
- even if the controls are implemented, they may not work effectively.

For example, supermarket managers may consider shoplifting an inevitable consequence of allowing the customers to have free access to the goods on the shelves. This acceptance would not deny that large numbers of security staff could be employed or that the stores could be redesigned, but these changes might make customers feel less comfortable and damage business so the stock losses are tolerated.

Controllable risks

The incidence and effect of some unacceptable risks can be reduced through the introduction of controls. The aim would be to limit the likelihood of loss and/or the criticality of the loss to the organization.

Transferable risks

Some of the risks may be transferred to third parties through negotiating insurance policies or indemnity agreements. The risks most often transferred in this way are less likely to occur but, if they were to arise, would cause high levels of loss to the organization (i.e. low probability and high criticality).

Critical risks

If possible, these risks should be avoided altogether. If the risks cannot be avoided, they should be transferred.

The aim of all security systems should be to provide realistic levels of protection to each organization. This involves devising and implementing practical safeguards against loss which will strike a fair balance between the level of exposure to loss and the cost of the controls necessary to minimize that loss.

This emphasizes the principle that the cost of prevention is usually less than the cost of recovering from the loss once sustained.

Protection

This is the sum of the practical means adopted by the organization to minimize its vulnerabilities and to reduce the risk of loss.

Security: project planning implications

Planning cycles

As part of the risk assessment process, the organization must review the likely effects of any disruption to the normal activities of the organization. Although it is impossible to be absolutely precise, managers should create disaster scenarios and estimate the costs both of repairing any damage and of any increase in overheads while the recovery is made. Once these figures are established, they must assess the level of expenditure and effort which is justified to minimize the risks of loss for each scenario. These policy decisions can only be made at a senior management level, and require significant and continuing commitment if the resulting decisions are to be implemented effectively. All management decisions have to be placed in their proper contexts, and they must be related to a realistic time planning schedule. Within all organizations, there are three major interactive planning cycles:

1 **Physical systems**. All organizations occupy buildings. These physical structures tend to have an expected utility of about 50 years. Each building is serviced through the primary services which include the heating, wiring, ventilation and air conditioning systems. These services have a normal life expectancy of about 15 years. Within the building, the fabric of occupation is coloured by the lighting system, decoration and furniture. This social environment is more dynamic and may experience the need for change on a more regular basis.
2 **Information systems**. In the same way that a building has a range of different life cycles which relate to its physical components, information systems have different timescales which relate to the level of capital invested in, and the technological capacities of, their various functional elements. These elements include:
   - the communications media and network control systems – these are constrained both by the software system and by the physical systems referred to above, for what designers may specify as a cabling system to produce a 'smart' building using the best of today's technology, may appear inadequate in an increasingly short time
   - the central processing units, workstations and peripherals
   - the software.
3 **Planning systems**. Business planning horizons rarely extend beyond a seven-year period. Within this overall period, organizations plan at a *strategic* level,

anticipating the future needs of the organization in its global, social and commercial environment. The planning then moves to a more detailed *tactical* level and, on a two- to four-year period, identifies specific goals and the resources currently available, together with the resources that will be required and the key factors that will affect the ability to achieve those goals. Finally, the planning moves to an *operational* level which actually commits resources to the achievement of very detailed short-term objectives. This part of the cycle may be between six and 18 months.

In contrast to the life cycles of the physical systems, organization planning has to be dynamic and constantly updated to reflect the prevailing conditions. However, the planning of information systems cannot be as dynamic because the process is constrained by the life cycles of the component elements. For example, the current wiring systems in the building reflect the technology horizons at the time of installation and may not support the desired management decision support goals. The same may be true of the capital invested in the multiplexers and operating software which support the present network. Unless the senior managers address the needs of the organization from the buildings up, it is impossible to ensure that each part of the organization anticipates and supports both the long-term and the short-term needs of that organization, and only senior management has the necessary overview of the whole organization to achieve adequate planning targets. One of the important tools in this review process is cost–benefit analysis given that decisions may have to be made to replace equipment while it is still working well according to its original specifications and before it has been fully depreciated.

Senior management's role in disaster planning

The whole process of disaster planning must be under senior management control because it directly affects all the people who are employed in the buildings occupied by the organization. Conflicts may therefore arise as political and cultural barriers are breached, and special interests that had been protected by the old departmental structures are threatened with change. Indeed, the result of any plan *ought to be* change and, because all organizations are based on the people who work for them, the management of that change must properly address the personnel issues within the overall practicality of the planning cycles.

In 1985, a survey revealed that only about half the 1400 UK computer installations surveyed had a disaster plan of any sort. This figure should highlight the proposition that disaster planning is likely to be ineffective if senior managers are not committed to it. Indeed, the probable reason for such a poor showing in the survey is organizational rather than any inherent difficulty in performing the risk analysis, evaluation and planning exercise. For example, decisions must be taken as to which departmental user functions are deferrable in an emergency and for how long – a decision that can only be taken if there is reliable evidence of the cost of that deferment. This cannot be accurately established unless the users provide basic information which can be validated. This is a senior management task requiring considerable sensitivity both because it involves making judgements about the merits of the claims made by the affected groups, and because it involves determining the relative importance between often competing interest groups. Moreover, without a formal policy which has been thought through from the top down, security and the auditing procedures to support it are likely to be ineffective. In reality, disaster planning often only takes place after an event when the awfulness of the consequences have been demonstrated. But whether before or after the event, only the most senior managers can assess the impact of disasters at a macro-organizational level and, without proper macro-guidelines, the micro-assessment achievable by individual departments is likely to be unco-ordinated and ineffective. The management should therefore consider:

- the full extent and financial effect of each interruption to computer services
- the extent of both direct and indirect financial loss likely to arise from the foreseen events
- the extent of any legal liability which may accrue to all those who may become involved.

The senior managers must also accept that there are likely to be real and continuing financial implications for the organization if an adequate plan is to be produced and kept operational. The plan should have the following elements:

- An overall statement of policy which makes it clear that responsibility for security is now an integral part of every employee's job.
- A series of general rules indicating how the policy is to be implemented: noting, for example, that because information is a valuable resource, it should only be disclosed if there is adequate value in return.
- More detailed measures to be taken and responsibilities to be assumed both by individuals and departments within the organization, and by third parties who relate to the organization.
- Mechanisms for the review and change of both rules and measures – information systems are dynamic and security measures must be kept up-to-date.

At a policy level, every organization ought to be able to identify baseline controls which can be developed to apply to all aspects of the organization. One problem, however, is that managers who know little or nothing about computers and the information systems which they support, can overreact and demand security measures from subordinates who have neither the organizational perspective nor the authority to respond effectively. For example, if left to the DP department, the organization will only get the controls for those risks that the DP managers identify, and that department will not be able to ensure that peer departments make the necessary changes to their procedures to produce a more secure system. The result can be irrelevant security procedures with the wrong people in charge. It can also lead to unnecessary and uneconomic complexity.

The real difficulty therefore comes in designing improvements to these obvious minimum levels. This evaluation should be carried out as a form of cost-benefit analysis to identify and justify security enhancements. For these purposes, a good (if surprising) opening assumption would be that all security measures are inherently undesirable! The reason for this perhaps surprising assertion is that many of the standard security measures will be expensive to install and, once installed, can significantly reduce performance levels.

Further, many systems will become less user-friendly and less popular with the staff. Then, whatever plans are approved must be given the funding necessary to achieve the expected upgradings in performance, and not only must that funding be given an adequate priority within the corporate plan, it must also be built into the staff training schedules so that the desired responses and countermeasures can be thoroughly integrated into the normal organizational procedures, e.g. most organizations will already have fire alarm procedures, etc. Detailed rehearsals must also be budgeted for, and pushed through against possible opposition – they serve the interests of the organization as a whole, but may be very disruptive to the immediate working of individual departments and their parochial interests.

The role of the security working party or team

To achieve the best results, each organization should review its own structure. Every organization has human resources which can assist in the solution of problems and it is important that the organization identifies what resources already exist, and plans to produce further resources through a sound education policy and awareness training. This examination may also lead to changes in organizational structure and a reallocation of responsibilities as the worth of individuals or departments is reappraised. Once this process is complete, the organization should consider whether to set up a fully representative working party to lay down the basic policy for the future. We emphasize that any review should always be prospective and not retrospective, and that whoever leads this process should have both a senior and a highly visible post.

For these immediate purposes, the security co-ordinator should be responsible both for guiding the pre-planning and for leading the full planning exercise, and senior management must be seen to support the role actively to allow the exercise to retain appropriate credibility. In the long term, the co-ordinator should be responsible for:

- managing all the security systems necessary to protect the organization's tangible and intangible resources
- developing and implementing new security procedures, including the retraining of staff
- monitoring the awareness and the commitment of the organization at all levels to the declared security policy and investigating all breaches of procedure.

The immediate task of the security team is to set the primary objectives and to identify the fundamental assumptions which will underpin the long-term security plan. The review carried out by the group could start with a historical analysis of the declared record of security performance. The difficulty is that many of the incidents will not be reported and the scale of the problem may be understated. It may be preferable to ask for the group's best guess as to what can go wrong based on their own experience. In principle those who are co-opted into the group should understand both the technical and the commercial problems likely to arise, and must represent the interests of all the major departments whose co-operation is essential if the plan is to made to work.

But in constituting the group broadly, there is a security issue. The problem with teams from several departments is that it teaches each member of the group what the vulnerable points are in each other's departments and what the controls are. If one person, having discovered where there are no controls, then abuses that information, there could be a major disaster. This is not the most secure way of maintaining security within an organization. The team should certainly be convened but, if there are concerns about the reliability of any member of the group, either its work should be kept at a level of generality, or its work should be dealt with through sub-groups to ensure that the people involved in each area only learn a little about each other's areas.

However it is organized, the most obvious first task for the team is to consider:

- which disasters are to be included in the plan?
- what are the critical resources and applications within the organization to be protected?
- what sort of security strategies are available to counteract each major classification of disaster and, following a disaster, which resources are most critical to the restoration of normal operations?
- what would be the extent of the possible losses, and the cost of the projected recovery measures?

The team should report directly to the chief executive of the organization and, with this information, the senior management ought to be able to make better decisions.

The primary security objectives

Whether the organization is commercial or non-commercial, its paramount concerns will include the need to:

- maintain client/customer services at an acceptable level
- protect the capital investment in buildings and plant
- provide a reasonably safe place of work for all employees and for those visiting each affected site
- keep operations running in a disaster situation with less than a specified number of hours loss of essential services and with an acceptable audit trail.

The identity of the representatives on the planning team

It is obvious that the security department (if any) must be actively involved. It may also be advantageous to have senior managers or directors sitting on the panel to make them aware of the essential issues. Thereafter, contributions should be expected from a number of corporate departments and consultancies:

- **The finance department** will be expected to provide detailed costings, appraisals and projections.

- **The internal audit department** should be actively involved, but their primary function is to review the plan and not to create it. Within an effectively functioning organization, audit controls are an essential part of the management's drive towards security because they enable the management to achieve proper levels of accountability. The rule should be that every employee should be seen to be responsible for each action taken. Audit controls are more important during a disaster than at any other time. During normal operation, enough back-up information will be available so that, if an application needs to be re-run, the data will usually be available. During a disaster, all computer-stored data may be lost. In planning the response, it should be remembered that disasters can be staged to cover up a fraud and to engineer the disruption to audit trails.
- **The legal department** will advise on the existing statutory requirements and the possible extent of third-party liability in the event of failure to act properly.
- **The public relations department** should make sure that the best presentation of information to the public is achieved during a crisis.
- **The industrial relations** and/or **human resource management departments** also have an important role to play. All aspects of the proposed assignment of duties or redefinition of safety procedures should be properly discussed with those who will be closely involved in the implementation of the plan, with the employees and with their representative unions (if any). Thus, for example, individual employees will have to be designated as recovery co-ordinators, logistics controllers (ensuring that support services are available), and hardware and software controllers who will assess the damage and the likely period of downtime.
- **The transport department** should give support as it will be vitally important to move both people and equipment during a major incident.
- **The engineering, production and building departments** can give positive guidance on critical issues in their areas of responsibility.
- **The management services department** and other groups can offer a decision support service to the organization.
- **Outside consultants** can be useful because they have a breadth of experience. This will often allow comparisons between the target organization and other installations which may help to produce a more rapid start by avoiding the more obvious mistakes. In appropriate cases, they may discuss details of other security systems which are already in operation (suitably altered to prevent identification), a practice which can help in-house decision-makers to be more objective about their own needs. On the other hand, in-house efforts to devise security systems keep knowledge within the organization. The other possible advantages are that:
  - the staff involved will have a better understanding of the plan
  - they can often draw up a more detailed plan than an outside consultant
  - because they have invested more effort in it, they are more likely to be committed to it.

In any event, making comparisons with other organizations can be misleading because even though organizations may be in the same line of business, each organization's structure and procedures will have developed as a response to the internal and external pressures which it has faced. The idea of transplanting the security solutions adopted by other organizations into the 'home' organization may therefore not be appropriate. Finally, whether there is an outside consultant or not, the team is more likely to get a better overview if the team leader and overall co-ordinator is an internal appointment.

The work of the security team

Whatever the final constitution of the team it should have a diversity of skills and backgrounds so that, subject to the security considerations referred to earlier in this chapter, each possible point of vulnerability can be considered from different perspectives and a more rounded view produced. The more detailed work which the members of the team can then be asked to undertake will be:

- **Gathering information and making preliminary decisions**. The first requirements are to obtain and evaluate:
  - the site and floor plans of the data processing facilities
  - details of the hardware configuration and of any networking, i.e. the system architecture
  - details of the placement of the existing warning systems and emergency controls, and of medical and first-aid facilities
  - details of the software applications and programs, processing requirements and schedules and of the database systems
  - organization charts and lists of the names, addresses and telephone numbers of key staff
  - a checklist of documentation
  - details of all subsisting maintenance agreements.
- **Evaluating the alternatives** based on the assumption that while all information services should be considered, a full risk analysis is only required for those services deemed critical.
- **Laying down the strategies and creating the plans**. The strategies selected must bear in mind the functional requirements which have been identified and accepted as vital by senior management, and which seek to optimize the recovery plans.
- **Engaging in the normal life cycle review of the plans**, leading to an updating where appropriate (if it is assumed that the team will have a continuing function).

Security in the software development life cycle

An inevitable part of the planning process will the commissioning and design of software systems to both support management's information needs and provide appropriate levels of security. As seen earlier, the purpose of the **software development life cycle (SDLC)** and the **software quality assurance process (SQAP)** is to provide structure to the development of software. For example, the SDLC is divided into a number of phases:

- In **the initiation phase** the user's needs are identified and tested for feasibility.
- **The development phase** starts with a translation of the user's needs into detailed functional and operational requirement which can be used to produce the detailed program specification. The software is then coded and the program acceptance tested.
- **The operations phase** involves implementation of the tested system and maintenance.

When it comes to placing security within the development life cycle, much of what needs to be done to incorporate or improve security is not clearly separable from what is needed to improve the utility and efficiency of the application itself. The aim should be to build security into the design process at every stage, ensuring that there is a separate evaluation of all the safeguards within an effective software system. The security activities are:

- determining the sensitivity of the application or the data to be manipulated
- determining the security objectives
- assessing the risks
- determining the feasibility of implementing safeguards
- defining the most cost-effective security requirements
- implementing the security requirements
- developing the test procedures
- evaluating test results and modifying practice accordingly.

Complexity in systems design

A good objective when designing any system is to avoid or minimize complexity. Long-term experience within the software industry has shown that the more complicated the original specification, the more likely it is that there will be errors in writing the code. Even though many of these 'bugs' will not actively prevent the software from running, the cumulative effect will make implementing and maintaining the software significantly more difficult. It is also more likely that the audit trails will not work satisfactorily. But if the designer aims for simplicity and makes the systems easy to use, the result may make those systems more helpful to the potential criminal. The problem is that computers have no judgement and cannot sense a criminal intent in the user. Operating systems allow the access to the applications or the data once proper authorization procedures have been complied with. Thus, if sensitive applications or data are involved, it may be wise to eliminate menu-driven systems and to restrict access to the system documentation. Similarly, access to embedded training and help programs should be restricted if this might help casual users to commit frauds. For these purposes, let us assume that there is some sensitivity in either the applications or the data – there are a number of general rules to be followed.

Rule 1: keep flexibility to a minimum

One of the buzzwords of the 1990s is 'empowerment'. In design terms, this means enabling the users to make more effective use of the technology's capacities and one way in which this can be achieved is to make different parts of the system work together more flexibly. The idea of security does not eliminate the opportunity to build in flexibility. It simply requires that the flexibility is made available in a way which promotes the needs of the organization and does not represent a significant vulnerability. So if there is real data sensitivity involved, it becomes important to plan all user interfaces on a 'need to use' basis. In practical terms, this means that each employee's needs are written into a profile which controls and limits logical access (see Chapter 17). If this is not done properly and the ways in which the different components of the system may work together are poorly defined, the result will be significant redundancy in the system. Consequently, not only will the users have to be given more training if they are to get the best out of the system (which may allow users to analyse the security precautions), there is also a greater possibility of misuse.

Rule 2: take account of human weakness

Human as well as software engineering is vital. Socially and organizationally, life is becoming increasingly complicated. In part, this is due to improved communications and data processing capacities. The effects of decisions made by organizations have also been speeded up so there is significantly less margin for error than in pre-automation times. Unfortunately, the capacity of the human mind has not been enhanced, and although modern managers may have acquired better education, this has not necessarily given them any greater wisdom than they had in the days of the quill pen. It is therefore important to recognize the limitations of the mind and always to design systems that are easy to understand and use. This can minimize the risk of error and enhance the chance that the user will use and respect the system rather than consider it slow and annoying. If complexity is not understood and kept within reasonable limits, people will not be the master of the information system they create and the benefits detailed during the design phase will never be realized.

Rule 3: 'small is beautiful'

The designer should consider the size of the system. The larger the system, the less likely it is that individuals will be able to understand the whole. This creates feelings of uncertainty and leads to errors when the users are trying to use the system to solve problems. Sometimes large systems simply 'grow' into being. Others are created from scratch. Complexity becomes a problem of *vulnerability* when the system is not properly understood. The vulnerability arises either because the system cannot be changed in an orderly or controlled manner, or because it cannot be protected effectively – writing the security routines is impossible if it is not known in detail what the system is doing and if the knock-on effects of each change cannot be foreseen. Yet the pace of technological development has encouraged an increasingly rapid rate of change in information systems without a corresponding increase in control. The result has tended to be an inadequately understood system which can be compromised before the users notice that anything is wrong.

Rule 4: think about the problem early

If possible, complexity should be avoided at the design stage. In part, this may be achieved by using development methodologies which take human limitations into account. Designers should also monitor current research into human decision making. This should help to reverse the trend which sees too many machine-based technical aids to decision making imposed on the organizational environment (whether by the work of in-house designers or by purchasing packages in the hope that they will support decision making). Thus, designs should reflect the fact that many human decisions are highly subjective and based on approximations and guesswork. It should be recognized that the quality of decisions will not be improved simply by giving the human decision-maker large quantities of accurate information. Moreover, even if decision-makers are made aware of their own limitations, this will not guarantee any improvement in the quality of the decisions. The task for system designers is therefore to strike a balance between the volume and the nature of the information offered to the decision-maker to support each particular type of decision.

Rule 5: give the decision-makers what they need

When analysing the generality of the information that may be relevant to each significant decision situation, it is obvious that there will be a number of elements or factors which appear to influence the outcome. Some of these factors will seem to be more important than others. If the designer is going to change the number of factors which are to be presented to the human decision-maker for consideration, judgements will have to be made about significance in the identification and ranking of the factors. The problem is that what may appear important to the designer may not be thought so significant by the end users. This emphasizes the need for detailed consultation between designers and users to ensure that there is the lowest possible risk of error in selecting the key factors to support each class of decision. Without this consultation, the designers may distort the decision-making process by arbitrarily excluding information from the automated decision support system which the users consider vital to support the decision or by including information which the users find misleading. The consultation should therefore aim:

- to achieve some degree of consensus about which of the factors are the most relevant and significant; and then
- to group these essential factors into classifications or modules.

Rule 6: avoid oversimplifying the problem

Following on from rule 5 there will sometimes be consensus, so clear-cut divisions are defined and groups of essential factors will be apparent. On other occasions, the same factors may appear equally relevant to several different classifications. Thus, if we take the classifications of accounting factors, quality factors and marketing factors as examples, is it really possible to identify factors which are exclusively connected to each classification, or will some of the marketing factors only be clarified when the pricing implications of new quality standards are quantified, a set of factors that can only be resolved when the cost implications are considered? However, the classes are defined and the factors allocated between these classes, the problem will always be to retain an understanding of the interrelationships between the factors in each classification or module. In effect, therefore, this means that the classification of factors which emerges from the consultation may be somewhat arbitrary (perhaps including many overlaps) and it will have to be used flexibly if good support is to be delivered to decision making. The alternative design strategy is to avoid rigid and potentially inflexible support, and to use the power of the computer to model or simulate the effects of each decision. The aim is to enable the human observer to explore the problem and to assess the probable effects of each decision by allowing the user to:

- define the problem
- specify the relevant and significant factors
- ask '*what if?*' questions by varying the values for each factor in the model.

Because computers have no natural language ability and can only execute tasks expressed in quantified terms, this inevitably involves a simplification of each decision so that it can be modelled. The consequent risk is that the problem is *over*simplified.

Whichever approach is adopted, the key to an effective design is to concentrate on the *data* and not on the programs and packages which may be highly obsolescent. The data are the long-term resources which have to be protected because the information will not change as quickly as the rules for processing it.

Rule 7: produce good documentation

Finally, one of the keys to avoiding complexity is clear and up-to-date documentation (both during the design and the implementation phases of the SDLC) because, if it can be written down clearly, it must be a reasonably accessible system.

An introduction to the Data Protection Act 1984

Civil liberties groups have expressed increasing concern about both the amount of information that can now be stored electronically, and the ease with which that information can be manipulated and exchanged. Indeed, more information about every member of society can now be accumulated and stored than ever before – so, for example, banking records, medical records and itemized telephone billing among many others, are now capable of being consolidated to show what purchases we make, where we travel, who we talk to and how well we are. Further, it is well known that information is traded commercially – say, to create mailing lists. But there are potential problems. Starting with the individual, suppose that a name is shown as a subscriber to a magazine with a particular political bias, is it proper for the police to infer that the subscriber holds the political view adopted by that publication? In this case, the worry lies not in the exchange of information, but in the use to which that information might be put, or how it may be interpreted. The information might be used to decide whether someone should get a job, or be given credit, or be called to the police station for interrogation.

Taking the perspective of the technology, there are two major issues. Because more and more computer systems can communicate with each other, it has become routine for an increasingly wide range of data users to exchange information. If there is any error in the data that are widely exchanged, it magnifies the extent of the possible damage to the affected individuals. Moreover, even if the error is detected and put right in one database, it cannot be guaranteed that the data will be changed in all those systems which took that original data. Secondly, because computer data take up comparatively little space and are cheap to maintain, storage can be more permanent. For that reason, an error made when the person was young may haunt that person for the rest of their life – so if a false entry appears in school records available to prospective employers, it might be impossible to get a job. If the record is accurate but fails to explain the context and justification for what occurred, no one would ever be allowed to start again fresh.

People say they want more information because they think it will enable them to make better decisions. Hence, insurance companies or banks need to have some basis on which to decide whether to insure someone, or to give them credit. However, increased information is only useful if it is relevant. Relevance, of course, is a matter of judgement. Thus, was it relevant for life assurance companies to know the sexual orientation of the proposer before AIDS became a problem and, given that the incidence of AIDS among heterosexuals is also now a problem, is it still relevant? Information gathering may be good if it leads to efficiency savings which are passed on to the consumer through better or cheaper products and services. Otherwise, data collection may be a cause for legitimate concern. It is not sufficient to say, 'If people have done nothing wrong, they have nothing to fear', unless there are very strong controls on the definition of what is wrong. The true test of acceptability for data collection and processing should be a clear set of rules which protect the rights of individuals.

In general terms, the law does offer some protection to the individual through the concept of confidentiality which has its origins in equity. As Lord Denning says in the case of *Seager v Copydex* [1967] 2 All ER 415, 'The law on this subject does not depend on any implied contract. It depends on the broad principle of equity that he who has received information in confidence should not take unfair advantage of it'. The Data Protection Act 1984 represents a statutory extension of this general protection, but it is regulatory and not prohibitory. This means that it does not prevent computer users from holding information about individuals or disclosing that information to others, but it controls the way it is done. To that extent, therefore, it may be possible to argue that our law fails the test stated in the last paragraph.

Basic definitions

Parliament gave the following definitions to underpin the working of the Act.

Data

This is 'information recorded in a form in which it can be processed by equipment operating automatically in response to instructions given for that purpose'. Despite the existence of document scanners and optical character recognition software that would allow any user to capture manual text and to process it electronically, this definition excludes all hand-written records such as index cards and accounting sheets where sequential entries are made from time to time. So all that a data holder needs to do in order to avoid the operation of the Act is to keep the more controversial information about individuals in a manual form. This information may be highly inaccurate or out-of-date, but no one at present has the right to intervene – this will change following the implementation of the 1995 EU directive in 1998. We should also note that the word 'computer' is not used in the definition. Instead, parliament chose the word 'equipment'. The idea was to produce the widest possible coverage since all the different types of machine or device in which information may be processed and stored can be described as equipment.

Data material

This includes all the documents or other material used in connection with the data equipment, e.g. technical manuals, hard copies or tapes of source or other codes.

Personal data

This is 'data consisting of information which relates to a living individual who can be identified from the information in the possession of the data user.' The Act only applies to individuals and so there is no protection for legal persons – limited companies, trade associations, trade unions or other groups of people – or things such as production or stock records. If a living person can be identified, the Act will then apply to all the factual and judgemental information about that person including:

- factual matters such as age, sex, marital status, race, religion, salary and union membership
- matters of judgement such as appraisal records at work, creditworthiness, etc.

One difficulty is that no protection is given for any information describing what the data user intends to do in the future. So, in theory, if the data user created records indicating an intention not to promote X or to refuse X credit, these would be private to the data user. Indeed, data users may try to hide a wide range of material information by recording it as a series of intentions. It is, however, very difficult to separate fact, from opinion, from intention. Thus, the decision not to promote X is likely to be based on judgements made about X's performance at work and, presumably, these judgements rely on factual evidence of X's timekeeping, performance in meeting commercial targets, and so on. The Data Registrar would then be forced into the difficult task of having to evaluate the substance of what has been written rather than following the literal word.

Data equipment

This includes both the equipment on which data are processed and on which the information is recorded before processing. The Act does not apply to those who do no more than collect information. The intention is to regulate those who intend to process that information automatically. How this processing is done is irrelevant although it is probably safe to assume that the Data Registrar would only really be interested in electronic rather than mechanical systems – in 1998 the EU directive will include manual processing in the expression 'personal data filing systems'.

Processing

This word includes the tasks of amending, augmenting, deleting or rearranging the data, as well as all the ways of extracting information from the data. To prevent the passage of time being used as a defence, the fact that the data user may not intend to process the data immediately is irrelevant. That the information is recorded in a way that would permit it to be processed in the future is sufficient. To fall within the scope of the Act, all these and other similar processes must be related to a data subject.

Data subject

This is the person who is the subject of the personal data involved. There is no minimum age, and it includes all those recorded in the system whether as individuals or in some capacity such as employees, customers or service receivers.

Data user

This is any person, whether company, building society, etc., who controls the content and the use of the data held as part of a collection where the intention is to process that data at some time (in 1998, this will change to 'data controller'). This definition applies no matter what the intended scale of use. Thus, it will apply to major national industries and to government departments in the same way as to a private individual with a personal computer in his or her sitting room unless the data are of a purely domestic character, e.g. a shopping list, recipes, etc., or excluded for some other reason. The test is whether the data are collected into a set so that it can be accessed by the user as required. In *Data Protection Registrar v Griffin* (*The Times*, 5 March 1993) the court held that accountants who used a computer to prepare accounts on behalf of clients for submission to the Inland Revenue and other agencies were data users and therefore were obliged to register under the Act. Note that it is not necessary for the data user to own a computer. The processing may be performed by a third party such as a computer bureau so long as it is at the direction of the data user.

It is a criminal offence under section 5(2)(b) for a data user knowingly or recklessly to hold personal data or to use that data for a purpose other than that described in the register entry. This offence was considered by the House of Lords in *R v Brown* [1996] in which a police officer used the police national computer to extract information at the request of a friend who ran a debt collection agency. But although he saw the information on the screen, he did not pass it on to his friend. The question for the Lords was whether this amounted to a 'use' of the data. One view is that data are used by being accessed and the user derives information from the screen. The other view is that it is necessary to do something with the data once accessed. Although retrieving data may be evidence of an intention to misuse the information, the reference to the purpose described in the register would be redundant if no infringing action takes place. By a majority, the Lords held that the word 'use' meant 'to make use of' or 'to employ for a particular purpose' and, on that basis, simply reading the information on the screen did not amount to a use. Lord Hoffman said, 'It would be strange if the Act was concerned only with what happened unseen in the computer and not what happened when the information became accessible to the human user'. In reaching this decision, the court would seem to defeating the ordinary person's expectation that the law will help to protect privacy.

A computer bureau

This is either an individual or a corporate body who provides another with services in respect of data (in 1998, the directive imposes the term 'processor' to cover the person who undertakes the processing on behalf of the controller). At present, this may either be a commercial arrangement for the processing of major batch processing, e.g. payroll applications, or it may be for disaster recovery purposes where the bureau offers the organization 'hot stand-by' facilities.

The data protection principles

At the operational heart of the Act are the eight data protection principles. They are derived from the Council of Europe Data Protection Convention which was signed by the UK in 1981 but they are expressed in rather general terms and so they are not directly enforceable through the courts. The means of application is through the Data Protection Registrar who has the duty of supervising the operation of the legislation. The first seven principles apply to all data users, the eighth applies to both data users and computer bureaux. Personal data must:

1. be obtained and processed fairly and lawfully
2. be held only for one or more specified and lawful purposes
3. not be used or disclosed in any manner incompatible with these purposes
4. be adequate, relevant and not excessive for their purpose
5. be accurate and, where necessary, kept up-to-date
6. not be kept for longer than is necessary for their purpose
7. be disclosed on request to the data subject at reasonable intervals and without undue delay or expense, with the individual being entitled, where appropriate, to have such data corrected or erased
8. be kept secure against unauthorized access, alteration, destruction, disclosure or accidental loss.

These principles are enforced through a system of compulsory registration for all data users and computer bureaux, the system being supervised by the Registrar and enforced through the criminal law (even against individuals employed in the private sector – in *Data Protection Registrar v Victoria Davidson* [1995] the branch manager of the Woolwich Building Society was held personally liable). But the more usual case will involve corporate data users. Thus, Principle 1 was considered in *Innovations (Mail Order) Ltd v Data Protection Registrar* [1994]. The Registrar had served an enforcement notice because the company did not make it clear in all its advertisements that it sold and rented out lists of the names and addresses of its customers. The issue was whether fairness requires that data subjects are notified of secondary data uses. The tribunal held that every individual ought to be told of any non-obvious use of the data before the data were obtained. If this is not possible, say, because the data user proposes a new use of existing data, every data subject's consent must be obtained.

The Data Protection Act was extended by the Criminal Justice and Public Order Act 1994 which made it an offence for a person to procure personal data knowing or having reason to believe that this obtaining would amount to a breach of the Data Protection Act. The first prosecution took place in July 1996 when a private investigator was convicted of procuring information from the Driver and Vehicle Licensing Agency (DVLA) by a deception. The Registrar has a number of powers:

- **To accept or refuse registration.** Only registered data users or bureaux may lawfully process personal data, and there are no limits on the court's ability to fine as the punishment for any unregistered processing.
- **To issue a range of notices,** namely:
  - **enforcement notices** if there is a breach of the Data Protection Principles. Thus, for example, on the 29 August 1990, the Registrar served enforcement notices on four of the main credit reference agencies requiring them to stop searching on address only when asked for creditworthiness data. Instead, all such searches should be on the basis of the name of the credit applicant and address. The aim was to prevent credit applications being blighted by 'third-party information', e.g. that a judgement debtor lived at that address some years earlier. Following hearings in 1991 and 1992, these four companies had until July 1993 to modify their search practices to conform to the notices
  - **de-registration notices** where enforcement notices have been ineffective
  - **transfer prohibition notices.**
- **To enter the premises of data users,** search them, and to inspect, examine, operate and test any data equipment to determine whether there has been a breach of the law.

Exemptions to the Act

In some cases, there is no real threat to privacy and so the data user is exempted from compliance. This includes:

- **Payroll, pension and accounting data** used for calculating entitlement to pay or pension, or for keeping records of ordinary business activity. Payroll and pension data are held for the benefit of both the data user and the data subject, so both have an interest is making sure that the right amount is paid and the correct amount of tax is deducted. Similarly, businesses must keep records of commercial transactions so that payments can be made or collected, and the financial health of the business monitored. Through the issue of payslips and invoices the data subjects can monitor the accuracy of the data held about them.

- **Membership details of clubs and name and address files**, e.g. to collect subscriptions and to circulate information to club members. However, the individual members have the right to object to the information being held electronically or the information being given to a third party, e.g. to add to a commercial mailing list.
- **Data held for statistical and research purposes**.

Equally, some government functions are excluded from the Act because it would not be in the public interest to allow the individuals access to that data, for example it would impede the investigation of a crime or would prejudice national security.

Remedies

A data subject also has a range of civil remedies to enforce the following entitlements:

- to be informed by the data user as to whether any personal data are held relating to him or her
- to be supplied with a copy of that data
- to be compensated for any damage or distress caused by any inaccuracy in the personal data
- to be compensated for any damage or distress caused by the loss or unauthorized disclosure of the data
- to apply for rectification or erasure of inaccurate data.

There is a defence to the claims for compensation if the data user can show that reasonable care was taken in acquiring, holding or processing the data.

Transborder data flows

The Data Protection Act is of direct relevance to the issue of electronic data interchange (EDI) since the information transmitted can be personal data. In commercial areas, developments such as the UNCID rules and the EDI Association Interchange Agreement are beginning to set standards, but the laws of the individual European states have not been keeping pace with the EDI explosion. Hence, in the context of transborder data flows, the UK Registrar may serve **transfer prohibition notices** to prevent the transfer of data to a specified country or countries outside the UK. Such notices may be issued where any data elements are to be transferred to countries not bound by the European Convention or without similar data protection legislation, and the transfer in question is likely to contravene any of the data protection principles. If such a notice was issued, the transmission of the data would have to be frozen while the Registrar investigated the complaint and/or until the Data Protection Appeal Tribunal had overturned the Registrar's decision. If it proved impossible to isolate the personal data elements from the whole, then all the data transfers from that source would have to be stopped. This would represent an example of supervening illegality to any contract between the transferor and transferee, and it would make any further performance of the contract impossible.

Within Europe, each country's data protection laws differ in the scope of the protection given to their citizens (in fact, only seven of the EU member states have enacted data protection legislation). Some of the differences between these laws are fundamental. Thus, for example, French law extends protection to manual records, whereas UK law only deals with automated data. Similarly, the Scandinavian countries (Denmark, Norway and Sweden) issue unique personal identity numbers to all their citizens, but in the UK, there is such a fear of increased surveillance by the state that not even law-abiding football supporters can be required to carry identification cards to help exclude the potentially rowdy from the football grounds.

A further difference is that UK law does not include limited companies in the definition of data subjects, whereas Denmark and Luxembourg give protection to all forms of legal person. Thus, although data about British and Danish companies might be collected and processed lawfully in this country, there would be problems in sending it to Denmark because its receipt might be unlawful in that country. Conversely, data about British or Danish companies could only be sent from Denmark to this country if Danish law were not broken (that is so even though its receipt would be lawful in the UK). Illegality under the law of either country of performance (whether sending or receipt) would make any contract of transfer unenforceable.

European developments

Within the present structure of the EU, the Commission has been studying the problem of harmonizing data protection laws. The problems in achieving this aim have been recognized. Thus, for example, in 1989 the Council of Europe published a study entitled *New Technologies: A Challenge to Privacy Protection?* which recommended changes in the law on telemetry systems, the interactive media and electronic mail systems. One of the major concerns was to produce much greater transparency in data storage facilities to ensure that data subjects are able to discover personal data holdings throughout a potentially European-wide networked system. As it stands, it would be difficult for any data subject to determine whether there were prejudicial data holdings held in other countries where there were fewer protections. This is particularly important given the pace with which the improving technology makes mass data storage, exchange and consolidation ever more feasible. In 1990, the Commission put forward a package of six proposals to deal with data protection and the problems of the 'data haven', i.e. the countries in which there is no data protection legislation:

1 An ambitious draft framework directive, intended to cover 'every situation in which the processing of personal data involves risk to the data subject', and representing the first supranational law on data protection.

2. A recommendation that the Community as a government institution adheres to the Council of Europe Convention on Data Protection 1981, e.g. to ensure the protection of personal data transferred to third countries, say, in eastern Europe.
3. A resolution to extend protection to all personal data held in the public sector that does not fall under present community law, e.g. crime and national security.
4. A declaration extending the data protection principles to all personal data held by community institutions and bodies.
5. A draft directive for the telecommunications sector, especially the integrated services digital network (ISDN) and the new value-added data services (VADS).
6. A draft Council directive to adopt a two-year plan in the area of security for information systems. This could lead to minimum European standards being developed and imposed on all businesses, e.g. to include manual data within the protection in all countries, to obtain the data subject's consent to the collection of the data, etc.

Directive 95/46/EC on the Protection of Individuals with Regard to the Processing of Personal Data and on the Free Movement of Such Data aims to protect the fundamental rights and freedoms of privacy for natural persons and the prevention of barriers to the free flow of personal data across the EU. This will require substantial amendments to the UK Data Protection Act no later than the end of 1998. However, the implementation costs to data users should not be too onerous given that many of the measures are good computing practices. After all, it is more economic to have good security and to avoid having data that are inaccurate or out-of-date.

Intellectual property rights in software

The Copyright, Designs and Patents Act 1988 (CDPA) as modified by the Copyright (Computer Programs) Regulations 1992 which came into force on 1 January 1993 to implement EU Council Directive 91/250 is the major source of law on the protections given to software, and section 3(1) confirms that computer programs are to be treated in the same way as any other literary works, but the Act does not contain any definition of the words 'computer', 'program' or 'software'. The conventional explanation for this omission is that it allows the courts considerable flexibility continuously to reinterpret the provisions of the law to keep them in line with the evolving technology. There is no doubt following the regulations that the initial specifications, flowcharts or 'preparatory design material' are protected in the same way as any other literary or artistic works. This copyright protection is automatic and attaches to the work as soon as it takes permanent form. This extends to any notation or code that might be used, and the means of recording is irrelevant (i.e. it may be on paper, on magnetic media or using some other technology) so long as it may be made available for a human to read. Thus, the protection includes both the source code and the object code even though the latter would not be easy to read as would a novel. The period of protection is during the life of the author and then 50 years except where the work was computer-generated, i.e. there is no life, in which case the protection is for 50 years only.

The protection of databases is problematic. For these purposes, a database is a body of information organized or arranged according to some basic principle of compilation that enables a user to retrieve and use particular items. General copyright protection is available under the Act for 'compilations of information' which rank as original literary works. But a computer database is distinguishable from the standard literary compilations such as bus or train timetables, telephone or trade directories because:

- it can be so easily reconfigured
- it can make data available more efficiently
- it can allow information to be extracted by inference.

Hence, if the database is updated on a daily basis, it would not be clear whether the protection is continuously recreated in the whole or applies only to the first complete version. There is no significant requirement of originality for any work to qualify for copyright protection if the work is generated by humans (there are some problems with computer-generated works). In this case, the protection is more for the effort invested by the database manager. Thus, if the manager invests thought in designing the file structures rather than simply adopting the standard file structures available in the package, the compilation will be deemed to have qualities of originality and would be protectable. The EU has now produced a draft directive which aims to give both electronic and paper database creators greater protection throughout the community for their investment of time and money. This protection will be valid for 15 years, subject to renewal when a new and substantial investment takes place. When in force, it will parallel copyright and allow the author to use a right of unauthorized extraction to prevent another from reusing the contents of the database for commercial purposes. In the meantime, English law as reflected in cases such as *Waterlow Publishers v Rose* (1991) will continue to struggle with issues such as ownership of database copyright if the file structure is computer generated.

The general protection given by copyright is to allow a remedy to the owner if someone makes an unauthorized copy of the original. For these purposes, section 17 defines copying as including the storing of the work in any medium by electronic means, even though the copy is transient and/or incidental to some other use of the work. This would, for example, include viewing a stored work on a VDU or hearing a sound recording played back through a multimedia computer system, as well as all necessary translations into or out of computer language or code to allow the program to run.

There has been considerable debate as to the extent of copyright protection. It has always been clear that the literal copying of another's work or simply adapting that work would amount to an infringement and give rise to a range of powerful remedies. The problem has arisen when the other has simply copied the logic and design concepts underlying the original work's success. Traditionally, the protection has only been given to the form the ideas took rather than to the ideas themselves. Thus, if I write a best-selling novel based on the hunt for a dangerous white whale and I call it *Moby Dick,* that does not prevent someone else from writing a book about a shark hunt called *Jaws.* Free competition therefore allows customers to benefit from the efforts of suppliers to enter the market with new products. In the USA, the courts have been developing the concept of 'look and feel' or the 'gestalt theory'. It may be an infringement of copyright even though there has been no literal copying of the original, if the second version has similar screen menus and outputs (and so looks the same), and similar file structures and processes (i.e. produces the same form of experience during use as felt when using the original). The leading American case is *Whelan Associates Inc. v Jaslow Dental Laboratory Inc.* (1987). It states that if there is only one way of achieving a particular effect, copying that would not be an infringement. But if there are several way in which the desired purpose could be achieved, copying the particular ideas would be an infringement. This is a direct blow against the so-called practice of reverse engineering where an expert will decompile the object code and construct different but equivalent source codes to produce similar results.

A European directive will now permit reverse engineering to enable the user to achieve interoperability, i.e. that the newly acquired software can be made compatible with the existing operating system and any other relevant programs. US cases also suggest that copying the relevant parts of a program to achieve compatibility of software is potentially a fair use of the first author's material.

In the USA, the Whelan principle is now under attack. Thus, in *Apple Computer Inc. v Microsoft Corp.* (1992) the Californian Court held that the similarities of the Macintosh interface and Windows did not suggest unlawful copying but 'standardization across competing products for functional considerations'. This does not mean that meaningful protection is not now available, but the days of the broad sweep of 'look and feel' are gone. It will be much more difficult to prove infringements. The most recent trend in the US courts suggests that a test of abstraction/filtration/comparison based on *Gates Rubber Co. v Bando American Inc.* (1993) will now be applied. The first step requires the court to dissect the program into its component elements:

- its purpose
- the program structure or architecture
- modules
- algorithms or data structures
- source code
- object code.

Once these levels of abstraction have been identified, the court must filter out all those elements that are not protectable by copyright. This will leave a core of protected elements that can be compared to the alleged infringing programs. If there is substantial and unjustified similarity between the two programs as compared, this will be evidence of infringement.

In March 1993, the High Court clarified the position in England. The case, *John Richardson Computers Ltd v Flanders and Chemtec Ltd* [1993] FSR 497 confirmed that an infringement can take place even though the computer code is different.

The court compared the two programs and found 17 points of similarity between the packages, nine of which were probably due to copying. Despite the limited nature of the copying, the court held that the second program infringed the original copyright. However, this is only a first instance decision and so not very authoritative, and it is framed in a somewhat limiting way. A later case is *Ibcos Computers Ltd v Barclays Mercantile Highland Finance Ltd* [1994] FSR 275 and it rejects the broad 'look and feel' approach of Richardson as being overcomplicated. It prefers a four-step test to apply the CDPA:

- what are the works claiming copyright?
- is the work original?
- is there copying from the work?
- is the copying a substantial part of the work?

In this case, two programs for agricultural dealers had similar features. The court began by confirming that there could be copyright in ideas so long as they were formulated in sufficient detail. On analysing the programs there was sufficient evidence of copying, but the appearance of similarity will not be enough on its own. It will always be for the plaintiff to particularize the exact way in which the defendant has reproduced the author's work. This will almost inevitably require detailed expert evidence so it is not certain that the UK will see litigation on the scale seen in the USA.

The boundaries between hardware and software are being blurred. Hardware implementation or 'hard-wiring' will execute algorithms as a single operation. This makes the execution fast, but makes the CPU more complex and so more expensive to design and manufacture. Programs written by using microinstructions are sometimes given the name 'firmware', for example an interpreter is usually embedded. In practice, whether an algorithm is executed by software or hardware is a trade-off between speed and cost. If the software is 'hard-wired', i.e. the electronic circuitry on the semiconductor chips is designed to produce signals which will make the computer run in the desired way, the European protection is provided by the Semiconductor Products (Protection of Topography) Regulations 1987. The chips are not programs in themselves, but the means which facilitate their functioning. It can take a long time (and therefore a lot of money) to get the design exactly right. Unfortunately, copying the design is quick and cheap. Under the regulations, a semiconductor product:

- is designed to perform an electronic function
- has two or more layers
- at least one of the layers is composed of semiconducting material
- at least one layer has a fixed pattern which is relevant to the electronic function.

Topography means the design which is fixed in or on one or more layers of semiconductor product. The topography right arises automatically when the design is complete, and it gives an exclusive right to the creator to exploit and reproduce the design. The period of protection is ten years from the end of the first year of commercial exploitation or 15 years from creation.

Under Regulation 4(2)(b), reverse engineering is permitted and, unlike copyright, a person who makes a new chip that will perform an equivalent function will not infringe the original topography right. It is not clear how this inconsistency with copyright law can be justified.

Summary

- The control of data quality and integrity has become critical to the successful operation of the automated office. Effective corporate security planning is therefore a significant priority, not simply in order to avoid loss, but to deter future threats and to bring about a good plan to recover from disasters if they cannot be avoided. Organizations must identify where they are most vulnerable, assess the probability that perceived threats will materialize and, if so, be aware of the critical operations that will be affected.
- The detailed security planning exercise must be built into the general planning process so that critical issues can be thoroughly addressed and decisions taken to achieve a satisfactory level of protection. This task must involve all the major departments of the modern organization, and all the major software development projects. Wherever possible, complexity should be avoided.
- Public concern over the volume of electronically stored information and the uses to which it might be put by unscrupulous persons has led to the enactment of data protection legislation. The UK's Data Protection Act 1984 requires the registration of data holdings, but gives few real rights to those who may be damaged by inaccurate information. Although there are moves in Europe to improve the protections given to data subjects, reform of the law is likely to be a slow process.
- Currently, no intellectual property system protects the idea behind the inventiveness, it only protects the form the idea takes. In this way, the law avoids giving absolute monopolies to the creative and encourages competition in the market place which benefits the consumer.

Self-test questions

1. Briefly identify the different roles that computers might have in criminal or fraudulent activities.
2. What are the main functions of a security system in the modern commercial organization?
3. Explain whether there are any broadly acceptable classifications for the increasingly wide range of risks faced by the modern organization.
4. How should designers plan to avoid complexity in their designs?
5. List the data protection principles and identify the main remedies available to a data subject.

Exam-style questions

1 ABC Stores Ltd is a trading company retailing a variety of goods from a number of stores in the south of England. All goods are supplied to the store outlets from a central warehouse adjacent to the company's head office, which contains the accounting, purchasing, personnel and marketing departments. Staff at the warehouse are responsible for stock control and for scheduling transport to the store outlets.

The computer-based information system the company uses has been developed over the years and is based on a mainframe computer sited at the head office with terminals in all of the functional offices. Data are held in a central database and all of the application programs are written in COBOL. Operation and maintenance of the system is carried out by specialist staff who are employed by the computing department.

The company has come to depend completely on its computer system to support its main business functions such as purchasing, accounting, stock control and order scheduling. Recently, the computing department has decided to replace the existing computer-based system with a new system based on a network of workstations.

As information systems manager you have been asked to investigate the security aspects of ABC Stores Ltd's information system. Write a report to the board of directors identifying and describing the areas of vulnerability to which the company is susceptible and the risks it is likely to incur.

2 CD plc is a financial services company with an information system based on a mainframe computer at a dedicated site in the centre of a medium-sized city in the Midlands. Most of the important business applications are computerized and it has been brought to the attention of the company's management that the loss of the computing facilities could have a disastrous effect on the company's trading position. The directors have asked you, as a consultant, to produce a disaster plan or contingency plan for the company's information service. As a preliminary to this process, produce a report making clear the role of senior management in the disaster planning process and describing suitable contents of a disaster or contingency plan.

3 XY Ltd is a large chemical company, highly computerized in terms of its primary business areas (such as production) and also its secondary or support areas such as the legal, financial, personnel and public relations departments. The company has a team of internal auditors trained in computer security procedures and can call on the services of external consultants. It intends to create a security planning team to investigate the security of XY Ltd's information systems and to produce a security plan for the company.

You are required to identify the tasks which members of the planning team would be expected to carry out in their particular business areas, and to describe briefly the detailed work which the security planning team would be expected to carry out in general.

(All answers on pages 568–569)

CHAPTER 15

Risk analysis

Introduction

It has been said that in today's business environment the only continuous element is change. The scale and pace of the changes that have affected organizations since the 1970s – in markets, technologies, resource management and other aspects of their life – require them to be adaptable, responding to pressures in the environment and remaining constantly alert to its dangers, including those that threaten their security systems.

Clearly, businesses that have heavy commitments to competitive strategies and new product/market development have a lot to lose. At one end of the spectrum, individual disaffection, in the age of the flexible workforce and the decline of traditional corporate loyalties, may manifest itself in data theft or corruption. At the other, corporate raiders stalk the business jungle, seeking underperforming companies for asset-stripping or successful enterprises for takeover and devouring all the relevant information they can find. And there are also natural dangers and disasters to be considered. Hence the value placed on risk management and its component, risk analysis, which help organizations to determine their vulnerable assets, security needs and protection routines, and to balance the cost of countermeasures against estimates of risk impact.

Our main objective in this chapter, following our discussion of security planning issues, is to help you understand the background and implications of these processes. We analyse the particular dangers presented by fraud – the kind of person likely to commit it, its current scale, and the reasons why so much criminal and fraudulent activity is not reported. We consider the key factors relevant to the preparation of cost estimates. We examine the various security decisions that need to be taken, the implications of security systems for networking and other electronic communications, and the contribution which insurance may make.

The use of threat scenarios in risk analysis

The aim of the scenario-based methodologies is to create a detailed understanding of the dangers to security faced by the organization. This is achieved by simulating reality. It is better to involve risk management experts in this process because simply asking the users for their opinions can produce highly subjective or superficial responses.

The first step in the standard methodology is to undertake **perpetrator analysis**. Here the aim is to identify those most likely to be able to damage the organization's ability to continue its normal operations, i.e. to maintain the availability of the information system and the integrity of the data it stores and processes. This analysis falls into two distinct parts. The first element involves two primary tasks:

- defining and quantifying the characteristics of those who may threaten the computer system
- trying to understand the motives for each type of attacker to make such an assault.

The second element requires the identification of the vulnerable areas of operation within the organization. Some targets will be relatively more attractive to different types of perpetrator. Their attractiveness will in part be determined by two key factors:

- the opportunities available to each class of perpetrator to exploit flaws in the software itself or in the security system
- the levels of knowledge and expertise, and of authority (if any) within the organization held by those individuals.

Once these targets and the potential perpetrators have been identified, the next step for the planners is to analyse different scenarios involving different types of perpetrator. The point of this line of enquiry is to direct the mind of the planners to the best safeguards – it is this phase of the methodology that gives the name of **threat scenario analysis** to the overall process, and it can be a vital part of the initiation study phase of the SDLC before entering into the more detailed feasibility study because, without this step, detailed security requirements and positive risk control strategies will not have been defined. The aim is therefore to:

- identify which of the vulnerabilities would be most likely to allow the attack to succeed
- quantify what the relative impact of attack by each type of perpetrator would be.

User needs

When formulating policy, the system designers need to remember that the users will only make some of their needs clear. This is because the users will tend to focus on the errors and difficulties which they know about or suspect and which are current. This reflects an important truth – that users are often naive. They tend to expect that, without ever mentioning their needs in the early discussions, comprehensive controls will be produced by the 'experts'. The designers must therefore prompt the users to make their real needs clear. This is not simply to confirm existing practice because that may be ineffective or based on manual systems which cannot match the standards achievable by automated means – standards of which they may be unaware. User functions and responsibilities should then be identified in relation to the security system, so that there is a clear understanding of the interaction between different user functions and the security system. This will help to disclose the real needs at each interface because the consequences of error or misuse can be more readily seen, and simple action can be taken to ensure that high-risk activities are checked and approved from another interface before being allowed to proceed.

Testing

Once it is in place, the security system must be tested. Testing the system must cover a number of important considerations:

- It must ensure that the security procedures are invoked when they are called for.
- It must show that the security procedures cannot easily be avoided.
- It must prove that the audit trails are reliable.
- It should demonstrate that the security procedures identified through the scenario analysis and now implemented actually represent a reasonable response to the threats given the degree of criticality to the organization for each of the protected objects and processes.

Penetration studies

The use of **penetration studies** should also be considered – in other words, individuals should be challenged to try to break the system. This may be carried out as a theoretical exercise through the use of scenarios and/or structured walkthroughs, or it may involve a practical exploration of the information system by experts in hacking. Naturally, the system should be fully archived before the exercise begins so that, no matter what damage the simulated hacking may cause, the system can be restored to its former state.

The kind of person likely to commit a fraud

Anybody, whether employed or not, may commit a fraud and there are no physical characteristics that will identify these people in advance. As always, the dividing line between honesty and dishonesty is simply a matter of opportunity and motivation. Employees may be motivated to act against their employer for a variety of reasons. These would include:

- envy and resentment of the success of other employees
- frustration that their own high expectations of rewards or recognition have not been achieved
- greed and selfishness (some staff consider this form of extra earning capacity to be a perk)
- some simply enjoy the intellectual challenge of beating the system, or simply want to have fun.

Naturally, the identification of motive assumes that the criminal has been allowed the opportunity to commit the crime. In this, the critical factors are the ability to access the relevant building and the accounting records, the requisite level of skill, and the time to plan and commit the fraud. This can only be measured on an individual basis. Indeed, one of the ways of identifying a criminal after the event is by identifying who had the ability both to commit the crime and to conceal its existence in the way selected.

Of all the factors, access is probably the most significant. Access to the relevant systems, or parts of systems, may either be authorized by the gullible employer, or it has been engineered by the would-be offender. Indeed, most offences are committed by people who have achieved positions of trust and who then abuse these positions. Further, the would-be offender must believe that there is a reasonable chance of concealing either the existence of the fraud itself, or their own identity. The act of concealment may:

- simply confuse the situation
- divert attention from the dishonest event
- delay its discovery
- actively prevent the discovery of the perpetrator's identity.

None of these devices can conceal the ultimate truth which is that the organization has sustained a net loss of worth and, in a well-run organization, it should not take too long before this truth surfaces.

Concealment

The pattern of fraud is usually incremental and it grows in scale from the first successes. Concealment is therefore essential if the fraud is to continue. Here, the perpetrator's greed is balanced against the general human instinct for self-preservation. The need is to prevent the organization's records from revealing the loss or, if that is unavoidable, there must be no clear record of responsibility. So, if property is to be stolen, the accounts must be manipulated by reducing or inflating the value of physical assets held so that the accounts appear to balance. This form of falsification actively prevents an auditor from discovering the loss.

All frauds have the tendency to reduce the net worth of the victim. In systematic frauds, the precise extent of the losses may be concealed. Frauds concealed in income or expense accounts are closed to the profit and loss account. They result in reduced profits and thus a reduced tax liability for the victim. Because they directly affect profitability, they are relatively easy to detect. Frauds concealed in assets or liability accounts are not closed to profit and loss, do not reduce profits and do not provide tax offsets for the amount defrauded. Such frauds are more difficult to detect. Most current frauds are aimed at financial applications systems within the computer but, increasingly, there is a threat to electronic funds and data transfers.

Defence strategies

The best form of defence is created by the communication of the security strategy from the top management to all levels of the organization. This must be backed up and consolidated by:

- the most senior managers being seen to comply with all the security procedures
- proper levels of training for all employees

- implementing and enforcing good controls
- through a clear deterrent policy operated by the employer in relation to all offenders, e.g. always prosecuting.

This is both a management and a communications problem. In relation to new recruits, employers must recognize that both honest and dishonest people may apply for the available jobs in the sensitive areas. Employers therefore have a responsibility to make proper checks on those considered suitable for appointment. In relation to existing staff, the statistics also show that a significant number of frauds are collusive. This allows low-level staff to share their resources in a way that either produces an opportunity that would not otherwise exist, or maximizes the resulting opportunity. Managers must therefore consider the range of personnel security strategies, such as functional separation which is discussed in a later chapter.

The reasons why people commit fraud

In addition to the motives that we noted earlier in this chapter, the following factors make for growth in both the frequency and scale of fraud.

- **Economic and political uncertainty**. In times of commercial recession, following boom years, previously honest people or organizations are more likely to consider fraud as a means of ensuring future survival and well-being.
- **Increasing materialism**. People are becoming more concerned with the acquisition of status symbols, and see greater loss of face in not achieving the external symbols of wealth and position. Further, more will put personal gain ahead of collective interests. This often first shows itself in decreased company loyalty.
- **Changes in social attitude**. There is arguably less respect nowadays for the property of others and more people challenge authority. This trend has been reinforced by a well-reported leniency in sentencing policy adopted by the criminal courts in crimes not involving violence. Criminals, particularly first-time offenders (often those who have not been caught before), have therefore found that, despite the best efforts of the Serious Fraud Office to secure convictions, there is little or no deterrent policy in operation against the pursuit of fraud. To that extent, 'white-collar crime' has achieved a degree of social acceptability.
- **Changing skill patterns**. Because of the increasing familiarity with computers which the young have, organizations are increasingly exposed to the activities of a younger technocratic breed of criminal which the older managers are ill-equipped to monitor.
- **Frustrated high flyers**. It may be suggested that some computer personnel have a different attitude of mind. Many are highly original problem solvers who find frustration in the more narrowly based management systems, or who lack respect for the managers who have inadequate or outdated technical expertise. The result is satisfaction in breaking the system or exposing the deficiencies of the more senior staff.

The volume of fraud

It is not clear how much fraud is being committed. The most recent security breaches survey published by the Department of Trade and Industry in 1996 suggests that computer-related theft is up by 60% and that the cost of a computer security failure has almost doubled since 1994. But all statistics based on reported and prosecuted crime are unreliable. Most computer crime goes unreported because:

- not all those involved may recognize that a crime has been committed
- the victim may regard the offence as too trivial to justify reporting it to the police
- the victim employer may not want to involve the known offender in the social consequences of prosecution
- the victim may have no confidence in the police or, in extreme cases, may even be antagonistic towards the police, say, because the employer has been engaged in tax evasion and may not relish any investigation of the organization's affairs
- the victim may be too pessimistic about the chances of either identifying the offender(s) and/or gaining a successful prosecution
- the victim may be too embarrassed to report the offence – e.g. public confidence might be affected as in the case of a bank, or the victim might prefer to be deceived than have to be seen as distrustful of colleagues
- the actual victim, the prospective victims, or the hardware and software suppliers might not want details of the mechanism of the fraud discussed in public because this might encourage 'copy-cat' crimes, or others might improve on the method once the countermeasures and detection systems have been explained
- the victim may be deterred by the threats of the offender, e.g. the victim has proof that the attacker can destroy vital data if the police are involved
- the offender may have disappeared.

Even if the offence is reported to the police and the offender is traced, it may be that no prosecution takes place because:

- The police may consider that a warning is sufficient – particularly when the offender has repaid the value of the loss caused or the amount involved is relatively trivial.
- The Crown Prosecution Service (CPS) may not consider the evidence sufficiently convincing to justify the expense of a trial – this is particularly important now that the courts may grant costs to the successful defendant out of public funds.
- The CPS may think the law unclear and the risk of acquittal high – sadly the law has not kept pace with technology.
- There may be jurisdictional problems – these arise if the alleged offender has operated across national boundaries.

Reasons for inaction

In some areas of organizational life fraud has become institutionalized as a perk. The problem is that fraud has a contagious quality. Hence, if small frauds such as expense claim fictions are not dealt with, they are likely to spread and grow. Alternatively, losses simply mount up, albeit in smaller amounts. It just takes that little bit longer for the victim to bleed to death. However, many organizations do not take action to control fraud. A wide range of excuses have been offered to explain this failure:

- Many managers never quantify the losses and simply live in the hope that most employees are honest.
- Like ostriches, many managers live with their heads in the sand, hoping that fraud always happens somewhere else.
- The decision has been taken that the implementation of controls would not be cost-effective. This may be an entirely rational decision based on researched information or it may just be an excuse for inaction.
- The managers have tried controls and they have proved ineffective. This simply proves that it is easy to design ineffective controls; good security is based on a well-founded appreciation of the risks and sound strategies to keep those risks within acceptable limits.
- Because controls are based on the assumption that employees cannot be trusted, some managers find the enforcement of security systems to be socially unpleasant.
- Some managers believe that the auditors will find all the most serious frauds, i.e. they do not perceive security as being a part of their immediate responsibilities. This attitude misunderstands the role of auditors (both internal and external) whose function is limited to testing whether the accounts are a fair and accurate statement of the company's performance.
- Many managers do not have the technical competence to check the work of the newly qualified technical staff, and therefore feel obliged to consider them honest until it is proved otherwise.

How to prepare cost estimates

The cost analysis process compares the cost of the proposed security measures with the possible cost of disruption to the organization. It is relatively easy to estimate the initial and revenue costs of security measures. It is more difficult to estimate actual losses if no action is taken, or the percentages of loss displaced if alternative measures are taken. The fact of difficulty should not deter organizations from attempting the exercise.

The best method of quantifying potential losses is to estimate under the following headings:

- loss of physical assets, e.g. buildings, hardware, etc.
- loss of intangible assets, e.g. goodwill, corporate image
- loss of data and recovery costs – in 16% of reported cases, it takes more than one week to restore the operation of systems affected by fraud

- legal costs, e.g. contractual late payment penalties, etc.
- personnel losses, e.g. death, injury, illness
- financial losses, e.g. uncollected receivables, delayed cashflow, loss of business, increased costs of working.

The organization should then undertake a complete asset inventory of facilities, contents and services, and calculate the current and replacement values of all the major assets. The next step is to examine the organization's accounts at a functional level, and to identify the income or services that are directly dependent on information handling. In taking this step, it is vital to talk to the users. They know what is likely to follow a disaster, and it is a good way of interesting the users in the problem of security. Independently, managers should be asked for their views. It is always revealing to compare views on the same topic from different parts of the administrative hierarchy. It is also useful to refer to the new IT Security British Standard BS7799 to raise awareness of the standard range of threats and solutions.

Probability

In finalizing the evaluation, all the assumptions which underpinned the probability assessment for each disaster should be stated, together with the predicted disaster costs, the priority of strategy, and the costs of implementation. To justify the effort of assessment, there must be a real probability of each disaster happening, or the losses involved must be substantial. You should remember from the definition of risk offered in Chapter 14 that:

$$\text{Risk} = \text{probability} + \text{criticality}.$$

So, the likelihood of a total loss of major facilities will be of relatively low probability, but disabling fires or the acts of the inattentive operators may cause difficulty on a more regular basis. It must be recognized that, cumulatively, the latter type of causes might produce greater losses than one major catastrophe. If the objection is that no one can accurately assess the probability that any given employee will steal the organization's property, this does not excuse a failure to take precautions. To justify the necessary measures, the managers must rely on their experience to value the probable loss from those classes of misbehaviour that are potentially controllable.

If managers devise several alternative strategies, the most cost-effective will be those where the economies of loss outweigh the costs of implementation. In other words, the organization must aim to save more than it spends on prevention. For each risk, the assessment of probability for each of the identified headings of loss occurring is increased by the number of vulnerability factors, and decreased by the security measures taken. The question is how to weigh the probability of occurrence as opposed to non-occurrence. If we take the question of fire in any given room: the more inflammable furniture, materials and equipment stored in the room, and the closer it is to a furnace, boiler or other source of fire, the greater the risk unless there are adequate fire walls, alarm and extinguisher systems, etc. By identifying all the evidence on which the risks of occurrence and damage might be enhanced or diminished, the organization is better placed to make a more objective assessment of the probability in the light of known values, rather than leaving it to an intuitive, and probably inaccurate, guess.

Prerequisites

It is also probable that the measures which offer the greatest displaced losses for the least cost, will be the inevitable preconditions upon which the implementation of the currently less cost-effective measures would be dependent. Hence, a positive statement of support by the most senior executive officer or managing director costs least, but is the essential prerequisite of effective action to follow. Equally, the helpful and flexible responses of a receptionist can be far more beneficial in creating an atmosphere where security procedures are followed, than the lumbering diligence of a guard on a door. Management's task is to consider which measures are most likely to beneficially affect the greatest number of possible threats.

Ensuring survival

Senior managers can be reluctant to commit funds when there is no immediate tangible return, or if funds are committed, it can be difficult to maintain the long-term interest of management in something which has no short-term payback (if it has a payback at all). Further, managers are more used to assessing cost against profit rather than against expected loss. Even if the decision is taken in principle to commit resources, what is proper provision against losses of, say, £500,000? This will in part be determined by the estimated frequency of loss. Thus, if the given disaster is only likely even 50 years, would an annual budget of £10,000 be cost justified? Computer suites are usually well protected and, from a statistical or actuarial point of view, there have not been enough disasters to form a trend. Senior managers will always ask for the cheapest measures that are consistent with the risks. However, these are mere guesses and cannot be binding financial bases for calculating performance. The only criterion is to ensure the survival of the organization. In hindsight, the level committed may be seen as overspending, but it will have been justified in psychological terms, if for no other reason, because it guaranteed peace of mind in the meantime.

Examining user claims

In reaching decisions, the probable costs of any disruption given by users will not be directly comparable since each will base their figures on different assumptions. Some users will plead importance, but will not want to pay for security. Others will underestimate the extent of the likely disruption. Yet more will ask for unnecessarily high reliability and will make funds available. Objective scrutiny of all the claims is required. This can be achieved through comparisons with other organizations. The problem is that many managers fear the possibility of bias in the advice which they may receive from the in-house computer experts who have already helped to produce this dependence on the DP resources. Managers therefore like to know what percentage of turnover is usually spent on security in comparable industries. Unfortunately, the answer to this question is not necessarily helpful because even organizations trading in the same commodity can be very different. Assessments should always be made on the basis of the organization as it is.

Evaluation

The first step should be evaluation of the loss on the assumption that current arrangements will not work. Thus, even if there are back-up arrangements, the 'worst case' scenario should be taken and the estimates should include items such as the full costs of the recovery and reconstruction of data from original source documents. The calculation should then proceed to cost the loss on the basis that current arrangements will work. Finally, the loss should be estimated on the basis of the desired levels of protection. This will give three figures against which to benchmark planning targets and later implementation performance. As a part of making all assumptions explicit, the following elements should also be stated:

- the time which it will take to recover or to replace the asset or data
- the estimates of the additional costs in running the organization immediately following the predicted disasters
- the loss resulting from the organization's inability to offer the normal services
- replacement costs of hardware and software should be itemized without reference to insurance sums which may be available (subject to the possible payment of increased premiums following a claim)
- rebuilding costs and/or relocation costs should be estimated and then all figures index-linked. (In this, we should remember that rebuilding may be less expensive than the restoration of damaged facilities.) The calculations should also include generous overtime figures for existing staff, and suitable sums to cover the hiring of temporary staff.

The combined end product should be a list of proposed and costed measures which are established in priority ranking order, reflecting the fact that:

- some measures will be considered *absolutely necessary*
- others will be considered merely *necessary*
- the remainder will be simply *desirable.*

Resource planning

Senior managers must then consider and decide what resources are available for implementation, assigning roles and appointing staff where necessary, but recognizing that the active and continuing co-operation of all employees is vital. This planning exercise must be seen in the light of Data Protection Principle 8 contained in schedule 1 of the Data Protection Act 1984 which states, 'Appropriate security measures shall be taken against unauthorized access to, or alteration, disclosure or destruction of, personal data and against accidental loss or destruction of personal data.' As the penalties for non-compliance may be severe, this means that computer security has to be examined from both a commercial and a legal point of view. In this, managers must consider the nature of the personal data held and the harm that would result from unauthorized access, alteration, disclosure or destruction. This involves both a consideration of the security measures programmed into the relevant equipment and the measures taken for ensuring the reliability of the staff who have access to the data. The Registrar may enforce compliance by issuing an enforcement notice under section 10. A failure to implement the security measures within the time specified would then result in a fine and/or the issue of a deregistration notice under section 11 which would require the data user to cease holding the data identified in the notice (and therefore in effect to cease trading). See Chapter 14 for a general discussion of the Data Protection Act 1984.

The range of security decisions to be taken

Each organization will need to take decisions about:

- **physical security** – physical access to buildings and terminals, and controls over the environment of the computer media (considered in detail in Chapter 16)
- **logical security** – controls which seek to regulate access to a system or to resources held within that system (considered in detail in Chapter 17).

Disaster recovery planning

If a serious incident does arise recovery will be more effective if there has been adequate pre-planning and the most likely countermeasures or responses have been fully rehearsed beforehand so that all those involved know their duties and responsibilities. However, this planning exercise should not be limited to the major disasters; it should address all those undesirable events which will affect the performance capacities of the organization in a real way. Hence, for example, at a purely physical level, the overall contingency plan is likely to include some or all of the following elements:

- **Manual fall-back systems** to operate during short disruptions and during the initial stages of a major disruption. Information flow has now become critical to the health of most organizations, and sufficient continuity must be maintained if those organizations are not to alienate or lose clients and customers. The ability to maintain cashflow, subject to the normal controls, is also fundamental. The plan should therefore address the issues of customer/client services and financial management so that the commercial competitiveness and/or the reputation of reliability of the organization can be maintained.
- **An arrangement with another user or bureau** which has compatible systems to use their machine(s) in an emergency. This is called a **hot stand-by scheme**, but few organizations will have a guaranteed level of free machine capacity so this arrangement can represent only a short-term solution and is likely to cover a limited amount of processing.

- **Plans for commissioning replacement facilities** as quickly as possible – the plan might call for the designation of a suitable room as an emergency computer room, and equipping it with the essential computer support equipment like air conditioning and suitable telecommunications equipment; or a subscription might be made to a **cold stand-by scheme** whereby access to an empty computer room is offered to subscribers in an emergency. There are also firms which provide *relocatable computer centres* – they are prefabricated rooms with built-in facilities but they can take time to erect. Planning is therefore essential to bridge the gap while the new working environment is achieved, so the hot standby schemes may be better value. Copies of essential files and software must survive the disaster for either of these latter schemes to be successful.

Decisions on reliability and availability

At a more mundane level, the data processing and user departments must agree on targets for reliability and availability. This involves deciding:

- the number of hours each day during which the service should routinely be operational
- the planned downtime for maintenance, where applicable
- the length of time that the system can be unavailable before business is seriously affected
- an estimate of fault frequency, probably based on past experience or information from the manufacturers.

Detailed decisions must also be taken to decide exactly what is to be made available both for normal operations and in disrupted operating conditions. For example, the following alternatives must be addressed:

- should the service aim to provide the required application programs at all the user terminals and subject only to the need to keep terminal response times within acceptable limits?
- or should the programs only be available to a proportion of the users at specified terminals?
- or should the programs simply be available on the host machine without preplanning the number of terminals at which access should be achievable?

These examples should serve to illustrate the diversity of matters to consider and explore when any organization addresses the security issue. The aim of this planning exercise should be to produce detailed manuals which lay down the organization's detailed disaster recovery plans which have been tested in a series of tests, drills and exercises. These tests and drills will also serve as staff training exercises.

The first stages of the planning process

The process should begin by defining the information resource management needs of the organization as a whole, and determining which range of standardized and compatible equipment will enable the organization to meet those needs. The creation of information centres, and the development of financial software packages for planning, trend analysis and other management tasks are all useful in producing management information which can be analysed and manipulated. But many managements pay little attention to the issue of information systems security. The first step is to consider what degree of security is required for the different types of information to be held on system. Without deciding which information is sensitive, little coherent planning can take place. Moreover, not all resources are equally important, nor are they equally likely to be harmed. The planning must therefore identify which system functions are supported by which resources, and demonstrate the susceptibility of each element to damage.

In the modern context it will be rare for larger organizations to be starting from scratch. Most will already have some form of automated system and few will be rash enough to ignore the capital invested in existing hardware, and the information which may be stored in its files. However, the appraisal must be objective and, if it is clear that the existing system cannot be upgraded to meet modern requirements, the organization must take the proper long-term investment decisions, such as the replacement of hardware.

Detailed decisions must also be made about the people who will develop, support and use the new information systems. New staff will have to be recruited with particular skills, and existing staff will have to have further training or be retrained. Indeed, in the first instance, the end users should have the responsibility for the security of their data, and if they are unhappy with the security system forced on them, it is unlikely to work.

Configurations

Ultimately, decisions will be made about the configuration of the system and this will define the nature of the security problems. If it is decided that a single mainframe system is to be established, it may be housed in a single building with access restricted to those present in the building. Alternatively, there may be several thousand terminals which are to be located in a variety of places as a wide area network, or there may be several computer installations linked together as a distributed system. The issue, whatever the system, is to provide cost-effective and operationally effective protection for both the hardware and the information which it processes. The historical irony is that the computerization of both public and private sector administrative systems has led to a centralization of data. This leaves many organizations with a legacy of danger because, through centralization, each organization has become more vulnerable to loss through accidental or malicious acts or omissions.

The main risks in networking

The greatest dangers to system security lie in linking machines together into networks. Organizations should not link machines together simply because it *can* be done. Instead, they should consider whether there are information flows which would be benefited by a network, or whether the same effect could be achieved by people talking with each other, or by exchanging pieces of paper or floppy disks.

The cheapest form of network is a local area network (LAN). LANs are usually self-contained and, at the lowest level, they are created by inserting interface cards with the appropriate communications software in each machine and then linking the machines together with cable.

The next stage development is a multi-user configuration where several machines share resources. These will usually be controlled by a central file server and the security software will be contained in the central machine. The problem is that if this central unit fails, the network fails. Further, as data move so rapidly through the most LANs, traffic management and error checking is vital. Should a collision occur as a result of two or more stations transmitting at the same time, data integrity will be lost.

The next option to deal with this problem would be a ring or loop system. Each node on the loop must contain the software security system. The control of data flows is then achieved by a token-passing system which avoids collisions. The most robust and flexible system is the *tree* or *bus* system which produces a distributed network of autonomous machines, connected to a common cable like the branches of a tree. This system will not collapse if one or more workstations break down and, if the receiving machine detects that data have been lost in transmission, the sending machine is directed to retransmit when the line is clear.

The advantages and disadvantages of a network

The main advantages of a network are:

- **Communication**. Communication between users is improved. Paper systems are slow whereas machine-based data transfer is virtually instantaneous, allowing management team consultation to be made more time-effective. It also avoids problems of trying to locate people by telephone since messages can be sent to the terminal where they have logged on.
- **Resources**. Large number of users can be given access to useful hardware and support software. This must be carefully costed because resource sharing can be more capital intensive. Thus, sharing laser printers can be cost-effective and site licensing is cheaper than paying fees for multiple copies of the same package, but if people are given redundant facilities because they are standard throughout the network, this is not cost-effective. The financial implications of staff training will also have to be considered if all are to get the best out of all the facilities made available.
- **Information**. If central databases are constructed this can produce better quality information. Too many organizations have allowed individual departments to produce their own records that may be difficult to consolidate into a useful central resource.

The possible problems of networking are:

- **The robustness of the hardware and software** – designs must aim to ensure that if one element in the system fails, the work can continue at the other locations.

- Adapting single user packages for network purposes can be difficult so completely **new software systems may have to be designed or purchased** if a network is to be installed.
- **Not all network software has built-in logical access controls**. It is also desirable to include some form of control to prevent the alteration of centrally held data and the changing of software. In planning decisions, it should be assumed that all information in a network is potentially *insecure*.
- **Implementation should be monitored** to ensure that information bottlenecking does not occur.
- Steps must be taken to ensure that, in a distributed system, **users are all given access to the most up-to-date data.**
- It can be **very expensive to make every single user's local database designs compatible** so that linking and data transfer can be made to work. To assist the linking process, the International Standards Organization (ISO) has drawn up a set of communication architecture standards called the **open systems interconnection (OSI)** model.

Network and communication facilities

The Telecommunications Act 1984 broke the British Telecom monopoly and allowed competition in the offer of services on the BT network, including the following:

Value-added network services (VANS)

The supplier of these services adds functions and capabilities to those necessary for simple data transmission, such as insurance brokerage systems which link to the major insurance companies, or ICL Tradanet which allows retailers and suppliers to transmit orders, invoices and other documents.

Viewdata

VANS will often be made available through viewdata, videotex and teletex systems. This is a cheap and efficient way of distributing information stored on a computer. Access is by the normal communication links and information is presented in frames, a frame being one screen of information. The central computer accessed either stores the frames requested or acts as a gateway to other computers where the information is stored. The public system is called PRESTEL, with an increasing number of systems being made available to private subscribers as a closed user group (CUG), for example in the stock exchange for share prices and in the travel trade for hotel and holiday bookings. Viewdata systems can also link to the range of telex, teletex, telesoft and electronic mail systems.

Viewdata is predominantly an information service, so most effort goes into maintaining system availability with good back-up and recovery systems. For security, most viewdata systems use terminal identifiers, ID codes and passwords. It is a standard operating procedure that accounts are frozen if there are unsuccessful attempts to log on. CUGs can control access, with different levels of security given to individual frames. Editing can only be carried out by the information providers (IPs) who are given special passwords. The number of people having editing powers needs to be controlled and their use of system privileges should be carefully monitored by the viewdata managers. Similarly, the special facilities which create and delete accounts should be monitored. The audit trails must also be good. If all the information is held on the same mainframe, the whole database could be at risk is security is breached. However, not to centralize is to give up the opportunity to integrate the database with other systems, and to give up the more sophisticated access controls that can be produced within a mainframe environment. Further, fewer users could access a system based on distributed minis. Users should also recognize that security on some of the commercial systems has been sacrificed because creating good controls takes time, and time is money. At a level of physical security, hardware design should reflect the fact than some viewdata terminals are often in public places and are therefore vulnerable to vandalism and theft.

Text communication

Teletex has been designed to link word processors together via the telephone network, but adoption and implementation by manufacturers has been slow. Nevertheless, commercial pressures have persuaded the manufacturers to provide some intermachine capabilities. An important feature of a teletex message standard is the **call identification line (CIL)** which identifies the sending terminal, the receiving terminal, and the date and time of the message, thereby providing a reasonable validation of the source of the message. If the right terminal has not been addressed, the message should abort. There should also be a final 'handshake' message to confirm the number of pages sent.

Alternatively, the text may take the form of **electronic mail** – that is an on-line computer system for the electronic exchange of information through a mailbox system. The speed and character set limitations of telex networks have left the market open for the development of good computer-based messaging systems. The public services are Telecom Gold, One-to-One and Mercury Link 7500. Many organizations have comparable in-house systems which provide terminal-to-terminal messaging facilities. Messages can be encrypted on Gold and Link. All three public systems are protected by passwords and have good security records.

Voice mail or messaging systems, such as BT's Voicebank, are similar in that each user has a personal voice mailbox which can be accessed by dialling the appropriate telephone number plus an optional password. There are some problems, however:

- the sender does not have the facility to review and change messages
- the system does not work when the recipient is using the telephone
- there is no integration with other systems
- although messages are usually short, the nuances of speech are retained which is only sometimes an advantage; it may be better to review and send a written document.

Word-processing facilities

If word-processing facilities are to be centralized within an organization, there may be greater problems of security and the system may become more vulnerable to failure. All users will have to be taught good disk management habits. The control of physical access to centrally located terminals should be through a central reception area to cut down the risk that outsiders will gain access to confidential documents. In creating adequate fire precautions, all user departments should agree how long to keep manual records so that electronically stored data can be recreated. A reasonable number of battery laptops or manual typewriters should also be kept so that, in an emergency, letters can still be written. Good logical access controls must be installed and the staff trained to maintain discipline. But, if successful, centralization will:

- overcome the problems of hardware and software compatibility between different users in the same organization
- make maintenance administratively more convenient, and it should produce economies in the negotiation of a single mainframe agreement with one reliable service provider
- allow the standardization of training to build up expertise across the organization
- allow the production of standardized documentation vital to support new users.

Desk-top publishing and phototypesetting

Now that problems of compatibility are being overcome, it is logical to connect word processors to laser printers (for the production of camera-ready copy) and typesetters. Manufacturers have taken security seriously. Most systems provide good back-up facilities to minimize the risk of not meeting publication deadlines. The print room in most organizations is usually organized on a limited access basis only. If the typesetter is networked, there should be a proper identification of every user, with good facilities built in to protect the integrity of the data. Where external lines are used, say, to permit a reporter to input data from a laptop computer, there must be good controls to minimize the risk of data corruption through noise on the line, or from a discontented journalist. It is always advisable to have a final proof-read before printing.

Telex and facsimile machines

These are now used routinely to transmit text, pictures and facsimiles of documents. Telex has been improved by the replacement of electromechanical telephone exchanges by the more versatile **stored program control**. This provides new message management facilities including the ability to store and forward messages to a single address or to a pre-recorded list of addresses, or to redirect calls, establish multiline facilities or user groups, etc. But the standard concerns remain. Thus, are telex staff trusted not to make unauthorized calls? Can temporary staff gain access to the system? Is it practical to use passwords? Should encryption be used on sensitive messages, or is it adequate that a message is not sent until an authorized person is in a position to receive it? Are paper copies of telexes kept and, if so, for how long? For audit purposes, are all messages traceable and accounted for?

Facsimile machines transmit and receive scanned images of documents through the telephone network. Unlike telex, facsimile machines do not usually interwork with other systems although this is changing as integration with e-mail and document image processing equipment becomes feasible. The security requirements for imaging systems are the standard, i.e. some form of CIL system to preserve integrity, the possibility of encryption to preserve confidentiality and an effective audit trail.

Closed-circuit television and teleconferencing

Closed-circuit television (CCTV) has been in regular use in the security industry for many years, linking different parts of a site or a building to a central control position. More recently, it has been used to broadcast information around a large site and to provide a **videoconferencing** system. The growth in cable TV technology is accelerating the trend. **Teleconferencing** is becoming increasingly common. **Voice conferencing** is well established. **Audiographics conferencing** allows the transmission of charts and diagrams (in other words, there is an integrated facsimile system). Videoconferencing has been the slowest growing because of the cost of the technology to transmit the video information but, as the cost falls, this is likely to become increasingly common in office-to-office link-ups, representing considerable savings in travel time and expense. There are, however, problems with electronic eavesdropping – see Chapter 17.

The role of insurance companies

One way in which losses can be reduced is through insurance. At its simplest level, insurance policies can guard against:

- the physical loss of assets through the occurrence of fire and other specified catastrophe perils
- those expenses incurred in recovering from one of the specified disasters, e.g. repair or investigation costs, etc.
- losses arising from the incidence of fraud and employee dishonesty.

Cover and policy types

Structure and contents insurance comprising fire, property damage and general liability (including all-risk policies against the more extreme contingencies such as flood and earthquakes, as well as business interruption cover and extra expense insurance) remains a reasonably competitive market. The extent of the cover can only be determined by senior management after a careful evaluation of the extent of likely losses in the event of each contingency occurrence, and decisions as to whether the insurance should cover replacement costs, or actual cash value for assets. However, the market for policies to compensate in the event of fraud (whether computer-based or not) is now becoming more demanding, with increasingly high premium rates and restricted terms reflecting the high risk nature of the cover. In one sense, the problem is that many potential victims do not know what losses they are likely to sustain. But even though the precise mechanics of the ultimate fraud or its scale may not be known, insurers have learned that the only real uncertainty is usually as to the extent of the losses to be expected. Reductions in premiums may nevertheless be negotiated if the organization is seen to have adequately addressed security problems by formulating sound policies and by installing good safeguards. Such market forces may encourage more hardware and software manufacturers to design more effective security systems from the outset. There are a further three basic types of policy now available from insurers:

1 **Fidelity** – where a breach of the normal standards or duties of care by a current employee results in loss. Guarantee bonds used to be available to cover the activities of named individuals in a position of trust. The market is now moving in the direction of blanket insurance as insurers come to acknowledge that many more employees could now cause loss, regardless of their formal position within the organization. The standard cover excludes liability for the activities of hackers, ex-employees and the employees of any other organization having access to the system. Part-time or contract staff may not even be covered.
2 **Electronic crime** – although all fraud is potentially criminal, it need not be. A crime is an intentional or reckless violation of the criminal law. Fraud causes economic loss to the victim but need not be criminal. For example, a breach of confidentiality may cause significant loss to the inventor of a process or the originator of information, but it is not criminal in itself. You should bear in mind that the police only respond to crime, so the victims of non-criminal fraud must look to their own resources for an investigation and pursuit of money or assets lost.
3 **Directors' and officers' liability** – this policy reflects the fact that all directors and senior company officers owe a fiduciary duty to the shareholders, creditors and other interested parties to take adequate care of the organization's assets.

Problems

In the larger organizations it is sensible to carry out an insurance audit. Overlaps in the cover negotiated are highly probable, particularly where several carriers are involved. One strategy is to negotiate an all-risks policy on specified items of hardware, but this does not necessarily cover computer applications, nor the consequential aspects of computing. In negotiating cover, it should be remembered that hardware may be rendered unavailable for a variety of reasons, e.g. it may be due to accidental or deliberate damage by an employee, or if air conditioning fails, the main computer environment may have to be shut down; in more extreme cases, access may be denied to the building because of a fire in the neighbourhood, etc.

Several problems need to be considered:

- Conventional policies insure on an indemnity basis – that is, either the current market price less an allowance for depreciation, or reinstatement, i.e. new for old. Many organizations insure at the original purchase price and expect to upgrade insurance to reflect expected higher replacement costs.

But, in the computer hardware world, real prices have been falling for equivalent capacity. In the event of a loss, the organization might be tempted to spend the total sum insured or buy new for old and, incidentally, improve the installation by acquiring the new hardware with its additional capacity and facilities. Unfortunately, this would fall foul of the rules on what is called 'betterment' unless the issue is expressly addressed in the policy. So, if system improvements were made without terms being included in the policy, the value of the enhancement would be deducted from the insurance money paid out.

- The insured should ensure that the policy includes the breakdown of hardware in the phrase, 'all risks of physical loss or damage'. It should also be noted that there may be conditions in the policy requiring that maintenance agreements are in force. In such instances, the insurance cover will only apply to breakdowns not covered by the maintenance agreements.
- Most policies do not cover software risks, and data risks may be limited. Full cover should include both accidental and deliberate erasure and corruption. However, even then there may be problems of interpretation. For example, does cover against consequential loss include the value of information and all those losses consequential on its loss, or is it limited to the cost of reinstating the lost data? Theoretically, if data and software have been properly backed up, it will simply be a case of returning to the last archive copy, so the losses should be minimal. But if the back-up copies have been lost, the costs of reinstatement could be substantial. This would particularly be the case if in-house generated software had to be recreated.
- In addition to the costs of reinstating the data, there are consequences to the lack of computer availability, or the inconvenience which occurs as a result of reduced services. Suppose that the organization could not meet contract performance deadlines, and was faced by an action claiming damages for breach. Suppose that the organization cannot fully reconstruct the debtor records, and is faced by a payment shortfall. If the policies are not worded to include all those losses naturally and directly flowing from the event, the loss must be borne by the organization. However, the quantification of those losses is not without difficulty. If the loss of data leads to an increase in the costs of running the organization or a loss of profit, how are these figures to be quantified, and what is the indemnity period to be? The period agreed must obviously allow the organization a reasonable opportunity to recover from the disruption, but the insurance market has been slow to recognize the increasing dependency of organizations on computer-generated information and it is therefore difficult to negotiate all risks cover in this area.

How the managers should approach their decision making

The legal and practical responsibility for maintaining security lies with the senior management of each organization. When losses are discovered, they carry ultimate responsibility. The nature of their responsibility will vary depending on whether the organization is incorporated, but to avoid or minimize that liability (whether practical in the sense of dismissal or legal in the form of a judgement in damages), they must be seen to have taken the following steps:

- to have acted with reasonable diligence to identify and quantify the risks of particular importance to their organization
- to have identified the most vulnerable assets and resources, to have set protection goals, and to have created a formal risk management strategy
- to have created implementation policies and assigned sufficient resources to ensure a reasonable likelihood of success
- to have monitored the detailed results of that strategy, and to have established a policy of enforcement for all the major security rules and procedures
- to have investigated any frauds both within the new regime, and within allied organizations, and to have taken reasonable steps to learn from all identified mistakes and breaches of procedure and
- to have shown reasonable diligence in seeking to recover money and assets lost.

Each organization ought to know its own operation well enough to be able to predict both how losses might arise and the extent of those losses, but experience shows that knowledge is rarely used in a systematic way. A mixture of instinct and guesswork is frequently preferred to the detailed investigation and planning exercise even though this is not the optimal approach to planning security measures.

Summary

This chapter has focused on the analysis of risk and vulnerability, on estimates of risk impact and on countermeasure planning. It has included the following key points:

- Fraud depends on motive and opportunity. The optimum risk avoidance strategy requires each organization to analyse its staff profile to determine which members of staff pose the greatest threat to security. Once the potential perpetrators are known, the organization may either direct them into non-sensitive activities or exercise greater supervision.
- The organization must estimate the potential losses in the event of security breaches and weigh those losses against the cost of installing adequate security measures. The most cost-effective measures will be those which produce the most secure environment in the most vulnerable areas.
- The organization must consider both physical and logical security, and make contingency plans to deal with the disasters which are most probable and will cause the greatest loss if quick action is not taken.
- Many organizations are now installing networks. While this may produce significant advantages, the organization must guard against hardware threats, threats to message integrity, data bottlenecks and unauthorized access.
- Every organization ought to consider whether to insure against physical and economic loss arising from a disaster.
- All managers must be seen to have taken care in making decisions about security.

Self-test questions

1 Explain what is involved in perpetrator analysis.
2 Describe the legal factors involved in setting the level of security for the data holdings.
3 What factors influence the setting of reliability and availability targets.
4 Explain why a person may not be prosecuted for fraud.
5 What are the main insurance policies?

Exam-style questions

1 The Midwest Bank has a sophisticated information system based on a centralized transaction processing system which is linked to a network of PCs running a variety of business software packages which are used by employees in all areas of the Bank. Midwest has a policy of encouraging end users to become more 'IT literate' and to develop their own applications which can interface with the main system. As chief auditor you are concerned that this policy may lead to the possibility of computer fraud going undetected.

   In order to bring this possibility to the notice of the management of the bank write a report identifying the factors which might motivate an employee of the bank to commit fraud and describe the steps which may be taken by the perpetrator to cover the existence of such a fraud.

2 You have produced a security plan and made recommendations for security measures to protect your company's information resources. Unfortunately, your plan has been opposed by the chief accountant, who feels that it is likely to prove too costly. You believe that she is acting more on intuition than informed judgement, and you propose to carry out a cost analysis exercise on your company to produce some 'hard facts'.

   Describe the factors which you would have to take into account when carrying out a cost analysis exercise.

3 A small manufacturing company for which you work is developing a contingency plan to ensure the continued operation of its computer-based information systems should a disaster occur. The managing director has asked you to supervise a small team which is to produce the plan, and an old friend who has experience of contingency planning has recommended that you use a 'checklist' approach to identify the decisions which the team would have to take when producing the contingency plan.

   Produce such a checklist, identifying and briefly describing the decisions in important and less important areas.

(All answers on pages 569–571)

CHAPTER 16

Threats to security

Introduction

The television has made us all more aware in recent years of the scale and cost of natural disasters. The most memorable images have perhaps been those of the 1980 eruption of the long-dormant Mount St Helens in north-western USA, the two near-hurricanes that caused much devastation in England in the 1980s, or the 1993 Mississippi river valley floods which brought damage to business and farming communities estimated in many billions of dollars.

No business can buy better weather or 100 per cent reliable meteorological forecasts. But organizations can and must guard against risks to security arising from many kinds of natural events – corporate information systems can be seriously damaged by far less newsworthy happenings than volcanic eruptions – or, for that matter, from human negligence and malice. The scale of destruction caused by terrorist action in the City of London in the early 1990s has shown that business premises can suffer the most disastrous effects from the use of quite easily procured explosives. The prevalence of information system viruses and the growth of computer crime present other threats against which system security managers must be on their guard.

In this chapter we begin to consider the extent of the main risks to the security of information systems. Our main focus is on the physical threats, with a survey of the most reliable countermeasures. We must therefore evaluate the threats represented by the weather, electricity, fire, water, temperature and dirt; appreciate the consequences of component malfunction; understand the project planning considerations for the detailed management of physical security. We also examine the mechanics of physical access control including the use of guards and receptionists, mechanical locking systems and automatic entry control systems such as smart cards, and consider the problem of equipment theft.

The main threats to security

The main threats to the security of business information systems fall into two primary groupings:

1. **Physical threats** to the buildings which contain the information systems such as fire, flood, wind, lightning, subsidence, and, in appropriate geographical areas, earthquakes, sand storms and hurricanes.
2. **People-based threats** – people are at the heart of all security systems and threats. The threats which they pose may arise from negligence or they may

have a political or criminal character, including accidental damage, theft and malicious damage, bomb threats, strikes, riots, terrorism and war.

The result of either form of threat may be:

- simple damage to the whole or part of the organization or its resources; or
- destruction of the whole or part of the organization or the total loss of critical resources.

To guard against these threats, countermeasures must be instituted. These must be:

- **People-related measures** – which may include ensuring the safety of staff and visitors or the control of movement within a building or a part of a building.
- **Resource-related measures** – whether to protect physical assets or to control access to resources.

Storing and accessing sensitive material

All threats of a physical nature may result in the loss of system availability and in the destruction of data and hardware. Organizations have always had the problem of protecting their information. In the past this requirement has meant the storage of physical records in lockable cabinets and safes. In more modern systems, data storage may take several forms. Inevitably, organizations will have hard copy materials, whether from outside sources or generated in-house. For these purposes, hard copy is taken to be material that is readable by humans without the need of computer support, whether it be material written or printed on paper, or recorded on punched cards, microfilm, etc. Care must be taken at all time, and this concern must include the disposal as well as the storage of hard-copy records. If data are still sensitive, the paper should be shredded or incinerated and not simply thrown out. Before disposal, the paper should be stored in a way which minimizes the risk of fire yet, ironically, for large-scale waste disposal, it is probably better to use a furnace. Information may also be temporarily displayed on VDUs. If there is a risk that sensitive data might be seen by unauthorized individuals, the screen should be kept in a secure room to minimize the risk of disclosure.

Magnetic media for the storage of information, such as tapes, disks and drums, can be used repeatedly and, in larger organizations, will usually be stored in libraries. Such storage media are vulnerable to corruption through exposure to magnetic fields (such as those generated by large electrical motors) and to fire (floppy disks have a lower ignition point than paper), so care should be taken in the siting of the storage facility and its construction. Access to the library or storage facility should be limited to authorized staff and, of course, access to the computers must be controlled.

Physical threats

The weather

The weather is the greatest natural threat to most locations. Wind, rain and storms can have dramatic effects on the buildings and their immediate environment both during the winter and, less predictably, at other times of the year. Alongside the physical threat of direct damage, lightning and electrical storms are sources of electromagnetic interference which can materially disrupt power supplies and, which, in turn, may indirectly damage equipment through power surges, etc.

Electricity

The electricity supply can be critical. Even nanosecond-long power surges can cause the misregistration of data and false logic, actual damage to sensitive circuitry or system crashes causing the wholesale loss of data. Power supplies can be affected by other environmental features, such as the high demand for power at certain times of the day, damage to power lines or switching gear at more distant locations, and so on. Equipment should therefore be protected against both current and voltage fluctuations. However, full-scale power protection can be quite expensive if it includes an uninterrupted and stand-by power supply system which will provide back-up in the event of power failure.

Uninterrupted power supplies (UPS) use the mains supply to charge stand-by batteries. These batteries power an inverter (direct to alternating current converter) which produces the main alternating power within the organization in the event of power failures or excessive fluctuations. The alternatives are:

- stand-by generators which will start up automatically in the event of a mains failure (leaving the problem of the time taken to achieve stable power output); or
- simple battery operation (this may not be able to meet modern power requirements in networked equipment, but will be satisfactory to maintain the telephone system).

Fire

The threat of fire through flames, heat and smoke contamination is well established. The causes vary from careless smoking, through faulty electrical wiring, to arson. The danger posed is not only to the hardware, but also to data records. Fire-resistant safes can save a proportion of the backed-up data, but it is better to prevent the fire in the first place, or detect it before it has caused too much damage. As to prevention, the best plans include the following elements to reduce fire risks:

- good employee recruitment and training practices in the use of all fire-fighting equipment and evacuation procedures (with the possibility of banning smoking or encouraging no-smoking policies in sensitive buildings)

- the use of building materials of low flammability (including the installation of fire doors) and the planning of electrical systems to minimize the risk of overloading – a common cause of fire
- the avoidance of wooden or flammable furniture and fittings
- the installation of good administrative controls over the use and storage of flammable materials (including good refuse disposal practices).

Similarly, automatic heat and smoke detection equipment and extinguishers (including gas flooding systems) should be installed at critical points in the building. When planning the optimum detection system, information system managers should remember that fires go through a recognized cycle:

- the first stage is normally ignition followed by smouldering
- open flames form, the temperature of the surrounding air rises and the flames then spread the fire by direct contact
- the final stage is the rapid spreading of the fire by heat radiation.

Photoelectric smoke detectors therefore help to detect fires before they are out of control, with thermostats to detect temperature changes as a second line of defence. Water is a cheap extinguishing material but neither water nor foam extinguishers should be used on an electrical fire unless it is necessary to prevent an established fire from becoming a major disaster. There are two gas-based systems which may be used to permeate the affected area:

- **halon (monobromotrifluoromethane)** is expensive but, because it does not displace the oxygen, it is not harmful to people in small quantities
- **carbon dioxide** is cheap and plentiful but 10 per cent by volume is harmful to human beings and 30 per cent by volume is required to extinguish a fire. Consequently, it should not be used until all the people have been evacuated.

Neither system can assist if the fire rekindles after the gas has been exhausted but, equally, gas does not harm the machines.

Water

Water, whether from flooding or fire fighting, represents a significant threat to buildings, and the resources (particularly documentary) stored there. If a building is sited in an area prone to flooding, some form of water defence system such as land drains and dikes, together with structural waterproofing should be considered. Similarly, equipment and sensitive records should not be sited on the ground floor or in the basement. Unfortunately, many wiring and telecommunications distribution systems still come into the building underground and so the communications system can be disabled by a flood in any event. In the planning exercise, the whole range of threats should be considered, it being essential to remember that water damage may come from burst pipes and spilled cups of coffee as well as the more dramatic storms. Thus, equipment and sensitive records should be sited away from water pipes and leaking roofs.

Temperature and dirt

Wherever possible, manufacturers' recommendations should be followed in supplying a reasonably stable temperature environment for the equipment. Air conditioning and purifying can be essential to keep mainframe operating temperatures down and air quality within manufacturers' tolerances. In a general office environment, micros and peripherals may require an auxiliary cooling system to supplement their own fans. Static electricity can, if not properly controlled, represent as much a danger as power surges. Organizations should therefore consider using antistatic carpeting, dehumidifiers and ion particle emitters. Further, quite apart from the improvement in working conditions for the ordinary office worker (and possible improvement in morale), it can be essential to filter dust particles and other contaminants out of the air which might damage the disks or the disk head readers. If the cost is disproportionate to the risks, vacuum cleaners should be used to suck dust and dirt away (using cloths will only stir up the dust and may promote static). Smoking deposits a film on surrounding objects that holds dust. It should be discouraged. Staff should also be encouraged to follow a 'clean desk' policy: working materials should be tidied away regularly, and eating and drinking at the desk should be discouraged.

Hardware threats

Component malfunction is not always immediately apparent to those operating equipment and so special measures are required. The need is to allow the system to check its own operation and to detect and, where possible, correct the detected errors. Some self-monitoring systems of this kind affect software performance and all affect cost, so few manufacturers have installed such systems. The result is that preventative maintenance is more effective than emergency cure. The past record of the machines should dictate the frequency and extent of maintenance. All faults should be recorded to build up a pattern of reliability. This should also dictate the stock of replacement parts held on-site.

Back-up procedures

No matter what the level of hardware reliability achieved, all organizations should encourage a good data back-up discipline. This means that users should not wait until the end of the day, but should copy anything important at regular intervals, preferably with the back-up stored in another location to the immediate user.

The optimum back-up scheme is called the 'parent–grandparent' system. This has three days' worth of data in rotation. At the end of the first day, all sensitive files are backed up with the copy stored off-site. At the end of day two, a further copy is made and stored in a secure location on-site. At the end of the third day, the copy is kept on-site and the day two copy is taken off-site. The day one copy is returned for making the copy on day four. The effect is therefore to have the oldest of the three copies off-site so that in an emergency which destroys the most recent copy, the organization will never lose more than two days' data.

Floppy disks are insecure both because they are so easily concealed and therefore easily removed from the work environment, and because they are easily damaged. It is difficult to devise a scheme to prevent staff taking sensitive information home on floppy disks. If micros are used in the system configuration, it is impossible to avoid using floppy disks for storage purposes. To a reasonable degree, employers must trust their staff, or if someone is suspect, the employer should monitor access to sensitive information generally. Security products are not a substitute for effective human resource management. There is also a risk of introducing viruses into the work environment if staff bring the organization's disks back to work having used them on a foreign machine or use their own disks in machines at work – see Chapter 17.

Physical communication problems

There are a range of transmission faults which may affect data integrity. Transmission media will either be guided or unguided. The most usual form of **guided media** are copper cable for low-capacity local connection, and *coaxial* or *fibre* optics for higher capacity connections. *Twisted pair* and *multiway* cabling is cheap and easy to install but neither can be used in electrically noisy environments because the signal is vulnerable to interference.

Unguided media such as microwave and satellite links are vulnerable to eavesdropping and may be affected by atmospheric conditions. Parity checks, error detection codes and polynomial check codes may detect whether there are end-to-end problems. If the messages may not have been transmitted in their entirety or there may be data corruption, the solutions may be to retransmit, to reroute the data or to use cryptography.

People and security

People are at the heart of all security systems and threats. The threat to an organization may come from employees or outsiders. An employee will have direct access to the buildings and to some or all the employer's records, whereas outsiders will have to take more risks to gain entry unless collusion with an employee can be arranged. As a general rule, a criminal will only attempt to exploit an opportunity to gain if there is a reasonable chance of avoiding detection. The probability of loss is therefore reduced if the target organization is alert. To set the tone of the organization, alertness is encouraged if senior managers act as role models and demonstrate their commitment to maintaining security standards. Hopefully, this commitment will filter down to all levels within the organization. Even if the filtering down is imperfect, enforcement of security discipline is achieved with less employee resentment if the managing director is also seen to follow the rules or face the same penalties.

Physical access controls

The fundamental rationale of the task of physical security is to control space. The purpose of access control is two-way:

- it may be used to protect people from known hazards, such as high voltages or radiation; or
- it may be to protect the installation itself.

In personnel terms, this requires that the management formally assigns responsibility for controlling space, and takes all measures necessary either to achieve practical control over the given area or to make it look as though security is effective. Before networking became established, physical security was achieved by restricting access to the mainframe computer room. As the computer-stored data were concentrated in that one room, physical access controls reduced the risk of an unauthorized person gaining access to the data. Modern physical access control has to be designed to allow entry to those people who have a legitimate right to be in the secure areas while denying access to all unauthorized persons. The identification and recognition of people is vitally important.

Identification means to determine (and hopefully prove) the identity of a person or thing. Humans are good at recognizing each other by sight or the sound of their voices. But recognition by a machine is an uncertain affair. Within an organization, friends and immediate colleagues do not generally represent a problem. The problem is how to recognize people in more anonymous surroundings. The usual identification systems depend on:

- something remembered such as a password
- something possessed like a key or token
- a physical characteristic with unique qualities such as a fingerprint
- an action performed such as a signature or speaking into a voice-recognition system.

Put simply, this means that identification techniques involve identifying a person by something he or she is, or has, or knows, or does, or by a combination of these things. But, whatever the system, the designer must try to minimize the number of false acceptances which can breach security, and false rejections which can be annoying and embarrassing.

Access control methods

There will be different security priorities if the public are allowed access either all the time, or for substantial parts of the day. However, the real problems emerge when access is to be limited to an identified class of person, whether constrained by time or not. In these situations, the management has to decide the extent to which:

- the class is definable in advance
- the class has a stable and predictable membership
- whether the membership can be compelled or persuaded to follow the access procedures.

If outsiders are to be allowed in, security has to be designed in the knowledge that it can be difficult to get these people to co-operate because they have no direct interest in promoting the site's security needs. There is also a real risk that outsiders will disclose the security systems. For employees, the duty to obey the prevailing security systems and to keep them confidential can be written into every contract of employment and this can be enforced through the standard disciplinary codes. But if an employee decides to break the contract by passing on sensitive data, employment-based remedies are of little value after the loss is sustained.

Entry control

If the security requirements are of a high order, precautions may have to start with a boundary or perimeter fence. Obviously, although this may be desirable, it may not be possible in many city centres either because of the lie of the land or because of local authority planning constraints. Once the site is established, it may be sensible not to label buildings and to design them so that function is not obvious to outside observation. Then, taking care not just to protect sensitive buildings, the external security controls should be highly visible as a deterrent to the casual intruder.

Decisions must then be taken about access controls for each building. In sensitive environments, each possible access point may have to be secured, including windows and air vents. Within the building, areas may require specific access controls. There are three basic ways to control a door or gate:

- by using receptionists and/or guards
- by using mechanical locks and keys
- by using electronic systems.

Receptionists and guards

A security guard can challenge all those who attempt entry, but people are an expensive way of controlling the environment, and they may be better used overseeing the correct working of other systems. This is not to say that a guard cannot perform a useful function. Guards are effective if properly trained and motivated, and they can challenge strangers or the apparently unauthorized and call for help if necessary. Indeed, one of the best forms of protection is to give the guard control over a self-locking door or gate. In the more sensitive buildings, the creation of a segregated area in the form of a pen or closed corridor is a good defence because intruders are unlikely to risk being held while their identities are checked. This assumes that the guard or receptionist is able to recognize legitimate users – typically, from a list with photographs, or from badges or passes. Indeed, requiring people to produce passes on a routine basis is useful, if only because it checks to see whether a pass has been lost or stolen. The better passes include a photograph and specimen signature so that, in cases of doubt over a photograph (where, for example, a person is wearing new glasses or has adopted a new hairstyle) sample signatures can be taken and can be compared with the specimen. This emphasizes the need to change passes regularly to keep the photograph and the sample signature up-to-date.

In setting staffing levels and defining duties, managers need to recognize that guards are only human. This means that they are readily distracted and may be diverted from the task in hand unless there are enough people to deal with each problem as it arises. Similarly, telephonists on busy switchboards who are also called on to act as receptionists are frequently unable to perform the security function well. For both guards and receptionists, the level of consumer satisfaction will tend to be set by the number of people claiming the right of entry. This reflects the fact that how people are welcomed to a site is a vital part of the organization's public relations function. If traffic is low, it may be possible to leave would-be entrants outside until their credentials can be validated. But the more likely it is that people will be delayed, the greater the need to provide a comfortable waiting area. Otherwise, adequate security staffing levels are essential if staff and visitor goodwill is to be maintained.

Mechanical locking systems

One view is that good security control is achieved through the use of tamper-proof locks on doors, but this strategy is inconvenient if the door is in regular use. Experience shows that conventional locks and keys are only suitable for small installations where a few people are employed. The difficulty is that whereas conscientious employees will accept the chore of locking and unlocking a door once or twice a day, they will find it intolerable for a door in regular use. As traffic increases, doors will simply be left open. In unmanned buildings, cheap locks give poor security, and good locks are useless in a poor door because the would-be intruder can easily attack the door and its hinges to get in. Because it requires less skill, most intruders will attempt to force the door rather than to pick the lock. However, it must not be assumed that those who wish to enter are without intelligence, and so all accessible windows and the accessible parts of the roof must be of a similar standard of security to avoid the expenditure on external doors being wasted.

Key control

The weakness of any locked door system lies in poor control of the keys. Staff are forgetful and often go home with keys or leave them in the wrong place unless there are set procedures for dealing with them. When the keys relate to sensitive areas, the better systems require that they are issued against a signature, or a tag card system shows who has particular keys. But no system is effective unless it is policed. A further concern is the availability of the blanks for both the ordinary keys and for the master key(s). Most ordinary keys are easily duplicated – a feature that could be considered useful since they are frequently lost or mislaid. But if the blanks are easily obtained by burglars and the locks are simple, duplicate keys may be cut for unauthorized use.

As an alternative to keys, cipher locks can be used. There are both mechanical and electronic versions of this type of lock. They usually have five or more buttons. To unlock the door, a code of between three and 15 digits must be entered, the buttons being pressed in the right combination to open the door. It is possible to break the code through trial and error, but these locks are relatively cheap to install and will probably be satisfactory for less frequently used routes. Too much traffic and they will probably be abused. The better models will sound an alarm in the event of tampering, and automatically lock the door after a predetermined number of false attempts, requiring a reset by the security supervisor. There should also be built-in facilities to restrict the ability of others to observe the code being punched in, and the locks should be reprogrammable in the event that the code falls into the wrong hands. Forgetful staff must also be persuaded not to jot the code down somewhere close to the door.

Electronic entry control systems

These are usually electric locks, with a battery supply which gives extra security in the event of a power failure. For additional security, a push-button keypad can be provided for supplementary coded input, but this is an inconvenience to staff and should only be used when absolutely necessary. Whatever the configuration, the combination of card reader, keypad and lock can control entry by testing the validity of the card and the identity of the person carrying it against the location and the hour and day. Many systems offer the option of time windows. This means that access is only permitted at certain times, so cleaners are only allowed entry between specified hours, while ordinary office staff are denied routine access outside normal office hours. But the management of detailed time profiles can have high costs because it creates administrative work.

Most employees also value *flexibility* in their working regime – for example, to be able to stand in for a sick colleague, perhaps at short notice. If the responsible substitute cannot quickly gain access because he or she appears to be on the wrong shift, the system is inconvenient and will damage employee goodwill. If it can be overridden by special access codes, it may be making extra work for the system administrators (and so increasing costs) or it may be easily abused (and so fall into disrepute). Moreover, if the system is clock based, the time may be wrong – after power problems, say, or the summer time change. If people are denied access at the proper time, user confidence and morale will be damaged. These potential problems should not be taken as a justification for not implementing such a system. In the best-run systems, effective staff monitoring and policing is possible and, if all breaches of time discipline are quickly (but sensitively) followed up by the individual's manager, staff morale can be maintained.

Badge and token reading

The constant risk in the use of keypads is that the entry of codes may be overseen by people standing nearby. If the particular door controls entry to more sensitive resources, automatic entry through cards carried by staff or through badges worn by the staff may be a better system. Cards and badges may be designed so that the significant information is in machine-readable form only. If the badge or the card is then lost but does not show precisely what is authorized, a casual finder could not easily make use of it. It also makes it more difficult for an impostor to read and alter that information. Whether manual or machine-readable, the badge or card can be clipped to clothing or carried around the neck on a chain. If the badges are passes, all must wear them prominently and the senior managers must set an example in this respect. Machine-readable tokens may take the following forms:

- **Punched cards**. These are sensed by mechanical probes, electrical contacts or light. They are cheap but easily replicated.
- **Plastic cards**. These are coded to infra-red by including a lamination that is opaque in ordinary light but transparent to infra-red.
- **Magnetic cards**. These incorporate small beads of magnetic material or thin wires or have stripes. They have to be encoded during manufacture. As a result, delivery time may be long.
- **Wiegand cards**. These use tiny individual wires for each bit of data that is to be coded. To read the data the card is moved rapidly through a strong magnetic field, producing a pulse in an adjacent sensing coil.
- **Stripe cards**. These are the most common, being the standard for the bank and credit card industry. There is a security problem in that data can easily be altered or transferred to other cards by using a skimmer.
- **Proximity cards**. These use radio signals to pass on information between the token and the access controller. The token can be active or passive. The active token transmits a signal continuously. It has the advantage that the user need do nothing other than carry the card to gain freedom of movement. It leaves the hands free, and avoids the need for the user to put the card into a slot or against a reader. These cards rely on rechargeable batteries and so the card must be left overnight on the premises in its coded slot to be picked up each morning on entry. Cards which are not recharged in this way will not open doors. There may be a problem because some cards will transmit through conventional walls. In congested sites, signal overlaps can therefore be a problem. The alternative passive card responds to a signal issued by the controller. The card must be held near the controller, but it avoids the problem of overlap.
- **Chip cards** (also known as 'smart cards'). These are any form of card that includes a microprocessor. These cards retain data and are programmed to disclose it only when the right signals are received.

Most of these systems need a free hand and so special arrangements must be made for the disabled or those recovering from an injury and who may perhaps be on crutches or in a wheelchair. Moreover, packages and trolleys will need to be moved about the site, and so wide (and high) doorways may be required. Big loads move slowly, so timing on locks and their alarms must be adjustable. The more sophisticated the system, the greater the cost so management must engage in proper cost–benefit analysis to ensure that additional expenditure will represent value for money.

Planning considerations

The first step is to define which areas are to be controlled and to what level of security. The perimeter needs to be defined in terms of physical features such as fences, walls, doors, etc. The designated area may be one zone, so that once inside, the user can move anywhere, or there may be a need for a **hierarchy of zones** to give greater protection to sensitive areas. Whatever design is adopted, it should aim for simplicity. It should also minimize the level of traffic that is to pass through the various areas. Work should be structured so that most people work within one zone and should not have to pass to other areas on a regular basis.

It is obvious that some classes of employee or visitor must be allowed to move around the site, but such individuals should be the exception rather than the norm. This means that when the layout of buildings is being considered, toilets, canteens, recreational facilities (if any) and any other commonly accessed facility should be located in such a way as to ensure that the staff do not need to move through other sensitive areas on a regular route to common facilities. Not only does this avoid heavy traffic at peak times, causing queues at controlled doorways which is irritating and wastes time, it may also lead to the abuse of 'tail-gating' where several people follow each other closely through barriers, creating the risk that unauthorized people might pass through at these times. If turnstiles and air-lock chambers are installed, managers should remember that their operation may be difficult for the disabled and embarrassing to large people and pregnant women. High levels of security may also make exit difficult in the event of a fire or other emergency.

Any access system must be practical or it will fall into disuse, and it must be acceptable to those who have to make it work. To maximize the chances of acceptance, the reasons for a new system should be explained, all the users should be consulted before the design is finalized, and some account should be seen to be taken of their views. Once in place, they must all be properly trained and the rules for using the system must be positively communicated. Deliberate misuse of any part of the system should be regarded as a disciplinary offence, no matter what the rank of the offender in the management hierarchy. All breaches should be followed up with a view to making breaches less common. In performing this function, employee goodwill may be more easily maintained if access entitlements are defined in each individual's job description, because there will be less cause for error through lack of understanding and therefore less sense of injustice if an employee is disciplined for breach. Provision must also be made for when staff leave, and procedures should be devised for tokens or passes lost or stolen.

The problem of equipment theft

The theft of equipment which is often left unattended in offices is becoming an increasing problem. In 1995, it is estimated that computer theft cost UK business £1 billion with the insurance industry reporting losses of £200 million for the theft of chips alone. The temptation has become all the greater because office equipment such as laptop computers and personal printers is increasingly portable and now more likely to be compatible with home equipment. Further, high-value components such as processors and RAM chips are being stolen. It can be difficult to prevent thefts, and there is a growing underground market for stolen equipment, with many thefts taking place to order. This form of activity is helped because comparatively few organizations consistently carry out checks on staff carrying packages from their premises, particularly where branch offices have few employees. Organizations should estimate the value of equipment likely to be pilfered and the replacement costs (including the loss of productivity and time), and measure those costs against the staffing implications for security personnel on all the main entrances and exits, and the premiums chargeable for insurance. The Loss Prevention Council has published a revised standard for the testing of computer security devices. The new specification LPS1214 – Issue 2 follows consultation between the police, insurance companies and manufacturers and provides two security approval classifications for:

- physically securing hardware to desks, walls or floors
- protecting components inside computers.

It is likely that compliance with this standard will become a common condition of insurance cover in the future.

Inventories and security measures

Real steps to contain the theft problem begin with the creation and maintenance of a detailed inventory. All the equipment and its location should be logged, and employees identified as responsible for the computers and peripherals in each area. Such ground plans are, of course, a risk to security in their own right because access to the plans would save the thief the trouble of looking for particular items. They should be carefully locked away. Marking serial numbers or ownership references with some form of security marker pen may also be useful because it may restrict the ability of the thief to resell the equipment on the legitimate open market. But if the equipment is leased, a check should be made to see whether the owner objects to identifying codes and labels being fixed permanently on.

The organization should then consider the installation of a burglar alarm system. Alarms are a way of trying to defend space. Visible systems on doors and windows begin the process of deterring intruders, with more sophisticated measures being taken to protect areas of particular sensitivity. In addition to the standard door/window sensors and pressure sensitive pads placed in rooms or under equipment, there are four basic types of alarm, all of which may be monitored by computer:

1. **Photo-electric**. These devices emit a beam. Any object breaking the beam triggers the alarm.
2. **Microwave**. Pulsing microwaves are transmitted throughout the area and monitored. Any changes in frequency or occurrence indicate the presence of an intruder.
3. **Ultrasonic**. Here sound is transmitted in the same way as microwaves in the previous example.
4. **Passive infra-red**. Every object radiates heat. The device measures the amount of heat in the protected area and reacts to radical changes in heat level – caused, say by a person walking into the area.

The most successful crime prevention policies depend on recognizing the risks and taking appropriate action. In this case, bolting equipment to furniture or the fabric of the building will make the theft more difficult. Sadly, this will not prevent the theft of components, and total enclosures may have to be considered where high-value chips are installed.

Physical attack and industrial espionage

All organizations must take account of the increasing danger of vandalism or malicious damage, with sabotage becoming a less uncommon part of industrial action (for example, damage was caused to the National Coal Board's computer installation during the coal miners' strike in 1984), and, in extreme situations, there is the possibility of terrorist attack and civil riot. Government departments are likely to recognize the risk of attack from radical or subversive groups. Other large commercial organizations such as banks may also be identified as political targets, as may air passengers and freight companies, while the manufacturers of pharmaceuticals and cosmetics come under threat from animal rights groups and other similar organizations.

The security frontier

Each organization should consider the location of its more sensitive facilities in the light of the prevailing state of society. Security experts should advise on the extent to which the site is defensible, the brief including the parking areas as well as the buildings. In addition to the more overt attacks, advice should be sought on the more covert forms of assault. Thus, individuals or rival organizations may seek to disrupt the normal working patterns. This may be done more overtly through strategems like bomb hoaxes, and more covertly through false answers to advertisements to tie up the sales force, planting inefficient or disruptive staff in the target organization, etc. This may be a form of unfair competition which may show itself in the forgery of product lines which are of inferior quality, or through psychological sabotage (e.g. circulating false rumours in the trade, reporting fictitious information to government or debt collection agencies, etc.). Rivals may also attempt to blackmail key employees to disclose trade secrets, or to underperform; or simply try to steal their expertise through headhunting. A recent example of this last problem is the movement of José Ignacio Lopez de Arriortua and three other senior executives from General Motors to Volkswagen in Germany which has led to the four being charged with the German offence of espionage for allegedly handing over confidential information about General Motor's more efficient production technology.

This reflects the basic truth which underpins the capitalist ethic of competition. All commercial organizations would like to be better informed about their competitors and, because of recent developments in technology, industrial espionage has become a growing problem. Note that the offence of theft only protects *physical* property. It does not apply to protect information, no matter how confidential it may be. Indeed, the criminal law is of little use in this area. The main countermeasures of good-quality alarms and locks have already been discussed.

Organizations should also take care of wastepaper and magnetic media disposal. (It is worthwhile remembering that the staff of the US Embassy in Saigon went to much trouble to shred their secret documents as the Viet Cong entered the city at the end of the Vietnam War in 1975 – but the incoming Communist authorities took even greater pains to reassemble the shredded material after the American evacuation.) Single-strike typewriter ribbons and old shorthand pads should also be disposed of carefully. The problem is accentuated because if discarded material is taken, its loss is unlikely to be noticed although, if detected, it will be theft. Further, many people are untidy and missing documents may simply be assumed lost. In their embarrassment, the employees may then assist the thief by covering up the loss, for instance, by creating a substitute document. Staff must be trained to report their own errors honestly.

If entry to the target building is too difficult, the spy may use binoculars and infra-red equipment, or laser beans to see who is speaking and to hear what is being said. Bugs planted in the building can relay conversations. Any communication system that uses the public telephone system, the postal system or relies on broadcast media is vulnerable. The UK's Interception of Communications Act 1985 makes it an offence to intercept the postal or public telecommunications system. This includes the bugging of telephones because this intercepts the message, but not bugging to monitor ordinary conversations.

Summary

The main focus of this chapter has been the threats presented by natural phenomena and human agency to corporate security and the countermeasures that organizations can employ.

- The main physical threats are the weather, fire, water, temperature and dirt. The organization must also protect the power supplies and take steps to eliminate direct threats to the hardware such as component failure, theft and sabotage. Once the level of danger under each heading has been identified, the organization must determine the probability and criticality of each substantial threat.
- No matter how good the physical security, people will always represent a threat. Steps must be taken to exclude non-essential staff from sensitive areas by physical access controls. The first step is to consider the building design and space allocation. Movement within the space is then considered. Access control is achieved through the use of personal vetting, mechanical or electronic systems. The range is from simple lock and key to sophisticated cards.
- All critical hardware and software must be protected from the risk of theft or damage.

Self-test questions

1 What are the main classifications of physical threat to security and what are the countermeasures?
2 Indicate the steps that can be taken to protect the power supplies to a computer installation.
3 Describe the parent–grandparent back-up scheme.
4 What action can an organization take to deal with the problem of equipment theft?
5 Indicate the scale of the problem of industrial espionage.

Exam-style questions

1 You work for a public utility which has an information system critical to its every-day activities, and which holds sensitive information. It is based on several mini-computers sited in the data processing (DP) department, in an area of the building often used by both staff and members of the public. A local area network (LAN) is linked to one of the mini-computers, acting as a server for a number of PCs in offices to which the public has occasional access. In addition, a wide area network (WAN) links the system to other public utilities throughout the country.

   The DP manager has gone to great lengths to protect the system with 'logical' controls against skilled hackers from breaking into the system from outside, but you feel that he has not paid sufficient attention to the more obvious physical threat from people having physical access to the building. Write a report to the DP manager, explaining the importance of physical access controls in a system like this one, and suggest *two* methods of physical access control which would be suitable for this application.

2 DC Ltd is planning to replace its ageing data processing (DP) system with a new system based on a mini-computer in a purpose-built DP facility. The management of the company has identified the move as an opportunity to create a zoned physical security area to protect the system from unauthorized access, as DC Ltd relies heavily on its DP system and stores commercially sensitive data.

   As you have experience of both IT and interior design, you have been asked to prepare a report describing the planning considerations you would have to take into account when designing the accommodation for the mini-computer and its ancillary systems.

(All answers on page 571)

CHAPTER 17

Data security

Introduction

Information is a precious commodity to businesses engaged in today's battle for market supremacy. Just as observers compare the strategies of commercial companies to the campaigns of generals and armies, so the enduring quest for competitive business information can be likened to the work of military intelligence – such as the success of World War II British cryptographers in breaking the Enigma machine cipher used for strategic communication by the German armed forces, or the American interception of Japanese naval ciphers which identified the Midway as the focus of Japan's fleet operations in 1942.

Again, just as warring nations must face the threat of espionage and treachery, so business organizations must accept that industrial spies and disaffected employees have a significant role to play in the corporate market place. In the 1980s, Kelloggs had to abandon their practice of encouraging tourist parties to visit their Michigan breakfast cereal plant when they found that rival food manufacturers were using this opportunity to study their production technology. More and more organizations with predatory strategies or substantial research commitments display notices in staff canteens warning against carelessness in handling communications. Today's businesses must recognize that they are vulnerable to data interception and must take steps to protect their information in order to maintain their competitiveness and ensure profitability and strategic success.

This chapter continues our discussion of the main threats to security by concentrating attention on the threats to the actual data. We begin by outlining the scope of the threat to data and the nature of the protection offered by logical access systems. We go on to appreciate the strengths and weaknesses of the password and to understand how password systems should be administered. The latter part of the chapter explains the nature of file access permissions and authorization procedures generally, and examines the use of flow and inference controls. We conclude with a discussion of encryption techniques, the threat represented by hacking and electronic eavesdropping.

Introduction to data security

Data are vulnerable to the following factors and activities:

- indiscriminate searching, whether by authorized or unauthorized individuals
- leakage to unauthorized individuals

- inference which breaches confidentiality
- the ease with which it may be corrupted or destroyed.

Data *security* is achieved by four basic types of control:

1 **Access**, which includes access to both data or software through a terminal or computer.
2 **Flow**, which regulates the movement of data from one file to another.
3 **Inference**. Statistical databases should not allow a user to extract confidential information through inference. It is difficult to eliminate the possibility altogether. The problem is that in databases, information may be held about many topics. An intruder can pose a series of questions which cause statistical reports to be made which, when correlated, may allow the inference of more detailed information.
4 **Cryptographic**: converting ordinary language into a form of code through the process of encryption may be a way of providing adequate protection.

Logical access systems

Just as in planning for the protection of physical assets, logical access planning requires the establishment of perimeters around both the data system at large and, more particularly, around sensitive component elements within the data. Data are exposed to the following dangers:

1 There may be **inaccuracies**. The problem is that the system will still continue to function apparently properly, but the answers produced will be seriously distorted on a cumulative basis and, if relied on as accurate information, will undermine otherwise sensible decision making.
2 The data may be **falsified** as part of a plan to obtain some advantage to the detriment of the organization or those dependent on it.
3 The data may be **disclosed** either to unauthorized individuals or to the public at large.
4 The data may be **lost** before, during or after processing.

Having assessed the risks, the organization should then classify data by deciding how sensitive each element would be in the wrong hands. In making these judgements, managers should also insert caveats and define the necessary clearances. Classification into categories such as 'secret' or 'confidential' is based on an attribute of the data, whereas *clearance* relates to attributes of the users, given caveats such as those groupings where access is discretionary on a need-to-know or similar basis. The classification might be based on:

- **Public data** – i.e. unrestricted and so all may have access to read or copy the data.
- **Limited access** – in other words, the data are considered private and confidential and, consequently, access clearance is to be restricted to specific users such as those in the personnel and finance department.
- **Private data** – the information is restricted and is only to be made available to identified individuals within the organization.

Once all the data have been labelled, the organization will have decided who should have access to what, and in which circumstances. The organization's managers should think carefully about its data vulnerabilities and the threats posed – ideally making use of methodologies such as **perpetrator analysis** (see Chapter 15). Thus, some users such as programmers may pose a greater threat because of their detailed knowledge of a particular application or system, or because they are able to access particular functions. It is therefore useful to limit or control access to system resources including terminals, applications programs, system utilities, disk files or datasets, and transactions within transaction processing systems.

The form of a logical access system

A logical access system will go through three stages:

1. It must identify the user, usually through the use of an ID code.
2. It must authenticate the user, usually through the use of a password.
3. It must ensure that proper authorization has been given for the proposed use of the data within the system.

The full access system must therefore have the following features:

1. It must be possible to uniquely identify and verify each individual user by a logical identifier. Each user's security profile will be expressed as a binary vector for each security domain – that is, each individual will be given authorizations to access only those sensitive areas which are relevant to their work. There will be one component for each security level and only if the values match will the user be allowed access to the level attempted.
2. It should then be possible to uniquely identify each individual terminal, accessing the system by a logical identifier which logs the physical location of that terminal as an additional check to ensure that the user is making access from an expected or required location.
3. In a network, there should also be a unique identification of each individual computer accessing the network, again by a logical identifier which logs the physical location of that computer. This also helps to verify the propriety of the attempted access.
4. It should then be possible, within the system, to control access to identified data and resources by individual users, terminals, computers and access type (for example, to read or update sensitive files).
5. It should be possible for auditing purposes to record the access to that data and usage of those resources by both authorized and unauthorized users, terminals and computers.

The best strategy is to create a comprehensive, integrated access control system, rather than a piecemeal system which might require users to remember different passwords to access different components within the system. Users of IBM's MVS operating system can incorporate Resource Access Control Facility, ACF2 and TOP SECRET, but such systems are only effective if properly supported by administrative and authorization procedures.

Access controls have the following elements:

1 **Fixed terminal identifiers**. These establish a link between the terminal's logical identifier and its physical location. The terminal ID can then be used to restrict the resources that can be accessed by, for example, restricting access to specific functions, to specific terminals or to identified terminals at specified times of the day when supervision is available.
2 **User identifiers and user authorities**. If users are clearly identified, all activities in the system can be traced back to them. Some users may be given special authorizations – for example, the system administrator who controls the allocation and authorization of resources, the operations management staff and the auditors.
3 **Passwords**. Most operating systems provide passwords to control access to resources, both to log on and at several points in the system, typically to control access to transaction processing systems.

The mechanics and administration of passwords

As in any security system, there is a trade-off between ease of use and security. Password controls may be inconvenient for the users, yet their co-operation is vital – so a user-friendly design is essential. A password or personal identification number (PIN) or formal access protocol represents secret knowledge. The password may be any combination of letters, numbers or symbols. The entry is usually in non-echo format so that the characters entered by the user do not appear on the screen or on a print-out. Access is therefore limited to those who have the appropriate knowledge. A minimum of six characters is probably required for a reasonable level of security, with whatever maximum might be required to strike a balance between the security needs of the organization and the ability of the user to remember the code. But remember that the password is only as secure as the users allow it to be. This means that users must be encouraged:

- not to write it down
- not to share their passwords (if, say, someone forgets their own number or temporary staff need access)
- not to use obvious words as the password, such as the names of a partner or of children.

Once they are entered into the system, passwords should always be encrypted one way, that is to say they should be *irreversibly scrambled* when stored. The password is then compared in encrypted form. This minimizes the risk of disclosure if an unauthorized person obtains a copy of the password file, but it does not exclude the possibility. If a user does obtain access to the encrypted password file, a more powerful computer might be able to break the code. If the storage encryption algorithm is known, the intruder might put suitable words through the algorithm to see whether any of the words match.

In general, passwords assigned by the system administrator are more secure than those that are unassigned. Some systems have a routine which generates passwords and notifies the users of each new word through a secure mailing system. If a password has been changed, the system may be programmed to accept a use of the old password but to notify security who can then monitor entry. System-generated words are hard to guess but may be equally difficult to remember and, if a hacker deduces the algorithm on which generation is based, the whole system may become insecure. If the created and assigned password is difficult to remember, the user may write it down which makes it equally vulnerable. Hence, some systems are programmed to produce pronounceable passwords to reduce the risk of amnesia or noting down, but the range of the words thus created must be wide. If the password is numeric, one scheme calls for the number to be divided into pairs, and each pair of numbers refers to one of 99 objects which are far more easily remembered. This allows the user a choice. If numbers are not easily remembered, the user should be able to remember the objects which can be translated into numbers by reference to a standard list.

Changing passwords

However the first password is selected, all users on sensitive systems can be forced to change their passwords regularly – the ideal frequency may be once a month. To ensure that the same password is not reused or that some other word (say, based on the month) is not used, best practice may require that the system allocates the words. As a fail-safe in the event of user amnesia, the system administrator must have the power to overwrite the user's password, but this power should be tightly controlled to reduce the administrator's opportunity to commit fraud.

In theory, the life expectancy of a password would be infinite, but if security is broken the problem for the system administrator is whether the password has been given away by the user or deduced by another. A standard countermeasure is to give passwords for a fixed period. In such systems, the quality of the security depends on the length of that period. Self-evidently, if the system is under attack, the longer the period of validity for the password the more likely it is that the password may be compromised. Further, if the password is breached, it may be some time before the hacker is detected and, during that time, considerable damage may be done. A possible defence is to have users notified of the last use of the system. This can be a useful control so long as users check the accuracy of this information – a habit that has to be encouraged through staff training.

The ultimate security system would only use a password once. Thus, even if a hacker gains information about one log-in, this will not be helpful. This may work in one of two ways:

- There may be rules, known to the users, which dictate what each new password will be. This system will remain secure until the attacker discovers which element changes and on what rules.
- The users are notified of each new password. If a user is supplied with a list of the next ten passwords, this is a vulnerable paper record which may fall into the wrong hands. One defence is to have the passwords listed in an order known only to the recipient.

System suppliers' passwords

When an installation buys or rents a system or package, there are standard passwords set up in the system, and usually published in the documentation. These are weaknesses that can be exploited by anyone who gains access to the system so they should be changed immediately. The supplier should also be questioned as to the existence of any backdoor passwords. These are sometimes used to speed up the diagnosis and correction of system faults and can confer global access privileges on the holder of that password. These passwords should either be deleted or changed to those known only to the administrator. Many of the operator commands can be controlled and protected by passwords, or may require the operator to enter his or her ID. This allows a record to be kept of user accesses to commands. Some systems allow the administrator to flag staff who are on holiday or ill. Any attempts to use the ID would be detected and reported as a violation. Similarly, a terminal can be locked out by using a password command. The terminal will then remain locked out until the same user resets it by entering the password. The terminal can also be locked out when it has not been used for a predetermined time.

Combating the hacker

If all the standard IDs and passwords have been changed, the hacker will then attempt the usual names and words. If all else fails, the intruder will program his or her computer to permutate alphanumeric characters until entry is achieved. If the password is long, this process will be time-consuming and expensive in telephone connect time, but if only four characters are used, only 10,000 permutations will not take long to try. It is therefore essential either to build in a delay after each unsuccessful log-in attempt, or to construct a trap to log-off the terminal or freeze the account if unsuccessful attempts at the password are made. The best systems automatically suspend the user's access authorization after two or three unsuccessful attempts. Fast and effective action is required for good security with access only restored after an investigation by the system administrator. For the more sensitive systems allowing remote access, manual switching through to the computer after voice verification may be appropriate, with dial-back if necessary to ensure that the call is coming from an acceptable source. Greater security is achievable through **handshaking**, which is an extended dialogue sequence rather than the entry of a single password. Here two computers or a user and the computer communicate with each other. In high-security environments, cards or tokens may be required as a precondition of log-on or, in the most extreme cases, dynamic signature verifications systems, retina pattern scanners and fingerprint analyses may be used to identify users.

Transaction or function authorization

A transaction in computer terms means a series of programs which carries out a related piece of processing. The data element involved in this processing is also called a transaction. Some systems will control the use of transactions from specific terminals by specific users, or control the use of terminals and functions by dates or days of the week and within certain time periods. If a user requires access to a function or other protected resource, this can be granted for a limited period of time. After the expiration of the set period, the authorization will automatically lapse.

Profiling allows the administrator to define common access requirements. Each user can then be linked to a given profile and given the permissions which it contains. Alternatively, combinations of users, terminals and functions can be stipulated for each user. Some permissions can be qualified, say, to allow permission to make use of the transaction facility, but only up to a specified value of commercial transaction.

Design features of access provision

Some users may be allowed access on the basis of 'least privilege' – in other words, they are only allowed to use the privilege to the extent necessary to complete the given job. This limits the damage which may be done by the inexperienced and by those who have yet to prove their trustworthiness. Any default will result in the immediate loss of system privileges. This can be a good way of controlling **Trojan horses** (a Trojan horse is either an individual or a program which appears to offer a legitimate service, but does so in a way which allows the collection of vital information and which might, for example, allow the impersonation of clients on other occasions). Overall, the designer should aim for economy of mechanism. It is better to implement a relatively simple mechanism which all staff are prepared to use, than to devise sophisticated features that are seldom used. All the mechanisms must be simple to use, but effective in performing the task of ensuring that every request for access has proper authorization. Further, security should not depend on the overall design remaining secret. Indeed, the designers should publish details as a deterrent to possible fraudsters who should recognize the likelihood that they will be caught. The corollary is that if the detailed principles underlying the security system cannot safely be described in open literature, it cannot be used with confidence.

File access permissions

All operating systems provide controls over access to disk files. These can incorporate passwords within the logical grouping of files as well as a system of access permissions. Access to either file data or its description can be granted in one of two ways – by quoting the *system password* for that group of files or the *user password*. Access modes can be created at different levels within the file organization systems, such as:

- read
- write
- exclude (this denies access to specifically named users)
- append (this allows users to add information to the end of a file)
- purge (this allows authorized users to release files or overwrite the released file data area with zeros)
- modify (this allows authorized users to list or modify file description details, e.g. file name, organization, size, access attribute permissions, etc.)

- lock (this allows authorized users to deny access under certain conditions, e.g. time, after a given number of accesses, on a program terminating abnormally, and so on).

Although tape-based systems are now being replaced by on-line disk systems, tape access controls may also be needed both for access, and for housekeeping and maintenance.

Authorization procedures

In access hierarchies, high-ranking subjects are automatically given the privileges of lower-ranking subjects. An authorization list or access controls can limit access to those authorized. Such a system is easy to implement and reasonably effective, although long lists can take time to check, and are not appropriate for accessing every aspect of functions and processes. When a user attempts to gain access, the lists are checked to ensure that the activity is authorized for the particular user. Other software modules will record or journal this activity and may charge for the resources consumed. At the top of the hierarchy, the operator or administrator mode overrides all protections within the operating system and allows the user to exercise responsibility for allocating privileges to new users, system maintenance, etc. It is the equivalent of a master key in a conventional mechanical locking system. At the next level down, users with high privileges can read the lists and directories set up for both their own and for the lower level operations. Those with low-level authorization can only access the files at that level.

Threats

There are two distinct threats faced by organizations with a heavy dependence on IT:

- Access to systems and resources may be abused within a person's authority level. The major losses are caused by employees. They succeed because of the general lack of security and the fact that there is a tendency to grant high-level privileges to too many people.
- Access to the systems may be contrived. Active penetration for commercial espionage and fraud usually requires a high level of skill. Passive breaking refers to those who accidentally breach security and then exploit the information gained. Although hackers are becoming more skilled, few are responsible for substantial losses.

Administration or authorization procedures

The structure of an organization is not limited at a conceptual level. Each organization will tend to develop dynamically, and the form of the management system will evolve to meet each organization's particular needs. Some organizations will have a *centralized* administrative structure, others will have a *distributed* structure with some centralized functions. Some systems permit a hierarchical type of administration, others will be modular. Within each management system, the creation and maintenance of good logical access controls needs good software and effective administration. For these purposes, the administration may be centralized in one section or department, or shared between several sections. This may be a division of function at the top of the organization structure – as, say, between the administrator and the internal audit department which scrutinizes the whole system, or at an intermediate point, for example, as between a DP department and a data control section.

Design and set-up issues

The first part of any control system must address the issue of control of inputs to access control software, for example, setting up the logical identifiers, or the user IDs and passwords, granting access to time sharing facilities, and to transactions in on-line systems. The authorization procedures which are established must take account of the value and vulnerability of the resource. If too high a level of authority is stipulated as a precondition of access and too many experienced staff are excluded, the effectiveness of the management which the information system is able to support may be substantially reduced.

The authorization levels eventually set must reflect the actual degree of responsibility held, and the normal and most desirable course of events in each work environment. To that end, a profile of the resources which each user will, and should, require access to should be drawn up and implemented. This process should be matched by a training programme which allows staff to make optimum use of their access to the resources.

User or applicant information

Once the system has been designed, the use of pre-printed request forms for resource allocation can be useful in a survey of function and information flow by obtaining basic information of each key individual's job, department and location. The forms should be kept simple, with the amount of written details being required from users kept to a minimum. When the form is received, it should be authenticated by the administrator. Details of the ID allocated and any initial password should then be transmitted to the applicant by a secure mailing system. The degree of control exercised should obviously reflect the risks involved in the particular resource or assistance requested. Further, the user's goodwill should be maintained wherever possible because, if a response is unhelpful, the user may be tempted to bypass the security controls, for instance, by asking a colleague if their ID and password can be borrowed. Some provision should also be made for the time when the system administrator forgets his or her key password. While this should be a rare occurrence, recovery could be a problem. Some administrators place the password(s) in a sealed envelope in a fireproof safe. Alternatively, a back-up system can be created with access separately passworded and held by another member of staff. This duplication of access may not be wholly desirable from a security point of view.

Reporting on system access

The second part of the control system regulates outputs from the information system. There may be *management* or *audit trail reports* – on some systems details of all transactions entered by the security master user are logged and reported on;

or *activity reports* – these can be divided into *systems access* and *exception reports*. The first of these sub-divisions may produce large amounts of print-out and is normally for reference only. The content and layout of reports will vary from one system to another, but monitoring functions must be created to ensure that only authorized users gain access to the resources which they are authorized to access. Unless unauthorized attempts to access resources are brought to the attention of the administrator, the latter may be lulled into a false sense of security. Selective or exception reporting is therefore a useful detective function to log interesting activity.

The effectiveness of these reports

The effectiveness of security reports is determined by:

- the frequency of report production
- the follow-up of detected breaches of security
- the rules which prescribe security systems.

The speed with which the system reacts to security breaches is crucial. The longer the delay, the less likely it is that the action will be effective. It is much easier to monitor short daily reports than trying to read through a long weekly print-out. If some events are deemed fundamental, they can be reported immediately to a security terminal. However, the nature of the response must be carefully thought out to minimize damage to industrial relations. If no action is taken, the system will almost certainly end up compromised. If insensitive action is taken to reprimand all who transgress, regardless of status, function or attitude, the staff will almost certainly resent the system's response and this could again lead to a loss of security.

The best route is through a continuous process of *staff education*. The preparation of guidelines and a code of practice can help to alert staff to the reasons for the various security measures. Once these are understood, the co-operation of staff can be more readily sought.

Control of flow

Although access control can be precise about who should access what, flow controls are necessary to specify the channels along which the information is allowed to flow. Information should be classified as either 'confidential' or 'non-confidential', and authority levels should be linked to the data thus classified. All information flows are then permitted save the confidential to the non-confidential. These controls can be established to validate all flows as they occur, or when the program is being compiled, i.e. before the program executes.

It can often be difficult to classify information and to determine who should have access. In a hierarchical system, for example, information flows down can always be prevented, but not those up the hierarchy. The placement of individuals in the hierarchy therefore assumes significance for each item of information, and may lead to information being hopelessly over-classified.

Inference controls

A medical information system may use a statistical database which is supposed to release statistical information without compromising individual patients' data. Unfortunately, summary reports contain traces of the original data, and information about a patient could be reconstructed from several summaries. For example, if an intruder has the physical characteristics of a patient as to height, weight, age, etc., the query might seek to establish how many patients with those characteristics have suffered various illnesses and infer the target's condition. Each query is a logical expression using the logical operators. The reply is a set of records that satisfy the requirements of the expression and is called the **query set**. Intruders often insert dummy records and then test the size of the query set necessary to obtain precise information. A filter based on the query set size is possible.

Where query sets overlap it is often possible to infer information by comparing the two. Suppose, for example, that the system contains information of employees' salaries but will not give out an individual's salary. The query could establish the number of men in a given department, the total of salaries for persons employed in that department, and the number of employees in that department. If it is known that only one woman is employed in that department, exact confirmation of her salary is now achieved. People may be tracked through age, status or other known variables stored in the databank. The problem with controls is that they may unreasonably limit answers to perfectly legitimate and useful queries. Any controls which are therefore inserted and which distort the data while giving replies, will only be valuable if the loss of confidentiality would represent a significant loss.

Encryption

Security risks at terminals

Ordinary users may not have expert typing skills and so an observer may be able read or guess the password through simple observation. Further, the password must not be displayed at the terminal, i.e. communication must be in 'non-echo' mode. However, although non-printing characters are used in some passwords, they can be observed in wire-tapping. The countermeasure used is *encryption* of the passwords during transmission but this is an expense to be justified according to the sensitivity of the information to be transmitted. In some systems, the passwords are printed out in logging files produced by the central system, even if they are suppressed by the terminal, so care should be taken to protect those files.

Electronic mail

There are two main concerns in the sending of messages:

- to provide a mechanism for the validation of the content
- to provide a mechanism the authentication of the sender.

Although some special authentication codes (sometimes changed daily) can be included in the message, some degree of encryption remains the best protection against fraud and dishonesty. Thus, for example, **digital signatures** can be added to the message as a unique identifier; for instance, the Swedish electronic seal system has been used since 1981 to protect banking transactions. The seal is applied to a plaintext message of any length. It is a cryptologically-based hash total of 18 digits which is appended to the message. A secret key of 35 digits is used in the seal algorithm, with the communicating parties free to agree any 35-digit key. The 18-digital seal is then computed using the secret 35-digit key. It uses non-linear permutations and exponential functions and is difficult to break.

Similarly, the authentication can be achieved by using the **public key systems**. Here there are two keys: one enciphers the text, using a special one-way function. A different key must then be used to decipher the enciphered text. User A therefore holds one private key and publishes his other key to all correspondents, together with the appropriate decryption rules. When they receive a message, supposedly from A, they can decipher it using the key. If it makes sense, it should have come from A for the ciphertext could only have been produced using A's key. The security of the system depends on having one-way functions – functions which are easy to do one way and difficult to undo.

Encryption methods

Hardware encryption systems work quickly and effectively and are easy to install (every terminal has a black box attached), but this can be expensive if sophisticated hardware is to be fitted to every terminal in a large system. Software encryption methods would potentially be more cost-effective in large systems because the software is installed wherever it is required in the processing configuration, and it can be adjusted to cater for any peculiarities in each organization's operating system or data. Standard algorithms are relatively cheap but tend to be slow to operate at the terminal end. This is inconvenient because users require good responsive speeds at the terminal. Experience shows that public key encryption can be very slow when implemented using a micro. The ideal solution would be true end-to-end encryption using an algorithm that is fast and small. It should be combined with hardware which has wired-in master keys, and properly sealed to prevent tampering. The combination of hardware and software would be more secure because software remains more vulnerable on its own.

Data encryption

Encryption is the technique or process for deriving enciphered text from *plaintext* (the term for readable text from which the encoded message is derived) and it is likely to become very important because:

- more sensitive information is now being transferred (e.g. electronic funds transfer, corporate planning, marketing and sales information, etc.)
- hackers are becoming more clever and have more sophisticated computers to aid their access to the data whether stored or transmitted.

Thus, the costs of encryption are easier to justify, and the commercial market has developed products which are increasingly effective in preserving data confidentiality. The rationale could not be easier to state. Even if data do fall into the wrong hands, they are useless because they cannot be read.

An encryption or decryption process consists of an algorithm and a key. The algorithm is controlled by the key. The procedure is usually symmetrical, i.e. it uses the same key each way. Early systems relied on a literal code: a vocabulary of words, for example, can be assigned arbitrary values (the word 'hidden' might be assigned the coded value '298', and 'meaning' the value '915'). If each end of the communication link has the code book, the words can be matched to the coded value and vice versa in a process of sending and translation. Self-evidently, the code is broken by discovering a copy of the code book, or being independently able to determine the contents of the message and thereby gain an insight into the vocabulary of the code.

Cipher systems depend on the processes of **substitution** and **transposition**, either individually or in combination. In basic substitution systems, another symbol replaces the original symbol in the plaintext so, quite arbitrarily, A, B and C can be replaced by F, L and Q. But this process is too easily broken because too many features of the original message remain (such as the relative frequency of letters). Similarly, transposition transformations (where the letters are rearranged according to a grid formula) are vulnerable because the original letters are simply jumbled up and may easily be rearranged to form coherent words using the tireless power of the computer. So sophisticated transformations are more commonly based on *polyalphabetic* or *polygraphic* substitutions, or on transposition systems which use different grid sizes.

The development of encryption standards

Computers have made the transmission of data more efficient. The communication protocols devised by the hardware manufacturers were published and networks were initially open to anyone who could obtain access. By the 1970s, users were beginning to feel the need for greater security. The earliest systems relied on an algorithm, but once the algorithm is known, all security is lost. The next step is for an algorithm and a key, the purpose of the key being to transform the data. The algorithm should be arranged so that each different value of the key produces a radically different transformation of the plaintext. The different values of the key should change the effect of the algorithm so radically that the transformation is entirely different in nature for each value of key. Then if the algorithm is compromised and one value of the key is discovered, all is not lost. The secrecy can be restored by using a different key. However, the yardstick of effectiveness is now measured by the effectiveness of the system if the attacker knows the algorithm.

The Data Encryption Standard

In 1977, the American National Bureau of Standards approved a standard for cryptographic transformations – the **Data Encryption Standard (DES)**. A satisfactory cipher should produce a result which is not detectably different from random, whether regarded as a function of the plaintext or the key. Hence, it should contain no real statistical information about the plaintext. The DES uses a product transformation of transpositions, substitutions and non-linear operations. They are applied for 16 iterations to each block of the message, the result being a 64-bit ciphertext. The key used is 56 bits taken from a 64-bit key which includes eight parity bits. Parts of the algorithm do produce regularities which slightly limit the utility of the standard, particularly in the multiple encipherment situation. Given increases in the computer power that could be brought to bear on decipherment, some now argue that a 128-bit key would be better.

Key security

Because the system is known, security depends on the security of the keys. The weakness in these systems is that they call for the transmission of the key. The problem is therefore to ensure that the key is only transmitted to the legitimate receiver and that the would-be decoder cannot gain access to it. The solution is that the key has to be held at both ends of the link. Distributing the keys can be a costly and complex overhead, with many having to be created, distributed and stored. Lost or forgotten keys may also mean that files of data may be inaccessible and, risking the users' memory failures, users must change the keys regularly. There is no room for complacency because the ciphertext looks unreadable. If someone has compromised the key, months or years of data communication may be read by an intruder.

The one-time pad

The so-called **one-time pad** is a classic method of encryption. The data are treated as a string of bits. The key is another random string of bits. The plaintext string and the keytext are added to produce the ciphertext. The keystring has to be as long as the message and is random, so the ciphertext ends up random. Analysis of the ciphertext produces no information about the plaintext. The computer version is based on the original paper-and-pencil version, where both ends of the communication link used the same pads printed with random sequences which were only used once and then destroyed.

The computing dimension

Computers allow the cryptanalyst to use techniques impossible by hand. Because the cost of hardware has fallen in real terms, the analyst can now bring far more computational power to decode text economically both in monetary and in time terms. Equally, the encoder can use greater sophistication to hide meaning. The decoder must weigh the economic advantages to be gained from cracking the code against the cost of the decipherment exercise. The encoder must try to ensure that the cost of decoding is high enough to discourage an attacker. The equation of encipherment and decipherment is also affected by the problem that the more sophisticated the algorithm and its key, the more slowly it may process the plaintext. Speed depends on the key size and the efficiency of the algorithm, and processing time is money. A number of recent incidents are instructive. A French student managed to decrypt a 40-bit (non-USA) Netscape key which had been posted on to the Internet as a challenge. He did it by brute force – he was able to harness two parallel processing supercomputers and a network of 120 other computers. It is significant that a student could get access to this amount of computer power and, given that the cost of raw computing power continues to fall, the only defence for users is continually to increase the length of the keys. A more serious incident involving Netscape encryption involved two students at the University of California at Berkeley who bypassed the encryption mechanism and accessed the random information generator from which the encryption key was generated. This meant that the students could generate all possible keys in a few minutes. Netscape say that the size of the random input has been increased to make this recreation process more demanding but the incident is alarming, prompting service providers to compete in developing more and more sophisticated key systems.

But there is a very real political problem as the use of ever more secure systems emerge for the electronic exchange of data. In many states, the police and other law enforcement agencies are given the power to tap telephone conversations both for the prevention of crime and for reasons of national security. As more people begin to use computer systems and those systems use cryptographic measures, it becomes more difficult for the state to monitor what is being done. This may actively prevent the detection of criminals, terrorists or other socially undesirable individuals. Consequently, the safety of the majority of citizens may be threatened by the dangerous few escaping detection. Many states therefore prohibit the use of some encryption techniques except for certain defined purposes or unless the means of decoding is supplied to the law enforcement agencies. At the time of writing, this issue is the subject of international discussion and it will be interesting to see what conclusions are reached.

Hacking

Hacking is the deliberate accessing of on-line systems by unauthorized persons. Many hackers do not act out of malice, but because they consider it to be fun. However, breaking into a confidential computer file is morally no different to someone who breaks into a locked office and reads confidential documents. In 1988, the House of Lords in *R v Gold and Schifreen* [1988] 2 All ER 186 decided that hacking into systems to change or amend data records is not the crime of forgery. This left the Telecommunications Act 1984 as the only possible crime which might be commit by the hacker: it is an offence under section 5 of the Act to connect any unauthorized apparatus to the licensed telecommunications system. Hackers might therefore be prosecuted for attaching an acoustic coupler or modem to the telephone system.

The security implications

The threat of hacking has become a more significant danger with the development of micros and modems. To break into a system from the outside, the system must have dial-up connections or be accessible from a system like PSS. Many systems have dial-up facilities as a matter of course because they are distributed systems, or because employees like sales representatives need to be able to access the computer, even from their customers' own premises. Even systems which have leased lines often have dial-up lines as a back-up in the event of line failure, or because the manufacturer's technical support staff want the ability to review the diagnostic or breakdown reports which the machine automatically accumulates. In fact, the practice of remote maintenance represents a security risk and the auditor or administrator should be aware that it is taking place and consider the implications. This will involve issues such as:

- the apparent reliability of the manufacturer's or contract maintenance company's staff
- whether disks with sensitive data can be taken off-line during maintenance
- whether the operating system can be reloaded from back-up if unauthorized amendments have been introduced.

If it is decided to allow the practice, it is useful to have a manual switch to connect outside lines for remote maintenance purposes rather than to leave such lines permanently open to the main systems. As a precondition to switching the alleged engineer through, proper verification procedures can be carried out which will, with luck, eliminate the hackers.

Accessing the system

Before a remote hacker can gain access to a computer system, the dial-up telephone number must be obtained. Sometimes a telephone bluff, say posing as a remote user, to the computer department will obtain the number. Some organizations publish the numbers fairly widely in an internal directory within the organization and risk hacking from ex-employees or the friends and associates of employees. Scavenging the wastepaper produced by an installation may show user IDs on the print-outs. The determined hacker will adopt a trial-and-error strategy. Professional hackers may try bribing employees either for the numbers themselves, or for discarded telephone accounts which show the numbers.

Another way of gaining access is through an autodialer. The dialling may be random or dial port numbers may be assumed to be in the same telephone area as the intended victim's voice lines. The hacker programs the micro to try a range of telephone numbers. When a data line is detected (after two or three rings, the call is answered with an identifiable computer-generated tone), the system records that number and may then attempt to detect the protocol. Hackers pass on discovered numbers through bulletin boards and electronic mail boxes (micros on an auto-answer modem). If a hacker obtains a sign-on screen display, a valid ID and password is normally required to gain access. Standard format IDs laid down by the manufacturers can be tried.

Password access

Unmodified computer systems will often accept an unlimited number of tries to input a correct ID without generating a warning or closing off the terminal. Note that once an ID code has been detected, the hacker may telephone the administrator, claim amnesia and ask for a new password. Most systems have standard IDs and passwords, e.g. sysman, admin, oper, etc., with similar IDs for engineers, programmers, etc. When the system is supplied, it often has these words as standard with passwords set as 'password' or the imaginative 'XXXXXX'. This information is often freely available in the manufacturer's documentation. If these standard IDs and passwords have not been changed, the hacker has an immediate toehold in the system. Discarded print-outs may also reveal account, program and file names or they may be guessed if the files are functionally named after the relevant aspects of the victim's business. Some hackers have adopted a decoy system (sometimes called *Trojan horses*) to gain information. Thus, for example, if the hacker has identified the legitimate users' communication channels, the hacker waits on the line. If an authorized user then begins the log-on procedures, the hacker will send a simulated response from the main system, i.e. the log-in frame. When the user attempts to log in, the hacker acquires a set of ID codes and passwords. The hacker will then put up an error message inviting the user to try again, triggering the main system to offer the real log-in frame to the user. If the hacker is lucky, the user will then re-enter ID code and passwords to the system, gain access and not realize the deception.

Access control disruption

Hackers with the right level of skill can disable the journal or console logs of the main CPU to suppress the records of their activities. Another strategy is to disrupt the access control system. The controls may become discredited to such an extent that obvious symptoms of fraud or illegal access are passed off as machine errors: if access control software can be made to malfunction so that legitimate users are denied access, it may be switched off and unauthorized users may then gain access without detection. Similarly, if back-up files can be removed from store, altered and returned, fraud would be achieved when the altered files or programs are loaded on to the prime system. It is particularly difficult to detect this method of fraud after the event. Similarly, some computers have front panel systems which allow direct accessing, and their use frequently leaves no trial on journal records.

Computer viruses

The computer virus is a small program that, once introduced into a system, becomes self-propagating, i.e. it is designed to spread itself to all parts of the system with the intention of disrupting both data and software. The potential for what viruses can do is limited only by the imagination of the programmer. As in the case of its biological equivalent, it replicates itself in such a way that it is impossible to detect its original source, and once a system is contaminated, the only remedy may be to recreate the system from back-up. But some viruses have been programmed to lie dormant for a while. This allows the infection to be spread to the back-up copies. In such a case, the entire system can be rendered permanently unusable. Some viruses hide in the optimum places to cause harm (the Lehigh virus lived in one of the fundamental operating system files, the COMMAND.COM file and was activated every time a user typed a DOS command), but the program can include any condition for the virus to apply to decide whether it should reveal itself and what it is supposed to do.

Preventive measures

Despite the creation of virus detection software as a guard against infection, it is almost impossible to protect a computer against a newly created virus – one that has yet to be incorporated into the detection software. Although software acquisitions can be restricted to reputable suppliers, and public domain and demonstration programs avoided, both hackers and disaffected employees can introduce the infection unless access control mechanisms and compliance monitoring is effective. A number of practical prevention strategies may help:

- the organization can provide its own disks, marked with a distinctive logo
- contracts of employment can make it a summarily dismissible offence for any employee to use unmarked disks
- all externally provided disks have to be inspected by the security department and the data or software transferred to marked disks before use
- the floppy drives on all PCs and workstations can either be locked or permanently disabled.

The problem becomes even more intractable in a large network situation because of the difficulty in preventing the bored or malicious employee from introducing a virus. Although security experts have now developed vaccine software which will limit or eradicate the known viral programs, these programs will not restore corrupted or lost data. Organizations should therefore carefully consider the wording of their insurance policies to determine whether data loss through viral infection is included.

Electronic eavesdropping

Line tapping is as easy as conventional telephone tapping. Transmitted signals can be recorded through a radio transmitter and replayed through an appropriate terminal or printer. Passwords will then appear in clear text. Alternatively, devices like the datascope can be connected and will allow text to be read. Wire tapping may lead to one or more of the evils of data insertion, modification and deletion. It may suit the plans of a fraudster to totally block the given transmissions – so that a debit to an account is delayed or stopped, or to modify the transmissions (thereby reducing the amount of the debit), to engage in forgery or perhaps the increasingly lucrative but simple activity of information gathering. The best protection is through encryption because the signal is protected during transmission.

Electronic equipment produces both **radio frequency interference (RFI)** and **electromagnetic radiation (EMR)** and eavesdropping the encoded digital information contained in EMR is possible up to 1 km from the target VDU. LANs are particularly vulnerable because, in many cases, the cabling acts as an aerial to enhance the signals. Initially, it was thought that it required sophisticated equipment to decode the signals, but work done at the Dutch telecom laboratories has shown that all that is required is a television receiver and the means to synchronize the frequencies of the signals received. The cost of the components required to construct the synchronizing device is minimal. Such systems therefore represent a major threat to data confidentiality. Data encryption is no defence because the text will be displayed in the screen in plaintext. The threat may come from a mere hacker, or it may be from professionals who want details of the target organization's sensitive plans and resources.

Shielding

To reduce the risk, standards have been developed to define the shielding to reduce the maximum radiation emissions from equipment for use in military or intelligence services. These standards are referred to by the American term, **TEMPEST**. They are not publicly discussed nor can the equipment be offered for sale on the open market, but some manufacturers are now incorporating shielding which is claimed to be of a comparable standard. This is a potentially serious threat to security, but organizations have proved unwilling to spend large amounts of money on countermeasures, for example special metallic foiling on the windows or shielding in front of the VDU screen or other radiating components such as the ROMAG system of laminated materials which helps to divert the radiated signals. The signals produced by flat-screen terminals may be more difficult to eavesdrop because a different system of data display is used, or the use of devices to broadcast masking spurious signals may be partially effective. The decision whether to shield the building or the terminals is a simple matter of cost–benefit analysis. The variables are:

- the sensitivity of the data
- the other consequences of the action taken (shielding the building may, for instance, make the use of radio pagers and portable telephones ineffective)
- the cost of the countermeasures.

Computer Misuse Act 1990

The modern law is supplemented in the UK by the Computer Misuse Act 1990 which was introduced as a private member's bill by Michael Colvin MP. It largely follows the recommendations of the Law Commission's Report No. 186 which undertook an investigation of the law in the light of general public concern following the acquittals in the House of Lords case of *R v Gold and Schifreen* [1988] when the defendants who managed to hack into the Duke of Edinburgh's e-mail on PRESTEL were held not to have committed offences under the Forgery Act 1981. One slightly odd feature about the legislation is that it does not define the words 'computer', 'program' or 'data'. Presumably, the intention is to allow the courts to give the current meanings without being restricted by definitions that may have dated. There are also uncertainties as to the nature of the intentions that have to be proved.

The criminal offences

The Act starts by creating three new offences:

1 The offence of **unauthorized access** to computer material is designed to criminalize hacking, whether by an employee who exceeds the authority given or by an outsider. It is committed if the person causes a computer to perform any function with intent to gain access to any program or data stored in the computer, knowing that the access is unauthorized at the relevant time.

   The offence is relatively minor and is triable summarily by the magistrates' court. It requires the accused to have done something more than merely read output (whether on the screen or in hard copy), electronically eavesdrop or passively achieve contact with the machine. But it is not necessary that the accused should actually have gained access or be successful in avoiding the security measures in force. Nor is it necessary for the accused to have any particular program or data in mind when trying to get the computer to respond. Thus, simply getting the computer to display a log-on menu or triggering a security system would constitute the offence even though the accused might have no idea what is stored on the computer. Anyone who supplies information, say through a bulletin board, which helps the accused to get the computer to respond would be liable as an accomplice.

   The main authority on the first two offences is the *Attorney General's Reference (No. 1 of 1991)* [1992] 3 WLR 432. In this case, the defendant was acquitted even though he had gained unauthorized access to a computer with the intention of obtaining a discount on goods to which he was not entitled. He was charged under section 1 and under section 2 with the ulterior intention of committing false accounting. The reason for the acquittal was that the trial judge misinterpreted the section 1 offence. The Court of Appeal now confirms that it is not a requirement of the offence that the defendant uses machine A to access machine B. The offence is complete when the defendant causes a computer to perform any function in relation to any program or data whether held on that machine or another.

2 The second offence builds on the first: the accused must achieve **unauthorized access with intent to commit and facilitate the commission of a further offence**. This is a more serious offence because the accused will intend to commit theft (for example, by diverting an electronic funds transfer) or blackmail (say, by gaining access to confidential information about the intended victim). For these purposes, it does not matter that the accused does not commit that more serious offence. Indeed, the offence will still be committed even though it was actually impossible to commit that offence, say because the electronic funds transfer was not made on that day or because the confidential information was not stored on that particular system. The range of penalties reflects the greater seriousness of the offence and it includes forfeiture of the equipment used for hacking, compensation orders for the victim, imprisonment of up to five years, etc.

3 The third offence is committed if the accused knowingly causes an unauthorized modification of the contents of any computer with the intention

of interfering with the operation of that computer, preventing access to a program or data, or interfering with the operation of the program or the reliability of the data. That the accused does not know what programs or data may be stored on the computer at the time of access is irrelevant. This creates a wide offence including all deliberate alterations and erasures of computer-held material. The offence would also include introducing a virus into a computer system if the effect was to use up the spare capacity of the machine and thereby interfere with the operation of the machine or if it corrupted or destroyed data. It will be no defence that the actual introduction was by an innocent user who places a disk containing the virus into the system. Liability attaches to the person who placed the disk into circulation.

Jurisdiction and search warrants

Because so many networks now cross national boundaries, it was necessary to define which courts might have jurisdiction to hear cases where the accused acts in country A to affect a computer, programs or data held in country B. To allow the English courts to hear a case under the Act, there must be a positive link between the accused and this country, i.e. that the misuse originates in this country or it was aimed at a computer in this country. The nationality of the accused is irrelevant and it is not necessary that the link should actually have been completed. It will sufficient to commit the second offence if D gains unauthorized access to a computer in, say, Holland intending to commit a further offence of fraud in England. The court will also have the power to deal with conspiracies and attempts on the same basis. However, there is a test of *double criminality*, i.e. the facts must give rise to criminal liability in both countries and, while several countries have legislation expressly dealing with computer abuse, there are not yet common. But all that is required is that there is some punishment for the misuse. It is not relevant how the offence is described under that law.

If there is evidence that an offence has been or is about to be committed, the English police may apply to a circuit judge for a search warrant to enter and search premises, and to seize evidence of an offence under the Act. The extradition laws also apply to the second and third offences so anyone accused of committing either or both offences could be moved from one country to another for the purposes of trial.

The effectiveness of the Act

Perhaps surprisingly, there has been very little real effort made to co-ordinate the communication of the results of the few cases prosecuted under the Act. A survey of newspapers suggests that there are a few prosecutions each year, but the courts are not developing a body of clear-cut principles which will underpin the development of this Act as a vital weapon in the armoury against computer abuse. Indeed, most prosecutions have failed. Thus, in March 1993, after a trial lasting 16 days, the first high-profile prosecution under the Act failed to produce a conviction. Despite a two-year investigation by British Telecom, Scotland Yard's special computer crimes unit and seven other police forces, a teenage hacker called Paul Bedworth walked free. Thus, if the intention of the Act was to close the loopholes in the law revealed in the case of *R v Gold and Schifreen* [1988], it would appear to have failed. In the short term, therefore, there would seem to be a need to review the Act and to tighten up the definitions, particularly with regard to the question of the intentions and how they are to be proved.

But this ignores the real question which is whether the criminal law is really the right way of approaching the problem. If this case has demonstrated anything, it is that our legislators have not been able to devise laws to deal with the hackers of the 1980s. It is doubtful that they would be any more successful in trying the capture the activities of the new generations of hackers in new laws. As mobile data communications and multimedia facilities become more of a reality, the scope for hackers to interfere with all forms of broadcasts will expand significantly. It may become a new form of intellectual 'joy riding', but as with cars, who should carry the responsibility for protection? Should the car manufacturers and the owners fit better locks and alarms on high-powered cars, or should the law threaten ever heavier penalties as a deterrent to the bored young? Similarly, should the IT industry not accept some responsibility for improving security? When cheap measures such as the automatic call-back device would make it more difficult for the remote hacker to gain access, there is a strong case for requiring computer manufacturers and users to put their own houses in order before the criminal law is involved. Indeed, in the case of *R v Vatsal Patel* [1993] the evidence that the computer system was so unprotected and unstable completely undermined the prosecution case that the defendant had sabotaged the software system by making unauthorized modifications while it was under development. Consequently, the jury had no sympathy for the complainant company and acquitted the defendant.

Summary

We have considered the issue of threats to data security in this chapter. These threats lie in unauthorized access to data, which may result in breaches of confidentiality or data corruption and loss. Organizations addressing these problems must first define the security risks and set a sensitivity level for each classification of data. Logical access controls can then be established where necessary to identify and authenticate each proposed user:

- A password or PIN limits access to those who know the word or number but, to be effective, the system of allocating or selecting that knowledge must be properly administered. The level of protection achieved is only as good as the people who are to make it work.
- Once the user has logged in, there may be further controls to limit access to files, transactions or functions. This allows the creation of tiers of authorization within the system, with each member of staff profiled to set an appropriate level of access for their particular job function.

- Control must also be established over data flows and the ability of users to draw inferences from the data stored. One of the main mechanisms of protection is encryption, where otherwise readable text is encoded. Thus, only the user with the correct key may read the data.
- Hackers now represent a real threat as more systems are distributed and networked. Other dangers are computer viruses and the capacity to electronically eavesdrop.
- The Computer Misuse Act 1990 has been designed to fill in gaps in the criminal law. A recent well-publicized first instance case suggests that juries may not find the activities of some hackers to be truly criminal.

Self-test questions

1. Identify the main elements of logical access control.
2. Outline the main features of inference controls.
3. Define hacking and explain the main practical dangers hackers represent to computer operations.
4. What is electronic eavesdropping?

Exam-style questions

1. There is evidence that 'hackers' have gained unauthorized access to the computer system at your place of work. This has led to discussion within the organization on ways in which password security might be improved, to some speculation as to how 'hackers' may try to gain access to the system in the future and to planning countermeasures to prevent such access.

   Prepare a report describing the common methods of improving the security of a password and identifying the most likely ways in which a hacker might attempt to gain unauthorized access to the system. Make suggestions for suitable countermeasures.
2. Your organization, part of the defence industry, is undergoing a thorough review of its computer security procedures. It uses a local area network (LAN) to handle large amounts of data, much of which are secret. The organization has established a set of physical access controls and also has a sophisticated system of passwords to control logical access. The next stage in its security plan is to apply data encryption techniques to all sensitive data which are carried by its LAN.

   You have been asked to research and to report briefly on five suitable methods of data encryption, indicating their relative merits, so that a final choice can be made.
3. Your company's computer system has been subject to a spate of 'hacking' by temporary clerical staff who have, it is suspected, copied customers' details which would be valuable to your competitors. They have also changed the data in the

general ledger so that a costly adjustment exercise is required to 'balance the books'.

Your boss, the chief accountant, who studied law some ten years ago (and is therefore not familiar with the Computer Misuse Act 1990), is bemoaning the fact that the law is powerless to deal with the culprits. You, however, are not so sure. Describe how you would explain to your boss the offences which were created by the Act and discuss whether they represent a real improvement to the law.

(All answers on pages 572–573)

CHAPTER 18

Security design and operation

Introduction

The old question, 'Who will guard the guards?' is even more significant in the electronic age than when a Roman satirist first posed it 2000 years ago. At a time when so much valuable information is not only held on computers but increasingly (through developments such as electronic data interchange) exchanged between them – and when so much of that information is related to confidential matters, such as financial strategies or R & D projects, or transferred internationally, as in securities trading – the design of security systems must clearly keep pace with advances in technology and with the opportunities which those advances may offer for industrial espionage or systems abuse.

After considering the risks that are presented to security systems and to the data they hold, we now turn to the fundamental points of system design and to the operational features necessary to produce an effective security system. In particular, we look at methods of controlling the data itself and of the manner of its processing; we discuss whether the risks become greater if decision and administration support systems are used to aid the data processing and decision making; and we consider the advantages and disadvantages of creating and running a distributed system. We go on to examine whether a microcomputer environment can be made secure and what happens when micros are turned into gateways either to a single mainframe or to LANS. Lastly, we turn to the matter of fraud, giving attention to the main methods of perpetrating fraud, the best ways in which to investigate suspicions of fraud and, regardless of whether the investigation is undertaken by the auditors or some other investigative group, what tests to apply to discover the nature of the fraud.

Internal data controls

The designers of effective data security systems adopt several basic principles as their starting point:

- First, the underlying design criteria should not be secret – there are two reasons for this:
  - a new system is improved if its detailed features are exposed to constructive criticism by a significant number of both designers and users
  - long as the system is effective, the more people are aware of the system,

the greater the potential deterrent value (however, if a flaw is detected, the greater the number of people who may get to know about it).

- Next, each interface between the software and the users should be kept simple and natural otherwise even the most tolerant of users will be tempted to bypass it.
- Every access ought to be checked to see if appropriate authority has been given. If access is in doubt, access should be denied because denial is preferable to unauthorized access.
- Lastly, the underlying design assumption should be that the final system will have to operate in a *hostile* environment where it will be exposed to frequent threats. The resulting 'worst possible case' system should be reasonably secure.

Human-based accounting controls

Within the overall ambit of the physical and logical security systems, detailed accounting controls over the data and over subsequent management reporting should be built into the various software applications to ensure that the data are properly and accurately processed. At an organizational level, perhaps the most important internal control is the positive **segregation of duties** among the staff. As a general rule, no single employee should have the responsibility for all the stages in the processing of a transaction. The aim is to produce a situation where it would always require at least two employees acting together to make a fraud possible. The most important aspects of segregation of duties are that:

- The tasks of preparation and validation of the input data should be performed independently of any check of the resulting output.
- Computer operators should not be allowed to amend the system software or data, and should be denied access to the detailed program documentation.
- Programmers and systems analysts should not be allowed unsupervised access to the computer.
- New programs should not be tested or checked by the team that wrote the code.
- Neither the operators nor the programmers should have responsibility for the operation of the library of programs and data back-up/archive copies and/or the system documentation.

These rules should be seen against the background of the main advantages of an on-line system which are that all users could be allowed to input data from the terminals in their own departments, and that each user department is potentially able to check the latest state of the data. If adequate security is to be maintained, these advantages may have to be compromised. Hence, the types of transaction that can be initiated and authorized by each department should be clearly defined and limited in the light of the known vulnerabilities. Moreover, all potentially sensitive data should be independently validated before the main system files are updated. This may require that all input is to be stored in a collection file and not merged into the main files until proper validation and authorization checks have been made. The main disadvantage of such a safeguard is that users cannot operate in real-time and be allowed access to the up-to-date data. Indeed, it is not unusual in the more sensitive applications to find that only the previous day's situation is available for consultation. This may not be suitable for a significant number of organization systems where an absolutely contemporary record may be required – for example, airline reservation and stock systems benefit from real-time processing.

In many systems, the data may be scheduled to pass through several stages in the input process. Errors, whether innocent or fraudulent and usually human, are always possible. One way of detecting errors is by comparing input to the output, transaction by transaction. This can be expensive in terms of time, but it may be the only effective way to prevent fraud in many situations. As you should be aware, batch controls may be effective, but they cannot work in real-time systems, so validation routines must be built into real-time systems to check each individual entry before the core files are amended. This would be in addition to post-process or post-input batching which allows the operator(s) to check batch totals after a given number of transactions have been processed. Then, if a discrepancy arises, for example if serial numbers are out of order or missing, a manual check can be made. To operate efficiently, such a system requires some form of input document, whether form or record, which should be kept in the department which submitted the transaction for processing. Without this, there is nothing to batch and so other compensating controls must be built in.

A system design

Let us consider, by way of example, an organization designing a teleordering system. The following human-based security features would be required:

- In the first instance, only orders from recognized customers would be accepted (with the additional safeguard that recognition should be given and monitored by someone other than the telesales operator).
- Then, order values would only be accepted up to predefined credit limits, with deliveries only made to authorized addresses.
- In general, procedures would have to be established which would create an audit trail back to the originator of the order. This would normally rely on a user ID, date and time, with the customer also required to give some form of password.
- Phone-back for formal confirmation of the order would then be made to prestored and authenticated numbers. In some organizations, where the unit cost of the items to be manipulated is high, it would be sound practice to tape-record all such telephone calls.

With such a system in operation, the organization could be reasonably confident that errors and abuses would either be detected, or would not cause excessive loss in the short term. The security arises from the degree of protection given to the individual component data elements and the ability to link transactions to identified employees and customers.

Automated controls

Simply creating manual systems which will enhance security is not enough. Organizations must also build in both general and particular software controls. So the first safeguard is that the programs, once validated, should not be changed. Assuming the validation confirms the proper operation of the programs, avoiding any changes will reduce the chance of introducing accidental bugs or fraudulent elements into the programs and so limit the danger of corruption to the data through software malfunction while the data items are being input or manipulated. This confirms and consolidates the fundamental objective of hardware security which is to protect the data which may become sensitive information if they fall into the wrong hands.

CPU operation

The designers must then turn their attention to the operation of the standard CPU. In real memory protection, the memory should be partitioned into a series of mutually exclusive areas to which access may be separately controlled. When a program is being executed in a controlled area, the program execution should abort if an error is detected. The same effect can be achieved through the creation of a *bounds register* which keeps track of the events taking place or proposed within a protected area. Some areas can be locked so that sensitive programs can only be executed if the user has a key for access. For these purposes, the system software has overriding rights over all the other software. Since library-based programs are not fixed to one area, their protection cannot be achieved by memory protection alone. The standard security systems therefore use *binary execution states* or *multiple execution states*. Each possible state will be classified so that the system will know whether it is executing in a privileged supervisory state or in a non-privileged state. In other words, only a user with the proper profile may access particular programs in each state and only a program user in a privileged state can issue privileged instructions. Multiple-state architecture allows programs to have a hierarchy of privileges and allows the sharing of resources under conditions of mutual mistrust.

Data verification

Similarly, despite the fact that the more detailed checking systems increase CPU time and reduce run times, individual data element validation by software ensures that the data input is within the predetermined parameters. In real-time systems, data which are rejected can be highlighted on the screen so that the terminal operator can review the item, and if the error has been caused by an obvious keying error, re-input the correct value for the variable. However, it may not be desirable to allow operators to change any of the data (because of security implications, perhaps, or because the operators are not known to be conscientious or alert) and, in those cases, the data should be referred back to the user for validation. In general, proper controls should be maintained over all data input rejections. Error reports are usually printed out and the record stored pending investigation. Regular review of this suspense file should detect regular errors or offenders. Data verification procedures should be followed to achieve a correct and complete transcription from data to machine-readable form. This is particularly important because errors not detected during this phase may cause loss of integrity and produce unreliable data for decision making. In general, processing controls are designed to prevent or detect the following types of error:

- the incomplete or duplicated processing of input transactions
- processing and updating the wrong files
- processing illogical, incomplete or unreasonable input
- loss or distortion of data during processing.

The main methods of **verification** are:

1. **Visual**, comparing the keyed version with source materials; as a method, this is error-prone and time-consuming but it may be the only option available.
2. **Key**, which involves keying the data in twice and then comparing the two sets of data; again, this is time-consuming.
3. **Internal software checks** for reasonableness, consistency and completeness – that is, validation checks:
   - **Data format checks** ascertain that:
     - all mandatory fields exist; or
     - the correct number and composition of alphabetic and numeric characters exist, i.e. that all information fields are complete and the fields contain data of the expected type; or
     - if it is an updating transaction, the target record is present.
   - **Limit or reasonableness checks** ensure that the data are within acceptable bounds; for example, if the number of hours worked in a given week exceeds a specified limit, claims for overtime can be investigated.
   - **A check digit control** is one in which numbers, usually account or stock reference numbers, are computed in accordance with a special formula to produce an extra digit for validation purposes. This provides good protection against transposition, transcription, omission or addition and the random errors which are likely if the operator is routinely typing in meaningless numbers.
   - **Cross-casting checks** can be applied so that the computer automatically validates arithmetic.
   - **Sequencing checks** ensure that the data elements are input in the required order (this is useful if it is coupled with the use of prenumbered stationery, but care is required to recover if an error is detected in the sequence).
   - **Batch controls**. At an early point in the system, independent totals of documents are accumulated by a control group, and are later matched against totals derived from the processing of the same documents by the DP department. The three most common types of batch total are the following:
     - *control total* – usually a meaningful money total such as the total of credit sales
     - *hash total* – a total that need not have any significance other than as a batch total, for example a total of customer account numbers
     - *record count* – a count of the number of documents or transactions processed.

The process of data validation is necessary both during data collection and data entry before any of the data are used within the application software, and continuously as new data are generated by the software. Output controls are therefore designed to ensure that:

- the processed results are accurate
- only authorized personnel receive the output.

Checking output

The psychology of users is important in this respect. Most lay, but computer-literate, users will judge the quality of an information system by its output. Output should therefore be checked as thoroughly as possible before being released to authorized users by the approved distribution routes. If the output is viewed as sensitive, the fact and manner of distribution should be logged. On receipt, the user should check the output as a matter of routine, and should report any errors. This discipline should be encouraged from the first day in the implementation stage of the system and the resultant feedback should help to build a more error-free system. (To maintain data security once validated, all data media when off-line should be kept in a secure place – the appointment of a competent data librarian is perhaps an advisable step in the larger organization where a reasonable quantity of sensitive material has to be stored.)

Verification

To some extent, this section has been written from a batch-processing perspective which is more periodic in nature. On-line systems do not require that data from source documents be transferred to machine-readable form before processing takes place. Indeed, it is not necessary that a source document be created for individual transaction elements when an on-line system is used. This difference does not change the security considerations underlying automated controls. While we should recognize the importance of limiting access to the terminals and having password controls on different types of editing functions, we should note that the effective machine-based verification systems outlined above remain vital. However, given the potential lack of physical documents, the creation of audit trails assumes primary significance. Thus, it may be expedient that all sensitive transactions and master file changes should be recorded on another set of files, accessible only to authorized personnel so that, in the event of error or fraud, transactions may be reviewed and the master files recreated.

Support systems and networks

The standard decision support systems include spreadsheet and database packages which may be used for sensitive operations such as corporate planning. The problem is how to guard against unauthorized access and retrieval. In multi-user environments, unauthorized staff may be able to oversee the screens or to use the relevant terminals without supervision. Separate terminal rooms with access limited to authorized personnel or with supervised usage may be the answer, or controls should be established within the packages which offer an acceptable level of security. Hence, it may be necessary to write macros to protect individual data items within the package, or to inhibit the more sensitive processes.

Administrative support systems include diaries, messaging and reminder systems, and telephone, network and other directories. Special function diaries can be created, say, to control room bookings. Modern systems tend to be menu-driven and user-friendly, and to be integrated with other office systems. Access to documentation on some of the more sensitive functions may have to be controlled. It should be the responsibility of the owners of personal diary systems to control access to them – legitimately, colleagues and secretaries will require access to them to arrange meetings, but other parts of the system should be passworded. Thus, if electronic mail systems are likely to carry sensitive information, the mail boxes should be properly protected.

Planning and consolidation

At the heart of designing a network lies the need to identify the present information flows and to make the reasons for introducing the automated systems explicit. The plan will list the existing hardware and software packages, and provide an outline guide as to what will be required to aim at ensuring an integrated system. The greater the degree of hardware and software compatibility that can be built up, the more likely it is that the organization will be able to generate real expertise in the particular systems. On the purchasing side, economies of scale may be achieved and maintenance should be more straightforward. The overall organization strategy needs to be broken down to a departmental level, allowing for logical connections and exchanges between departments as required. The objective of the plan should be to encourage and consolidate the basic and natural information flows between departments. In this, the departments should play a direct role in the design exercise. This will help to encourage good morale.

The chain of security

In any distributed system, the best control systems operate hierarchically. Thus, local controls should be organized so that the feed of information into the central control system and into peer systems is clearly identified and provides an adequate level of security at each major interface. This will allow the maintenance of a proper data trail whenever data are transferred from one location to the next, and should permit the identification of all those who have been involved at each stage of the transmission. This cannot of itself eradicate errors, but it allows warnings and/or training to be targeted at the staff most at fault. Indeed, mistakes are always more likely to arise if the responsibility for data input is not given to a core of well-trained and motivated staff.

The problem of intrusion

All the major applications rely on a foundation of system software, including the operating system. This is a complex and comprehensive set of program modules which allows the applications software to use the resources of the computer, e.g. input and output system, executive program to initiate and terminate application programs, accounting and statistics functions, etc. An operating system must also be able to identify each user and the resources uniquely. The security problem is that penetration of the operating system potentially allows access to all the other resources which it supports and controls. This form of intrusion requires specialist knowledge and appropriate opportunity for access both physical and logical.

To safeguard information in a distributed system, one of the standard strategies is that of **intrusion avoidance**. This can be difficult to implement successfully because:

- sometimes there is significant geographical separation of the component parts which can make it so difficult to defend all the physical access points
- the resultant complexity of the configuration can make it difficult to design comprehensive and effective logical access controls.

Further, once the system has been penetrated by an unauthorized person, all the intrusion avoidance controls are useless. Encryption can be used to defend the data once someone has gained entry, but the effectiveness of this strategy depends on good key management and the processing capacity of the intruder to decrypt the protected data. Generally, in the design of distributed systems, there is a conflict between data security techniques and techniques to promote reliability and availability. For example, if the designer reduces the number of access points for security purposes, several parts of the system may tend to become redundant. However, if parts of the system are isolated from each other, this can become the basis of the alternative strategy of **intrusion tolerance**. Here, the philosophy is to accept that intrusion is likely at some time during the system's life cycle and to take steps to minimize the effect of that intrusion – for example, by fragmenting the data throughout the system and only allowing reconstitution to those who have authority to enter the file management system which holds a directory of fragment locations.

Micro security issues

More and more businesses have become dependent on micros and the personal computer as the cost of suitable hardware and software has fallen. Yet the advertised virtues of these machines as accessible and user-friendly actually indicate the reality of the security problem.

The first step in securing a highly portable piece of equipment is to limit physical access to it, locking it away at night. All the back-up disks should be stored in a safe place. The risks from the staff should also be considered and good office habits encouraged: there should, for instance, be no eating and drinking near the computer or the disks. For planning purposes, managers must start with the recognition that, regardless of the size of the organization or of the computer system, all dependence increases vulnerability. Unfortunately, manufacturers tend to ignore security in the designs of small machines. Indeed, the pace of development in hardware terms, has forced the development of more sophisticated operating systems which can now permit multitasking and make access to all the machine functions easier. These machines are marketed with the boast that it is possible to provide effective memory organization and disk management. But security requires that all privileged facilities should be protectable and it should be difficult, if not impossible, to alter the operating system files. This must be carefully considered when purchasing machines for sensitive uses.

Micro-systems are most vulnerable during the input phase because data may easily be altered, lost or damaged – most of the manufacturers' internal data controls are weak and allow users to introduce false data. Even if the users enter genuine data, most micros tend to leave that data poorly protected, and all systems are vulnerable to software bugs whether accidental or malicious. Similarly, virus programs can be introduced (whether innocently or not) but then do considerable damage. In a sense, therefore, the manufacturers' failure to remedy the inadequacies of the standard operating systems presents the users with the opportunity to circumvent all the other controls which may have been introduced by the security conscious manager.

The micro as a gateway

The maintenance of access controls becomes more difficult if the user uses the computer as a gateway to another machine or network. Users should think carefully whether it is desirable to establish a link between the microcomputer and a mainframe, or whether a link with a network is really required. If a link is made, the use should have some system to impose security on downloaded data to prevent misuse or theft. Internal software controls can be supplemented by physical systems to prevent copying on to non-approved disks. Similarly, internal controls on data uploaded to the mainframe can try to ensure data integrity on that machine. These controls will also help to maintain proper audit trails, but all networks are only as secure as its weakest link.

Methods of fraud

The manipulation of computer systems for financial gain must result in the creation of false accounting records. Thus, to conceal a shortage, the book value of assets must be adjusted to correspond with the post-loss situation. This apparent agreement can be achieved either by simply misrepresenting the value, or by manipulating the accounting records. In general, the main methods of fraud include:

- **False input** – suppressing or falsifying transaction data before or as it is input. This may be achieved:
  - by entering additional data
  - by failing to enter valid data
  - by simply altering the data.

- **False data** can be created at one or more of several points:
  - at the data preparation stage
  - on manual entry
  - through the use of false bar codes or some other automated means
  - a wide range of corruptions and errors can trigger the computer into non-acceptance of the data – this facility can be exploited so that, when rejected into a suspense account, the data can be fraudulently manipulated.
- **False output** – output can be destroyed or withheld to conceal the impact of the fraud, for example to reduce liabilities or improve performance. The basic devices rely on the fact that output can be reprocessed or reprinted with the originals destroyed or by editing files while they are in the buffer awaiting printing. Output may also be inflated by double printing.

The failure to enter valid data is the most difficult to detect because there will not be an audit trail to show any later alterations. The common types of transactions used for this purpose involve the creation of false purchase or sales details, the incurring of expenses, additions to the payroll, etc., and each of these transactions is likely to be allocated an entry code which will signal a sequence of events: so, for example, a cash sale code might require the preparation of an invoice, debiting the cash account, crediting the cash sales account and adjusting the stock inventory. The most vulnerable codes are those which allow the movement of goods or funds and managers should introduce audit checks to ensure that the relevant sequences of event have taken place as required by the system.

Fraud strategies

Fraud is nothing more than a deception that causes a loss and it can be aimed at a wide variety of possible targets including shareholders, customers, suppliers, bankers and external auditors. Frauds against shareholders and people outside the organization will almost certainly include producing false accounts. The motive may be simply to conceal losses or, more deviously, to pull in more investment money or loans where the quality of the investment does not justify it. Frauds against employers include:

- bribery
- extortion (for example, threats to poison products or to destroy computer records)
- pirating copyright or patented information or commercial espionage
- manipulation of electronic funds transfer systems or in-house data or the more crude theft of goods or cheques, and so on.

The most effective frauds will involve one or more of the following strategies:

1. **The manipulation of master files** such as the payroll master, which will contain details of the employees and their salary and commission rates, or the sales master, which contains details of prices, discounts, approval of customers and credit limits. These manipulations may be immediate to cover particular transactions, or long term. They usually affect pricing and are often collusive with buyers – for example, to sell stocked goods at an excessive discount, posting debits to a separate discount file to conceal the loss.

2 **The misuse of suspense accounts.** It is standard practice that all rejected and unallocated data are held pending clarification in an edit/error cycle or is posted to suspense accounts for later review. At its lowest level, this allows managers to monitor the accuracy of those responsible for keying in the data. More seriously, it acts as a fraud filter. But there is always an opportunity to commit a fraud if entries which should be posted to personal accounts are posted to a suspense account, or vice versa. The opportunity arises if the data held in a suspense account can be altered before being inspected and allocated by the auditing staff.
3 **The misuse of restricted utilities.** These are the powerful software tools used by programmers to fix faulty systems and to assist in housekeeping. They are normally (but dangerously) kept on a systems disk and are invoked by using the appropriate password. Because these utilities can be used for a variety of data checking and amendment purposes, the scope for fraudulent use is significant and particularly tempting because most do not leave an audit trail.
4 **The introduction of program patches.** These can divert data into a fraudulent routine. The switch from a legitimate to a fraudulent routine will be triggered by a conditional jump statement. The trigger may be a customer name or by any other identified transaction: it is, then, a conditional statement requiring a modification of the standard system, either to accept or reject the data, or to manipulate it in some way. Such traps can be placed anywhere in the system. To be able to write and place the patch the fraudulent programmer must:

   - know exactly what the program does
   - have access and the time and skill to be able to change it
   - be able to test the patch and conceal it, etc.

   High levels of skill are required to create patches, but the rewards are that patches usually leave no trace of their operation and they are not detectable by the ordinary auditing techniques (in any testing of the system by introducing dummy data, the patch will never be detected unless the auditor accidentally matches the dummy data to the conditional statement). Program patches can be introduced into the software at any time either during the initial writing, or later during maintenance or updating.
5 **The manipulation of job control (JCL) instructions.** Job control or *executable* programs direct the process of a computer application: they tell the computer which program to execute, which data to read and where to make the output. JCL is a high-level language which interfaces with the operating system and automates much of the work of the operators. JCL instructions are usually held on-line on a systems disk, and may be patched to divert processing to a fraudulent program or master file. Making successful changes to an operating system calls for high skill and time, so the use of this method is rare.
6 **The conversion of assets.** This is the process whereby the data manipulation is turned into a financial gain. Hence, although the manipulation of accounts and stock records may have led to the delivery of goods to an address, these goods must then be sold in a way which does not give rise to suspicion.

The manipulation of *incoming* data can be the most difficult to identify. So, for example, incoming cheques may be omitted from the cash book and ledgers, but either included in the banking returns to cover previous cash shortages or (if not crossed) simply endorsed and negotiated through a third party outside the victim's records. Equally difficult to detect is the conversion of disbursement cheques through the alteration of the payee names or (if the cheque is not crossed) endorsement to third party. This type of fraud is made very difficult to investigate if the fraudster is able to destroy all cheques after their return through the banking system. Finally, the significant growth in the volume of electronic funds transfers has made the system vulnerable to the one-time smash-and-grab frauds where the criminal simply changes the destination account number or otherwise alters the payment instructions. It is usual to divert the funds to tax haven countries in which follow-up investigations will be difficult.

The insurance safety net

It is clear that any company may become the victim of fraud, whether electronic or not. But, in statistical terms, only a small number of these frauds will cause significant loss. It has been the custom to consider passing the risk of loss through fraud on to others through insurance as a safety net – not only where more significant losses are likely to be sustained, but also where it is not possible to make the controls wholly adequate. But managers should also consider whether self-insurance would meet their needs. In general, insurance through external carrier will only be of marginal assistance at best, even if it should be obtainable at an economic rate. Managers should therefore install the best possible security controls and make a provision against losses in each year's accounts. Over a period of time, the aim would be to build up a substantial buffer fund against potential losses. Thus, formal insurance would only be considered when other forms of risk management seem ineffective and where the consequences of those strategies failing would be unacceptable. There is no justification for purchasing irrelevant insurance cover, or insurance cover for its own sake. If organizations do decide to approach the insurance market, it should only be with a clear specification of their needs and a determination not to be distracted, or in a spirit prepared to make a critical evaluation of the advice received. Carriers are usually prepared to amend and extend coverage to suit the needs of each proposer. It is simply a matter of negotiating what is required and nothing more.

What to do when a fraud is suspected

If a fraud is suspected, the organization should maintain absolute secrecy. Unless this is done, the criminals involved will be forewarned, documents may disappear and witnesses may be discouraged. It is advisable for organizations to have a formal policy, laying down the standard procedures to be followed in each of the anticipated situations. Sadly, many investigations fail because managers cannot decide what they want the immediate outcome to be.

The first question to decide is whether the organization should have a policy of always prosecuting identified criminals. The factors to bear in mind are:

- the automatic prosecution of all those detected may be a deterrent to others
- the conviction can be used as a basis on to claim a compensation order, or it will shift the burden of proof in any subsequent civil action to recover money and assets taken
- prosecution, regardless of outcome, may be a condition of the insurance policy
- failing to prosecute gives the thief an unfair advantage when applying for another job where the same crime may be repeated.

In deciding to refer the matter for investigation by the police and possible prosecution, there are three considerations:

- fraud trials may be difficult for juries to understand and the law requires that if there is any doubt in the mind of the jury, the defendant(s) should be acquitted – the managers may therefore go through an expensive and potentially damaging exercise, and not get the satisfaction of a conviction
- whether or not there is a conviction, the evidence of poor security systems may lead to criticism of the complainant organization and its management by shareholders, banks and institutional investors
- trials are open to the public so criminals may attend to hear the evidence, or the press coverage of the trial may reveal details of the method of fraud for other criminals to learn from.

But to fail to refer the matter to the police for their investigation is to encourage more fraud. In all cases, dishonest employees should leave their employment. The certainty of dismissal is a deterrent to others and sympathy for the criminal's spouse and family should not obscure this long-term truth. Weak policies in this whole area are self-defeating. Further, a useful by-product of the investigations, internal and external, should also be consideration of how the defences may be improved for the future so that the organization learns from its mistakes.

Investigation

When the objectives for the investigation have been agreed, the investigation itself may move forward. The victim should consider the mechanics of the suspected fraud:

- the number and identity of those involved
- the likely methods of fraud used
- which documentary and computerized records will have been falsified
- the scale of the probable losses involved
- why the fraud was not detected earlier.

The investigation should never be based on the assumption that the alleged wrongdoers have only committed one fraud. The organization should always plan for the worst possible case. Plans should then be made to catch the criminals with the best chance of getting good-quality evidence of their dishonesty. The first priority is to identify what documentary or computerized records might be destroyed by the criminals if they wished to hide their activities and move rapidly to secure them. In seizing records, it is always advisable to take all the documents that may be relevant. Those which prove irrelevant can be returned later. At this stage, the organization should seek positive legal advice on how to search for and seize other evidence. If people are to be arrested while working, a stand-by team of trusted operators should stand by and move in quickly when the suspects are arrested.

Once the physical evidence has been collected, the analysis of documents and computer records must begin. The investigators should aim to identify all deviations from the known procedures. All fraud depends to some extent on modifications to the accepted practice so all possible explanations for each identified deviation should be made. This will be added to the forensic and expert evidence (as to how the computer systems work or ought to work, the methods of manipulation, authorship of documents, and so on), the interviews with the suspects and other pretext investigations (such as test purchases from a suspected pirate or fence, undercover operations to infiltrate the group suspected, asset tracing, and so on). The end product should be the preparation of schedules of evidence so that otherwise complex evidence can be presented in a way more easily understood. In the case of long-term frauds, schedules of loss should be cross referenced to the documents. Building up the case in this way will make it more likely that a jury can understand what has happened and make the conviction more certain.

Auditing steps

Accounts are designed to show the immediate profitability and net worth of a business. But as well as meeting the information needs of the management, accounting procedures must operate within a number of constraints:

- the need to preserve commercial confidentiality while maintaining shareholder confidence
- the need to comply with statutory reporting requirements
- professional accounting standards
- the desire of the Inland Revenue to take the proper proportion of tax on behalf of the state.

In order to achieve a meaningful overview, the organization must start by keeping proper records of each transaction on a daily basis. These are then summarized and consolidated into records representing a longer time span until an annual account is achieved. There are a number of interdependent ratios which can then be applied to assist in measuring the performance of a commercial enterprise. Without resorting to illegality, these ratios can be improved through commercial manipulation: for instance, by arranging to pay off some of its liabilities before accounts are finalized, the organization can favourably adjust the current ratio which is often used as one of the criteria in deciding whether to offer credit facilities.

Modern accountancy depends on the double-entry system. Hence, for each credit entry, there must be a corresponding debit and vice versa. When an asset is removed, a related account should be debited with its worth. The point of any manipulation is therefore to conceal the debit:

- by suppressing it altogether
- by creating a false credit; or
- by posting it to a safe account.

If debits must ultimately appear, they may either reduce profitability or overstate net worth (suppression of sales, for example, affects profits while theft of cash reduces net worth), but if the cash shortage is concealed by posting the debits to the accounts of the customers, the loss is hidden in the balance sheet. In all instances, the effect of these concealment methods is cumulative and may covertly destroy the worth of the business. The extent of the problem will be dictated by the number of loosely controlled accounts within the personal and nominal ledger structure, and the number of people having access to them. Within the accounts, the following divisions will be found:

- **Personal accounts** which relate to individual customers, suppliers, and so on.
- **Nominal accounts** which summarize assets, liabilities, expenses, and so on.
- **Real accounts** which relate to physical assets.
- **Suspense accounts** which hold entries which cannot be posted to one of the other accounts. The fact that these accounts cannot immediately be reconciled makes them vulnerable to fraud.
- **Control accounts** which summarize and check on the accuracy of individual postings to ledgers. The assumption is usually that if the control accounts agree, the accounts from which they are derived must also agree.

When attempting to assess the reliability of an organization's reporting and accounting system, the following records are essential reference materials:

- stock records which show current inventory
- invoices, delivery notes, and so on
- transportation records, for example routing sheets and drivers' logs
- management reports which summarize sales and purchases against targets or previous year's figures
- vouchers, expense claim forms, and so on.

The main verification tests

A number of strategies can be used to test the veracity of documents and the reliability of persons and other organizations in relation to suspected fraud.

Customer or client verification

One of the more obvious ways by which to defraud organizations is to hide the loss of value by recording the supply goods and/or valuable services on credit to fictitious customers or clients. It is therefore essential to verify the persons, firms and organizations which are listed as receiving value from the organization. It is also prudent to appraise the creditworthiness of a random list of customers and clients.

The master files should be checked to identify accommodation addresses, Post Office boxes and anything else which might suggest a false address for delivery purposes – for example, the addresses of present or ex-employees. Equally, names which might easily be altered should be identified on the files used to produce disbursement cheques – for instance, the initials IBM are easily changed to IB Marshall.

Invoice verification

Another common method of fraud is to insert false invoices into the system for payment. It is usual for the accounts to reflect services rather than goods because the missing value does not show up on stocktaking or as a loss of profit expectation. The first step is to identify invoices which do not have a telephone or VAT registration number, or which appear to use an accommodation address. Auditors should be suspicious of invoices that are copies rather than originals, or which are unfolded and so may not have been sent through the post. It is also sensible to investigate invoices which appear to have been altered or modified in some way, or where a complete numerical invoice sequence has been sent – it would be quite unusual for a business to have only one customer.

Ledger verification

If all that investigators do is to assume that the basic ledger structure is accurate and so merely check debit and credit entries from supporting documentation, there is very little chance of detecting fraud. Investigators should examine accounts opened after the appointment of individuals who occupy sensitive jobs, typically those who act as buyers or as authorized signatories to purchase orders and invoices. They should also look for changes in trends. Fraud distorts the usual organization patterns and even the most careful criminals find it impossible to guarantee long-term stability and consistency. The best tests would compare the current year's with one or more of the previous year's purchase ledger and budgetary cost centre records, so that any unusual trends in the volumes passing through an account would become apparent. One sign of fraud may be that individuals consistently authorize payments to the same payees close to their authority levels. These tests should be combined with perpetrator analysis (see Chapter 15) or job sensitivity analysis (see Chapter 19). Credit cards issued in the organization's name as well as those used by individual employees and managers are also vulnerable.

Tests to detect possible corruption

Bribery is a fairly common problem and, potentially, it involves all those employees and managers who are in a position to influence a decision in favour of a third party. The organization is particularly vulnerable in the areas of purchasing and procurement. If the organization uses competitive tendering, it should routinely check the background of a sample of those tendering to see whether there is any evidence of links between them. Even though the best value tenders may have been accepted, this does not mean that the best price will be paid. Investigators should check published price lists if the products to be supplied are in common use. If the contracts are for labour or services, or the price will be based on third-party invoices, investigators should check to see whether labour costs appear to be above industry norms or whether the invoices may be verified independently. In this way, it should be possible to identify those cases in which inflated prices have been paid. As a further check against bid rigging, it may be useful to check the ownership of suspected companies and their associates.

Tests to detect the conversion of outgoing cheques

A random sample of cheques cleared through the banking system should be examined to discover and check the propriety of:

- any endorsements to third parties
- cheques paid through building society accounts rather than business accounts
- cheques made payable to non-commercial customers
- any renumbering or other alteration, etc.

Any such cheques may evidence possible fraud.

Tests to detect the theft of incoming cheques

This is one of the more difficult frauds to detect. The success of any investigation depends on whether the organization was expecting payment to arrive, and on the way in which the cheques would be handled when received. Investigators should examine the bank paying-in slips. Often unrecorded or improperly recorded cheques will be used to conceal thefts of cash, or differences in the dates of payment in may be used to delay the discovery of the loss, say, by adjusting time and manipulating credits on a group of accounts to make it appear that the residual debits on each account are within credit limits. This is part of the more general problem that money from one customer can be paid into the accounts of others to conceal previous thefts, so it is advisable to trace sample entries to make sure that this is not happening. Further, the investigators should write to a randomly selected sample of customers asking for details of all payments made to the organization in a given time period (it may be necessary to pay the costs of the customers contacted for extracting this information from their accounts). So long as there is no collusion between the in-house criminal and the third-party firms, this is a foolproof way of detecting suppressed income.

Tests to detect frauds in sales and marketing

The standard frauds are based on suppression, the aim being to acquire goods or services without being charged for them or to convert incoming payments. The need is therefore to detect uninvoiced sales, underpriced sales or the adjustment of posted entries. The creation of false sales credits and cancelled orders is also common way of hiding a theft, but it may be detected because the thieves may not be able to create the false source documents to support these entries. Delivery notes and invoices should also be checked for any signs of alteration. This will detect frauds such as recording a sale to a third-party customer as if it was an interbranch transfer of stock; once the invoice is created and the goods priced, the name and/or the delivery address on the invoice is simply changed. Investigators should also randomly attempt to inspect goods which have been:

- sent to remote warehouses
- placed ready for sale or scrap

- used for advertising or promotional purposes
- sent to other premises without being invoiced.

All entries of this in the stock control accounts are commonly used to hide fraud.

Tests to detect stock, asset and inventory losses

Any goods which are portable can be carried out of the premises in bags or briefcases. Bulky items may have to be removed more openly by creating false documentation to trigger delivery to 'safe addresses'. If the organization is to install an effective system for the control of the inventory, it must create an interlocking documentary system which accurately shows:

- when and where specific goods arrive
- who accepted responsibility for the delivered goods matching the invoices
- where the goods are stored before, during and after any required processing
- the date and destination of their delivery out.

All organizations are at risk at the beginning of this recording process because suppliers or dishonest delivery drivers may deliver short quantities or goods which are of a poorer quality than the price requires. Only identified individuals should be allowed to accept goods on behalf of the organization and there should be formal controls to verify the quantity and quality of the deliveries. Quite apart from helping to ensure the honesty of suppliers, it will also help to preserve the buyer's right if short quantities and unmerchantable goods are identified and rejected immediately. Once on the premises, random spot checks can then test to see whether the expected goods are where the records claim they should be. However, physical counting is only useful if it is paralleled by other paper-based controls such as those targeted on other vulnerabilities such as sales suppression, purchase inflation, etc.

In this battle against theft and fraud, the annual stocktaking is particularly important. Before deciding which sites to visit and which product lines to focus on, the auditors should consider the reasonableness of the alleged stock holding in the light of the storage space known to be available in each site and in relation to the turnover recorded. Hence, if the rates of return on capital invested on highly portable lines of stock are low, this would be suspicious. Similarly, the auditors should identify those product lines which appear to have the longest shelf life. The obvious problem for any thief is that fictitious stock can never be sold. Stock actually removed from the premises must be recorded as a book asset and appear to be under-utilized capital. So if a check of the documentation shows that the classification of stock has been changed from fast turnover lines to lines known to be very slow moving, this will be seen as a ploy to delay the discovery of the loss. It will also be particularly suspicious if adjustments are made to book stock just before, or as a result of, stock checks.

The employees' work records just before or during the stocktaking may also indicate fraud. To conceal stock losses, for example, it may be necessary to move stock from one warehouse to another so that it can be counted twice. This type of activity would show up as unusual levels of time recorded or as a sudden increase in the demand for internal transport. But bold thieves may subcontract this work, so invoices from independent carriers at the relevant time should also be investigated. Finally, it is a sound policy to make sure that all fully depreciated assets are still held. If it is proposed to scrap such assets, they should be independently appraised.

Tests to detect fraud in the general accounts

The tests may be general and aim to identify trends or they may focus on individual employees. A detailed statistical analysis of the main components of the accounting system may reveal interesting patterns of behaviour from which fraud may be inferred. To take sales accounts as an example, the statistics may show changes in the accounts of a groups of customer whose volumes of purchases have declined against the normal commercial trend but the levels of cancelled orders and returned goods have increased. This may show that these customers are now receiving stolen goods, with balancing credits being written off as returns. A full analysis of the accounting system should also aim to identify all the suspense accounts and to verify a selection of the postings into and out of those accounts. It may be advisable to verify a sample of all interaccount transfers.

When looking at the performance of individual employees, an examination of the ratio of successful to unsuccessful calls made by the sales representatives can be an indicator or fraud. Of course, it may just show nothing more than inefficiency or lack of commitment, but it may equally show a conflict of interests. The best strategy is to apply job sensitivity analysis (see Chapter 19) to identify the most vulnerable transactions: those where discretions are involved – in relation to, say, levels of discounts or the issuing free samples, or where there are elements that would normally not be closely controlled, such as repairs to office furniture, office cleaning costs, local advertising costs, expense accounts, and so on.

Tests to detect fraud in the payroll

Large payroll frauds are uncommon because too many outside agencies are likely to be involved in the verification of the record keeping. Thus, sooner or later the Inland Revenue and the Department of Social Services will require tax returns and pension details for each false employee created. However, one or two modestly paid false employees can be a steady drain on revenues, so investigators should check the details of the most recently recruited employees. This would involve tracing a random selection of names from the payroll records to the personnel files, telephone directories and voters' registers to detect ghost employees. It may also be helpful to look for employees who do not take holidays, or who take only infrequent holidays. Theoretically, criminals rarely take holidays in case their frauds are discovered in their absence, but in practice, most take extremely expensive holidays.

Tests to detect interference with control machinery

All those processes which enable the organization to measure the quantity or volume of materials for pricing and valuation purposes, should be treated as vulnerable – for example, all the weighbridges, meters and scales used by the organization to control inventories or the despatch or receipt of goods should be checked regularly. If employees are tampering with critical measuring devices, there may be evidence in the repair and service records which might show that early trials broke the device or produced readings so odd that the machine had to be represented as broken.

Tests to detect fraud in the transport system

All the aspects of transportation can represent a significant component element in the variable costs of an organization, whether as a drain on capital or revenue, or as a drag on profitability. One of the problems is that a significant number of situations are not under the direct control of the organization, but depend on the accuracy of the reporting procedures from the employees involved. Many frauds relate to the supply of new vehicles and of spares and replacement parts. It is therefore advisable to check a random sample of vehicles to ensure that they are as described in the sales invoices and inventory. Similarly, checks should be made in the service and maintenance records for reasonableness given the declared age and level of use. It is also useful to check the industry norms for, and the actually claimed petrol/diesel of the fleet vehicles – this should help to detect short deliveries of bulk fuel as well as agency credit card frauds.

Tests to detect computer abuse

There is a wide range of possible computer abuses, from the theft of machine time by employees using their employer's system for their own private gain, to the complete loss of data integrity through fraud or malice. The level of activity in this area depends on the degree of perceived risk. The auditors should, for example, appraise the methods of control over the issue and use of passwords, and of all the more critical parts of the logical access system. Detailed audits of the back-up library will help to uncover cases of deliberate damage. If there is a real possibility that unauthorized amendments have been made to more sensitive resources, the auditors should make object code comparisons, seeking to reconcile the source program with the current version to check for any signs of program manipulation. If there is evidence that outside hackers may have been active, British Telecom may be able to trace the hacker on-line through the new digital exchanges.

Audit trails

Each of the individual tests described in this section of the chapter must also be placed into a proper organizational context. Indeed, to conduct an auditing investigation only on the basis of constituent elements and without verifying the interrelationships between the elements for internal consistency, would be to court disaster. The first step is to produce a series of audit trails.

An audit or information trail is produced by using flowcharting techniques to detail the links between the different elements in a given transaction. The end product can be described as a chain of evidence provided through coding, cross references and documentation connecting account balances and other summary results with original transactions and calculations. For example, in a manual system individual cash receipts would, in the first instance, be linked to remittance advice notes and to receipts listings, say shown on a till roll or other recording system. Such entries would then lead to the cash receipts journal and be tied to a bank paying-in book and the bank statements which could be the subject of reconciliation checks. Ultimately, there would be postings to the customer's account to show the current state of indebtedness and to the general sales ledger. The preparation of adequate audit trails is important because:

- it is required by law as a part of the general duty to maintain proper accounting records for reporting and taxation purposes
- the management of any organization needs to be able to trace source documents, typically, to enable proper answers to be given to queries from customers or suppliers and
- as a part of the reporting requirements under the Companies Act 1985, the rules of the Stock Exchange relating to member firms' accounts, and the statutes regulating insurance companies, building societies, friendly societies, etc., the auditor should be in a position to certify that the information presented in the final accounts gives a true and fair view of the organization's trading position, and the only way to be sure is by tracing a representative sample of the source documents.

The auditor should subject the audit trails to extended compliance tests. Documents should be selected from the various stages in the system so that they may be verified in depth (sometimes called *cradle to grave* testing). Thus, an entry for issues of stock in the stock records should be supported by sales order, despatch note, sales invoice, etc., and the sales invoice should be supported by sales order, sales despatch note, entry in stock records, entry in debtor's ledger and subsequent payment, and so on.

In a computer system, the cash receipts data are likely to be transformed into machine-readable form soon after the transaction occurs. In some systems, the data may be transcribed from a remittance advice (a form of source document) to a magnetic tape storage device or disks. The data appear as output in the form of computer print-out, representing a combination of a sales journal and a cash receipts journal. The general ledger data may be stored on magnetic tape or disks. In other systems, the data may be transformed into machine-readable form and processed into a general ledger entry as the cash receipts transaction occurs.

In a manual system, the trail may be relatively easy to follow because the recording of transactions is split into discrete actions, but in a computer system there may be many breaks because:

- data no longer considered necessary may be deleted to save space in the memory
- data may be kept on magnetic files only and may therefore not be immediately human-readable
- source documents may be sorted by computer, making it unnecessary to hold them in easily accessible order
- reports may contain summary information only, giving no reference to source documentation

- transactions may be initiated by the computer program itself (for example, in an automated JIT system, purchase orders may be prepared automatically when minimum specified stock levels have been reached).

Thus, in a computer system a sales ledger may be updated by a sales invoice to create an open entry in the ledger held on computer file. If the sales ledger were to be printed out at this time, the trail would be intact. When the debtor pays the invoice, the computer is likely to remove the open entry from the file and, if the auditor were then to take a copy of the file, the trail would be broken. If the system has been designed without consultation with the auditor, the solution is either:

- to make more frequent visits to the organization to be audited, taking more hard copies of the files and reconciling the transaction records; or
- to attach identification codes to selected transactions with a view both to tracing them through the system, and to obtaining satisfactory evidence that they have been properly processed.

If the auditor has been involved in the initial design of the computer system, proper controls and tests of accuracy can be built in from the outset. In real-time or on-line systems it is often neither reasonable nor practical to take hard copy of every transaction. The answer is therefore to create special audit files where records of the sensitive transactions are recorded.

Detection methodology conclusions

This last group of methodologies must be seen against the background of *tolerance*. Some victims are prepared to tolerate small losses, possibly because it is believed that the frauds are institutionalized and cannot be stopped, or because it is considered that the organization will benefit in some way by allowing it to continue. Yet, even on a small scale, condoned crime creates an environment in which employees can begin the process of rationalizing major dishonesty: it is the thin end of the wedge. All the methods for the detection of fraud we have listed rely on a series of simple propositions:

- The one who most needs to conceal a fraud is the one whose guilt would otherwise be obvious.
- All those thefts which are opportunist in nature have little likelihood of detection unless effective security checks always show the identity of people in each area so that loss can be tied to presence.
- The more violent smash-and-grab theft tactics rely either on fast escape and/or being able to preserve the anonymity of the robbers.
- Most frauds leave traces which careful auditing can detect. Thus, for example, the conversion of cheques can be achieved in a variety of ways, including the following:
  - the cheque can be cashed by opening an account in the name of the payee and paying it in for later encashment

- if the cheque is not crossed and marked 'A/c payee only', it can be endorsed as if by the payee and paid into a safe account
- the thief can simply alter the name of the payee.

But the cheques, stamped by the collecting bank, can be returned to the drawing organization in the ordinary course of events. Scrutiny of the cheques can detect irregularities. But this emphasizes the need to separate administrative functions. It would be fatal if the person who diverted the cheque on the way out could dishonestly destroy the evidence after its return through the clearing system.

- Most long-term frauds rely on collusion. Thus, for example, it is easier to explain account credits or stolen goods if the receiver is already a customer or client of the victim organization. It is a natural part of a commercial organization's function to make credits for goods returned. Similarly, it is easier to explain the delivery to, or the presence of goods in, a given warehouse or store if those facilities belong to an existing customer.

Summary

In this chapter we have focused on questions of system design and essential features in relation to the need to maximize security. Our key points are:

- The best security designs are those which have been exposed to constructive criticism and reviewed by all who will be involved in the design and in the use of the system and which have been ergonomically designed.
- The best human controls depend on separation of function both between individuals and between departments. Automatic controls rely on checking the arithmetic and the internal consistency of the input.
- Distributed systems may have significant operational advantages, but security is a real problem. If intrusion cannot be prevented, the organization must consider producing an intrusion tolerant system.
- Although microcomputers have become powerful devices at an economic price, they create significant security problems both as stand-alone machines and as terminal gateways into a distributed system.
- The auditor's primary duty is to check on the effectiveness of the controls within the systems and to validate the data which the systems contain.
- Fraud inevitably depends on the creation of false accounting records. Every organization is therefore obliged to undertake a series of tests to determine whether fraud may be taking place. If a fraud is suspected, evidence should be collected with a view to prosecution.

Self-test questions

1 Outline the main principles for data security system design.
2 List the main techniques for input data verification.
3 Identify the stages of the auditing function.
4 What are the main methods of fraud?

Exam-style questions

1 FG plc is a financial services company which employs over 200 people at its office in a prestige business park. For several years, it has followed a policy of encouraging 'end-user' computing, and every worker throughout the organization has his or her own PC or workstation, with full access to the corporate database and a range of software packages. In addition, employees are encouraged to develop their own applications and to write their own programs in the company's standard fourth-generation language.

Discuss the problems which the management of FG plc might have in reconciling the concept of the corporate data holding with free access to data by all users. Describe the problems the company will have faced in adopting this policy of 'end-user' computing.

2 As a junior member of your company's audit team you have been asked to prepare a plan of action to be followed in the event of fraudulent access to the computer system being detected. Identify the requirements of such a plan and describe the steps which should be followed when a case of computer fraud is suspected.

(All answers on page 573)

CHAPTER 19

Personnel and back-up issues

Introduction

Peter Drucker remarks that 'the test of a healthy business is not the beauty, clarity or perfection of its organizational structure ... It is the performance of people'. Since people operate systems and effectively form part of them, good systems performance requires good people performance. And if the individuals operating a system do not perform well – through ignorance, indolence, negligence or ill-will – that system will be defective or may even fail completely. The special needs and concerns of security systems make particular demands in regard to staff loyalty, efficiency and cohesion, and impose quite severe requirements for the planning, control and monitoring of the human input. These priorities must be addressed by an organization's security managers and the related issues of team commitment and ethical behaviour must be seen to be important in its corporate culture.

This chapter therefore concentrates on the personnel issues implicit in the development and maintenance of an organization's security systems. We focus on the need for each organization to establish both a practical and an ethical framework within which security is to be maintained. We discuss the fact that the practicality of fraud detection and investigation is a phenomenon which may prejudice labour relations and examine the value of job sensitivity analysis for establishing vulnerabilities. We then look at the role of the auditor in the modern world of the automated information system. Lastly, we focus on the main strategies which an organization should consider to enable it to recover from a disaster.

The planning framework

Every person in a modern society has the right to protect his or her property, income, safety and security. Sometimes duties of protection are given to employers, but no matter what the law may require, all organizations have a direct interest in promoting security-based duties to protect not only their own capital and revenue, but also the safety and economic well-being of their employees. This arises because security is inevitably allied to profitability in the commercial sector, and to efficiency and cost accountability in the public sector. As well as laying down a policy on practical matters, each organization should also set the moral and ethical tone of the employment. This means that, wherever relevant, certain minimum standards should be established for behaviour in situations where, for example, there may be:

- a conflict of interest
- an opportunity for insider dealing
- the abuse of confidential information, etc.

These standards should be effectively communicated to the employees, which means that the employees must be encouraged to meet those standards. Simply writing policies down cannot solve even the simplest security problems, but they are important in setting the ground rules and expectations of those involved. More detailed provisions allocating appropriate levels of professional and personal responsibility should therefore be included in all employees' contract of employment and/or job descriptions, and in any contracts with third parties where there is an identifiable element of risk.

Security management

When planning the administration of security matters, the organization should identify a specific individual who is to have the responsibility for advising on and maintaining security. This should be a senior management post, visibly supported by the most senior managers. The function should be to advise both horizontally and vertically within the organization, and to assume overall responsibility for the enforcement of obligations at all levels within the organization and against third parties. The creation and support of such a post will, in the event of subsequent legal action, show that the management was acting prudently. But the appointment must not be in a vacuum. It should be made with very specific responsibilities for the post holder in respect of the:

- organizational procedures for the screening and appointment of staff
- criteria of confidentiality for the classification and protection of information
- commercial and ethical screening of new investment opportunities both internal and external to the organization
- prevailing statutory and professional data protection standards
- strategies for contingency planning
- practice of incident reporting within the organization.

The depth and detail of these responsibilities will, of course, vary with the size and complexity of organization involved.

There also has to be significant commitment to education and training at every level within the organization so that the process of change can be properly managed. All those actually or likely to be affected by changes in working practices must understand the new systems and the problems of using them efficiently. Even after these changes have been introduced, employees who do not begin using the systems immediately will need refresher courses, and those who have regular practice should be shown how to consolidate and improve upon their skills and be updated in any amendments to the systems. It is a good policy to ensure that all relevant staff are well versed in the standard operating procedures. This will allow for covering if colleagues are absent from work for any reason, and for a good response in the event of an emergency when flexibility of response from employees may be the key to a successful recovery.

The importance of understanding the system

When planning the training of staff, it is important to consider face-to-face consultations, discussions and briefings between groups of employees and their managers. Although meetings can disrupt normal working schedules, the benefit lies in the opportunity for people to ask questions and to feel that they are, to some extent, in control of the process of change. Once the staff feel that they have some ownership of the concepts underlying the new systems, it is sensible either to prepare accessible documentation which assumes nothing and is regularly updated, or to provide computer-based training (CBT) systems whether stand-alone, or embedded in the operating system or the resources themselves. In theory, staff will then be able to rapidly familiarize themselves with the relevant procedures. In practice, however, help-lines and readily available people to advise are essential if difficulties and prejudices are to be overcome.

This desire to train people and to produce flexible and effective employees must be seen against the need, in some organizations, to control and restrict general access to information about the operating procedures. If some procedures and facilities are sensitive, the answer is that all these procedures should be designed bearing in mind the level of security required in each aspect of the office environment. But the levels of security specified for the design must be realistic. Hence, levels of security appropriate to mainframe operations in a sensitive government establishment will not be appreciated nor be appropriate in a conventional commercial office. Moreover, whatever the overall system in operation and the level of security considered appropriate, the staff should understand why things are to be done, what policies underpin those procedures, and what the likely effects of applying those procedures will be to them. People are generally more supportive if they understand the reasons for the system. Finally, the organization will consolidate the loyalty of its staff if it is seen to meet the moral and statutory requirements of providing a working environment which is both healthy and safe.

Security planning for people

To commit a computer fraud, the criminal must have access to the computer so both physical and logical access must be controlled, and planning must take account of known vulnerabilities. Once access has been achieved, most frauds depend on the falsification of input – these additional data, for example, are entered or suppressed to make accounts appear to balance (see Chapter 18).

Most frauds have obvious symptoms, and the principal detection strategies rely on noticing deviations from the norm. Once management suspicions have been raised, a good rule is to follow the asset and to ignore the apparent records.

Similarly, if documents are missing, the auditor should suspect the person who would have been suspected had incorrect documents been found. In the short term, the bonus expected from the investigation is recovering part or all the assets lost in the immediate fraud. But the main objective in prosecuting all detected fraud is long-term deterrence. To that extent, being seen to engage in the investigative process is an aspect of the ongoing function of personnel management and it is intended to affect staff attitudes. It should not be seen as a mere by-product of standard auditing.

To give it the necessary independence and authority within the organization auditing is a function that requires separate resourcing. Once established, the auditor's first task is to identify and watch all the vulnerable points. This can usually be done discreetly, say by analysing historical trends or by testing reasonableness in comparisons between branches or with other similar companies. The aim should always be to avoid any prejudice to employer/employee relations. But checks can never be restricted to statistical methods. Detailed sampling checks should always be made on individual items, regardless of the possible threat to labour relations. Hopefully, if the auditing staff have been properly trained, and the staff to be investigated have a constructive view of the process, there should be minimum friction arising from the disruption to the established routines.

The conduct of the audit

Because all audits disrupt the normal working routines, they should be carefully planned to maintain a good level of staff morale and to avoid appearing either provocative or overly paranoid. In this, the manner and attitude of the auditing staff is a critical factor. Those recruited for the task should not be the regular employees in the area(s) under review. The expectation is that outsiders are more likely to be objective, to see through plausible excuses and to avoid friendships which might colour judgements. Once the team has been recruited and the audit planned, it is best to carry out checks by surprise even though this may introduce a confrontational element between the audit team and the affected employees. Further, the team should not examine too large a part of the organization over too long a period of time, because this may disrupt the operation of that area too much. But if a close supervision can produce a fraud-free period of operation, this will be a vital basis for later comparisons. Such audits are expensive and depend on the effectiveness of the auditing staff. A period of about 14 days is a useful target. There are a variety of reasons for this:

- thieves often live up to their incomes and may need to continue the fraud to meet newly acquired commitments
- they may be arrogant enough to believe that the fraud is not detectable
- they may consider the investigation a challenge and enjoy the game of continuing the fraud while under scrutiny
- they may recognize that if the fraud stops, the operational pattern will change, thus revealing the existence and method of the fraud.

Such factors may lead to catching the person in the act.

Fraud potential

One way of focusing the investigation is to recognize that each job in every organization has a different potential for fraud. The actual level will depend on factors such as:

- the ability of each member of staff to gain access to critical resources
- the skills of those involved
- the amount of time available to plan and execute the fraud.

Job sensitivity analysis is a modification of *perpetrator analysis* (see Chapter 15). It is a review of all the management systems to identify risks by examining the operation of the organization from the point of view of the potential thief. Each security department in all organizations should identify those assets at risk and list them in order of probability of damage or loss, making decisions as to the likelihood that anyone might want to steal each class of asset. In part, this will be determined by how attractive each item will be to thieves; cash, for example, has high value and, as a low bulk item, it is very attractive to thieves. It should then be possible to identify who would have the ability to take each class of asset with a good chance of success. This analysis should include both one-off opportunities and all the standard methods of fraud. Once it is known which employees are able to acquire each class of asset, it is possible to define the level of *criticality of function* for each job. This means that a list of sensitive activities will be created for each employee to show when they represent the greatest risk to the organization. With this list in mind, the investigators should examine the written contract of employment which may have formed the basis of the original security system, and compare it to the actual tasks performed by each employee once a managerial routine has been established. This form of evaluation is based on a number of general propositions:

- the more senior the employee, the greater his or her discretion to operate outside normal controls
- it is easier for fraud to occur when supervisory managers are under pressure
- many subordinates now have greater skills than the managers
- branch offices, single occupancy offices or travelling employees represent a greater risk.

Observation of employee behaviour

Security staff should then look for danger signs from the employees such as:

- sudden wealth which might show itself through high cash spending, gambling, drinking or drug abuse
- social connections with other organizations which might evidence possible conflicts of loyalty (an inferential sign may be the sudden effectiveness of competitors which might indicate one or more breaches of confidentiality or that there is commercial espionage)
- a general lack of loyalty to the organization may be seen in poor time-keeping, disregard for instructions, dissatisfaction over lack of promotion or unreasonable self-importance.

If staff showing these danger signs or who do not conform to other operational norms are identified, the individuals should be observed and perhaps informally interviewed. If reasons or explanations are given for any deviations from the expected behaviour, the security manager should consider how reasonable the explanation might be and whether it was evidenced in any way. This would be particularly important if the employee(s) had access to high-risk procedures.

Professionalism

One element in this review of employee function will be that some staff with access to high-risk procedures will be considered to have achieved a professional status. As professionals, staff owe a series of interconnected duties:

- to their employers – this will either be contractual or it will be governed by the common law duty of loyalty
- to their clients – staff may be employed to assist clients; again this relationship will either be contractual or it will be regulated by the professional standards in force at the time
- to fellow professionals in their capacity as professionals
- to society.

Whether or not staff have become professionals, the growth of all organizations depends on mutual trust. Trust is required both between staff members horizontally and vertically within the organization, and between the organization and peer organizations, customers or service-receivers. If computer professionals could not be trusted, the risks of system abuse would be so great that computers could not be widely used. Although employers could try to control matters through a contractual framework of disciplinary proceedings, unthinking and routine resort to the legal big stick is always likely to sacrifice working relationships in the long run.

Expectations of conduct

The burden is on the professional to establish and maintain quality in their decision making and credibility in their decision support. This requires that the professional remains faithful to the employer and does not breach confidentiality, maintaining proper standards of professional integrity. This is particularly important during a computerization project. Most of those responsible for taking the final decision of whether to buy and install particular computer equipment will have little direct knowledge of what the operational problems are likely to be, yet the purchase may have a profound effect on their organization. Thus, if the organization buys a good management tool, it may substantially improve profitability and/or efficiency. But if the organization acquires a system which is defective, it may inflict real damage before the likely effects of the faults are fully appreciated.

When it is obvious that the final decision-makers lack critical expertise, the issue is what it is fair to expect the computer designers and manufacturers, the marketing firms and the in-house computer managers to do. Between them, they have the ability to cause the decision-makers to take either a good, a bad or an indifferent decision. The senior managers will expect the in-house managers to take responsibility for advising on and installing the information system. Legally, these professionals may be responsible for any losses which are sustained if they have not used the state-of-the-art standards for their profession. This can be particularly important in deciding whether there should be litigation and, if so, who should be involved as parties. The general sale/supply relationship works well when the seller/supplier is honest with the customer during the precontractual negotiations. Honesty for these purposes means that reasonably accurate information is given which allows the buyer to take a properly informed decision on whether to enter into the contract. If problems arise in such a case, it will be because the in-house professional drew up the wrong specification at the design stage or made errors in the installation. This will usually justify dismissal but litigation is not generally appropriate because employed professionals rarely carry their own insurance cover and cannot pay any damages that might be awarded.

When selling, it is obvious that the seller/supplier should not attempt to deceive the customer, but it is not necessarily so clear how much of the truth should be told. Sales staff, particularly those paid on commission, can be economical with the truth. The in-house professional should have the experience and the expertise to ask the important questions to protect the buyer's interests. If the seller/supplier continues to mislead the buyer and this induces the contract, the buyer will have a good case against the seller to recover damages (so long as the seller was insured or has sufficient assets to make it worth suing). However, too much information may be just as confusing to the inexperienced buyer, so the real legal issue is the degree of relevance and salience in the information given. If the professional cannot see the wood for the trees and so protect the decision-makers, the professional will be at fault and is likely to become personally involved in any case that follows.

Systems staff

Once the computer hardware is installed, the systems staff are in a particularly privileged position because their work gives them a detailed knowledge of many operational aspects critical to the organization. Moreover, they have considerable freedom of access to both physical and system resources, and become familiar with staff, data and procedures throughout the organization. All this knowledge and these relationships are essential if the professional staff are to work towards achieving full system synthesis. If the risk of threats from the designers or the systems staff to the emerging system are to minimized, security must start during the design phase. The most common motives for staff disloyalty are greed, revenge and anger, but other factors like professional arrogance or ignorance can contribute. The results can be positive errors or omissions or general shortcomings in the design, poor documentation, etc. If there is poor control over staff and they are encouraged to work on their own or outside normal office hours, the dangers of both accidental or deliberate threats become more real. To keep proper control, organizational procedures should therefore separate systems staff from programming and operations staff in the execution of their duties, so that each group will represent a check upon the other, and an intelligently administered supervisory regime is maintained.

Other internal staff

In addition to the systems staff, threats from within the organization by function may be as follows:

- **Applications programmers**. As in the case of systems analysts and designers, there is a need to divide responsibilities, set standards and maintain an effective authorization system. The possibility of errors or omissions passing through the development phase into the working programs must be reduced to acceptable levels. In this sense, the programmer is more vital than the analyst. Detailed testing can help to reduce the risk but, following the detection of an error, any amendments to software while it is a formative state may cause unforeseen knock-on effects. Real supervision is therefore necessary to ensure that all the relevant amendment procedures are observed, and that proper records are maintained.
- **Operating staff** receive data for processing and are responsible for disseminating the results to the appropriate users. Any breach in security potentially prejudices data integrity and confidentiality, and may result in the loss of availability of both services and data. One operator working unsupervised can accidentally or deliberately undermine the best security system. Further, the use of powerful system commands can mask the operator's activities so independent control must be exercised.
- **Users** will have a detailed knowledge of the business or operating procedures which could be manipulated to make fraud work, so their activities must be carefully audited and controlled in the same way as operators.

External staff

Threats may also be posed by external staff:

- **Independent contractors.** Contract maintenance and cleaning staff can prejudice confidentiality and the availability of services. All externally employed staff should be supervised when they come on the premises as if they were internal staff. Security can be breached by maintenance and other engineers by substituting hardware components, by disabling control mechanisms or by using the powerful software tools on their diagnostic disks to read protected files. All their activities should be monitored by competent staff.
- **Third-party action**. There could be problems if, for example, the delivery of stationery were to be stopped by suppliers, say, during a strike. To minimize the risk of loss of system availability, the organization should maintain adequate stock of critical documentation. Similarly, if the electricity supply was disrupted, the organization would discover whether it had invested in adequate generator back-up facilities.

Using an outside agency

It is essential for the organization to select and retain honest and efficient staff, whether on a full-time or contract basis. The costs of choosing the wrong candidate can be enormous. Job sensitivity analysis will help to decide the level of care required in each interview and selection procedure. The rigour of checking will be determined by the sensitivity of the job. In sensitive jobs, the task of verifying information given on application forms should be given to an outside agency to reduce the risk of collusion in the appointment process.

Personnel issues

People represent a threat even if only through their inexperience, incompetence, negligence or curiosity. For these purposes, it is irrelevant that users and their managers may have been made explicitly responsible for maintaining security. If security systems are going to succeed, the active co-operation of all those involved is required at all times during the routine of the work. But people are always a weak link and even the most conscientious of employees may forget to log-off or allow an unauthorized person through temporarily abandoning a terminal.

The dynamics of change

The installation of an information system can represent a significant act of modernization for any organization. This can be good for morale if it is properly managed. In the best cases, employees draw great confidence from the fact that they are seen to be involved in a progressive organization, and this stimulates all those affected to be creative and productive. However, the prospect of change can also be demoralizing with staff afraid for their jobs. In the worst cases, this results in a lack of co-operation or even outright opposition to the proposed changes, so the first priority is to establish proper lines of communication with all the staff likely to be affected. The aim should be to agree a set of organizational goals, with plenty of opportunity built in for consultation and feedback. If staff feel that they are able to influence the outcomes in a real way, they are more likely to support the changes. From the goal-setting stage, the management team then moves to the planning stage where more detailed consultation with the prospective beneficiaries of change should lead to the creation of properly defined, costed and scheduled arrangements.

Once decisions have been taken, people will accept change more readily if it is implemented in a structured fashion, one step at a time, to allow each person to become familiar with each new phase of the operation before the next step is taken. Consequently, because change can affect many departments and third parties with whom the organization interacts, it is better for all personnel matters to be co-ordinated at a senior level. Adequate liaison with all interested parties during the creation and implementation of plans for change is essential, and because peer organizations may be affected, the active participation of senior managers is vital throughout the exercise.

Helping new users

Everyone involved in the process of change needs to know who to ask about the risks involved. With a new system, there is a chance to get everything right from the start, so it is important to have a good, security-conscious person in charge during the development phase. To help users who may never have had to deal with computers before, there should be a help-line. This should also provide a central record of the problems experienced and help to target training time. For this purpose, the computer services unit team should have a blend of computer and of organization experience. If they have a reasonable level of experience, they should be able to dispel the usual fears and misconceptions. They should therefore be good communicators and be prepared to service the end users.

Security issues

No matter how good the training, the possibility of accidental error is always present, and this may allow major systems failures to arise. As a result, all reasonable steps must be taken to protect the data. But it is uneconomic to protect all the data all the time except in the most sensitive applications. In general, human error is more common than dishonesty but, since error may conceal dishonesty, the reduction of error incidence is essential to maximize auditing effectiveness. It is a typical 'wood for the trees' problem. Thus, once it is acknowledged that all people-based threats cannot be prevented, designers should build in detection systems to allow rapid intervention to limit damage. All security design must be based on good psychology and sociology. This is because, in the final analysis, security issues are not simple technical problems. It is inevitable that people will be vital component parts of the system, but they cannot be programmed as if they were machines. In deciding what steps to take, planning teams must consider and reflect upon the fact that people:

- may be the source of risk
- may be at risk from others
- may need protection.

Planning needs to take account of the full range of threats that may be present in the working environment from full disasters to minor damage to data integrity. The concept of employee protection should be sufficiently flexible to include all those factors which may affect the quality of work produced by the workforce. This may include damage to health from causes as diverse as the air conditioning (Legionnaire's disease), and the ergonomics of the office layout. Staff are vital, if not irreplaceable assets to the organization, so all should be cared for. Good working conditions, supplemented by the communication of a well-structured plan for the protection of staff, help to reduce sickness, absenteeism and staff turnover, and may also reduce industrial relations problems. Staff morale can also be affected by the intangible quality of the environment, which includes the level of sensitivity with which staff are counselled, appraised or security vetted. It also includes the way in which staff are treated if they make mistakes. The burden is therefore on the personnel department to co-operate in the production of a safe and paranoia-free workplace.

Functional separation as a security control

Fortunately, most employees are honest, but a standard safeguard is that employees should not be allowed to gain exclusive control over vulnerable functions. The risks, as Baring's Bank found out to their cost in Singapore, are significant so, wherever possible, duties should be separated. This means that, at a practical level, the care of assets and of the records which describe and list those assets should be in different hands. Similarly, separation by function or by transaction ensures that no one person has control over the whole of an administrative system (see Chapter 18). Indeed, any fraud is more likely to be discovered if jobs are performed jointly or there is some form of job covering or rotation. There are three separate strands of argument:

1 The health of the employee is important and this may be enhanced through rest or a change of activity.
2 Change in personnel helps to uncover frauds which may require continuity of activity or presence to maintain secrecy.
3 However, job rotation will be impractical in many cases because retraining may be uneconomic and inefficient.

Equally important is that staff should not be allowed to give up their holidays. Organizations should not be hypnotized by the appearance of conscientiousness and should not be tempted to let their 'star performer' work on. Toshihide Iguchi, the trader who concealed losses of $1.1 billion from the Japanese Bank Daiwa, was famous for rushing back to work after only one or two days holiday. The fraud was discovered when US regulators demanded that the bank impose a mandatory two-week holiday on all staff. In the UK, the Midland Bank now requires staff to take at least two consecutive weeks, Lloyds/TSB have a similar system for all staff while UBS and BZW ask the same of staff who handle money. There is no sign that British regulators will follow the US line and require that holidays be taken but some insurers are now writing the requirement into their policies.

A stepped approach

The best security controls to protect administrative systems divide sensitive tasks into a series of interdependent steps which must all be performed before the task can be completed. If different people are responsible for each step, this increases the chances of an honest employee noticing the error. Before deciding how functions are to be separated, the security staff should first impose general practical controls. For example, authority limits can be imposed on the amounts which employees can manipulate. Then in sensitive environments, access to information can be restricted on a need-to-know basis, regardless of the status or rank of the staff members who ask for details. Further, it should be considered normal for a person designated as superior in the management hierarchy to supervise the work of subordinates so that each employee works under the continuous observation of a supervisor who knows the employee and who may be able to spot unusual behaviour.

Given a system incorporating these protections and good functional separation, any employee who wants to break into the whole system should find it impossible to do it alone and will be forced into collusion with other employees. This increases the chances of detection. But in any organization, there are always some people who must be trusted – the security officer, say, or the senior systems analyst – and so there will always be people who can prejudice the system if they want to. Designs should take account of this fact. Designers should also recognize the difficulty of achieving satisfactory separations of duties in the small organization where only a limited number of people are employed. In such situations, urgent tasks are frequently undertaken by the ones with the time rather than by fixed role. Within sensible limits, therefore, all hands that may be called to the pumps must be trusted to do the jobs honestly.

User documentation and training

System manuals and both user and programming specifications can also be a weak link because a potential criminal can quickly discover how the documented system is supposed to work. But without good documentation, serious difficulties can arise. Good and clear documentation and the use of checklists can:

- significantly reduce the number of errors and omissions which people make
- ease communications between departments
- help to ensure operational continuity – a prime objective of security safeguards to deal with problems of equipment failure and personnel turnover.

If any documentation is considered sensitive, it should therefore be kept in a secure place and only made available to identified individuals on a need-to-know and time-constrained basis. This requires the documentation to be written in discrete elements which match system functions and processes. In this way, the organization can prevent its employees from gaining an overview of the system and, in parallel with the logical access system, each employee's security profile will dictate whether access may be made to any given documentation element.

One problem which regularly faces the users of stand-alone micros is illness. If there are only a limited number of people trained to use the machines for each function, any prolonged period of absence may cause a serious disruption to that function. Training should therefore always include all those who might be called on to cover for absent colleagues. If only one or two staff have the expertise, care should be taken to prevent them from either personalizing the system, or choosing idiosyncratic places in which to store the back-up copies, unless there is very good documentation of what they have done. Any failure to leave accessible information of practice can cause chaos if those staff suddenly leave or are ill, because those who are to replace them will have no idea how to make the system work. Indeed, the irony is that without adequate documentation, people really are irreplaceable.

Finally, training should persuade or condition everyone to respond to anything which is unusual as a security variance. But, if such events are not to be ignored, there must be a procedure for reporting suspicious incidents. It must be recognized that staff will not report things when their friends are involved. To encourage the proper response, it may therefore be advisable to permit reports to be made in confidence and with no stigma attached to the reporter, regardless of the outcome. All levels of employee must be encouraged to see themselves as security safeguards, the overall aim being to create a secure environment in which employees are aware of their responsibilities and are not tempted to misbehave.

Direct employment policies

As a priority, every organization should formulate a detailed policy for:

- recruitment and selection
- staff assessment and appraisal
- termination of employment.

It is well known that disgruntled and under-used employees are the most likely to breach security. Good personnel management is therefore essential to maintain morale and to produce effective training. This should include proper career progression so that people can achieve their legitimate aspirations within the organization. If staff are happy, with plenty of task variety and stimulation, they are likely to stay. But whatever the conditions under which people work, no employing organization can assume that its staff will remain loyal. People's attitudes change and, depending on the circumstances, they may leave, they may become susceptible to bribery or they may take information with a view to selling it to a competitor. Each organization should therefore consider a key person policy which decides how expertise is to be replaced, or how the organization is to be restructured to compensate for its loss. Should it become necessary to terminate employment, adequate security procedures should be devised. The employees who are to be removed should be excluded from sensitive areas immediately. Arrangements should be made for the immediate return of security sensitive items such as manuals, keys, ID badges, and all passwords and logical access authorizations should be cancelled.

The key personnel issues may therefore be summarized as follows:

- tempered by job sensitivity analysis, the organization should have effective pre-employment screening and background checking to reduce the possibility of appointing an untrustworthy person into a post of responsibility
- all staff should be trained to recognize and act on deviations in behaviour seen in their colleagues which could be warning signs of likely fraudulent behaviour
- there should be strict guidelines following a dismissal or other termination to reduce the opportunity for vengeful behaviour by a disgruntled individual
- there should be a well-defined policy on non-disclosure of confidential information
- staff should be given well-defined channels to air their grievances, and there should be regular personnel reviews
- morale is maintained by having a safe and well-appointed environment in which to work.

The role of the auditor

The traditional role of the auditor has been described as a watchdog. The role is therefore not actively to search for and detect fraud, but merely to see whether the system appears to be working as designed and producing accurate data.

Naturally, if a material irregularity is discovered which would make a significant difference to the reliability of the accounts, the dog will bark to call attention to it.

The external audit will normally take place annually, and its purpose to allow the auditor to test the credibility of the accounts before they are published. This cannot be an exact test because the accounts may be a summary of thousands of transactions which cannot all be reviewed in the time available. It would also not be economical to pay for every last entry in the accounts to be verified. The best that to auditor can do is to form an opinion as to whether the organization's financial statements appear to be a fair representation of the operation as on the date of publication. The auditor should be professionally qualified and must be both competent and independent – someone other than the preparer of the accounts and those people likely to gain directly from the use of the information.

Definitions in this area cannot be based solely on the functional proposition that the auditor has to act in accordance with the relevant statutory provisions. To do so misses the public policy issue of the need to provide interested parties with reasonably credible information on which to base their decision making. Many different people need information about organizations. In relation to a commercial company, a bank wishes to set credit limits before lending money to it, a prospective investor needs to appraise the company before buying shares in it, and so on. The market place needs to be able to have a reasonable degree of trust in the accounts. But no matter how searching that annual audit may be, the primary responsibility for the detection and eradication of error lies with the directors or senior managers and their internal staff. In practice, the increase in the number of computer systems and the rise in the crime rate is exerting more pressure on the management and consequentially on the auditing profession to look for fraud more actively. If there is evidence that the auditors have relied too much on the internal accounts, say, because they wanted to keep the client company happy and ensure the auditing contract for the next year – the courts have begun to award damages against the auditing firms in favour of anyone who can show that they relied on the accounts to their detriment.

Functions of auditors

The main responsibility of the internal auditors is to evaluate and identify opportunities to strengthen the administration and the control which it can exercise. For these purposes, a control system sets standards, records performance, compares performance with targets, and takes appropriate action to bring the organization's performance levels up to standard. The modern auditor therefore has the following functions:

- to review the critical applications to ensure maximum data integrity
- to consider proposed software developments to ensure that good data controls and audit trails are maintained – it is more cost-effective that this input should be made at the design stage rather than after the event
- to review the administrative, operational and security procedures in all departments

- to complement the activities of the organization's external auditors by reviewing financial procedures on a regular basis
- to review and test disaster recovery plans.

The function of auditing should be authoritative within the organizational hierarchy, and auditors should report directly to the senior management. To achieve the best results, the auditors should be free from local or departmental political commitments, and should have wide experience in review work. The practice of auditing has had to match the evolution of accounting from traditional paper systems to information systems, so the auditor's review of the design, methods and procedures for system modification has become an essential step in producing an environment in which both legal and management requirements are met. The aim is to produce and maintain a sufficient level of overall control so that it is possible to assess the effectiveness of the component controls. This means that it is no longer acceptable for auditors to lack awareness of computer technology and information systems, and there are significant training implications for all accountants who might wish to enter the auditing side of the profession.

Auditing system controls

Internal auditors should not be content with a yearly assessment of risk, but should review all record-keeping systems, including the computerized data store, on a regular basis to ensure the adequacy of the controls. In this, approved members of the audit management team can use the established management information system and decision support systems (DSSs) to manipulate the sometimes large quantities of data through the technique of modelling to detect changes or suspicious trends in the whole. DSSs usually have good software tools with which to interact with the data and to prepare reports on the data environment. Such systems can easily be modified to support the auditing function. The resulting tests could be scheduled on a regular or routine basis, but there are dangers in being too predictable because this allows the criminals the chance to have the data in a good state by the time the known inspection is to be made. Equally, if the tests are too infrequent, they may fail to detect control degradation or the system violations which take place between tests. Alternatively, audit testing could be used to follow up an apparent failure in the controls by attempting to detect the cause or to ensure that previously detected deficiencies have been corrected.

Ensuring data security

Generally, auditors seek to ensure data security by:

- monitoring computer activity including the exception reports (unauthorized attempts to access files or procedures), console logs (to look for unusual activities), the system management facility which records which operations have been performed, and so on
- checking all changes to the system including additions to the system library as well as changes to source codes.

Application software is at the heart of the information system. For this software to operate effectively, security controls are necessary within the software and at the interface between the software and other components of the information system. The security measures implemented must reflect the needs of that system and be consistent with the sensitivity of the data processed by the system. The software most likely to be involved includes:

- the financial and asset management systems such as payroll and stock management
- those systems which provide process support for the organization's operations, such as CAD/CAM, CIM
- the automated decision-making systems, such as stock re-ordering, maintenance scheduling, and so on.

In good design, security is built in from the outset. For this to be achieved, a systematic approach to design is required (see Chapter 9). However, no matter how good the design may be on paper, an information system can only be secure if it is a part of an organization with a positive attitude towards security. It is therefore vital that those in a position of authority ensure that the standards of best practice are incorporated into the management of the organizational environment. The aim must be to make the optimum selections of security goals and strategies, and to design effective security safeguards. This requires a blend of foresight and experience, but the best results can only be achieved when decision making is based on a holistic view of the organization and its systems. Only an all-embracing overview allows the construction of appropriate security measures to meet the known vulnerabilities.

Finally, when taking design decisions, managers should recognize that there is a difficult balancing of factors to achieve, namely that although automated controls are less costly to operate and more consistently applied than their manual equivalents, the automated systems that fail to take account of the people who are to operate them are likely to be ignored or by-passed. More often than not, a compromise will be required to accept slightly less than optimum security in return for a more friendly interface which the employees are likely to accept and operate.

Auditors and the organization

In organizational terms, the role of the auditor has become increasingly fundamental. Even applying ordinary common sense, the organization will be able to identify the most probable threats and vulnerabilities. Managers will be able to see that, if threatened by determined criminals, an automated system will be more vulnerable if it has been inadequately developed and incorporates a poor defensive design. The problems will grow in scale if access is to be made by many users, making the application of input controls difficult. So most organizations accept that there is a positive need for good auditing advice and facilities during the design and implementation phases. At its best, this will be based on a detailed mapping of the information system and of the human interfaces with it. At each human interface, the auditors should consider the likelihood and consequences of error. Not only can automated countermeasures be put in place, but the human resource development team can also be advised to devise training schedules that will improve the preparation of source data and promote individual accountability at each data flow interface.

Once the system has been installed, there will be dangers in all program modifications and file changes if poorly trained staff are allowed to make them, so it is up to the auditors to liaise with the systems analysts to ensure rigorous testing before any amended software is allowed into the working environment. Both static and dynamic testing should be encouraged. During the tests, the analysts should judge the extent of the program which has been exercised and attempt to judge whether the unexercised code is an unauthorized insertion such as a program patch. In this way, the auditors give themselves the best chance of maintaining system integrity as the system develops.

Recovery strategies

If the organization is to survive a real emergency situation, it must plan to be able to keep going and then to recover to full strength. When analysing possible disasters, it will become obvious that not all the data processing tasks which the organization performs are necessary to the continued functioning of the organization during an emergency. The restoration of many of the routine and everyday routines can be delayed. If the organization is to act responsibly, it must set priorities and assess criticality by considering each program or application and asking:

1. what are the legal requirements? These will be both positive, to require the organization to act, and avoidance-based to limit the potential liability of the organization to employees and third parties.
2. what do the customers or service-receivers require so that satisfaction and/or loyalty are maintained?
3. what are the public relations requirements to maintain general confidence in the organization?
4. what are the losses and costs by hour/day, and how long can each source of loss be tolerated before serious damage is caused?

There is no need for the priority list to be absolute, and it will be sufficient to batch the programs and resources in approximate priority groupings. A list of priorities must also be drawn up to detail the order in which the data are to be restored. This will involve identifying which hardware will be required, and the necessary back-up and documentation which will include original invoices, and so on, to support the operation.

The first reaction to a disaster

The organization must first plan its initial response to any potential disaster situation. During the day, when the majority of the key personnel are likely to be on site, the decision-making problems should be readily resolved. But during an off-peak period, when a night watchman, security guard or other employee detects an apparently dangerous situation, detailed decisions must be made as to who should be called in and in what order. Those who first formally attend the scene on behalf of the management, are responsible for appraising the situation and for deciding which sections of the disaster plan to implement. The first team must have the competence to be able to make an accurate assessment of the actual or potential extent of the damage, so that appropriate damage limitation action can be taken without delay. Disaster recovery teams with specific responsibility will be listed for call-up, but alternative personnel must always be available in case the first nominated team members cannot be reached. Much work can be achieved if each team engaged on the job is well trained, and can act both independently and in parallel.

But the authority level of that first team must be considered. It would be unreasonable to involve the most senior managers for every incident, no matter how trivial. A graduated scale of response will have to be made, depending on the apparent severity of the situation, with more senior managers being called in for the more serious events. It may be felt necessary to limit the scope of the action which each grade of decision-maker can authorize, depending on the level of consequential risk involved. Thus, if the first response team feel that the extent of the disaster is within their authority levels, all relevant steps can be taken. Otherwise senior management must be called in to authorize the appropriate response, e.g. to use water to quell a fire near the main computer installation.

Alternative hardware provision

Commercial computer bureaux (acting as time brokers) offer a service by making time available on their own systems in the event of an emergency. This is called a **hot stand-by scheme**. The first step is for the organization to sign an agreement with one of the bureau and then, as a customer, to receive access codes, information and training so that the organization's software can be modified to make it portable on to the bureau's systems. Detailed tests will then have to be run to prove system compatibility, and the relevant applications and recent data will be stored on their facilities. At this point, a rental of storage space and support fees becomes payable. This solution to the problem can be relatively costly to maintain as an ongoing commitment, which will include fees for regular system test time. It also includes the expense of system modifications which may be necessitated by any changes in the bureau's operating environment, and if the organization wishes to amend its own software, the designers will have to allow for the bureau's needs when modifying all the stored applications. However, this strategy is good for the standard high-volume payroll and other similar applications.

Reciprocal agreements and contingency centres

A number of organizations near the larger towns may decide to pool their resources to save money. These **reciprocal or mutual aid agreements** work by allowing one member access to the hardware of another during an emergency, and they are likely to be particularly attractive in those industries which have accepted common hardware standards. Both software and data must be portable between the different member's facilities, and in evaluating the practicality of the scheme, rehearsals can be helpful even though they can be expensive, and generate unwelcome disruptions to the back-up organization. But if tests are to be effective, the full critical applications must be put up and made to run realistically. It is difficult to make mutual aid agreements totally reliable. Few organizations have a guaranteed level of free machine capacity so the arrangement is usually only for short-term relief and often covers only a limited amount of processing. Changes in either system will jeopardize the practicality of the agreement, and changes in management policy may cause the withdrawal of one member without notice so it can be a high-risk strategy because participants may only discover that promised aid is not available when an emergency arises. For these reasons, mutual aid agreements have high risks attached to them and may not be practical in the real world.

Equipped contingency centres are relatively rare because they are capital-expensive to create and demand for the service is relatively low. If an organization proposes to use this strategy, it should first ensure hardware compatibility and check all the communications linkages. If the technical problems are overcome, the organization pays a subscriber fee for the right to use the facility in an emergency. The cost of declaring an emergency may be great because, once the decision is taken to move to the back-up site, the hardware rental fees are payable. The organization should also carefully consider whether there are any security problems if other organizations are using the facility. The question of storing sensitive materials (whether on system or not) at the contingency centre should be discussed if, say, trade competitors are likely to be using the same resources.

The organization should also consider the level of availability of the facilities at the centre for rehearsal. It is fundamentally important that the staff at both ends of the transfer are fully familiar with all the problems which are likely to occur, and detailed training schedules should be drawn up and executed to raise staff awareness to a proper level. Further, the centre itself should disclose the number of subscribers so that there can be an intelligent guess made as to the likely odds of another subscriber needing the facility at the same time. The logistics of transfer should then be calculated starting with simple factual matters such as the distance from the organization to the centre – recovery at the original site may be slowed if key personnel are too far removed in the back-up centre. Finally, as with the bureau system, the planners must recognize that membership of these schemes limits the development of home sites to those changes which are compatible with the back-up site.

Other emergency facilities

Some organizations have constructed **empty rooms** or **shells**. This is called a **cold stand-by scheme**. In the event of a disaster, the client organization is allowed access to assemble a back-up system. The scheme is significantly less expensive than the equipped room system, but suffers from the disadvantage that it is slower to start up. Co-operative interfirm provision of empty rooms, spreads the costs. As with the hot stand-by systems, there must be careful consideration of the number of clients likely to want access at any given time, but overall, such schemes represent a good system for less critical back-up because it is not essential to maintain full system compatibility. There are also firms which provide **relocatable computer centres** – these are prefabricated rooms with built-in facilities but they can take time to erect. Planning is therefore essential to bridge the gap while the new working environment is created, so the hot stand-by schemes are more effective in this respect. Obviously, for any of these schemes to work, copies of essential files and software must survive the disaster. Adequate back-up power systems should therefore be installed so that the in-house system can be archived and brought down gracefully in the event of a major loss of power during the disaster.

The in-house hardware considerations

The first question is whether there are manual fall-back systems which will allow the organization to operate during short disruptions and during the initial stages of a major disruption. For example, the organization should check to see whether there are any manual typewriters and a suitable stock of documentation for recording sales and accounting transactions. Hardware can be easily replaced if it is of recent manufacture or still in stock. Some manufacturers will give priority of supply to those affected by a disaster. However, different suppliers have different policies and it essential to discuss disaster recovery with the suppliers at an early stage. Some hardware suppliers will, for example, make demonstration computers available to bridge in the event of disaster. These are usually showcase computers, but they are likely to have poor security, and it is possible that they have been constantly updated with the most recent software releases, so system compatibility may be a problem. It will also be hard to replace customized hardware or hardware produced in small quantities or on demand. This will inevitably be the case if the manufacturer has discontinued the line or has ceased trading. If this fact is recognized during the lifetime of a contingency plan, it should be modified to allow time to find a second-hand system, or to recreate the system using new hardware. When drawing up and maintaining the contingency plan, adequate time should be allowed for the delivery, installation, testing and commissioning of the replacement processors. In this, the size and complexity of the communications network can be a major factor. Although the telephone system may be swiftly reconnected, the supply and fitting of modems and multiplexers may be time-consuming and there may be substantial systems work required to allow for the new configuration – for example, for access to become remote during repairs.

Data and documentation considerations

With considering the data themselves, a whole series of decisions must be taken. The first and most serious possibility is that some or all of the source data have been destroyed. This may happen if there is disruption during processing. The organization should therefore decide:

- What kind of back-up files should be routinely created.
- How many generations of back-up are needed to ensure rapid recovery.
- How much data must be stored in geographically remote sites.

The organization must aim to produce data which are accurate, complete, timely and authorized; and to create a system whereby, with minimum effort, it is possible to reconstruct transactions from the relevant source documents. With both these facilities, organizations should be able to make decisions based on the best information, to create a good audit trail and to recover quickly from disasters. The DP and user departments have joint responsibility in this respect. It is also vital to consider which functions are most important to the continuing operation of the business, and priority should be given to the restoration of those functions.

Planning document storage

This should be undertaken alongside **records retention analysis**. In some cases, there will be legal requirements to retain documentary evidence of transactions, say, for the Inland Revenue and Customs & Excise. Similarly, there will be processing requirements, (e.g. to restart processing from source data if the computer malfunctions during processing), which require documents to be preserved. Each organization should analyse its documentation to identify which documents are critical. It is then advisable to microfilm, fiche or put on CD the most important and to store them on a remote site. Documents may be stored on different sites on a cyclical basis depending on their age so long as recovery can be made quickly to permit the recreation of the electronic data. Finally, user manuals tend to be kept in offices where fire damage may easily occur. Back-up copies should be stored at remote sites. Copies of the disaster plan itself should be distributed throughout the organization and should be easily available at protected locations. Some copies should be kept at the homes of the key personnel who will be contacted if the disaster occurs.

Conclusions on back-up strategy

The complete relocation of the organization to another site is rarely good logistics or economical. Further, it is seldom necessary, no matter how major the emergency. But if relocation is considered a possible option, it would be sensible to plan it alongside other plans for the expansion of the organization. In that way, the alternative site can be prepared in a way which supports the existing operations, but would have the whole infrastructure of communications, power and environmental controls installed in case relocation was required. This makes a more cost-effective scheme than a cold stand-by arrangement which may leave capital tied up with no return. But with competent management on hand, local operations are always easier to manage than remote operations.

With this in mind, the creation of multiple DP facilities ought to be considered. The smallest location should always be large enough to carry the critical work of at least one other location during the projected recovery time. This involves the physical dispersion of computer resources into two or more sites with each centre undertaking economically useful work at all times to get the most of the capital employed. Any additional or redundant capacity built in is justified by the additional security given in-house, and by the fact that each computer system has room within which to grow and develop. It is generally accepted that only about 20 per cent of each computer installation's use is critical, so the excess capacity to handle transferred processing can be kept to a minimum.

If the organization is not going to move all its operations, it should plan for the following:

- The ideal is to preserve the best possible configuration of hardware following the disaster. This will probably mean that the information service will operate at reduced efficiency. This may be acceptable over a limited period of time for some user departments where there is reduced dependence on computerized information handling or where reversion to manual systems is still possible, perhaps supported by calculators or personal computers.
- If limited processor time can be reallocated to priority departments this may allow the organization to continue efficiently.
- Manual methods may be better than nothing if there is a choice between operation and no operation.
- Some departments may not have to perform their work immediately, e.g. long-range planning, which will allow the limited processor time to be used by the priority users.
- Very few organizations need full and rapid back-up of their entire system.
- Some applications can wait weeks, others months. These systems do not need to be handled by the same strategies. Some accounting packages could be back-up within hours, others might move to a bureau the next day or be dealt with on a time share basis as and when required.
- Other facilities might be made available at a co-operating organization at low peak, off-shift times. Others might not run until another facility is prepared or the original site restored.
- In an emergency, it is the people who provide the flexibility, availability and versatility needed to meet an unexpected situation and to adapt the plans to the reality. Everyone must therefore be well trained and be motivated to give of their best.

Summary

Long-term profitability relies on installing realistic security systems. This must be more than a paper exercise and must involve all the employees in setting and achieving effective performance standards. This involves giving particular attention to the following aspects of security planning:

- Because the auditing activity disrupts the operation of the organization, all audits must be sensitively handled. But the auditor is not a criminal investigator. The primary task is to monitor and verify corporate activity which, incidentally, may reveal symptoms of fraud.

- The use of techniques such as job sensitivity analysis will assist an organization to identify both the vulnerable assets and resources and the employees with the opportunity to cause loss or damage.
- It is important for all organizations to define the status and role of each member of staff – the more critical roles are the systems staff and applications programmers. Professional staff must be encouraged to achieve state-of-the-art standards. All staff can be protected from themselves through functional separation.
- The power to make changes within the organization depends upon ability to persuade the staff to abandon the known procedures.
- If the organization is to make an effective recovery from a disaster, appropriately detailed plans must establish initial responses and lay down lines of authority for managing the damage limitation and recovery exercise.

Self-test questions

1 Identify the basic types of security audit check.
2 What is the process of job sensitivity analysis?
3 Which internal job holders represent threats to security?
4 What are the problems in security vetting at the staff appointment stage?

Exam-style questions

1 As a member of an audit team you suspect that unknown persons within your organization are perpetrating some kind of fraud which involves 'siphoning off' money from accounts within your company's computer system. The team has decided to try to identify the perpetrators by carrying out a security audit.
   (a) Explain the main points of how you would go about producing a security audit plan.
   (b) Discuss the problems your company may face in prosecuting the fraudsters when they are identified.
2 PG Ltd is a trading company which has grown rapidly and has developed a computer-based information system which covers most areas of the business. The company is now seeking to employ an internal auditor which special responsibility for ensuring the security and integrity of its information system. You have been asked to assist in preparing a job specification so that a suitable auditor may be recruited.
   (a) Describe the main areas of responsibility of an internal auditor that your company will need to include in the job description for the post.
   (b) Describe a suitable role for the proposed appointment of an internal auditor within your company.
3 You work for a medium-sized company which relies heavily on its computer-based systems to carry out its business activities. You have been instrumental in producing a disaster plan and designing physical security measures for your

organization's systems, and now you are required to make sure that the company will have alternative hardware provision ('back-up') in the event of the destruction of its computing facilities.

Write a report to the management of your company identifying and evaluating the alternative methods by which alternative hardware provision or 'back-up' may be provided for your computer-based systems.

(All answers on pages 574–575)

CHAPTER 20

Integrative case studies

Introduction

The aims of this chapter are briefly to review the material covered in this book and to introduce you to one of the approaches to handling questions formulated in a case study scenario.

The initial part of the chapter will explain why many teachers consider case studies to be a useful way of improving understanding of complex and practical concepts such as information systems in the organization. We will then review the general approach to handling case studies and their associated questions, listing the points of good practice as well as the points that you should avoid. Following this initial explanation, the remainder of the chapter works through three short case studies. These case studies will show you what you may encounter in the examination room. We suggest that you attempt to write answers to each of the case studies and associated questions before studying the outline solutions, but you are warned that the suggestions which follow each of the case studies do nothing more than illustrate the elements that would be expected by the examiner. The answers that we provide are not intended to be comprehensive.

Why use case studies?

Management education at almost all academic levels now uses case studies in the teaching and assessment of many areas of management theory, accounting and information systems. This recognizes that both students and working managers benefit from being encouraged to place information in a context. Simply reading dry facts in a book does not of itself communicate a sense of how relevant and useful each piece of information is. This understanding comes from studying how knowledge may be used and what the outcomes may be in different situations. Although case studies are inevitably very simplified versions of reality, their value lies in providing you with a vehicle in which you can travel around a subject and get better idea of how it works. It is also a more useful form of examination assessment because it avoids testing rote memory and gives you an opportunity to practice the skills you are likely to be asked to use in future employment. Case studies therefore:

- illustrate the application of concepts and knowledge through the study and understanding of a practical situation
- demonstrate that the organizational and human factors which need to be considered if successful new systems or processes are to be implemented, are inherently complex

- provide an opportunity for you to recognize relationships between different pieces of information and, hopefully, to integrate the related issues or elements into potentially useful packages for real-world application
- test your ability to identify and analyse the relevant and important factors in each scenario and, through that analysis, to recognize the range of possible approaches to solving the problems
- require you to provide a reasoned justification for the more appropriate solution strategies.

In general terms, therefore, the case study provides a sharper tool for testing whether you really understand the relevant principles and can apply that knowledge in a practical setting. The conventional essay which used to appear as the most common form of question on examination papers was frequently linear. This meant that the question would include a number of key words which were intended to trigger the recycling or repeating memorized lists of points taken from a text or manual. Pass marks were given for doing nothing more than demonstrate the ability to memorize. Top marks were awarded if the examinee was able to comment on the facts recited. The consequence was that pass qualifications could be given to people who did not actually need to understand anything of what was written. But in the real world, employers require a practical understanding of the subjects studied. The characteristics which demonstrate real understanding involve the:

- organization of knowledge (in this instance, of management information systems and its associated areas) so that the relevance of the underlying principles to different types of situation is recognized, and the means and consequences of applying those principles is understood
- identification of the key issues and relevant principles to apply in the particular scenario
- development of an analysis of the situation described so that the problems and concerns of the interested parties are clarified
- outlining of possible strategies for solving the problems and meeting the concerns identified
- explanation and justification of the various strategies proposed
- recognition of the shortcomings of the strategies and suggestions for the steps most likely to give favourable (or least unfavourable) outcomes to those involved.

As will now be apparent, this approach to case study assessments requires a new set of skills and these can only be perfected by practice. But before looking at some case studies and their suggested solutions, a fuller explanation of the approach to handling case studies is required.

Approaching a case study

When used as an assessment vehicle rather than a learning tool, examiners tend to focus case studies on particular areas of the syllabus rather than writing one long and detailed scenario which would allow you to introduce material from the whole syllabus. This does not deny the potentially open-ended nature of every case study – no factual account is every so self-contained that the ingenious examinee could not fill in the gaps with material that will make every known principle relevant. Thus, it is usual for the examiner to follow the scenario with specific questions which are designed to limit your responses to the facts as given and to elicit particular information. Unlike the older style of essay question, these questions are likely to involve the integration of a number of different areas of the syllabus at the same time. Even so, the examiner will expect a disciplined answer which analyses and discusses the situation coherently.

The cases themselves are usually hypothetical scenarios, albeit based around the sort of real-life situations that will arise in most types of business or organization. Similarly, the ordinary rules of cause and effect will apply. When creating the underlying factual background, the author will inevitably simplify the situations described. The reasons for this are that:

- in an examination, you cannot be expected to read the equivalent of a novel before beginning to write the answer – the facts you are given must be focused on those elements most likely to target the particular parts of the syllabus to be tested
- you may not have any practical experience of the situation described, and so cannot be expected to fill in any gaps in the story from knowing what would probably be happening – the scenario must therefore strike a balance between reflecting what would be happening in the real world and providing you with a fair opportunity at your level of academic attainment to show off what you know to the best advantage
- the author will have a number of likely outcomes in mind and will design the case data around them
- the author will almost certainly mix different sections from the syllabus together – the intention is to limit the 'question spotting' approach to revision and to encourage you to revise the whole syllabus
- in describing the scenario, the author will aim to provide sufficient data to enable you to identify what you have to do
- the examiner will describe a set of rules for answering the questions, such as denying marks if you supply additional data concerning the industry or sector and warning that marks may be lost due if you fail to fully address the issues posed in the case.

The steps that you should take

The following list summarizes the key stages in formulating and presenting a good answer. Each of these points is developed further after the summary.

- Read the case study from start to finish at least once without making notes.
- Read and understand the questions asked.
- Note the main problems or issues in the case raised by the questions asked.
- Review these problems and identify which are the most important.
- When planning the answer to each question, try to provide a logical structure.
- Apply your knowledge, recognizing that you may need to draw on different parts of the syllabus for each question.

- Never simply assert something as the answer, but always analyse, explain, reason and justify your answers.
- Finally, develop conclusions or recommendations as required by the question, noting any problems that these may leave unresolved.

Read the case study

Time pressure is greater in a case study examination because there is so much more factual material to read than in the convention examination. One of the most common mistakes when working against the clock in the examination room is to pick up the first issue or problem encountered as the only relevant material and, substantially, to limit the answer to that material without reading the case study fully and understanding the total situation. The dangers are that:

- this will only represent a small part of what is required to produce a complete answer; or
- it devotes too much effort to one aspect of the complete answer; or
- even worse, it answers a question that was not asked.

So when you read the case study for the first time, try to keep your mind in neutral until you reach the end. Do not judge the significance of any of the facts given until all the facts have been assimilated. Only then can you really begin to judge which are the most important and how they relate to each other.

Read and understand the questions

The basic rule of all examinations which follows from the last point is that you should always read the questions carefully and get a comprehensive view of all that is required. This is even more important in case study assessments because the scenario almost always offers far more information than in the more conventional set of essay questions, but not all that information is completely relevant or equally significant to all the questions asked. It is therefore common to find that people either misread the questions or misinterpret them in the light of a superficial reading of the case study. This trap is easy to fall into because many concentrate their revision on those parts of the syllabus which they hope will appear (it is always tempting to read questions in a way that will allow you to introduce the material you have studied well) and because of the natural nervousness most feel at the start of any examination.

Note the main problems or issues

Part of the skill necessary to analyse a case study is sorting out the more important or relevant data from the less relevant. Each question will offer some guidance but there is a 'chicken and egg' problem (should you read the scenario or the questions first) and its resolution really depends on your own judgement. The examiner is interested in your ability to see relationships between data given at different points in the case study and to draw inference both from what is written and from what is left unsaid. The first step should therefore be to note what you think the main problems or issues to be before reading the questions. If none of the questions then seem to make sense, this may suggest that you have not correctly identified the main problems and issues. If the problems you have noted are matched by the questions, this is vital confirmation of the keys to the subsequent analysis and answering of the questions.

Apply your knowledge

Although identifying the problems is a good indication of the level of your understanding, the main part of the assessment of your abilities is that you can apply what you know to resolve those problems. Because the examiner is likely to include a fairly generous factual statement of the situation, this will tend to make knowledge gained from different parts of the Information Analysis syllabus relevant in answering any specific question. You should always worry if you can only see one problem to resolve, and you should work on the basis that there is never ever one correct answer to any question. A good starting point for any answer is always 'It depends ...'. By being prepared to argue for different possible strategies and different outcomes, you create the opportunity to show off your knowledge.

Review the problems

This stage involves creating a logical format or structure for the answer. Although it is never bad to give a general statement of relevant principles, the distinctive quality of a good answer goes beyond abstract contents and coverage, and continuously demonstrates the purpose and immediate relevance of each statement of principle. The reader should be left in no doubt that you have a detailed understanding of how to link and apply each principle to each aspect of the problem scenario. If the relevance of a statement of principle is not demonstrated, it looks like padding and may indicate that you have included the material 'on the off chance' that it is relevant. Any failure to provide a logical and coherent justification for each element of the answer to the question posed suggests some degree of failure in understanding the subject, the case situation or the question being posed.

Analyse, explain, reason and justify

To improve the chance of the examiner being impressed by form and content, it is a good idea to write in the form of an essay and never to include large volumes of data as lists of points. Quality is measured by the ability to explain, reason, analyse and justify the points made, and their relevance to the questions posed. You must then go on to develop conclusions or recommendations for the interested parties nominated in the questions. But this must not be done blindly. It is important that any answer shows how these conclusions and recommendations develop from the previous analysis and a separate justification should demonstrate how and why they are derived. Try making the word 'because' one of the most common that you use.

What you should avoid

Before concluding this section and proceeding to the case studies themselves it may be appropriate to repeat some of the problems you should avoid in answering your case study questions:

- Do not rush – you have to take your time in reading the case study and the questions to make sure that you have grasped exactly what you are supposed to do.

- Answer the questions asked by the examiner and not those that you believe they are or wish they were. Just because you know what some of the most common problems are, does not mean that those are the ones to talk about.
- Read the case objectively – do not close your mind to the case scenario, even though you may find some elements difficult to believe. Just deal with the facts as they are given to you.
- Do not try to find an answer for every issue or problem in the case – establish priorities and be guided at all times by the questions posed. Do not provide answers which simply reproduce the facts or lists of data that you have memorized. Make sure that everything you write is directly relevant to, and supports your arguments for, the identification and resolution of the problems.
- Do not try to pack everything you have remembered into the answer – superfluous and irrelevant material will often lose you marks because it may obscure the important and relevant parts of your answer.

Case study A

Wiltminster plc is located to the south of Birmingham in the UK and, for almost 100 years, it has specialized in the production of high-quality woven carpets, distributing to customers both at home and overseas. In the early part of the century, the company expanded its sales quite rapidly and, at its peak, it employed over one thousand people in three factories. But the combination of increased competition and the development of new manufacturing technologies has resulted in the company's decline. Consequently, the company now employs only 350 people in a single factory, supplying carpets to two main types of customer:

- the large carpet superstores (such as Allied Maples and Carpet-World) who operate on the out-of-town retail parks and who represent the largest proportion of its sales at 70% of volume
- the smaller independent carpet and furniture retailer typically operating in the high streets of most towns.

The sales team recognizes that each customer has different needs which have to be met by different types and levels of service and support. Not unnaturally, this variability in costs affects the profit margins available in each sale. Because of their buying power, the large superstores continuously strive to drive down the prices they pay while seeking to retain a high level of service. They are likely to maintain low levels of stock of a wide range of Wiltminster plc carpet rolls in their stores at any time (operating a form of just-in-time system). Each store has delegated power to place orders directly with Wiltminster plc and speed of delivery on these orders is considered as a crucial part of the service that is offered. The normal period for the delivery of an order is expected to be between two and seven days from receipt of the order. The superstores normally telephone or fax the orders direct to Wiltminster plc with order confirmation by post. Wiltminster plc then processes the order by cutting the lengths from the rolls of carpet in the warehouse and arranges delivery to the appropriate superstore. Distribution to all locations within the UK is managed from a single warehouse. This facility is also responsible for arranging the despatch of all export orders.

The specialist furniture and carpet retailers are more likely to enquire about the availability of particular carpets by telephone and then to place orders by post. In most cases, these retailers will work from pattern books of various carpet samples. Their customers browse through the complete range of carpets and make their selection. Although delivery is an important part of the service which they offer to their customers, they are less concerned with the speed of delivery and more with ensuring that Wiltminster plc meets the agreed dates and provides the correct size and specification.

Wiltminster plc has an automated sales order processing system. It was installed nearly five years ago as a turnkey system and it replaced the manual system that had operated substantially unchanged since the company began trading. In adopting this system, the company acted on the advice of a local computer systems supplier, who had experience in installing the system in many local small businesses. The system is based on a standard sales order processing package which drives a central PC with four networked terminals in the sales office. The central PC maintains the customer database, stock records and other elements of the sales order processing files and software. This installation had two apparent advantages. Because it was 'off the shelf', it was cheap, and because the sales office staff already had keyboard skills, they could be trained to operate the new system within a short period of time. Some of the bolder sales staff and their immediate managers raised questions at the time of installation, criticizing both the lack of any serious analysis or investigation of the system requirements and the failure to propose alternative solutions to the existing problems. But the speed with which the new system became operational and the lack of complaints from the customers concerning the system or level of service from the sales office led the senior managers to believe that these criticisms were unwarranted.

The four sales office assistants receive orders via the telephone, fax or post and enter the relevant details into the system. If the customer has not exceeded the credit limit and the necessary carpet is in stock, a multipart order is printed out and sent to the warehouse for processing. One of the copies from the multipart set is despatched by post to the customer to confirm the receipt of the order, the order details and the availability of carpet from stock. If the carpet is not available in stock the multipart order set is forwarded to production planning who note on the copies the expected date of availability based on the planned production schedule. The delay associated with carpets not in stock may be as long as six weeks depending on the production cycle and the level of demand for particular patterns. Once stock is received from production, the warehouse administrative staff are responsible for scheduling the orders for delivery to all customers. The delivery of a large order or of several smaller orders to the same large superstore is usually a straightforward task. But the delivery of single small orders to a large number of independent specialist retailers requires careful planning and scheduling to ensure maximum efficiency in using the fleet of transport vehicles. Several days may be added to the delivery time for a particular order from stock while the staff consolidate orders from each area to make up an economic load for delivery.

Stuart Denholme, the marketing director, who joined the company three years ago has complained that the system does not provide a range of information to support the marketing and sales functions. The main thrust of the criticism is that the system is designed simply to process orders efficiently and is little more than a glorified printer of dockets and forms. He argues that the customer database and the ordering system could provide invaluable information about the company's customers and markets. More immediately, Global Carpets plc, one of the company's largest superstore retailers operating throughout the UK and also in many countries of the European Union, is pressing Wiltminster plc to institute a new sales ordering system which will operate on an electronic data interchange (EDI) basis. Global believes that EDI will facilitate a more effective ordering system, and it has already established compatible systems with over 50 per cent of its other suppliers. It is now threatening all its other suppliers that unless they are prepared to offer this facility it is unlikely that Global will continue to offer their carpets for sale. Other superstore customers have already discussed this with Wiltminster but this is the first evidence of a possible loss of business due to failure to provide the facility. Denholme confirms that the present system cannot be made compatible with the standard EDI platforms and that a completely new software package will be required.

Questions

1 Explain the contribution that a comprehensive sales order processing system could have made to the strategic development of Wiltminster plc.
2 What was wrong with the approach taken by Wiltminster plc to the development of an automated system?
3 Describe how Wiltminster plc might have improved the analysis of the automation issue.
4 Analyse the demands that the introduction of an EDI facility are likely to have on the company's management processes.
5 In particular, explore the issues and problems that this will create for meeting the needs of the different types of retailer.
6 If an integrated sales order processing and EDI system was produced, identify the different types of information that could be provided by the system.
7 Analyse how the marketing function might benefit from enhanced information quality.

Case study A: outline solutions

The outline solutions provided are only intended to cover the main elements that would be expected in answering each question. They are not exhaustive answers and there is always scope for you to incorporate new or innovative insights into the answers. The solutions also seek to provide some guidance on the structuring of the answer which was indicated earlier as an important factor in developing a good-quality answer.

1 Information systems have the capacity to add value to the business at the operational, tactical and strategic levels. In the medium to long term, the intention of all competent management teams would be to use all available information to increase the company's efficiency in resource usage, to improve competitive advantage and to enhance profitability. In this case study,

Wiltminster plc places a high value on the speed of response of each customer's order. As a manufacturer, the company is at the head of a vertical supply chain. Hence, the better the quality and efficiency of the service that it can offer, the better the service that those retailers can pass on to their customers. The factor that is intended to deliver this quality service is the sales order processing system. It exists to provide the vital interface between the organization and its customers. If that interface can be made to work at an optimal level, the strategic benefits may be classified under a number of headings:

- *Market-related*: as part of the marketing mix, offering improved service through a speedy response to both existing and new customers' orders will enhance customer loyalty and build competitive advantage.
- *Stock control*: an effective and more timely monitor of sales patterns will enable the company to achieve a more efficient use of resource stocks, reducing both slow moving stock lines and the percentage of circulating capital tied up in stock holding, and achieving more efficient warehousing operations through dealing with fewer fast-moving stocks – the results should be a better service to the customer in terms of quicker delivery times and a more productive use of capital.
- *Manufacturing*: information which provides more accurate and quicker responses on the customer orders (i.e. for different patterns or qualities) should enable the production schedulers to plan to meet the immediate needs. At a tactical and strategic level, it will also improve the company's capacity to respond more effectively to changing market trends.
- *Financial*: the effect of reducing stock holdings and achieving higher stock turnover rates is both to realize the working capital and added value tied up in stock and to reduce the direct financing costs of that capital. This may give rise to an opportunity cost in terms of the return that could be generated from the released capital if it was in more immediately productive use. Similarly, a faster response to orders and a more accurate invoicing may reduce the debtor recovery periods and eliminate some of the costs associated with this and bad debts.
- *Marketing*: providing better-quality information to the marketing function enables the business to respond more effectively to changes in demand patterns, prices and the types of support services required.

This indicates the range of potential benefits that might be achieved by Wiltminster plc but a cautionary note needs to be added. Although the information system itself provides the potential for these strategic benefits, it is the organization and the personnel involved who will be responsible for actually realizing this potential. The system design must therefore 'fit' the organization – it must match the structure and processes of the organization. Unless this fit is achieved, the benefits of improved quality of service to customers and reduced costs will be not realized.

2 The senior managers' approach to the development of the existing system was both illogical and unstructured. Instead of analysing the company's present and future IT needs, it seems that the managers were driven primarily

by the convenience of cheaply available technology and software. Their intention was therefore to fit the organization's processes to the needs and limits of the package, and the limited effect has proved to be the automation of only one aspect of the company's operational requirements. The outcome seems to be that the system produces multipart hard copy output which just gets added to the mass of paper in the organization's other manual systems. This means that none of the potential advantages identified in the answer to question 1 have been delivered.

Because they failed to go through a real consultation process, the managers could not actually be certain that they were addressing the real problems experienced both by their own employees and by their customers. The fact that the managers were pleased with the speed of implementation is a serious indictment of their attitude. If there had been a proper approach, the company would have moved through a phased changeover to ensure that the staff were trained and the system performed up to the design specification. The result has been the creation of major problems, namely that the 'black box' is an inflexible stand-alone which not only fails to meet the function's changing needs, it also fails to address the needs of other parts of organization and does not reflect the needs of customers. More seriously, the scenario also hints that the operational staff have become alienated because their criticisms were ignored. This dangerous situation has been allowed to fester because the senior managers failed to carry out any form of post-implementation review to check that the system was actually meeting quality standards. By any standards, therefore, the money saved in buying an off-the-shelf product was not cost-effective.

The better approach would have been the development of the sales order system as part of an overall systems review to identify the company's IT needs at strategic, tactical and operational levels – evaluating the information needs to support decisions in other functions and providing sufficient interdependence of support rather than this piecemeal effort which is run by demotivated staff.

3 There are three main schools of information systems development methodology, namely, process-driven, data-driven and user-driven. But no methodology should ever be used on its own. Each methodology should be slotted into the systems development life cycle in which the first step is a proper investigation of the present situation so that a requirements specification can be produced (so by seeing what you have, you can say what you need). Hence, Wiltminster plc should have drawn up an IT strategy by matching their potential IT needs to the business plan. This would have enabled managers to identify which possible applications would give them the best opportunities.

The managers had the right idea in seeking outside help. Unfortunately, they chose to rely on a supplier with only limited local experience in small companies. The consultant should have been able to draw up a data and a systems architecture for the company so that everyone could see how all the different processes or systems of processes were intended to fit together to allow the company to operate successfully. The most effective designs allow a clustering of the most interdependent data files because the most efficient organizations rely on having the most used data readily available when and where it is needed. Since the sales order processing system should interface with many other systems within the organization, the needs of the sales/ marketing, manufacturing and finance divisions should have been considered together so that the distribution of, and responsibility for, the sales order data could be planned. Once a feasible system had been designed, the managers could have proceeded to the activities of project selection and justification. If the sales order processing project was selected, the practical design could be managed under the methodology considered most appropriate. The advantages of each of the three methodologies are as follows:

- *Process-driven* – the intention is to capture and describe the existing organizational processes, and then to make them work more efficiently.
- *Data-driven* – because the nature of the company's data is likely to be more stable than the dynamics of people interacting together, it is better to focus on what is processed and not how it is processed.
- *User-driven* – because the success of any system depends on the skills and commitment of the people who are to use it, real and continuing consultation with them is a good idea.

4 Because EDI introduces the reality of what is called 'paperless trading', the design and installation involves far more than just the installation of a new technology. In order to reap the potential benefits, it requires a complete review of the information strategy and associated systems for Wiltminster plc. It also requires new relationships with its retail customers – it requires the establishment of a culture of greater trust between the company and its retail customers, and the mutual development of new internal systems to facilitate the effective flow and use of the information exchanged. There are profound cost implications and many of the smaller retail customers may not wish or be able to afford the cost of EDI. But the strategy now being followed by Global is a positive sign that not using EDI may result in loss of customers.

In the conventional manual system, either the customer submits an order in writing or the seller issues invoices to confirm an oral order. Thus, there is always a piece of paper which will begin the audit trail for each transaction. In a paperless environment, all of the major processes are triggered and managed without the need to create manual records (and often without the direct intervention of a human being). This has real implications for both buyers and sellers. At a practical level, orders can be raised immediately the need is established. This can be particularly important if the buyer is operating an automated JIT system and wishes to place orders the moment critical stock levels are reached. But if this is to produce a rapid response from the seller, new internal systems are required so that the seller can act on the orders when they are received. This means that warehouse stock levels must be checked – if the relevant goods are available in appropriate quantity, their despatch must be authorized and a sales invoice raised; if the stock is not available, production must be authorized and confirmation that the order has been accepted must be transmitted to the buyer. There are a number of problems for the seller, the most important of which are:

- *Stock control*: because buyers now want to reduce the amount of capital tied up in their stock (hence the popularity of the JIT system), this may require the seller to carry a larger buffer stock both of raw materials and of finished goods to meet orders quickly when they arrive. This will tend to drive up the cost of capital.
- *Production*: scheduling becomes more demanding because, in a fully integrated system, the buyers' orders may be received in the production department fractions of a second after they have been received by the organization's computer and inadequate stock levels are confirmed.
- *Legal*: lawyers are particularly interested in defining when and where each contract is made. This becomes difficult when no human beings have been involved. It will also be necessary to decide whether the contract is made using the standard terms of the buyer or of the seller. There may also be implications raised by the Data Protection Act 1984 if any of the data held are personal data. Organizations should also begin the consider the implications of the European Directive 1995/46 which will require changes before the end of 1998.
- *Security*: the key issues are putting in place safeguards to prevent the seller's entire stock being sent to a criminally inclined hacker, and specifying procedures to limit the opportunities for anyone to alter any of the electronically-held data.
- *Goodwill*: queries on orders and invoicing may be harder to resolve unless the relationship between buyer and seller becomes more co-operative in spirit.
- *Auditing*: under a manual system, cradle-to-grave auditing is possible, albeit expensive; paperless trading can only be audited by verifying the software systems and the associated security provisions. The seller's auditors should be positively involved in the design of the security system.

If Wiltminster plc is to respond constructively to Global Carpet plc's request, it must commit an appropriate amount of capital to the IT budget and begin an immediate Total Systems Analysis. If we assume that an integrated EDI system is feasible (in this, the loss of such an important customer is likely to make it cost-effective in the middle to long term), then detailed discussions must begin with all the existing customers about EDI issues. In particular, security protocols must be agreed to reduce the opportunities for unauthorized orders to be placed and copies of orders must be kept in both buyers' and seller's systems to support auditing (the auditors and lawyers of both the seller and the buyers should be consulted about system design). Similarly, the terms of all contracts must be clarified and acceptance procedures agreed. There should also be detailed disclosure by the buyers of their likely future needs so that Wiltminster plc's raw materials acquisition, production and stock holding can be smoothed to more predictable patterns of demand. In short, the introduction of EDI will require different levels of communication and trust between the seller and the buyers.

5 Although Global Carpets plc appears keen to move forward with the introduction of an EDI system, not all Wiltminster plc's customers will wish to follow suit. The customers are likely to fall into the following groups:

- small organizations that have not automated and have neither the capital nor the inclination to introduce modern technology
- medium to large organizations that have not automated or that do not have the level of automation that would be compatible with an EDI system
- organizations that have a level of technology that would permit them to interface with an EDI system.

If the number of small organizations that did not wish to join in an EDI system did not represent a significant volume of business, Wiltminster plc could consider making its use of its EDI system a precondition of business. But there are two dangers in this. All goodwill is important to an organization and, even though only a small number of customers might be lost in the short term, other customers might consider Wiltminster plc's inflexibility to be worrying and not commit themselves to Wiltminster plc, fearing that they might fall victims of future arbitrary changes. Further, new small customers may be deterred from approaching Wiltminster plc and, in the long term, this may represent a significant loss of business. Thus, some form of parallel running between a manual and an automated system should be arranged. The retention of manual ordering would become highly desirable if large customers rejected the idea of EDI. But the willingness of large numbers of customers to adopt EDI is not trouble-free. The key question is the extent to which Wiltminster plc might wish to take account of their customers' declared needs or suggestions in the design of their own system. The greater the number of differences between their customers' needs, the more difficult it may be to produce a universally acceptable system. But if problems can be overcome, it may speed up the quality of the service that Wiltminster plc is able to offer to its customers, if only by reducing the time spent in dealing with paperwork. It should improve stock turnover and it should enhance cashflow by faster invoicing and better debt management.

6 The different types of information that could be provided include:

- customer spending behaviour – detailed by customer or geographic region, level of credit outstanding, different patterns demanded, levels of support that may be required, frequency of ordering, etc.
- product demand patterns overall – changes in total demand, type of demand, and so on.
- responses to changes in marketing policies – monitoring the effects of price changes, new product lines and advertising/in-store promotions, assists planning at the strategic, tactical and operational levels.

7 The marketing department would have access to information that would allow it to monitor and appraise the effectiveness and efficiency of the existing relationships between Wiltminster plc and its customers. Thus, it would have the power to search the database and to produce the information detailed in the answer to question 6. At an operational level, customers who have not placed an order for some time may be flagged for a visit by a sales representative or for involvement in some form of sales promotional activity. Similarly, at a tactical level, analysis would allow the company to identify the different patterns in ordering and to identify the level of support necessary to optimize sales. This may involve increasing the number of staff involved in the activity or changing the training given to staff in the hope that their performance will improve sales. Equally, at a strategic level, if Wiltminster plc decided to change any of its policies, it becomes easier to monitor consumer behaviour before and after the change to measure effectiveness. Thus, if pricing structures or discounts are changed, it is easy to detect changes in sales volumes of the products (and customers) affected. If more money is spent on advertising or in-store promotions, customer reaction can be more directly measured. Trend analysis may also help in the design of new products or the more effective exploitation of existing product lines.

Case study B

Merston Vehicles plc is a major distributor of cars and it operates three sites in a single urbanized region of about 30 square miles. Each site has a sales showroom and garage facilities for the maintenance and repair of vehicles. To maximize its market opportunities within the area, the company has negotiated separate agencies to sell the cars of three different manufacturers. The terms of each agency agreement are that each manufacturer's new cars are exclusive to each site. The company deals with both the individual customer and the business or fleet buyer. The resulting sales business divides into the following annual proportions:

- used vehicle sales representing 50 per cent of the total car sales
- sales to the business/fleet user representing 40 per cent of the new car sales
- sales to the private buyer representing 10 per cent of new car sales.

The other major dimension of the company's business is car servicing and repair which is carried on at each of the three sites. The company services all new cars under the warranty schemes offered by each of the manufacturers, and offers guarantees with all the second-hand cars sold. This represents a core of tied customers, each of whom is known to the company. The company hopes to retain each customer's loyalty when the warranty or guarantee runs out, but it does not advertise the garages as service centres to the general public. Each site does have some repair trade from people who live or work nearby, but this is not considered a major part of the business.

The company has had a successful history in the use of computer systems to support the work at all three sites. Some of the development work was provided by each of the car manufacturers as turnkey systems. These are standard packages to maintain databases for the following sets of records:

- an inventory and the cost of spare parts held in store
- the manufacturer's complete spare part catalogue by model and year
- the manufacturers' current price lists both for new vehicles and their spares
- the service records of the customers' cars.

Each of these systems have been developed separately using different hardware and software facilities, and they will not interoperate without substantial modification. The company has not contacted the manufacturers to see whether they would consent to these modifications being carried out and so the systems are either accessed separately on the same hardware, or they are used on stand-alone machines supplied by the manufacturers. Nevertheless, all these systems have proved robust and have proved to be reasonably effective in supporting the work of the service centres. Each of the sales offices has on-line access to the manufacturers' or national distributors' systems which enables the sales staff to establish the availability of cars by model, colour and additional features such as spoilers, sun roof, leather upholstery, etc. Once cars are located, they can be ordered directly but none of the sites has an internal system which stores data on new products or customers. Instead, they rely on manufacturer's brochures and a card index system.

The company operates a standard financial accounting system which is operated in isolation at each of the three centres. Although the garages use the same system and produce the same outputs in terms of invoices, statements and monthly financial reports, there has been no attempt to link the systems together. This makes the consolidation of the three sets of monthly accounts for the management team a time-consuming problem because it has to be undertaken manually each month from the print-outs produced at each centre. The personnel function has also been denied an integrated and automated system. Each site has a director in charge and that director assumes responsibility for local personnel management. This hands-on approach has been considered reasonably effective and, with the exception of the payroll system, the management has not thought it necessary to centralize and automate any personnel data.

As a result of a general economic down-turn, Merston Vehicles plc has been experiencing considerable pressure on its profit margins. This has affected all aspects of its business. The directors have been reviewing their strategies, and their response has been to recognize that it is necessary to:

- improve efficiency
- reduce overheads
- become more responsive to market demands
- achieve greater synergy between the operations of the three sites.

It was obvious from an early stage in this review that the development of a more coherent information system would play a critical role in the achievement of the business strategic plans. The chief executive, Tom Merston, decided to seek the advice of a local consultancy organization, Value Adding Systems. Following a preliminary three-month investigation of the business situation and the information system requirements, these consultants have recommended that Merston develop and install an integrated database system capable of supporting all the major functions at all three sites. In hardware and software terms, this would produce a distributed system. Each site would have a local area network and the integration into a wide area network could either be achieved through the public telephone system or through the local cable television company which also offers a packet switching facility. The consultants have identified a number of obstacles to overcome, but have convinced Tom Merton that the business cannot continue in the medium to long term without an integrated systems approach.

Questions

1 Value Adding Systems use SSADM in their consultancy work. Describe this methodology.
2 Explain how the use of this methodology may assist Merston Vehicles plc.
3 Identify the general problems that will have to be resolved before application-specific files or an integrated database system can be created.
4 What specific problems might arise from the proposal to automate the personnel function?
5 Security is an important consideration for any system. What general concerns does this proposal raise?
6 What immediate practical steps should be taken to plan the security system?

Case study B: outline solutions

1 The Structured Systems Analysis and Design Method (SSADM) is a hybrid methodology which contains features from three previously separate approaches, namely:

- process-driven
- data-driven
- event-driven.

The method is now in its fifth version and it contains precisely defined stages and support documentation. It contains four types of elements:

- the structure of the methodology
- the techniques which describe how the various steps are to be carried out
- the procedures to define the project management activities
- the dictionary which contains the expected output models and documentation.

There are five stages within the structure:

- Feasibility study – this evaluates the proposed system before any significant resources are committed to implementation. It incorporates decisions on the objectives of the proposal, the criteria of performance and success, and the boundaries between the different systems both existing and proposed.
- Requirements analysis – a detailed investigation of the present systems data, functions, operations and events which highlights the objectives of the proposed system in terms of the users' needs.
- Requirements specification – this builds on the system overview which has now been produced and analyses the detail of what will be required. In doing so, it may be appropriate to use prototyping techniques.
- Logical system specification – this is the detailed specification of the processing and human–computer interaction requirements.
- Physical design – this converts the logical design into real design for the programs and data storage requirements that will make up the complete system.

2 This is a general purpose methodology which aims to produce the effective standardization of techniques and documentation throughout an organization. The immediate advantage is that training can be centralized and co-ordinated with a rapid improvement in provable quality standards realistically to be anticipated. From the point of view of the directors of Merston Vehicles plc, the first two stages will give them an opportunity to gain an understanding of how the company actually works now so that the benefits of any changes can be better identified. Such an understanding is an essential precondition to the use of techniques such as critical success factors and cost–benefit analysis. The company has actually been running as three separate divisions within a holding company framework. Each site has been the domain of a single director, responsible for promoting the sales of a unique manufacturer's products. This has encouraged the development of completely independent and largely incompatible systems. Hence, it is likely that Stages 1 and 2 will necessitate a top-down appraisal of present reality so that the directors can decide which among the best of each site's systems ought to be preserved and incorporated into an integrated system. This appraisal will have to be carried out in an egoless atmosphere in which the directors genuinely commit themselves to work together for the benefit of the company. Because the subsequent stages of the methodology separate the logical specification and the physical design, the directors will move from an overview of what is required to the more detailed planning exercise without having to be bound by their understanding of how they do things now, i.e. the current system is the baseline and only defines the environment into which the new systems must be placed.

3 Application-specific files group records according to common purposes. Hence, for example, stock files will contain details of all the product lines held in stock. There are four main types of file:

- masterfiles which either contain permanent data such as names and addresses, or data subject to update (e.g. sales to date)
- transaction files which contain temporary records of values and amounts
- look-up files which contain reference materials such as price lists
- archive files which contain historical data.

It would be convenient for each file to allow access to its data about the number and models of car held available for sale, and about the identity and price of the spares stored so that customers wishing to buy cars can be given a wider choice, and spares can be exchanged between sites where this would save money. This data could be held on-line in look-up files or in a database. A significant proportion of the software and data dealing with spares has been supplied by the manufacturers and distributors. Each of these packages will be protected by copyright. In principle, this means that the company cannot make a copy of any material part of any of the turnkey software packages supplied to it. But if the packages already have the capacity to export data, this may be exploited to transport processed data to in-house systems, subject to any copyright in the contents that might exist in the data contained in any database included within the package, for example each item listed in a database of spares might be protected against copying.

But if the software works well, a European directive currently permits users to decompile the software and to modify it so that it interoperates with any in-house software. Although this European provision is directly effective and would give the company rights overriding the English rules, Merston Vehicles plc should be cautious about its use. The fact that a law may permit something does not change the need to maintain the goodwill of the suppliers and it would be sensible to include the manufacturers and distributors in any discussion to establish whether a collaborative venture is possible. The copyright holders might take the view that any amendments or enhancements that may lead to increased turnover of their products should be encouraged and, perhaps, supported financially. There are a number of dangers in using several application-specific files, namely that:

- data may be duplicated which is wasteful of storage space
- there are problems in ensuring that data integrity and consistency between files is maintained so common data held in each of the files must all be updated in the same way and at the same time
- multiple access to each file may be difficult to manage, particularly if read and write processes are being attempted simultaneously – for example, spare parts may be deducted from stock for use in repair work with write operations for each spare part to a transaction file for subsequent invoicing to the customer and to all other files in which that spare part may have been recorded while one or more other interrogations of stockholding are taking place.

It may therefore be better to regard all data as a corporate resource rather than as three site-specific holdings to be shared. If this intellectual step can be taken by the directors, a full database management system could be installed. A typical DBMS will include record, access and security controls which should provide a more flexible, informative and secure environment. The immediate benefit would be that the directors could have a better corporate view of performance. Indeed, decision support systems and expert systems could be added to allow data to be used more effectively in strategic decision making. This assumes that the culture of decision making will tolerate the change in availability of data and transparency of individual performance (not something that can be taken for granted). The development of a DBMS is a more radical project. It will therefore require more effort to design and greater changes on the part of all users. So before taking the go/no-go decision, the company should think very carefully about the costs, both tangible and intangible. It may be better to opt for a more piecemeal integration and enhancement of existing systems than to aim to produce a total system design.

4 The issues and problems encountered by Merston Vehicles plc in developing a system to support the personnel management function are of the same type that would be encountered in developing any system. The differences would lie more in the significance of particular issues (so, for example, the privacy of personal information may be a significant issue in a personnel system). The development of a personnel system like any other system needs to be incor-

porated within the overall systems development strategy for the organization, given the potential common use of certain data elements. Hence, the personal details of each member of staff are required for the payroll system and may be required for invoicing repair customers if different hourly rates are applied depending on the experience and competence of each mechanic. Similarly, design should reflect the fact that users may need to access more than one system giving rise to the need for common human–computer protocols.

The development of the system should start with a review and analysis of the needs of users at the strategic, tactical and operational levels, including the types of information required and the nature of the access necessary to support decisions at each of these levels. The particular problem for Merston Vehicles plc would be the development of a common approach to personnel management across its various sites. The previous development of different policies and systems would make the development of a computer system extremely difficult. Another issue of particular concern is the nature of the data that are likely to be stored within such a system. The storing of personal details concerning its employees may not only raise concerns about the privacy of the individual but also concerns about access and security. The legal requirements to provide users with a copy of the information stored may assist in resolving some of the concerns about privacy. Staff will wish to have assurances concerning those permitted access to this data and the steps taken to ensure unauthorized access. The organization would need to discuss such issues with staff directly or through their representatives.

The problem of maintaining the accuracy of the data held in the system and ensuring that it is also up-to-date is one that is shared with most systems. However, given the sensitivity of data elements within the personnel field this would require particular attention to ensure the validity and correctness of the data to avoid embarrassment to the individual. Like all other systems, the key to developing a successful system is not only to undertake a logical and planned approach to the development but to undertake a review of the performance of the system against the design criteria established at the outset.

5 The basic issues for a WAN are in principle the same as for any other form of networked system including the:

- number of users
- frequency and type of access required by each class of users
- degree of centralization or distribution of the database files
- nature of the communications systems to be employed (whether public/private cables or some form of broadcast media)
- geographic distribution of the system and the consequent vulnerabilities to disruption
- sensitivity of the data held within the system.

In general terms, a WAN is exposed to the normal threats to the security of the system and the data but, because of the communication links between the different parts of the system, the risks are greater. The advantages and disadvantages to be weighed would include:

- Physical security in terms of preventing damage from fire, flooding and theft in a much wider range of different locations, many of which may be outside the direct control of the company.
- If the system is operated on a more distributed basis then the consequences of a single incident may prove less severe. So, for example, damage to hardware at one site is unlikely to prevent the other sites from continuing normal levels of service availability providing they hold the appropriate data files locally.
- Reductions in the risk of data corruption or loss because of faults in the system's hardware and software may be achieved by backing-up the system regularly to ensure that the loss of data and transaction processed is minimized – say, by taking copies of the key files at the end of each day or more regularly if appropriate and storing those copies at the other two sites.
- The major threat to data integrity and confidentiality arises from the possibility of unauthorized access by persons both internal and external to the organization. Developing a WAN substantially increases the opportunities for this to occur because hackers may exploit the communication links in their efforts to penetrate the more sensitive parts of the system. The standard approaches to addressing this type of problem involve the use of passwords, priority codes, access logs for particular files or for the system as a whole, read-only files to prevent data corruption and, in extreme cases, physical locking devices on the input terminals.

6 A security working party or team should be created as a part of the SSADM exercise. It should be headed by one of the most senior managers to send a message to all employees that real changes are to be made. The working party's brief should be to implement all the security systems necessary to protect the company's tangible and intangible resources. This will include retraining the staff and monitoring the commitment of the staff at all levels to the new security measures. Membership of the working party should draw on all the main functions within the organization and include the company's auditor and lawyer. The first step should be to undertake a risk management audit to consider the extent to which the company has insurance cover against the range of likely perils or, if the company decides to self-insure entirely or to carry a part of the risk on a given peril, whether full and detailed plans are in place to deal with each peril should it arise. Thus, the working party must identify the points of vulnerability in the existing and proposed systems, and rank the risks in terms of their probability and criticality. Some risks will be acceptable (for example minor stock loss through the occasional incident of pilfering by a mechanic); some risks will be controllable; some risks will be transferable. The remaining critical risks must be the subject of a contingency or disaster planning exercise. At an early stage, the team must collect data on the financial effect of each possible interruption to computer services, and on the baseline of performance required from the affected functions in order to keep the business running. Hence, for example, if fire damaged the accounting data, it would be critical to maintain the credit and debt management systems to maintain some cashflow. Proper archiving

procedures should therefore ensure that no more than one day's data are ever lost and that there is always enough spare processing capacity in one of the remaining sites to be able to keep the billing function running.

Case study C

Bison Tools plc manufactures and distributes hand tools (such as hammers, saws, pliers and screwdrivers) for use by the professional and by the do-it-yourself user. The company manufactures a range of almost 200 products which are designed for both the home and export markets. With accelerating speed over the last 20 years, there has been increased competition from manufacturers overseas. There are two main reasons for the success of foreign firms. First, hand tools are relatively 'low tech' and, although there have been improvements in the technologies associated with both the materials and the processes used to manufacture tools, these changes have been reasonably obvious and they have been copied without penalty. Secondly, consumers have grown more demanding and now expect better-quality tools for lower prices. This has fuelled substantial market penetration by manufacturers in countries where materials and labour costs are lower than in western Europe (particularly from China and some of the old Communist countries). Many of the traditional companies have ceased trading, finding that the prices charged by some of the new market players matched their costs. The only reason that Bison Tools plc has been able to survive is that it had a well-established reputation for quality and consumers have been prepared to pay a little bit extra to get that perceived added value. Nevertheless, the company's workforce has fallen from a peak of 1200 employees in 1986 to its current level of only 450.

At its simplest level, this reduction in direct labour costs was a necessary reaction to competitive forces and made the survival of Bison Tools plc more likely. The strategy was to prune the product range so that, wherever possible, the company focused its production on those tools where a high degree of automation with fewer components was possible. The engineering department also took the opportunity to review the factory environment and it identified a number of significant bottlenecks. So, in designing the new technology, the shop floor layout and the nature of some of the processes were changed to maximize the flow of materials. This has been a capital intensive strategy and the company has struggled to write off this investment during a period of reduced turnover due to the increased competition. The management of these changes has also placed considerable strains on the individual employees who have been expected to become multifunctional. At a time when almost two thirds of the workforce were made redundant, the survivors have been required to accept major changes in their working practices and in the culture of the organization. All those who remain work long hours and, because they have given up pay increases for the last five years, they have accepted a reduction in pay in real terms. This has left them with little sense of job security, some desperation and not a lot of loyalty for the company.

The company has operated a computer-based system of production scheduling and control for many years with some success. The system works by creating a schedule for the following week based on orders received and sales forecasted. This scheduling system is controlled by the manager of the production department and he is responsible for distributing the computer output to all the affected departments on the Thursday of Week A ready for operation on the Monday of Week B. This includes a listing of the raw materials requirement which is distributed to the stores responsible for providing the materials requested at the start of each day. Low levels of raw materials required are reported to the production manager and, after consultation with purchasing department, the production schedule is amended on a daily basis in the light of expected delivery times.

Despite this scheduling system, Bison Tools plc has found it difficult to guarantee customer delivery dates and this has begun to affect sales. After researching the market, the directors have decided to commission a new manufacturing resource planning system called MRP 2. This system will require a fundamental change to the current processes associated with capacity planning, inventory control, product costing, shop floor control, finance, marketing, engineering and human resource management. Because this is a top-down system, it is likely that the nature of many jobs will change and these changes in roles and responsibilities may also require changes in the organization structure to ensure the effective use of the system. The completed system will have the following elements:

- a master production schedule (MPS) to provide a full interface between the sales/marketing activities and production – the intention is to build in shipping dates for the customers and controls for made-for-stock orders
- a central database to provide information on the quantities and lead-times of the materials required to make each line of finished goods
- an inventory file to show the amount and location of stocks of all raw materials, components and finished goods
- the materials requisition planning system (MRPS) breaks down the MPS into a time-phased requirements schedule for raw materials and components, compares that schedule to the inventory and sets the timing of all procurement
- the production activity control system (PACS) controls the release of work to the shop floor and its subsequent flow.

At this stage in their analysis, the directors have recognized that this system will have to have a monitoring and feedback function to cater for delays and waste in the purchasing and manufacturing activities. They also understand that it must be able to react to changes in the products and manufacturing technology.

Questions

1. The implementation of any new system requires careful thought. Identify the main factors that you consider Bison Tools plc should address in the proposed new system and recommend the steps that should be taken.
2. There are a number of approaches to the implementation of a system. Evaluate the benefits and difficulties that Bison may encounter in using a parallel running method of implementing its new system.
3. Assessing and reviewing the performance of any new system is important. Evaluate the reasons for the need to assess performance and suggest approaches that would be applicable in the case of Bison.

Case study C: outline answers

1 When evaluating any proposed system, all organizations should focus on three key dimensions, namely:

- *System-related issues* – this involves deciding which methodology to use in assessing the hardware and software proposals and setting the 'go/no go' criteria; subsequently, it will be necessary to decide how the system is to be implemented and tested, what security and recovery plans will be needed, and how the system is to be supported and customer goodwill maintained while the inevitable teething problems are resolved.
- *Internal organization issues* – many systems such as that proposed by Bison Tools plc will require some degree of reorganization and changes in working practices. All these changes will require pre-planning and detailed consultation with the people affected. Once implementation procedures have been agreed, careful monitoring and flexible support will be required during the changeover. In this, the training of both the users and the support staff will be a critical factor in ensuring the effective implementation of the system.
- *External interfaces* – the impact of any system, particularly during the implementation phase, on both suppliers and customers should not be ignored. If the system and all associated changes were to be implemented by Bison Tools plc it would have a significant impact on the working relationships with the larger customers and suppliers. It is therefore essential for all the affected parties to be involved in a real consultation process so that the likely impact and the timing of the changes can be discussed and mutually acceptable strategies agreed on how some of the potential difficulties may be overcome. Needless to say, it would not be sensible to proceed with the new system if the majority of the external parties have not confirmed their active support.

The following key elements require careful consideration when planning the implementation of a new system: establishing effective lines of communication to internal and external parties, positively involving all interested groups in the planning process, the timing and phasing of the implementation, the effective training and development of staff resources, and the establishment of the necessary support services which will operate during the implementation and post-implementation stages.

Coming to the specific problems for Bison Tools plc, the company has already met three of the essential preconditions to a successful MRP system, namely:

- it appears to have rationalized its product lines
- to some extent, it has optimized its production technology
- it has forced its workforce to begin confronting the process of becoming truly multifunctional.

But to achieve optimal results, the system as proposed must be integrated fully into the organization as a whole. If Bison Tools plc takes the time to produce an integrated system, the outcomes will include the reduction of waste in the form of materials handling, queuing, machine set-up and down-times, leading to simple products flowing through short production lines with good communication and a flexible workforce. This means that the implications of MRP 2 for each of the major business functions must be established. For these purposes, we will briefly consider the purchasing and marketing functions. It is taken as read that there is more to purchasing than placing orders and demanding fast delivery. This planning system would enable the company to introduce a JIT system to support the cost-effectiveness of the production technology. But, put simply, no supplier can meet JIT requirements if the buyer has no proper controls over fluctuations in demand. The problem for Bison Tools plc would be exploit the MRP 2 in a way that would make its input requirements less erratic and more predictable. If this can be done, JIT becomes a realistic opportunity for both buyer and seller.

Similarly, there is more to selling than taking orders. Marketing embraces a wide range of strategies to improve sales from promotions in individual stores through to reserving manufacturing capacity for priority customers. If the MPS is going to become an effective tool, it must be able to reflect commercial reality as well as manufacturing logic. A balance has to be struck between the economics of small production runs for individual product lines and the need to be able to maintain customer confidence in being able to order advertised goods against guaranteed delivery dates. So if marketing wishes to plan a sales initiative (say, by a national advertising campaign for additional discounts on particular products for a limited period of time), it must be able to determine whether production capacity can meet the expected increase in demand for the products to be promoted and what level of discount to offer. Obviously, this level of decision making will require something more than a simple short-term production rescheduling exercise. The assumption must be that all affected functional departments must be able to access a centralized system for planning and control purposes. The elements that will need to be considered include price, quality, production volume flexibility, delivery lead-time, after-sales support and stability (all customers and suppliers need to have confidence in the long-term service performance of Bison Tools plc).

The successful operation of a fully integrated system will require a substantial redistribution of power within the company and much greater transparency of decision making. Given that the staff are already highly stressed, this level of change will have to be very carefully managed if any degree of success is to be achieved and maintained. Because the overall impact of implementation will be top-down, we would advise that the directors and senior managers undergo specific training before any other step or action is taken. Only when it is apparent that these individuals clearly understand what the current problems are and how the MRP system will affect them, should the company begin planning the implementation of MRP 2.

2 Parallel running means that the old and the new systems run alongside each other until the new system has established sufficient reliability to be trusted to replace the old. It is most usually adopted when one or more of the following conditions are met:

- the application is sufficiently critical to the organization that no interruption to the availability of the service can be tolerated
- the new system uses untried technology or operating methods which require full testing before being accepted as reliable
- the new system will change the organization's methods or business processes so radically that the existing processes cannot be maintained once they have been abandoned.

The approach may be justified on the grounds that the changeover to the new system is as effective as it can possibly be. It will give Bison Tools plc's staff the opportunity to learn about the new system in a 'safe' way before having to rely on it totally. The drawback is the cost. It is the most expensive of the three changeover methods but it is the most secure. To operate both the old and the new systems means that the existing staff will have to work longer hours (this will be so even if temporary staff are drafted in to continue running the old system because the existing staff must train and then supervise the new staff for as long as the old system runs). There are also technical problems associated with the changeover. So, for example, when new orders are received and a schedule is produced under the old system, how are any differences between that schedule and the output from the new production activity control system to be resolved? Production planning and inventory control cannot simultaneously be organized under two different systems. So the directors should not mechanically opt for parallel running because it is reputed to be the safest method. The best solution may involve a combination of pilot running and parallel running so that relevant parts of the system are allowed to operate in less sensitive functional areas while the critical parts of the system are not acted on until the effectiveness of the output has been verified over a predetermined period of time. The key factor is the predicted cost of loss. If the system failed and the development and implementation costs had to be written off, this will represent a significant loss for the company. This means that MRP 2 is a high-risk project. Further, the more the new system is allowed to replace the old, the greater the costs of restoring the old (and the more disruption there may be to the suppliers and customers with consequent damage to goodwill). The directors should therefore adopt the system of weighted ranking to decide which elements of the system should be introduced, in what order and over what timescale.

In deciding the strategy, the human aspect is particularly important. It seems that the company has already produced a 'culture of fear' in which the surviving staff work longer hours for less money. Building staff confidence to make sure that the implementation is a success will be a severe challenge for those given the task of training and managing the changeover. Moreover, if we assume that the company decides to adopt a JIT system (which would be a logical development) this will involve building up the trust of the suppliers before all those involved feel it safe to let the system go live. Establishing external lines of communication and being prepared to disclose otherwise sensitive data about future raw materials and components needs are big steps for a company that may have been used to tradition management hierarchical structures and the conventions of commercial confidentiality.

3 The performance evaluation of a new system is usually carried out by undertaking a post-implementation or post-audit review after the system has been working normally for a predetermined time. The aims of the review are not to find excuses for any elements of poor performance in the system. The true purpose is to enable the company to learn from its experience. The elements to be considered are therefore to:

- ensure that the new system is able to handle the volume of data and transactions which the company needs to be able to process under varying conditions
- check that the new system is secure and that records are being maintained correctly
- make sure that the objectives of the system as defined in the statement of goals or terms of reference are being met – this could include a check that predicted cost–benefit patterns are being achieved
- ensure that the new system is capable of matching the user requirements specified in the initial development stages
- evaluate the quality of the interaction between the user and the system to ensure that the appropriate standards are being achieved.

The review should be carried out in as open a way as possible. Everyone must be encouraged to give honest appraisals of the system as it is working without fear of penalty (i.e. even though this may mean criticizing colleagues and managers). If people react defensively, the company is unlikely to learn anything useful from the review. Further, the review should not be seen as a one-off activity but as part of an ongoing programme to enhance efficiency and effectiveness within the organization. There are several approaches that could be appropriate to the Bison Tools plc situation. The two most useful are:

- Critical success factors (CSF) – this analysis focuses on the evaluation of those key performance factors which the system is intended to address, such as stock levels and sales delivery performance.
- Benchmarking – this sets the levels of performance considered acceptable such as processing speed or sales delivery times, and then measures actual performance against the benchmark figures for the range of transaction over a number of days or weeks under as wide a range of circumstances as possible.

The evaluation of performance depends on a wide range of factors and the directors should accept that differences in the way in which users define terms and perceive value may lead to problems in interpreting all feedback, whether from questionnaires or less formal means. It should also be accepted that there is rarely a single reason for poor performance. Most problems arise from interaction between a number of variables and, although CSF and benchmarking may give rise to interesting data, the directors should never treat the resulting data as able to identify causes or to allocate blame with any degree of certainty. The results are simply a part of the evidence which may form the basis of future planning to improve performance.

Further reading

Aalders, J. C. H., Herschberg, I. S. and Van Zanten, A., *Handbook for Information Security. A Guide Towards Information Security Standards*, North Holland, 1985.

Anthony, R. N., *Planning and Control Systems: A Framework for Analysis*, Harvard University Press, 1965.

Ardis, P. M. and Comer, M. J., *Risk Management. Computers, Fraud and Insurance*, McGraw-Hill, 1987.

Ashworth, C. and Slater, L., *An Introduction to SSADM Version 4*, McGraw-Hill, 1993.

Avison, D. E. and Fitzgerald, G., *Information Systems Development: Methodologies, Tools and Techniques*, Blackwell, 1988.

Beer, S., *Diagnosing the System for Organisations*, John Wiley, 1981.

Benjamin, R. I., Rockart, J. F., Scott Morton, M. S. and Wyman, J., Information technology: a strategic opportunity, *Sloan Management Review*, Spring, 1984.

Brumm, P., *The Micro to Mainframe Connection*, TAB Books, 1986.

Camrass, R. and Smith, K., *Wiring Up the Workplace: A Practical Guide for Management*, IBC Technical Services, 1986.

Cash, J. I. and Konsynski, B. R., IS redraws competitive boundaries, *Harvard Business Review*, March/April, 1985.

Cashmore, C. and Lyall, R., *Business Information: Systems and Strategies*, Prentice Hall, 1991.

Clifton, H. D., *Business Data Systems*, Prentice Hall, 1996.

Comer, M. J., *Corporate Fraud*, McGraw-Hill, 1985.

Cronin, D. J., *Microcomputer Data Security, Issues and Strategies*, Prentice Hall, 1986.

Douglas, I. J. and Olson, P. J., *Audit and Control of Computer Networks*, NCC Publications, 1986.

Driver, M. J. and Mock, T. J., Human information processing, decision style theory and accounting information systems, *The Accounting Review*, July 1975, pp. 490–508.

Earl, M. J., *Management Strategies for Information Technology*, Prentice Hall, 1989.

Earl, M. J. and Hopwood, A. G., From management information to information management. In: Lucas, Land, Lincoln and Sapper (eds) *The Information Systems Environment*, North Holland, New York, 1980, pp. 3–13.

Edwards, C. and Savage, N., *Information Technology and the Law*, Macmillan, 1986.

Elbra, R. A., *Computer Security Handbook*, Blackwell, 1992.

Ellison, J. R. and Pritchard, J. A. T., *Security in Office Systems*, NCC Publications, 1987.

Eva, M., *SSADM Version 4: A User's Guide*, McGraw-Hill, 1992.

Feeny, D., Creating and sustaining competitive advantage with IT. In: Earl M. J. (ed.) *Information Management: The Strategic Dimension*, Oxford University Press, 1988.

Flood, R. and Jackson, C. M., *Critical Systems Thinking*, John Wiley, 1995.

Flynn, D. J., *Information Systems Requirements: Determination and Analysis*, McGraw-Hill, 1992.

Fraga, J. and Powell, D., A fault and intrusion-tolerant file system. In: Grimson, J. B. and Kugler, H.-J. (eds) *Computer Security: The Practical Issues in a Troubled World*, North Holland, 1985, pp. 203–18.

Grimson, J. B. and Kugler, H.-J., *Computer Security: The Practical Issues in a Troubled World*, North Holland, 1985.

Hirschheim, R., *Office Automation: A Social and Organisational Perspective*, John Wiley, 1985.

Hodkinson, K. and Wasik, M., *Industrial Espionage, Protection and Remedies*, Longman Intelligence Reports, Longman, 1986.

Johnson, D. G., *Computer Ethics*, Prentice Hall, 1985.

Kroenke, D., *Management Information Systems*, McGraw-Hill, 1992.

Lane, V. and Step, J., The formidable – if not insurmountable problems of disaster recovery planning. In: Grimson, J. B. and Kugler, H.-J. (eds) *Computer Security: The Practical Issues in a Troubled World*, North Holland, 1985.

Lane, V. P., *Security of Computer-based Information Systems*, Macmillan, 1985.

Law, D. and Longworth, G., *Systems Development: Strategies and Techniques*, NCC Publications, 1987.

MacCrimmon, K. R., Managing decision making. In: McGuire, J. W. (ed.) *Contemporary Management: Issues and Viewpoints*, Prentice Hall, 1977, pp. 445–95.

Palmer, I. and Rock-Evans, R., *Data analysis*, IPC Publications, 1981.

Panki, R. R., *End User Computing: Management, Applications and Technology*, John Wiley, 1988.

Porter, M. E., *Competitive Advantage*, Free Press, New York, 1985.

Ritchie, R. L. and Marshall, D. V., *Business Risk Management*, Chapman & Hall, 1993.

Robson, W., *Strategic Management and Information Systems*, 2nd edn, Pitman, 1997.

Senn, J. A., *Analysis and Design of Information Systems*, McGraw-Hill, 1989.

Simon, H. A., *The New Science of Management Decision*, Prentice Hall, 1977.

Skidmore, S., *Introduction to Systems Design*, 2nd edn, NCC Blackwell, 1997.

Spencer, D. D., *Computers: An Introduction*, Merrill, 1986.

Stern, N. and Stern, R. A., *Computing With End-user Applications*, John Wiley, 1990.

Ward, J. and Griffiths, P., *Strategic Planning for Information Systems*, John Wiley, 1997.

Wong, K. K., *Computer Disaster Casebook*, BIS Applied Systems, 1987.

Wong, K. K. and Farquhar, W. F. N., *Computer-related Fraud Casebook*, BIS Applied Systems, 1986.

Wong, K. K. and Farquhar, W. F. N., *Computer Crime Casebook*, BIS Applied Systems, 1987.

Worthington, T. K., Chainer, T. J., Williford, J. D. and Gundersen, S. C., IBM Dynamic Signature Verification. In: Grimson, J. B. and Kugler, H.-J. (eds) *Computer Security: The Practical Issues in a Troubled World*, North Holland, 1985, pp. 129–54.

Zwass, V., *Management Information Systems*, W. C. Brown, 1992.

Answers to end of chapter questions

Chapter 1

Self-test questions

1 The text indicates that the nature of any organization's environment involves a diverse range of elements. Different elements are likely to influence to different degrees, depending on the nature of the organization. There are, however, certain elements that are likely to influence most organizations, and these are listed with an example of data items related to each:

- *Economic*: inflation rates, employment levels, interest rates, exchange rates.
- *Political*: strength of party in parliament, policies of parties, influence on economy.
- *Markets*: consumer tasks, distribution channels, growth rates in sales.
- *Competitors*: pricing policies, marketing activities, strategies for growth.
- *Technology*: new product information, new material developments, improved manufacturing, regional variations.
- *Social*: changes in social structure (e.g. family unit), social policies and supports.
- *Legal*: new consumer legislation, EU laws and regulations.

As discussed in the chapter, the organization may view many of these factors at the local, national or international level. Also, the data need not necessarily only take the form of quantified measures but may equally be represented as subjective value judgements by those involved in assessing the environment.

2 Information represents a shared resource within the organization. It is difficult to think of any item of data in any organization that is used by only one individual or for one single activity. Using an example of the customer ordering a particular item from the organization, the basic order request data may be used by the following functions in the organization:

- *Sales department*: record the sale and update customer sales record.
- *Operations department*: process the order to manufacture/schedule/order materials/inspect the goods required.
- *Cost accounts department*: record the costs of the order transaction throughout the organization and monitor/control these.
- *Warehousing/despatch department*: arrange delivery of the order to the customer as required.
- *Financial accounting department*: initially record the order request and subsequently produce the financial documentation associated with receiving payments for this.

There are many examples you could use and the example provided could be elaborated in much more detail. The essential point to note is that data provide a key source for the operation of many parts of an organization, each requiring the same element of data (e.g. order request data in above example) to perform different tasks or functions.

3 The process of strategic management is concerned primarily with the long-term development of the whole organization. Information supports this process in a number of ways:

- It improves knowledge and understanding of the environment.
- It identifies potential threats to the business in the long term.
- It identifies potential opportunities for the business through new markets or changes in technology.
- It assists in the evaluation of sources of added value and the potential competitive advantage of these (e.g. through market research studies).

- It monitors strategies and policies of competitors.
- It identifies and evaluates potential sources of improved efficiency in the operations of the business.
- It monitors the effectiveness of existing strategic and tactical plans (e.g. through internal monitoring systems).

This list could be extended, although the key point to recognize is that the information provided relates to both external and internal factors. The chapter indicates that the balance of the information used will be externally oriented.

4 It is important to recognize the distinction between terms 'data' and 'information' to answer this question. The factors which are identified in the text include:

- prior knowledge of recipient to understand what the data means
- quality of the data provided initially (i.e. rubbish in = rubbish out)
- quality of the processing activities used to manipulate and communicate the data
- appropriateness of the time at which the data are received
- effectiveness of the communications media used
- presentation of data to the user in a meaningful way
- the nature of the interface between the user/recipient and the technology providing the data.

These points could be developed further, although the key point to remember is that the conversion of data to information is not an automatic process, and the whole field of systems development and operation is designed to improve the efficiency and effectiveness of this conversion process.

5 Data exist within an organization in four broad forms, including:

- written or documentary
- oral, resulting from meetings and discussions
- visual, reflecting the actions or reactions of people in the organization
- subconscious, based on the knowledge, views, experiences etc. of the individuals and groups.

While much of the formal data processing activities involve the first of these forms, it should be recognized that the other forms are equally valid forms of data and will influence significantly the operations and decisions of the organization.

Exam-style questions

1 One way of viewing the information system is as a series of activities which are broadly encompassed in the following stages:

- Identify data needs (the reason for which the data is needed or used). This may be a permanent requirement, e.g. regular postings to an accounts ledger, or a response to a transient problem, e.g. to combat the effects of a strike. Not all data needs can be predicted.
- Data capture (how data are captured to meet the given need). The design of the data capture system must reflect the timing and the processing requirements.
- Data processing and communication (how the data are processed, that is how data items are turned into information or made useful). This will include storage, access, calculating, sorting and presentation, for example exception reports, levels of detail.
- User data processing. The users of the system (or its information) are the people who add value to the data or achieve benefits. If items (1) to (3) are primary data processing, then item (4) onwards is secondary information processing. The way in which an accountant will interpret or modify information produced by a computer is an example of this. New developments in information system technology, such as expert systems, are focused on this area.
- Usage of information (the results of the user having the information, e.g. improved knowledge, actions, decisions or any change in behaviour). Often these will be intangible. Information has no intrinsic value. Its value lies only in the results which it can bring about.
- System feedback and control (the control or feedback of results which is applied to the system, often from the user). This may modify the behaviour of the system to better achieve the needs of the user, e.g. improved methods of stock control.

The activities and stages outlined above are those that apply to most forms of system, and are covered in more detail in the chapter dealing with systems theory.

2 This question concerns the relationship between an organization's objectives and practical performance criteria. The five dimensions would be:

- *Environment*: the things outside the organization with which it interacts, e.g. local people, the trade community, the government. To some extent this is a public relation's dimension.
- Competitive edge or distinctive competence: the way in which the management decide to differentiate its products or services in terms of price, quality of reputation.
- Marketing thrust: how the organization seeks to promote itself through advertising, sponsoring, etc. A measure of effectiveness may be the size of the client base or turnover.
- Operating efficiency: this is determined by the ratio of internally generated costs to income. Ultimately, control of these costs (labour, overheads, stock, etc.) affects profitability.
- Human factors. The organization will seek to create and maintain a humane image for the benefit of employees, consumers generally and potential customers.

These five factors will influence the objectives of most organizations. The extent to which a particular factor will influence the objectives will depend on the situation of the organization. For example, during an economic recession when markets are in decline or stagnant, the primary objectives may be oriented more towards survival through improved cost efficiency and operating efficiency. Hence, changes in each of these factors may result in a change in the nature of the objectives pursued and the relative importance of each one. The determination of the objectives of an organization is a very complex process involving internal and external factors, which are liable to change dramatically in the short to medium term.

Chapter 2

Self-test questions

1 Information technologies provide a range of potential benefits to the organization, including:

- Improved efficiency: saving the time taken and the costs involved by employing human processing.
- Improved quality: more accurate, more detailed, more readily available data.
- Improved effectiveness of communications, both with the organizations and to outside agencies.
- Enhanced ability of users to specify and receive information in the format and quality they require for their purposes.

These are all potential benefits. Their realization depends on the quality of the information system that is developed and on the ability of users to interface with the system effectively.

2 An effectively integrated organization is one in which the activities, processes and decision making at different levels and different parts of the organization are working in unison towards the achievement of the common objectives. This may be reflected in:

- early identification of problems and issues
- rapid access or response to the decision-makers' data needs, to analyse such problems
- quick and effective decision making
- rapid and effective communication of decisions throughout the organization
- effective co-ordination of the diverse activities throughout the organization
- responsiveness to change in systems, structures, procedures, etc. and the ability to develop and implement these quickly and effectively
- high-quality performance measurement and control systems at all levels to ensure rapid response to deviations from planned performance.

The basis for generating most of these attributes of an effectively integrated organization rests with the development and operation of an effective information system to provide the necessary support.

3 Programmable decisions are typically those that (a) occur frequently and (b) are relatively well structured in terms of the parameters involved and the criteria necessary to make the decision. The contrary type of decision is the non-programmable variety, which occurs less frequently and is more difficult to structure in terms of the parameters or the decision criteria to be used.

Typically programmable decisions include: stock ordering, production scheduling, delivery scheduling and credit rating.

Typical non-programmable decisions include: developing a marketing plan, decisions on the location of warehouses, strategic decisions on future products and markets, decisions relating to development of human resources in the organization.

4 Examples of data items that would be recorded in the sales transaction processing system include:
- customer name and address
- delivery address and details
- product codes or references
- quantities ordered
- pricing details and discounts
- credit and payment details.

Each of these elements will in itself contain a number of items of data for processing.

5 It is often assumed that the increasing use of information technologies will result in improved efficiency and effectiveness in the organization. Evidence suggests that this is not the case and that the main dangers to achieving such improvements result from:
- Reduced selectivity: users become accustomed to receiving whatever data they request and often request data that is rarely if ever used – resulting in high levels of redundant data and, consequently, higher processing costs than necessary.
- An increased gap between the users of the system and the specialists employed to design and develop the system, who may produce a very sophisticated system which fails to meet the needs of the users.
- The technical complexity of the interfaces between the system and the user, which may reduce the practical effectiveness of the system owing to lack of user knowledge or skills in relation to the technology.
- Increased usage and greater decentralization of the system may pose increased problems for the management of the system and for maintaining common standards or quality of service.
- Security issues may also become more significant as more data are stored on common databases and accessed by more users within the organization.

Exam-style questions

1 The general process of decision making should be seen as a sequential process, usually undertaken as a group activity and comprising both a planning and a reactive quality. The stages are as follows:

(a) a trigger or event which starts the activity – usually the input of data or information, e.g. a stock level report or quality control reject

(b) problem definition or analysis: the identification of the cause of problems and the separation of cause and effect

(c) problem structuring, during which a mathematical or conceptual model is structured (e.g. linear programming) and the objectives of the decision process are defined

(d) information requirement definition: the decision as to the data which must be captured and processed in order to solve the problem

(e) information analysis using mathematical techniques, e.g. regression analysis or the application of qualitative preferential criteria. (One possible result of this stage may be the decision whether enough information of the right quality is to hand or whether further data capture is required)

(f) the decision itself – the selection of a course of action, change in behaviour or commitment of resources.

The decision-making process is often carried out under less than ideal conditions, e.g. with inadequate information, insufficient time or uncertain priorities.

2 The issues to be discussed here – the development of information technology, its application to information systems and its resultant effect in organizations – involve the sociotechnical systems.

(a) Benefits
- greater efficiency, money savings, enhanced human resources
- better decision making through higher information quality
- increased flexibility and responsiveness, e.g. better use of query languages
- data sharing across organization boundaries, e.g. the use of a database
- increased involvement of users in information systems development, e.g. user computing and prototyping
- better communications, internally and externally.

(b) Dangers
  - data redundancy and lack of consistency due to poor system design
  - installing excessively expensive technology
  - systems which are too complicated for the intended users
  - lack of user involvement in systems, leaving the experts to take over
  - security problems and the possibility of fraud or accidental information loss
  - sub-optimality, i.e. parts of the system are managed to achieve their individual objectives at the expense of the whole system – also known as 'islands of automation'.

Chapter 3

Self-test questions

1 The informal organization structure within any organization represents an important element of the overall information and communications system. The incorporation of this element within the systems development programme is problematic, owing to the following factors:
- The transient structure changes continuously with changes in personnel and in relationships.
- It is difficult to identify, as members are often reluctant to acknowledge that it deals with only part of the non-routine information flows and is often focused on the more sensational aspects.
- It may prove ineffective and inefficient, as the motives of the individuals involved may result in distortion or delays in the communications.
- It can be unpredictable in terms of the operation of the system, as it may depend on the presence of particular individuals to provide the necessary links and processing.

Despite the problems of incorporating the informal organization structure and information systems within the planned development process, the system developers should be fully aware of the contribution that such systems can make.

2 Transaction processing refers to the activities and decisions at the operational level in the organization. The broad groups of transaction processing activities would typically encompass:
- sales order processing
- purchasing
- goods received and stock control
- production operations and scheduling
- warehousing and distribution
- after-sales service and support.

3 The information requirements of any organization will be dictated by the structure that the organization develops to manage and control its resources and operations to provide goods and services:
- Each organization will select the most appropriate means to organize its resources, primarily human, to achieve efficiency and effectiveness.
- The information system provides the inputs for the organization to assess the market/environment needs and to develop objectives, strategies and plans to meet them.
- The communication of objectives, policies and plans throughout the organization is achieved by the information system.
- The information system supports the processes of performance monitoring, control and subsequent decision making.
- The outline of the organization and the methods it uses to manage and control will be reflected in the structure of the information system.
- A significant point of a contingency view of organization structure and information requirements suggests that there is no single information system ideal for all organization structures; rather, that the appropriate information system is determined by particular needs of the organization.

4 The attributes which are used in identifying the quality of the information provided in a system include:
- the level of detail
- the degree of accuracy
- ease of accessing
- current or historic nature

- completeness
- relevance to user needs
- the degree of bias
- the extent to which it may be verified
- the level of uncertainty
- clarity of expression/communication.

As identified in the chapter, each of these qualitative values may be measured over a range of potential values. The position of the data on this range of values should not be viewed as preferable for all situations; certain decisions may require a highly accurate form of the data, whilst other users may be satisfied with lower levels of accuracy for their particular decisions.

5 Two of the three broad levels of decision making are:

(a) tactical, characterized by:
  - concern (primarily) with the medium term
  - interface between strategic (long-term) and operational (short-term) concerns
  - relation to particular functions or groups of activities
  - semi-structured forms of decisions
  - moderate degrees of risk and uncertainty
  - the fact that information needs may be predicted to some extent.

Examples of this decision include product prices, setting stock levels, budgetary control decisions, etc.

(b) strategic, characterized by:
  - concern with the long term (primarily)
  - relation to the total organization
  - typically unstructured and novel types of decisions
  - (usually) high levels of risk and uncertainty
  - specific information needs which are usually difficult to predetermine.

Examples include new technology development, acquisition of a competitor and the development of new markets.

Exam-style questions

1 A matrix structure is one in which the responsibilities for the development, management and control of the business's operations are divided in more than one way. Typically this would be both on a functional basis and on a product/service basis. A team of staff from various functional areas would then have the responsibility for managing a particular product or group of products, each member contributing particular specialist skills.

This structure is argued to be more responsive to change, more market-oriented, providing greater responsibility to all employees and improving co-ordination, communications and control. Whilst such benefits may be potentially available, the key to achieving them is through the supporting information system, which needs to be:

- more flexible to the changing needs of the organization
- responsive to the often less predictable demands of the teams and individual members
- adaptable to changes in the strategy of the business
- providing data across a wide spectrum of functional areas to a range of different users
- efficient in terms of the response time and access time to support effective team working, which is a key feature of matrix structures
- capable of using a common database which permits access by all users, as opposed to restricted access to users in a particular function.

Arguably, many of these features would be present in a more conventionally structured functional organization. However, their importance in terms of the overall effectiveness and efficiency of the information system is even more critical in the matrix style of operation. The nature of the interaction and integration of the human resources relies heavily on the quality of the communications and information systems supporting the teams involved.

2 The question refers to the difference in the decision types (and therefore the information requirements) which apply at different levels in the organization. Conventionally, a three-level model of management is accepted:

- strategic or top management
- tactical or middle management
- operational or supervisory management.

It should be stressed that it is the implication of the decision, not the job title, which places the decision-maker at a particular level. The boundaries are therefore not hard and fast. (Figure 3.1 illustrates the model.) The character of the decisions could be as follows:

- Strategic decisions:
  - very long-term horizon, e.g. five to ten years
  - radical implications for the whole organization, e.g. new products, new markets
  - high risk, e.g. investment in overseas markets
  - non-routine, e.g. setting up a new company
- Tactical decisions:
  - medium time horizon, e.g. less than five years
  - implication for a function under control, e.g. accounting or production
  - moderately uncertain outcome involving the possible use of forecasting techniques and information technology
  - possible routine decisions, e.g. quarterly budgets
  - moderate risk, as the level of investment is smaller and the decisions are more predictable, e.g. in regard to manning levels.
- Operational decisions:
  - short timescale, e.g. one day to one week
  - routine and specific outcomes, e.g. achievement of production targets
  - low levels of risk with much decision support
  - predictable, well-documented information requirements, e.g. office procedures.

While a distinction has been drawn between these three levels, one should recognize that in practice it is often difficult to allocate a particular decision clearly to one category as opposed to another.

Chapter 4

Self-test questions

1 The main elements present in any system include:

- *Inputs*: receipt of resources from the environment in the form of energy, people, materials, finance or information, depending on the nature of the system in question.
- *Process*: activities which typically modify or change the resource inputs: recording, storing, machining, assembling, and so on.
- *Outputs*: the completion of the processing activities will result in the delivery of outputs to the environment. Such outputs may reflect tangible resources (e.g. motor cars, balance sheets) or less tangible outputs (e.g. knowledge gained or changes in perception).

The precise composition of the three elements will depend on the particular system under discussion. A particular system may input multiple types of resources, perform a variety of processes on these resources and produce a range of different resource outputs to the environment.

2 The discussion in the text on the presence of sub-systems within systems highlighted a problem: there is an almost infinite level of sub-systems present in any organization. Equally, the determination of the system boundaries, where two systems interact (i.e. one sub-system's outputs providing the inputs to the next sub-system) is also difficult to determine in many situations. The system developer needs to find practical approaches to structuring the group of sub-systems to facilitate their analysis and the subsequent development of the information support systems. The factors that are typically incorporated in this approach are:

- the nature, scope and purpose of the analysis (and hence the level of detailed analysis required)
- the stage in the overall development process: earlier stages may require consideration of groups of sub-systems, although the later design stages may require these to be examined individually
- the importance of data input or output quality (greater quality will require more detailed assessment)

- the degree of integration and interaction between the sub-systems that is required.

The key issue involves the requirement for the systems developer to apply the concepts of systems and system boundaries into the practical context in a way that is both meaningful and helpful to the activities in hand at that time.

3 The question addresses the organization at micro-level, proposing five layers:
- corporate (relating to strategic management decisions, e.g. corporate plans, budgets)
- unit level or division, differentiated by product, geography or management structure
- functional (relating to middle management), including organizational sub-systems, e.g. financial planning, manpower planning, etc.
- departmental, at the level of tactical activities, e.g. quality management
- operational – the day-to-day activities, e.g. adding to and withdrawing from stock.

4 Externally-oriented sub-systems are those elements of an organization which are primarily concerned with interfacing or conducting transactions without agencies in the external environment. Examples of such systems include purchasing, marketing, sales, distribution, after-sales service, wage payments, and research and development.

Internally-oriented sub-systems are primarily involved in the activities and processes required to support the operations, decision making, management and control within the organization. Examples of internally-oriented sub-systems include management accounting, cost accounting, production scheduling and budgetary control.

Although a sub-system may be primarily externally or internally oriented, this does not mean that it has no interaction within or outside the business. Each sub-system will have a combination of internal and external inputs and outputs. The classification into a particular group of sub-systems depends on whether the majority of these interactions are internally oriented or externally oriented.

5 The question relates to the different categories of control system operating within a system. The distinction is drawn between two forms of feedback and control systems:

(a) An open loop control system is one where:
- there is no feedback of performance back into the system
- the system is therefore not responsive to the environment or changes in the environment
- the system is unlikely to adapt to changes over time
- (in essence) the system is under a process of self-control.

(b) A closed loop control system is one where:
- there is a mechanism for feeding back the performance of the system
- the system responds to information
- the operation of the system will be adapted in the next cycle to respond to changing needs.

Although the open loop system is rarely found in practice, it should also be recognized that in closed loop control systems responsiveness to changing needs in the environment may vary substantially. Certain systems may respond almost immediately to changing needs, whilst others may take months or years to respond. Many information systems fall into this latter category and changes are not effected until a major review of the system is undertaken.

Exam-style questions

1 The quality and reliability of the interface between different sub-systems is dependent on the effectiveness of the communication links between them. The key factors influencing the quality of the communications are:

(a) the quality of the original data being transferred, in terms of accuracy, data redundancy, timeliness, etc.

(b) the quality of the transmission/reception mechanisms: their ability to transmit or capture data accurately, reliability of performance, and sensitivity in detecting abnormalities in the data (e.g. absence of particular data elements)

(c) channel quality relating to the media used to carry the data from one sub-system to the other. (Although we might consider physical data carriers such as cables or post systems, the human carrier or channel is equally common in many systems.) (Absence of distortion and of interference or noise are the elements to be looked for in a high-quality carrier)

(d) the quality of the feedback loops which is often of considerable significance in the assurance of the quality of system interfaces. (Various methods may be used to correlate the data received by the sub-system with the data originally transmitted, e.g. message checking and repetition, batch totals, check digits, etc.)

A final observation relates to the importance of maintaining quality in the system interfaces. If reliability is of particular importance, the organization can employ a variety of means to ensure this. If lower levels of reliability are acceptable, it may be able to adapt different approaches to achieve the desired level of quality and reliability.

2 The question can be answered by naming and describing six elements met in the analysis and design of information systems:
(a) inputs:
- information quality and content
- interfaces with other systems
- the need to capture or produce data

(b) processes:
- conversion of input to output
- system protocols and interaction
- standards and quality

(c) output:
- users' information requirements
- media choices
- messages sent to other sub-systems

(d) environment:
- other sub-systems
- monitoring output

(e) channels:
- choice of channel/media
- overcoming interference, noise and distortion

(f) feedback:
- use of system control loop(s)
- predicting situations where control is required.

Chapter 5

Self-test questions

1 This is a straightforward question requiring an identification and a brief description of each of the stages.
(a) Initiation: usually an organization's first attempt at computerization. Usually driven by operational (typically, cost reduction) factors.
(b) Contagion: as the demand from a wide range of users increases. Often the (newly formed) information systems department is unable to meet the demand and an 'applications backlog' occurs.
(c) Control: usually exerted as a management response to the unsatisfactory stage 2. New posts (e.g. information manager) and processes (e.g. structured system development method) will be introduced.
(d) Integration: control begins to be effective. Organization-wide ISs are developed (e.g. a corporate database) and 'islands of automation' are joined.
(e) Data administration: information is a shared resource and is carefully managed. Users exploit their own applications development by 'end-user computing'. IS planning is introduced.
(f) Maturity: there is a close link between the business and IS strategies.

2 A strategic information system (SIS) should have facilities for supporting top-level executive decisions. Some examples:
(a) Decisions on new products and services.
(b) Decisions to move into new markets.
(c) Pricing and costing decisions (e.g. CUP analysis).
(d) Decisions regarding the movement of stock and share prices.
(e) Merger and takeover decisions.
(f) Decisions regarding the acquisition of resources.

The types of decision (characteristics) are:
(a) unstructured (i.e. wicked problems)
(b) non-routine or one-off decisions
(c) having a high risk factor
(d) involving a long timescale
(e) involving major external information sources.

3 The structure of an IS will be influenced by:
(a) The organizational structure: a centralized organization (one where the decision-making process is centred) will probably use a centralized IS.
(b) The type of business: the need for a rapid response to environmental changes (e.g. market factors) will tend to produce an IS in which the users have more autonomy.
(c) The management style: informal types of organization with a 'flat' span of control will tend to develop IS with a high degree of autonomy and flexible central control.
(d) The extent to which information is important to the everyday running of the organization (i.e. the 'information intensity').

4 A comparison of two types of IS and their roles requires you to say in what way they are different:
(a) A decision support system (DSS) contains mathematical models of a situation. An expert system (ES) contains rules to guide choices.
(b) A DSS can be used for a variety of decisions by changing the internal model. An ES is usually specific to one problem domain (e.g. stock control).
(c) An ES simulates the decision which a human expert would reach in a given situation. It is capable of heuristics, whereas a DSS tends to operate with statistics.
(d) The DSS does not make the decision – it provides the user with the information with which to make the decision. An ES is capable of making a decision.
(e) An ES has a knowledge base and a DSS has a database.

Exam-style questions

1 This question relates to Cash's view that the development of IS has passed through three eras and that these have become 'fixed' in organizations, being typified by different levels of ISs. The eras and their typifying ISs are:
(a) The data processing era, which is typified by DP or transaction processing (TP) systems. DP-centred companies usually have a single IS department which has a big influence upon the development of ISs because it has the IT expertise. The objective of most DP systems is to automate manual/clerical processes and to achieve higher levels of operational efficiency.
(b) The management information systems (MISs) or management support era in which information was extracted from the DP/TP systems in order to support the management decision-making processes. Most organizations have provision for such MISs, and some have taken a further step by encouraging users to develop their own MIS. This is often termed 'end-user computing' (EUC) and involves the use of packages and fourth-generation languages. At the same time, in some organizations, management will seek to control EUC by using data administration and information centres.
(c) The strategic IS or competitive strategy era marked information as a major corporate resource and the IS as a competitive weapon. An organization which has strategic and executive information systems will justify the use of these in terms of market share, profitability and position in relation to the competition. There are fewer examples of IS from this era as it is a relatively recent development in practical terms.

An alternative way to answer this question would be to quote the three phases of technology assimilation; innovation, incorporation and exploitation, and to relate them to DP, MIS and IS development.

2 This is a straightforward question which requires a brief description of systems in context.
(a) A management information system (MIS) could produce information from detailed shopfloor production records on which shop loading and machine scheduling decisions could be made. The highly detailed and historical data (e.g. the number of products produced per machine in the last week) could be analysed for trends and compared with stock-in-hand and orders.
(b) A decision support system in a manufacturing environment could contain a mathematical model of

the market for the company's products including the levels of demand, the price elasticity of products, and the policies of its rivals. This could be used to simulate the effects of changes in costs, prices and levels of production in a more sophisticated way than would be possible with a spreadsheet.

(c) An expert system could contain the rules which would make up the knowledge of an engineer or metallurgist. Often such human expertise is in short supply, and yet the knowledge which experts have may be useful in several areas of the business, from design to customer complaints. The use of an ES shell would enable this knowledge to be replicated and made more widely available.

(d) A strategic information system could come in two forms. First would be a system which supported the strategic decision-making needs of executives in the company (e.g. an executive information system). Second would be a system which gave the company some strategic advantage over its rivals. An example of this would be a just-in-time (JIT) system which would share a stock-control/order processing system with the firm's suppliers, thereby creating switching costs which would inhibit them from supplying the firm's rivals with components.

Chapter 6

Exam-style questions

1 The availability of information and the quality of the information system are often important sources of competitive advantage for most organizations. Competitive advantage is essentially the ability of the organization to operate more effectively and profitably in the market place than its competitors. The sources of potential advantage to Scribe plc may be grouped into three broad categories:

(a) Product service attributes or values – developments or elements which enable the company to deliver greater value to the customer than competitors. These elements may originate from technical features in the product or the means of manufacture. The developments of TQM by Scribe plc would provide enhanced quality, often through improved manufacturing processes. The development of support services, technical services or after-sales services may also offer an opportunity for added value and competitive advantage. The information system is required to provide the information resource to assist in the research and development, manufacture and delivery of the product.

(b) Improved efficiency. Improvements in efficiency resulting in reduced costs provide scope for competitive advantage through offering greater opportunities to compete effectively on price. The information resource at all these levels of decision making in Scribe (i.e. strategic, tactical and operational) provides the essential inputs for the planning, management and control of performance to enhance efficiency. Specific references in the case study to the management accounting sub-systems is a good example of the type of information sub-system supporting the organization's management.

(c) Corporate market intelligence is the third element which may enhance the company's competitive position – the quality of the external information to support decisions at all three levels. The ability to research and feedback market and competitor information will aid the company to respond effectively to market needs and competitor actions. At the operational level, the development of EDI by Scribe plc will also provide effective links with customers in the market place and provide a source of competitive advantage.

The approach that we have adopted in this answer is to outline the broad sources of competitive advantage and provide only a few examples from the case of each of these. There are many more examples for each of the three categories and at different links of decision making.

2 There are a number of ways in which an organization such as Scribe plc can encourage a more supportive attitude in its employees towards new computer systems. The key to most of these approaches is the recognition that all employees need to be consulted or actively involved in the development process, so that they feel a sense of joint ownership of the system. The typical approaches that could be used include:

- the development of clearly stated objectives, policies and strategies related to IT and the articulation of related business benefits
- involvement of representatives of the staff in the early stages of identifying and specifying the priorities of system development

- approaches to the analysis of user needs which seek to identify real needs rather than those that are merely perceived
- incorporation in the design of system interfaces that are sympathetic to the users and enable them to interact effectively with the system
- removing, wherever possible, technical or specialist jargon which may confuse users rather than enlighten them
- development of regular and effective communication channels between the system development team and the users in the organization
- initiation of effective training programmes for all users of the system in advance of implementation
- establishment of ongoing help and support facilities to provide users with technical or even moral support once the system has been implemented.

None of these actions would alone be sufficient to ensure a more supportive attitude, but the willingness of all members of the management team to provide full backing to the changes will help to ensure a greater chance of success.

Chapter 7

Self-test questions

1 This question relates to the types of software which the company has. You are not required to give different examples of a type (e.g. database, spreadsheet and word-processing packages). The two categories of software are:

(a) Applications software, which for this type of organization will probably consist of:
   - generic off-the-shelf packages which are capable of being used in a number of roles for different tasks in several areas of the business. Spreadsheets (e.g. Lotus 123) word processors (e.g. WordPerfect) and databases (e.g. dBase IV) are such packages;
   - specialized packages which will have one role and will probably be used in only one area of the business for a defined task, such as a stock control or accounts package;
   - bespoke software, created individually for a special purpose to the end-user's specifications. This would involve the development cycle of analysis, specification and design and would probably use a third-generation language (3GL), although a 4GL is a possibility.

(b) Systems software, which would consist of:
   - utility programs providing service facilities to those who use the system, such as an editor, a sort program, file maintenance and dumping programs, debugging and virus detection
   - operating system programs, providing the user interface and controlling the peripherals and applications programs (MS-DOS, UNIX and OS/2 are examples of operating systems)
   - compilers and interpreters to convert a high-level programming language into a more efficient machine code.

Most of this category of software is invisible to the everyday system user, yet it is of vital importance.

2 The company is likely to apply the following criteria of software effectiveness when selecting or specifying applications software:

- Accuracy: the software should give the desired results under any expected operating conditions. This could be ensured (as much as is practicable) by the correct analysis, specification and design and thorough testing of the software. These practices form part of what is called 'software engineering'.
- Flexibility: the ability of software to be changed as the application changes, with new functions being added or larger volumes of transactions being processed. Also in this category could be portability – the ability of the software to be used on different versions of the operating system or to accept upgrades. This therefore includes a criterion of 'maintainability'.
- Performance: the effectiveness of the software and its ease of use. This would include not only the processing time and response (to a query) time factors but also the controls which should be built into the system to prevent unauthorized access, accidental errors and loss of data. The ability of the software to interface with other systems could be included in this category.

Other criteria which may be important, but which do not relate to the software directly, include the reputation of the manufacturer and the level of support which could be expected from the supplier.

3 The uses to which an end user may put a fourth-generation language (4GL) include:
- report generation, by setting up a form or report layout and extracting data from the database (with limited manipulation) to fill it
- applications generation, by creating simple programs which store, output or manipulate data
- database querying and reporting on data extracted from the database via a DBMS (database management system)
- prototyping or developing new systems by producing 'trial' programs or simulations of programs or applications, which may later be turned into functioning programs.

4 The main factors which should influence the choice of applications programming language are:
- Ease of use. The easier a language is to use, the more likely programmers are to work accurately and to achieve quality.
- Flexibility. The language should be capable of being used in a variety of applications to be efficient.
- Portability across different hardware platforms so that the user is not tied to one type of computer.
- Security and error handling.
- Supplier characteristics, such as documentation and provision of upgrades.

Factors which will influence the selection process are:
- The performance characteristics of the system.
- Future policy on systems development (contractor or in-house programming).
- The system development budget.

5 A successful LAN installation should meet the following criteria:
- High speed of communication, to ensure a high data transfer rate. The ability to communicate a large amount of data is called a high bandwidth.
- Low latency (the delay between the sending of a message and the message being acted on).
- High reliability and low error rate from the LAN and the software which controls it.
- Cost-effectiveness, particularly the fixed costs of maintaining the LAN in relation to its use.

Exam-style questions

1 A decision support system (DSS) is a piece of general purpose software which may be used to solve problems or to predict outcomes in a wide range of applications As such it should be capable of handling different types of data presented in varying volumes. It should be capable of containing a number of different statistical or simulation modes.

As a typical DSS will be used by a wide variety of end users, it should be easy to use with a powerful and flexible interface. Although the internal model may be set up by an expert (programmer or OR specialist) or obtained from a library of models, the user must be able to extract and to manipulate the data without having to learn a complex interface. The results of 'what if?' calculations should be clear and output statistics should be displayed in graphical or tabular form.

To aid the process of interrogating the database, a fourth-generation language (4GL) maybe a part of the interface, or a query language may be used. The data storage and handling capacity of the DSS should be sufficient for all foreseen applications.

The factors which are involved in the choice of DSS software are basically those which apply to any type of software. A comparison should be made of the costs of acquisition, including licence fees. The compatibility of the DSS software with the user's existing hardware and operating systems 'platforms' should be assessed. It is important in some applications that the DSS integrates with existing applications software.

The DSS software is obviously an important factor in making the DSS powerful, flexible and easy to use. A comparison of the 'user-friendly' aspects of a piece of software can be carried out by demonstration or by loan of the software packages which are under consideration.

Also important are the vendor-related factors, such as the technical support and the arrangements for future updates to the software.

These factors could be built into a 'weighted ranking' exercise to compare alternative DSS packages.

2 (a) 'Weighted ranking' is a method of comparison which can be used to evaluate a number of resources (e.g. hardware, software packages, development methods) with a view to recommending them in order of greatest suitability. The feature which distinguishes it from other methods of selection, such as feature analysis or financial appraisal, is its ability to 'weight' the features of the resource in terms of their importance to the application.

First, the features which the applications packages must have to be effective will be identified. These typically include ease of use, cost and vendor rating. Then the features are assigned weightings to reflect their importance. For instance, in a typical accounting application, 'ease of use' might be given a rating of 0.8 out of 1 to show its importance, as the system will be used almost constantly by non-expert users,

The packages are then tested by the eventual end users under the guidance of experts (e.g. from the information systems department or an information centre). Each package is assigned a score out of 10 in terms of its performance in relation to that feature.

The score is then multiplied by the weighting factor to give a rating (e.g. 0.8 × 8 = 6.4) out of 10, adjusted for the importance of the feature. The ratings for each of the packages would be totalled, and the package with the highest total rating would rank first.

(b) An integrated applications package is one which combines several types of functionality which would normally by separate in 'stand-alone' packages. For instance an integrated office package might contain a word processor, graphics package, database and spreadsheet in one piece of software. Microsoft Works is an integrated office package.

The advantages of such integrated packages include the fact that the user need not 'quit' the package when changing from one function to another (e.g. from word processor to graphics). This saves time and effort, cuts out a source of possible errors and makes 'cutting and pasting' an easier proposition.

Another function which relates to ease of use is the consistency of the interface. Three stand-alone packages (e.g. word processor, database, spreadsheet) by different suppliers might have different commands and screen layouts, which can make using the different packages confusing and harder to learn and is another source of possible errors.

A third factor is cost. Usually an integrated package which offers a word processor, spreadsheet and database will cost less than three separate packages. Upgrades are usually cheaper where integrated packages are concerned.

Chapter 8

Self-test questions

1 The SDLC may be typified by the following phases:
- The feasibility study, which involves a problem analysis, leading to a feasibility report, leading to a 'go/no-go' decision about the proposal.
- Systems analysis, a detailed fact-finding exercise which will produce a logical method of the system in terms of its data, processes and events, expressed as a specification.
- Systems design will take the specification and turn the logical model into a physical one which will include program design, file design, hardware specification and operational (e.g. security) guidelines.
- Implementation will convert the physical design into an actual working system. It will involve program coding, file/database conversion and changeover to the new system. Testing and training will be a part of this phase.
- Review and maintenance will measure the extent to which the system meets the design criteria and maintain the system for the rest of its working life.

2 The feasibility study types are as follows:
- Technical feasibility, which is concerned with matching the system requirements with the performance of the hardware and software.
- Operational feasibility, which concerns the organizational and human factors of system design and includes matters of policy.
- Economic feasibility, which attempts to measure the costs and benefits that may derive from a system and to estimate the return from the project.

3 The more common fact-finding techniques are:
- interviewing a range of knowledgeable staff in key roles and recording the results of the interviews as structured facts
- observation of physical processes, such as record accessing or communicating with other people

- questionnaires, which are an alternative to interviewing or observation where the population under analysis is large or is distant
- record/document sampling, involving the examination of files and documents to find out their source, contents and destination.

4 The main techniques of economic analysis are:

- Breakeven analysis, which attempts to analyse the cost patterns which will be involved in the system in terms of fixed and variable costs. Comparison of the total of these with the total benefits will give a breakdown point, beyond which the system will give a financial return. The method gives only a 'snapshot' of the cost pattern at one time, and relies on accurate cost–benefit estimation.
- 'Payback' is a method which attempts to measure the time at which the benefits or returns from a proposed system recoup the initial investment in the system. The method stresses short-term profitability and fails to take into account changes in the value of money over time.
- Discounted cashflow (DCF) methods such as net present value and internal rate of return adjust the value of cash streams which are identified with the proposed system in relation to future time and the cost of capital. The method produces either a value (NPV) or a rate (IRR) and therefore can be used to compare the system with other investments.

Exam-style question

1 The company could expect the following types of cost and benefit from its management information system (MIS):

System costs include:

- Development costs, such as the costs of carrying out the detailed analysis and design of the MIS. This would include the time which the users spend as part of the fact-finding exercises.
- Implementation costs, such as the writing of program code, acquisition of hardware and software, setting up databases, file conversion, etc. This would include the costs of recruitment (of new or temporary staff) and training.
- Running costs, such as maintenance, consumables and insurance costs for the system. Salaries may be included in this category, particularly where they are extra to the original manual system.

System benefits may be classified as:

- Direct benefits, such as the reduced costs when compared to producing the management information by hand. Also the increased turnover which is expected to come from the better, more timely decisions.
- Indirect (or intangible) benefits, such as the freedom to produce more innovative ideas and better qualities of working life.

Chapter 9

Self-test questions

1 'User-driven' development refers to a class of methods which concentrate on the behavioural aspects of information systems design. Whereas other 'hard' development methods involve the user as a subject of application expert, it is the technical staff (analysts/software engineers) who make most of the decisions.

In user-driven development methods, the technical staff act as facilitators and advisors and the users make most of the decisions. The methods therefore seek to overcome apparent user dissatisfaction with technically developed systems by recognizing the importance of end-user involvement and encouraging active participation in the analysis and design process.

Some examples of user-driven development methods are soft-systems method (SMM) and joint applications design (JAD). Both are often used as part of an evolutionary systems development approach which is an extension of prototyping.

2 Entity analysis concentrates on identifying the things (entities) which are important to the organization (system) and about which data is stored. The way in which the entities relate to one another is identified and the facts (attributes) which are held about the entities are described. The resulting entity-relationship model or logical data structure (LDS) is an important part of the logical model and forms the basis of the database design.

Function analysis examines the processes or activities which occur within the system under study. The functions are represented on data flow diagrams (DFD) in SSADM and form the basis of functional decomposition – a hierarchy of functions in increasing detail at lower levels. The functions on the DFDs form the basis of the specifications on which the program designs are based.

Exam-style questions

1 The company should consider development methods from the following two categories:

- Process-driven development, emphasizing the tasks or functions which are carried out within the system. The way in which these tasks (e.g. the updating of stock records) are carried out is examined in detail and a system is specified which will carry out the same tasks in a more efficient manner. This is the typical justification for many office automation projects. The emphasis is on improved efficiency. Systems which are designed in this way often use structured development methods and are implemented in third-generation languages (3GLs). They tend to be inflexible, or poor at coping with changes in the application.
- Data-driven methods assume that the data (upon which the processes act) is the most important part of the system, as it will be stable even if the processes (or ways of doing things) change. A stock control system will always deal with the same data items (e.g. stock items, reorder levels, withdrawals) no matter how these are handled and by whom. The data view of systems centres around the use of databases and fourth-generation languages (4GLs). Although relatively inefficient, such systems are flexible.

  Some system development methods (e.g. SSADM) use techniques for describing processes (i.e. dataflow diagrams or DFDs) and data (i.e. logical data structures of LDS). A comparison is made between the process and data models of the system to check correctness and completeness at various stages of analysis and design.

2 Your answer to this question should be in report format (i.e. it should include a summary and, possibly, terms of reference) and should identify the typical phases of the systems development life cycle (SDLC) as follows:

(a) Project selection
An operational problem is identified or an idea for an opportunity for improvement is put forward and the analysis team (or systems analyst) carries out a preliminary study. The objectives of the proposal are drawn up, alternative outline solutions may be generated (e.g. a centralized or a distributed system) and 'terms of reference' agreed.

(b) Feasibility study
The alternative proposals (and, possibly the existing system) are examined in terms of technical, economic and operational feasibility. In particular, a cost–benefit analysis on the proposals will be conducted. The result will be a recommendation (of a suitable system) to management.

(c) Systems analysis
This is the detailed investigation of the existing system. The purpose is to understand the existing processes or tasks and to identify the properties of the data which the company uses. The objectives for the new system (from Phase 1) and the results of the detailed analysis are used to form a full requirements specification for the new system.

(d) System design
The requirements specification will be separated into two types of design and specification: logical design of the data and processes, and physical design of programs, database and human–computer dialogue. The output from this phase is the final system specification (i.e. a complete set of logical and physical designs).

(e) Implementation
This phase will involve writing and testing the programs, acquiring new hardware and software (if required), training staff and putting into action a plan for changing from one system to the other.

(f) Review
This is a follow-up phase which is carried out after implementation to ensure that the new system meets the evaluation criteria which were part of the objectives set at the beginning of the project.

Chapter 10

Self-test questions

1 A WIMP interface is a type of graphical user interface which is intended to be easy to use, powerful and capable of being learned intuitively. The system is based on:
- Windows, or predefined work areas which contain icons or applications and which may be opened, closed, expanded and moved as requested.
- Icons, which are symbols representing files or functions of the system and which may be used to open or close windows and applications.
- A mouse, which can be used to 'click' on icons which appear on the screen without using the keyboard.
- A pointer, which appears on the screen to indicate to the user the movements of the mouse.

2 Computer-aided systems engineering (CASE) tools seek to automate or to provide support in the development of complex systems. They do this by providing the basic steps of the chosen development method and by providing the tools (for instance, graphical modelling techniques). By guiding the analyst through the stages of the method and aiding the modelling process, CASE tools seek to simplify the process of development. The volume of data will be handled by using a data dictionary as part of the CASE tools.

3 The key factors involved in computer dialogue design are:
- There should be sufficient guidance from the dialogue itself to aid the user and to make it clear what response is required.
- The appearance of the dialogue should be consistent.
- Commands (from the mouse or keyboard) should be acknowledged on the screen.
- Verification and validity checks should be carried out on all data and error messages should be clear and self-explanatory.

4 Graphical specification techniques are particularly suitable for specifying complex logic and showing under what circumstances a task is to be carried out. They tend to lack detail, and are therefore less useful for specifying dialogue design. The main graphical specification methods are decision tables and decision trees.

Exam-style question

1 To: The Manager
From: Accountant

Report describing systems analysis techniques

Terms of reference

To report on the techniques which may be used by the analysts during a system design project.

Findings

The techniques which can possibly be used include the following:

- entity models
- decision tables.

The report will describe each of these techniques.

Entity models. An entity model (or entity-relationship model, or logical data structure) is produced during the data analysis stage of system development. The entity model describes the data which the system uses, some facts about that data and the relationships between data items.

An entity is something which is of importance to the application about which data is stored. Entities may be 'real' things such as products or customers or abstract things, such as appointments or tests. An organization's entity model tends therefore to be unique to that organization, and describes it at a fundamental level.

This 'data-driven' description of an application is said to be more stable than one which describes processes (like a program flowchart) and is less subject to future changes. The entity model may be used to complement or cross-reference the dataflow diagrams (which include processes) to give an overall view of the system. The conventions of an entity model are typically those shown in the following diagram:

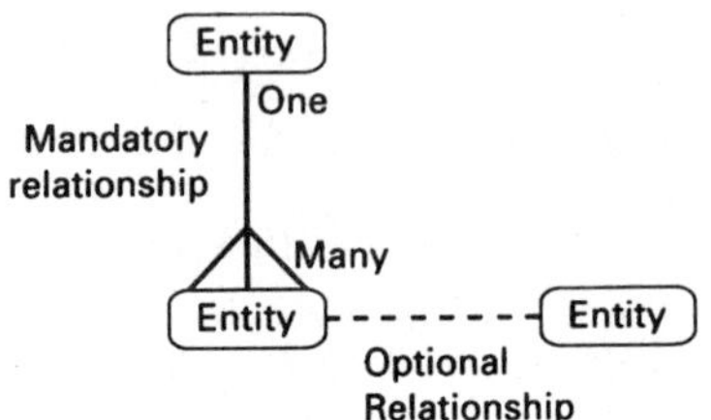

Decision tables. A decision table is most often used to specify the logic or functioning of a process (such as updating a stock record) at the stage of system design. The technique links actions (things that must be done) with preconditions (states that exist). Therefore the table describes rules of action (often called 'business rules') which can be used to create software. Decision tables are a communication between the systems analyst and the programmer or software engineer.

The decision table is constructed by matching the actions and the conditions by stating whether or not rules apply to certain cases. When complete, a decision table may be used to see the alternative actions which can result from complicated preconditions such as granting or refusing an application for credit or giving discount for a customer order.

The diagram below shows a typical layout for a limited-entry decision table.

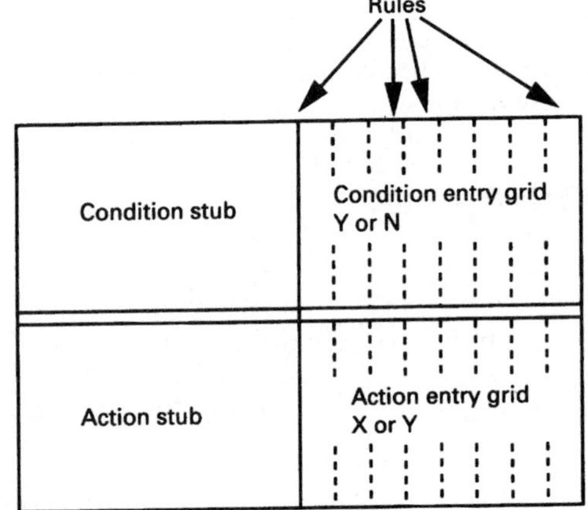

Chapter 11

Self-test questions

1 The three possible routes for changeover from one system to another are:

- Direct changeover, where the old system simply ceases to function and the new system takes over immediately. The files will have been set up in advance and the programs will have been tested. This route is risky, as the new system may fail, and is only suitable for proven technologies or non-strategic systems. It is, however, cheap.
- Phased changeover or pilot running introduces the new system gradually, function by function or department by department. This reduces the risk and gives inexperienced users a chance to become familiar with the system. It is a compromise in terms of cost and risk.

- Parallel running has the two systems operating alongside one another, the old system only being 'switched off' when the effectiveness and reliability of the new system is proven. This route is very 'safe', but very costly in terms of effort and finance.

2 The invitation to tender is a document which is drawn up by an organization that is seeking to acquire a large-scale computer system. It is sent to a range of possible suppliers and asks them to produce a specification and price for the hardware and software for the proposed system. It will include:
- a specification of the physical system
- the functions which the system is to perform
- the environment in which the system will operate
- the timescale for changeover
- the volume of data, records, performance requirements, etc.

3 A post-implementation review or audit is an exercise which is carried out after a new computer-based system 'goes live' and has worked for a time. Its purpose is to evaluate the performance of the system in terms of:
- the degree to which the design criteria have been met
- the attitude or degree of satisfaction of the staff with the system
- the way in which the operating procedures of the organization have changed
- the benefits of the system which have been gained in terms of better information and decision making.

4 The factors which lead to an organization changing its information systems are:
- the system development strategy and system planning process
- changes in the operating environments, such as legislation or market opportunities
- efficiency drives and cost-reduction programmes or 'downsizing'
- responses to competitive pressures and the actions (possibly computerization projects) of rival companies.

Exam-style questions

1 To: Chief Executive, BC plc
From: Management Accountant

Report on software maintenance

Terms of reference

To report on the types of software maintenance which may be encountered when operating a computer-based system.

Maintenance of software can be categorized under three general headings:

- corrective maintenance
- adaptive maintenance
- perfective maintenance.

The report will describe two of these.

Corrective maintenance. This category covers maintenance which is needed to put right programming errors and other faults which may appear in the software. It will include the following:
- Routine 'debugging' of newly produced or recently amended software as part of the testing process before the software 'goes live'.
- Emergency error correction as a response to faults detected during the running of a piece of software. These may be relatively minor or may cause the system to 'crash'.
- Restarting the system after system failure to ensure that the data is still accurate and that the restarted programs will perform correctly.

Adaptive maintenance. This covers the changing of software to meet new or changed circumstances. It will include the following:

- Changes to software resulting from the restructuring of a database or files, such as may occur when changes to the system require new types of data to be held.

- Alterations which are made necessary due to changes in users' operating procedures, reflecting the dynamic nature of applications in many organizations.
- Changes caused by the introduction of new versions of software, either an operating system or an applications program or package. New versions may require changes to be made to interfacing programs.
- Amendments to software which are caused by changes in hardware as a result of updates or improvements. Such changes would include those necessary to run software on a network which previously ran on a stand-alone system.

  A third category which you could have included would be:

Perfective maintenance. This covers attempts to make the software operate more effectively. It will include user requests for enhancements, as possibilities which were not realized at the initial design stage style etc. to ensure achievement of the objectives set.

Chapter 12

Self-test questions

1 The objectives of the project management process, whether in an information system or any other context, may be classified under two broad headings:
  (a) Effectiveness – ensuring that the projects or systems developed achieve the objectives established at the outset:
    - specified needs of users
    - agreed quality standards
    - degree of integration with existing systems, structures and processes
    - flexible and responsive to changing needs and situations
    - provides appropriate support at all levels to decision makers.

  (b) Efficiency – ensuring that the project or system developed is undertaken with the most appropriate use of resources and timescales available, including:
    - use of the specialist human resources
    - use of user resources in assisting the development process within the time constraints specified for each stage and the project as a whole
    - using the resources of outside suppliers and contractors as efficiently as possible
    - utilizing the hardware, software and other associated IT resources as fully as possible.

    In any project management process, there will be a continuous need to manage trade-offs between effectiveness and efficiency (storing data in a certain type of file structure may be more effective but less efficient in disk space terms), and within the objectives of effectiveness and efficiency themselves (development costs may be reduced by slowing down the pace of the system development and implementation).

2 The nine project management activities are:
  - planning
  - analysis
  - communication
  - co-ordination, integration and co-operation
  - monitoring, evaluation and control
  - trouble-shooting
  - quality assurance
  - leadership and motivation
  - managing interfaces.

  These are not a sequential set of activities, and most of these are taking place continuously and concurrently. Indeed, in many respects they are mutually supportive (the practice of effective leadership and motivation will often assist in trouble-shooting or in assuring improved quality).

3 There are a number of stages in the project management process. There is often no clear distinction between the phases as they are put into operation, and many operate concurrently:

- Outline planning: converting overall aims, objectives or strategies into a broad plan for the development and implementation.
- Detailed planning: taking each broad element of the plan and analysing and designing the activities necessary to achieve these.
- Implementation: putting the detailed plan into action, often requiring changes to the plan as problems are encountered.
- Progress review: monitoring the progress of the implementation against the detailed plans and the objectives established.
- Control: taking steps to correct potential problems anticipated in the future.
- Post-audit review: review, analysis and evaluation of the project once completed, seeking to establish the performance of the system in relation to the effectiveness and efficiency objectives.

4 The process of project management is similar to most types of management activities in organisations, and may be subdivided into three levels:

Strategic: overall view of the project, emphasis on the objectives and contribution of the system to the total organization. May focus on issues of structure, policies, resource allocation and management style, etc. to ensure achievement of the objectives set.

Tactical: concentrates on the short- to medium-term issues of project management, involving periodic review of the progress in all aspects of the project and the initiation of corrective action to resolve problems or to improve performance.

Operational: deals with the day-to-day management problems with the emphasis on tackling the more immediate aspects of the plans, often requiring skills in supervision and motivation of staff and higher levels of technical competence and experience.

5 Typical tactical actions that a project manager would undertake include:

- motivating particular staff
- monitoring and supervising performance
- advising on technical problems or issues
- ensuring maintenance of quality/standards
- trouble shooting
- progress chasing with internal and external suppliers
- team building
- reporting progress to senior management.

Exam-style questions

1 The question addresses the issues of efficiency and effectiveness in the planning and control of projects:

(a) Efficient utilization of:

Time – a key parameter. There will be an overall project deadline and, within this, milestones at which specified deliverables will be required. Failure to achieve completion of these dates will incur resource costs.

Resources – may be material or human. Material resources (hardware and software) entail acquisition and production decisions. Human resources require recruitment, management and training decisions and facilities.

Costs – will be influenced by factors 1 and 2. Cost management will entail forecasting and estimating, monitoring and rescheduling project activities to meet budgetary constraints.

(b) Types of judgements and decisions:

Time management – may involve decisions on simplifying project tasks, acquiring extra resources (e.g. extra staff or overtime) and reducing non-productive activities.

Quality management – often a decision trade-off between cost, time and the effectiveness of the completed system or software.

Resource management – often decisions involve trying to optimize the use of resources with constraints of cost and time.

Cost management – central to decisions on time, cost, quality and resources.

Although listed separately, the management of these aspects should be balanced and integrated.

2 The effective operation of teams is often a prerequisite for the successful achievement of many tasks within business organizations. This is equally true of the task of information systems development.

Without the effective interaction and integration of the various people with specialist skills, knowledge and experience, the system produced will be inferior to what may be achieved and will often fail to attain the objectives established. The major factors contributing to the effective operation of teams include:

- Development of a common or shared perception of the objectives and the means of achieving these.
- Encouraging mutually supportive environment to share workloads, discuss problems openly and aid other members in resolving problems.
- Developing mutual respect for professional skills of various members and engendering a sense of self-confidence by the team.
- Developing sound interpersonal skills and relationships between all team members.
- Sharing responsibility for the development of the project and achieving the necessary performance levels in terms of costs, quality and time.

While such factors may contribute towards the effectiveness of team working, the ultimate success will depend on the willingness and contribution of all members of the team, and the management to provide the necessary support.

Chapter 13

Self-test questions

1 The system evaluation process involves a number of stages:

- determining the objectives and performance criteria for the system (e.g. response time, quality of data, operating costs) to provide a basis for comparative evaluation
- measuring performance against objectives and other criteria. (This may involve both quantitative (e.g. cost data) and qualitative (e.g. user perceptions) measures)
- comparison of actual performance against planned performance, seeking to identify deviations that have already occurred or more particularly to identify future potential deviations in performance
- analysis of the nature, scale and reasons for any deviation from planned performance and assessing whether corrective action is required
- identification and evaluation of potential solutions to the deviations and assessment of their likely consequences
- taking a decision and implementing it, monitoring the effects of the corrective action taken and implementing any further controls or corrective actions necessary.

2 Criteria for evaluation of a system's performance at the strategic level would include:

- the ability of the system to provide good-quality information relating to the external environment
- provision of the appropriate internal information to support the needs of decision-makers and to complement the external data
- capacity to support the decision-makers' needs in terms of analytical models, tools, techniques and the necessary data quality
- the ability to provide opportunities for the organization to gain competitive advantage through the improved effectiveness or efficiency generated by the information system.

3 Measuring the effectiveness of an information system from the organization's perspective would incorporate the following types of criteria:

- effectiveness in supporting decisions at the strategic, tactical and operational levels in all functions and for all types of user
- the quality of the information provided and its appropriateness to the needs of the users involved
- the effectiveness of the human–computer interactions and the ease with which users may input and access data and manipulate tools from the system
- the ability of the system to achieve the necessary levels of security on data files and to permit access only to appropriate users internally and externally.
- the reliability of the system in supporting the needs of the users in the organization
- achieving value for money, in the sense that the organizational benefits gained outweigh the costs. This refers not only to the financial costs but equally to the human costs and benefits of systems and change.

4 The main groups of expenditures in relation to an information system include:

- development costs associated with the design, analysis and implementation, including hardware, software, training, etc.

- operational or direct running costs, salaries of the operators and maintenance staff, consumables and software maintenance costs
- overhead costs relating to the operation of the information system, its associated facilities, staff and other resources
- user costs arising from the need for users to provide data, verify data, process data, and access data, etc., plus the emotional costs and problems associated with change in working practices.

5 The evaluation of performance of a system may be assessed from a variety of different perspectives. The perspective of the provider of data to the system may focus on issues such as:

- system reliability
- speed of response time
- ease of using the system
- level of technical knowledge/training required
- quality of the data input/data capture devices and the consequent need for verification.

These issues may be addressed in terms of the example of the hotel booking system used in the text, or indeed in terms of almost any system which requires the output of volumes of data to maintain the system.

Exam-style questions

1 The term 'optimum' is frequently used in the fields of operations management and information systems. It refers to the system which achieves the maximum possible level of performance in relation to either a single criterion or multiple criteria. Usually, if one seeks to optimize against a number of criteria, the net result is that the achievement in relation to each criterion has to be sacrificed to achieve a balanced performance overall. For example, the optimizing of information quality may be at the expense of both the time taken to produce the information and the costs involved. Redressing the level of quality may also aid in achieving the other performance criteria of faster response time and lower costs.

The problems that would typically be encountered are:

- multiple performance criteria, which require some form of prioritization or ranking
- the need to achieve a balance across multiple criteria
- the problem of measurement of qualitative criteria user perceptions of performance varying from user to user and for the same user over time.

Whilst the term 'optimum system' is useful as a conceptual tool, it poses severe problems when we are seeking to apply the concept to practical systems.

The organization and the system development team require a clear understanding of the criteria involved, the ranking of these criteria and the level of performance required in each to obtain the desired 'optimum' performance.

2 Since an information system is typically used by a variety of users at different levels of the organization, within different functions and for different purposes, (e.g. data input or data retrieval), there are a variety of different perspectives on the term 'system effectiveness'.

Users from different perspectives will often seek very similar criteria on which to measure effectiveness, but may wish to rank or weight these differently in their overall assessment. For example, all users may seek a fast response time from the system. However, the user who is continuously inputting or retrieving data may weight this as more significant than the user who makes less frequent enquiries. Similarly, the question of cost effectiveness may be of significant importance to the manager or the financial/management accountants, but of less significance to the normal users of the systems. A further difficulty is that the perceptions of users concerning effectiveness may vary over time or according to their particular situation and use of the system. The sales order processor who regards the system as effective in supporting routine sales operations may consider the same system as very ineffective in responding to the less routine type of enquiry.

The key issues that need to be addressed are the following:

- The criteria used in determining effectiveness need to be identified.
- The level of performance in each of those criteria needs to be agreed by the organization.
- The weighting or ranking of each of the performance criteria also needs to be agreed by the organization.
- There is no unique definition of system effectiveness, hence the need to establish an agreed measure of this for a system.

Chapter 14

Self-test questions

1 Computers may either be the objects of the crime – for example, the criminal wants to steal or damage the computers in some way – or the means whereby the crime is to be carried out or concealed.

2 Since the aim of a commercial organization is to meet the needs of its customers and thereby to make a profit, the managers must introduce security measures that will maintain customer services at an acceptable level in all but the most severe emergencies. The main security system functions are therefore:
- to protect the capital (both physical and human) employed in the organization's operations
- to avoid or prevent threats to the critical systems
- to provide for the quick recovery of systems if they are lost
- to identify the causes of the loss of systems so that the risk of a repeat loss maybe reduced.

3 Risk arises where there is a likelihood of undesirable consequences flowing from conditions where there are uncertain factors. Nevertheless, some risks will be classified as acceptable (say), where the probability of loss is low. Where the prospect of the risk cannot be tolerated, some risks will be controllable or avoidable. Others may be transferred, perhaps through insurance. Where the loss cannot be avoided or transferred, planning may keep the losses within reasonable boundaries through loss reduction strategies. Risks may also be classified by reference to their source.

4 Unless it is necessary for the particular application, designers should not build too much flexibility into the system. Equally, designers should not expect too much from the users – so that, with training, users may be masters of their information systems. This would also suggest that designers should not attempt applications of excessive size, in order that all of the system's parts can be understood by those who must use them. This will be enhanced by providing clear support documentation. The designs should also concentrate on making the data accessible, as the information is the long-term resource of the organization.

5 Personal data must:
(a) be obtained and processed fairly and lawfully
(b) be held only for one or more specified and lawful purposes
(c) not be used or disclosed in any manner incompatible with these purposes
(d) be adequate, relevant and not excessive for their purpose
(e) be accurate and, where necessary, kept up-to-date
(f) not be kept for longer than is necessary for their purpose
(g) be disclosed on request to the data subject at reasonable intervals and without undue delay or expense, with the individual being entitled, where appropriate, to have such data corrected or erased
(h) be kept secure against unauthorized access, alteration, destruction, disclosure or accidental loss.

A data subject also has a range of civil remedies to enforce the following entitlements:
- to be informed by the data user as to whether any personal data is held relating to him or her
- to be supplied with a copy of that data
- to be compensated for any damage or distress caused by any inaccuracy in the personal data
- to be compensated for any damage or distress caused by the loss or unauthorized disclosure of the data
- to apply for rectification or erasure of inaccurate data.

Exam-style questions

1 This question asks you to write a report which identifies the factors to be considered when designing the systems that will make up the organization's information and physical systems. Under the heading of vulnerability, you should consider the circumstances in which a system or the data contained might be wrongly used. Things which place a system at greater risk include the ability of people to access the hardware, and whether the system is centralized or distributed. Further factors would be whether logical access can be achieved without leaving a trace (say) in an access log, and whether any centralized DP facility is located in a high-risk area. The recruitment and turnover of staff is also an important factor in increasing vulnerability.

Under the heading of risk, analysis techniques are available to begin the process of classifying and quantifying an organization's exposure to threats. The quantification is based on an assessment of the probability of an unwanted event occurring, the cost of avoidance and the cost of loss if the event does occur. Risk factors are often classified by source (i.e. internal/external) or by the method of control (i.e. acceptance, avoidance or transfer through insurance).

2 This question tests your understanding of contingency planning. The senior managers role is central because a disaster plan should not be limited to the specialist DP staff (if any), but should affect most of the people employed in the organization. It is up to the senior management to sponsor and promote the disaster plan. This will involve establishing priorities to the various user functions in the event that system capacity is reduced by the emergency. Thus, managers would have to decide whether sales order entry is more important than invoicing, and soon. The effect of each possible disaster must be assessed at a strategic level. Moreover, senior managers are in the best position to assess the true cost of business interruption, direct loss and the extent of any legal liability.

A disaster plan should contain the following main elements:

- a statement of policy and terms of reference for each job holder
- rules on implementing the policy
- responsibilities and actions to be taken by employees and third parties in the event of a disaster
- mechanisms for review and update.

3 The planning activity should draw on the specialist experiences of a wide range of staff. Although there are risks in pooling information about threats to security, a team approach would normally be preferred and would draw people from departments as follows:

- the finance department should provide castings and appraisals
- the internal auditors should review all security proposals
- the legal department should identify possible exposures to liability
- the personnel department should advise on changes in jobs, etc.
- the public relations department would need to draft press releases and advise on bow best to protect the corporate image
- the production department would advise on how to keep the plant working or to produce the most efficient recovery
- outside consultants would provide the benefit of their advice and experience.

The detailed work of the team would include:

- fact-finding and a security audit of the hardware distribution, storage, software requirements and system controls
- producing and evaluating alternative disaster scenarios, with risk analysis performed for critical applications
- laying down strategies to cope with the requirements of disaster scenarios, and producing recovery plans
- monitoring and reviewing the plans.

Chapter 15

Self-test questions

1 Perpetrator analysis is one of the scenario-based methodologies used to assess the level of risk faced by each operation and function of the organization. It aims to identify the knowledge, abilities and opportunities that would be required for a person to threaten the operation of each part of the systems in use. Some targets will be more attractive to different classes of perpetrator; those with authority and expertise, for example, may be able to threaten more critical systems.

2 Data Protection Principle 8 contained in Schedule 1, Data Protection Act 1984 states that 'Appropriate security measures shall be taken against unauthorized access to, or alteration, disclosure or destruction of, personal data and against accidental loss or destruction of personal data'. A full security audit should therefore consider all the major threats which might result in unauthorized access and the other hazards to personal data. Taking reasonable steps to avoid these hazards would be a defence to a Deregistration Notice issued by the Registrar. This would involve setting authority levels for logical access and introducing and policing confidentiality clauses in contracts of employment.

3 Each department must assess its needs and decide how many hours each day the computer service should routinely be available. Naturally, this will include planned downtime for maintenance, bearing

in mind the fault frequency demonstrated. It will also be necessary to show how long the departments could survive without the system, in the event of an emergency, before the business would be seriously affected. At a level of individual applications, it will be necessary to show who should have access and over what period of time.

4 If we assume that the person is identified as the possible wrongdoer, there are several factors that may prevent prosecution. Because the criminal courts will now award costs to successful defendants, the CPS will not now prosecute if the evidence of wrongdoing is not clear. There are also problems in the definition of some of the offences involving computer misuse, and acquittal rates may also deter prosecutions. Further, the introduction of new guidelines leads the police to use cautions where the offender has made good the loss of where the amount involved is small.

5 Insurance policies are a way of transferring the risk of loss to another. The main classes of risk covered are fidelity, where any lack of care by an employee results in loss, electronic crime which makes good losses sustained through crime, and directors' and officers' liability where breach of fiduciary duties causes loss.

Exam-style questions

1 This tests your knowledge of fraud in computer-based information systems. People may be motivated to commit crimes for a variety of reasons including:

- the intellectual challenge of beating the system
- greed and selfishness
- high levels of debt due to poor management or more aberrant reasons such as excessive gambling, drug/alcohol addiction, etc.
- resentment arising from a perception of poor rates of pay
- jealousy of others seen as more successful.

Apart from the 'smash and grab' criminals who simply run away after the theft, most of those who commit fraud do so on a long-term basis and believe that they will get away with it, i.e. that their method will prevent or delay detection. Fraud may be concealed by some or all of the following methods:

- confusing the situation, e.g. by causing a system crash
- diverting attention from the fraud, e.g. by planting evidence of fraud elsewhere in the system, perhaps implicating another person
- delaying the discovery – by breaking the audit trail, for example
- preventing discovery, typically by destroying evidence.

2 The most cost-effective strategies will be those where the organization achieves economies of loss which exceed the costs involved in implementing the security procedures and recovery plans. The factors that may affect the cost analysis process include:

- The probability of a disaster occurring, and the likelihood of a significant loss. Any difficulty in producing precise quantification for these variables should not be used as a justification for a failure to set up countermeasures.
- The unwillingness of management to invest in security. The reason sometimes given is that no direct return can be seen on money invested in security when the possible disasters do not occur.
- The lack of a reliable basis upon which to compare costs, both between different departments in the same organization and between different organizations.

The fact that some departments may not be completely honest about the degree of their reliance on the DP function – or the fact that different departments may base their estimates of loss and disruption on different assumptions, which may produce considerable uncertainty.

3 The decisions that must be made within an organization involved in setting up security procedures are in the areas of physical and logical security. The main decision areas would be:

- failback systems and continued manual operation
- alternative hardware provision
- recommissioning and restart facilities.

More detailed decisions within these areas would include:

- the likely duration of the disruption before critical damage to the business was sustained
- whether a full service should be provided to a restricted or rotating number of users

- whether to allow a partial service to all users
- whether to make mutual arrangements with another user running a similar configuration or a bureau
- the setting-up of emergency facilities.

Chapter 16

Self-test questions

1 Physical threats may be classified as being either asset-based or people-based and the countermeasures therefore depend upon which assets are to protected and to what degree of security, and what protective or defensive measures the organization decides to take in regard to those who work in or visit the premises.

2 Full-scale power protection for all equipment against current and voltage surges is expensive. Critical systems are therefore identified and may be protected by back-up power supplies which will be available in the event of violent fluctuations or failure of supply.

3 This works on a three-day cycle. On day 1, data is backed up and stored off-site. On day 2, a copy is made and stored in a secure location on-site. On day 3, the copy is kept on-site, the day 2 copy is taken off-site and the day 1 copy is returned ready to make the back-up copy on day 4. In this way, there is always one copy off-site in a secure location and the organization should never lose more than two days' data.

4 The preventive measures begin with the possibility of bolting portable equipment to desks or tables. Alarms and locks may then defend the rooms in which the equipment is used or stored. All staff should be trained to be security-conscious and to report suspicious movements of equipment.

5 Because competition becomes less risky when you have information about the intentions of your competitors, there is pressure to find out what is planned. This may be by direct intervention, such as burglary or bribing employees, or by electronic surveillance (the recent BA/Virgin Airlines case shows the damage that may be caused).

Exam-style questions

1 (a) This question highlights the importance of people to the design of security systems. Physical access controls depend upon the control of space, allowing access only to those who have been authorized to enter. The principle is two-way in that physical access may be used, either to protect the installation itself or to protect users or employees.

(b) The methods of access control may include:

- human control systems, i.e. receptionists or guards
- automatic entry control systems, using machine-readable tokens or cards
- mechanical locking systems – a conventional key (for example) or a combination lock.

2 In designing physical space control systems, the main planning considerations start with a definition of the perimeter which is to be controlled. This may be a single zone, or there may be a hierarchy of zones with increasing levels of security. Within each zone or group of zones, planners must then decide what level of security should be implemented. This may depend on the ability to be able to control movement between different zones or to monitor different activities in each zone. If movement is to be controlled, the layout of the whole site must be considered to ensure that staff movements for common purposes, such as using the canteen, will be routed away from the more sensitive parts of the site. Some security facilities will be positively required for the detection and control of fires, security doors and similar purposes. These must be designed with the need for staff to be able to evacuate the site quickly in the event of a disaster. It would be unfortunate if security personnel could not access the scene of a crisis if the only entry was blocked by staff slowly passing out through a turnstile security gate. Training and rehearsals are important, not only to maximize the chance that staff will react well in an emergency but also as a practical test of the planning.

Chapter 17

Self-test questions

1 The users must be identified and the systems must ensure that each user has the appropriate authorization for the proposed use of application or data. Each user and terminal must therefore have an identifier to ensure that the right person is attempting access from the expected place. The system should then check the security file to see whether that individual has authority to access the given application or data.
2 By sequential searches through a database, it is possible to formulate query sets that will allow the user to infer unstated facts about data elements in the database. The difficulty in formulating controls for limiting searches is that it may well prevent legitimate and useful searches. The designers must therefore decide whether the requirements of data confidentiality outweigh the benefits of free searching.
3 Hacking is intervention by an unauthorized person achieving access to a computer system. Once entry has been made, the person may then cause damage to the system itself or to the data which it contains. The confidentiality of the data may also be compromised.
4 Electronic eavesdropping is the use of electronic means to gain information about the contents of messages during their transmission or while they are being displayed on the screen of a VDU. The standard defence to eavesdropping during transmission is encryption. To guard against the scanning of electromagnetic radiation is expensive and depends on building shielding into the fabric of buildings where sensitive data may be viewed on VDUs.

Exam-style questions

1 (a) This is a general question about access control. Three ways in which password security might be improved would be:
   - a duress password, meaning one which causes an alarm (or at least a record) when used. (This not only covers the possibility of the password being stolen, but also means that the user is forced to use it)
   - machine-generated passwords, which are communicated to the user through a secure mailing system
   - changing passwords at regular intervals – say, every month.

   (b) Three ways in which a hacker might gain access:
   - using a microcomputer and a modem (with an appropriate decoy program) to capture the system password on callback
   - wire trapping or electronically intruding into a legitimately logged-on terminal link. (This is particularly likely if a terminal is left logged on but unused)
   - access to highly secure parts of the system gained from less secure parts by using a program which simulates the log-on screen. (In attempting to log into this, the user reveals his or her password.)

2 This question refers to the straightforward methods of data encryption for security. The methods are:
   - hardware encryption (permanent but expensive)
   - cipher systems using algorithms and a key
   - substitution or transposition methods of cipher
   - mixed transformation methods, such as DES
   - one-time pad systems using message and key on separate media.

3 This question asks you to consider the scope of the Computer Misuse Act 1990 and its relevance to the problems encountered by commercial organizations. The three new offences are:
   - the anticipatory offence of unauthorized access
   - the aggravated form of the first offence, which requires proof that some other offence (theft, for example) is intended following access
   - modification of the data in some way following entry.

   Before the Act came into force, there was no real offence of hacking. Although some academics speculated that various existing offences could be reinterpreted to cover computer-based crimes, the courts were unwilling to extend laws into activities not envisaged by parliament when the laws were made. Thus, efforts to extend criminal damage, forgery, etc. were largely unsuccessful. Parliament therefore responded to calls from the commercial and industrial worlds to produce these three new offences. In theory, these offences should allow the courts to criminalize many misuses of computers, but recent cases suggest that the courts may still not be able to offer much more protection than before. Computer users should therefore continue to act in self-defence and take steps to make their systems more secure. That the Act does not deal with eavesdropping as an offence should encourage computer owners to urgent action.

Chapter 18

Self-test questions

1 The design should be discussed by as many people as possible to ensure that its effectiveness is recognized by all and is a deterrent. Within the overall requirement that the system should be as user-friendly as possible to encourage all users to follow the security procedures, the safety-first rule should be that if there is doubt, authorization to access or manipulate the data should be denied.

2 The main steps are, first, the human control of visually comparing the keyed version with the source materials. Data may be keyed twice by different operators and the two versions compared for consistency. There may also be internal software checks to ensure that data are in the right format and within reasonable limits.

3 The role of the auditor begins during the design of software systems, to ensure that adequate security procedures are built in from the outset. Once the design has been validated and implemented, the auditors will ensure that the controls are working effectively and that the data contained within the system represents a fair view of the operation of the organization. If defects in the security system are detected, the senior management should be alerted.

4 Fraud depends on one or more of the following manipulations of data records. First, there may be false input whether by entering false data or by suppressing valid data. Secondly, existing data records may be altered or destroyed. Finally, output can be destroyed or withheld.

Exam-style questions

1 The problem of security becomes increasingly complex as organizations move to desk-based systems rather than centralized facilities and all managements must consider how to reconcile the concept of corporate data holdings with the possibility of reasonably free access by all users. The following problems need to be addressed:

- physical limitations on access to some terminals or workstations where more sensitive access or manipulations may be performed
- improved data security procedures if more sensitive activities may be undertaken by individuals
- security procedures that are effective while remaining user-friendly
- training that will allow the majority of users to get the best out of the systems
- establishing good communications links between the different parts of the system.

2 The detection of fraud requires rapid but considered action by management. The actions that may be taken include:

- maintaining secrecy to prevent the suspected offender from being warned off
- taking decisions on whether to involve the police. (There may be a policy on whether to prosecute, either to deter offenders or to meet the terms of an insurance policy)
- obtaining evidence of the nature and scale of the suspected fraud, and taking copies of all the relevant records and output
- soliciting evidence from third parties such as customers, suppliers, the Inland Revenue, etc.
- analysing the data to produce a schedule of evidence for submission to the prosecution authorities.

Chapter 19

Self-test questions

1 Security audit checks begin with the design of the software systems, both pre- and post-implementation. The software must be integrated into the overall accounting system and all audit trails must be validated. The auditors then look for signs of fraud, checking all the controls on the most sensitive applications and monitoring computer activity. Proposed modifications to the system must be vetted and the disaster recovery plans tested on a regular basis.

2 Job sensitivity analysis aims to identify risks by analysing the organization from the point of view of the potential thief. Thus, each class of assets will tend to be vulnerable to attack from different classes of thief. By identifying who would have the opportunity and the ability to steal each type of asset, the organization may take better decisions on how to protect itself.

3 All employees represent a possible threat to security. However, the greatest danger comes from those who have the greatest privileges within the security system: systems staff, applications programmers and the operating staff. Similarly, those senior managers with higher-level authorizations may access all the more sensitive records.

4 To check every prospective employee may not be cost-effective because many who break security are first-time offenders. If the applicant is a determined criminal, the information presented in support of the applicant is likely to be internally consistent and to appear valid in a superficial check. Even if previous employers are contacted directly, they may not wish to disclose previous fraudulent activities.

Exam-style questions

1 (a) Audits tend to disrupt the work of the departments under review and so they should be carefully planned to keep disruption within reasonable bounds. A security audit plan may include the following:
- Staff selection: the staff must be as knowledgeable as those to be audited but must normally be recruited from another department.
- Some checks should be scheduled at random to create the maximum surprise.
- The location and duration of the check should be decided, making the task of an appropriate size given the degree of risk represented by the particular department to be checked.
- The selection of the type of audit comparison to be made, e.g. historical or intercompany.
- After carrying out the audit, managers should maintain the controls for some weeks after the event.

(b) Problems in prosecutions may occur because:
- A jury may not understand the technical details of the case.
- Sentences for non-violent fraud may be too lenient and not be a deterrent to others.
- The image of computerized records may prejudice juries and public opinion against the organization and in favour of the defendants.
- The organization may fear adverse publicity through revealing the vulnerability of their systems.
- Details of the fraud raised in court may inspire copycat crimes.

2 (a) The responsibilities of an auditor include the following:
- Assisting in drawing up, reviewing and testing the disaster plans.
- Liaison with external auditors during financial audits which involve the organization's computer system.
- Helping to design and review security measures.
- Assisting in the specification of software and data storage in the area of controls and audit trails.
- Helping to maintain data integrity, in collaboration – say, with the database administrator.

(b) The organization's security auditor should be in a position of authority, possibly in a senior management position. Data security is about the design and operation of the information system. The auditor will be involved in the development of new applications throughout the system development life cycle. The auditor will be involved in the development of new applications throughout the systems development life cycle.

- The auditor will be particularly involved at the feasibility study phase in the definition of security objectives, at the design stage in developing controls and countermeasures, and at the post-implementation stage in ensuring conformity with procedures.
- The auditor will monitor the day-to-day operation of the system, including logs and exception reports.
- The auditor will check and approve proposed enhancements and amendments to the system and its software.

3 The ability to restore computing service depends on the replacement of any hardware which may be lost in a disaster. Alternative methods of hardware provision include:

- Drawing up a contingency agreement with a bureau (a time broker): this option will involve detailed testing to ensure system compatibility and may be economically viable only for high-volume DP operations.
- Arranging a mutual aid agreement with other user organizations having a nearly identical system. Although this is potentially cheap and may be superficially attractive, such agreements may be fraught with difficulty. The organization may not be able to change its system easily (e.g. by introducing a new operating system), because of the need to maintain compatibility with the other system. The disruption to DP operations which would be suffered by an organization offering aid may be intolerable. Such agreements are therefore difficult to negotiate and maintain.
- Maintaining a fully equipped computer centre in duplication of existing facilities (a contingency centre or hot stand-by). The centre may be shared by several organizations or be operated as a commercial venture by a third party on subscription. Although the full cost only becomes payable when an organization is exercising the option to use the centre, there are problems of standardization and security where data are stored on site.
- The empty shell or cold stand-by centre is similar to the above. An organization using this facility would need special agreements with manufacturers to supply replacement hardware at very short notice. This may prevent the option being used for critical operations, but the constraints on system change do not apply to the same extent.

All these methods of hardware provision rely on the successful back-up of data and software in the event of a disaster.

Glossary

Added value The term applied to describe the satisfaction of consumer or aspirations, i.e. the consumer's motive to select one supplier rather than another is governed by the perception of the additional value to be derived from the supply of goods or services. Value may be added by appearing to provide better quality or currency through the brand name; organizations generally seek to enhance the value delivered as a key platform of their competitive strategy.

Algorithm A sequence of predefined rules, procedures and selection criteria which may be applied to resolve problems with a predictable structure.

Applications software Programs designed to process data for particular user needs, such as payroll application, spreadsheet.

Artificial intelligence (AI) The application of computer-based technologies to mimic certain problem-solving abilities of humans, usually related to structured or semi-structured problem situations.

ATM A type of network protocol in which 'packets' or cells of data are routed independently to their destinations.

Automatic teller machines (ATMs) Computerized systems employed in banks and other financial services institutions to issue cash and to offer other customer services.

Bandwidth The ability of a communications medium to carry large amounts of data at one time.

BASIC (Beginners All-purpose Symbolic Instruction Code) A high-level programming language designed to facilitate the use of relatively simple English-type instructions to create programs.

Batch processing Aggregating similar types of of data requiring similar processing into groups or batches and processing these batches together rather than individually, thus deriving economies of scale and increased security and control.

Batch total A security check to ensure that all records submitted for processing have been processed, usually involving a total of the number of records or source documents in the batch.

Baud rate A measure of the speed at which data travels – the number of signal pulses per second.

Business process re-engineering (BPR) A radical redesign of business processes in order to increase productivity or effectiveness. Usually enabled by the use of IT.

Browser Software for finding and viewing pages on the World Wide Web (WWW). Also 'web-browser'.

Buffer Either an insert to separate one block of data from another, or an area of storage (e.g. in a printer or other peripheral device) which is used to store transitory data. For example, a CPU can supply data to a printer faster than the printer can operate, hence the CPU transmits blocks of data for printing to the printer's buffer (or memory store) and the printer 'reads' the data from the buffer store as required.

Byte A sequence of eight bits of data. A unit of measurement of computer memory or processing.

CAD/CAM (computer-aided design and computer-aided manufacture) A generic term applied to the development and design of systems to support design work and to control manufacturing operations.

CASE (computer-aided software engineering) tool A software tool for helping to automate all or parts of the software development process.

Cathode ray tube (CRT) A visual communication device based on television technology providing the major element of the human–computer interface in modern systems.

CBT (computer-based training) Vocational training systems which exploit computer technology to present and explain the instructional materials.

CD-ROM Compact disk read-only memory. An optical storage device of large capacity used in multimedia applications.

Central processing unit (CPU) A main unit of the computer system which holds the operating system software instructions and data, performs the execution of these instructions and controls all the associated peripheral devices.

Chief information officer (CIO) The person responsible for managing IT and IS in an organization.

Client–server architecture A computer network configuration in which certain devices are dedicated to providing services (e.g. printing, data management) for other devices which run user applications. A flexible and powerful way of building extendable networks.

Closed system A system which has no interaction with its environment.

COBOL (Common Business-Orientated Language) A high-level programming language primarily designed for the development of commercial or business data processing applications and, despite its antiquity, still used extensively.

COM (computer output microfilm) A computer storage device employing microfilm technology, used primarily for backing and off-line storage.

Compiler Systems software which translates high-level program code into machine code for execution.

Conceptual schema The overall structure of a database expressed in logical terms and used in database design development.

Console The interface unit between the user and the computer, typically in the form of a typewriter keyboard but also employing other ergonimically efficient devices, such as a mouse or light pen.

Cost–benefit analysis (CBA) Techniques for estimating and comparing the cost of an IT project with the projected benefits.

CPU See 'central processing unit'.

Data administration A part of the organization responsible for an organization's plans and policies with regard to data and information usage.

Data dictionary A structured file of details (e.g. contents, structure, location and relationship to other data elements) of data held within a database, otherwise known as 'metadata'. A part of most database management systems (DBMS).

Database A collection of structured data in the form of records, usually appropriate to a number of user applications, which are organized and managed in a single form and are accessed and updated by different data users.

Database administration A part of the organization responsible for the technical aspects of developing and maintaining the corporate data resource.

Database machine A computer dedicated to running DBMS software to provide fast access to a large database. Part of a client–server system.

Database management system (DBMS) The software used to build, maintain and control database files and user access to them.

Data definition language (DDL) A part of the DBMS software which defines data items in a database.

Data flow diagram (DFD) Diagramatic tools used in a numbers of systems analysis and design methods to indicate logical flows of data between processes, entities and data stores within an information system.

Data dictionary system (DDS) Software designed to control a data dictionary.

Data manipulation language (DML) The part of the DBMS software which controls access to data items, is used to change their value and delete them.

Decision support system (DSS) Software whcih is designed to aid decision-makers by modelling data and evaluating and selecting appropriate solutions to problems.

Decision table A charting tool used in systems analysis and design which models decision situations by decomposing situations into potential conditions and indicating consequent actions forming 'rules'.

Desk-top publishing (DTP) system A system which is capable of producing camera-ready near-typeset quality copy.

Distrubuted database A database in which the data are stored in several locations.

Distributed data processing A number of computers linked by a network, with each computer or workstation capable of storing and processing a part of the workload in isolation from the network or providing access to resources within the network.

Electronic data interchange (EDI) The direct transmission of data relating to business transactions (e.g sales) between IT systems in different organizations, replacing paperwork and eliminating repeated data entry.

Electronic fund transfer (EFT) The transfer of financial balances by electronic means through appropriate computer networks (the related term EFTPOS – electronic funds transfer at point of scale, involves the automatic debiting of each customer's account at the time of purchase without using a cheque).

Electronic mail (EMS or e-mail) Communication of messages between users through a computer network.

End user A person who uses IT in support of his or her everyday work.

End-user computing An approach to IT management which allows end users to acquire and develop their own IT systems within certain guidelines.

Entities A term used in context diagrams and logical data structures or entity-relationship models to refer to individuals, groups or organizations involved in the system, both internally and externally. Also logical data structure (LDS).

Entity-relationship model (ERM) A systems analysis tool designed to assist data analysis in terms of entities, attributes and relationships.

EPOS (electronic point of scale) Automatic systems for the capture of product and pricing data, using barcodes and electronic sensors to avoid the need to key in prices; used extensively in retailing.

Executive information system (EIS) A decision support system intended to support high-level managers. The information is aggregated and presented in a summarized form.

Expert systems Systems designed to apply knowledge and problem-solving rules derived from applying human reasoning to mimic human expertise (often termed knowledge-based systems or KBS).

External schema The user's view of the structure and contents of the data elements in a database, applied in database construction and development.

Fibre optic High-capacity telecommunications medium using a strand of glass fibre down which light pulses are sent. Fibre optic links have a high bandwidth.

Firewall A secure gateway to a network.

Flowchart Diagrammatic tool using standard symbols and lines to illustrate the logical flow in the operations of a system or a program.

FORTRAN (FORmula TRANslator) A high-level programming language used primarily for mathematical computations.

Fourth-generation language (4GL) A programming tool which is end-user-orientated and which is declarative (rather than procedural) in that the program instructions are generated automatically by describing the input and output formats in simple statements.

Front-end processor A computer which handles data on behalf of a larger computer (a 'host') in a network, (e.g a client–server system).

Gateway A point at which two or more IT networks connect (typically a server with appropriate security software – a 'firewall').

Graphical user interface (GUI) A WIMP-type interface.

Groupware Software which is intended to support group or collaborative business functions. (Also computer-supported collaborative work CSCW.)

Heuristics Experiential, intuitive or 'rule-of-thumb' approaches to problem-solving.

Hierarchical database A method of structuring a database which has a tree-like structure with levels and branches defining the association of data items.

Host A computer which handles the applications software in a computer network (e.g a client–server system).

Hypertext transfer protocol (HTTP) The protocol which governs use of the Internet.

Hypertext mark-up language (HTML) A simple language with which WWW pages are created and linked.

Human–computer interface (HCI) The interaction between the users of IT and the IT systems. The study of techniques for designing and implementing such interfaces.

Hypermedia A type of database in which 'pages' of text are linked.

Hypertext The content of hypermedia.

Information centre A location within an organization which is intended to give information, help and advice to end-users about acquiring, developing and using IT systems.

Information resource management The planning, management and control of an organization's information and technology resources.

Information technology (IT) Computing and communications technology applied to information processing.

Interactive processing The use of a computer system which gives a direct and immediate response to the users' commands – an alternative to batch processing.

Internal schema The definition of the internal physical structure or organization of constructed.

Internet The world-wide virtual communications network.

Interorganizational information systems (IOS) Systems which are shared by several organizations.

Interpreter Software which translates a high-level language into machine code *one statement at a time* for execution immediately after translation. Contrast with compiler.

KB systems See *expert systems*

Kilobyte, K or Kb Refers to multiple of approximately 1000 bytes of data or characters, usually relating to storage capacities of devices or CPUs.

Knowledge engineering The process of acquiring and structuring knowledge about a domain of operation and convertig into a knowledge base.

LAN (local area network) A network of computer devices within a close geographical area, usually within the same part of the organization or building.

Megabyte, M, Mb or Meg Refers to multiples of 1,000,000 bytes or characters, relating to storage capacities of devices.

Management information systems (MIS) Manual or computer-based systems designed to provide managers with appropriate information to aid decision-making and control of the operations of the organization.

MIPS A unit of measurement to indicate the number of instructions that can be executed by the processors comprising the CPU, i.e. one million intructions per second. See also KOPS (one thousand computing operations per second).

Modem A modulator–demodulator deveice which converts digital signals into an analog signal for transmission over non-digital telecommunications media.

Multi-access A term applied to computer systems which allow simultaneous access to files or processing by more than one user.

Network A system of communication channels interconnecting users at different locations.

Network database A database which contains data items which are structured in a network of associations.

Neural networks Systems which 'learn' (i.e. apply artificial intelligence) from a large number of examples how to recognize patterns in data in a way which is similar to human learning.

Normalization A term applied in relational database design, referring to the process of simplifying the logical relationships within the database structure.

Object-oriented technology (OOT) A variety of IT which is based on objects, which contain both data and instruction code. OOT includes object-bases and object-oriented programming languages.

Office automation systems Systems designed to support office tasks with IT.

Optical character recognition (OCR) A system of data capture which 'reads' special characters on documents.

Optical mark recognition (OMR) A system of data capture which 'reads' special markings on documents.

Open systems interconnection (OSI) model A standard for protocols to operate in a network 'open systems' environment.

Outsourcing 'Buying-in' IT services or resources, includes 'facilities management'.

Packet switching network A telecommunications system which splits messages into packets which are transmitted to their destination independently.

Peripheral A computing device which can be linked to a CPU (e.g. a printer or scanner).

Protocol A set of rules or standards governing the format and methods employed in the transmission of data which are necessary when communicating between computers or systems which are not similar.

Prototype The initial software model of a system to be developed. A prototype may be developed into the 'real' system or may be abandoned (used as a design only).

Relational database A database which structures the data items in tables (or relations) which are connected logically by relationships.

Query language A programming language designed to interrogate a database: a fourth-generation language.

SDLC See system development life cycle.

Server A 'host' computer which provides data to other 'client' computers in a network.

Service provider An organization which offers computing facilities or which operates a value-added network.

Sequential access A method of accessing records in a file which involves a record-by-record search search of the file in order until the record is found.

Spooling The use of secondary storage devices (e.g. disk drives) to act as a buffer store between input and output peripherals (e.g. a keyboard) to reduce processing delays due to the difference in processing speeds between such devices. A 'print queue' is an example of a spooling device.

Strategic information system (SIS) An IT application which is of strategic importance to an organization.

Structured query language (SQL) A fourth-generation language intended for use in interrogating relational DBMSs.

Systems flowchart A graphical tool used in systems analysis and design to record and communicate the logical data flows and operations. Such charts are not used much today.

Systems development life cycle (SDLC) The stages involved in the initiation, analysis development and implementation of an information system.

Tally systems Typically, hand-held or laptop data recording devices used to monitor stock levels in retail outlets or details of orders by salesmen. Data are downloaded to the main computer periodically by connecting into the network.

Teleworking The use of IT to operate from a remote location (usually from home,.includes 'telecommuting' and 'teleconferencing'.

Timesharing A common variety of operating system within a computer which time rotation to each user for the slice of sharing of time is effected is typically such that users are unaware of the process in operation, believing they access.

Topology The configuration of an IT network.

Unique resource location (URL) The 'address' of a WWW site.

VANS (value-added network services) available over public networks; often of a specialist nature, e.g. share price movements or airline flight and holiday booking information.

Videotex A system for offering information (e.g. weather and travel) and services (e.g. shopping and banking) via a TV or terminal.

Voice mail A messaging system which uses speech recordings which can be communicated asynchronously (i.e. messages can be 'left' in a 'mailbox').

WAN (wide area network) A telecommunications network connecting systems and users which are geographically separated.

Web page A 'page' of data on the WWW.

Web site A collection of pages on the WWW at one 'location'.

WIMP interface A computer interface which uses 'windows' technology for its HCI. WIMP stands for 'windows, icon, mouse and pointer'.

Workbench A software tool used to support the work of software engineers and systems analysts in developing systems and generating code. See also CASE tool and IPSE.

Workstation A very powerful computer with appropriate peripherals (e.g. a high-definition monitor) which is capable of running the most sophisticated software (e.g. CAD/CAM). Workstations are often linked in networks.

World Wide Web (WWW) All of the web pages at all of the web sites on the Internet.

Index

32770642
WITHDRAWN
from
STIRLING UNIVERSITY LIBRARY